The Psychedelic Rock Files

By Jerry Lucky
2002 Edition

D1738750

Dedication

To my family, Sue and Rachel

All rights reserved under article two of the Berne Copyright Convention (1971).
No part of this book may be reproduced or transmitted in any form or by any means,
electronic or mechanical, including photocopying, recording, or by any information storage
and retrieval system without permission in writing from the publisher.
We acknowledge the financial support of the Government of Canada through
the Book Publishing Industry Development Program for our publishing activities.
Published by Collector's Guide Publishing Inc.
Box 62034, Burlington, Ontario, Canada, L7R 4K2
Printed and bound in Canada
The Psychedelic Rock Files
by Jerry Lucky

Copyright © 2003 C.G. Publishing / Jerry Lucky ISBN 1-896522-97-1

The Psychedelic Rock Files

By Jerry Lucky
2002 Edition

Contents

Acknowledgements

A project like this fails or succeeds based on the contributions form a wide assortment of people. I might have been able to write something about the psychedelic genre on my own but it would have paled to insignificance had it not been for the help of a good many individuals who assisted me because of their love for the psychedelic genre and music in general.

First off, thanks to Steve Johnson at Lyles Records for providing a mighty stack of psychedelic CDs early in this project. These CDs not only gave me the opportunity to re-acquaint my self with the well-known psychedelic bands but also and more importantly opened my ears to many of the more obscure psychedelic bands.

Thanks also go out to a number of others for their help in bringing this project to a successful completion. San Francisco photographer and author Gene Anthony for inviting me into his home to talk about the sixties, and for taking all those great photographs that record the psychedelic era in San Francisco so well. Ray Anderson creator of the Holy See Light Show who now is the proprietor of Grooves Record Shop in San Francisco who shed even more light on the world of light shows. Psychedelic poster historian Eric King for sharing thoughts over a great Thai lunch in Berkeley. Fred Walker for his comprehensive poster price guide. And Gary Anderson at the Turntable in Fan Tan Alley in Victoria for keeping the psychedelic light on.

Finally a special thank you goes to Rob and Ric at Collectors Guide Publishing for seeing some value in creating this series of Rock Files books. I'm not sure if they know it or not, but it's fulfilled a dream. Thanks guys.

Introduction

In many ways this book has fulfilled a life-long goal. And interestingly enough, it was a goal I was aware of. Not only have I completed a volume devoted to psychedelic music, but also I now sit in a room with walls full of original psychedelic posters from San Francisco. My wife being a minimalist is struggling with the overall business of my den. But little did I ever expect I would see these posters let alone embark on a quest that would allow me to own a few and even stand on the corner where it all happened, Haight-Ashbury.

I had just turned 13 when the Summer of Love occurred in 1967. It was June 2nd and the Beatles had just released **Sgt. Peppers Lonely Hearts Club Band.** I was a teenager, raised in a musical family and I was in touch with what was happening musically ever since the Beatles had entered my life in early 1964. But I couldn't participate in the "hippie" movement even if I wanted to.

Still as I look back at that first order of albums from the record club, it's clear to me now that the world of psychedelia had already affected me. It included among other LPs, Jimi Hendrix's **Are You Experienced**, **The Doors** first and their second release **Strange Days**, the Grateful Dead's first LP and the Electric Prunes. I saw something I liked in this psychedelic movement. I even created my own version of a lightshow. Well actually all I did was replace my bedroom light with a red one, which seemed to cast a "psychedelic" glow on everything and everyone who entered.

And the posters…well after four years of art in high school, Wes Wilson's Fillmore posters put a headlock on me I couldn't get out of. When I saw the **Life** magazine from September 1st 1967 with a cover story on the new poster craze I was hooked. I even designed a High School drama night poster in 1970 that bore all the hallmarks. It's funny, the city I grew up in, Saskatoon even had it's own poster shop located on Broadway Avenue called the Blown Mind. I remember standing outside the place, looking up into the windows of this second floor shop, with walls covered in the latest psychedelic creations. But I vaguely recall my apprehension about going in. For one thing, I probably didn't have much money and hey, remember I was only 13. When I finally overcame all my fears and did go in, I remember being in awe, overwhelmed at the images around me.

1967 was a pretty exciting year in more ways than one. I remember the local AM radio station CKOM, where I eventually got my first radio gig, took time out to play the whole **Sgt. Pepper Lonely Hearts Club Band** album from start to finish. As a matter of fact, that station went psychedelic in a big way. Not only employing, according to local legend, real draft resisters, but also the announcers took exotic names such as Dylan Thomas, Alfie, and my favourite the Psychedelic Banana.

This was an exciting time because of what you could hear on the radio. Even though it was AM they dedicated a few hours in the evening to playing everything from Pink

Floyd to Frank Zappa. It was also a very prolific period musically. In many cases bands released one or more albums in any given year. There was a constant stream of new music. Just take a look at the Beatles output. In the two-year spread between December of 1965 and December of 1967 they released **Rubber Soul**, **Revolver**, **Sgt. Pepper** and **Magical Mystery Tour**, plus a number of singles and EPs. Today bands take breaks between recordings longer than two years and sadly the quality of writing many times falls short of the Beatles output under such pressure.

I don't think you can write about the psychedelic scene without standing on the corner of Haight Street and Ashbury Avenue, so part of this book was written there. Being in San Francisco, trying to "connect the dots" of the sixties scene, I was struck by how spread out the psychedelic community really was. In my mind the Fillmore Auditorium and the Avalon Ballroom were just a stones-throw away from Haight-Ashbury, but in fact the Fillmore was a good distance away from the centre of hippie-dom. And the Avalon was clear across town, although its long gone replaced by a cinema complex. Add to this what was happening across the Bay on Telegraph Avenue in Berkeley, and it's clear that there was a lot more going on than met the eye. From what I had seen in the media, or read in other books, it seemed that the musical and social underground was confined to just the small neighbourhood of Haight-Ashbury, but in fact it's impact was felt throughout all the Bay area.

As I walked up and down Haight Street many times over the time of my stay, I was struck by how it has in some ways changed and yet how in some ways it is very much the same. Apart from the McDonalds that sits at the foot of Golden Gate Park's "hippie hill", the tiny record shops like the Psychedelic Shop have been replaced by the enormous Amoeba Records still selling posters, records, CDs and paraphernalia. The head shops are still there but now they carry a good supply of souvenirs. The restaurants and drinking establishments still dot the street but "Love Burgers" are not as prominent. Designer fashion shops have replaced the craft and sandal stores. It's obvious that the fundamental communal hippie spirit has been replaced by a keen sense of consumerism.

Observing the people walking up and down Haight-Ashbury, you might be forgiven if you think you had gone back in time to the sixties. The fact is there are still many of the same characters there. They're older now, but they've grown older with the community. There are many young people in the community as well, some looking every bit like their hippie ancestors. Some still look lost and searching for something, others just living the life of the community. Unlike the sixties, you are just as likely to see mixed in this group the punkers, the Goths and plenty of tourists. What's interesting, is that while the "collective-idealism" that sparked the sixties counterculture may have driven out by competing commercial forces, many of these people are there still looking for something. Those who live there are trying to experience the essence of what the sixties came to represent. And those visiting are there hoping to at least momentarily touch or feel what it was that caused a small neighbourhood community in San Francisco to have such an impact not just on their lives but on the world. There is no question that a very important part of the counterculture movement was the music.

This the second book in my "Rock Files" series, and it was only natural that I go back and take a closer look at the music that most influenced the creation of the progressive rock genre. The truth is, if it hadn't been for the experimentation of the psychedelic sixties, progressive rock music would not have even happened.

This book is part encyclopaedic, part reference, part story telling. It is designed to be a comprehensive overview for the beginner and provide a handy reference tool for the more sophisticated psychedelic music fan. For the beginner, just discovering the genre, there is a history, which includes not only the San Francisco scene but looks at different cities and countries and compares what was happening elsewhere. The history is aided by a detailed timeline or chronology that goes day-by-day from early 1965 through to the end of 1971. There is also a discussion describing and defining what psychedelic music is and how it came to be. For those who weren't there at the time and wondered why it went away, we explore some of the inner workings of the business side of rock as it grew to maturity at the close of the sixties. Then, for those wanting to find out more we look more closely at psychedelic music today and discover how easy it is to fill out that library and record collection. Lastly there is the A-Z listing of psychedelic bands or artists with brief bios and discographies.

More than anything creating this book has brought me to a better appreciation of what those wacky, psychedelic sixties were all about and what they meant to a lot of people. There are of course some things about the sixties that we all wish we could forget. On the other side there are many things that I think deep down inside we wish, we could have really changed when we had the chance. The collective idealism that ran rampant through the growing counter-culture helped bring about many substantive adjustments in the way we view life today. Sadly for most, it lost momentum and the dashed idealism of the sixties gave birth to the social excesses of the seventies and ultimately to the greed of the "me" decade of the 1980s.

My goal is to put everything in one place, in one handy volume. This is a book for those just getting into the psychedelic genre and looking for some background, but also a book where someone who experienced the period first hand might look at the timeline and gain even further perspective as they reminisce. A book that allows the reader to find more than a little detail about the period but also discover other sources to explore the period in even more detail at a later time. In the end, I hope this book helps you acquire a deeper appreciation for what the psychedelic era was all about and in the process of exploring the A-Z band listing to also substantially add plenty of undiscovered music to your listening library.

If any of the above happens this book will have met its purpose.

Jerry Lucky,
August 2002

File No. 1

The History Of The Psychedelic Era

It's not always easy to see why a certain artistic style, cultural trend or fashion movement comes together where it does. It's undoubtedly a melding together of many different elements to form whatever that "new thing" is. It can be as simple as having the various individual components nearby causing the almost obvious combination to occur, or it may be much more complicated drawing upon matters of politics, timing and even events happening elsewhere for that new idea or way of thinking to come about.

It's much the same way with music. It's always a combination of things that leads to the creation of new musical trends. It's this combination of elements that gives certain musical styles a home. In Chicago it's the blues. In Liverpool it's the Mersey Sound. In New Orleans it's jazz. In Philadelphia it was the smooth "Philly" sound. In Seattle it was "grunge". Think of Nashville and you think of country music. In Detroit it was "Motown" and in San Francisco it was the sound of psychedelic rock music.

The psychedelic era is without question one of the most creative musical periods in the history of modern pop and rock music. In an interesting see-saw of influences, it was the American Motown and blues artists that influenced the Beatles bringing about the British Invasion, who then influenced the San Francisco and Los Angeles psychedelic bands like the Byrds and Jefferson Airplane, who then went on to influence the British psychedelic bands moving many of them in the progressive rock direction. The swings of musical influence never cease to amaze.

The roots of the psychedelic sound grew out of the British Invasion of the early sixties. In fact, there were many bands that straddled the line from late 1964 through to 1966 before LSD took over and changed people's perspective. Bands such as the Beau Brummels, the Knickerbockers or the Gants and many others were born in garages across the United States in the wake of the Beatles conquering America. Others such as the We Five or the Vejtables took the folk vocal style of groups such as Peter Paul & Mary or the Seekers and added a slight electric feel to produce a more contemporary folk-rock style. These bands typified the less-is-more musical ethic. A couple guitars, a drum kit and maybe an organ and that was all you needed. Listening to their efforts one is struck by the similar harmonies and song structures. This is not to demean their efforts; rather it's to identify the spirit more than anything else. And everything was going fine through the early sixties. You could write a short two and half minute song in the traditional style of verse, chorus, verse, chorus, middle eight, verse, chorus, chorus and fade out, and you know what? You even had a pretty good shot at getting played on your local radio station, because back then far more emphasis was placed on looking to homegrown talent. Then about 1965 everything began "shifting off the page" so to speak. One reason for the shift was the introduction of LSD. Psychiatrist Humphry Osmond coined the actual term "psychedelic" in 1957. It was while researching the therapeutic value of the drug LSD that he needed a word to describe its mind-altering affects. The roots of the term psychedelic refer to a "mind-expanding" or "mind-manifesting" experience. When the term "psychedelic" came into use among the sixties youth culture it's meaning was quickly extended to include not only the effects of the drug, but also the music, posters, lights, clothing, even lifestyle.

Writing in **High Art: A History of the Psychedelic Poster**, Ted Owen puts forth the notion that LSD basically provided a certain freedom to the arising youth culture. And in many respects the drug did provide a rallying point of experience for a group who were very much as Owen writes, *"disillusioned with the war in Vietnam, racism, class distinctions and parental and governmental controls."* In generations past there may have been some youth unhappy with their lot in life, but never before in history had so many shared the same ideals. As if to provide an outlet for the built up frustration with the events happening around them, the youth vented their frustration in experiencing new drugs such as LSD, and the new psychedelic music being created in conjunction with its use.

The musicians of the day, with "minds expanded" by various hallucinogens looked to other musical influences, typically in folk music, the blues, jazz, swing, jug-band, East Indian and even some country. LSD changed the way the Beatles wrote and that in turn changed the way everyone else wrote. It changed the way you played as well. Not everyone took LSD. As a matter of fact that was very much an issue. The Grateful Dead expected you to take it with them in much the same fashion that certain tribes share their wealth with befriended strangers. And they might be put out if you didn't. Which is ironic since "Pigpen" their founding keyboardist was more a connoisseur of the alcohol kind. He and Janis Joplin had the blues and alcohol in common. As a result, some in the psychedelic community considered them on "the other side". Hard drinkers like Janis Joplin found it difficult to feel a part of the crowd when alcohol was looked upon as passé. But that's another story.

The folk music influence was born out of the protest-folk era populated by individuals like Pete Seeger. This particular strain of folk music not only brought the acoustic element to the music but it also instilled the concept of expressing dissent in thought and words. This protest attitude was soon mixed with an even more revolutionary utopian ideal. In short, order the blues came to be the harder-edge electrified focus of the musicians. For influences, you could point to any number of individuals from Chuck Berry, John Lee Hooker, Lightnin' Hopkins and many others who'd found fame in Chicago. Psychedelic music did have other lesser influences. Some of the bands fit into the scene really well with elements of country or jug-band, some relied on even older turn of the century sounds, and many continued to rely on Beatles influenced harmonies, albeit modified to fit the growing musical consciousness. This is discussed in more detail later.

You can't begin to discuss psychedelic music without thinking of two places: San Francisco and London. It's like the whole psychedelic style started in those two cities first and almost simultaneously. While it's unfair to suggest that these two cities were the only place the psychedelic scene flourished, its unavoidable to talk about the genre

without acknowledging these two centres as the focal points. That being said, there were thriving psychedelic scenes in many parts of the United States including, Los Angeles home of the Doors, Detroit with its thriving Grande Ballroom, Austin, Texas birthplace of the 13th Floor Elevators and even for a brief time New York. Recent CD compilations have also demonstrated that there were thriving beat, garage and psychedelic music scenes in countries around the world and many of these diverse musical communities produced their own takes on psychedelic music. It is now possible to listen to psychedelic bands from Turkey, Sweden, Holland, Germany, Mexico, Japan and Brazil to name but a small group.

It's fair to ask why San Francisco?

It's easy to see how the "Swinging London" of the sixties was also home to a growing psychedelic scene, but it's fair to ask, Why San Francisco? After all, what was it about the "city by the Bay" that should cause it to be singled out? It doesn't take too much digging to discover that San Francisco has an historical reputation for attracting unique characters that lived in a variety of unorthodox lifestyles. And if it weren't for the fact that the Beat poets and authors of the late fifties had settled there and called it home, psychedelic music may not have had a chance, because it was that strange blend of attitudes that allowed for the musical freedom and expression to blossom. Bob Weir of the Grateful Dead, quoted in **Guitar Player** magazine said, *"San Francisco's always had a real liberal bent. Its anything-goes atmosphere goes way back to the Barbary Coast in the 1800s, and then the Bohemian scene started back in the '30s and came to flower in the late '40s and '50s. San Franciscans have always had a willingness to put up with ethnic diversity – and even embrace it. And we were direct descendants of all that."* It didn't hurt that the acid-king Owsley Stanley III made his home there. Family Dog founding member Luria Castell was interviewed by Ralph J. Gleason for the **San Francisco Chronicle** in October of 1966 where she said, *"San Francisco is a pleasure city."* And then she added the telling comment, *"San Francisco is the only city in the U.S. which can support a scene. There's enough talent here, especially in the folk field. We don't have any particular group to present, just a plan to get started, to acquire knowledge and information and have fun and a rock & roll sound. We have plans to improve the rock & roll sound."* Words that I'm sure were fuelled by the heady success of the Family Dog's first major dance-concerts.

In the years following World War Two individuals known as "Beats" made the coffee houses and bookstores part of their turf. These places generally thick with cigarette smoke, and the sound of jazz and poetry reading were breading grounds for those who chose to dress predominantly in black or dark colours. It was in this environment that revolutionary social thinking was explored. The primary leaders of this movement, if you could actually call them leaders were Allen Ginsberg, Jack Kerouac and William S. Burroughs. They set the tone with their highly politicised writing. Kerouac even provided the group's identity and ethic with his 1958 play **The Beat Generation**.

By the early to mid-sixties a younger generation was on the scene. The Beats described them as "trying to be hip" or "hippies" for short. The term was not meant to be complimentary. Still the younger crowd took the name "hippie" and wore it proudly. Unlike the Beats, hippies didn't wear black. In fact they went 180 degrees the other direction and tended to dress as outlandishly, colourfully or as expressively as they could. While the Beats chose the North Beach as their stomping grounds the hippies settled in a more working-class neighbourhood called Haight-Ashbury. And instead of jazz, which the Beats listened to, the music of the hippies was rock-n-roll. Additionally, the sheer number of youth worldwide allowed for organization as a community. There were never enough Beats to make much of an impact other than on the local scene. But this new youth movement was fed by thousands of "baby boomers" born shortly after World War Two. It was this sense of community that drove the hippie movement into the public consciousness and created a "counter-culture".

For many the whole idea of a counter-culture was born in San Francisco even though in actual fact it manifested itself in other areas as well. For our purposes, it's important to remember that San Francisco is the home of Berkeley. And Berkeley has a long history of counter-culture and revolutionary thinking. It is after all the home of the free speech movement. That being said the hard-core politicos found they had little in common with the drug-taking hippies. They always felt the pop scene was trivial and shallow, while the mellowed out musicians and hippies couldn't understand why the Berkeley crowd was always so uptight. It wasn't until the Human Be-In, the so-called gathering of the tribes that the two sides attempted to focus on a similar vision. But even after that the miss-trust remained. It's no wonder that Haight-Ashbury gave us the hippies while Berkley gave us the Yippies; two groups with the same general ideal in mind, a revolution, but with two very different methods of bringing it about.

Quicksilver Messenger Service guitarist Gary Duncan quoted in **I Want to Take You Higher**, describes the early San Francisco scene this way, *"What was really going on* *in San Francisco in the early sixties was a whole other thing most people don't know about. The underground scene was really a lot heavier than what was publicized and what people think happened…You'd go to say 1090 Page Street, open up the door and there'd be a fourteen bedroom Victorian house with something different going on in every room: painters in one room talking to each other, musicians in another room. It was really cool, and to all outward appearances, there was nothing happening. It was like a secret society…There was a while when the place was just totally free… As soon as the spotlight came on and there was money to be made, it went the way of all things."* The house referred to at 1090 Page Street was home to Big Brother and the Holding Company and it was in the basement that hundreds would crowd to watch the band rehearse and hone their chops before their ballroom appearances.

One of the elements that seemed to stimulate the music scene in San Francisco was the fact that it was a "band" or "ensemble" market. San Francisco has been the home to very few successful solo artists. Virtually every single major artist to arise out of the San Francisco scene has been part of a band. But more than that these were bands where every instrument played its part rather than the rhythm section providing a backdrop for standout soloists. That's not to say there weren't solo spots but again they were there as part of the musical style. It was a sound unlike New York where the rhythm section of drums and bass would dominate, or a sound like L.A. where session players would provide strings or brass to the latest pop songs. In San Francisco it was all about the band. This made it easy for many of varying degrees of skill to merge and create a sound where the sum of the parts exceeded the individual efforts. It was this environment that encouraged participation allowing the music scene to flourish. In addition to the above, there were plenty of places to play regularly. At first it was the many free events or benefits. You have to remember that all of the bands were from the community and were motivated to participate in activities that directly affected their neighbourhoods. Talking to those who were there, they all remember how a week couldn't go by without a free benefit or dance in the park for some cause. The burgeoning number of halls soon superseded this, and the many ballrooms took over staging that were originally called "dance-concerts" every weekend. This live, participatory environment was very forgiving to the musician's lack of technical ability. It wasn't until the advent of the recording contracts that many of the bands found themselves wanting. But that would come for those who survived.

There is no question drugs were instrumental in creating the psychedelic scene of the sixties. While many in the San Francisco community were smoking marijuana, which was inherited from the Beat community of the late fifties, the drug of choice for the "enlightened" sixties was LSD. Lysergic acid diathylamide or "acid" for short was seen as the vehicle through which the new hippie consciousness was best achieved. This hallucinogenic drug produced very different affects from marijuana, having more in common with ancient natural substances that have been used for centuries by various tribes around the world. It's been said that LSD is like an amplifier for the nervous system. It turns on every single nerve and allows for things to be seen, heard, felt and even thought that without it we're incapable of. With it, some said you could see the aura of neon that is totally invisible to regular sight. You could hear frequencies the non-acid ear was deaf too. We've all heard the stories about arms looking like rubber, or rooms changing perspective like a living-vertigo. Small insignificant events take on apocalyptic dimensions. LSD, among other things seemed to slow down the passage of time making it shift and bend. Anyone on a high would hear music more as a flow of tones as opposed to hearing specific notes or events of the musical piece. LSD could even make time stand still, and the right music simply enhanced the euphoric state-of-mind as the listener was now able to hear the rich musical panorama in microscopic detail. Nothing escaped...it was sensory overload. And therein was the danger. Not all trips were pleasurable and happy. George Harrison relates the story of when he and John Lennon were given their first dose of this new drug. Harrison's dentist administered it to them in their tea. After consuming it the group went to a night-club and it was in the ride in the elevator that the powerful hallucinogen started to have it's effect. As George relates the tale, the tiny and insignificant red light of the elevator suddenly became a giant all consuming fire, and when the doors of the elevator opened, the club goers were treated to the sight of George, John, the dentist and their partners all screaming and clamouring to escape the fiery flames of hell. Imagine what you could write under that influence. Well the Beatles went on to learn and so did many in the San Francisco music community.

The ties to the drug-culture are well documented. It was a period of experimentation with much more than just music and sowed the seeds for many aspects of today's music scene. Many of the sixties dance-concerts were all-night affairs, especially in England, and were events flooded with pulsating lights, everyone dancing with everyone else, and more than a little drug use. A scene not at all unfamiliar to today's Rave culture.

In summation it's also worth pointing how influential San Francisco really was on music in general. In his book **San Francisco Rock**, Jack McDonough lists a startling number of firsts including; higher royalty rates paid to the artists based on minutes-per-side rather than songs-per- side and more studio and artwork control. Previous to this time artists were paid royalties based on the number of songs they recorded. Hence most LPs contained approximately 10 or 12 songs five or six per side. But when the Grateful Dead began creating longer compositions limiting the number of actual songs that could fit on an album, they fought for compensation based on the number of actual minutes of music. In a short time they won their case, and bands, especially those inclined to writing longer compositions have benefited ever since. San Francisco was the birthplace of underground FM radio, a format that spread across the United States and eventually Canada. This new style of radio broke from the Top 40 convention of playing only a limited number of pop hits to playing a wide variety of longer rock and pop music. Sadly it soon was co-opted by the industry and eventually converted back into nothing more than glorified jukeboxes with the advent of the official AOR (Album Oriented Rock) formats. San Francisco, home to facilities like the Fillmore and the Avalon quickly set the standard for full-stage production of lights and sound for rock shows. This encouraged other facilities and bands to take more interest and control in the overall presentation of their live performances. On the recording front it was home to the first computerized recording studio. Rock music journalism was given credibility with the birth of **Rolling Stone** in November of 1967. And let's not forget that San Francisco was the birthplace for the new style concert poster that has gone on to influence graphic arts in all areas. These are just a few of the more influential areas where San Francisco has more than played its part in the creation of the psychedelic music scene.

The Trip Overview:

The history of this musical period has been well documented in a number of books, many of which are listed in the back of this volume. To provide some sense of chronology, I've created a detailed day-by-day timeline outlining many of the key events of the psychedelic period of 1965 through to 1971. The time-line covers not only the music, but also certain key political or social events that shaped the day. I've always found it fascinating to look at time in this manner. To be able to select certain key events and see what else was happening provides a unique perspective. The chronology appears in it's own section of this book. But it might be good to provide the brief overview here.

To start at the beginning we travel back to June 1965 to a place called the Red Dog Saloon and a band called the Charlatans whose music was a mixture of folk, blues and jug-band. This San Francisco group started by George Hunter caught wind of a musical opportunity in Virginia City, a mere three hours drive from the Bay. Hunter had left Los Angeles in 1962 and had settled in Haight-Ashbury and started attending design classes at California State University although he never actually registered. While there he gained a reputation for always being on the edge of fashion and street trends. He was a self-appointed trendsetter and he was also into an art nouveau "headspace". Some have said he was actually the first hippie, although that may be a bit of stretch. In the wake of the British Invasion, perhaps it was only a matter of time before he put together a band. Everybody else was. Hunter teamed up with Mike Ferguson who was running San Francisco's first head shop called the Magic Theatre For Mad Men Only. The two of them along with Dan Hicks, Mike Wilhelm and Richie Olsen initially called their group George and the Mainliners, but soon changed the name to the Charlatans.

The Red Dog Saloon had recently been refurbished to wild-west standards and now resembled a typical B-movie saloon. There, high on acid, they auditioned and got the gig. Dressed in their finest western gear they not only fit the look but their rag-tag playing style even added to the rough and tumble feel of the place. In fact, it's been said the band was hired more for their appearance than their musicianship. Now truth be told, none of these individual elements spoke to the psychedelic genre, however it was a combination of them all mixed with the LSD everyone was taking that created the convergence. Hunter and Ferguson even drew up the poster used to promote their appearance, and that too had its impact on the coming psychedelic style. As time went on these posters became an important promotional and social tool. Radio and TV was too expensive and not many in the sub-culture were reading the newspaper, but since they all lived in the near vicinity and prowled the streets, posters were a cheap and economical way of getting the message out. These posters soon set the tone for the whole psychedelic scene. Wildly colourful, nearly impossible to read in some cases, they advertised coming bands in their own trippy style. Bill Graham tells the story of how early in the Fillmore days he would be out putting up posters on his scooter, and as he looked back down the road, he saw people taking them carefully off the

telephone poles to add to their collection. If the posters were being collected so quickly he knew then he was on to something.

The adventure at the Red Dog Saloon lasted only a little more than two months, but the Charlatans returned to San Francisco as heroes of a new scene. This creative-spark combined with the growing psychedelic influence in the Beatles music as well as the combining of folk and rock in the sound of the Byrds was all it took to start the ball rolling. As word of the Charlatan's success spread other bands formed. The Grateful Dead, Big Brother and the Holding Company, the Great Society, Quicksilver Messenger Service, the Jefferson Airplane, Country Joe and the Fish and others were taking over from the more acoustic British Invasion sounding bands of the earlier era. Bands like the Beau Brummels, and others who had actually made it to vinyl on Autumn Records, a label started by two San Francisco disc jockeys, one being Tom Donahue. The new bands for the most part were into experimenting, not only with drugs, but with combining musical styles as well. They took what had gone before, added to it and created something new. For many it was a concerted effort to not sound like the all those other bands of the British Invasion. This new musical sound was borne out of a live environment with song structure being a much looser element, allowing compositions to become extended jam sessions designed to flow with the evening's activities.

The same month the Charlatans made their appearance at the Red Dog, Britain got it's first taste of psychedelia with the Poets Of The World/Poets Of Our Time reading at the Royal Albert Hall, London. Some 7000 early styled flower children, many high on LSD were in attendance to hear readings from 18 leading counter-culture poets including Allen Ginsberg, Lawrence Ferlinghetti and Gregory Corso. This event sent shock waves through the British underground and became a rallying cry for the new psychedelic scene. Soon, through the efforts of individuals like Michael Hollingshead, LSD was readily available through coffee shops and bookstores like Indica Books. It was Hollingshead who had first introduced LSD to Timothy Leary and he returned to his homeland on a mission. In possession of copies of **The Psychedelic Experience**, **The Psychedelic Reader** and loads of LSD, Hollingshead's mission was to "turn-on" as many of his countrymen as possible, which he proceeded to do from his newly opened World Psychedelic Centre. Remember LSD was still considered legal, with no law on the books to prohibit its use. It wasn't long before British bands began exchanging their more subdued shirts, ties and suits for the more colourful psychedelic fashions and changing their musical approach as well.

The Grateful Dead, who got their start under the name the Warlocks, were soon playing at a variety of Acid Tests put on by Ken Kesey and the Merry Pranksters.

These tests began in 1965 in the San Francisco area and were staged-events to try and get as many people high on LSD as possible. The Prankster's brightly painted bus would roll into a community, posters would be up to advertise the event and the people gathered for an evening of tripping, lights, readings, music and general zaniness. The Grateful Dead were quickly adopted as the resident travelling acid band. On a more traditional note, Marty Balin convinced some buddies to buy an old pizza joint on Fillmore Street, together they created one of the first official San Francisco psychedelic clubs called the Matrix. This club opened in August of 1965, a mere two months after the Charlatans opened the Red Dog Saloon. The room was small, seating just over 100 but it was an opportunity for his new band, the Jefferson Airplane to play on a regular basis. Soon the club was booking everyone from Big Brother to the Doors.

Unlike San Francisco, which tended to be all-scene and no-hit songs or London which was equal parts scene and hit songs, Los Angeles was just about hits with no real psychedelic scene to speak of. 1965 in Los Angeles was very different from what was happening in the Bay area. The recording industry was firmly established with any number of movers and shakers. Clubs began turning up like the Action, the Trip, the Troubadour, and perhaps most importantly the Whisky A-Go-Go patterned after the French club of the same name. Interestingly, the common connection here was the Byrds who had already made an early appearance in San Francisco at the Peppermint Tree club in 1965. The Byrds, with their synthesized blend of folk and rock had quite an effect on the recording industry in Los Angeles. This was a musical style that had truly taken a British Invasion sound and moulded into something new again. But then while the Byrds were on tour in Britain, Los Angeles being the town it was, quickly looked elsewhere and turned to Sonny and Cher and the Beach Boys who were soon working on **Pet Sounds** influenced by the easy access to pot and LSD. This was also the year that the Mothers of Invention made their presence known by taking shots at the establishment with their unique satirical approach.

The San Francisco "ballroom" era was not far off. In fact, it was around this same time that Chet Helms, who'd originally come to San Francisco from Texas with Janis Joplin in 1963, began charging fifty cents a head for people to attend impromptu jam sessions with Big Brother and the Holding Company in the basement ballroom of an old Victorian mansion at 1090 Page Street. This was the very first of the San Francisco ballrooms. The house was actually managed by Peter Albin of Big Brother and he rented the 20 rooms to all sorts of musicians, artists and transients. As word spread in the community of Haight-Ashbury more and more people began filling the ballroom, which held about 300 people at best. Helms saw the need to expand. In attendance at many of these formative shows was a group of individuals who lived on Pine Street as a communal group called the Family Dog. Why they choose the name Family Dog is the stuff of legend. Some say it was because they were living in a place called the Dog House managed by light show pioneer Bill Ham, some say it was simply because there were so many canines around the place, and still others make reference to the fact that one member's dog had recently been run over. Whatever the true story, the name seemed somehow fittingly appropriate for the times. The key players were Luria Castell (a local political activist), Ellen Harmon (an ex-Red Dog Saloon employee),

Alton Kelley (who helped build the Red Dog Saloon) and Jack Towle. They along with Helms saw an opportunity to stage larger events and set about making that happen. The Family Dog borrowed money and staged their first large scale event on October 16th, 1965 at the Longshoremen's Hall on Fishermen's Wharf. It was called "A Tribute to Doctor Strange" and featured the Jefferson Airplane, the Great Society and the Charlatans plus all sorts of other artistic goings on. It was a smashing success. More than anything this first Family Dog event provided the opportunity for all the pockets of budding counter-culture bohemians to congregate in one spot and realize they were part of something bigger. It was an event staged at perfectly the right time and the right place. Ralph Gleason later wrote in his book from the era **The Jefferson Airplane and the San Francisco Sound** that it was like going to a Halloween party. Everyone was dressed like they were going to a costume party. The Family Dog was always interested in attaching names to their dances so the next two events carried on the idea with, "A Tribute to Sparkle Plenty" featuring the Lovin' Spoonful and "A Tribute to Ming the Merciless" with Frank Zappa and the Mothers of Invention as the headliner.

Around this same time transplanted New Yorker Bill Graham who was managing the San Francisco Mime Troupe ran into some legal issues, which resulted in the leader of the Mime Troupe being arrested. Graham ever the showman struck on the idea of having a dance-concert appeal to raise legal funds. Graham eventually ran three appeal shows, the first of which occurred on the same night as the Family Dog's third event, the "Tribute to Ming the Merciless". Graham's shows were also a huge success. Once again, it was the right type of event occurring at the right time in history. Over this short period of three weeks the original leaders of the Family Dog had pretty much faded from the scene leaving everything in the hands of Chet Helms and Alton Kelley who had been doing the posters for each show. Helms and Graham agreed to work together, with Helms providing the musical talent, Graham providing the Fillmore auditorium and organization. It seemed like a good idea, but after only two shows their conflicting styles clashed head-on. The two had a major falling out after the performance of the Paul Butterfield Blues Band. Helms had booked the show and was impressed with the San Francisco response. So much so he planned to book the Butterfield Blues Band for more San Francisco shows. Graham, who'd never been into rock & roll, was also impressed with the band, and even more impressed with the ticket sales. Never one to miss an opportunity, Graham woke up at dawn the next day to contact the band's manager, Albert Grossman in New York and worked out a deal for all future San Francisco performances to be handled exclusively by Graham. Helms ever the idealistic hippie was shocked that Graham would go behind his back and do such a thing. Graham for his part explained it away by simply saying that to stay in business you have to get up early, and he liked getting up early. In any case the two worked together for one more show before going their separate ways.

Meanwhile in London England, they were going through their own musical rethink. Word was getting back to them of the psychedelic happenings in San Francisco and there was a concerted effort to mirror or incorporate what was happening in America in the new British underground music scene. British poster artist, Nigel Weymouth explains, "*Suddenly, things like Fellini and the Beatles and the Stones and pop art all came busting out. There was a sort of liberation and idealism. It was pretty naïve by today's standards, of course, but at the time we thought we were going to change the world. And this was how we illustrated it. We designed the clothes and put up the posters and left it to the rock stars to make the music."* With the prominence of the Beatles, the English media was monitoring their every move. And in a small country that's not too difficult. So when it was reported the Beatles had dropped acid, the multi-coloured light bulb went on all over the musical landscape. Soon bands across the country formed with the sole mission of taking the already well-established English musical style and stretching it in directions not yet seen. Fashion combined with attitude. Mary Quant created the mini-skirt, which in its own way provided young girls the opportunity to show their independence and rebellion against the old styles. Unless the older styles were, say Edwardian, then that was cool. Clubs that had been the homes of rockabilly or R&B saw the new opportunity and quickly began booking the new psychedelic bands. In March of 1966, the London Free School was created as a counter-culture home base for change. Funding for the school came from a series of performances by Pink Floyd at All Saints Church Hall in Powis Gardens. It was during these dances that Pink Floyd's colour and sound experimentation originated. In late 1966 the London underground paper the **International Times**, **IT** for short, had a huge launch party at the famous London Roundhouse featuring the cream of the crop of London's burgeoning psychedelic scene. Bands like Soft Machine, Arthur Brown and Pink Floyd performed to a crowd of 2500 and for many it was their introduction to a rudimentary psychedelic light show which the Floyd were now carrying with them to their live performances. This all night rave would not be the last time this cold and dank facility was used in the services of rock music.

SUBSCRIBE TO IT !

NAME. . . . .

ADDRESS . . . .

RATES FOR 1 YEAR'S SUBSCRIPTION
UK . . . . £3.0.0d.   OVERSEAS SURFACE £3.0.0.
US AIR . . . £9.0.0d.   OTHER AIR RATES ON
                                    APPLICATION

Send cheque or postal order
to IT, 27 Endell St., London WC2

AN AD FOR INTERNATIONAL TIMES NEWSPAPER

Following up on the success of the **IT** launch party, Sunday afternoons opened up at London's famed Marquee Club and impromptu happenings called the Spontaneous Underground were staged. These mostly unstructured events played host to poets, artists, light shows, films, crafts, people hanging around and of course the bands. Pink Floyd had settled in as the house band, sharing some weekends with another new outfit called the Soft Machine. Looking back now, there were only five of these Spontaneous Underground events with never more than fifty people in attendance, but their impact was far reaching. These non-alcoholic styled affairs were quickly adopted by other clubs; the most-trendy underground spot soon became UFO. Clubs such as UFO were doing something revolutionary. Not only were they not serving alcohol, but they were providing a place for many of the new underground bands to perform away from the traditional constraints of the pop clubs. In these new underground clubs the bands may have played two sets but they were usually songs all joined together with few gaps, which is kind of unheard of now other than at rave shows, but then that's what these were. Soon Pink Floyd and Soft Machine, both psychedelic bands on the fringe of mainstream at the time were installed as house-bands at UFO.

The Psychedelic Shop opened in January 1966 at 1535 Haight Street in the Haight-Ashbury. Run by brothers Ron and Jay Thelin, sons of a Woolworth's store manager, the Psychedelic Shop in a short time became the centre of the hippie universe in San Francisco. The store sold books, records, head supplies, posters and basically any other odds and ends that suited the hippie lifestyle. It not only sold all the paraphernalia but was also the place to meet, post messages on the community bulletin board and generally "be". In the back was a meditation room for interested parties to calmly chill out, and in the front window the brothers installed three theatre seats for anyone to sit and look out at the world on Haight Street. Quoted in Gene Anthony's **Summer of Love**, Ron Thelin said, *"Our window was a live display of whoever was sitting there looking out at the people looking in on them. It blew a lot of minds. Our display was a kind of mirror image of the street action outside."* Not long after it's opening, the Thelin brothers became involved with the **Oracle**, Haight-Ashbury's very own news flyer. The flyer was created by Allen Cohen and acid-evangelist Michael Bowen as the voice of the hippie or counter-culture community growing in the Haight-Ashbury. While it focused on issues the **Oracle** was not like the more politicised **Berkeley Barb**, in that it never dealt with day-to-day matters choosing instead to deal with news matters from a more philosophical angle. The **Oracle** also broke new ground in both content and layout, as each of the 12 issues produced grew more and more psychedelic, sometimes reflecting the art of the concert poster scene. Around the same time Dr. David Smith opened the Haight-Ashbury Free Clinic, primarily to deal with the growing number of acid casualties. It was a safe haven for those needing help, and it was always busy. The hippie's based on shear numbers were coming together as a community for better and for worse.

The next significant event that drew the Haight-Ashbury community together took place the weekend of January 21st – 23rd 1966 and was called the Trips Festival. This three-day extravaganza was initially suggested by Ken Kesey and was staged once again at the Longshoremen's Hall. It not only featured Kesey's Acid Test but also was a communal gathering of all things avant-garde and psychedelic, a mixture of arts and music. For example, besides the many people wandering the hall dressed in wild costumes there was a psychedelic store selling books, there were Trips Festival t-shirts and all sorts of obscure publications. At least five movie screens were hung on the walls showing old movies and short films of the most unusual kind. Over all this were large splashes of coloured lights. In addition to those lights there were strobes and even traffic lights blinking away. On stage the music for the event was provided by none other than the Grateful Dead and Big Brother and the Holding Company. Bill Graham was asked to run the event and it was an opportunity for him to find out first hand what the growing scene was all about. In amidst all the psychedelic pandemonium many remember seeing Graham flit about with his trusty clipboard trying to keep everything under control. The key to the Trip's Festival success was that everyone participated. Like the previous Acid Tests and various benefits the audience became a part of the activities and if they participated they assured themselves of having a great time.

Suitably impressed, it was two weeks later that Bill Graham took all he had learned from the earlier Trips Festival and staged his first dance-concert at the Fillmore appropriately entitled the "Sights and Sounds of the Trips Festival" featuring the Jefferson Airplane. And true to form the show featured the music, the lights and even the right amount of atmosphere. More to the point Graham was able to capture all the elements and package them in a way that worked. Graham was able to reproduce the psychedelic euphoria in a more manageable fashion. More than one person has credited him with the ability to make things work. The growing hippie community seemed to love it as they packed the Fillmore every weekend.

Following his distasteful experience sharing a ballroom with Bill Graham, Chet Helms opted to go it alone and opened the Avalon Ballroom to run in direct competition to the Fillmore. Both ballrooms had great acoustics, permanent light show facilities and room for roughly a thousand paying customers. The Avalon was always seen as the true hippie ballroom, it was considered by many the place to be and tended to stick to more traditional rock and blues line-ups. In fact, it was the place many of the bands preferred to play. The Fillmore on the other hand was a tight ship run by Graham and he paid well. Graham, who personally preferred Latin and salsa music, felt it was a mission to expose his audiences to new musical styles and it was this sense of mission that caused him to create some very unique line-ups. Quoted in **Billboard** magazine in April of 1967 Graham explained his booking philosophy, *"Blues groups should be here. You don't just give them what they want, but you go beyond that by giving them what you think they might like."* Interviewed in **Exposure** magazine in 1988 Graham went on to explain, *"When we began the sixties, we could prepare a bill like a well rounded meal. Along with a rock headliner, we'd put a side order of blues or jazz on the menu – a B.B. King or Howlin' Wolf. Or we'd co-bill the Grateful Dead with Miles Davis. It was a righteous thing to do. It was educating the audience."* The Avalon and Fillmore plus other facilities such as the Continental, Winterland, California Hall, Carousel Ballroom, Longshoremen's Hall etc. provided ample opportunity for bands to find places to play and build the local music scene. It wasn't long before the growing acid-rock community overtook the folk scene.

Across North America bands were springing up in garages like mushrooms to create their own mutated versions of the British Invasion sound. These three or four piece combos consisting of usually a guitar or two, bass and drums and just perhaps a small organ created a sound that was raw, simple, energetic, electric, loud, and hopelessly naïve. Not quite psychedelizised, these groups gave birth to the first "punk" or "garage-band" era. In short order many of these bands began to feel the effects of the growing psychedelic movement either due to the spreading use of LSD or simply hearing the musical results. The bands most of us remember are those that came from Los Angeles; the Seeds, the Standells, the Chocolate Watch Band, the Leaves, Music Machine, the Knickerbockers and Love. Love founder, Arthur Lee had seen the Byrds in early 1965 and knew from that moment what direction he wanted to take, adding a little Rolling Stone feel to the folk-rock feel of the Byrds all blended together with a heavy dose of the growing psychedelic sounds. For a variety of reasons, Love's two albums have become highly prized mementoes of the psychedelic era, but the band never made it. Perhaps in a more nurturing environment like San Francisco Love could have been huge, but as author Greg Shaw has noted, *"There were great punk records made in LA but the bands were never able to free themselves from the presence of the industry. There was always one eye on the possibility of making money from this."* It was this mercenary aspect of the music business that offended those in San Francisco the most. They were not about hits. In 1966 they were about the scene.

The psychedelic rock ballroom concept, which was born in San Francisco, soon spread to other cities. The ballrooms, many of which had been built in the '30s or '40s were originally used for ballroom dancing, hence the name. Many had been put to other uses, others remained empty until the mid sixties where they were seen as the perfect venue, size wise to stage psychedelic dance-concerts. They were a facility whose use was reborn of a new age. Ralph Gleason offers this assessment, *"The reason the ballroom scene could flourish in San Francisco was that urban renewal had not yet taken hold. San Francisco was still lingering on the edge of the nineteenth century and the city was full of old buildings."* In time however most would fall to the wrecking ball.

Many saw what was happening the Bay area. Russ Gibb had visited San Francisco during the summer of 1966 and even attended a few events at the Avalon Ballroom. He liked what he saw. He also saw an opportunity. Returning to Detroit Gibb opened up the Grande Ballroom in the Fall of 1966 and patterned it after what he saw happening in San Francisco. Of all the psychedelic operations outside of the Bay area, his was the one that most closely resembled the San Francisco scene. And while the bands may not have been as strong or have as much depth, he more than made up for it in the look of the posters. Gibb's operation more than most mirrored the West Coast psychedelic scene and became a regular part of the underground rock circuit. In Boston Ray Riepen opened up the Boston Tea Party, a smaller club seating only about 750, but it became the leading underground spot for Bostonians.

The blossoming poster scene benefited from the number of venues as well. Given the fact that the music scene in San Francisco was very much a street level affair, people walked, talked and stopped to read the posters of upcoming events. Given the number of venues it was possible to see upwards of five or six new posters every weekend, with each artist attempting to outdo the other. With each attempt the psychedelic posters became more and more outlandish and more and more visually descriptive of what was happening in San Francisco. But while the posters epitomized what was happening with the youth movement specifically, there was much more to it than that. In general everywhere you looked the artistic temperament was changing. It wasn't just the posters or the music it was deeper than that. Ted Owen writing in **High Art** about the mood of the day summed it up this way, *"To the counterculture of the 1960s, Art Nouveau became a vehicle through which the participants could express their new-found freedoms. Fashions became fluid and flowing, hair was worn long and dresses, such as those designed for Biba by Barbara Hulanicki, imitated early* *twentieth century styles. Art Nouveau opulence and decadence fitted ideally with the tastes of the Flower Children of the 1960s."*

In England a vibrant and energetic psychedelic music club scene was shaping up with places such as the already mentioned UFO, the Marquee Club, Middle Earth and other smaller clubs. American Joe Boyd who'd arrived in London in 1965 to open a branch office for Elektra records (home of the Doors etc) recalls, *"The first night of UFO was December 23rd, 1966 and in three months the club went from being non-existent to being the club that defined which groups were hot, which groups would go down well on the university concert circuit; by spring 1967, Pink Floyd was already on the record charts."* In less than a year the psychedelic genre had become part of the mainstream pop music industry in Britain.

1967 and the Summer of Love

As 1967 dawned San Francisco played host to the first Human Be-In. This event was a gathering of some 10 - 20,000 individuals in peaceful co-existence on a warm January day. It was a beautiful scene that inspired the community to believe nothing was impossible if you put your mind to it. The word had been spread throughout the Bay area that this "gathering of the tribes" would take place at the Golden Gate Park and while the event was scheduled to begin at 1pm, people began arriving in the early morning hours and by mid-day the park was packed. The event featured a variety of bands, poets and artists all gathered to send a peaceful message of coexistence. This message of harmony was directed at both the Haight-Ashbury hippies and the more radical Berkeley group. In simple terms the Berkeley crowd felt the hippies were too superficial, to interested in just taking drugs and listening to music, while the Haight-Ashbury group were nervous of the radical political stance taken by the Berkeley crowd. Both groups distrusted the other and while the day ended well the hoped for union never came about. All in attendance were treated to poetry readings from the likes of Michael McClure, Alan Ginsberg and Gary Snyder along with the music of all the popular local bands such as the Grateful Dead, Quicksilver Messenger Service, Big Brother and Jefferson Airplane. Word of the success of the Human Be-In spread across the country like wildfire, and soon that word touched down in counter-culture communities on other continents overseas. San Francisco and Haight-Ashbury became a magnet to all those looking for a different lifestyle or hope of change in their lives.

In England the police were cracking down, raiding the offices of the **International Times** removing every stitch of paper in hopes of finding something incriminating. The raid led to an appeal-benefit billed as the 14 Hour Technicolor Dream, an event similar to the Mime Troupe appeals staged in San Francisco. The all-night rave was held in April 1967 at the Alexandra Palace featuring a veritable who's who of the psychedelic music scene. Inside the cavernous building two stages were erected, one at either end along with the largest array of lights and sound system yet seen in

14 Hour TECHNICOLOR DREAM
8 pm Saturday APRIL 29 onwards
ALEXANDRA PALACE N 22

Alexis Korner* Alex Harvey* Creation* Charlie Browns
Clowns* Champion Jack Dupree* Denny Laine* Gary
Farr* Graham Bond* Ginger Johnson* Jacobs Ladder
Construction Co* Move* One One Seven* Pink Floyd*
Poetry Band* Purple Gang* Pretty Things* Pete Townshend
Poison Bellows* Soft Machine* Sun Trolley* Social Deviants
Stalkers* Utterly Incredible Too Long Ago Sometimes

INTERNATIONAL TIMES

£1 advance tickets only

FROM HIP SOURCES & BOOK SHOPS

Shouting at People* Young Tradition* Lincoln Folk Group*
Noel Murphy* Dave Russell* Christopher Logue* Barry
Fantoni* Ron Geesin* Mike Horovitz* Alex Trocchi* Mike
Kemshall* Yoko Ono* Binder Edwards & Vaughn* 26Kingly
St* Robert Randall* love from Allen Ginsberg* Simon
Vinkenoog* Jean Jacques Lebel* Andy Warhol* The Mothers
of Invention* The Velvet Underground* and famous popstars
who cant be mentioned for contractual reasons* guess who*

Britain. Close to 10,000 people showed up including John Lennon and Paul McCartney. For many the event was the climax of the growing underground scene.

In amongst everything else going on in Los Angeles there were a number of interesting psychedelic things happening. The Beach Boys, in particular Brian Wilson was working on psychedelic songs such as "Good Vibrations" and "Heroes and Villains" both of which were going to be a part of the ill fated **Smile** project. The Byrds and Love were playing weeklong stints at local clubs and other bands such as the Association, the Electric Prunes, Peanut Butter Conspiracy, West Coast Pop Art Experimental Band, Kaleidoscope and Strawberry Alarm Clock came along for the ride. The Strawberry Alarm Clock even provided a number one hit with "Incense and Peppermints". Nineteen sixty-seven was the year that the Monkees hit it big on television and in their own way spread the look and feel of psychedelia to millions of teenyboppers across North America. And clubs like the Whisky A Go Go, Brave New World and the Kaleidoscope with its circular revolving stage provided the opportunity for live gigs. The Doors and the Monterey Pop Festival were not far off.

The Canadian Psychedelic Scene

Meanwhile in Canada the roots of the psychedelic scene were growing out of a strong and vibrant folk-music scene most notably in the community of Yorkville located in Toronto, Ontario and Vancouver, British Columbia. Yorkville, with its dozens of musical coffee houses and folk clubs was the first to see the seeds of the counter-culture to take root. Bands such as the Ugly Ducklings, Three's A Crowd, the Cryin' Shames, the Paupers all were involved in a healthy local and live music scene. Within months individuals from surrounding communities descended on Yorkville. Looking to greener pastures Neil Young loaded up his 1953 Pontiac Hearse and moved to Los Angeles in 1966 with fellow Canadian Bruce Palmer to become two-fifths of Buffalo Springfield. They soon hit the charts with the classic summer anthem *For What It's*

Worth. Then there was John Kay and the band Sparrow who also made the trek West and evolved into Steppenwolf. The Canadian influence was also felt in Denny Doherty of the Mamas and the Papas, Zal Yanovsky in the Lovin' Spoonful, and the Pauper's Brad Campbell who helped form Janis Joplin's Full Tilt Boogie Band just to name a few.

However it was the music scene in Vancouver that most closely resembled what was happening in San Francisco. Once again it was a combination of the music, posters, clubs, light shows and general West Coast attitude that contributed to this. Clubs such as the Afterthought and Retinal Circus not only regularly featured local psychedelic acts such as the Collectors, My Indole Ring, Painted Ship, Mother Tucker's Yellow Duck and a host of others, but they also showcased performances from many of the Bay area bands including, the Grateful Dead, Country Joe and the Fish, Steve Miller Blues Band and the Jefferson Airplane.

In early 1967 Chet Helms traveled overseas to take a look at the burgeoning psychedelic scene in London. He also had a thought of extending his empire and opening up an Avalon Ballroom in the swinging city. It never came together and Helms returned home. But Helms was not the first from the San Francisco scene to visit London. That distinction lies with light show pioneer Ray Anderson of the Holy See. Anderson's visit in January of 1966 saw the London Underground's introduction to the classic San Francisco "liquid light" show. Anderson was asked to provide the lights for "The Million Volt Rave" at the Roundhouse. Upon entering the facility Anderson was struck by it's cold, bleakness. There wasn't an inch of reflective white-space on which to shine a light show. He and his crew frantically searched London for appropriate material that was available in sufficient quantity. After much scrambling they settled on sheets of vinyl, similar to that used for waterbed lining. The crew lined the Roundhouse with the plastic and even though the light set up was grossly under illuminated, they introduced a true San Francisco light show to London's underground community.

While the overseas Family Dog idea never came about Helms did open a second ballroom under the Family Dog name in Denver later in the year. This dance hall was plagued with problems from the very beginning, and was targeted by the authorities as an unwanted facility. It eventually closed before the year was out. The Denver experiment ended up costing a lot of money and in the end the Family Dog lost $85,000. Meanwhile, bands in both the Avalon and the Fillmore played regularly and soon record companies started eyeing them up. Festivals provided ample opportunity to A&R guys to see the talent at work in a live environment and sample the sounds.

As the summer of 1967 approached all was not rosy in Los Angeles. For one thing, the Byrds were starting to fall apart. David Crosby was spending more time with Stephen Stills and Buffalo Springfield than with his own band. For its part Buffalo Springfield was having its own ego battles. Neil Young decided for the sake of his metal health he needed to go off on his own. Rumours of David Crosby's rampant drug use abounded and fuel was added to the fire as he began spending more and more time in San Francisco jamming with the bands in Haight-Ashbury. At the same time

Crosby more than most understood the fundamental difference between Los Angeles and San Francisco. The attitude is best described by writer Carl Gottlieb himself a former member of the satirical troupe the Committee quoted in **Waiting For the Sun**, *"You would have to say that San Francisco had the jump on L.A. in terms of drugs and Psychedelia. Up in San Francisco, we felt quite superior because we were actually living it. In L.A., then as now, people dressed up and acted it out."* Added to this was a distinct lack of "political-engagement" in Los Angeles, and it's easy to see why the hippies in the Bay area held Los Angeles in such low esteem. It was a city that never seemed real to them. But there were efforts to change that.

The Monterey Pop Festival

In 1967 the Beatles released three of their most psychedelic singles; in February *I Am the Walrus*, in July *Baby You're a Rich Man*, and in November *Strawberry Fields Forever*. This was also the year labelled as the "Summer of Love", and two of the Beatles, Paul and George made a special point of visiting San Francisco. Then at the beginning of June the Beatles released an album that forever changed the face of pop and rock music, **Sgt. Pepper's Lonely Hearts Club Band**. In many respects **Sgt. Pepper** and the follow-up **Magical Mystery Tour** were the culmination of the Beatles travels into the world of psychedelia.

One of the most significant events, as far the psychedelic music scene was concerned was the Monterey International Pop Festival, which was staged in an attempt to bring the divergent musical scenes of San Francisco, Los Angeles and London all together. Lou Adler and John Phillips of the Mama and the Papa's eventually put the festival together. Needless to say the Haight-Ashbury crowd who'd always considered Los Angeles as a "synthetic" scene viewed the event with more than a little suspicion. Leading up to the weekend the event was fraught with planning difficulties. At first the San Francisco bands didn't want to sign away the royalties for the movie being shot, then one-by-one they acquiesced. The lone holdout was the Grateful Dead and as a result they never appeared in the finished film. Following a powerhouse performance Janis Joplin and Big Brother were signed to Columbia Records. Manager Albert Grossman realizing the benefits of having Joplin included in the film, and negotiated with the promoters to schedule Janis and Big Brother for a second performance the next day. That second performance was filmed and included in the final document. From a business perspective, the Monterey Pop Festival was an extremely successful event and brought about a number significant record deals for the Haight-Ashbury bands. Most notably, Janis Joplin and Big Brother and the Electric Flag who were snapped up by Columbia, and Steve Miller Blues Band, and Quicksilver Messenger Service who were shortly thereafter signed to Capitol. Already out there with a disc, was the Jefferson Airplane who had signed with RCA in late 1966 getting $25,000 up-front, an unheard of sum for a new rock band. Soon others followed. Steve Miller set the music business on notice when they signed a record deal consisting of a $50,000 advance plus bonuses. In total the deal amounted to $750,000, a staggering amount of money for 1967. The Quicksilver Messenger Service recording deal included a $40,000 advance. And this was just the start. The psychedelic scene had started to go mainstream.

Unfortunately what few realised was that it was also the beginning of the end for the psychedelic cultural phenomenon. Barney Hoskyn's writing in **Waiting For the Sun** correctly points out that *"What Monterey really represented was the transition from Pop to Rock – from toe-tapping teen discothèque music to FM Art for young adults."* In the end there was perhaps good reason for the suspicion felt by the San Francisco psychedelic scene. Fred Goodman writing in **Mansion On The Hill** summed it up this way, *"The Monterey Pop Festival wound up serving primarily as a commercial showcase for the record companies. Executives flocked there, and the price for bona fide underground San Francisco bands skyrocketed."* After the Monterey Pop Festival it became a lot easier to be heard at the record company level. Record companies now seemed to be accepting the psychedelic bands with out-stretched open arms. The trade-off to this acceptance was that bands started to relinquish control of their lives as recording demands took over and longer tours began keeping bands away from their neighbourhoods for longer periods of time.

The political climate of the day was not always love and flowers, charged as it was with the goal of seeing an end to the Vietnam War. Anti-war marches were becoming commonplace. There was even an attempt to levitate or exorcize?? the Pentagon! Many cities across America began seeing race riots, with arrests and deaths. The committee that had been created in San Francisco to promote 1967 and the Summer of Love as an event unto itself failed to see the downside to such an influx of people. Unfortunately the community of Haight-Ashbury was ill prepared for the massive onslaught of transient youth.

The music scene was changing as well. In the beginning the dance-concerts at the many ballrooms were all participatory events. The crowds were a mass of movement as people danced and rarely sat down. Poster artist and one of the founding members of the Family Dog, Alton Kelley comments, *"The audience was as good as the bands. The only people sitting down were the ones worn out from dancing."* They were one-with-the-music so to speak. But by the end of 1967, even the bands were noticing a difference. People were now watching more than participating. In addition the hero worship was starting, as bands could play a good set and a bad set but still hear the same applause in response. So while the crowd was hearing they didn't seem to be listening. Many were there because it was the place to be. Gone were the days when the band would interact with the audience from a low stage and know many in the crowd because they lived down the street from most of the people there. Now they were becoming rock stars. For some it was distasteful and disheartening. Others adapted and grew into the new status.

The Aftermath of The Summer of Love

Following the Summer of Love, the whole psychedelic scene really took a turn for the worse. While the rest of the world was just catching up, in San Francisco things weren't the same anymore. Many of the bands no longer lived in the neighbourhood. As a matter of fact the whole neighbourhood of Haight-Ashbury was now a tourist Mecca as thousands of sightseers travelled to witness first hand the world of the hippies. Worse still thousands of runaways descended on the scene. The United States was rocked with race riots and antiwar demonstrations. By the Fall of 1967, Haight-

Ashbury was starting to show signs of burnout. Some 75,000 young people had invaded the community over the summer and no one was prepared for the influx of people. With the crowds came the down side of overcrowding, homelessness, and over-the-top drug use. Many who made the trek were sincerely looking for some magical utopia they'd heard about, but there were plenty of others who's interests were more self-serving. Soon "free love" verged on rape and drug usage turned hard and ugly with the influx of heroine and cocaine. In a desperate attempt to signal a change or provide a call for help, San Francisco hippies staged the "Death of Hippie and Birth of the Free Man" march in October. The march ended with the removal of the sign for the Psychedelic Shop. The sign was more than symbolically buried. The Thelin brothers closed up shop and moved to the country. The disillusionment had set in. The Psychedelic Shop that had come to be a beacon for the San Francisco underground closed for good. Many of the older hippies who were instrumental in charting the course of Haight-Ashbury took their cue from the Thelin brothers and began fleeing the community they created.

In England, the psychedelic scene also peaked over the summer of 1967 and in the trendy, mercurial environment of England's pop music world, everyone was moving on to the next trend or fad. There too the political climate was becoming charged and police had their hands full dealing with protesting youth. The psychedelic time in England flowered and blossomed into a mere nine months of mind-altering bliss. It was short, but sweet.

There was a new awareness running through the community. While Berkeley had maintained its radical stance, now the underground papers in both San Francisco and London took on more of the issues. Papers like the **International Times**, the **Oracle**, the **Berkeley Barb**, and **OZ** were competing with the traditional press in getting information into the hands and minds of patrons. Bridging the gap between news, music and social commentary, **Rolling Stone** was born in late 1967 and soon spread the issues of youth across the United States.

Bill Graham opened up Fillmore East in New York to take advantage of the growing interest in psychedelic music on the East Coast. He had spent much of 1967 and well into 1968 using both the Fillmore in San Francisco and the larger Winterland roller-rink down the street. Most weekends were split affairs with bands performing one night at the Fillmore and then two nights at the Winterland. Graham and his small crew could be seen most weekends shuttling sound and lightshow equipment across the street by hand. Part way through 1968, as a result of racial tension Graham decided to move to new facilities in San Francisco. Taking over the old Carousel Ballroom located on the corner of Market Street and Van Ness Avenue he renamed it Fillmore West. Russ Gibb was booking weekly shows at Detroit's Grande Ballroom and mirroring the success in San Francisco. Halls everywhere were in operation: the Kaleidoscope and Whisky A-Go-Go in Los Angeles, the Kinetic Playground in Philadelphia, the Vulcan Gas Company in Austin Texas, the Bank in Torrance, California the Retinal Circus and Afterthought in Vancouver, Canada and plenty of other lesser-known venues. The weekends were still jam packed with musical entertainment. Business was still good, but the soul was changing.

To quote Hoskyn's *"Nothing was the same after Monterey."* And there's a strong case to be made that as a scene it was all-downhill from that point on. Take the Doors for example who had released their first two albums by 1967. Yet by the release of their third LP in 1968, **Waiting For the Sun**, they too began to lose direction. Their No. 1 single, *Hello I Love You* tended to sound more pop than the rock band they were.

By the end of 1968 the Avalon Ballroom closed down due to noise violations. Helms reopened for a while as the Family Dog on the Great Highway in a building situated across the street from the Pacific Ocean. Interviewed in **Rolling Stone** years later Helms recalled the experience in one word, *"Cold."* While Bill Graham was still doing very well, running headline acts and turning a nice profit, Helms reverted to more of a showcase club featuring unknown bands and charging low admission prices. Being ever community minded he opened up the facility to various local community groups. All was for naught, the Family Dog on the Great Highway closed for good in August of 1970. Ironically the old Avalon Ballroom carried on for a few more gigs into 1969 with new promoters going under the name 'Sound Proof Productions'.

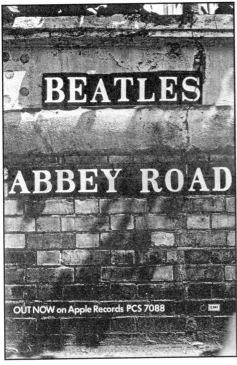

In 1969 the Beatles released their last album **Abbey Road** and then split up for good. In England a number of giant music festivals had taken place, but plans were in place to top them all and in August 1969 Woodstock happened for three days in Max Yasgar's farm. The event may have taken place in the East, but the feel was all West Coast. It was a happening place and for three days all seemed well with the world. But in the end it was that final bright flicker before the candle goes out. The year ended in a surrealistic drugged-out haze at a speedway outside of San Francisco called Altamont. Hells Angel security resulted in the stabbing death of one member of the audience at the foot of the stage while the Rolling Stones performed.

By the late sixties and early seventies the music was changing. And so too were many of the cultural elements that created the underground scene. It was perhaps predictable. The fashions that had gone to such extremes of the height of the summer of love were now moving in other directions looking for something else new. It was no longer odd to see men with long hair and many adults were now listening to rock music. People were now freely talking about living a different lifestyle, sometimes more communal sometimes not. What had started as a small, almost "secret" little scene back in San Francisco in 1965 had grown into the counter-culture movement and now had finally come full circle to be pretty much mainstream.

Likewise the pop music that had melded with folk and Motown and then turned into the Beatles and then mutated into the psychedelic world of feedback, distortion, and volume was going through changes. First the move was back to more of a blues influenced style and then as if going full circle, folk was back as a dominant thread creating an overall more roots-based rock best exemplified by groups such as the Band with their release **Music From Big Pink**. Bob Dylan's **John Wesley Harding** and the Byrds' **Sweethearts of the Rodeo** also exemplified the return to a more basic sound style. Speaking of the Byrds, within a short time after the **Sweethearts** release, two members went off to form the Flying Burrito Brothers. Around the same time two members of Buffalo Springfield split to form Poco. The country rock genre was blossoming. Then in early 1970 the Grateful Dead returned to their country and bluegrass roots and released **Workingman's Dead** and **American Beauty**. Both of these releases are actually cited as the Dead's most satisfying LPs. But all this was sending out a clear message about the psychedelic genre. Crosby Stills Nash & Young and the Eagles were not far off.

The London psychedelic club UFO and Middle Earth had closed and the others that continued like the Marquee changed their musical focus. By the seventies the psychedelic sixties were a thing of the past. Young people who'd frequented the hippie ballrooms were all in the twenties and even thirties now, and strange as it may seem, they were settling down into familiar routines. Families, work and bills were becoming part of their lives; heading out to the clubs was slowly becoming a thing of the past as priorities changed.

But perhaps the most sobering aspect of the decline of the psychedelic era was how much Haight-Ashbury and other hippie communities had changed. Whole neighbourhoods became infested with harder drugs like heroine and cocaine. These drugs and the change in character that ushered in their arrival literally sucked the life out of a whole movement. And then like a black cloud rolling in we all witnessed the premature deaths of many of the era's key figures. First Brian Jones of the Rolling Stones was found dead in his pool in July of 1969, then in September of 1970 Hendrix died of drug related causes and the following month Janis Joplin overdosed on heroine. Then Jim Morrison was found dead in a bathtub in Paris in July of 1971. All were in their late twenties.

By late 1970 many of the intimate weekly hippie ballrooms that had sprouted up across the United States began running into financial problems. The costs involved in running halls that seated fewer than 3000 people was clashing with the inflated amounts now being asked by the top bands of the day. The Aragon Ballroom in Chicago closed up in October 1970, the Electric Factory followed suit in December and soon after the Boston Tea Party. The monetary structure of the rock music industry was changing and the power was swiftly moving away from producer's pockets into the band's hands and in some cases unscrupulous managers.

After six years, the Matrix closed down in 1971 and for a time turned into a singles bar with entertainment provided by a jukebox. In June 1971 Bill Graham announced he was closing the Fillmores. Times had changed. Bands were costing too much; the halls needed to be bigger to recoup the investment and in the process were losing the intimacy that had created the scene in the first place. It was the end of an era. In the early days the events were labelled as dance-concerts and through 1965 and 1967 it would have been difficult to find anyone sitting at a Fillmore or Avalon event. These dance-concerts were a place to be, to talk, take drugs (quietly) to dance and yes to listen to the band. But by 1968 the band took precedence over the event. They became the rock stars and the idea of just being there to participate had lost its meaning. After a time Graham resorted to booking some of these larger shows and would go onto become involved in many large scale Woodstock type events staged for specific causes until his untimely death in a helicopter accident in the nineties.

Coming Down: The End of the psychedelic era . . .

Some would say the end came with the closing days of the Summer of Love with the Death of a Hippie march and the closing of the Psychedelic shop. Others would say it came when Woodstock changed the face of concert promotion. Others will point to the disaster of Altamont and the death of the spirit of the counter-culture movement. Clearly each of these events played a part in the demise of the whole psychedelic movement.

If we look at the San Francisco or West Coast scene as representative of the genre in general a number issues came to a head early that predicted the demise of the genre. The most obvious is the commercialisation of psychedelia. By the end of 1967, those who had been involved with forging the movement gained a new perspective. The Grateful Dead's Bob Weir, *"By the time the press had found San Francisco and declared the Summer of Love, the scene was over. Those of us who'd grown up in it got out. One reason in particular was bathtub methedrine. I knew plenty of musicians who were screwed up by methedrine. They lost their teeth; they lost their sense of humour. Some of them turned to crime. It did a nasty number on a lot of people, because methedrine had a nasty comedown and many users turned to heroine."* The cases of more serious narcotic abuse in the wake of the experimentation with psychedelics are plentiful. But there were other elements that had changed.

One of the central reasons the psychedelic communities in both San Francisco and London grew was because they were part of the local community. This has already been discussed earlier, but as the musicians grew in stature they began to be removed from that local community. Soon they were stars and in the eyes of some even more than that. Country Joe's Barry Melton observes, *"When the media was looking to package the whole phenomena, the musicians got singled out for better treatment."* So while all of the other aspects of the communal experience were generally ignored the musicians became the focus. The dancing had stopped. The participatory nature of events stopped. The audience began to stand and stare. The dance-concerts became simply concerts. Bob Weir observes, *"It became concerts and that point personalities started to emerge. Of course the star-maker machinery was more than happy to lend its weight there."* Lastly there was the touring. While the communities thrived on having local heroes, especially heroes who were a part of the community, by 1968 many of those heroes had moved out of those local neighbourhoods. Some had moved out to the country but virtually all of them were now spending more and more time on extensive tours that are a part of the star maker machinery. Country Joe McDonald interviewed in 1997 reflected on the changing times, *"By 1968 everyone had left the Bay Area and discovered the horror of the road. Work, that's what happened – work and work and work and work. It took creativity and smashed it to pieces. Then came contracts – one record every six months – and then one-nighters and airplanes. We thought the world was as big as the Bay Area, and we found out it was gigantic."* The pitfalls of selling one's soul can be told over and over again but it always comes with the same results.

The music industry changed during the sixties. The people changed as well. We'll explore this aspect of the era in more detail later. For better and for worse, the music industry grew up and so did the counter-culture generation. A number of insightful, retrospective and reflective quotes on the psychedelic sixties era are found on the videotape series, the **History of Rock 'n' Roll**. David Crosby who was instrumental in driving the psychedelic movement into the spotlight with his involvement in the Byrds and Crosby Stills and Nash, had this to say, *"We were right about civil rights, we were right in that love is better than hate, we were right in that peace is better than war...ah, we, it turns out weren't right about drugs."* In a similar tone looking back on what the sixties had wrought, Joni Mitchell offered her assessment on the changing sexual mores of the era, *"The free sexuality was an interesting experiment that failed."* And perhaps Paul Kantner of the Jefferson Airplane summed it up best with the comment, *"For two weeks in the middle of 1967, Summer – it was perfect!"*

File No. 2

The Psychedelic Music Timeline

The timeline I've created for this book spans the period of 1965 through to 1971. The dates pretty much speak for themselves. This day-by-day approach attempts to cover many of the key events or dates that had an impact on the psychedelic rock genre. Because so much of the movement revolved around the politics of the day, many of the pivotal news or political events of the day are included. The timeline primarily covers the growing scenes in San Francisco and London, although there are other locations included where they help flesh out the story. Not every performance from every band is identified; instead I've randomly selected events to help provide a representative overview of the time. In particular while I've chosen to list all performances from the two Fillmore Auditoriums, and the Avalon Ballroom, I've been more selective with the Marquee dates. I have attempted to include the first appearance of certain bands to help set the stage, but again this is not a comprehensive listing of every performance. Where known I've listed the first appearance of many of the British psychedelic bands from the era along with notes regarding interesting aspects to the band's futures. Of note for those following the Fillmore dates, virtually all of the Sunday performances were afternoon shows that ran from 2pm till 7pm and in some cases there were even different Sunday evening line-ups. It's also worth pointing out that the British dates, at the Marquee for instance tended to be one-niters, while in the United States bands performed over a couple of days. Where possible the actual dates of performances are shown. One final thing, many of these dates come from advertised posters and flyers and some times performances were cancelled or artists substituted. Where this is known I've made the changes, but there will be some that slipped through un-checked.

My intention with this chronology is to provide the reader with the big picture of the events of the psychedelic era as they unfolded and as they were linked together. More than anything you get a sense of the interaction between the various pockets of psychedelia. You get to observe what was happening in San Francisco while Jimi Hendrix was climbing in popularity in London and vice-versa.

The beginnings of the psychedelic era occurred in about 1965 and then metamorphosed into the rock & roll industry through the late sixties. It's safe to say by the early seventies it hardly resembled its beginnings. The dates and performers listed towards the end of the chronology bear testimony to the changing nature of bands and live performances. In particular many of the bands that had been influential in starting the psychedelic era no longer played in the smaller ballrooms and auditoriums. They were now being booked into the larger arenas and stadiums. The point made through out this book is that rock grew up over this period, but by that analogy some might also conclude that it grew into a spoiled adolescent who'd forgotten it's humble beginnings and now honestly believed the earth revolved around it. Sure it's happened before. Fame is a treacherous friend.

Psychedelic History Timeline 1965 -1971

February - 1965
• John Lennon and George Harrison become the first two Beatles to experience LSD as a result of their drinks being spiked at a party held by George's dentist. LSD still not illegal had become the recreational drug of choice and was seen as the latest "thing".

1st February – 1965
• The Marquee Club in London features the Yardbirds and the Mark Leeman Five on Monday the 1st.

8th February – 1965
• The Marquee Club in London features The Who on Monday the 8th.

11th February - 1965
• New U.S. President Lyndon Johnson orders the first sustained bombing campaign against the Vietnamese forces.

11th February – 1965
• Donovan is signed to Pye Records. The soon to be psychedelic folkie will eventually record such psychedelic hits as *Mellow Yellow, Sunshine Superman and Atlantis*.

21st February - 1965
• Malcolm X is shot and killed at a rally New York.
• Police raid acid king Owsley Stanley's pad in Berkeley. All his lab equipment is taken. No finished drugs are found on the premises so he is set free. Stanley sues the authorities to have his lab equipment back and it's later returned.

8th March - 1965
• The first wave of U.S. Combat troops enter Vietnam.

21st March - 1965
• Martin Luther King leads a civil rights march in Alabama. Twenty five thousand march from Selma to Montgomery, Alabama.
• The No.1 Pop album in the United States is the soundtrack from the latest James Bond movie, **Goldfinger**. It stays at the top spot for 16 weeks!

26th March – 1965
• Jeff Beck replaces Eric Clapton in the Yardbirds. Clapton quit over the commercial direction the band was heading in with songs such as *For Your Love* and *Heart Full of Soul*.

2nd April – 1965
• Ken Kesey soon to come into prominence with his Merry Pranksters is arrested for marijuana for the first time.

5th April – 1965

- While filming scenes for the movie **Help**, George Harrison watches the East Indian musical group practice and becomes interested in the sounds of the sitar.

5th May - 1965

- The first gig by the Warlocks takes place at Magoo's Pizza Parlor in Menlo Park. At the time the Warlocks who later changed their name to Grateful Dead, consisted of Bob Weir (guitar), Bill Kreutzmann (drums), Ron "Pigpen" McKernan (keyboards), Dana Morgan Jr. (bass) and Jerry Garcia (guitar). The band's musical style initially borrowed much from the Rolling Stones with its electric R&B style.

14th May – 1965

- Radio Station KYA, known as "The Boss of the Bay" presents in concert, the Rolling Stones, the Byrds, Beau Brummels, Paul Revere and the Raiders and the
- Vejtables on Friday the 14th at the San Francisco Civic Auditorium.

3rd June – 1965

- American astronaut Edward White becomes the first U.S. citizen to walk in outer space.

11th June - 1965

- Poets Of The World / Poets Of Our Time reading is staged on Friday the 11th at the Royal Albert Hall, London, England. What is now regarded as the official beginning of the British Psychedelic scene, this legendary meeting of 18 poets including Allen Ginsberg, Lawrence Ferlinghetti and Gregory Corso was a turning point that effectively gave birth to the entire UK underground scene. The audience was handed flowers as they arrived and many people were high on LSD. Approximately 7000 early style "flower-children" with faces painted and handing out flowers tripped on the poetry and collectively came to the realization that they were the beginnings of a new movement.

18th June – 1965

- The Grateful Dead changes their lineup as Phil Lesh replaces Dana Morgan Jr. on bass, at a gig at Frenchy's in Hayward California. The band gets fired the next night.

21st June – 1965

- The Charlatans play at the Red Dog Saloon, Virginia City, truly a massive milestone in the entire West Coast music scene! Formed by George Hunter, it was his idea to have a band playing a mixture of blues and country styled folk songs wearing a mixture of either western or Edwardian style outfits. In an effort to try and put some distance between their style and the recent British Invasion they incorporated such standards as *Alabama Bound* and Wabash Cannonball. Even though the band was seriously impaired by acid, all the elements came together from the audition through to the actual stay at the Red Dog Saloon. It worked and over their stay in

THE FRONT OF THE RED DOG SALOON

Virginia City, many from the burgeoning San Francisco scene came to check them out including the likes of Darby Slick, John Cipollina, Rick Griffin and future Family Dog creators Chet Helms, Ellen Harmon and Alton Kelley. Their residency at Red Dog eventually turned out to be three and a half months.

- To promote the initial event Hunter and pianist Mike Ferguson created their own promotional poster. The poster later became known as "the Seed", and is acknowledged as the first of the legendary psychedelic posters from the era. The original poster listed the opening dates as June 1st to 15th, but in reality a second version was changed to reflect the true opening, which was Monday the 21st 1965.

26th June – 1965
- Pink Floyd are entered in the annual **Melody Maker** National Beat Contest but fail to progress to the finals.

4th July – 1965
- Local radio disc jockeys Tom Donahue and Bobby Mitchell open what some have described as America's first real psychedelic discothèque called Mothers. Period author Gene Sculatti called it "a pulsating ultraviolet cavern doing weird business along the topless Broadway sin-strip in North Beach."

5th July – 1965
- The Marquee Club in London features the Animals and Jimmy James and the Vagabonds on Monday the 5th.

10th July - 1965
- *Satisfaction* by the Rolling Stones is the No.1 single in the U.S. charts. The Beatles hold the No.1 album position with **Beatles IV**.

20th July – 1965
- The Marquee Club in London features the first appearance of the Spencer Davis Group and the Mark Leeman Five on Tuesday the 20th.

24th July – 1965
- Bob Dylan's *Like A Rolling Stone* enters the charts.

25th July - 1965
- Traditional folk music fans boo Bob Dylan when he plays on Sunday the 25th at the Newport Folk Festival using amplified guitars for the first time. Dylan is booed off stage after three songs, only to return for an acoustic encore. As a harbinger of what

was to come of his acoustic career he fittingly sings *It's all Over Now, Baby Blue* and ends with *Mr. Tambourine Man*.

28th July – 1965
- The U.S. combat presence in Vietnam is now at 125,000 soldiers and to meet the growing need for combat troops the number being drafted doubles.

29th July - 1965
- The Beatles movie **Help** premiers in London at the Pavilion Theatre to a sell-out audience.

August – 1965
- Marty Balin approaches Paul Kantner with the idea of starting band. With a folk background, Balin had heard the Byrds and was keen on creating his own folk-rock group. Kantner, who was living in a Fillmore commune jumped at the idea. They fleshed out the group with Bob Harvey (bass), Skip Spence (drums), Jorma Kaukonen (guitars) and Signe Toly (vocals). Thus Jefferson Airplane was born. Balin then began working on his roommates to partner up with him and buy a pizza parlor on Fillmore Street with the idea to turn it into a music club.
- Taking a break from the embryonic band he'd just put together, the Pink Floyd Sound, Syd Barrett and school chum Dave Gilmore go busking in the south of France. While there they get arrested.

6th August – 1965
- The 5th National Jazz & Blues Festival is held on Friday, Saturday & Sunday the 6th, 7th & 8th in Richmond, England featuring, the Yardbirds, the Who, the Moody Blues, the Graham Bond Organization, the Animals, Spencer Davis, Steam Packet, Brian Auger's Trinity and a host of others.

11th August - 1965
- Race riots erupt in L.A.'s Watts district, 200 million dollars worth of damage is caused and during the following week 34 people are killed as a result of the rioting.

12th August – 1965
- John Lennon tries out a Mellotron for the first time, and instantly falls in love with the rudimentary sampling keyboard. It would later be put to good use in songs such as *Strawberry Fields Forever* and *I am the Walrus*.

13th August - 1965
- Marty Balin opens the Matrix club in San Francisco on Friday the 13th. The converted pizza parlor located in the Marina district at 3138 Fillmore Street hosts the first live gig from Balin's newly formed Jefferson Airplane. Their set consists of mostly electrified blues and folk cover versions with a few band originals as well. In the audience that night are Grace and Jerry Slick.
- The left-wing student newspaper, the **Berkeley Barb** is born.

15th August – 1965

- The Beatles perform on Sunday the 15th at Shea Stadium, New York in front of 56,000 screaming fans. It's the largest single crowd ever gathered to see a rock concert. Later on in the evening the Beatles hang out with Bob Dylan.

27th August – 1965

- To drive home the point he'd moved on, Bob Dylan released his second electric LP entitled **Highway 61 Revisited**. He performs at the Forest Hills Tennis Stadium, with a band that includes Robbie Robertson and Levon Helms, both of whom would go on to form The Band. This time the crowd warms to Dylan's new sound.

31st August – 1965

- The burning of draft cards becomes illegal. With the escalation of the war in Viet Nam, the resistance movement grows within the younger generation.
- The Beatles perform the last night of their third U.S. tour at San Francisco's Cow Palace on Tuesday the 31st. It turns into a "mad-house" as fans rush the stage. It's rumored that many Kesey's Pranksters were not impressed and left half way through.

September - 1965

- The World Psychedelic Center is opened in Pont Street, London by Michael Hollingshead, spreading the gospel of Psychedelia by selling copies of **The Psychedelic Experience** and **The Psychedelic Reader,** fresh from Timothy Leary's Millbrook Center in New York. As well as these items, Hollingshead also brought with him 5000 doses of LSD. After introducing LSD to Leary 4 years earlier, Hollingshead set out to "Turn On London", which he succeeded in with fine chaotic style. During its brief time open the World Psychedelic Centre attracted many interested people including a long list of celebrities such as William Burroughs, Roman Polanski and Paul McCartney. Within three months the Centre had taken on a seedy appearance as its owner Hollingshead was overindulging in LSD, Speed and DMT. Tabloid articles appeared exposing this seedy side the public and Hollingshead was in short order arrested on a 'minor narcotics charge' and jailed for 21 months in an attempt to suppress his attempts to spread the gospel of LSD.
- **The San Francisco Examiner** runs an article reporting on "A New Haven For Beatniks". This is perhaps the first article on the new breed of hippies invading the San Francisco area.
- Syd Barrett takes his first LSD trip in a friend's garden.

1st September – 1965

- The Beatles having just completed their third U.S. tour go to Los Angeles and spend some time with the Byrds.
- The Marquee Club in London features Al Stewart for the first time on Wednesday the 1st. He would go on to make 29 more appearances at the Marquee.

5th September – 1965

- San Francisco writer Michael Fallon in his article describing the growing counter-culture uses the term "hippie" for the first time. The term shows up in an article describing the Blue Unicorn coffeehouse where LEMAR (Legalize Marijuana) and the Sexual Freedom League meet and references "hippie" houses.

21st September - 1965

- Lightning Hopkins and Jefferson Airplane play from Tuesday the 21st to Sunday the 26th at the Matrix Club, San Francisco.

25th September – 1965

- Barry McGuire's "Eve of Destruction" is at the top of the U.S. charts.
- The Beatles half-hour Saturday morning cartoon show debuts on television in the United States. Strangely actors are used for the voices, none-the-less the show would run on the air till September 7th 1969.

14th October - 1965

- 14,000 protestors arrive outside the Oakland army camp to stage an Anti-War demonstration.

15th October - 1965

- The Great Society make their debut on Friday the 15th at the grand opening of the Coffee Gallery in San Francisco. The Great Society was formed by Grace and Jerry Slick shortly after seeing the Jefferson Airplane perform at the opening of the Matrix.
- San Francisco State College holds a special Vietnam Day Committee Teach-In on Friday the 15th at which Country Joe and the Fish perform. The band introduces the "I-Feel-Like-I'm-Fixen-To-Die-Rag" performed on a variety of jug band instruments and electric guitar. 14,000 marchers show up.

16th October - 1965

- A fledgling collective called the Family Dog present "A Tribute to Dr. Strange" on Saturday the 16th at the Longshoremen's Hall, San Francisco, featuring Jefferson Airplane, the Charlatans, the Marbles and the Great Society. The event was billed as a "Rock n Roll Dance and Concert" and in many respects was an opportunity for a number of underground factions of the hippie community to come together for the first time. This event proved to be the springboard for much of what would come later. This was the Jefferson Airplane's first gig outside of the Matrix Club and exposed their folk-rock style to a wider community. Grace Slick lead singer of the Great Society was seen for the talent she was and it was also the evening that brought together a young Jann Wenner and a seasoned journalist by the name of Ralph Gleason, a meeting which ultimately led to the Creation of **Rolling Stone** magazine. It was also the event that led to the meeting of three musicians who would later become the Quicksilver Messenger Service. The importance of this event on the future of the San Francisco psychedelic scene is not to be under estimated. Chet Helms and Janis Joplin had journeyed to San Francisco in 1963 and worked themselves into various musical scenes before Joplin ended up having a nervous breakdown only to return to Texas, while Helms survived shooting methamphetamine. In time, Helms came in contact with Luria Castell who helped him get off meth by introducing him to LSD. The two of them joined forces with a loose collective of prominent hippies including Ellen Harmon, the Charlatans, artists Alton Kelley and Stanley Mouse, photographer Herb Greene and future Grateful Dead manager Rock Scully and the group started calling itself the Family Dog.

- On the same day as the Family Dog event, there was a massive anti-war protest in Berkeley, with thousands marching from the campus into Oakland. The Berkeley students didn't look favorably upon the so-called hippie movement, thinking them too apolitical and certainly not serious enough to make a difference in the world. Berkeley after all was the home of the "Free Speech" movement. Ken Kesey's pranksterish appearance at the march didn't win over many converts to the new acid movement happening elsewhere in San Francisco.

24th October - 1965

- "A Tribute to Sparkle Plenty", the second Family Dog event is held on Sunday the 24th at the Longshoremen's Hall. The Loving Spoonful and the Charlatans entertain. Following the rave reviews of the first dance, this second Family Dog dance-concert was an even bigger success.

5th November – 1965

- The Who release the song *My Generation*. It will eventually reach the No.2 spot in England, but only No.74 in the United States.

6th November - 1965

- The Family Dog's third event "A Tribute to Ming the Merciless" is held on Saturday the 6th at the Longshoremen's Hall. On the bill were the Mothers and the Charlatans. Many of the more peaceful elements show up at the competing Mime Troup Appeal party, leaving this event to draw many non-regulars and a rougher element. The event ended up in a series of fights.

- The San Francisco Mime Troupe holds an appeal party for one of its members on Saturday the 6th at the Calliope Ballroom at 924 Howard Street. Amongst the various people appearing were The Grateful Dead, The Fugs, Laurence Ferlingetti and the Jefferson Airplane. The event like others of the time featured films on walls, lots of flashing lights and the prerequisite acid spiked kool-aid. This was the first prominent event staged by Bill Graham. Already in his thirties, Graham had a theatre background back east, but had been working at Allis-Chalmers. On the side he kept his hand in the arts by promoting the San Francisco Mime Troupe. The mime Troupe were a radical group of actors whose specialty was skits that pointed fingers at what they considered was a non-thinking society. By 1965 Graham had quit Allis-Chalmers and was promoting the Mime Troupe full time. When the troupe was busted and it's leader arrested for staging a live performance without a permit, Graham went into high gear and staged an appeal to generate some cash to pay for the legal fees. The sight of the long line of people stretching around the corner on Howard Street was an inspiration to Graham. In addition, the event raised over four thousand dollars and from that point forward Bill Graham set his sights on bigger things. Graham said this was the most significant evening of his life in theatre.

22nd November – 1965
• Bob Dylan marries Sarah Lowndes and then moves to Woodstock, New York. He keeps the ceremony a secret until February of 1966.

27th November - 1965
• The Mystery Trend perform on Saturday the 27th at the Peter Voulkos Studio, Berkeley.
• The first Acid Test is held on Saturday the 27th in Santa Cruz by *One Flew Over the Cuckoo's Nest* author Ken Kesey. Kesey and the Merry Pranksters as they were called ensured that what started off as just a party ended up a full-on assault on the senses, with LSD, lights, films and music provided by the Warlocks. Garcia later described the events as "ordered chaos" and the Warlocks became the house band of the Acid Tests. Soon after they changed their name to the Grateful Dead. The notoriety these events received helped introduce psychedelia into the public consciousness.

3rd December - 1965

• The Beatles release **Rubber Soul**, which reflects their growing interest in psychedelia, notably in the stylized lettering on the cover.

4th December - 1965
• The second Acid Test is held on Saturday the 4th in San Jose after "Can You Pass the Acid Test?" invites are handed out at a Rolling Stones gig at the San Jose Civic Auditorium. An estimated 400 people arrive at the Acid Test in a house in San Jose, where once again the Grateful Dead perform.
• With the British Invasion in full

swing, there is a rush to define an American sound. Garage-rock bands spring up all over America, many influenced by the growing psychedelic awareness. One such band, the Knickerbockers enters the charts with *Lies* a song that would eventually reach the No.20 spot of the U.S. charts.

10th December - 1965

- San Francisco Mime Troupe Second Appeal Dance takes place on Friday the 10th at the Fillmore Auditorium 1805 Geary Street, featuring the Great Society, Jefferson Airplane, the John Handy Quintet, Mystery Trend and Sam Thomas and the Gentlemen's Band. The Fillmore had a history of presenting R&B revue shows since 1952. Most of those shows were attended by mainly black audiences. However on this night the Fillmore was filled with mostly white kids. It was noted San Francisco writer Ralph Gleason who made the suggestion to Graham about using the Fillmore.

14th December – 1965

- The Marquee Club in London features Action and the Mark Leeman Five on Tuesday the 14th. Action would go on to make 24 appearances at the Marquee.

18th December – 1965

- The next Acid Test is held at Muir Beach Lodge in Marin Country on Saturday the 18th. In attendance is LSD guru Owsley Stanley III. Unfortunately he blames a bad-trip forever after on none other Ken Kesey.

TIMELINE - 1966

January – 1966

- Nigel Weymouth opens the hippest clothing boutique in London called Granny Takes A Trip. It becomes the first shop to sell men's and women's clothes side by side on the same rack. Lots of bright colourful clothes in velvet and other exotic fabrics made it the place to shop for the growing psychedelic community.

1st January – 1966

- An Acid Test Saturday the 1st at Sound City becomes the sixth in the series.

3rd January – 1966

- The Psychedelic Shop opens Monday the 3rd at 1535 Haight Street. Run by brothers Ron and Jay Thelin, sons of a Woolworth's store manager, the Psychedelic Shop soon became the center of the hippie universe in San Francisco. It not only sold all the paraphernalia but was also the place to meet, post messages and generally "be". Not long after it's opening, the Thelin brothers became involved with the **Oracle**, Haight-Ashbury's very own news flyer created by Allen Cohen and acid-evangelist Michael Bowen. Around the same time Dr. David Smith created the Haight-Ashbury Free Clinic. The hippie community really came together and lived as one. There was a feeling they could change the world if everyone did like the Youngblood's song said, "Smile on your brother, everybody get together. Try to love one another right now".

7th January – 1966
- The Grateful Dead perform Friday the 7th at the Matrix Club for the first time.

8th January - 1966
- KYA Super Harlow A Go-Go present the Vejtables, Baytovens, Just Six and William Penn and His Pals on Saturday the 8th at the Longshoremen's Hall, San Francisco
- The Acid Test comes to San Francisco Saturday the 8th. This marks the seventh event and 2,400 people show up for an Acid Test at the Fillmore Auditorium, lightshows, camera equipment and Time-Lag audio equipment create a mind blowing audio/visual feast. The Grateful Dead provide the music and the LSD flows like water. Noted for the first time is a new style of dancing, a relaxed, flowing style that almost followed hypnotically the music's ebb and flow. To many observers it seemed that everyone was stoned and whole room seemed to move in a coordinated effort. Later observers note that the Rave culture started on this day. In attendance was the Charlatan's manager Rock Scully and it was while watching the Grateful Dead perform, he realized this was the band he wanted to manage. Not the Charlatans. Scully realized more than most that the Dead were musically in tune with the growing drug culture. In a matter of weeks Scully divested his shares in the Family Dog and devoted his efforts to the Grateful Dead. City regulations required a 2 am curfew but no one was looking at the clock so the Acid Test was eventually broken up by police.

13th January - 1966
- Big Brother and the Holding Company, Moby Grape and Morning Glory perform on Thursday the 13th at the Santa Venetia Armory, San Rafael.

14th January – 1966
- A third and final Mime Troupe Appeal dance-concert was held Friday the 14th at the Fillmorc, with performances from the Great Society, Gentlemen's Band, Mystery Trend and the Grateful Dead. Interestingly, Graham insisted the Dead be identified on the poster as "formerly the Warlocks" given the status the "Dead" had already achieved under their old name, and their's is the only photo missing. Given the success of this third event, it's likely Bill Graham began to see the opportunity to spearhead the psychedelic music scene in San Francisco. His organizational skills would prove instrumental in shaping the hippie music movement.
- Captain Consciousness Productions presents Vancouver's First Dance-Concert featuring Jefferson Airplane and the Tom Northcott Trio performing Friday, Saturday & Sunday the 14th, 15th & 16th at the Kitsilano Theatre in Vancouver, British Columbia.

21st January - 1966
- Ken Kesey and the Merry Pranksters hold a Trips Festival on Friday, Saturday & Sunday the 21st, 22nd & 23rd at the Longshoremen's Hall, 400 North Point St., San Francisco. This 8th Acid Test was seen as the culmination of the previous tests and

Mime Troupe appeals. Organizers brought together all elements of the artistic community to make this a multimedia psychedelic experience, it featured theatre, mime, lightshows, readings, films, the Grateful Dead, Allen Ginsberg, Big Brother and the Holding Company, Loading Zone, Ron Boise, Neal Cassady, lots of LSD and many more strange and bizarre happenings. Prankster Ken Kesey wandered around in a space helmet, while Neal Cassady made his way through the crowd of over two thousand individuals in a gorilla costume. While this is Big Brother's first official gig it seems that most commentators better remember the sight of Bill Graham walking through the writhing sea of bodies with his clipboard in hand. Graham was hired to maintain order and was forever taking notes. Jerry Garcia of the Grateful Dead said, "The first time I ever saw Bill was when the Acid Test moved to the Trips Festival at Longshorman's Hall. And there's this guy running around with a clipboard…in the midst of total insanity. Everybody in the place was high except Bill." Graham later wrote he was more than a little scared by what he saw happening around him. To everyone's surprise the event turned a profit of $16,000, but more importantly according to writer Tom Wolfe, "the Haight-Ashbury era began that weekend."

23rd January - 1966

• The Mystery Trend and the Great Society play Sunday the 23rd at the Gate Theatre, Sausalito.

28th January – 1966

• "A Million Volt Rave" takes place on Friday the 28th at the Roundhouse in London, featuring the Tonics, Soft Machine, Electric Poets and the New Vaudeville Band. Lights by Ray Anderson of San Francisco's Holy See light show.

29th January - 1966

• Guerilla Lovefare is staged on Saturday the 29th at the Grande Ballroom, Detroit featuring the Spikedrivers, MC5, Livonia Tool & Die Company, Detroit Edison White Light Band, Lyman Woodward Ensemble and the Joseph Jarman English Spangler Jazz Unit with lightshows by the High Society and the Bulging Eyeballs Of Guatama.
• The **International Times** 'Uncommon Market' a strange bring-and-buy sale happening is staged on Saturday the 29th at the Roundhouse, Chalk Farm, London.

30th January - 1966

• Spontaneous Underground opens its doors Sunday afternoon the 30th at the Marquee in Wardour Street. Performers include Donovan, Graham Bond, Mose Allison and the Pink Floyd Sound. LSD and pot are in abundance. Some 20 people are in the audience to witness Pink Floyd's debut. These events were loosely organized and intended more as a happening, showcasing whoever might show up. The Spontaneous Underground events take place on Sunday afternoon when the club would normally be closed and was a showcase for everything from fashions, to makeup to arts to music. In short order it became the focal point of the growing London underground scene.

February - 1966

- Barry Miles, John Dunbar and Peter Asher open Indica Books in Masons Yard, London. Paul McCartney, who at the time was going out with Peter Asher's sister, Jane, was heavily involved with Indica to the point of helping them paint the walls and even designing and printing their original wrapping paper.

4th February – 1966

- Bill Graham presents "The Sights and Sounds of the Trips Festival" on Friday, Saturday & Sunday the 4th, 5th & 6th at the Fillmore, 1805 Geary Street featuring the Jefferson Airplane. This event was promoted with the first of almost 300 posters and is now listed BG1. The poster also indicates admission is by a suggested donation of $2. By this time the Jefferson Airplane were playing regularly in venues throughout San Francisco and were featured by Ralph Gleason in his newspaper article entitled "San Francisco – The New Liverpool". For this event bed-sheets had been hung around the auditorium on which to project the light show images. These images included slide shows, films, lights, wet show projections, black lights etc. Record labels were taking notice, and the Airplane were soon signed to RCA Victor for an unprecedented advance of $25,000. As was typical for the time, the band saw very little of the money thanks to Matthew Katz their manager at the time.

11th February - 1966

- Stray Cat present the Great Society, Charlatans, Mystery Trend, Family Tree and the Skins on Friday the 11th at the Fillmore Auditorium.

12th February - 1966

- Peace Rock is held on Saturday the 12th at the Fillmore Auditorium with the Great Society, Wildflower, Quicksilver Messenger Service, Our Lost Souls and Big Brother and the Holding Company. The event was a benefit performance for Democratic congressional candidates and the Vietnam Study Group.
- An event called Lincoln's Birthday Party is held Saturday the 12th at the Firehouse the former location of Engine Company 26 and Truck Company 10, 3767 Sacramento Street. Performing are Sopwith Camel and the Charlatans.

14th February - 1966

- The Purple Earthquake and Zephyr play on Monday the 14th at Berkeley High School, Berkeley, California.

19th February - 1966

- The Family Dog presents a Tribal Stomp on Saturday the 19th at the Fillmore Auditorium featuring the Jefferson Airplane and Big Brother and the Holding Company. This was the first of three events the Family Dog was to produce with Bill Graham. Chet Helms was always the real hippie while Bill Graham was the businessman from New York transplanted into the hippie scene. As such Helms was always more interested in creating and being a part of the experience because of what it was. Graham on the other hand was prepared to present the experience for what it produced, a good time and a profit. This partnership eventually blew apart when Graham appeared to behind Helm's back and secured the Paul Butterfield Blues Band for his own presentations.

- The Wildflower and Sopwith Camel perform on Sunday the 19th at the Firehouse in San Francisco.

26th February - 1966

- The Family Dog presents the King Kong Memorial Dance Saturday the 26th at the Fillmore featuring the Great Society, Grassroots, Big Brother and the Holding Company and Quicksilver Messenger Service.
- Bob Dylan plays Saturday the 26th at the Island Garden, New York.

27th February – 1966

- The second Spontaneous Underground is staged on Sunday afternoon at the Marquee Club. Once again Pink Floyd take to the stage.

28th February – 1966

- Liverpool's Cavern Club, famous for being the home of the Beatles on their rise to fame, closes.

4th March - 1966

- The Charlatans, the Electric Chamber Orkustra and Lynne Hughes play on Friday the 4th at the Sokol Hall, 739 Page Street, San Francisco.

6th March - 1966

- London Free School launched by John "Hoppy" Hopkins and activist Rhaunie Laslett in Notting Hill. In order to change the world, some in the underground felt it would only happen through a relearning, hence the LFS was opened to re-educate. Issues such as race relations and other social issues were high on the list of studies. Such notables attended for a time as Peter Jenner who later went to manage the Pink Floyd, and Graham Keen who went on to run the **International Times**. The LFS was located in a basement flat at 26 Powis Terrace, rented from Black Power activist Michael X.

11th March - 1966

- The Hedds, Styx and the Pussycats play on Friday the 11th at the California Hall, San Francisco.
- The "Rag Ball" at the University of Essex, England is staged on Friday the 11th and features Pink Floyd, Marianne Faithful, Swinging Blue Jeans and Jimmy Pilgrim & the Classics. This is the first live setting where Pink Floyd perform in front of a "moving" light show with students of the university projecting moving films on the band during the show.

12th March - 1966

- The Charlatans, Alligator Clip, Sopwith Camel and Duncan Blue Boy & His Cosmic Yo-Yo appear on Saturday the 12th at the Firehouse, Sacramento Street, San Francisco.
- The Pico Acid Test is held Saturday the 12th at the Danish Centre in Los Angeles, California.

13th March - 1966

- Soft Machine in one of their first early line-ups perform on Sunday the 13th at the Spontaneous Underground at the Marquee Club, Wardour Street, London. While the band played a young woman had her long hair trimmed on stage while other revelers rolled around in Jell-O.

15th March - 1966

- The Great Society perform on Tuesday the 15th the Matrix Club.

18th March – 1966

- Bill Graham presents the three-night "Batman" dance-concert featuring on Friday the 18th the Mystery Trend, Big Brother and the Holding Company and Family Tree, on Saturday the 19th Quicksilver Messenger Service, Family Tree and the Gentlemen's Band and on Sunday the 20th Quicksilver Messenger Service, Great Society and the Skins at the Fillmore Auditorium in San Francisco.

19th March - 1966

- Big Brother and the Holding Company perform on Saturday the 19th at the Firehouse in San Francisco with lights by Elias Romero. Sgt. Barry Sadler, was originally slated to entertain, but could not attend.

21st March - 1966

- The Rock Garden presents Big Brother and the Holding Company and Love on Monday the 21st at 4742 Mission Street, San Francisco.

22nd March – 1966

- The Sopwith Camel perform on Tuesday the 22nd at the Matrix Club in San Francisco.
- The Marquee Club in London features the first appearance of the Small Faces and the Summer Set on Tuesday the 22nd.

25th March - 1966

- The Family Dog presents the Paul Butterfield Blues Band and Quicksilver Messenger Service Friday, Saturday & Sunday the 25th, 26th & 27th at the Fillmore. It was following one of these performances that Bill Graham became so taken by the Butterfield Blues Band and their ability not only to perform but to draw a crowd. He is said to have awoken at sunrise to call their manager Albert Grossman in New York to secure the band's future San Francisco appearances. Helms saw this as an underhanded approach not in keeping with his "brotherly" approach. Graham's defense was simply "I get up early".

- Vietnam Day Committee Peace Trip on Friday the 25th at the Harmon Gym, University of California, Berkeley with Jefferson Airplane, and the Mystery Trend.
- The All Night Harmonica Store presents the Grateful Dead and Tiny Tim on Friday the 25th with lights by Del Close at the Troupers Club at 1625 La Brea in Los Angeles.

27th March - 1966

- The Spontaneous Underground is staged on Sunday the 27th at the Marquee Club, Wardour Street, London featuring Pink Floyd.

April – 1966

- Autumn Records, the label started by DJs Tom Donahue and Bobby Mitchell to promote the burgeoning early "San Francisco Sound" of bands like the Beau Brummells ran out of money and closed its doors.
- **Time** magazine declares "Swinging London" the capital city of the world. The article also says a million doses of LSD will be consumed through the course of the year.

1st April - 1966

- Stray Cat presents a dance concert with the Friendly Stranger, Family Tree and the Hedds on Friday the 1st at the California Hall in San Francisco.
- The Marquee Club in London features Gary Farr and the T Bones and the first appearance of the Move on Friday the 1st. The Move will make an additional 26 appearances at the Marquee.

4th April - 1966

- Big Brother and the Holding Company play the Matrix in San Francisco on Monday, Tuesday & Wednesday 4th, 5th & 6th.

7th April - 1966

- Chemical giant Sandoz makes the corporate decision to stop supplying LSD to researchers.
- City Lights Books present Andrei Voznesensky reading poetry on Thursday the 7th at the Fillmore. Lawrence Ferlinghetti translated the poetry and Jefferson Airplane performed following the intermission.
- The final Spontaneous Underground event is staged at the Marquee Club in London.

8th April – 1966

- The Family Dog present Love, Sons of Adam and the Charlatans at the Fillmore on Friday & Saturday the 8th & 9th. This would be their last partnership with Bill Graham. Lights by Tony Martin.
- Jefferson Airplane and Quicksilver Messenger Service play Friday the 8th at the

California Hall on Polk Street in San Francisco.
- The Marquee Club in London features the T-Bones and Sands Friday the 8th. The Sands will make an additional 21 appearances at the Marquee.

9th April - 1966

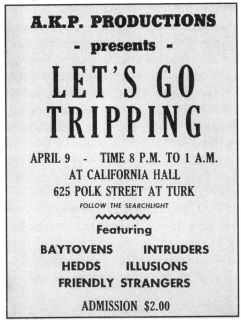

A.K.P. PRODUCTIONS

- presents -

LET'S GO TRIPPING

APRIL 9 - TIME 8 P.M. TO 1 A.M.
AT CALIFORNIA HALL
625 POLK STREET AT TURK
FOLLOW THE SEARCHLIGHT

Featuring

BAYTOVENS   INTRUDERS
HEDDS   ILLUSIONS
FRIENDLY STRANGERS

ADMISSION $2.00

- A.K.P. Productions present Let's Go Tripping on Saturday the 9th at the California Hall, San Francisco with the Baytovens, Intruders, Hedds, Illusions, and the Friendly Strangers.
- Week of the Angry Arts - Vietnam Mobilization Benefit on Saturday the 9th at the Longshoremen's Hall with Sopwith Camel, Quicksilver Messenger Service, Big Brother and the Holding Company, Country Joe and the Fish and the Grateful Dead with lights by Dan Bruhns. Of note is the fact that the Grateful Dead had been in Los Angeles for the past few months staying with acid guru Owsley Stanley, who was not only keeping them supplied with acid but was also providing them with new musical equipment. By the time they returned to San Francisco, their legend had grown and manager Rock Scully was able to command $350 per performance! More importantly the Dead's ability to perform as a tight and cohesive musical unit had grown measurably. Regardless of how stoned they were the band was able to communicate musically on stage to perfection.

15th April – 1966

- Bill Graham presents the "Blues Rock Bash" featuring the Paul Butterfield Blues Band and Jefferson Airplane at the Fillmore Auditorium on Friday, Saturday & Sunday the 15th, 16th & 17th. The evening of the 16th was performed at the Harmon Gymnasium on the Berkeley campus.
- 5th Annual three day Folk Festival held on Friday, Saturday & Sunday the 15th, 16th, and 17th at San Francisco College with performances by Mark Spoelstra, Malvina Reynolds and Dick and Mimi Farnia.

16th April - 1966

- The Charlatans, Wanda and her Birds, Mystery Trend and the Haight St. Jazz Band play Saturday the 16th at the California Hall, San Francisco.

22nd April – 1966

- Bill Graham presents the Grassroots, Quicksilver Messenger Service and Family Tree on Friday 22nd and Saturday 23rd at the Fillmore Auditorium. Lights provided by Tony Martin's Light Show.
- The Family Dog presents its first show at the Avalon Ballroom on the corner of Sutter and Van Ness on Friday & Saturday the 22nd & 23rd. On the bill are the Blues Project and the Great Society. Free to run their own shows in the manner they chose the Family Dog maintained a long string of performances for over two years featuring the cream of the psychedelic bands of the era. Over this time anyone who was anyone either played the Fillmore or the Avalon. While Bill Graham always tried for a more eclectic blend of performers, Helms and the Family Dog seemed to be more in tune with the whole San Francisco sound and stayed closer to the rock side of the musical spectrum. The competition between the two venues also spurred the development of the musical light shows and psychedelic posters that have become synonymous with the era.

29th April - 1966

- Bill Graham presents Jefferson Airplane and Lightning Hopkins and the Jaywalkers on Friday the 29th, and Quicksilver Messenger Service, Lightnin' Hopkins and the Jay Walkers on Saturday the 30th at the Fillmore Auditorium.
- The Family Dog presents the Grass Roots, Sons of Adam and Big Brother and the Holding Company Friday & Saturday the 29th & 30th at the Avalon Ballroom.

6th May – 1966

- Bill Graham presents Jefferson Airplane and the Jaywalkers on Friday & Saturday the 6th & 7th at the Fillmore Auditorium.
- The Family Dog presents Daily Flash and Rising Sons at the Avalon Ballroom. Big Brother and the Holding Company perform on the 6th, while the Charlatans perform on the 7th.
- The Mojo Men, Vejtables and the Hedds play at Winterland in San Francisco on Friday & Saturday the 6th & 7th.

13th May – 1966

- Bill Graham presents the New Generation, Jaywalkers and the Charlatans at the Fillmore Auditorium on Friday & Saturday the 13th & 14th.
- The Family Dog presents the Blues Project, Sons of Adam and Quicksilver Messenger Service at the Avalon Ballroom on Friday & Saturday the 13th & 14th. Lights by Bill Ham.

15th May – 1966

- A huge Anti War demonstration takes place in Washington DC. Ten thousand show up to express their resistance to the war.

19th May - 1966

- The Straight Theater Reading and Dance-Concert is staged on Friday the 19th at the

Avalon Ballroom. Playing are Wildflower and the Grateful Dead, also on the bill is Michael McClure and Ed Bullins. Lights by Reginald. This is the Grateful Dead's first appearance at the Avalon.

20th May – 1966
- Bill Graham presents Quicksilver Messenger Service and Final Solution on Friday & Saturday the 20th & 21st at the Fillmore Auditorium.
- The Family Dog presents Love, Captain Beefheart and His Magic Band and Big Brother and the Holding Company on Friday, Saturday & Sunday the 20th, 21st & 22nd at the Avalon Ballroom. This event was actually cancelled, and the groups did not perform.

27th May – 1966
- Bill Graham presents "Pop-Op Rock" featuring Andy Warhol and his Plastic Inevitable, Velvet Underground and Nico and the Mothers Friday, Saturday & Sunday the 27th, 28th & 29th at the Fillmore Auditorium.
- The Family Dog presents the Leaves, Grassroots and the Grateful Dead on Friday & Saturday the 27th & 28th at the Avalon Ballroom. This is the Grateful Dead's first Family Dog performance.

29th May - 1966
- The LEMAR (Legalization of Marijuana) Prohibition Ball Benefit is staged with the Grateful Dead and the Charlatans on Sunday the 29th, with lights by Ted Ball.

30th May - 1966
- The HALO (Haight Ashbury Legal Organization) Benefit is staged on Monday the 30th at the Winterland with Jefferson Airplane, Big Brother and the Holding Company, Quicksilver Messenger Service, Charlatans and the Grateful Dead

2nd June – 1966
- The Marquee Club in London features the Move and Triad on Thursday the 2nd.

3rd June – 1966
- Bill Graham presents Quicksilver Messenger Service, Grateful Dead and the Mothers at the Fillmore Auditorium on Friday & Saturday the 3rd & 4th.
- The Family Dog presents the Grassroots and Big Brother and the Holding Company at the Avalon Ballroom on Friday & Saturday the 3rd & 4th.

4th June - 1966
- The Jefferson Airplane, E Types and William Penn and His Pals play on Saturday the 4th at the Civic Auditorium, San Francisco.

5th June - 1966
- Black activist James Meredith is shot and wounded in Mississippi. His shooting will be one more element that galvanizes the Civil Rights movement.

10th June – 1966

- Bill Graham presents Jefferson Airplane, the Great Society and the Heavenly Blues Band at the Fillmore Auditorium on Friday & Saturday the 10th & 11th.
- The Family Dog presents the Grateful Dead, Quicksilver Messenger Service and the New Tweedy Brothers at the Avalon Ballroom on Friday & Saturday the 10th & 11th.

16th June – 1966

- The Marquee Club in London features John Mayall's Bluesbreakers and the first appearance of the Amboy Dukes on Thursday the 16th. The Amboy Dukes would play the Marquee another five times.

17th June – 1966

- Bill Graham presents the Wailers and Quicksilver Messenger Service at the Fillmore Auditorium on Friday & Saturday the 17th & 18th.
- The Family Dog presents Captain Beefheart and his Magic Band and Oxford Circle at the Avalon Ballroom on Friday & Saturday the 17th & 18th. Lights by Bill Ham.
- The Grateful Dead and the Jaywalkers play at the Veterans Hall, San Jose on the 17th & 18th.

19th June - 1966

- The Steve Miller Blues Band and Curly Cooke's Hurdy Gurdy Band play on Sunday the 19th at The Ark, Sausalito.

21st June - 1966

- The Great Society perform on Tuesday the 21st at the Matrix Club in San Francisco.

22nd June – 1966

- The Family Dog presents Jefferson Airplane on Wednesday the 22nd at the Avalon Ballroom.

23rd June – 1966

- Bill Graham presents Them and the New Tweedy Brothers on Thursday the 23rd at the Fillmore Auditorium.

24th June – 1966

- Bill Graham presents Lenny Bruce and the Mothers of Invention at the Fillmore on Friday & Saturday the 24th & 25th. Graham was not impressed by the lack of professionalism shown by Bruce and was glad the Mothers were actually able to save the show. It would be Bruce's last public performance as he was dead six weeks later.
- The Family Dog presents Big Brother and the Holding Company and Quicksilver Messenger Service at the Avalon Ballroom on Friday & Saturday the 24th & 25th.

Lights by Bill Ham. Big Brother and the Holding Company play for the first time with new lead vocalist, Janis Joplin. Chet Helms had persuaded her to return to San Francisco, reassuring her that it was a very different town since she was last there. And in fact it was. Joplin who was also being courted to sing lead in the Texas psychedelic outfit 13th Floor Elevators chose instead to take another shot at San Francisco. Everyone agreed that 23 year old Joplin was not only looking better, but also she was singing better than ever. Her style now more infused with a rich and even more heartfelt blues style.

- Radio Station KFRC presents the Beach Boys Spectacular on Friday the 24th at the Cow Palace. Also on the bill were Jefferson Airplane, Lovin' Spoonful, Chad and Jeremy, Percy Sledge, the Byrds and Sir Douglas Quintet.

26th June – 1966
- The Rolling Stones perform on Sunday the 26th at the Cow Palace. Opening acts included Sopwith Camel and Jefferson Airplane.
- Leander Productions present Them, the Association, Grassroots, Baytovens, Wildflower, Harbinger Complex and William Penn and His Pals on Sunday the 26th at the Oakland Auditorium Arena.
- Grand Opening of the Mod Hatter on Sunday the 26th at the Strawberry Town & Country Village, Mill Valley with the Great Society plus other bands.

29th June - 1966
- U.S troops bomb Hanoi in North Vietnam.

July - 1966
- Notting Hill Fair and Pageant is revived by the London Free School and is held in London's Notting Hill, in later years it becomes known as the Notting Hill Carnival. From its humble beginnings of roughly 2000 revelers, it has grown to one of the largest outdoor festivals in Europe now held every August.

1st July – 1966
- Janis Joplin and the members of Big Brother and the Holding Company and their wives and girl friends move into a house in Lagunitas in the San Geronimo Valley.
- Bill Graham presents the "Independence Ball" featuring Quicksilver Messenger Service, Big Brother and the Holding Company and the Jaywalkers on Friday the 1st; the Great Society, Sopwith Camel and the Charlatans on Saturday the 2nd; and Love, Grateful Dead and Group B on Sunday the 3rd, at the Fillmore Auditorium.
- The Family Dog presents the Grassroots, Daily Flash and Sopwith Camel on Friday, Saturday & Sunday the 1st, 2nd & 3rd at the Avalon Ballroom.

2nd July - 1966
- Karma Productions & Brotherhood of the Spirit presents Big Brother and the Holding Company, Quicksilver Messenger Service and the Gladstones with Bill Ham's Light Show on Saturday & Sunday the 2nd & 3rd at the Monterey Fairgrounds Dance Hall, Monterey.

3rd July - 1966

- The Ninth Berkeley Folk Festival is staged on Monday the 3rd at the Pauley Ballroom, Berkeley with Jefferson Airplane, Pete Seeger, Robert Pete-Williams, John Fahey and Ralph Gleason.
- The National Jazz and Blues Festival in Windsor features one of the first performances of Eric Clapton, Jack Bruce and Ginger Baker playing together as a trio.

6th July – 1966

- Bill Graham presents the Turtles and Oxford Circle on Thursday the 6th at the Fillmore Auditorium.

8th July – 1966

- Bill Graham presents the Mindbenders and the Chocolate Watch Band on Friday & Saturday the 8th & 9th at the Fillmore Auditorium.
- The Family Dog presents the Sir Douglas Quintet and Everpresent Fullness on Friday, Saturday & Sunday the 8th, 9th & 10th at the Avalon Ballroom. Lights by Bill Ham.

10th July - 1966

- National Farm Workers' "Giant Delano Strike Benefit" takes place on Sunday the 10th at the Fillmore Auditorium, with Quicksilver Messenger Service and the San Andreas Fault Finders.

12th July – 1966

- The Marquee Club in London features Action and the first appearance of Creation on Tuesday the 12th. The Creation would play the Marquee an additional four times.

14th July - 1966

- San Francisco Calliope Co. presents the Hindustani Jazz Sextet, Grateful Dead and Big Brother and the Holding Company on Thursday the 14th at the Fillmore Auditorium with lights by Elias Romero.

15th July – 1966

- Bill Graham presents Jefferson Airplane and Grateful Dead on Friday, Saturday & Sunday the 15th, 16th & 17th at the Fillmore Auditorium. While performing "Midnight Hour" the Grateful Dead are joined on stage by Joan Baez and Mimi Farina.
- The Family Dog presents Love and Big Brother and the Holding Company on Friday & Saturday the 15th & 16th at the Avalon Ballroom. Lights by Bill Ham.
- The Marquee Club in London features the Summer Set and Majority on Friday the 15th. The Majority would perform at the Marquee two more times.

16th July – 1966
- In London, Eric Clapton, Jack Bruce and Ginger Baker, having played together for one of the first times at the recent National Jazz and Blues Festival in Windsor officially form Cream. They would go on to become one of the most influential bands of the sixties.

17th July – 1966
- The A.R.T.S. Benefit takes place on Sunday the 17th at the Fillmore Auditorium. Performing are Allen Ginsberg, Sopwith Camel, S.F. Mime Troupe, S.F. Dancers Workshop, Bob Clark and Group, Mosa Kaleem Quartet and others. Lights by Bill Spencer and Romero.

22nd July - 1966
- Bill Graham presents the Association, Quicksilver Messenger Service, Sopwith Camel and the Grassroots on Friday & Saturday the 22nd & 23rd at the Fillmore Auditorium. Wes Wilson poster BG18 featuring the group names in a fiery plume, red letters on green background is one of Wilson's more memorable efforts.
- The Family Dog presents Jefferson Airplane and the Great Society on Friday & Saturday the 22nd & 23rd at the Avalon Ballroom. Lights by Bill Ham.
- The Rolling Stones play the Sacramento Memorial Auditorium on Friday the 22nd. Also on the bill are the Standells, McCoys and Tradewinds.

24th July – 1966
- Bill Graham presents the American Theatre performing "The Beard" by Michael McClure on Sunday the 24th at the Fillmore Auditorium.

28th July – 1966
- The Family Dog presents Bo Diddley and Quicksilver Messenger Service on Thursday, Friday & Saturday the 28th, 29th & 30th at the Avalon Ballroom. Lights by Bill Ham.

29th July – 1966
- Bob Dylan crashes his Triumph 55 motorcycle and is rushed to hospital with several broken vertebrae in his neck, a concussion and plenty of facial lacerations.
- Bill Graham presents Them and Sons of Champlin Friday & Saturday the 29th & 30th at the Fillmore Auditorium.
- The three-day Electric Media Trips Festival takes place Friday, Saturday & Sunday the 29th, 30th & 31st at the PNE Garden Auditorium, Vancouver, British Columbia. This is the Grateful Dead's first performance outside of the United States or even outside of California for that matter.

2nd August - 1966
- Jefferson Airplane, Big Brother and the Holding Company and the Great Society play on Tuesday through Friday the 2nd – 5th at Losers South, San Jose.

POSTER FOR THE ELECTRONIC TRIPS FESTIVAL

5th August – 1966

• Sliding further into the world of psychedelia, the Beatles release **Revolver** in Britain. It's released in North America 4 days later.

• Bill Graham presents Love and Everpresent Fullness at the Fillmore Auditorium on Friday & Saturday the 5th & 6th.

• The Family Dog presents Big Brother and the Holding Company and Oxford Circle on the 5th and Bo Diddley and Sons of Adam on the 6th at the Avalon Ballroom. Lights by Bill Ham.

6th August – 1966

• San Francisco plays host to a Vietnam War Peace march up along Market Street.

7th August - 1966

• Third annual Children's Adventure Day Camp Benefit is staged on Sunday the 7th at the Fillmore Auditorium. On the bill are Quicksilver Messenger Service, Big Brother and the Holding Company, Grateful Dead, Grassroots, Sunshine, SF Mime Troupe and the Jook Savages. Lights by Tony Martin, Ben Van Meter and Dan Bruhns.

9th August - 1966

• The Great Little Walter and Quicksilver Messenger Service play on Tuesday the 9th at the Matrix Club in San Francisco.

10th August – 1966

• Bill Graham presents Sam the Sham and the Pharaohs along with the Sit-Ins on Wednesday the 10th at the Fillmore Auditorium.

12th August – 1966

• Bill Graham presents Jefferson Airplane and the Grateful Dead on Friday & Saturday the 12th & 13th at the Fillmore Auditorium.
• The Family Dog presents Bo Diddley and Big Brother and the Holding Company Friday & Saturday the 12th & 13th at the Avalon Ballroom. Lights by Bill Ham.

13th August – 1966

• The Marquee Club in London features the Soul Agents and the Game on Sunday the 13th.

16th August – 1966

• The Marquee Club in London features the first appearance of Cream and the Clayton Squares on Wednesday the 16th. Cream will make an additional six appearances at the Marquee Club.

17th August - 1966

• The Mod Hatter presents a Psychedelic Fashion Show on Thursday the 17th at the Fillmore Auditorium. As well as the fashion show, tarot card readings and other surprises. Mimi Farina, Jefferson Airplane and Quicksilver Messenger Service play music.

18th August - 1966

• The P.H. Phactor Jug Band perform on Friday, Saturday & Sunday the 18th, 19th & 20th at Cedar Alley (between Polk & Geary), San Francisco.

19th August - 1966

• Bill Graham presents the Young Rascals and Quicksilver Messenger Service Friday & Saturday the 19th & 20th at the Fillmore Auditorium.
• The Family Dog presents the Grateful Dead and Sopwith Camel on Friday & Saturday the 19th & 20th at the Avalon Ballroom. Lights by Bill Ham.

23rd August – 1966

• Big Brother and the Holding Company begin a four-week stint in Chicago at Mother Blues. The band has fired Chet Helms as their manager and is now managed by Bob Shad who refuses to give them an advance on their forthcoming album even airfare back to San Francisco. The LP is recorded in Chicago as well as Los Angeles, but Shad doesn't even permit the band in the studio during the final mix. The recording is eventually released following Big Brother's successful appearance at the Monterey Pop Festival in June 1967. The band fires Bob Shad.

25th August - 1966

• Teens 'n' Twenties present the Yardbirds, Harbinger Complex, Peter Wheat & the Breadmen and the Just V on Thursday the 25th at the Carousel Ballroom, San Francisco. The Carousel used to be called the El Patio Ballroom and was located on the second floor, above a car dealership on the Southwest corner of Market and Van Ness. This show also took place on the 26th August at the Rollerena, San Leandro.

26th August – 1966

• Bill Graham presents the Great Society, Country Joe and the Fish and Sopwith Camel on Friday & Saturday the 26th & 27th at the Fillmore Auditorium. This was Country Joe's first appearance at the Fillmore as they were a substitute for the non-appearing 13th Floor Elevators.
• The Family Dog presents Captain Beefheart and his Magic Band and the Charlatans

on Friday & Saturday the 26th & 27th at the Avalon Ballroom.

- Tour Del Mar Bicycle Race and Folk-Rock festival at the IDES Hall, Pescadero, California. This unusual three-day event takes place on Friday, Saturday & Sunday the 26th, 27th & 28th and featured lots of bike racing and between the various events the Grateful Dead, Quicksilver Messenger Service and the Colossal Pomegranate all performed.
- The Marquee Club in London features the T-Bones and the Syn on Friday the 26th. The Syn will make an additional 35 appearances at the Marquee and eventually evolve into Mabel Greer's Toyshop.

27th August – 1966

- The Marquee Club in London features the Soul Agents and the first appearance of Episode Six on Saturday the 27th. Episode Six included pre-Deep Purple members Ian Gillan and Roger Glover and will make an additional seven appearances at the Marquee Club.

29th August - 1966

- The Beatles play their last public concert on Monday the 29th in San Francisco's Candlestick Park. Supporting bands included the Cyrkle, the Ronettes, and the Remains. Psychedelic poster artist Wes Wilson designs the official poster now worth many hundreds of dollars.

September – 1966

- Jefferson Airplane record their first album in a mere seven days entitled, **Jefferson Airplane Takes Off**.
- Timothy Leary holds a press conference in New York announcing the formation of his Psychedelic religion, "League for Spiritual Discovery" or simply L.S.D. and then he proceeds to hold nightly presentations at the Village Theatre. Leary's famous phrase "Turn On, Tune In, Drop Out" is coined and reverberates through the counter culture.
- The Grateful Dead move into an old Victorian house at 710 Ashbury Street in San Francisco. The house will soon become a rallying point for the Haight-Ashbury hippie community.

2nd September – 1966

- Bill Graham presents Jefferson Airplane, PH Phactor Jug Band and Andrew Staples on Friday & Saturday the 2nd & 3rd. The Grateful Dead, Quicksilver Messenger Service and Country Joe and the Fish preform on Sunday the 4th (this is the Grateful Dead's first headline performance at the Fillmore). Martha and the Vandallas with Johnny Talbot and De Thangs play on Labour Day Monday the 5th at the Fillmore Auditorium.
- The Family Dog presents the 13th Floor Elevators and the Sir Douglas Quintet on Friday & Saturday the 2nd & 3rd at the Avalon Ballroom. Lights by Bill Ham.

3rd September - 1966

- *Sunshine Superman* by Donovan reaches No.1 in the U.S singles charts. In England, the Beatles album **Revolver** is going into its 4th week at No.1 on the LP charts.

7th September - 1966

- The Blues Project perform on Wednesday the 7th at the Matrix Club in San Francisco.

9th September – 1966

- The cover of **Life** magazine proclaims "New Experience that Bombards the Senses: LSD Art." The new art, whether it be on posters, advertising or record album covers is designed to stand out from the traditional graphic styles and therefore have greater impact. New styles of lettering and new mixtures or blending of colors combine to bombard the senses.
- Bill Graham presents the Mothers of Invention and Oxford Circle on Friday & Saturday the 9th & 10th at the Fillmore Auditorium.
- The Family Dog presents Quicksilver Messenger Service and the Great Society on Friday & Saturday the 9th & 10th at the Avalon Ballroom.

10th September - 1966

- Trip City on Saturday the 10th at the Skate Arena, San Francisco with the Charlatans and Country Joe and the Fish.

11th September - 1966

- BOTH/AND Club Benefit is staged on Sunday the 11th at the Fillmore Auditorium, among the many artists featuring are "Big Mama" Thornton, Elvin Jones, Jon Hendricks Trio, Joe Henderson, the Jefferson Airplane, the Great Society and the Wildflower. Following this performance Jack Cassidy approached Grace Slick to join the Jefferson Airplane. Grace told her husband of the offer and considering the turmoil the Great Society were going through he advised her to take the deal. Her contract was bought out for $750!
- The Blues Project and Country Joe and the Fish play on Sunday the 11th at Tilden Park, Berkeley.

12th September – 1966

- The Monkees television show debuts depicting life in a pop band. Labeled everything from the "pre-fab four" to "a waste of time" the concept of the Monkees worked well on TV, providing an introduction to the world of psychedelia to a younger generation. They would also have many No.1 singles and sell millions of records.
- The Marquee Club in London features the VIPs and the Syn on Monday the 12th.

14th September – 1966

- George Harrison goes to India for six weeks to study the sitar with Ravi Shankar.

16th September – 1966

- The Family Dog presents the Grateful Dead and Oxford Circle Friday & Saturday the 16th & 17th at the Avalon Ballroom. The poster designed by Stanley Mouse and

Alton Kelley promoting this performance is the first to use the "skeleton & roses" image that would become a Grateful Dead trademark in the years to come.

- Bill Graham presents the Byrds, Wildflower and a play by Le Roi Jones entitled The Dutchman Friday & Saturday the 16th & 17th at the Fillmore Auditorium.

17th September – 1966

- A Freak Out featuring the Mothers of Invention, Little Gary Ferguson, Factory, Count 5 and the West Coast Experimental Pop Art Band takes place on Saturday the 17th at the Shrine Exposition Hall in Los Angeles. Light show by Nirvana.

20th September – 1966

- The first edition of the **San Francisco Oracle** is published. The flyer was created by Allen Cohen and acid evangelist Michael Bowen. Editor Cohen promises the magazine will "confront its readers with a rainbow of beauty and words ringing with truth and transcendence."
- While in India, George Harrison becomes the first Beatle to meet the Maharishi Mahesh Yogi.

21st September – 1966

- Jimi Hendrix and manager Chas Chandler arrive in London. Chandler discovered Hendrix playing in New York and convinced him to fly to London where he would find a more receptive audience to his reworking of the blues. While on the flight over it's said that Jimmy changed his name to Jimi.

23rd September – 1966

- Bill Graham presents "The Sound" series of dance concerts featuring Jefferson Airplane and Muddy Waters on Friday & Saturday the 23rd and 24th at the Winterland. The Wes Wilson poster designed for this show, BG29 truly marks the epitome of the San Francisco psychedelic poster art style.
- The Family Dog presents Howlin' Wolf and Big Brother and the Holding Company on Friday & Saturday the 23rd & 24th at the Avalon Ballroom.
- The Grateful Dead and Experience play Friday & Saturday the 23rd & 24th at the Pioneer Ballroom, Suisun City with lights by Diogenes Lantern Works.

25th September - 1966

- Bill Graham presents "The Sound" series of dance concerts featuring the Paul Butterfield Blues Band on Sunday the 25th at the Fillmore Auditorium.

27th September – 1966

- Riots erupt in San Francisco after a white police officer shoots and kills a black youth.
- The Marquee Club in London features Cream and the Herd on Tuesday the 27th.

30th September - 1966

- Bill Graham presents "The Sound" series of dance concerts featuring Jefferson Airplane and Muddy Waters on Friday & Saturday the 30th and 1st at the Winterland.

- The Family Dog presents the 13th Floor Elevators and Quicksilver Messenger Service on Friday & Saturday the 30th & 1st at the Avalon Ballroom.
- Andrew Staples performs Friday – Sunday the 30th, 1st & 2nd at the Matrix Club in San Francisco.
- A three-day Acid Test takes place at the San Francisco State College commencing on Friday the 30th with the Grateful Dead performing on the evening of October 1st.
- San Bruno A-Go-Go presents the 13th Floor Elevators, Inmates and the Westminster 5 on Friday the 30th at the National Guard Armory, San Bruno.
- The Grand Opening of the Afterthought in the Kitsilano Theatre in Vancouver, British Columbia featuring the United Empire Loyalists and the Nocturnals on Friday the 30th.
- London Free School 'Celebration Dance' with Pink Floyd at the All Saints Hall, Powis Gardens, London. Pink Floyd perform *Pink Theme*, *Snowing*, *Flapdoodle Dealing* and *Let's Roll Another One* for the first time.

2nd October – 1966
- Bill Graham presents "The Sound" series of dance concerts featuring the Paul Butterfield Blues Band on Sunday the 2nd at the Fillmore Auditorium.

6th October - 1966
- Possession of LSD outlawed in California. The change in the law was commemorated by an event called the "Love Pageant Rally" organized by **Oracle** publishers Allen Cohen and Michael Bowen. The official invitation said the event was to "overcome the paranoia and separation with which the state wishes to divide and silence the increasing revolutionary sense of Californians." Performing in support were the Grateful Dead and Big Brother and Holding Company who played

for free in the Panhandle. The success of this event led to discussion regarding a much bigger event, to be called "a gathering of the tribes". Two days later LSD is declared illegal in the rest of the country.

- Big Brother and the Holding Company move back into San Francisco at the suggestion of their new manager Julius Karpen.

7th October - 1966

- Bill Graham presents the Paul Butterfield Blues Band, Jefferson Airplane and the Grateful Dead on Friday & Saturday the 7th & 8th at the Winterland.
- The Family Dog presents the Jim Kweskin Jug Band, Big Brother and the Holding Company and Electric Train Friday & Saturday the 7th & 8th at the Avalon Ballroom.
- The San Bruno A Go-Go presents the Chocolate Watch Band, Generations and the Sit Ins on Friday the 7th at the National Guard Armory, San Bruno.
- Russ Gibb presents in Detroit a dance-concert featuring MC5, Chosen Few and Magic Theatre. Detroit's first participatory Zoo dance on Friday & Saturday the 7th& 8th at the Grande Ballroom.

8th October - 1966

- 1st Congressional District Write In Committee For Phil Drath and Peace featuring Bola Sete, the Grateful Dead, Quicksilver Messenger Service, Ed Keating and Don Duncan on Saturday the 8th at Mt. Tamalpais Outdoor Theatre, Marin County.

10th October - 1966

- Country Joe and the Fish play on Monday the 10th through Sunday the 16th at the Jabberwock, Berkeley.

14th October - 1966

- Bill Graham presents the Paul Butterfield Blues Band, Jefferson Airplane and Big Mama Mae Thornton on Friday, Saturday & Sunday the 14th, 15th & 16th at the Fillmore Auditorium. This performance marks Grace Slick's first appearance with the Jefferson Airplane.
- Pink Floyd play at the London Free School, Powis Gardens, London. At the request of their manager Peter Jenner, Pink Floyd remove all their R&B influenced material and for the first time play their first full set of 'underground' material.

15th October - 1966

- The Black Panther Party is launched by Huey Newton and Bobby Seale in Oakland, California.
- The Family Dog presents their "One Year Anniversary Dance-Concert" with Big Brother and the Holding Company and Sir Douglas Quintet performing Saturday & Sunday the 15th & 16th at the Avalon Ballroom. Lights by Ben Van Meter and Roger Hillyard.
- Artists Liberation Front Free Fair on Saturday & Sunday the 15th & 16th at the Panhandle, Golden Gate Park in San Francisco.

- The Purple Earthquake, Just V and 5th Dimension play on Saturday the 15th at the Maple Hall, San Pablo.
- The launching of the **International Times**, a counter-culture newspaper is celebrated with an "All Night Rave" and "Pop Op Costume Masque Drag Ball Et Al" on Saturday the 15th at the Roundhouse, Chalk Farm, London with performances from Pink Floyd and Soft Machine. Twenty five hundred people showed up for this coming out party for both the newspaper and Pink Floyd. The **International Times**, **IT** for short is launched in part by John "Hoppy" Hopkins and Barry Miles and is modeled after American papers such as **The Village Voice**. The party takes place in an abandoned old engine shed that was freezing cold and had only two bathrooms. Everyone who showed up was handed a sugar cube and while they weren't actually spiked with anything it wasn't too long before everyone in the place was. People showed up in all sorts of costumes, Paul McCartney showed up dressed an Arab. The crowd of 2500 or so is the largest audience yet for both Pink Floyd and Soft Machine. It was also the first time most in the audience had experienced a full-blown psychedelic light show with films and lights.

18th October – 1966
- The Jimi Hendrix Experience play their first gig together in Paris, supporting French pop star Johnny Halliday on Tuesday the 18th. Upon returning to England the reviews are spectacular and he is immediately adopted by the British rock aristocracy and labeled by the media as the "next big thing".

19th October – 1966
- Love and Sons of Adam perform from the 19th through the 30th at the Whisky A-Go-Go in Los Angeles.

20th October – 1966
- The Family Dog presents Daily Flash and Country Joe and the Fish on Thursday & Friday the 20th & 21st at the Avalon Ballroom. Lights by Ben Van Meter and Roger Hillyard.

21st October - 1966
- Bill Graham presents the Grateful Dead, Lightning Hopkins and Loading Zone on Friday & Saturday the 21st & 22nd at the Fillmore Auditorium.
- Teens 'n' Twenties present the Byrds, Peter Wheat & the Breadmen, Baytovens and Jack and the Rippers on Friday the 21st at the Rollerena, San Leandro.
- Pink Floyd play at the London Free School, Powis Gardens, London on Friday the 21st. Pink Floyd play to their first capacity crowd! They are paid 15 Pounds or about $45.

22nd October - 1966
- Big Brother and the Holding Company, Grateful Dead and Quicksilver Messenger Service play on Saturday the 22nd at Winterland.

23rd October – 1966

- Bill Graham presents the Yardbirds and Country Joe and the Fish Sunday the 23rd at the Fillmore Auditorium.

24th October - 1966

- Jefferson Airplane perform Monday through Thursday the 24th – 27th at the Matrix Club in San Francisco.

27th October - 1966

- The Western Front Dance Academy presents the Charlatans, Triple AAA and Frumious Bandersnatch on Thursday & Friday the 27th & 28th.

28th October - 1966

- Bill Graham presents Captain Beefheart and his Magic Band, Chocolate Watch Band and Great Pumpkin on Friday, Saturday & Sunday the 28th, 29th, 30th at the Fillmore Auditorium.
- The Family Dog presents Quicksilver Messenger Service and Sons of Champlin on Friday & Saturday the 28th & 29th at the Avalon Ballroom.
- Wildflower perform Friday, Saturday & Sunday the 28th, 29th & 30th at the Matrix Club in San Francisco.
- Jefferson Airplane, Patty Philips and the Chosen Four play on Friday the 28th at St. Mary's College, Moraga, California.

30th October - 1966

- Larry Hankin and Jefferson Airplane play on Sunday the 30th at the University of California, Berkeley.
- Country Joe and the Fish play Sunday & Monday the 30th & 31st at the Jabberwock, Berkeley.

31st October – 1966

- The Acid Test Graduation takes place after much trial and tribulation at the intimate Colliope Company Warehouse on Monday the 31st. Ken Kesey and his group of Pranksters had realized or were made to realize that it was time to move on. Their brand of awareness was losing favor with virtually everyone in San Francisco. Originally booked in the Winterland and to be promoted by Bill Graham, it all came apart when Graham was alerted to the potential problems associated with his involvement. He quickly backed away, as did the Grateful Dead. In the end, the graduation was a small affair, which then saw various pranksters scatter to Oregon, California and New Mexico. Neal Cassady eventually turned up dead in Mexico in February 1968. Kesey went to jail serving 90 days behind bars and then five months in a work farm, after which he joined his family in Oregon.
- Bob McKendrick presents a Dance of Death costume Ball on Monday the 31st at the California Hall in San Francisco, with the Grateful Dead, Quicksilver Messenger Service and Mimi Farina. Light and sound by Calliope.

November – 1966

- The Steve Miller Blues Band forms in Berkeley. Originally from Texas, Miller demonstrated his ample guitar playing ability and within a week the band were performing at the Forum on Telegraph Hill, and shortly after that were tagged by Chet Helms to play the Avalon Ballroom. Miller's first love was the blues, but he found it easy to blend the various psychedelic influences to create a potent and unique style that would survive for many years to come.

1st November – 1966

- Big Brother and the Holding Company perform Tuesday the 1st through Sunday the 6th at the Matrix Club in San Francisco.
- Country Joe and the Fish play Tuesday 1st through Thursday the 3rd at Jabberwock, Berkeley.
- The Marquee Club in London features the Spencer Davis Group and Episode Six on Tuesday the 1st.

4th November – 1966

- Bill Graham presents Muddy Waters Blues Band, Quicksilver Messenger Service and Andrew Staples on Friday, Saturday & Sunday the 4th, 5th & 6th at the Fillmore Auditorium. Bill Graham is quoted saying, "There are two or three names in the business that are on the top ten list of every musician I know. Muddy Waters was one of those people."
- The Family Dog presents the Grateful Dead and Oxford Circle Friday & Saturday the 4th & 5th at the Avalon Ballroom.
- Uncle Russ Travel Agency presents in Detroit a dance-concert featuring Southbound Freeway, MC5 and the Bossmen on Friday & Saturday the 4th & 5th at the Grande Ballroom.
- Pink Floyd play at the London Free School, Powis Gardens, London on Friday the 4th.

5th November – 1966

- Ten Thousand people show up in New York for the Walk For Love, Peace and Freedom.
- The Monkees' first single release *Last Train to Clarksville* becomes the No.1 single in the United States, unseating *96 Tears* by ? and the Mysterians.
- Pink Floyd play at Wilton Hall, Bletchley, Buckinghamshire.
- The Marquee Club in London features the Herd and the Crazy World of Arthur Brown on Saturday the 5th.

6th November - 1966

- The Associated Students of San Francisco State College present an Edwardian Ball on Sunday the 6th at the Fillmore Auditorium featuring Jefferson Airplane.
- Country Joe and the Fish play Sunday through Thursday the 6th – 10th at Jabberwock, Berkeley.

8th November - 1966

- Ronald Reagan is elected governor of California and vows to stamp out anti-war

protestors and obscene publications. He defeats the incumbent Governor Brown by almost one million votes.
- Pink Floyd play at the London Free School, Powis Gardens, London on Saturday the 8th.

9th November – 1966
- John Lennon meets Yoko Ono at the Indica Gallery during a private preview of Yoko's show entitled "Unfinished paintings and Objects".

11th November – 1966
- Bill Graham presents Bola Sete, Country Joe and the Fish and Buffalo Springfield on Friday, Saturday & Sunday the 11th, 12th & 13th at the Fillmore Auditorium.
- The Family Dog presents the 13th Floor Elevators and Moby Grape on Friday & Saturday the 11th & 12th at the Avalon Ballroom.

12th November - 1966
- The Old Cheese Factory presents an Anniversary Party on Saturday the 12th featuring the Grateful Dead and Andrew Staples with lights by Bill Ham.
- The Hells Angels motorcycle gang presents Big Brother and the Holding Company and Ken Kesey and the Merry Pranksters on Saturday the 12th at the Sokol Hall, San Francisco.

13th November - 1966
- Zenefit - Zen Mountain Center Benefit featuring the Grateful Dead, Big Brother and the Holding Company, and Quicksilver Messenger Service with lights by Bill Ham on Sunday the 13th at the Avalon Ballroom.

15th November - 1966
- The Psychedelic Shop in Haight-Ashbury, San Francisco is raided by police looking for what was identified as obscene literature in the form of a book of poetry entitled **The Love Book**.
- Pink Floyd play at the London Free School, Powis Gardens, London on Tuesday the 15th.

18th November - 1966
- Bill Graham presents the Grateful Dead, James Cotton Chicago Blues Band and Lothar and the Hand People on Friday, Saturday & Sunday the 18th, 19th & 20th at the Fillmore Auditorium.
- The Family Dog presents the Daily Flash, Quicksilver Messenger Service and Country Joe and the Fish on Friday & Saturday the 18th & 19th at the Avalon Ballroom.
- Pink Floyd play at the "Philadelic Music for Simian Hominids" on Friday the 18th at the Hornsey College of Art, London with a full light show by Joe Gannon.

19th November - 1966

- The Monkees' first album simply called **The Monkees** is the No.1 LP in America. It will eventually spend 12 weeks at the top, only to be unseated by the Monkees' second LP release entitled **More of The Monkees.**
- The Beach Boys' *Good Vibrations* is the No.1 song in the U.K. for 2 weeks.
- The Special Events Committee presents the Righteous Brothers, April Stevens and Nino Tempo on Saturday the 19th at the University of San Francisco.
- Teens 'n' Twenties present the Beau Brummels, Tame Greens and the Daytrippers on Saturday the 19th at the Rollerena, San Leandro.
- Pink Floyd play at Canterbury Technical College, Canterbury, Kent on Saturday the 19th.

20th November - 1966

- Student Non-Violent Coordinating Committee (SNCC) Benefit on Sunday the 20th at the Fillmore Auditorium featuring the James Cotton Chicago Blues Band, Quicksilver Messenger Service, Grateful Dead and Johnny Talbot & De Thangs.

22nd November - 1966

- Pink Floyd play at the London Free School, Powis Gardens, London on Tuesday the 22nd.

25th November – 1966

- Bill Graham presents Jefferson Airplane, James Cotton Chicago Blues Band and Moby Grape on Friday, Saturday & Sunday the 25th, 26th & 27th at the Fillmore Auditorium.
- The Family Dog presents Quicksilver Messenger Service and Big Brother and the Holding Company Friday & Saturday the 25th & 26th at the Avalon Ballroom.
- The Jimi Hendrix Experience comprised of Hendrix, drummer Mitch Mitchell and bassist Noel Redding, make their London debut on Friday the 25th at the Bag O' Nails Club. Among those in attendance are John Lennon and Paul McCartney.

26th, November – 1966

- The Yardbirds enter the Hot 100 charts with the psychedelic *Happenings Ten Years Time Ago*. It eventually peaked at No.30.
- The Lynch Mob presents the "Turkey Blimp" featuring music from City Lights, Hobbit and L.A. Tymes on Saturday the 26th at the Lynch Building in Santa Monica.

28th November - 1966

- The Grateful Dead and Jerry Pond perform Monday through Thursday the 28th – 1st the Matrix Club, in San Francisco.

29th November – 1966

- Pink Floyd play at the London Free School, Powis Gardens, London on Friday the 29th.

December – 1966

- Cream releases their first LP entitled **Fresh Cream**. Eric Clapton, Jack Bruce and Ginger Baker solidify their psychedelic style with the release of their first recording.

1st December – 1966

- The Print Mint opens at 1542 Haight Street in the Haight-Ashbury just a few doors down from The Psychedelic Shop. As the name implies The Print Mint specializes in books, posters and other psychedelic printed matter.

2nd December – 1966

- Bill Graham presents Love, Moby Grape and Lee Michaels on Friday, Saturday & Sunday the 2nd, 3rd & 4th at the Fillmore Auditorium.
- The Family Dog presents Buffalo Springfield and Daily Flash on Friday & Saturday the 2nd & 3rd at the Avalon Ballroom.
- The Afterthought in Vancouver, British Columbia presents United Empire Loyalists and the Unforeseen on Friday & Saturday the 2nd & 3rd at the Kitsilano Theatre on 4th Ave. Lights by Trans-Euphoric Light Show.

3rd December - 1966

- Pink Floyd and the Ram Holder Messengers play at "Psychedelphia vs. Ian Smith" Giant Freakout on Saturday the 3rd at the Roundhouse, Chalk Farm, London. This event was promoted by a group called Majority Rule for Rhodesia and was held in protest to the then Governor of Rhodesia, Ian Smith's policy of white minority rule. As such the event featured underground films, poets and other spontaneous events. The Pink Floyd's light show by this time had gained some notoriety with its multiple slides, films and colored lights all moving in time with the ebb and flow of Floyd's music.
- The Marquee Club in London features the Herd and John's Children on Saturday the 3rd. Marc Bolan would join John's Children a few months after this gig.

6th December - 1966

- Moby Grape perform Tuesday, Wednesday & Thursday the 6th, 7th & 8th at the Matrix Club in San Francisco.

9th December – 1966

- Bill Graham presents the Grateful Dead, Big Mama Thornton and Tim Rose on Friday, Saturday & Sunday the 9th, 10th & 11th at the Fillmore Auditorium.
- The Family Dog presents Big Brother and the Holding Company and Oxford Circle on Friday & Saturday the 9th & 10th at the Avalon Ballroom.

10th December – 1966

- The Marquee Club in London features the Herd and Neat Change on Saturday the 10th. The Neat Change will make an additional 39 Marquee appearances. The band's guitarist was Peter Banks at one point.

12th December - 1966

- "You're Joking" - A Benefit for Oxfam is staged on Monday the 12th at the Royal Albert Hall, London featuring Peter Cook & Dudley Moore, Paul Jones, the Alan Price Set, Chris Farlow, Barry Mackenzie, Peter & Gordon, and Pink Floyd.

13th December – 1966

- The Marquee Club in London features Eric Burdon and the Animals and the Syn on Tuesday the 13th.

16th December – 1966

- Polydor Records releases *Hey Joe* by Jimi Hendrix in the U.K. The song will peak at No.6 on the charts, but won't get released in the U.S. until showing up on the first album.
- Bill Graham presents Jefferson Airplane, Junior Wells Chicago Blues Band and Tim Rose on Friday, Saturday & Sunday the 16th, 17th & 18th at the Fillmore Auditorium.
- The Family Dog presents the Youngbloods, Sparrow and Sons of Champlin on Friday & Saturday the 16th & 17th at the Avalon Ballroom.

17th December - 1966

- A Benefit for Legalization of Marijuana (LEMAR) is held on Saturday the 17th at the California Hall in San Francisco with Country Joe and the Fish and the Only Alternative and his Other Possibilities.

18th December - 1966

- Ralph & Al Pepe presents Carol Doda, Styx, Morning Glory and Sun Flowers with light shows on Sunday the 18th at the Santa Venetia Armory, San Rafael.
- Pink Floyd perform at an event called "The Night Tripper" on Sunday the 18th at the Blarney Club in Tottenham Court Road. The next week the club is renamed UFO and the Pink Floyd become regular performers.

20th December - 1966

- Bill Graham presents Otis Redding at the Fillmore Auditorium. Support bands for each respective night are the Grateful Dead – Tuesday 20th, Johnny Talbot – Wednesday 21st, and Country Joe and the Fish – Thursday 22nd. Graham would later write, "There was an ultimate musician everyone wanted to see. Everybody said, 'this is the guy. Otis. Otis Redding. He was it.' That was the best gig I ever put on in my entire life. I knew it then. Otis for thee nights at the Fillmore. That was as good as it got."

21st December - 1966

- The Jimi Hendrix Experience perform on Wednesday the 21st at the Blaises Club in London. In audience were Pete Townsend, Roger Daltry, John Entwhistle, Chas Chandler and Jeff Beck. Chris Welch in writing the review said; "Jimi has great stage presence and an exceptional guitar technique which involved playing with his teeth on occasions and no hands at all on others. Jimi looks like becoming one of the big club names of '67."

22nd December - 1966

• Pink Floyd and the Ivey's play on Thursday the 22nd at the Marquee Club, Wardour Street, London. This is Pink Floyd's first headlining appearance at the Marquee not counting their appearances at the Spontaneous Underground. They would headline a total of five times.

23rd December – 1966

• The Family Dog presents the Grateful Dead and Moby Grape on Friday and Saturday the 23rd & 24th at the Avalon Ballroom.
• The UFO club opens at 31, Tottenham Court Road, London on Friday the 23rd. The promoters were Joe Boyd, Barry Miles and John 'Hoppy' Hopkins. The first two events were called 'UFO Presents Night Tripper' before the club became just 'UFO' (Underground Freak Out). The first band to play on the opening night was of course Pink Floyd, who pretty much became the house band. For the first two and half months Pink Floyd and Soft Machine perform on alternating weekends. The UFO became the center of London's underground music scene.
• The Afterthought in Vancouver, British Columbia presents the Tom Northcott Trio and William Tell and the Marksmen on Friday & Saturday the 23rd & 24th at the Kitsilano Theatre on 4th Ave. Lights by Trans-Euphoric Express Light Show.

26th December - 1966

• The Grope For Peace Benefit is staged on Monday the 26th at the Ark, Sausalito with the Charlatans, Big Brother and the Holding Company, Congress of Wonders, Lynne Hughes and the Final Solution.
• The Jimi Hendrix Experience perform on Monday the 26th at the Upper Cut club. The story is that Hendrix wrote the song *Purple Haze* in the dressing room of the Upper Cut.
• The Afterthought in Vancouver, British Columbia presents Don Crawford and the Right People and the Northwest Company on Monday the 24th at the Kitsilano Theatre on 4th Ave. Lights by Trans-Euphoric Light Show.

28th December - 1966

• Goathead Limited presents the Grateful Dead, Quicksilver Messenger Service on Wednesday the 28th at the Beaux Arts Ball, Governors Hall, Sacramento.

29th December - 1966

• Ralph & Al Pepe presents the Grateful Dead, Moby Grape and Morning Glory on Thursday the 29th at the Santa Venetia Armory, San Rafael.
• Pink Floyd and the Syn play on Thursday the 29th at the Marquee Club, Wardour Street, London.

30th December - 1966
- Prominent underground activist John "Hoppy" Hopkins is arrested for marijuana possession. He is sentenced to nine months in jail.
- Bill Graham presents a "New Year Bash" featuring Jefferson Airplane, Grateful Dead and Quicksilver Messenger Service on Friday & Saturday the 30th & 31st at the Fillmore Auditorium.
- The Family Dog presents a "New Years Dance-Concert" featuring Country Joe and the Fish, Moby Grape and Lee Michaels on Friday & Saturday the 30th & 31st at the Avalon Ballroom.
- Pink Floyd and Soft Machine play on Friday the 30th at the UFO club, London.

31st December - 1966
- New Years Eve All Night Rave, "Psychedelicamania" on Saturday the 31st at the Roundhouse with the Who, the Move and Pink Floyd. Of note is that Pink Floyd had played an early evening New Years show the same night at the Cambridge Technical College.

TIMELINE - 1967

1st January – 1967

- The Hell's Angels hold a thank-you party in Panhandle Park celebrating the bailing out of Chocolate George. The party is called the New Year's Wail and features performances by the Grateful Dead, Big Brother and the Holding Company and the Diggers' band, Orkustra.

5th January - 1967

- Pink Floyd and Eyes of Blue play on Thursday the 5th at the Marquee Club, London.

6th January - 1967

- Bill Graham presents the Young Rascals, Sopwith Camel and the Doors on Friday, Saturday & Sunday the 6th, 7th & 8th at the Fillmore Auditorium. Ray Manzarek is quoted as saying, "We played the Fillmore for the first time the weekend before "The Human Be-In". It was the Young Rascals, Sopwith Camel and that group from LA that nobody knows – the Doors. The place was packed. We went onstage and opened with *When The Music's Over*. I had my left and right hands playing contrapuntal melodies against one another on the keyboard. San Francisco had never heard this kind of music before."
- The Family Dog presents Quicksilver Messenger Service and the Steve Miller Blues Band on Friday & Saturday the 6th & 7th at the Avalon Ballroom.
- Dica Productions present Freak Out Ethel at the Seymour Hall, London with Pink Floyd, Ginger Johnson's African Drum Band, Waygood Ellis & The Zone, Rich St. John, Alexandra Trocchi, Karma-Sigma, plus light shows, films and slides.
- The Afterthought in Vancouver, British Columbia presents the United Empire Loyalists and Winter Green at the Kitsilano Theatre on 4th Ave.

6th January - 1967

- The Golden Sheaf Bakery presents Country Joe and the Fish, Wildflower and John Fahey on Saturday the 6th with lights by Bill Ham, at the Finnish Brotherhood Hall, Berkeley.

10th January – 1967

- The Marquee Club in London features Cream and Catch 22.

11th January – 1967

- Pink Floyd are in the studio for two days to record "Interstellar Overdrive", "Arnold Layne" and "Let's Roll Another one". This version of "Interstellar Overdrive" will eventually be used in the soundtrack to the film **Let's All Make Love In London** and released in early 1968.

13th January - 1967

- Bill Graham presents the Grateful Dead, Junior Wells' Chicago Blues Band and the Doors on Friday, Saturday & Sunday the 13th, 14th & 15th at the Fillmore Auditorium.

- The Family Dog presents Moby Grape, Sparrow and the Charlatans on Friday & Saturday the 13th & 14th at the Avalon Ballroom.
- CNP (Community for New Politics) present a "Peace Fest" at the Ligure Hall, Oakland with performances from Maybe Tomorrow and Loading Zone.
- Ralph & Al Pepe present Big Brother and the Holding Company, Moby Grape and Morning Glory at the Santa Venetia Armory, San Rafael.
- Pink Floyd and Giant Sun Trolley play at the UFO, Tottenham Court Road, London.
- The Afterthought in Vancouver, British Columbia presents the Seeds of Time and the Unforeseen at the Kitsilano Theatre on 4th Ave. Lights by Trans-Euphoric Express Light Show.

14th January - 1967

- The Human Be-In "A Gathering of the Tribes" is held Sunday the 14th at the Polo Grounds in Golden Gate Park, San Francisco. This event was seen as a turning point in the new psychedelic scene. On the bill were Timothy Leary, Richard Alpert, Allen Ginsberg, Laurence Ferlingetti, Gary Snyder, Michael McClure and music was provided by the core San Francisco bands including the Jefferson Airplane, Grateful Dead, Big Brother and the Holding Company, Loading Zone and Sir Douglas Quintet. On the scene were elements from all factions of the psychedelic scene. Everyone was encouraged to bring flowers, beads, costumes, flags and of course food to share. The Human Be-In was also an opportunity to bridge the differences between the politically oriented Berkeley crowd and the more laid back hippie community. Berkeley distrusted the Haight-Ashbury scene pointing out their lack of commitment to politics while the hippies felt the Berkley crowd were too interested in fomenting disorder. Berkeley favorites Country Joe and the Fish performed in an effort to bring the factions together. The hoped for union was never consummated but for one day at least, close to 20,000 strange and unusual people wandered happily through the Golden Gate Park. The Human Be-In is without question one of the pivotal events of the hippie generation. It was a non-violent meeting with no purpose other than "to be". The significance of this counter-cultural event cannot be overstated. The Human Be-In was more successful than anyone had imagined. Noted poster authority Walter Medeiros has said, "It was a call for community and declaration of identity, and it resounded across the nation to energize millions of young people. It inspired the mass migration to San Francisco for the Summer of Love, live music in city parks, and, ultimately Woodstock."
- Pink Floyd undertake a hectic British tour that takes them over the next few months to just about every corner of the country including Reading University, Portsmouth and weekly gigs at the UFO in London. By now many in the traditional press were quite vocal about the sheer volume at Pink Floyd gigs.

16th January - 1967

- Pink Floyd play at the Institute of Contemporary Arts, Dover Street, London. As an interesting twist, after the show, they stayed to discuss their performance with members of the audience.
- The Marquee Club in London features the Herd, Richard Henry and the first

appearance of Timebox. Timebox would go on to make 42 appearances at the Marquee and eventually evolved into Patto.

17th January – 1967
- Big Brother and the Holding Company perform at the Matrix Club in San Francisco.
- The Boston Tea Party, the East Coast's first big ballroom opens its doors.
- Pink Floyd play at the Commonwealth Institute, Kensington, London. The event was billed as "Music In Colour" by the Pink Floyd.

19th January – 1967
- The Jimi Hendrix Experience perform at the Speakeasy in London.
- The Marquee Club in London features Pink Floyd and Marmalade on Thursday the 19th. Marmalade would go on to make an additional 41 appearances at the Marquee.

20th January - 1967
- The Monkees' TV show premiers in the U.K. Through the month of January the Monkees' hold down the No.1 spot on both the U.S. and U.K charts with *I'm a Believer*. Their psychedelic phase is yet to come.
- Bill Graham presents the Paul Butterfield Blues Band and Charles Lloyd Quintet on Friday, Saturday & Sunday the 20th, 21st & 22nd at the Fillmore Auditorium.
- The Family Dog presents the Steve Miller Blues Band and Lee Michaels Friday & Saturday the 20th & 21st at the Avalon Ballroom.
- Pink Floyd play at the UFO, Tottenham Court Road, London. They are named the house band and Granada TV is on hand to film the group performing for a documentary.

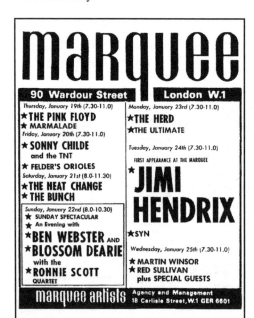

21st January - 1967
- Pink Floyd play on Saturday the 21st at Portsmouth, Hampshire, England.

22nd January - 1967
- Big Brother and the Holding Company perform on Sunday the 22nd the Matrix Club in San Francisco.

24th January – 1967
- San Francisco Police Chief Thomas Cahill comes up with the term, "the Love Generation".
- In Detroit, White Panther Party leader, and manager of the MC5, John Sinclair is arrested and charged with possession of two joints. He is

eventually convicted and sentenced to nine and a half years in jail.
* The Marquee Club in London features the first appearance of the Jimi Hendrix Experience and the Syn on Tuesday the 24th.

26th January - 1967
* Womb and Santana Blues Band play on Thursday & Friday the 26th & 27th at the Ark, Sausalito.

27th January - 1967
* Bill Graham presents the Paul Butterfield Blues Band and Charles Lloyd Quintet on Friday & Saturday the 27th & 28th at the Fillmore Auditorium.
* The Family Dog presents the Grateful Dead and Quicksilver Messenger Service on Friday & Saturday the 27th & 28th at the Avalon Ballroom. Lights by Roger Hillyard and Ben Van Meter.
* A Cinema Dance Concert is staged at the Golden Sheaf Bakery in Berkeley on Friday & Saturday the 27th & 28th featuring Berkeley with Lee Michaels, Melvyn Q. Watchpocket and the Justice League.
* Pink Floyd play on Friday the 27th at the UFO, London.

28th January - 1967
* Pink Floyd play Saturday the 28th at the University of Essex, Essex, England.
* A Million Volt Rave at the Round House, Chalk Farm, London, with lights by Binder Edwards-Vaughan is staged on Saturday the 28th.

ONE OF THE MANY STRANGE COVERS FOR OZ

29th January - 1967
* Krishna Consciousness event Sunday the 29th at the Avalon Ballroom featuring Swami Bhaktivedenta, Allen Ginsberg, Grateful Dead, Moby Grape, Big Brother and the Holding Company. Billed as a 'Mantra and Rock Dance'.
* Sunday the 29th At the Saville features the Koobas, Jimi Hendrix Experience and the Who.

31st January - 1967
* Big Brother and the Holding Company play Tuesday the 31st the Matrix Club in San Francisco.

February - 1967
* The first edition of **Oz** hits the streets of London. This colourful hippie newspaper was created by transplanted Australian Martin Sharp, fast becoming a prominent

figure in London's underground community. Because it was published monthly it rarely if ever carried listings of events as they'd likely be out of date by the time the paper hit the streets. But unlike the **International Times** it was in full colour and was able to better portray the colourful hippie scene and soon became the paper of choice by many in the underground.

2nd February - 1967

- A fashion show is staged at the Blushing Peony in Haight-Ashbury and even the San Francisco papers are there to report on the event.
- Pink Floyd play at Cadenna's, Guildford, Surrey. They make it official and turn professional.

3rd February - 1967

- Bill Graham presents Jefferson Airplane and Quicksilver Messenger Service with Dino Valenti on Friday, Saturday & Sunday the 3rd, 4th & 5th at the Fillmore Auditorium.
- The Family Dog presents Country Joe and the Fish, Sparrow, Kaleidoscope on Friday & Saturday the 3rd & 4th at the Avalon Ballroom.
- The Hell's Angels Motorcycle Club present a Benefit for Hairy Harry with Big Brother and the Holding Company and Blue Cheer with lights by Head Lights at the California Hall, San Francisco.
- Pink Floyd play at the Queens Hall, Leeds, Yorkshire. This all night rave also featured Cream, go-go dancers and a barbeque.

4th February - 1967

- Buffalo Springfield release *For What It's Worth*. The song is inspired by the recent riots in Los Angeles and also draws attention to the growing generational divide and the violence that was sweeping the nation.

7th February – 1967

- Granada TV in England air their documentary on the London underground scene, which includes footage of Pink Floyd performing at the UFO.
- Monkees' drummer Micky Dolenz arrives in London for a promotional tour and spends some time with Paul McCartney,

9th February - 1967

- Pink Floyd play at the New Addington Hotel, Surrey, England.

10th February - 1967

- Bill Graham presents the Blues Project, Jimmy Reed and John Lee Hooker on Friday, Saturday & Sunday the 10th, 11th & 12th at the Fillmore Auditorium. Lights by Head Lights.
- The Family Dog presents the Steve Miller Blues Band, Lee Michaels and the Peanut Butter Conspiracy on Friday & Saturday the 10th & 11th at the Avalon Ballroom.
- The Transaction, in association with Bob McKendrick presents A Tribute to J. Edgar Hoover at the California Hall in San Francisco with the Jook Savages, Congress of

Wonders, Blue Cheer and the Mojo Men, with lights by Head Lights.
- The Funny Co. presents a dance-concert with the Sparrow, Wildflower, Living Children and the Immediate Family at the Regency Ballroom, Leamington Hotel, Oakland.
- Big Brother and the Holding Company and Country Joe and the Fish perform Friday & Saturday the 10th & 11th at the Golden Sheaf Bakery. This is the weekend where Janis Joplin meets Country Joe MacDonald. They move in together shortly after this meeting.
- The UFO Club in London presents a Love Festival.
- The Afterthought in Vancouver, British Columbia presents Martha Mushroom's Fantastic Sensations, the United Empire Loyalists and Painted Ship on Friday & Saturday the 10th & 11th at the Kitsilano Theatre on 4th Ave. Lights by Trans-Euphoric Express Light Show.

11th February - 1967
- Pink Floyd along with the Alan Bown Set, Wishful Thinking and Russells Clump play on Saturday the 11th at the Sussex University, Brighton, Sussex

12th February - 1967
- KMPX-FM launches the first 'underground radio show', hosted by Larry Miller. It runs from midnight to 6am on weekdays. Miller avoids the usual Top 40 fare and focuses instead on music coming out of the underground scene in San Francisco.
- Police raid Keith Richard's house in Sussex, England. The 15 police involved find various substances of a suspicious nature, but no arrests will be made until later in the year.
- Bill Graham presents 'Abe Lincoln's Birthday Party' benefit for the Council for Civic Unity on Sunday the 12th at the Fillmore Auditorium. On the bill are the Grateful Dead, Moby Grape, Sly and the Family Stone and the New Salvation Army.

13th February – 1967
- The Beatles release *Penny Lane* b/w *Strawberry Fields Forever* in the United States. This is their first single since Revolver and in some ways foreshadows their next album **Sgt. Pepper**, with its full use of studio technology and psychedelic flavor. The British release is on the 17th.
- The Blues Project perform on Monday the 13th at the Matrix 3138 Fillmore Street in San Francisco.

14th February - 1967
- The Love Conspiracy Commune presents the Peanut Butter Conspiracy and the Doors on Tuesday the 14th at the Whisky A-Go-Go, 568 Sacramento Street, San Francisco.

16th February - 1967
- Pink Floyd were to play on Thursday the 16th at the Southampton Guildhall, Southampton, Hampshire, but the event was cancelled due to concerns over drug use.

A POSTER FOR WHISKY A-GO-GO

• The Afterthought in Vancouver, British Columbia presents Country Joe and the Fish, Martha Mushroom's Fantastic Sensations, Painted Ship and the United Empire Loyalists on Thursday, Friday & Saturday the 16th, 17th & 18th at the Kitsilano Theatre on 4th Ave. Lights by Trans-Euphoric Express Light Show.

17th February - 1967
• The London School of Economics holds a "Daffodil Protest" march.
• Bill Graham presents the Blues Project, the Mothers of Invention and the Canned Heat Blues Band on Friday, Saturday & Sunday the 17th, 18th & 19th at the Fillmore Auditorium.
• The Family Dog presents Big Brother and the Holding Company and Quicksilver Messenger Service on Friday & Saturday the 17th & 18th at the Avalon Ballroom.
• Pink Floyd along with Bob Kidman, Alexis Korner's Blues Inc. and the Pearl Hawaiians play on Friday the 17th for the St. Catherine's College Valentine Ball at the Dorothy Ballroom, Cambridge.

18th February - 1967
• The Mojo Men, Harpers Bizarre and Chocolate Watch Band play on Saturday the 18th at the Continental Auditorium, Santa Clara with lights by The Light House.
• Pink Floyd, the Equals and Two of Each play on Saturday the 18th at the California Ballroom, Dunstable, Bedfordshire.

19th February - 1967
• Port Chicago Vigil Benefit is staged on Sunday the 19th at the California Hall, San Francisco with Country Joe and the Fish, Steve Miller Blues Band, San Francisco Mime Troupe, Robert Baker and the Magic Theatre light show.
• The Marquee Club in London features the Bonzo Dog Do Dah Band on Sunday the 19th.

20th February - 1967
• Pink Floyd play at the Adelphi Ballroom, West Bromwich, Warwickshire, England.
• The Marquee Club in London features the Birds, Birds and the Majority. The Birds, Birds featured Ron Wood on guitar on Monday the 20th.

23rd February - 1967

• Lovescream presents Big Brother and the Holding Company and the Human Beings in a benefit for the Valley Peace Center on Thursday the 23rd at the Ark, Sausalito

24th February – 1967

• Bill Graham presents Otis Rush and his Chicago Blues Band, Grateful Dead and the Canned Heat Blues Band on Friday, Saturday & Sunday Afternoon the 24th, 25th & 26th at the Fillmore Auditorium.
• The Family Dog presents Moby Grape and the Charlatans on Friday & Saturday the 24th & 25th at the Avalon Ballroom. Lights by Van Meter and Hillyard.
• Pink Floyd play an early show at the Ricky Tick Club in Berkshire and then head over to the UFO, London for a late show with the Brothers Grimm.
•   The Afterthought in Vancouver, British Columbia presents Joe Mock, No Commercial Potential and Jabberwock Friday the 24th at the Kitsilano Theatre on 4th Ave.

25th February - 1967

• Pink Floyd play at the Ricky Tick Club in Hounslow, Middlesex.

26th February – 1967

• Bill Graham presents B.B. King, Moby Grape and the Steve Miller Blues Band Sunday evening the 26th at the Fillmore Auditorium. B.B. King has said, "Fillmore audiences were the best I ever played for. They participated, and when you pleased them, they let you know it."

27th February - 1967

• Pink Floyd record *Arnold Layne* at Sound Techniques Studios, Chelsea, London. The single does well on the British charts but fails to have any impact in America.

28th February - 1967

• Pink Floyd and the Majority play Tuesday the 28th at Blaises Club, London.

March – 1967

•   Jefferson Airplane releases **Surrealistic Pillow** with Grace Slick on lead vocals. The album in many ways is representative of the all that is flourishing in the psychedelic movement and contains two Top 10 singles *Somebody to Love* and *White Rabbit*. The Grateful Dead's Jerry Garcia sat in on the sessions and not only assisted on some of the band's arrangements but is said to even had a hand in the LP's title. The recording was released with much fanfare and confirmed the Airplanes status as one of the premier psychedelic San Francisco bands.

• Pink Floyd sign with EMI records and receive a £5,000 advance or roughly $12,000.

1st March – 1967

• Pink Floyd play at Eel Pie Island, Richmond, Surrey.

3rd March - 1967

• The **Berkeley Barb** prints a letter claiming that you could get high by smoking the white fibre inside a banana peel. A run on bananas ensues.
• Bill Graham presents Otis Rush and his Chicago Blues Band, the Mothers of Invention and Morning Glory on Friday, Saturday & Sunday the 3rd, 4th & 5th at the Fillmore Auditorium.
• The Family Dog presents the Doors and Sparrow on Friday & Saturday the 3rd & 4th at the Avalon Ballroom.
• The First Annual Love Circus presented by The Love Conspiracy Commune with the Grateful Dead, Moby Grape, Loading Zone and the Blue Crumb Truck Factory with lights by Commune at Winterland, San Francisco. This is the Grateful Dead's first Winterland gig, and they perform while outside there are picketers protesting the high ticket price of $3.50.
• Pink Floyd and Tuppence the TV Dancer play at Market Hall, St. Albans, Hertfordshire, England.
• The Afterthought in Vancouver, British Columbia presents the Carnival, William Tell and the Marksmen and Seeds of Time on Friday & Saturday the 3rd & 4th at the Kitsilano Theatre on 4th Ave. Lights by Trans-Euphoric Express Light Show.

4th March - 1967

• The Poly Rag Ball 1967 is held on Saturday the 4th at Regent Street Polytechnic, London featuring Pink Floyd and the Minor Birds.

5th March - 1967

• Bedrock One is staged on Sunday the 5th at the California Hall, San Francisco. Amongst the many artists performing are the Steve Miller Blues Band, Dino Valenti, Orkustra, the Rada Krishna Temple, San Francisco Mime Troupe, the Diggers plus poetry and other surprises. Lights for the event were by the Lysergic Power & Light Company.
• Pink Floyd, Lee Dorsey, the Ryan Brothers and Jeff Beck play Sunday the 5th at the Saville Theatre, Shaftsbury Avenue, London.

6th March – 1967

• Pink Floyd preview their forthcoming single *Arnold Layne* on ITV's new pop music television show The Rave. The Move are featured in a 30-minute segment on this first episode intended as a replacement program for Ready Steady, Go!

7th March - 1967

- The Doors play Tuesday the 7th through Saturday the 11th at the Matrix Club in San Francisco.
- Pink Floyd play Tuesday the 7th at the Malvern Big Beat Sessions, Worcestershire, England.

9th March - 1967

- **International Times** offices raided in London. Police enter the premises with warrants looking for obscene material.
- Pink Floyd and Thoughts play on Thursday the 9th at the Marquee, London.

10th March - 1967

- Bill Graham presents Jefferson Airplane, Jimmy Reed, John Lee Hooker and the Stu Gardner Trio on Friday & Saturday the 10th & 11th at the Winterland. The afternoon performance on Sunday the 12th was performed at the Fillmore.
- The Family Dog presents Quicksilver Messenger Service and the Steve Miller Blues Band on Friday & Saturday the 10th & 11th at the Avalon Ballroom.
- Uncle Russ Travel Agency presents the Poor Souls, We Who Are, Fruit of The Loom, Southbound Freeway and Passing Clouds on Friday & Saturday the 10th & 11th at the Grande Ballroom, Detroit.
- Pink Floyd play on Friday the 10th at the UFO, Tottenham Court Road, London. They screen their promotional film for their debut single *Arnold Layne*.

11th March - 1967

- Pink Floyd release *Arnold Layne* b/w *Candy And A Current Bun*. The band also performs at the Technical College, Canterbury, Kent, England.

12th March - 1967

- Sunflower-Phoenix Dance Benefit at the Fillmore Auditorium featuring Quicksilver Messenger Service, Big Brother and the Holding Company, the Steve Miller Blues Band, Country Joe and the Fish and the Dan Bruhns Light Show.
- Pink Floyd and Mike Raynor & the Condors play Sunday the 12th at the Agincourt Ballroom, Camberley, England.

16th March - 1967

- Pink Floyd's *Interstellar Overdrive* is produced at Abbey Road Studios. In the days following Pink Floyd would once again tour the English countryside.

17th March – 1967

- The Grateful Dead release their self-titled debut album. Recorded in Los Angeles it's at best a compromise between their early bar band sound and the "new-improved" tripped out style. The overall sound wasn't helped by production from individuals outside the hippie scene. The album was recorded in a total of three days!

- Bill Graham presents Chuck Berry, Grateful Dead and Johnny Talbot and De Thangs at the Winterland. The Sunday 19th afternoon performance was at the Fillmore Auditorium.
- The Family Dog presents Big Brother and the Holding Company, Charles Lloyd and Sir Douglas Quintet on Friday & Saturday the 17th & 18th at the Avalon Ballroom.
- The Charlatans and Quicksilver Messenger Service perform on Friday, Saturday & Sunday the 17th, 18th, & 19th at the Matrix Club in San Francisco.
- The Afterthought in Vancouver, British Columbia presents the Steve Miller Blues Band and the Collectors on Friday, Saturday & Sunday the 17th, 18th, 19th at the Kitsilano Theatre on 4th Ave. Lights by Trans-Euphoric Express Light Show.

18th March – 1967

- Steve Winwood, formerly of the Spencer Davis Group, forms his new group soon to be called Traffic. The group consists of Jim Capaldi, Chris Wood, and Dave Mason. They spend six months away from the public eye working on new material.
- The Beatles *Penny Lane* b/w *Strawberry Field Forever* reaches No.1 in the U.S charts.

19th March - 1967

- After weeks of arresting people the city of San Francisco agrees to provide pastel chalks for individuals to create psychedelic designs on the sidewalks.
- Sonoma State & KLPS present the Animals on Sunday the 19th at the Santa Rosa Fairgrounds.

21st March - 1967

- Eric Burdon & the Animals play on Tuesday the 21st at the San Francisco Civic Auditorium.
- Ralph & Al Pepe present Quicksilver Messenger Service, Freedom Highway and a battle of the bands with the Knaves, Michaels Way and the Emergency Broadcasting System at the Santa Venetia Armory, San Rafael.
- The Marquee Club in London features Cream and the first appearance of Family. Family will go on to make an additional fifteen appearances at the Marquee.

22nd March – 1967

- The Family Dog presents Quicksilver Messenger Service, John Lee Hooker and the Steve Miller Blues Band on Wednesday & Thursday the 22nd & 23rd at the Avalon Ballroom.

23rd March - 1967

- Bill Ham's Light Sound Dimension presents Easter Voyage at the Fillmore Auditorium.
- The Afterthought in Vancouver, British Columbia presents the return of Country Joe and the Fish along with the United Empire Loyalists on Thursday, Friday & Saturday the 23rd, 24th & 25th at the Kitsilano Theatre on 4th Ave.

24th March - 1967

- Bill Graham presents Moby Grape, Chambers Brothers and the Charlatans on Friday, Saturday & Sunday 24th, 25th at the Winterland. The Sunday afternoon show of the 26th was performed at the Fillmore.
- The Family Dog presents the Grateful Dead, Quicksilver Messenger Service and Johnny Hammond and his Screaming Nighthawks on Friday, Saturday & Sunday the 24th, 25th & 26th at the Avalon Ballroom.
- Uncle Russ Love Agency presents Landeers Henchmen, Born Blues, City Limits and MC5 on Friday & Saturday the 24th & 25th at the Grande Ballroom, Detroit.

25th March - 1967

- The Doors release their self-titled debut album. The album contains the hit single *Light My Fire* written by guitarist Robbie Kreiger as well as the psychedelic epic *The End*.
- Jefferson Airplane's second LP **Surrealistic Pillow** enters the US charts. It contains two hit singles, *Somebody to Love* and *White Rabbit*.
- Both the Who and Cream, virtually unknown in the United States start U.S. tours. The two bands appear near the bottom of a series of dates billed as a Rock and Roll Extravaganza presented by New York disc jockey Murray the K.

- Teens 'n' Twenties present Eric Burdon and the Animals, the Association, the Bola Sete Trio, Harbinger Complex, Baytovens and Sly and the Family Stone on Saturday the 25th at the Oakland Coliseum, Oakland.

28th March – 1967

- The Chambers Brothers play Tuesday, Wednesday & Thursday the 28th, 29th & 30th at the Matrix Club in San Francisco.
- The Marquee Club in London features Geno Washington and the Ram Jam Band and the Amboy Dukes on Tuesday the 28th.

29th March – 1967

- Jim Salzer presents the Grateful Dead, the Doors, UFO and Captain Speed on Wednesday the 29th at the Earl Warren Showground's in Santa Barbara California.
- Pink Floyd perform on Wednesday the 29th at Eel Pie Island, Richmond, Surrey.

30th March – 1967

- The cover for the Beatles' **Sgt. Pepper** LP is photographed at Michael Cooper's studio.

31st March - 1967

- Bill Graham presents the Byrds, Moby Grape and Andrew Staples on Friday & Saturday the 31st and 1st at the Winterland. The Sunday afternoon show of the 2nd was performed at the Fillmore.
- The Family Dog presents Big Brother and the Holding Company and Blue Cheer on Friday & Saturday the 31st & 1st at the Avalon Ballroom.
- Baldwin & Berner present Fluxfest at the Longshoremen's Hall, in San Francisco on Friday the 31st with performances from Retinal Circus, Cosmic-Concrete, San Francisco Mime Troupe, Wildflower and Quicksilver Messenger Service.
- Jimi Hendrix performing at an event in London sets his guitar on fire for the first time. This stunt gets so much publicity for the guitarist it will form the climax to virtually all of his shows for the next two years.

1st April - 1967

- The Yellow Brick Road perform on Saturday & Sunday the 1st & 2nd at the Matrix Club in San Francisco.

3rd April – 1967

- Paul McCartney visits San Francisco and then Denver and Los Angeles over a 10-day period, the 3rd – 12th.

4th April - 1967

- The Chambers Brothers perform Tuesday, Wednesday & Thursday the 4th, 5th & 6th at the Matrix Club in San Francisco.

5th April – 1967

- The Gray Line Bus Tour Company begins offering tours for tourists of the hippie community in Haight-Ashbury. It's called "The Hippie Hop" and is advertised as "the only FOREIGN tour within the continental limits of the United States." Word had spread across the country of what was happening and the enterprising tour company saw an opportunity to cash in.

6th April - 1967

- Pink Floyd appear on Top Of The Pops Thursday the 6th for the first time.

7th April - 1967

- Tom Donahue joins Larry Miller on KMPX-FM, playing even more of the underground music on an earlier evening shift. Donahue inaugurates a whole new era in broadcasting. This new style of "progressive FM radio" is vastly different from regular Top 40 fare, in that the emphasis is on the music, it avoids the inane disc jockey chatter and pacing. Here the announcers are more low-key and they play predominantly album cuts regardless of the length or chart placing. By the Summer of 1967 the station was playing hippie music 24 hours a day.
- Bill Graham presents the Chambers Brothers, Quicksilver Messenger Service and

Sandy Bull on Friday, Saturday & Sunday the 7th, 8th & 9th at the Fillmore Auditorium.

- The Family Dog presents the Charlatans, Sparrow and Canned Heat on Friday & Saturday the 7th & 8th at the Avalon Ballroom. Lights by the North American Ibis Alchemical Co.
- St. Ignatius High School presents Jefferson Airplane and Buffalo Springfield on Friday the 7th at the University of San Francisco with Jerry Abram's Head Lights.
- Wilderness Conference takes place Friday, Saturday & Sunday the 7th, 8th & 9th at the Hilton Hotel, San Francisco.
- The Afterthought in Vancouver, British Columbia presents the United Empire Loyalists, Unforeseen and William Tell and the Marksmen on Friday & Saturday 7th & 8th.

8th April - 1967
- Pink Floyd, Flies, Earl Fuggle, Electric Poets, Block and others perform on Saturday the 8th at the Roundhouse, Chalk Farm, London.
- The Marquee Club in London features the Syn and Love Affair on Saturday the 8th.

9th April – 1967
- Paul McCartney joins the advisory board planning the up coming Monterey Pop Festival and his first recommendation is to book the Jimi Hendrix Experience.

10th April – 1967
- Paul McCartney visits Brian Wilson and ends up participating in the recording of some "munching" sound effects for the track *Vegetables* intended for the LP **Smile**.
- "Peace and Freedom" Benefit featuring Country Joe and the Fish, Cleveland Wrecking Company, Loading Zone, Mount Rushmore and the Sons of Champlin on Monday the 10th at the Fillmore Auditorium. Lights by Garden of Delights.
- The Marquee Club in London features the Herd and Fleur De Lys on Monday the 10th. Of note, is that Jimmy Page produced Fleur De Lys' first two singles.

11th April - 1967
- The Rock Garden located at 4742 Mission presents the Electric Chamber Orkustra and Buffalo Springfield on Tuesday the 11th with lights by Light Environment.

12th April - 1967
- Ken Kesey is arrested on drugs charges.
- A San Francisco Mime Troupe Benefit is staged on Wednesday the 12th at the Fillmore Auditorium featuring Jefferson Airplane, Grateful Dead, Quicksilver Messenger Service, Moby Grape, Andrew Staples and Loading Zone.

14th April – 1967
- Bill Graham presents Howlin' Wolf, Country Joe and the Fish and Loading Zone on Friday, Saturday & Sunday the 14th, 15th, 16th at the Fillmore Auditorium.

- The Family Dog presents the Doors and the Steve Miller Blues Band on Friday & Saturday the 14th & 15th at the Avalon Ballroom.
- Country Joe and the Fish perform in the Panhandle of the Golden Gate Park on the eve of the peace march.
- Russ Gibb presents in Detroit "Mind Zap" featuring Changing Tymes, Weeds, Sum Guys, One Way Street and Thyme Gang on Friday & Saturday the 14th & 15th at the Grande Ballroom.
- International Kaleidoscope presents the Jefferson Airplane, Grateful Dead and Canned Heat on Friday, Saturday & Sunday the 14th, 15th & 16th at the all-new Kaleidoscope in Los Angeles.

15th April – 1967

- Some 100,000 people march in protest against the Vietnam War. Vietnam vet David Duncan gave the keynote speech, while the protesters marched from Second and Market to the Kezar Stadium at the Golden Gate Park.
- 400,000 people march from Central Park to the United Nations building to protest against the Vietnam War.
- The Kinetic Arena – K4 Discothèque is staged in the Main Ballroom of the West Pier, Brighton, England with a performance from Pink Floyd.

16th April - 1967

- The Charlatans, Mystery Trend and Haight St. Jazz Band perform on Sunday the 16th with the Aurora Glory Alice light show at the California Hall in San Francisco.
- Big Brother and the Holding Company and the New Breed play on Sunday the 16th at the Stockton Civic Auditorium.

18th April - 1967

- Howlin Wolf performs Tuesday, Wednesday & Thursday the 18th, 19th & 20th at the Matrix Club in San Francisco.

19th April – 1967

- The Grateful Dead perform on Wednesday, Thursday & Friday the 19th, 20th & 21st at Thee Image, 18330 Collins Avenue, Miami Beach, Florida.

21st April - 1967

- Bill Graham presents Howlin' Wolf, Big Brother and the Holding Company and Harbinger Complex on Friday, Saturday & Sunday the 21st, 22nd & 23rd at the Fillmore Auditorium.
- The Family Dog presents Quicksilver Messenger Service, John Hammond and His Screaming Nighthawks and Charles Lloyd on Friday & Saturday the 21st & 22nd at the Avalon Ballroom.
- Sierra Banana presents Spirit and Peter & His Group on Friday & Saturday the 21st & 22nd at the American Legion Hall, Truckee, California.
- Pink Floyd perform on Friday the 21st at the UFO, Tottenham Court Road, London.

22nd April – 1967
- Pink Floyd's *Arnold Layne* b/w *Candy And a Current Bun* enters the British charts at No.20.

23rd April - 1967
- The Green Joynt Project present the Charles Lloyd Quartet, Big Brother and the Holding Company and Wildflower with lights by Aurora Glory Alice on Sunday the 23rd at the California Hall in San Francisco.

25th April - 1967
- Sons Of Champlin, Rose and Amber Whine play on Tuesday & Wednesday the 25th & 26th at the New Dream Bowl, Napa Valley just outside of San Francisco. Lights by Deadly Nightshade.
- Big Brother and the Holding Company play on Tuesday, Wednesday & Thursday the 25th, 26th & 27th at the Matrix in San Francisco.

28th April - 1967
- Bill Graham presents Buffalo Springfield and the Steve Miller Blues Band on Friday, Saturday & Sunday the 28th, 29th & 30th at the Fillmore Auditorium.
- The Family Dog presents the Chambers Brothers and Iron Butterfly on Friday & Saturday the 28th & 29th at the Avalon Ballroom.
- Green Joynt Project present Big Brother and the Holding Company and Big Mama Thornton with Aurora Glory Alice lightshow and Organic food and refreshments by Far Fetched Foods on Friday & Saturday the 28th & 29th.
- The Rock Garden present the Charles Lloyd Quartet, Grateful Dead and Mystery Trend on Friday the 28th.

29th April - 1967
- An Easter Sunday "Love-In" staged at Elysian Park in Los Angeles draws a crowd of 4000.
- The Pretentious Folk Front present the First Annual Hippie Fair and Bazaar at the Hearst Gym, University of California, Berkeley with performances from Country Joe and the Fish, the S.F Mime Troupe and much other strangeness.
- **International Times** '14-Hour Technicolour Dream' is held at Alexandra Palace, London. Featured artists included: Yoko Ono, Pink Floyd, Alexis Corner, Pretty Things, Purple Gang, Champion Jack Dupree, Graham Bond, Savoy Brown, Flies, Ginger Johnson's Drummers, Crazy World of Arthur Brown, Soft Machine, Creation, Denny Lane, Block, Cat, Charlie Browns Clowns, Christopher Logue, Derek Brimstone, Dave Russell, Glo Macari and the Big Three, Gary Farr, Interference, Jacobs Ladder Construction Company, Lincoln Folk Group, Move, Mike Horovitz, 117, Poison Bellows, Pete Townsend, Robert Randall, Suzy Creamcheese, Sam Gopal, Mick and Pete, Giant Sun Trolley, Social Deviants, Stalkers, Utterly Incredible Too Long Ago To Remember, Sometimes Shouting At People, Barry Fantoni, Noel Murphy and all sorts of utter strangeness. Pink Floyd perform to a crowd of 10,000 people as dawn breaks. Admission is 1 UK Pound!! In attendance is John Lennon.

2nd May – 1967

• Capitol Records announces the Beach Boys' **Smile** project is no longer in the works. Brian Wilson masterminded this long fabled project in an effort to stay in step creatively with the challenge from the Beatles.

3rd May – 1967

• A "Cosmic Love-In" is held Wednesday the 3rd at New York City's Village Theatre, coincidentally this same theatre would eventually be renamed the Fillmore East by Bill Graham.

5th May - 1967

• Bill Graham presents the Grateful Dead, Paupers and Collage on Friday & Saturday the 5th & 6th at the Fillmore Auditorium.
• The Family Dog presents Big Brother and the Holding Company, Sir Douglas Quintet and the Orkustra on Friday, Saturday & Sunday the 5th, 6th & 7th at the Avalon Ballroom.
• Golden Star Promotions present Country Joe and the Fish and Baltimore Steam Packet on Friday the 5th at Fairfax Park, Fairfax, California.

6th May – 1967

• Scott Mackenzie's "San Francisco (Be Sure to Wear Flowers in your Hair)" is released. By June it's a Top 10 hit reaching the No.4 slot on the U.S. Charts. It'll be No.1 in the U.K. by August 14th. The song was written by Los Angeles based John Phillips of the Mamas and the Papas.
• Also on this day, the Grateful Dead's first self-titled LP enters the album charts.

7th May - 1967

• Jefferson Airplane and the Steve Miller Blues Band perform Sunday the 7th at the University of California.

10th May - 1967

• Mick Jagger and Keith Richards in court on drugs charges, Brian Jones arrested at home.

11th May - 1967

• Vanguard Records presents a celebration of Country Joe and the Fish's first LP at the Fillmore Auditorium. Also playing are Big Brother and the Holding Company.

12th May - 1967

• Bill Graham presents Jefferson Airplane and the Paupers on Friday, Saturday & Sunday the 12th, 13th & 14th at the Fillmore Auditorium.
• The Family Dog presents the Doors and Sparrow on Friday & Saturday the 12th & 13th at the Avalon Ballroom.

- Medicine Show at the Irwin Street Warehouse, San Rafael with the Jook Savages, the Vast Majority, the Charlatans and the Old Grey Zipper on Friday & Saturday the 12th & 13th.
- Games For May at the South Bank Queen Elizabeth Hall with Pink Floyd. The first quadraphonic sound system in the U.K is used. Unfortunately the device invented by EMI technicians was stolen after the show. Pink Floyd would revive the idea of moveable quadraphonic sound in 1969. None-the-less this multi-media event inspires Syd Barrett to write the event's theme song, which becomes *See Emily Play*.

14th May - 1967

- The San Jose Human Be-In, is held on Sunday the 14th in San Jose, California.
- The Pink Floyd appear on the new BBC Television program "The Look of the Week" and perform two non-single tracks entitled "Pow R Toc H" and "Astronomy Domine." Following their performance Syd Barrett and Roger Waters engage in a musical debate with music critic Hans Keller who describes their music as "terribly loud".

15th May – 1967

- The Gray Line Bus Company cancels their "Hippie Hop" tour through Haight-Ashbury.

18th May - 1967

- Jefferson Airplane, Rainy Daze, Acapulco Gold, Chocolate Watch Band and the Lewis & Clark Expedition play on Thursday the 18th at the Civic Auditorium, San Jose.

19th May - 1967

- The BBC bans the Beatles, *A Day In The Life* single.
- Bill Graham presents Martha and the Vandellas and the Paupers on Friday & Saturday the 19th & 20th at the Fillmore Auditorium. Lights by Dan Bruhn's Fillmore Lights. Martha and the Vandellas have the current No.1 record on the R&B charts with *Jimmy Mack*.
- The Family Dog presents Quicksilver Messenger Service and Country Joe and the Fish on Friday, Saturday & Sunday the 19th, 20th & 21st at the Avalon Ballroom. Lights by the North American Ibis Alchemical Co.
- Jefferson Airplane play on Friday the 19th at the California Polytechnic State University, San Luis.
- Golden Star Promotions presents the Charlatans and Universal Joint on Friday the 19th at Fairfax Park, Fairfax with lights by That Blinkin' Light Co.
- Erich Langmann presents "At the Happening" featuring the Nomads and Zoo on Friday the 19th at the Zap Palace on Sunset Blvd in Los Angeles.

20th May – 1967

- It's "Flower-Power Day" in New York City.

- Jimi Hendrix signs his first U.S. record deal with Reprise Records.
- The Grateful Dead, Real Thing and Autumn People play on Saturday the 20th at the Continental Ballroom, Santa Clara with lights by Marsh Mellow Cannon

21st May - 1967
- The "Youth for Peace in Vietnam" rally is held in Trafalgar Square, London.

22nd May – 1967
- The "Toronto Love-In" is staged in Queen's Park, Toronto, Canada. The event is organized by an offshoot of the Haight-Ashbury Diggers and much like their San Francisco counterparts; the Toronto group was dispensing food and clothing to the hundreds of young people who were flocking to Yorkville, the psychedelic center of Toronto.

23rd May - 1967
- *See Emily Play* by Pink Floyd is recorded at Sound Techniques.

24th May – 1967
- The Electric Garden Club in London opens and closes the same night. It reopened for a brief time, and many thought the Garden would be THE place to be, unfortunately it was not to be. The timing was not yet right. However the club would soon have new management brought in and be renamed Middle Earth.

25th May – 1967
- John Lennon takes delivery of his Rolls Royce, which has been repainted in glorious psychedelic colours and swirls.

26th May – 1967
- As might be expected, the U.S. Food and Drug Administration reports there are no mind-altering substances in banana peels.
- Bill Graham presents Big Brother and the Holding Company and the Steve Miller Blues Band on Friday & Saturday the 26th & 27th at the Fillmore Auditorium.
- The Family Dog presents the Charlatans, Salvation Army Banned and Blue Cheer on Friday, Saturday & Sunday the 26th, 27th & 28th at the Avalon Ballroom.
- Russ Gibb presents in Detroit a dance-concert featuring the Southbound Freeway and Cowardly Thangs, with lights by High Society on Friday & Saturday the 26th & 27th at the Grande Ballroom.
- Pink Floyd play on Friday the 26th at the Empress Ballroom, Blackpool, England as part of their ongoing nationwide tour. They are supported by the Koobas, Johnny Breeze & the Atlantics and the Rest.
- The Move play on Friday the 26th at the UFO Club, Tottenham Court Road, London

27th May – 1967
- Two of the biggest record labels in the United States, Columbia and RCA announce they are raising the list price of Mono LPs by $1 on June 1st. This is the first price

increase on mono records since 1953! Both companies claim that now that stereo records are more popular, mono production is an added expense.

- The Vancouver British Columbia "Trips Festival" featuring Jefferson Airplane, Collectors, Magic Fern, Painted Ship and others is held on Saturday the 27th at the Richmond Arena.

28th May – 1967
- Jefferson Airplane, the Byrds, P.H. Phactor and Magic Fern perform on Sunday the 28th at the Memorial Coliseum, Portland Oregon.

29th May – 1967
- "Barbecue 67" is staged at the Tulip Bulb Auction Hall, Spalding, Lincolnshire, England with performances from Pink Floyd, Jimi Hendrix Experience, Cream, Geno Washington & the Ram Jam Band, Zoot Money & His Big Roll Band and Sound Force Five.

30th May – 1967
- A benefit is staged at the Winterland on Tuesday the 30th for the Haight-Ashbury Legal Organization with a performance from Jefferson Airplane.

1st June – 1967
- Activist John "Hoppy" Hopkins begins a nine-month sentence for marijuana possession.
- The Beatles **Sgt. Pepper Lonely Hearts Club Band** LP is released in Britain on Friday the 1st and American on Saturday the 2nd. The album would have a revolutionary impact on recording from that point on, not only from the standpoint of studio production but from the shear composition bravado. And to think it was all done with just a four-track studio. **Sgt. Pepper** was also one of the first, if not THE first pop LPs to come with the lyrics printed on the sleeve. By the end of the week it was the No.1 LP on the U.K. charts and would stay there for 20 weeks. In the United States it knocked of the Monkees third LP **Headquarters** by the end of June and stayed at the No.1 spot for 12 weeks.
- The Family Dog presents the Steve Miller Blues Band and the Doors on Thursday, Friday Saturday & Sunday the 1st, 2nd, 3rd & 4th at the Avalon Ballroom.
- The Grateful Dead perform on Thursday through Saturday the 1st – 10th at the Café A-Go-Go in the Greenwich Village, New York. This is the Grateful Dead's first East Coast tour.
- Pink Floyd play on Friday the 1st at the UFO Club, Tottenham Court Road, London

2nd June - 1967
- Mick Jagger and Keith Richards are in court on drugs charges.
- Bill Graham presents the Jim Kweskin Jug Band, Peanut Butter Conspiracy and Sparrow on Friday & Saturday the 2nd & 3rd at the Fillmore Auditorium.
- Ramlala presents Big Brother and the Holding Company, Country Joe and the Fish and Quicksilver Messenger Service on Friday & Saturday the 2nd & 3rd at the

California Hall, San Francisco.

- Pink Floyd perform in front of the largest crowd yet at the UFO, Tottenham Court Road, London on Friday the 2nd. The crowd was so large the box office was closed twice to allow some to leave. In attendance were Jimi Hendrix, Chas Chandler, Pete Townsend, Eric Burdon and many other prominent figures of the blossoming psychedelic scene. Also on stage was Soft Machine, John Hopkins reading poetry and the Hydrogen Jukebox.

3rd June – 1967

- The Doors release *Light My Fire*. In two months it will be No.1 and be instrumental in launching the Doors to national popularity.
- The KFRC "Fantasy Fair and Magic Mountain Music Festival" is staged on Saturday & Sunday the 3rd & 4th at Mt. Tamalpais Mountain Theatre, Marin County featuring the Miracles, the Byrds, Wilson Pickett, the Seeds, Blues Magoos, Jefferson Airplane, the Doors, Country Joe and the Fish, Hugh Masekela, Tim Hardin, Mojo Men, Moby Grape, Tim Buckley, Kim Weston, Sparrow, Roger Collins, Grassroots, PF Sloan, Merry Go Round, Loading Zone, Smokey and His Sister and Every Mothers Son. Benefit proceeds went to the Hunters Point Child Care Centre. This event stands as one of the first Sixties–style rock festivals.

5th June - 1967

- Moby Grape release their first LP **Moby Grape** in the U.S. Partly as a joke from the band and partly as a publicity gimmick the record label releases five singles all at once.

8th June - 1967

- *A Whiter Shade Of Pale* by Procol Harum reaches No.1 in the UK charts.
- The Family Dog presents Big Brother and the Holding Company and Canned Heat on Thursday, Friday, Saturday & Sunday the 8th, 9th, 10th & 11th at the Avalon Ballroom.

9th June - 1967

- **Surrealistic Pillow** by Jefferson Airplane reaches No.3 in the U.S album charts. This makes them the most successful San Francisco band so far, if success is measured by placings on the music charts.
- The Haight-Ashbury Free Clinic opens. Created by Dr. David Smith, the Haight-Ashbury Free Clinic, opened on the corner of Haight and Clayton primarily to deal with the growing number of acid casualties. It is the first free clinic of its kind in the United States.
- Bill Graham presents the Doors and the Jim Kweskin Jug Band on Friday & Saturday the 9th & 10th at the Fillmore Auditorium. Lights by Dan Bruhn's Fillmore Lights.

10th June - 1967

- County Joe and the Fish release their first LP **Electric Music for the Mind And**

Body. The cover itself let alone the music captured the psychedelic experience.
- The "Muhammad Ali Festival" featuring (among others) the Steve Miller Blues Band, Loading Zone, Haight St. Jazz Band, Charlatans, S.F Mime Troupe and the Committee is held on Sunday the 10th at Hunters Point, San Francisco.

12th June – 1967
- The Marquee Club in London features Procol Harum and Timebox on Tuesday the 12th.

15th June – 1967
- The Family Dog presents the Youngbloods and the Siegal Schwall Blues Band on Thursday, Friday, Saturday & Sunday the 15th, 16th, 17th & 18th at the Avalon Ballroom.
- Pink Floyd and Episode Six perform a Free Concert on Thursday the 15th at Abbey Wood Park, London, England.

16th June – 1967

- Bill Graham presents the Who and the Loading Zone on Friday & Saturday the 16th & 17th at the Fillmore Auditorium. Lights by Dan Bruhn's Fillmore Lights.
- The "Monterey International Pop Festival" is staged Friday, Saturday & Sunday the 16th, 17th & 18th featuring the Who, Otis Redding, Janis Joplin, Jimi Hendrix, Country Joe and the Fish, Grateful Dead, Canned Heat, Al Kooper, Steve Miller Blues Band, Moby Grape, Simon and Garfunkel, Quicksilver Messenger Service, Paul Butterfield Blues Band, Mike Bloomfield, the Byrds, Blues Project, Jefferson Airplane, Mamas and Papas and Electric Flag. The event was seen by many of the San Francisco contingent as a slick opportunity for the LA crowd to co-op the scene and exploit the music for their own purposes. Northern California saw Southern California as an inferior imitation of the real thing. It was perhaps not coincidental that the festival took place at the Monterey Fairgrounds just 100 miles south of San Francisco. The event's overall stated intent was to bring together best

"international" talent. Many of the San Francisco bands were even offended by the pretentiousness of some in the LA crowd who were seen to be the "business" side of things, whereas the Haight bands actually lived in amongst the scene. They felt much more a part of it. Many turf battles ensued in the hours leading up to the event, most were settled. Although a number of the San Francisco bands refused to sign off on the film rights and never appeared in the famous film of the event. In an unusual twist, Janis Joplin with Big Brother and the Holding Company were asked to perform a second time because following their first performance they were signed to Columbia Records who felt appearing in the film would be a major career benefit. One thing was for sure, Monterey was the birth of the rock industry we know today. On the plus side, the event led to record deals for both Quicksilver Messenger Service and the Steve Miller Blues Band later in the year.

- The Crazy World Of Arthur Brown and Soft Machine play on Friday the 16th at the UFO Club, London.
- The Beatles appear on the cover of **Life** magazine. The article inside quotes Paul admitting to using LSD.
- Pink Floyd perform with Sugar Simone on Friday the 16th at the Tiles Club in London.

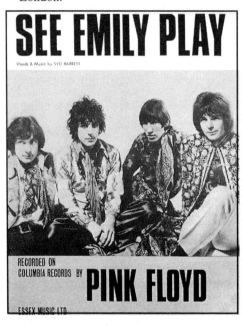

- Pink Floyd release *See Emily Play* b/w *Scarecrow*. The song eventually reached the No.6 spot on the British charts.

18th June – 1967

- Trans-Love presents Sun Ra and his Myth Science Orkestra in concert with MC5 at the Community Arts Auditorium on Sunday the 18th at Wayne State University, Detroit, Michigan.
- The "Radio London Motor Racing & Pop Festival" is held on Sunday the 18th at Brands Hatch Race Track. Performing are Pink Floyd, Chris Farlow & the Thunderbirds, Episode Six and the Shell Shock Show.

19th June – 1967

- A story runs in one of the UK's newspapers, **The Daily Mirror** where Paul McCartney admits to taking LSD.

20th June – 1967

- Bill Graham presents the "Opening of the Summer Series" with the Jefferson Airplane, the Jimi Hendrix Experience and Gabor Szabo performing Tuesday – Sunday the 20th – 25th at the Fillmore Auditorium. Lights by Dan Bruhn's Fillmore

Lights. Bill Graham said, "Jimi came to San Francisco right after Monterey Pop and played at the Fillmore with Gabor Szabo and Jefferson Airplane. Jimi took the town by storm. He was supreme."

21st June - 1967
- Summer Solstice celebrations on Wednesday the 21st launch "The Summer of Love" in San Francisco's Golden Gate Park with free performances from the Grateful Dead, Big Brother and the Holding Company and Quicksilver Messenger Service.

22nd June - 1967
- The Family Dog presents the Charlatans and 13th Floor Elevators on Thursday, Friday, Saturday & Sunday the 22nd, 23rd, 24th & 25th at the Avalon Ballroom.

23rd June - 1967
- A "Peace March" is held in Century City, Los Angeles on Friday the 23rd.
- The MC5, Charles Moore Ensemble and the Spikedrivers perform on Friday & Saturday the 23rd & 24th at the See, 3929 Woodward in Detroit Michigan. Lights by the Magic Veil.
- The UFO Club presents a "Liverpool Love Festival" on Friday the 23rd.

24th June - 1967
- Jim Salzer presents the Chambers Brothers, Steve Miller Blues Band and Canned Heat on Saturday the 24th at the Santa Monica Civic Auditorium.

25th June - 1967
- The Beatles *All You Need Is Love* is broadcast live by satellite around the world.

27th June – 1967
- Bill Graham presents "The Summer Series – Week 2 " featuring Chuck Berry and Eric Burdon and the Animals on Tuesday – Sunday the 27th – 2nd at the Fillmore Auditorium. Lights by Headlights. This was Eric Burdon's first visit to America.

28th June - 1967
- The Western Front Grand Opening on Wednesday through Sunday the 28th – 2nd with the Siegal Schwall Blues Band, Congress of Wonders, Charlatans, Big Brother and the Holding Company and Quicksilver Messenger Service with the Light Sound Dimension by Bill Ham.
- Teens 'n' Twenties present the Young Rascals, Grateful Dead, Country Joe and the Fish, Sons of Champlin, Sparrow and Grass Roots, with lights by Bob Holt Light Productions Wednesday the 28th at the Oakland Auditorium, Oakland.
- The Electric Circus opens Wednesday the 28th in New York City.

29th June - 1967
- Mick Jagger and Keith Richards are sentenced to 3 months and 1 year respectively

for drug possession (Jagger) and letting pot be smoked at his house (Richards).
- The Family Dog presents Quicksilver Messenger Service, Mount Rushmore, Big Brother and the Holding Company and Blue Cheer on Thursday, Friday, Saturday & Sunday the 29th, 30th, 1st & 2nd at the Avalon Ballroom.

30th June - 1967
- There are now 448,000 American troops in Vietnam.
- The MC5 and the Charles Moore Ensemble play Friday the 30th at the See in Detroit, with lights by The Magic Veil.

July - 1967
- Jim Haynes, a director of the **International Times**, opens the Arts Lab in London. This hippie directed learning facility focused on the full spectrum of art, from painting to sculpture, music to poetry and absolutely everything in between. It was a place to come and creatively express yourself.
- While it's the "Summer of Love" in San Francisco, it's turning into the summer of rioting in many other American cities, such as Chicago, Brooklyn, Cleveland and Baltimore.

1st July – 1967
- The Beatles **Sgt. Pepper's Lonely Hearts Club Band** LP hits the No.1 spot on the charts.
- The editor of the **London Times** writes an editorial entitled "Who Breaks A Butterfly On A Wheel?", criticizing the drug related sentences handed out to Mick Jagger and Keith Richards suggesting the sentences were harsher to the rock stars, than had they been anonymous citizens.
- Charles Moore Ensemble and Billy C and the Sunshine play on Saturday the 1st at the See in Detroit, with lights by the Magic Veil.

2nd July - 1967
- Billy C and the Sunshine and Seventh Seal play Sunday, Monday & Tuesday the 2nd, 3rd & 4th at the See in Detroit, with lights by the Magic Veil

4th July – 1967
- Bill Graham presents "The Summer Series – Week 3" featuring Bo Diddley, Big Brother and the Holding Company (Tues. Wed. Thurs.), Quicksilver Messenger Service (Fri. Sat. Sun.) and Big Joe Williams Tuesday – Sunday the 4th – 9th at the Fillmore Auditorium. Lights by Headlights.
- The Family Dog presents Quicksilver Messenger Service and the Siegal Schwall Band on Tuesday the 4th at the Avalon Ballroom. Lights by the North American Ibis Alchemical Co.
- International Kaleidoscope presents Canned Heat, Sly and the Family Stone and the Sons of Champlin on Tuesday & Wednesday the 4th & 5th at the Kaleidoscope in Los Angeles.

6th July – 1967

- Pink Floyd make their second appearance on **Top of The Pops** on Thursday the 6th and perform *See Emily Play*. Syd performs dressed in a collection of dirty rags.
- The Family Dog presents the Steve Miller Blues Band and the Siegal Schwall Band Thursday, Friday, Saturday & Sunday the 6th, 7th, 8th & 9th at the Avalon Ballroom.

7th July - 1967

- The Beatles release *All You Need Is Love* b/w *Baby You're a Rich Man* in Britain.
- **Time** magazine publishes a cover story on the burgeoning sub-culture with the front page banner saying "The Hippies: The Philosophy of a subculture."
- Space Age present Blue Cheer and Sopwith Camel with lights by Bob Holt on Friday & Saturday the 7th & 8th at the California Hall in San Francisco.

9th July - 1967

- Ramlala presents the Steve Miller Blues Band and Sparrow on Sunday & Monday the 9th & 10th at the California Hall in San Francisco with lights by Aurora Glory Alice.

10th July - 1967

- A benefit for the "American Indian Well-Baby Clinic" is held on Monday the 10th at the Avalon Ballroom, San Francisco. Performing are Quicksilver Messenger Service and the Ace of Cups.

11th July – 1967

- Bill Graham presents "The Summer Series – Week 4" featuring the Paul Butterfield Blues Band, the Roland Kirk Quartet, New Salvation Army Band (Tues. Wed. Thurs. only), and Mount Rushmore (Fri. Sat. Sun. only) Tuesday – Sunday the 11th – 16th at the Fillmore Auditorium.
- The Move perform on Tuesday the 11th at the Marquee Club, London, England. The support act is Winston's Fumbs featuring Tony Kaye on keyboards.

12th July - 1967

- 26 dead and 1500 injured during race riots in Newark, New Jersey.

13th July – 1967

- The Family Dog presents the Charlatans and the Youngbloods on Thursday, Friday, Saturday and Sunday the 13th, 14th, 15th & 16th at the Avalon Ballroom.
- The Grateful Dead, Daily Flash, Collectors and Painted Ship perform Thursday, Friday & Saturday the 13th, 14th & 15th at Dante's Inferno in Vancouver, British Columbia.

14th July – 1967

- The Grand Opening of the Continental Ballroom, in Santa Clara is held on Friday & Saturday the 14th & 15th with Big Brother and the Holding Company,

Quicksilver Messenger Service, Freedom Highway and Heather Stone.
- The Who begin their first full scale U.S. tour on Friday the 14th with Herman's Hermits as the opening act.
- Space Age presents the Steve Miller Blues Band, Sunshine Co. and the Anonymous Artists of America, with lights by Bob Holt Friday & Saturday the 14th & 15th at the California Hall, San Francisco.
- Arthur Brown and Alexis Corner perform dusk-to-dawn on Friday the 14th at the UFO Club, London

16th July - 1967
- The "Legalize Pot Rally" is held at Speakers Corner in Hyde Park, London on Sunday the 16th. It's called "The Putting Together Of The Heads"
- The Grateful Dead, Daily Flash and Magic Fern play Sunday the 16th at the Eagles Auditorium, Seattle.

17th July - 1967
- The Joint Show opens at the Moore Gallery, 535 Sutter Street San Francisco. The show features the artwork of the era's most prominent poster artists. On display is the work of Wes Wilson, Stanley Mouse, Victor Moscoso, Rick Griffin and Alton Kelley. The artists produce 5 different posters promoting the show in their own unique style.
- The Monkees begin a U.S. tour with a performance in New York City with Jimi Hendrix as the opening act! Hendrix would play less than a half dozen of these tour dates, before being replaced by Vanilla Fudge.

18th July – 1967
- Bill Graham presents "The Summer Series – Week 5" featuring Sam & Dave, James Cotton Blues Band, Country Joe and the Fish (Tues. Wed. Thurs. only) and Loading Zone (Fri. Sat. Sun. only) Tuesday – Sunday the 18th – 23rd at the Fillmore Auditorium.

19th July – 1967
- Andy Warhol's Velvet Underground and the Muffins perform on Wednesday through Saturday the 19th – 22nd at The Trauma, 2121 Arch Street in Philadelphia, Pennsylvania.

20th July – 1967
- The Family Dog presents Big Brother and the Holding Company and Mother Earth on Thursday, Friday, Saturday & Sunday the 20th, 21st, 22nd & 23rd at the Avalon Ballroom.
- The Doors, Collectors and Painted Ship perform on Thursday the 20th at the Memorial Arena in Victoria, British Columbia.

21st July – 1967
- The Grand Opening of the Straight Theatre on Haight St. in San Francisco is held

on Friday, Saturday & Sunday the 21st, 22nd & 23rd with performances from Mt. Rushmore, Quicksilver Messenger Service, New Salvation Army Band, Mother Earth, Country Joe and the Fish, Charlatans, Blue Cheer, Freedom Highway, Phoenix, Wildflower, Grateful Dead and Big Brother and the Holding Company. The Straight Theatre was conceived as a more community-oriented hippie-run alternative to the Avalon and Fillmore Ballrooms.
- Space Age presents "Strange Happenings" at the California Hall in San Francisco on Friday & Saturday the 21st & 22nd with the Youngbloods, Magic Fern, Wildflower and the Northern Lights lightshow.
- Tomorrow and the Bonzo Dog Do Dah Band perform dusk-to-dawn on Saturday the 21st at The UFO Club, London
- The Doors, Collectors and Painted Ship perform on Saturday & Sunday the 21st & 22nd at Dante's Inferno in Vancouver, British Columbia.

22nd July - 1967
- The Beatles, *All You Need Is Love* reaches No.1 on the British singles charts.
- Jim Salzer presents the Yardbirds, Moby Grape, Captain Beefheart and Iron Butterfly on Saturday the 22nd at the Santa Monica Civic Auditorium.

23rd July – 1967
- A giant "Love-In" is held on Sunday the 23rd at Griffith Park in Los Angeles.
- According to a number of sources this was the evening Neal Cassady gave his famous rap at the Straight Theatre with back up from the Grateful Dead.
- 43 people die, 2000 injured and 5000 homeless as a result of a week of riots in Detroit, Michigan.

24th July - 1967
- A full-page Legalize Pot advertisement is published in the **London Times** on Monday the 24th, signed by various celebrities including the Beatles. The headline reads "The Law against Marijuana is immoral in principle and unworkable in practice." The editorial on the page attempts to balance the paranoia and fear surrounding the dangers of marijuana.
- The Jefferson Airplane's second album **Surrealistic Pillow** is certified Gold.

25th July – 1967
- Graham presents the Yardbirds plus James Cotton Blues Band and Richie Havens on Tuesday, Wednesday & Thursday the 25th, 26th & 27th at the Fillmore Auditorium.

26th July – 1967
- Andy Warhol's Velvet Underground and the Muffins perform on Wednesday, Thursday, Friday & Saturday the 26th, 27th, 28th & 29th at The Trauma, 2121 Arch Street in Philadelphia, Pennsylvania.

27th July – 1967
- The Family Dog presents Blue Cheer and Captain Beefheart and his Magic Band on

Thursday, Friday, Saturday & Sunday the 27th, 28th, 29th & 30th at the Avalon Ballroom.

28th July - 1967

- Bill Graham presents the Doors, James Cotton Blues Band and Richie Havens on Friday, Saturday & Sunday the 28th, 29th & 30th at the Fillmore Auditorium.
- Sandy Bull and the Rock Shop play on Friday, Saturday & Sunday the 28th, 29th & 30th at the Matrix Club in San Francisco.
- Space Age presents Big Brother and the Holding Company and the Charlatans, lights by Northern Lights Friday, Saturday & Sunday the 28th, 29th & 30th at the California Hall in San Francisco.
- Pink Floyd play on Friday the 28th at the UFO, Tottenham Court Road, London for the final time. Supporting acts for the evening were Fairport Convention and Shiva's Children. This proved to be the final evening for the UFO at this address as the following week the landlord gave manager Joe Boyd his notice citing a recent article in the **News of The World** newspaper reporting on the goings-on in the club. The club was moved to The Roundhouse where UFO continued to operate until closing for good in October of 1967.

29th July - 1967

A POSTER FOR THE LOVE-IN FESTIVAL, LONDON

- San Ramon High School presents the Yardbirds, Sir Douglas Quintet and Loading Zone on Saturday the 29th at San Ramon High School Stadium.
- An all-night rave entitled the "Love-In Festival" takes place on Saturday & Sunday the 29th & 30th at the Alexandra Palace in London featuring Eric Burdon and the Animals, Pink Floyd, Brian Auger and Trinity, Crazy World of Arthur Brown, Creation, Tomorrow, and Blossom Toes.

31st July - 1967

- Mick Jagger and Keith Richards' sentences are remanded. An appeals-court finds the earlier court ruling to be in error.
- The Door's *Light My Fire* is No.1 in the United States. In Britain the Beatles are No.1 with *All You Need is Love*.
- Big Brother and the Holding Company, the Charlatans and Blue Cheer play a benefit for the Haight-Ashbury Free Clinic.

- Bill Graham presents "The San Francisco Scene" at the O'Keefe Centre, Toronto, Canada, featuring Jefferson Airplane, the Grateful Dead and local favorites Luke and the Apostles with the Head Lights lightshow. **The Toronto Telegram** newspaper ran the headline, "Flower Power Takes Over" and went on to call the event a "cultural revolution". The six-day tour ran from the 31st to the 5th and was a smashing success. It also proved to be the final event for Luke and the Apostles who split immediately after, only to have Luke Gibson asked to join Kensington Market, who've been labeled as Canada's answer to Jefferson Airplane.

1st August – 1967
- Bill Graham presents Muddy Waters, Buffalo Springfield and Richie Havens on Tuesday – Sunday the 1st – 6th at the Fillmore Auditorium. Lights by Dan Bruhns Fillmore Lights.
- The UFO Festival is staged at the Roundhouse, Chalk Farm, London, England for the first time. Performing over the two night affair are Pink Floyd, Arthur Brown, Tomorrow, Fairport Convention, the Nack, and on the second evening Pink Floyd again with the Move, Soft Machine, Fairport Convention, the Nack, and Denny Laine.

2nd August – 1967
- Beacon Street Union and the Mandrake Memorial perform on Wednesday, Thursday, Friday & Saturday the 2nd, 3rd, 4th & 5th at The Trauma, 2121 Arch Street in Philadelphia, Pennsylvania.

3rd August - 1967
- The Family Dog presents Charles Lloyd Quartet and the West Coast Natural Gas Company on Thursday, Friday, Saturday & Sunday the 3rd, 4th, 5th & 6th at the Avalon Ballroom.
- The Byrds, Stone Pony's and Sky Blue play Thursday the 3rd at the Berkeley Community Theatre with lights by Seventh Ray.

5th August - 1967
- KACY and Jim Salzer presents the Doors, Lavender Hill Mob, Joint Effort and Captain Speed with lights by the Family Cat on Saturday the 5th at the Earl Warren Showground's, Santa Barbara.
- The Flamin' Groovies play the Matrix Club in San Francisco on Saturday, Sunday & Monday the 5th, 6th & 7th.
- Pink Floyd release their first album **The Piper At The Gates Of Dawn**. Recorded just down the hall at Abbey Road studios at the very same time the Beatles were recording **Sgt. Pepper**, Pink Floyd's release would have an even greater impact on the psychedelic music world. Containing not only the shorter psychedelic pop singles, this album contained longer spacey, trippy instrumentals that would go a long way in establishing Pink Floyd's psychedelic reputation.

7th August – 1967
- Pink Floyd set off on a tour of Denmark.

8th August - 1967

- George Harrison visits the "tourist trap" that is now Haight-Ashbury. Little known at the time, but Harrison's observations of the drug-culture clash with his "romanticized" expectations and would lead to him renouncing drugs as a means to enlightenment in the years ahead.
- Bill Graham presents the Electric Flag American Music Band, Moby Grape and South Side Sound System on Tuesday & Wednesday the 8th & 9th at the Fillmore Auditorium.

9th August – 1967

- Beacon Street Union and the Mandrake Memorial perform on Wednesday, Thursday, Friday & Saturday the 9th, 10th 11th & 12th at The Trauma, 2121 Arch Street in Philadelphia, Pennsylvania.
- Pink Floyd embark on a weeklong Scandinavian tour, followed by a brief tour of Ireland.

10th August – 1967

- Bill Graham presents the Electric Flag American Music Band, Steve Miller Blues Band and South Side Sound System on Thursday through Sunday the 10th – 13th at the Fillmore Auditorium.
- The Family Dog presents Moby Grape, Canned Heat and Vanilla Fudge on Thursday through Sunday the 10th – 13th at the Avalon Ballroom.

11th August - 1967

- Big Brother and the Holding Company, Charles Lloyd Quartet, Morning Glory and Mt Rushmore play Friday & Saturday the 11th & 12th at the Continental Ballroom, Santa Clara.

14th August - 1967

- The British Government enacts legislation that effectively closes down pirate radio stations broadcasting underground music to Britain's youth. Perhaps the only station still in operation, Radio Caroline closes down for good. These stations were operated usually in boats anchored just outside of British waters were playing all kinds of underground music that the BBC was not, and they were favorites of the underground community.
- Scott McKenzie's Summer of Love anthem *San Francisco (Be sure to wear Flowers in Your hair)* is the No.1 song in the U.K.

15th August – 1967

- Bill Graham presents Chuck Berry, Charles Lloyd Quartet and the Steve Miller Blues Band Tuesday, Wednesday & Thursday the 15th, 16th & 17th at the Fillmore Auditorium.

16th August – 1967

- The Wildflowers and Mandrake Memorial perform on Wednesday, Thursday, Friday

& Saturday the 16th, 17th, 18th & 19th at the Trauma, 2121 Arch Street in Philadelphia, Pennsylvania.

17th August – 1967
• The Family Dog presents Quicksilver Messenger Service and the Other Half on Thursday through Sunday the 17th – 20th at the Avalon Ballroom.

18th August – 1967
• Bill Graham presents the Young Rascals, Charles Lloyd Quartet and Hair on Friday & Saturday the 18th & 19th at the Fillmore Auditorium.

19th August - 1967
• The Beatles' *All You Need Is Love* reaches No.1 on the U.S charts.
• Jim Salzer presents the Jimi Hendrix Experience, Moby Grape, Tim Buckley and Captain Speed with lights by Omega Eye Saturday the 19th at the Earl Warren Showground's, Santa Barbara.

20th August – 1967
• Dolby noise reduction is developed as a means of reducing noise during the recording process.
• Police in Toronto, Ontario attempt to "clean-up" the hippie community of Yorkville and provoke a sit-in. For three days and nights, hundreds gather to protest. Sixty-one people are arrested and this would provoke more unrest within the counter-culture community.
• Bill Graham presents Count Basie and his Orchestra and Charles Lloyd Quartet on Sunday & Monday the 20th & 21st at the Fillmore Auditorium.

21st August – 1967
• Midway through a tour of Germany Syd Barrett goes missing and Pink Floyd are forced to cancel the rest of the tour.

22nd August 1967
• Bill Graham presents the Paul Butterfield Blues Band, Cream and South Side Sound System on Tuesday through Sunday the 22nd – 27th at the Fillmore Auditorium. Lights by Headlights.

24th August - 1967
• Patti Harrison convinces George and the rest of the Beatles to attend a London lecture of the Maharishi Mahesh Yogi
• The Family Dog presents Big Brother and the Holding Company and Bukka White on Thursday, Friday, Saturday & Sunday the 24th, 25th, 26th & 27th at the Avalon Ballroom.

25th August – 1967
• The Wildflowers and Mandrake Memorial perform on Friday & Saturday the 25th & 26th at the Trauma, 2121 Arch Street in Philadelphia, Pennsylvania.

- Western Maintenance presents Dave Van Ronk, Mimi Farina and Fred Neil on Friday & Saturday the 25th & 26th at the Berkeley Community Theatre.
- The "Festival of The Flower Children" is held on Friday, Saturday & Sunday the 25th, 26th & 27th at Woburn Abbey featuring Marmalade, Alan Price and the Bee Gees.

26th August – 1967

- Jimi Hendrix's first LP **Are You Experienced** is released.
- Following the lecture by the Maharishi Mahesh Yogi two days previous, the Beatles attend a news conference with the Yogi where Paul announces they have given up drugs, saying "It was an experience we went through. We don't need it anymore. We're finding different ways to get there." Following the news conference the Beatles and others leave for Bangor, Wales to continue studying under the Maharishi.

27th August - 1967

- Brian Epstein dies as a result of alcohol and barbiturates. The Beatles were in Bangor, North Wales studying with the Maharishi when they were given the news. The coroner will eventually rule the Epstein's death as accidental.
- The Jimi Hendrix Experience, Tomorrow and the Crazy World Of Arthur Brown play at Sunday the 27th At The Saville, Saville Theatre, London.

29th August - 1967

- Bill Graham presents Cream, Electric Flag American Music Band and Gary Burton on Tuesday through Sunday the 29th – 3rd at the Fillmore Auditorium. Featuring the Dan Bruhns lightshow.

30th August - 1967

- Country Joe and the Fish play Monday through Friday the 30th – 3rd at Jabberwock, Berkeley.

1st September – 1967

- Guitarist and vocalist Boz Scaggs joins the Steve Miller Band in San Francisco. The two are actually old friends having met in high school in Texas. Scaggs would stay with the band for their first two LP recordings before going off on a solo career.
- **Life** magazine runs a cover story entitled, "The Big Poster Hang-up – Walls and Walls of Expendable Art" focusing on the San Francisco psychedelic poster

explosion. The article includes many photos of the posters and the artists involved.

- The Family Dog presents the Steve Miller Blues Band, Mother Earth and Bukka White Friday, Saturday & Sunday the 1st, 2nd & 3rd at the Avalon Ballroom.
- The Straight Theatre presents Big Brother and the Holding Company on Friday, Saturday & Sunday the 1st, 2nd & 3rd with support on each day (respectively) by Freedom Highway, Colours and Phoenix, with lights by Reginald and Straight Lightning.
- Russ Gibb presents in Detroit a dance-concert featuring the Chambers Brothers, MC5 and Thyme on Friday & Saturday the 1st & 2nd at the Grande Ballroom.

2nd September - 1967

- The Cosmic Car Show benefit for Delano Grape Strikers is staged on Saturday the 2nd at Muir Beach, Marin County with Charley Musslewhite Band, South Side Sound System, Mt. Rushmore, Mother Earth, Second Coming and others performing.
- The Magic Music Benefit for SCA is held on Saturday & Sunday the 2nd & 3rd at Cabrillo College, Santa Cruz featuring the Grateful Dead, Canned Heat, Leaves, Andrew Staples, Sons Of Champlin, New Delhi River Band, Second Coming, New Breed, Gross Exaggeration, Yajahla, Tingle Guild, People, Jaguars, Art Collection, Morning Glory, Ben Frank's Electric Band, New Frontier, Chocolate Watch Band, Other Side, E-Types, Mourning Reign, Imperial Mange Remedy, Omens, Ragged Staff and Talon Wedge with lights by STP.

3rd September - 1967

- An LSD demonstration takes place at Speakers Corner, Hyde Park, London.

7th September – 1967

- Bill Graham presents "The Opening of the Fall Weekend Series" featuring the Byrds, Loading Zone and LDM Spiritual Band on Thursday, Friday & Saturday the 7th, 8th & 9th at the Fillmore Auditorium. Lights by Holy See.

8th September – 1967

- The Family Dog presents South Side Sound System and Freedom Highway on Friday, Saturday & Sunday the 8th, 9th & 10th at the Avalon Ballroom.
- The Family Dog presents the "The Denver Grand Opening" with Big Brother and the • Holding Company and Blue Cheer on Friday & Saturday the 8th & 9th at the Family Dog Denver, Colorado. Lights by The Diogenes Lantern Works
- The Marquee Club in London features Denny Laine and his Electric Band and the Gods on Friday the 8th. the Gods would go on to make 14 more marquee appearances.

10th September – 1967

- Eric Burdon and the New Animals, Denny Laine and the Electric String Band perform on Sunday the 10th at the Saville Theatre, Shaftsbury Avenue, London.

11th September – 1967

- An article in the New York Times points out how record companies are increasingly using younger producers and younger independent companies that in their view are more attuned to the growing teenage market.
- The Beatles begin filming the **Magical Mystery Tour**.

14th September – 1967

- Bill Graham presents the Electric Flag American Music Band, Mother Earth and LDM Spiritual Band on Thursday, Friday & Saturday the 14th, 15th & 16th at the Fillmore Auditorium.

15th September – 1967

- The Family Dog presents the Youngbloods, Other Half and Mad River on Friday, Saturday & Sunday the 15th, 16th & 17th at the Avalon Ballroom.
- The Straight Theatre presents the Steve Miller Band, Billy Roberts, Sopwith Camel and Notes From the Underground on Friday & Saturday the 15th & 16th with lights by Reginald.
- The Wildflower and Bagatelle perform on Friday & Saturday the 15th & 16th at the Boston Tea Party, 53 Berkeley Street in Boston.
- Bill Graham presents "The San Francisco Scene in Los Angeles" featuring Jefferson Airplane, Grateful Dead and Big Brother and the Holding Company on Friday the 15th at the Hollywood Bowl. Lights by Headlights.
- The Family Dog Denver presents the Charlatans and Quicksilver Messenger Service on Friday & Saturday the 15th & 16th at the Family Dog Denver, 1601 West Evans Street.
- Ten Years After perform on Friday the 15th at the 5th Dimension Club in Leicester, England.

16th September – 1967

- Chris Farlowe performs Saturday the 16th at the 5th Dimension Club in Leicester, England.

17th September - 1967

- The Doors appear on the Ed Sullivan show and perform *Light My Fire* and *People are Strange*. Sullivan requests that the line "Girl we couldn't get much higher" be changed, but Morrison sings it anyway.

- The Straight Theatre presents Little Richard and an all-soul revue with lights by Reginald and Straight Lighting on Sunday the 17th.
- John Mayall's Bluesbreakers, Long John Baldry Show and Peter Green's Fleetwood Mac play at Sunday At the Saville, Saville Theatre, London.

21st September – 1967

- Bill Graham presents Blue Cheer, Vanilla Fudge and the Sunshine Company on Thursday and Saturday 21st & 23rd at the Fillmore Auditorium. The evening of the 22nd the Fillmore was closed for the Donovan show at the Cow Palace.
- The Bringers Of Light & The Straight Theatre present The Equinox Of the Gods with Kenneth Anger, the Congress of Wonders, Charlatans, San Francisco Mime Troupe and the Duncan Company, with lights by North American Ibis Alchemical Company on Thursday the 21st.

22nd September – 1967

- Bill Graham presents Donovan on Friday the 22nd at the Cow Palace in San Francisco.
- The Family Dog presents the Charlatans and Buddy Guy on Friday, Saturday & Sunday the 22nd, 23rd & 24th at the Avalon Ballroom.
- The Family Dog Denver presents the Grateful Dead and Mother Earth on Friday & Saturday the 22nd & 23rd at 1601 West Evans Street.
- Dantalions Chariot, Social Deviants and Exploding Galaxy play on Friday the 22nd UFO At The Roundhouse.
- The Amboy Dukes and Wildflowers perform on Friday the 22nd at the 5th Dimension Club in Leicester, England.
- Pink Floyd play on Friday the 22nd at Tiles, Oxford Street, London, London.

23rd September – 1967

- The Jefferson Airplane, Youngbloods and Magic Fern perform on Saturday the 23rd at the Seattle Centre Coliseum. Lights by Glenn McKay's Headlights.
- Teens 'n' Twenties present the 13th Floor Elevators and Elements of Sound on Saturday the 23rd at the Rollerena, San Leandro.
- The Mothers of Invention perform on Saturday the 23rd at the Royal Albert Hall in London, England.
- Middle Earth in London features Denny Laine's Electric String Band, Piccadilly Line and Tyrannosaurus Rex on Saturday the 23rd.

24th September - 1967

- First UK appearance of Traffic at Sunday At the Saville, Saville Theatre, London.
- Middle Earth in London features the Graham Bond Organization, Third Ear and Shemains Woorlitza on Sunday the 24th.
- The Marquee Club in London features the Orange Bicycle and Pandemonium on Sunday the 24th.

25th September – 1967
• Middle Earth in London features Fairport Convention and Doc K's Blues Band on Monday the 25th.

27th September - 1967
• Pink Floyd play on Wednesday the 27th at Fifth Dimension Club, Leicester, England.

28th September – 1967
• Bill Graham presents Jefferson Airplane, Mother Earth and Flamin' Groovies on Thursday, Friday & Saturday the 28th at the Fillmore Auditorium. The evenings of the 29th and 30th were performed at the Winterland.

29th September - 1967
• The Family Dog presents Vanilla Fudge and the Charles Lloyd Quartet on Friday, Saturday & Sunday the 29th, 30th & 1st at the Avalon Ballroom. Lights by the North American Ibis Alchemical Co.
• The Straight Theatre in San Francisco presents the Grateful Dead and Sons of Champlin, with lights by Reginald and Straight Lighting on Friday & Saturday the 29th & 30th.
• The Family Dog Denver presents the Doors and Lothar and the Hand People on Friday & Saturday the 29th & 30th at 1601 West Evans Street.
• Jeff Beck, Ten Years After and Contessa Veronica perform at the UFO Friday the 29th at the Roundhouse with lights by Mark Boyle's Sensual Laboratory.

1st October - 1967
• A Benefit for the Economic Opportunity Program presented by U.C Berkeley Associated Students is held featuring Charles Lloyd, Grateful Dead and Bola Sete on Sunday the 1st at the Greek Theatre, Berkeley.
• Pink Floyd play at Sunday the 1st At the Saville, Saville Theatre, London with Tomorrow, the Incredible String Band and Fairport Convention. The New Music Expressed summarized their review by saying the new light show was an, "integral part of their [Pink Floyd] music, which was very loud and mainly instrumental."

2nd October – 1967
• The Neiman-Marcus Poster Show takes place at Exhibition Hall in Dallas, Texas. Victor Moscoso designs the large psychedelic poster advertising the event.
• The Grateful Dead are busted for drugs in San Francisco and charged with possession of marijuana. Police raid the Dead house at 710 Ashbury while Jerry Garcia is away at a grocery store, but charge band members Bob Weir, Phil Lesh and Ron "Pigpen" McKernan. After being held in jail for 6 hours they are released on bail.
• The Marquee Club in London features the first appearance of the Nice and the Nite People on Monday the 2nd.

4th October – 1967
- The Incredible String Band perform Wednesday the 4th at the Queen Elizabeth Hall in London England.

5th October – 1967
- Bill Graham presents Quicksilver Messenger Service, Grassroots and Mad River on Thursday, Friday & Saturday the 5th, 6th & 7th at the Fillmore Auditorium.

6th October - 1967
- The "Death Of Hippie" procession takes place in San Francisco on Friday the 6th and signals the beginnings of the end of an era. The Diggers organized the march along Haight Street and it ended with the burial of the Psychedelic Shop sign. Taking down the sign and ritually burying it was meant to symbolize a passing of much of what the original hippie movement was thought to originally stand for. In a couple months the Psychedelic Shop owners, the Thelin brothers had packed up and left the Haight-Ashbury, along with **Oracle** founders Cohen and Bowen. Many of the Diggers moved on to the country as well as the once vibrant community began to shrink.
- The Family Dog presents Blue Cheer, Lee Michaels and Clifton Chenier on Friday, Saturday & Sunday the 6th, 7th & 8th at the Avalon Ballroom. Lights by the North American Ibis Co.
- Police close down the Matrix Club in San Francisco on Friday the 6th during a performance by Big Brother and the Holding Company.
- The Family Dog Denver presents Buffalo Springfield and Eight Penny Matter on Friday & Saturday the 6th & 7th at 1601 West Evans Street.
- British authorities close down the UFO club on Friday the 6th. After moving from its original site into the newly restored Roundhouse, the original spirit of the original venue failed to travel with the change of address. The spirit of communality was starting to dissipate. British music paper **Melody Maker** runs a headline asking "Who Killed Flower Power?"

7th October - 1967
- Uncle Russ Love Agency presents Scott Richard Case, Billy and the Sunshine, MC5 and Odds And Ends on Saturday the 7th at the Grande Ballroom, Detroit.

8th October - 1967
- The "Haight-Ashbury Medical Clinic Benefit" featuring Big Brother and the Holding Company, Quicksilver Messenger Service, Freedom Highway, Mother Earth, • Ace Of Cups, Congress Of Wonders and Mad River is held on Sunday the 8th at the Family Park, San Jose.
- The Jimi Hendrix Experience, Crazy World Of Arthur Brown and Cryin' Shames play on Sunday the 8th at the Saville Theatre, Shaftsbury Avenue, London

11th October – 1967
- Bill Graham presents the "Haight-Ashbury Medical Clinic Benefit" featuring

Jefferson Airplane, Charlatans and Blue Cheer on Wednesday, Thursday the 11th & 12th at the Fillmore Auditorium and Friday & Saturday the 13th and 14th at the Winterland. Lights by Glenn McKay's Headlights.

12th October – 1967
• Big Brother and the Holding Company's **Cheap Thrills** LP featuring Janis Joplin is at the top of the album charts.

13th October - 1967
• The Family Dog presents Buddy Guy and Captain Beefheart and his Magic Band on Friday, Saturday & Sunday the 13th, 14th & 15th at the Avalon Ballroom.
• Moby Grape, Big Brother and the Holding Company and Sons Of Champlin play on Friday & Saturday the 13th & 14th at The Ark, Sausalito with lights by Funny Co.
• Western Front Dance Academy presents, Morning Glory and the Indian Head Band on Friday & Saturday the 13th & 14th.
• The Family Dog Denver presents Van Morrison and Daily Flash on Friday & Saturday the 13th & 14th at 1601 West Evans Street.
• Uncle Russ presents in Detroit a dance-concert featuring Cream, MC5, Rationals and the Apostles on Friday, Saturday & Sunday the 13th, 14th & 15th at the Grande Ballroom in Detroit Michigan.

15th October – 1967
• Junior Walker and the All Stars perform on Sunday the 15th at the Saville Theatre, Shaftsbury Avenue, London.

16th October – 1967
• The Marquee Club in London features the Nice and Studio Six on Monday the 16th.

19th October – 1967
• Bill Graham presents Eric Burdon and the Animals, Mother Earth and Hour Glass on Thursday, Friday & Saturday the 19th, 20th & 21st at the Fillmore Auditorium. Lights by Holy See.
• Jefferson Airplane perform on Thursday the 19th at the Loew's Warfield Theatre on Market Street in San Francisco.

20th October – 1967
• The Family Dog presents Van Morrison, Daily Flash and Hair on Friday, Saturday & Sunday the 20th, 21st & 22nd at the Avalon Ballroom.
• Russ Gibb presents in Detroit a dance-concert featuring Pack, MC5, Gold, Gang, Our Mothers Children and Billy C and the Sunshine on Friday & Saturday the 20th & 21st at the Grande Ballroom.
• The Family Dog Denver presents Canned Heat and Allmen Joy on Friday & Saturday the 20th & 21st at 1601 West Evans Street.

21st October - 1967
- The "Exorcism of the Pentagon, Washington D.C, march" takes place with 55,000 people arriving to make the trek. Over 600 arrests are made in an anti-war protest that lasts 2 days.

21st October – 1967
- The Marquee Club in London features Neat Change and Open Mind on Saturday the 21st. The Open Mind would go on to make another 18 appearances at the Marquee.

22nd October – 1967
- The Who perform on Sunday the 22nd at the Saville Theatre, Shaftsbury Avenue, London.

24th October – 1967
- Pink Floyd's first United States tour begins.
- The Marquee Club in London features the Nice and the Jimi Hendrix Experience on Tuesday the 24th.

26th October - 1967
- Bill Graham presents the first U.S. appearance of Pink Floyd also on the bill are Lee Michaels and Clear Light on Thursday, Friday & Saturday the 26th, 27th & 28th at the Fillmore Auditorium. Unfortunately Pink Floyd never showed as immigration authorities delayed their work permits.

27th October - 1967
- The Family Dog presents Quicksilver Messenger Service and Sons of Champlin on Friday, Saturday & Sunday the 27th, 28th & 29th at the Avalon Ballroom.
- The Straight Theatre presents a "Kinetic Event Dance Class" with the Charles Musslewhite Band, Wildflower and Preston Webster & Company on Friday & Saturday the 27th & 28th.
- The Family Dog Denver presents Allmen Joy and Lothar and the Hand People on Friday & Saturday the 27th & 28th at 1601 West Evans Street.
- The "Grand Opening" of the Vulcan Gas Company, 316 Congress in Austin Texas, on Friday & Saturday the 27th & 28th features Conquerod and Shiva's Head Band.

28th October - 1967
- Big Brother and the Holding Company play on Saturday & Sunday the 28th & 29th at the Peacock Country Club, San Rafael, California.

29th October - 1967
- A Proposition 'P' Benefit is held on Sunday the 29th at the Fillmore Auditorium featuring Jefferson Airplane, Mother Earth and Mad River with the Holy See light show.

30th October - 1967

• Brian Jones arrested on drugs charges.
• KPFA "Halloween Costume Ball Benefit" is held on Monday the 30th at the Fillmore featuring the Incredible Fish, Pink Floyd, Sopwith Camel and the Collectors. Once again Pink Floyd were not part of the show because of the immigration mix-up.
• Pink Floyd perform for three nights Monday, Tuesday & Wednesday the 30th, 31st & 1st at the Whisky A Go Go, Sunset Strip, Los Angeles. These are their first gigs on U.S. soil.

31st October - 1967

• Trip or Freak Halloween Ball is held on Tuesday the 31st at Winterland with Quicksilver Messenger Service, Grateful Dead and Big Brother and the Holding Company, lights by Head Lights.

1st November – 1967

• British band Family comes on the scene with their first live concert. The band includes Rick Grech who will eventually join Eric Clapton in Blind Faith in the months ahead.

2nd November – 1967

• British psychedelic band the Move is in court over a promotional post card used to advertise their single "Flowers in the Rain". The offending post card depicted then British Prime Minister Harold Wilson nude in bed. The court eventually finds in favour of the Prime Minister and the Move are fined and ordered to destroy all remaining copies of the post card.
• Bill Graham presents Big Brother and the Holding Company, Pink Floyd and Richie Havens on Thursday the 2nd at the Fillmore Auditorium, and Friday & Saturday the 3rd & 4th at the Winterland. Lights by Glenn McKay's Headlights.
• The Marquee Club in London features the Syn and Quik Friday the 2nd.

3rd November – 1967

• The Family Dog presents Canned Heat and Lothar and the Hand People on Friday, Saturday & Sunday the 3rd, 4th & 5th at the Avalon Ballroom.
• The Family Dog Denver presents Blue Cheer and Superfine Dandelion on Friday & Saturday the 3rd & 4th at 1601 West Evans Street.
• Russ Gibb presents in Detroit a dance-concert featuring the Paupers, Thyme, Gang and MC5 on Friday, Saturday & Sunday the 3rd, 4th & 5th at the Grande Ballroom.
• The Marquee Club in London features the first appearance of Wilde Flowers and Ten Years After on Friday the 3rd.

4th November - 1967

• Big Brother and the Holding Company, Baltimore Steam Packet and Moby Grape play Saturday the 4th at the Ark, Sausalito.

5th November – 1967
- Pink Floyd appear on the Pat Boone Show and perform *See Emily Play*. Syd Barrett fails to answer any questions posed and fails to even attempt to lip-synch to the pre-recorded track. Later that evening Pink Floyd performed two sets at the Cheetah Club in Venice Beach, Los Angeles.

6th November – 1967
- Pink Floyd's second U.S. TV appearance is recorded on this day for Dick Clark's American Bandstand and was just as disastrous as the first. The group mimed to *Apples & Oranges* and *See Emily Play*.

7th November – 1967
- The Family Dog Denver presents Jefferson Airplane and the Other Half on Friday & Saturday the 7th & 8th at 1601 West Evans Street.

9th November - 1967
- The first edition of **Rolling Stone** is published. This was a counter-culture publication that dealt with serious issues as well as music. Photos of the Grateful Dead drug bust appear in the first issue. John Lennon is on the cover along with headlines which reads, "The high cost of music and love: Where's the money from Monterey?" and "Airplane high, but no new LP release".
- Roger McGuinn fires David Crosby from the Byrds and replaces him with Gene Clark. Crosby takes his settlement money and sails with it until getting together later in 1968 to form Crosby Stills Nash and Young.
- Bill Graham presents Procol Harum, Pink Floyd and H.P. Lovecraft on Thursday the 9th at the Fillmore Auditorium and Friday & Saturday the 10th & 11th at the Winterland. Lights by Holy See. This was Procol Harum's first appearance at the Fillmore. Lead vocalist Gary Brooker said, "The Fillmore was the absolute making of our whole style."
- The Marquee Club in London features the Tages and Tuesday's Children on Thursday the 9th.

10th November – 1967
- The Family Dog presents the Youngbloods and Mad River on Friday, Saturday & Sunday the 10th, 11th & 12th at the Avalon Ballroom.
- The Family Dog Denver presents the Other Half and Sons of Champlin on Friday & Saturday the 10th & 11th at 1601 West Evans Street.
- Pinnacle Concerts presents "Amazing Electric Wonders" on Friday & Saturday the 10th & 11th at the Shrine Exposition Hall in Los Angeles featuring Buffalo Springfield, Grateful Dead and Blue Cheer.
- Russ Gibb presents in Detroit a dance-concert featuring the James Cotton Blues Band, MC5 and Billy and the Sunshine on Friday & Saturday the 10th & 11th at the Grande Ballroom.
- In Paris, France a two night "Love-In" takes place on Friday & Saturday the 10th &

11th featuring music from the Soft Machine, Spencer Davis Group, Dantalion's Chariot, Keith West and Tomorrow and others.

12th November – 1967

- Pink Floyd perform the last night of their first U.S. tour at the Cheetah Club in New York City.

14th November - 1967

- The North Face Ski Shop presents "The Rite Of Winter" with the Steve Miller Blues Band and Jesse Fuller on Tuesday & Wednesday the 14th & 15th with lights by Bill Ham and Aspen Lights.
- The Marquee Club in London features the Remo Four and the first appearance of Traffic on Tuesday the 14th.
- Jimi Hendrix Experience, Pink Floyd and the Move perform on Tuesday the 14th at the Royal Albert Hall in London, England. This tour in support of Hendrix exposed Pink Floyd to many new fans. **Disc & Music Echo** praised the Floyd, "Possibly the most interesting act was Pink Floyd, fresh from playing the hippie emporiums on America's West Coast, with what must be the best light show yet seen in this country and very inventive music."

15th November - 1967

- The Jimi Hendrix Experience, the Move, Pink Floyd, Amen Corner, the Nice, Outer Limits and Eire Apparent tour England from the 15th through the 5th performing in Bournemouth, Leeds, Liverpool, Nottingham, Portsmouth, Bristol, Cardiff, Manchester, Belfast, Chatham and Brighton.

16th November – 1967

- Bill Graham presents the Doors, Procol Harum and Mount Rushmore on Thursday the 16th at the Fillmore Auditorium and Friday & Saturday the 17th & 18th at the Winterland. Lights by Glenn McKay's Headlights.

17th November – 1967

- The Family Dog presents Bo Diddley and Lee Michaels on Friday, Saturday & Sunday the 17th, 18th & 19th at the Avalon Ballroom.
- The Family Dog Denver presents Chuck Berry and Sons of Champlin on Friday & Saturday the 17th & 18th at 1601 West Evans Street.

23rd November – 1967

- Underground disc jockey Tom Donahue is quoted in **Rolling Stone** magazine as saying, "Top Forty radio, as we know it today and have known it for the last ten years, is dead, and its rotting corpse is stinking up the airwaves."
- Bill Graham presents Donovan, H.P. Lovecraft and Mother Earth on Thursday the 23rd at the Fillmore Auditorium and Friday & Saturday the 24th & 25th at the Winterland. Lights by Glenn McKay's Headlights.
- The Family Dog hold a Thanksgiving "Turkey Strut & Trot" featuring Big Brother

and the Holding Company and Mt. Rushmore on Thursday, Friday & Saturday the 23rd, 24th & 25th at the Avalon Ballroom.

24th November – 1967
- The Beatles release *Hello Goodbye* b/w *I am the Walrus* in Britain.
- Russ Gibb presents in Detroit a dance-concert featuring the Fugs, MC5, Gang and Ashmollyan Quintet on Friday & Saturday the 24th & 25th at the Grande Ballroom.

25th November - 1967

- Strawberry Alarm Clock's *Incense & Peppermints* reaches No.1 on the U.S charts offering evidence that psychedelic music had gone mainstream.
- Jim Salzer presents the Youngbloods and Canned Heat on Saturday the 25th at the Earl Warren Showground's in Santa Barbara, California.

27th November – 1967
- The Beatles release the **Magical Mystery Tour** LP in the United States. A very different two-disc EP version of **Magical Mystery Tour** containing only the new songs from the film is released the first week of December in Britain.

30th November – 1967
- Bill Graham presents the Nitty Gritty Dirt Band, Clear Light and Blue Cheer on Thursday, Friday & Saturday the 30th, 1st & 2nd at the Fillmore Auditorium. Lights by Holy See.
- The Family Dog presents from Nashville's Flatt and Scruggs and the Lewis and Clark Expedition on Thursday, Friday & Saturday the 30th, 1st & 2nd at the Avalon Ballroom.

December – 1967
- Forty antiwar groups across the United States band together to start the "Stop The Draft" movement.

1st December – 1967
- The Straight Theatre presents Mad River and Santana Blues Band with lights by the Puppy Farm on Friday, Saturday & Sunday the 1st, 2nd & 3rd.
- Russ Gibb presents in Detroit a dance-concert featuring the Chambers Brothers on Friday & Saturday the 1st & 2nd at the Grande Ballroom.

- The Family Dog Denver presents the Jim Kweskin Jug Band and Solid Muldoon on Friday & Saturday the 1st & 2nd at 1601 West Evans Street.

2nd December – 1967
- The Jimi Hendrix Experience, Pink Floyd, the Move and the rest of the package tour perform on Saturday the 2nd at the Dome, Brighton, England. This evening's performance, it's said, was the first time Dave Gilmore filled in for a missing Syd Barrett.

5th December – 1967
- The Marquee Club in London features the Open Mind and Electric Prunes on Tuesday the 5th.

7th December - 1967
- The Beatles open the Apple Shop at 94 Baker Street, London. A psychedelic mural on the outside wall (painted by The Fool) causes outrage.
- Bill Graham presents the Byrds, Electric Flag and B.B. King on Thursday the 7th at the Fillmore Auditorium and Friday & Saturday the 8th & 9th at the Winterland. Lights by Holy See.

8th December – 1967
- Otis Redding records *Dock on The Bay*
- The Family Dog presents the Jim Kweskin Jug Band and Sons of Champlin on Friday, Saturday & Sunday the 8th, 9th & 10th at the Avalon Ballroom.
- The Family Dog Denver presents Canned Heat and Siegal Schwall Band on Friday & Saturday the 8th & 9th at 1601 West Evans Street.
- The 13th Floor Elevators, Shiva's Head Band, Swiss Movement and South Canadian Overflow perform on Friday, Saturday & Sunday the 8th, 8th & 10th at the Vulcan Gas Company 316 Congress Austin Texas.

9th December – 1967
- Cream's second LP entitled **Disraeli Gears** enters the American charts. The LP is 100% psychedelic from the cover designed by British poster artist Martin Sharp to the fuzz guitar of the hit single *Sunshine of Your Love* or the strange images in *Tales of Brave Ulysses*.
- Jim Morrison of the Doors is arrested in New Haven, Connecticut for mouthing off to a policeman.
- The Mothers of Invention and Tim Buckley perform in Los Angeles on Saturday the 9th at the Pasadena Civic Auditorium.
- The Marquee Club in London features Neat Change and the first appearance of Mabel Greer's Toyshop on Saturday the 9th. The 'Toyshop' will make an additional 3 appearances at the Marquee Club.

10th December - 1967
- Otis Redding dies in a plane crash when the plane he's traveling in crashes into a

frozen lake in Wisconsin. He was 26 years old at the time of his death.
- San Francisco regulars, the Steve Miller Blues Band are signed to Capitol Records for the unheard of sum of $750,000. The first thing the Steve Miller Blues Band does is drop the word "Blues" for their name.

11th December – 1967
- The Marquee Club in London features Simon Dupree and the Big Sound and Jon on Monday the 11th. Simon Dupree and the Big Sound would go to two more Marquee appearances. They would also hit the charts with "Kites" and then evolve into Gentle Giant.

13th December – 1967
- The Grateful Dead perform on Wednesday the 13th at the Shrine Auditorium in Los Angeles. This gig is significant for Dead fans because it is the first known performance of the Grateful Dead classic *Dark Star*.

14th December – 1967
- Bill Graham presents the Mothers of Invention, Tim Buckley and Chambers Brothers on Thursday the 14th at the Fillmore Auditorium and Friday & Saturday the 15th & 16th at the Winterland. Lights by Glenn McKay's Headlights.

15th December - 1967
- The Family Dog presents Quicksilver Messenger Service, Charlatans and Congress of Wonders on Friday, Saturday & Sunday the 15th, 16th & 17th at the Avalon Ballroom.
- The Shiva's Head Band and Lost and Found perform on Friday & Saturday the 15th & 16th at the Vulcan Gas Company, 316 Congress in Austin Texas.
- The Family Dog Denver presents Soul Survivors and the Box Tops on Friday & Saturday the 15th & 16th at 1601 West Evans Street.
- Pink Floyd supported by Fusion Fluff play on Friday the 15th at a new psychedelic club, Middle Earth, Covent Garden, London.

16th December – 1967
- The Monkees are riding high in the charts with the No.1 single in the United States *Daydream Believer* and the No.1 LP **Pieces, Aquarius, Capricorn and Jones, Ltd**.
- In the U.K the No.1 single is the Beatles *Hello Goodbye*.
- The Second-Annual Grope for Peace is staged at the Straight Theatre.
- The Xmas Show is held on Friday & Saturday the 16th & 17th at Winterland with Quicksilver Messenger Service, Big Brother and the Holding Company, Congress of Wonders, Great San Francisco Earthquake Dancers and the Loving Impulse with lights by Light Lives Co.
- A "Saturday Spectacular" is held on Saturday the 16th at The Penthouse, Birmingham, England with performances by Pink Floyd, Gospel Garden and the Rare Breed.

19th December – 1967
- The Marquee Club in London features Eric Burdon and the Animals and the first appearance of Eire Apparent on Monday the 19th.

20th December – 1967
- In England, two former members of the John Evan Blues Band, namely Ian Anderson and Glenn Corick form Jethro Tull.

21st December - 1967

ROLLING STONES - THEIR SATANIC MAJESTIES REQUEST

- The Rolling Stones release **Their Satanic Majesties Request** in response to **Sgt. Pepper** and it's their most psychedelic effort yet. The LP features a 3-D cover showing the Stones all decked out in the trippy wizard outfits.
- Bill Graham presents the Buffalo Springfield, the Collectors and Hour Glass on Thursday, Friday & Saturday the 21st, 22nd & 23rd at the Fillmore Auditorium. Lights by Holy See.
- The Family Dog presents the Siegal Schwall Band and Blue Cheer on Thursday, Friday & Saturday the 21st, 22nd & 23rd at the Avalon Ballroom.

22nd December – 1967
- Acid king Owsley Stanley III is busted yet again. This time he closes up shop and stops making acid. Stanley is in possession of 868,000 trips, with an estimated street value of $4.3 million.
- The "Christmas On Earth Revisited" event is held on Friday the 22nd at the Olympia, London with Jimi Hendrix, the Move, Soft Machine, the Who, Tomorrow, Eric Burdon & the Animals and Pink Floyd. Syd Barrett quickly losing touch with reality stands on stage and stares failing to play a note. Everyone is worried and Roger Waters makes it known that the band cannot go like this.

26th December – 1967
- The Beatles one-hour film **Magical Mystery Tour** is shown on British television and is generally given a thumbs-down. The psychedelic travelogue is primarily the brainchild of Paul McCartney and is a series of short vignettes all tied together under the guise of a bus trip.
- Bill Graham presents "Six Days of Sound" featuring the Doors, Chuck Berry and

Salvation on Tuesday, Wednesday & Thursday the 26th, 27th & 28th at the Winterland.

- The Grateful Dead perform for the first time at New York's Village Theatre, which in the months to come will be known as the Fillmore East.

28th December – 1967

- The Family Dog presents the Jim Kweskin Jug Band, Country Joe and the Fish, Lee Michaels and Blue Cheer on Thursday, Friday & Saturday the 28th, 29th & 30th at the Avalon Ballroom.

29th December – 1967

- Bill Graham presents "Six Days of Sound" featuring Chuck Berry, Big Brother and the Holding Company and Quicksilver Messenger Service on Friday & Saturday the 29th & 30th at the Winterland.
- The Seeds, Buffalo Springfield, Smokestack Lightnin' and Lollipop Shoppe perform on Friday, Saturday & Sunday the 29th, 30th & 31st at Cheetah's in Venice, California.
- The Family Dog Denver presents the Doors and Allmen Joy on Thursday, Friday & Saturday the 29th, 30th & 31st at 1601 West Evans Street.

31st December – 1967

- Radicals Abbie Hoffman, Jerry Rubin, Paul Krassner, Dick Gregory and others band together under the name of "Yippies"
- Bill Graham presents "New Years Eve" featuring Jefferson Airplane, Big Brother and the Holding Company, Quicksilver Messenger Service and Freedom Highway on Sunday the 31st at the Winterland.

TIMELINE - 1968

1st January – 1968

- For the first time in history album sales outstrip the sale of singles.
- The Marquee Club in London features the Nice and Mabel Greer's Toyshop on Monday the 1st.

4th January – 1968

- Bill Graham presents Vanilla Fudge, Steve Miller Band and Sonny Terry & Brownie McGee on Thursday the 4th at the Fillmore Auditorium and Friday & Saturday the 5th & 6th at the Winterland. Lights by Holy See.

5th January – 1968

- The Family Dog presents the Youngbloods and Ace of Cups on Friday, Saturday & Sunday the 5th, 6th & 7th at the Avalon Ballroom.

6th January - 1968

- Big Brother and the Holding Company, Creators and Walking Flower play on

Saturday the 6th at the Sacramento State College with lights by Simultaneous Avalanche.

7th January - 1968

- A "Stop the Draft Week Defense Fund Benefit" is held on Sunday the 7th at the Fillmore Auditorium. Performing are Phil Ochs, Loading Zone, Blue Cheer, Mad River, Mt. Rushmore and the Committee.

8th January – 1968

- The Marquee Club in London features the Nice and Human Instinct on Monday the 8th.

11th January – 1968

- Bill Graham presents the Chambers Brothers, Sunshine Company and Siegal Schwall Blues Band on Thursday, Friday & Saturday the 11th, 12th & 13th at the Fillmore Auditorium with lights by Holy See.

12th January – 1968

- The Doors second LP **Strange Days** goes Gold.
- The Family Dog presents Quicksilver Messenger Service, Kaleidoscope and Charley Musselwhite on Friday, Saturday & Sunday the 12th, 13th & 14th at the Avalon Ballroom.
- Pink Floyd perform for the first time as a five piece with Dave Gilmore as a permanent member. The performance took place on Friday the 12th at the University of Aston, Birmingham, England. Dave Gilmore is brought in to assist with guitar duties in Pink Floyd for a rapidly declining Syd Barrett. Barrett having taken huge amounts of acid over the previous year was becoming less and less coherent, and would simply strum the same chord over and over again during live performances.

16th January – 1968

- Youth International Party or as they're more commonly known the Yippies is officially founded.

17th January - 1968

- The Grateful Dead, Quicksilver Messenger Service and Jerry Abram's Head Lights perform on Wednesday the 17th at the Carousel Ballroom, San Francisco. This "alternative" ballroom was created to counter the growing trend towards the idolization of the rock star and was operated for a short time by the Dead and the Jefferson Airplane. Many individuals in the tightly knit San Francisco scene had noticed how the dancing had stopped and patrons were now standing in almost idle worship not wanting to miss one single drum stroke. No longer was the event a participatory affair. The music scene was changing and the musicians were becoming distant from their fan base. No longer could Jerry Garcia lean off stage in the middle of a set and converse with a friend. The times they were a changin…Unfortunately the lease deal on the Carousel Ballroom was a horrendous deal and the bands were quickly edged out as the Carousel was taken over by Bill Graham and re-christened it the Fillmore West.

18th January – 1968
- Bill Graham presents the Paul Butterfield Blues Band, Charles Lloyd Quartet and Ultimate Spinach on Thursday, Friday & Saturday the 18th, 19th & 20th at the Fillmore Auditorium with lights by Holy See.

19th January – 1968
- The Family Dog presents Genesis and Mother Earth on Friday, Saturday & Sunday the 19th, 20th & 21st at the Avalon Ballroom.

20th January – 1968
- The Great Northwest Tour featuring the Grateful Dead and Quicksilver Messenger Service begins on Friday the 20th in Eureka, California. The tour will run through February 4th.
- Pink Floyd and Beaufords Image perform on Friday the 20th At Hastings Pier, Hastings, England. Most Floyd historians cite this as Syd Barrett's final live appearance with the band.

25th January – 1968
- Bill Graham presents Big Brother and the Holding Company, Electric Flag, Youngbloods and the Ultimate Spinach on Thursday the 25th at the Fillmore Auditorium and Friday & Saturday the 26th & 27th at the Winterland with lights by Glenn McKay's Headlights.

26th January - 1968
- The Family Dog presents Country Joe and the Fish, Charlatans and Dan Hicks and his Hot Licks on Friday, Saturday & Sunday the 26th, 27th & 28th at the Avalon Ballroom.
- Boyd Grafmyre presents the Grateful Dead and Quicksilver Messenger Service on Friday & Sunday the 26th & 27th at the Eagles Auditorium, Seattle with lights by Jerry Abrams' Headlights.
- British music paper **Melody Maker** reports that Dave Gilmour has officially joined Pink Floyd and will play guitar on their forthcoming first European tour in February.

30th January – 1968
- The Marquee Club in London features Traffic and Spooky Tooth on Tuesday the 30th.

1st February - 1968
- Bill Graham presents the Jimi Hendrix Experience, John Mayall's Bluesbreakers and Albert King on Thursday the 1st at the Fillmore Auditorium with lights by Holy See.

2nd February - 1968

- Bill Graham presents the Jimi Hendrix Experience, John Mayall's Bluesbreakers and Albert King on Friday & Saturday the 2nd & 3rd at Winterland with lights by Glenn McKay's Headlights.
- The Family Dog presents Electric Flag and the Fugs on Friday, Saturday & Sunday the 2nd, 3rd & 4th at the Avalon Ballroom.
- Boyd Grafmyre presents Charles Lloyd Quintet and Shyamadas with lights by Retina Circus on Friday & Saturday the 2nd & 3rd at the Eagles Auditorium, Seattle.
- The Grateful Dead and Quicksilver Messenger Service perform on Friday & Saturday the 2nd & 3rd at the Crystal Ballroom in Portland Oregon as part of their "Tour of the Great Pacific Northwest." Headlights by Jerry Abrams.
- The Marquee Club in London features the first appearance of Jethro Tull and Savoy Brown Blues Band on Friday the 2nd. Jethro Tull will make an additional 18 appearances at the Marquee Club.

3rd February – 1968

- The Lemon Piper's *Green Tambourine* is the No.1 hit single in the United States.

4th February - 1968

- Bill Graham presents the Jimi Hendrix Experience, John Mayall's Bluesbreakers and Albert King on Sunday the 4th at the Fillmore Auditorium with lights by Holy See.

8th February - 1968

- The Jimi Hendrix Experience and Creators play on Thursday the 8th at the Sacramento State College, Sacramento with lights by Simultaneous Avalanche.

8th February – 1968

- Bill Graham presents John Mayall's Blues Breakers, Arlo Guthrie and Loading Zone on Thursday, Friday & Saturday the 8th, 9th & 10th at the Fillmore Auditorium. Lights by Holy See.

9th February – 1968

- The Family Dog presents the Siegal Schwall Band and Hour Glass on Friday, Saturday & Sunday the 9th, 10th & 11th at the Avalon Ballroom.

10th February – 1968

- Pinnacle Concerts presents the Jimi Hendrix Experience, the Soft Machine, the Electric Flag and Blue Cheer on Saturday the 10th at the Shrine Auditorium in Los Angeles. Visuals provided by Thomas Edison Lights and Acme Cinema.
- The Marquee Club in London features the Gods and Taste on Saturday the 10th.

11th February - 1968

- Pink Floyd appear on Top Gear, BBC Radio One. They perform Syd's new tunes, *Vegetable Man* and *Scream Thy Last Scream*.

14th February - 1968

- A "Valentine's Day Dance" is held on Wednesday the 14th at the Carousel Ballroom featuring the Grateful Dead and Country Joe and the Fish with lights by LSD.
- The Marquee Club in London features Human Instinct on Wednesday the 14th.

15th February – 1968

- The Beatles head off to Rishikesh in India to study under the Maharishi. They stayed for two months and wrote many of the songs that would appear on the **White Album**, including John Lennon's attack on the Maharishi in a song called *Sexy Sadie*.
- Bill Graham presents the Paul Butterfield Blues Band, James Cotton Blues Band and Albert King on Thursday the 15th at the Fillmore Auditorium and Friday & Saturday the 16th & 17th at the Winterland with lights by Holy See.

16th February – 1968

- The Family Dog presents the Youngbloods and Mount Rushmore on Friday, Saturday & Sunday the 16th, 17th & 18th at the Avalon Ballroom.

17th February - 1968

- Big Brother and the Holding Company play their first gig in New York on Saturday the 17th at the Anderson Theatre. The band gets great reviews.
- Baba Love Co. presents Country Joe and the Fish and Grateful Dead on Saturday the 17th at the Selland Arena, Fresno.
- Pink Floyd begin their first European tour, which lasts two weeks.

22nd February - 1968

- Bill Graham presents the Who, Cannonball Adderly and Vagrants on Thursday the 22nd at the Fillmore Auditorium and Friday & Saturday the 23rd & 24th at the Winterland. Lights by Glenn McKay's Headlights.
- The Grateful Dead and Morning Glory play on Thursday, Friday & Saturday the 22nd, 23rd & 24th at the Kings Beach Bowl, Lake Tahoe, with lights by The North American Ibis Alchemical Company.

23rd February – 1968

- The Family Dog presents Quicksilver Messenger Service and Son House on Friday, Saturday & Sunday the 23rd, 24th & 25th at the Avalon Ballroom.
- Pinnacle Concerts presents Jefferson Airplane, Charlie Musselwhite, Ceyleib People and Clearlight on Friday & Saturday the 23rd & 24th at the Shrine Auditorium in Los Angeles.
- Russ Gibb presents in Detroit a dance-concert featuring the Jimi Hendrix Experience, Soft Machine, MC5 and the Rationals performing on Friday the 23rd at the Masonic Temple, the corner of Cass and Temple in Detroit Michigan.
- The Dove Inc. presents Blue Cheer, Wedge and the Indian Head Band on Friday,

Saturday & Sunday the 23rd, 24th & 25th at the Civic Auditorium in Honolulu, Hawaii with lights by Paanic Light Circus.

26th February – 1968

- The Marquee Club in London features the Nice on Monday the 26th.

27th February – 1968

- The Marquee Club in London features the Move and Attack on Tuesday the 27th.

29th February – 1968

- Bill Graham presents Cream, Big Black and Loading Zone on Thursday, Friday & Saturday the 29th, 1st & 2nd at the Winterland with lights by Glenn McKay's Headlights and Sunday the 3rd at the Fillmore Auditorium with lights by Holy See.

1st March – 1968

- The Family Dog presents Blues Project and Genesis on Friday, Saturday & Sunday the 1st, 2nd & 3rd at the Avalon Ballroom.
- Russ Gibb presents in Detroit Big Brother and the Holding Company, MC5, Pink Peech Mob, Tiffany Shade and the Family Dumptruck on Friday & Saturday the 1st & 2nd at the Grande Ballroom.
- The Retinal Circus in Vancouver, British Columbia features 3's A Crowd and the Seeds of Time on Friday & Saturday the 1st & 2nd with lights by Addled Chromish. This is the first show since the name change from Dante's Inferno.

2nd March - 1968

- It is officially announced that Syd Barrett has been asked to stop touring with Pink Floyd but to continue contributing songs.
- The Marquee Club in London features the Gods and Glass Menagerie on Saturday the 2nd. The Glass Menagerie will make an additional 16 appearances at the Marquee.

3rd March – 1968

- After witnessing the slow deterioration of the Haight-Ashbury community, the Grateful Dead see the writing on the wall and decide to give a farewell performance on Sunday the 3rd before moving out to the country, Marin County in fact. The performance on Haight Street consists of four numbers and is performed on the back of a flatbed truck.

4th March – 1968

- The Marquee Club in London features the Nice and New Nadir on Monday the 4th.

7th March – 1968

- Bill Graham presents Cream, James Cotton Blues Band, Jeremy & the Satyrs and Blood Sweat and Tears on Thursday the 7th at the Fillmore Auditorium and Friday,

Saturday & Sunday the 8th 9th & 10th at the Winterland with lights by Glenn McKay's Headlights.

8th March - 1968

- Bill Graham takes over an abandoned movie theatre on Second Avenue and Sixth Street in New York City and opens the Fillmore East with this first performance Friday the 8th. Big Brother and the Holding Company, Tim Buckley and Albert King, perform with the Joshua Light Show. The Fillmore East has seating capacity for 3000.
- The Family Dog presents Love, Congress of Wonders and Sons of Champlin on Friday, Saturday & Sunday the 8th, 9th & 10th at the Avalon Ballroom. Lights by Jerry Abrams Headlights.
- The Retinal Circus in Vancouver, British Columbia features Papa Bears Medicine Show, Yellow Brick Road and My Indole Ring on Friday & Saturday the 8th & 9th with lights by Addled Chromish.

11th March - 1968

- Silva Productions presents Cream and the Grateful Dead on Monday the 11th at the Memorial Auditorium, Sacramento with lights by Light Brigade.
- The Marquee Club in London features the Nice and Attack on Monday the 11th.

12th March – 1968

- The Marquee Club in London features Procol Harum and Spooky Tooth on Tuesday the 12th.

14th March – 1968

- Bill Graham presents Traffic, H.P. Lovecraft, Blue Cheer and Mother Earth on Thursday the 14th at the Fillmore Auditorium and Friday & Saturday the 15th & 16th at the Winterland with lights by Holy See.

15th March – 1967

- The Family Dog presents Blood Sweat and Tears and John Handy on Friday, Saturday & Sunday the 15th, 16th & 17th at the Avalon Ballroom.
- Jefferson Airplane and the Grateful Dead play on Friday, Saturday & Sunday the 15th, 16th & 17th at the Carousel Ballroom in San Francisco with lights by the North American Ibis Alchemical Company.
- Pinnacle Concerts presents Cream, James Cotton Blues Band and Mint Tattoo on Friday & Saturday the 15th & 16th at the Shrine Auditorium in Los Angeles.
- The Charlatans and Valley Fever play on Friday & Saturday the 15th & 16th at the Marigold Ballroom, Fresno, California. Lights by UFO.
- Family perform at Middle Earth, 43 King Street, London, England on Friday the 15th.
- The Retinal Circus in Vancouver, British Columbia features Fat Jack, Mother Tuckers Yellow Duck and Hydro Electric Streetcar on Friday & Saturday the 15th & 16th with lights by Addled Chromish.

16th March - 1968
- Otis Redding's song *Sitting on the Dock on the Bay* posthumously reaches the No.1 slot on the singles charts.
- Pink Floyd play at Middle Earth, 43 King Street, Covent Garden, London, on Saturday the 16th. They were supported by Junior's Eyes and the event featured the Explosive Spectrum Light Show.
- The Marquee Club in London features the Gods and Sunshine Garden on Saturday the 16th.

18th March – 1968
- The on-air staff of Radio Station KMPX go on strike. Outside the studios on Green Street, Jerry Garcia joins Traffic in an impromptu jam session.
- The Marquee Club in London features the Nice and Exception on Monday the 18th.

21st March – 1968
- Bill Graham presents Moby Grape, Traffic, Lemon Pipers and Spirit on Thursday the 21st at the Fillmore Auditorium with lights by Holy See and Friday & Saturday the 22nd & 23rd at the Winterland with lights by Glenn McKay's Headlights.

22nd March – 1968
- The Family Dog presents the Siegal Schwall Band and Kaleidoscope on Friday, Saturday & Sunday the 22nd, 23rd & 24th at the Avalon Ballroom.
- Bill Graham presents the Doors, Ars Nova and Crome Syrcus on Friday & Saturday the 22nd & 23rd at the Fillmore East. Lights by the Joshua Light Show.
- International Kaleidoscope presents Jefferson Airplane, Canned Heat and Buffalo Springfield on Friday & Saturday the 22nd & 23rd at the Kaleidoscope. Lights by Omega's Eye.
- The Vernal Equinox Festival, Lime Kiln Creek, Big Sur is staged Friday, Saturday & Sunday the 22nd, 23rd & 24th.
- Russ Gibb presents in Detroit Eric Burdon and the Animals, Grateful Dead, Eire Apparent, the Apostles and Jagged Edge on Friday & Saturday the 22nd & 23rd at the Michigan State Fair Coliseum.
- The Moody Blues perform at Middle Earth, 43 King Street, London, England on Friday the 22nd.

23rd March – 1968
- The San Diego Happening No.6 featuring the Byrds and Brain Police is held on Saturday the 23rd at the Community Concourse in San Diego.
- The Nice perform at Middle Earth, 43 King Street, London, England on Saturday the 23rd.

24th March – 1968
- The Grateful Dead perform on Sunday the 24th at the Fountain Church in Grand Rapids Michigan.

25th March – 1968
- The last episode of the Monkees airs in the United States. After two successful seasons and 58 episodes the series is cancelled.
- The Marquee Club in London features the Nice and Still Life on Monday the 25th.

28th March – 1968
- Bill Graham presents Country Joe and the Fish, Steppenwolf and Flamin Groovies on Thursday, Friday & Saturday the 28th, 29th & 30th at the Fillmore Auditorium. Lights by Holy See.

28th March – 1968
- The Retinal Circus in Vancouver, British Columbia features the Siegal Schwall Blues Band, United Empire Loyalists, My Indole Ring and the Seeds of Time on Thursday, Friday & Saturday the 28th, 29th & 30th. Lights by Addled Chromish.

29th March – 1968
- The Family Dog presents Jerry Steig and the Satyrs and Sons of Champlin on Friday, Saturday & Sunday the 29th, 30th & 31st at the Avalon Ballroom.
- The Grateful Dead, Chuck Berry and Curly Cooks Hurdy Gurdy Band with lights by the Edison Light Co. perform on Friday, Saturday & Sunday the 29th, 30th & 31st at the Carousel Ballroom in San Francisco.
- Pinnacle Concerts presents Traffic and Quicksilver Messenger Service on Friday & Saturday the 29th & 30th at the Shrine Auditorium in Los Angeles.
- Bill Graham presents Richie Havens, United States of America and the Troggs on Friday & Saturday the 29th & 30th at the Fillmore East. Lights by the Joshua Light Show.
- International Kaleidoscope presents Bo Diddley, Peanut Butter Conspiracy and Clearlight on Friday, Saturday & Sunday the 29th, 30th & 31st at the Kaleidoscope. Lights by Omega's Eye.
- The Crazy World of Arthur Brown perform at Middle Earth, 43 King Street, London, England on Friday the 29th.

30th March – 1968
- John Mayall's Blues Breakers perform at Middle Earth, 43 King Street, London, England on Saturday the 30th.

April – 1968
- George Hunter is kicked out of the Charlatans! The band had tried to ascend to the same level as their peers and failed one too many times. Dan Hicks went off to form the Hot Licks, Mike Ferguson was fired and it just pitifully unraveled from there.

1st April – 1968
- M&A Enterprises presents the Palm Springs Pop Festival featuring Jeff Beck, John

Mayall, Paul Butterfield, Moby Grape, Lee Michaels, Canned Heat, Buddy Miles and Savoy Brown on Monday & Tuesday the 1st & 2nd. Lights by Dry paint.
- The Marquee Club in London features the Nice and Glass Menagerie on Monday the 1st.

4th April - 1968
- Martin Luther King is assassinated in Memphis, Tennessee, which starts 2 weeks of rioting and looting all over America. The racial tension is even felt around Bill Graham's Fillmore. Graham considers calling it quits. In fact over the next few months' events would play themselves out for Graham to move the Fillmore by taking over the Carousel Ballroom in July.
- Bill Graham presents Eric Burdon and the Animals, Quicksilver Messenger Service and Sons of Champlin on Thursday the 4th at the Fillmore Auditorium with lights by Holy See and Friday & Saturday the 5th & 6th at the Winterland with lights by Glenn McKay's Headlights.

5th April - 1968
- Bill Graham presents the Who, Buddy Guy, Free Spirits and the Joshua Light Show on Friday & Saturday the 5th & 6th at the Fillmore East, New York.
- The Family Dog presents the Blues Project and It's a Beautiful Day on Friday, Saturday & Sunday the 5th, 6th & 7th at the Avalon Ballroom.

6th April – 1968
- KACY and Jim Salzer presents Electric Flag, Traffic and Steppenwolf with lights by Omega Eye on Saturday the 6th at the Earl Warren Showground's, Santa Barbara.
- Family and a "People Show" perform at Middle Earth, 43 King Street, London, England on Saturday the 6th.

8th April – 1968
- International Kaleidoscope presents an Easter Show featuring Canned Heat, Evergreen Blue Shoes and the Travel Agency on Monday through Thursday the 8th – 11th at the Kaleidoscope in Los Angeles.

9th April – 1968
- Barry Berwin presents the Palm Springs Pop Festival featuring Eric Burdon and the Animals, Blue Cheer, Sweetwater and the Collectors on Tuesday the 9th with lights by Piccadilly Light Show.

11th April – 1968
- Bill Graham presents Big Brother and the Holding Company, Iron Butterfly and Booker T and the MGs on Thursday the 11th at the Fillmore Auditorium with lights by Holy See and Friday & Saturday the 12th & 13th at the Winterland with lights by Glenn McKay's Headlights.
- The Marquee Club in London features the Nice and Staks on Thursday the 11th.

12th April – 1968

- Pink Floyd release *It Would Be So Nice* b/w *Julia Dream*.
- Bill Graham presents the Paul Butterfield Blues Band, Charles Lloyd Quartet and Tom Rush with the Joshua Light Show on Friday & Saturday the 12th & 13th at the Fillmore East, New York.
- The Family Dog presents the Fugs and Ace of Cups on Friday, Saturday & Sunday the 12th, 13th & 14th at the Avalon Ballroom.
- Moby Grape, It's A Beautiful Day and Sweet Rush play on Friday & Saturday the 12th & 13th at the Carousel Ballroom, San Francisco.
- International Kaleidoscope presents their First Anniversary Dance-Concert featuring H.P. Lovecraft, James Cotton Blues Band and Mint Tattoo on Friday, Saturday & Sunday the 12th, 13th & 14th at the Kaleidoscope in Los Angeles. Lights by Omega's Eye.
- Arlo Guthrie performs at Middle Earth, 43 King Street, London, England on Friday the 12th.

13th April – 1968

- The Soft Machine perform at Middle Earth, 43 King Street, London, England on Saturday the 13th.

17th April - 1968

- Russ Gibb Presents MC5, Jagged Edge and the Psychedelic Stooges on Wednesday the 17th at the Grande Ballroom, Detroit.

18th April - 1968

- Bill Graham presents Love, the Staple Singers and Roland Kirk on Thursday the 18th at the Fillmore Auditorium and Friday & Saturday the 19th & 20th at the Winterland. Lights by Holy See.
- Russ Gibb presents Scot Richard Case, Thyme and the Ashmollyan Quintet on Thursday the 18th at the Grande Ballroom, Detroit.
- The Retinal Circus in Vancouver, British Columbia features Papa Bears Medicine Show, Black Snake Blues Band, Mother Tuckers Yellow Duck and Seeds of Time on Thursday, Friday & Saturday the 18th, 19th & 20th with lights by Ecto Plasmic Assault.

19th April – 1968

- The Beatles leave India two weeks before the completion of their studies with the Maharishi. Later all four of the Beatles will renounce their association with the Maharishi.
- The Family Dog presents Steppenwolf and Charley Musselwhite on Friday, Saturday & Sunday the 19th, 20th & 21st at the Avalon Ballroom.
- Erma Franklin, the Santana Blues Band and Frumious Bandersnatch play on Friday, Saturday & Sunday the 19th, 20th & 21st at the Carousel Ballroom in San Francisco with lights by the North American Ibis Alchemical Company.

- Baba Love Company presents Big Brother and the Holding Company and Mint Tattoo on Friday the 19th at the Selland Arena, Fresno, California.
- Bill Graham presents the Mothers of Invention and the James Cotton Blues Band with the Joshua Light Show on Friday & Saturday the 19th & 20th at the Fillmore East in New York City.
- Russ Gibb presents Cream, Children, Poor Richards Almanac, the Rationals, Frost, James Gang and the Psychedelic Stooges on Friday, Saturday & Sunday the 19th, 20th & 21st at the Grande Ballroom, Detroit.
- Brian Auger and Trinity perform at Middle Earth, 43 King Street, London, England on Friday the 19th.

20th April – 1968
- The Fairport Convention perform at Middle Earth, 43 King Street, London, England on Saturday the 20th.
- Deep Purple make their debut performance on Saturday the 20th at a concert in Denmark.

23rd April – 1968
- The Marquee Club in London features the Who on Tuesday the 23rd.

25th April – 1968
- Bill Graham presents Albert King, Electric Flag American Music Band and the Collectors on Thursday the 25th at the Fillmore Auditorium and Friday & Saturday the 26th & 27th at the Winterland with lights by Holy See.

26th April – 1968
- The Family Dog presents Quicksilver Messenger Service, the Charlatans and It's a Beautiful Day on Friday, Saturday & Sunday the 26th, 27th & 28th at the Avalon Ballroom.
- The Steve Miller Band, James and Bobby Purify and Sons of Champlin play on Friday, Saturday & Sunday the 26th, 27th & 28th at the Carousel Ballroom in San Francisco with lights by the North American Ibis Alchemical Company.
- Bill Graham presents Traffic, Blue Cheer and Iron Butterfly on Friday & Saturday the 26th & 27th at the Fillmore East, lights by the Joshua Light Show.
- The Marquee Club in London features the Nice and Black Cat Bones on Friday the 26th.

27th April – 1968
- A Peace march and rally is held in San Francisco.
- The Marquee Club in London features the Beanstalkers and Pandemonium on Saturday the 27th.

29th April – 1968
- The rock musical HAIR opens on Monday the 29th at the Biltmore Theatre on Broadway.

30th April – 1968

- The mixed-media club the Kaleidoscope opens in Los Angeles on the Sunset Strip. Opening night features the Jefferson Airplane, Canned Heat and Fever Tree.

May – 1968

- Jefferson Airplane purchase a 17 room mansion at 2400 Fulton Street and transform the Victorian mansion into the ultimate hippie palace. While this was happening Casady and Kaukonen were putting together a side project that eventually surfaced under the name of Hot Tuna. Marty Balin the meantime was slowly being squeezed out of the picture. From his perspective it was more a matter of everyone else not giving their-all and he began losing interest.

2nd May – 1968

- Bill Graham presents Moby Grape, Hour Glass and the United States of America on Thursday Friday & Saturday the 2nd, 3rd & 4th at the Fillmore Auditorium. Country Joe and the Fish performed in place of Moby Grape on Saturday the 3rd. Lights by Holy See.
- The Marquee Club in London features the Nice and the final appearance of Mabel Greer's Toyshop on Thursday the 2th. In June they would be reborn as Yes.

3rd May - 1968

- Left Wing students attempt to overthrow the French Government. Riots, strikes and civil unrest ensue for the following month until the French army is brought in to quell the unrest.
- The Family Dog presents Junior Wells and Canned Heat on Friday, Saturday & Sunday the 3rd, 4th & 5th at the Avalon Ballroom.
- Thelonious Monk, Dr. John the Night Tripper and the Charlatans play on Friday, Saturday & Sunday the 3rd, 4th & 5th at the Carousel Ballroom in San Francisco with lights by The North American Ibis Alchemical Company.
- The Cultural Arts Board of San Diego State College presents, Buffalo Springfield, Mike Bloomfield and the Electric Flag and Jello's Gass Band on Friday the 3rd at the San Diego State College. Lights by Crystal Focus.
- Pinnacle presents Big Brother and the Holding Company, Albert King and Pacific Gas & Electric on Friday & Saturday the 3rd & 4th at the Shrine Expo Hall. Lights by Single Wing Turquoise Bird.
- Bill Graham presents Jefferson Airplane and the Crazy World of Arthur Brown, with the Joshua Light Show on Friday & Saturday 3rd & 4th at the Fillmore East, New York.
- Russ Gibb presents the Yardbirds, Frost, the MC5, Stuart Avery Assemblage and Odds And Ends on Friday & Saturday the 3rd & 4th at the Grande Ballroom, Detroit.

5th May – 1968

- Buffalo Springfield, wracked with internal dissention, play their final gig in Long

Beach, California on Sunday the 5th.
- The Grateful Dead, Jefferson Airplane and the Paul Butterfield Blues Band perform on Sunday the 5th in New York's Central Park.
- Pink Floyd perform on Sunday the 5th at the poorly managed and attended First International European Pop Festival in Rome, Italy. The event ran from the 4th through the 10th and only 400 individuals show up to watch the Floyd, Donovan, Julie Driscoll and a number of lesser European groups. Police storm the stage at the Pop Festival on the night of the 7th when the Move set off explosives as part of their act.

8th May - 1968
- The Fire Dance, otherwise known as the Alton Kelley Benefit is held on Wednesday the 8th at the Carousel Ballroom in San Francisco featuring the Charlatans, Dan Hicks Hot Licks, Steve Miller Band and Jefferson Airplane. Lights by Brotherhood Of Light.

9th May – 1968
- Bill Graham presents the Loading Zone, Crome Syrcus and H.P. Lovecraft on Thursday, Friday & Saturday the 9th, 10th & 11th at the Fillmore Auditorium. Lights by Holy See. Special guest on Thursday & Friday was Tiny Tim.
- The Retinal Circus in Vancouver, British Columbia features the Collectors, Mock Duck, My Indole Ring and Black Snake Blues Band on Thursday, Friday & Saturday the 9th, 10th & 11th with lights by Addled Chromish.

10th May - 1968
- Bill Graham presents the Jimi Hendrix Experience, Sly and the Family Stone and the Joshua Light Show on Friday the 10th at the Fillmore East, New York.
- High Torr presents the Mothers of Invention, Charley Musselwhite Blues Band and Sweetwater on Friday & Saturday the 10th & 11th at the Shrine Auditorium in Los Angeles. Lights by Thomas Edison Castle Lighting.
- The Family Dog presents Quicksilver Messenger Service and Ace of Cups on Friday, Saturday & Sunday the 10th, 11th & 12th at the Avalon Ballroom.

11th May – 1968
- Bill Graham presents "Group Quake" featuring Autosalvage, Group Therapy, Joyfull Noise, Status Cymbal on Saturday the 11th at the Fillmore East in New York City. Lights by the Joshua Light Show.

12th May – 1968
- Jimi Hendrix is arrested for possession of hashish and heroin coming into Canada for concerts. He claims the drugs were planted and is later exonerated.

14th May – 1968
- The Marquee Club in London features Traffic and Taste on Tuesday the 14th.

15th May - 1968

- The Hells Angels present Big Brother and the Holding Company and the Youngbloods, with lights by the Brotherhood Of Light on Wednesday the 15th at the Carousel Ballroom, San Francisco.

16th May – 1968

- Bill Graham presents Country Joe and the Fish, the Incredible String Band and Albert Collins on Thursday, Friday & Saturday the 16th, 17th & 18th at the Fillmore Auditorium. Lights by Holy See.
- The Retinal Circus in Vancouver, British Columbia features the Collectors, Glass Harp, Hydro Electric Streetcar, Pacific Nation, Papa Bears Medicine Show and Yellow Brique Road on Thursday, Friday & Saturday the 16th, 17th & 18th with lights by Ecto Plasmic Assault

17th May - 1968

- The Family Dog presents Junior Wells and Santana on Friday, Saturday & Sunday the 17th, 18th & 19th at the Avalon Ballroom.
- Electric Flag, the Dan Ellis Orchestra and Pacific Gas & Electric play on Friday, Saturday & Sunday the 17th, 18th & 19th at the Carousel Ballroom, in San Francisco with lights by the North American Ibis Alchemical Company.
- Big Brother and the Holding Company play on Friday the 17th at the University of California.
- Jefferson Airplane play on Friday the 17th at the Memorial Auditorium, Sacramento with lights by the Light Brigade.
- Pinnacle presents the Grateful Dead, Steve Miller Band and Taj Mahal on Friday & Saturday the 17th & 18th at the Shrine Expo Hall. Lights by Single Wing Turquoise Bird.
- International Kaleidoscope presents Moby Grape, Hourglass and Mount Rushmore on Friday & Saturday the 17th & 18th at the Kaleidoscope.
- Bill Graham presents the Byrds, Tim Buckley and the Foundations on Friday & Saturday the 17th & 18th at the Fillmore East in New York City. Lights by the Joshua Light Show.
- Pink Floyd with Alexis Korner and Free play at Middle Earth, Covent Garden, London on Friday the 17th.
- The Marquee Club in London features Jethro Tull and Taste on Friday the 17th.

18th May - 1968

- The Northern California Folk Rock Festival is held on Saturday & Sunday the 18th & 19th at the Santa Clara County Fairgrounds with the Doors, the Animals, Big Brother and the Holding Company, Electric Flag, Jefferson Airplane, the Youngbloods, Kaleidoscope and Country Joe.

23rd May – 1968

- Bill Graham presents the Yardbirds, It's a Beautiful Day and Cecil Taylor on

Thursday, Friday & Saturday the 23rd, 24th & 25th at the Fillmore Auditorium. Lights by Holy See.
- The Retinal Circus in Vancouver, British Columbia features the Family Tree, Tomorrow's Eyes, Seeds of Time and Mock Duck on Thursday, Friday & Saturday the 23rd, 24th & 25th with lights by Ecto Plasmic Assault.

24th May – 1968
- The Family Dog presents the Youngbloods and Kaleidoscope on Friday, Saturday & Sunday the 24th, 25th & 26th at the Avalon Ballroom.
- Big Brother and the Holding Company, Clara Ward Singers and H.P. Lovecraft play on Friday, Saturday & Sunday the 24th, 25th & 26th at the Carousel Ballroom in San Francisco.
- The Straight Theatre in Haight-Ashbury presents Charlie Musslewhite, Savage Resurrection and Dan Hicks and his Hot Licks on Friday & Saturday the 24th & 25th.
- The Electric Flag and Cream perform at the Robertson Gym on Friday the 24th at the University of California in Santa Barbara. Lights by Dry Paint.
- Pinnacle presents the Chambers Brothers, Velvet Underground, Pinnacle, Salvation and Dr. John the Night Tripper play on Friday & Saturday the 24th & 25th at the Shrine Auditorium, Los Angeles with lights by Single Wing Turquoise Bird.
- International Kaleidoscope presents Them, Incredible String Band and Sons of Champlin on Friday & Saturday the 24th & 25th at the Kaleidoscope in Los Angeles.
- Bill Graham presents Ravi Shankar on Friday the 24th at the Fillmore East in New York City.

25th May – 1968
- The 1968 edition of the Monterey Pop Festival is cancelled. At the same time $52,000 is discovered missing from the previous years profits and the bookkeeper is nowhere to be found.
- Bill Graham presents Country Joe and the Fish and Blue Cheer on Saturday the 25th at the Fillmore East in New York City. Lights by the Joshua Light Show.

26th May - 1968
- An **Oz** Benefit is held at the Middle Earth Club, Covent Garden, London. Pink Floyd perform on Sunday the 26th.

29th May – June – 1968
- Bill Graham presents a "Memorial Day Weekend" featuring Buffalo Springfield, Chambers Brothers and Richie Havens on Wednesday & Thursday the 29th & 30th at the Fillmore Auditorium and Friday & Saturday the 31st & 1st at the Winterland. Lights by Holy See.

30th May - 1968
- The Grateful Dead and the Charlie Musslewhite Blues Band play on Thursday, Friday & Saturday the 30th, 31st & 1st at the Carousel Ballroom, San Francisco.

- A Teen Drop-In Center Benefit is held on Thursday the 30th at Acalanes High School, Lafayette with the Steve Miller Band, Loading Zone, Country Weather and Frumious Bandersnatch.
- The Retinal Circus in Vancouver, British Columbia features John Handy, My Indole Ring, Black Snake Blues Band and the United Empire Loyalists on Thursday, Friday & Saturday the 30th, 31st & 1st with lights by Addled Chromish.

31st May – 1968

- The Family Dog presents Taj Mahal and Creedence Clearwater Revival on Friday, Saturday & Sunday the 31st, 1st & 2nd at the Avalon Ballroom.
- Pinnacle presents the Yardbirds, B.B. King and the Sons of Champlin on Friday & Saturday the 31st & 1st at the Shrine Expo Hall. Lights by Single Wing Turquoise Bird.
- Bill Graham presents Moby Grape and the Fugs on Friday & Saturday the 31st & 1st at the Fillmore East in New York City with the Joshua Light Show.

5th June - 1968

- Robert F. Kennedy after having just won the California primary is assassinated by Sirhan Sirhan.
- The Jefferson Airplane, Jim Jones & the Chanteys and Zackery Thaks perform Wednesday the 5th at the Municipal Auditorium in San Antonio Texas. Light Show provided by the Electric Kiss.

6th June – 1968

- The Marquee Club in London features the Nice and Red Light District on Thursday the 6th.

6th June – 1968

- Bill Graham presents the Mothers of Invention, B.B. King and Booker T & the MGs on Thursday the 6th at the Fillmore Auditorium and Friday & Saturday the 7th & 8th at the Winterland.

7th June – 1968

- The Family Dog presents Iron Butterfly and Velvet Underground on Friday, Saturday & Sunday the 7th, 8th & 9th at the Avalon Ballroom.
- Jefferson Airplane, the Grateful Dead and Fleetwood Mac with Glenn McKay's Head Lights play on Friday, Saturday & Sunday the 7th, 8th & 9th at the Carousel Ballroom in San Francisco.
- The Steve Miller Band, Alexander's Timeless Blooze Band and Baptized By Fire perform Friday & Saturday the 7th & 8th at the Hippodrome in San Diego.
- Bill Graham presents Electric Flag, Quicksilver Messenger Service and Steppenwolf on Friday & Saturday the 7th & 8th at the Fillmore East in New York City with lights by the Joshua Light Show.
- The Retinal Circus in Vancouver, British Columbia features Allmen Joy, Black &

White Power, Seeds of Time and Pacific Nation on Friday & Saturday the 7th & 8th with lights by Addled Chromish.

11th June – 1968
- The Marquee Club in London features Family and Granny's Intentions on Tuesday the 11th.

13th June – 1968
- Bill Graham presents Big Brother and the Holding Company, Crazy World of Arthur Brown and the Foundations on Thursday the 13th at the Fillmore Auditorium and Friday & Saturday the 14th & 15th at the Winterland. Lights by Holy See.

14th June - 1968
- The Family Dog presents Frumius Bandersnatch and Clear Light on Friday, Saturday & Sunday the 14th, 15th & 16th at the Avalon Ballroom.
- The Straight Theatre in Haight-Ashbury presents the Charlatans, Cleveland Wrecking Company and Uncut Ballroom, with Straight Lighting on Friday & Saturday the 14th & 15th.
- The Velvet Underground, Clover and Maya perform on Friday & Saturday the 14th & 15th at the Hippodrome in San Diego.
- Bill Graham presents the Grateful Dead, Albert Collins and Kaleidoscope on Friday & Saturday the 14th & 15th at the Fillmore East with lights by the Joshua Light Show.
- Pink Floyd perform on Friday the 14th at the Midsummer Ball, staged at the University College London, London, England.

15th June - 1968
- Golden Star presents the Doors on Saturday the 15th at the Memorial Auditorium, Sacramento.

16th June – 1968
- A "Matrix Benefit" is held at the Fillmore featuring Big Brother and the Holding Company, Steve Miller Band, Sandy Bull, Dan Hicks and Santana on Sunday the 16th.

18th June – 1968
- Bill Graham presents the "Summer Series" featuring the Chambers Brothers, It's a Beautiful Day and the Crazy World of Arthur Brown on Tuesday, Wednesday & Thursday the 18th, 19th & 20th at the Fillmore Auditorium. Lights by Holy See.

19th June - 1968
- "Soul Scene" benefit dance for Blackman's Free Store is held on Wednesday the 19th at the Carousel Ballroom in San Francisco.

20th June – 1968
- Iron Butterfly's **In-A-Gadda-Da-Vida** enters the album chart. The revolutionary 17-minute title track becomes a staple of underground radio stations across the country. The album eventually hits the No.1 spot selling over three million copies.

20th June – 1968
- The Marquee Club in London features the Nice and Thackery on Thursday the 20th.
- The Retinal Circus in Vancouver, British Columbia features Easy Chair, United Empire Loyalists, Mock Duck, Paisley Rain on Thursday, Friday & Saturday the 20th, 21st & 22nd with lights by Ecto Plasmic Assault.

21st June - 1968
- Bill Graham presents the "Summer Series" featuring Quicksilver Messenger Service and Sly and the Family Stone on Friday, Saturday & Sunday the 21st, 22nd & 23rd at the Fillmore Auditorium. Lights by Holy See.
- The Family Dog presents Mother Earth and Kaleidoscope on Friday, Saturday & Sunday the 21st, 22nd & 23rd at the Avalon Ballroom.
- Bill Graham presents Vanilla Fudge, James Cotton Blues Band and Loading Zone on Friday the 21st at the Fillmore East with lights by the Joshua Light Show.
- Pink Floyd play at Middle Earth, Covent Garden, London on Friday the 21st. The other bands performing on this night include Hurdy Gurdy, Easy Moses and Dexasterous.
- The Marquee Club in London features Taste and the first appearance of Free on Friday the 21st.

23rd June – 1968
- Big Brother and the Holding Company perform on Sunday the 23rd at the Carousel Ballroom in San Francisco.

25th June – 1968
- Bill Graham presents the "Summer Series" featuring Albert King, Loading Zone and Rain on Tuesday, Wednesday & Thursday the 25th, 26th & 27th at the Fillmore Auditorium. Lights by Holy See.

27th June – 1968
- The Retinal Circus in Vancouver, British Columbia features the Velvet Underground, Seeds of Time, Black Snake Blues Band, My Indole Ring, Papa Bears Medicine Show and Don Thompson Trio on Thursday, Friday, Saturday & Sunday the 27th, 28th, 29th & 30th. Lights by Addled Chromish.

28th June – 1968
- Bill Graham presents the "Summer Series" featuring Ten Years After, Canned Heat and Dan Hicks and his Hot Licks on Friday, Saturday & Sunday the 28th, 29th & 30th at the Fillmore Auditorium. Lights by Holy See.

- The Family Dog presents the Youngbloods and It's a Beautiful Day on Friday, Saturday & Sunday the 28th, 29th & 30th at the Avalon Ballroom.
- Pinnacle Concerts presents the Who, Peter Green's Fleetwood Mac and the Crazy World of Arthur Brown on Friday & Saturday the 28th & 29th at the Shrine Auditorium in Los Angeles.

29th June - 1968
- Pink Floyd release their 2nd LP, **A Saucerful Of Secrets** on EMI Records on Friday the 29th.
- The first Free Concert in Hyde Park organized by Blackhill Enterprises featuring the Rolling Stones, Blind Faith, Jethro Tull, Tyrannosaurus Rex, Roy Harper and Pink Floyd takes place on Friday the 29th. Noted music and radio personality John Peel is quoted as saying, "I always claim that the best outdoor event that I've ever been to was the Pink Floyd concert in Hyde Park."

1st July – 1968
- Radio Station KSAN Stereo Radio 95 presents a Family Freakout on Monday the 1st at the Avalon Ballroom with music supplied by Creedence Clearwater Revival.

2nd July – 1968
- Bill Graham presents the "Summer Series" featuring Creedence Clearwater Revival, Steppenwolf and It's a Beautiful Day on Tuesday, Wednesday & Thursday the 2nd, 3rd & 4th at the Fillmore Auditorium. Lights by Holy See.

3rd July - 1968
- The Straight Theatre in Haight-Ashbury presents Initial Shock, Allmen Joy, Phoenix and the Indian Head Band on Wednesday the 3rd.

4th July - 1968
- The Family Dog presents Iron Butterfly and Indian Head Band on Thursday, Friday, Saturday & Sunday the 4th, 5th, 6th & 7th at the Avalon Ballroom.
- Spirit, Pyewacket and Stillborn Time play on Thursday & Friday the 4th & 5th at the Sound Factory, Sacramento with lights by Jerry Abrams Head Lights.

5th July – 1968
- Bill Graham presents the "Summer Series" featuring the Butterfield Blues Band, Ten Years After and Truth on Friday, Saturday & Sunday the 5th, 6th & 7th at the Fillmore Auditorium. Lights by Holy See.
- International Kaleidoscope presents an Independence Day Spectacular featuring live animals and Showgirls on Friday the 5th at the Kaleidoscope in Los Angeles.
- Eric Burdon and the Animals perform Friday the 5th through Monday the 8th at the Whisky A-Go-Go in Los Angeles.

6th July – 1968
- The No.1 Pop LP in the U.K. is the Small Faces' **Ogden's Nut Gone Flake**. It will stay at the top spot for four weeks.

- The Retinal Circus in Vancouver, British Columbia features the Hydro Electric Streetcar on Saturday the 6th with lights by Addled Chromish.

7th July – 1968

- The Yardbirds announce their breakup, leaving guitarist Jimmy Page to fulfill the remaining dates, which he does first as the New Yardbirds and then as Led Zeppelin.

8th July – 1968

- Pink Floyd begin their second U.S. tour with a performance on Monday the 8th at the Kinetic Playground, Chicago, Illinois. This tour runs all through July and August.

9th July – 1968

- Bill Graham presents the "Blues Bash" featuring the Electric Flag, Buddy Guy and Freddy King on Tuesday, Wednesday & Thursday the 9th, 10th & 11th to start the week of close out the performances at the original Fillmore on Geary and Fillmore Streets. Lights by Holy See.
- The Retinal Circus in Vancouver, British Columbia features the Yellow Brique Road and Winter Green on Tuesday the 9th with lights by Addled Chromish.

10th July – 1968

- The British psychedelic/progressive rock band the Nice are banned from future performances at the Royal Albert Hall for trampling on the American flag during a rendition of Leonard Bernstein's "America".

11th July – 1968

- The Marquee Club in London features the Beanstalkers and Dream Police on Thursday the 11th. The Dream Police will make an additional 23 appearances at the Marquee before evolving into the Average White Band.

12th July – 1968

- Bill Graham presents the "Blues Bash" featuring Blue Cheer, Ike & Tina Turner and Freddy King on Friday, Saturday & Sunday the 12th, 13th & 14th to close out the performances at the original Fillmore on Geary and Fillmore Streets. Lights by Holy See.
- The Family Dog presents the Steve Miller Band and Howlin' Wolf on Friday, Saturday & Sunday the 12th, 13th & 14th at the Avalon Ballroom.
- Pinnacle Concerts presents the Paul Butterfield Blues Band and Sly and the Family Stone on Friday & Saturday the 12th & 13th at the Shrine Auditorium in Los Angeles.
- Russ Gibb presents in Detroit Pink Floyd with Thyme and Jagged Edge on Friday the 12th at the Grande Ballroom, Detroit Michigan.
- The Retinal Circus in Vancouver, British Columbia features My Indole Ring and Genesis on Friday the 12th. Lights by Addled Chromish.

15th July – 1968

- Pink Floyd perform on Monday, Tuesday & Wednesday the 15th, 16th & 17th at Steve Paul's The Scene in New York City.

16th July – 1968

- Bill Graham presents Big Brother and the Holding Company, Richie Havens and Illinois Speed Press on Tuesday, Wednesday & Thursday the 16th, 17th & 18th at the new Fillmore West, at Market and Van Ness formerly the Carousel Ballroom. Having opened the Fillmore East in New York, Graham now spends almost as much time in the air commuting between San Francisco and New York. Needless to say his marriage and family life suffers greatly.

17th July – 1968

- The new Beatles' movie **Yellow Submarine** premiers in London.
- The Retinal Circus in Vancouver, British Columbia features Black and White Power, Mock Duck, United Empire Loyalists and Black Snake Blues Band on Wednesday, Thursday & Friday the 17th, 18th & 19th with lights by Ecto Plasmic Assault.

19th July – 1968

- Bill Graham presents Sly and the Family Stone, Jeff Beck Group and Siegal Schwall on Friday, Saturday & Sunday the 19th, 20th & 21st at the new Fillmore West. Lights by Holy See.
- The Family Dog presents Tim Buckley and Velvet Underground on Friday, Saturday & Sunday the 19th, 20th & 21st at the Avalon Ballroom.
- Bill Graham presents Jefferson Airplane and H.P. Lovecraft with Glenn McKay's Head Lights lightshow on Friday & Saturday the 19th & 20th at the Fillmore East, New York.

20th July – 1968

- Iron Butterfly's **In-A-Gadda-Da-Vida** enters the U.S. LP charts. The title track would quickly gain notoriety for its seventeen minute running time and the drum solo.

23rd July – 1968

- Bill Graham presents Moby Grape, Jeff Beck Group and Mint Tattoo on Tuesday, Wednesday & Thursday the 23rd, 24th & 25th at the Fillmore West. Lights by Holy See.
- The Family Dog presents Country Joe and the Fish and Pacific Gas & Electric on Tuesday, Wednesday & Thursday the 23rd, 24th & 25th at the Avalon Ballroom.
- The Retinal Circus in Vancouver, British Columbia presents ExPop 68 featuring John Handy and the Good Shepherds from Tuesday the 23rd through Saturday the 3rd with lights by Addled Chromish.

24th July – 1968

- The Philadelphia Music Festival is staged on Wednesday the 24th at the John F. Kennedy Stadium in Philadelphia, Pennsylvania. Performing bands include the Who, Pink Floyd, the Troggs and Mandala featuring the Joshua Light Show.

25th July – 1968

- Janis Joplin and Big Brother and the Holding Company release **Cheap Thrills**. The album eventually reaches the No.1 slot in October and stays there for eight weeks. Despite the success, Janis was tiring of her relationship with the band and would soon form another backing unit.

26th July – 1968

- Bill Graham presents the Charles Lloyd Quartet, Herd and the James Cotton Blues Band on Friday, Saturday & Sunday the 26th, 27th 28th at the Fillmore West. Lights by Holy See.
- The Family Dog presents Quicksilver Messenger Service and Dan Hicks and his Hot Licks on Friday, Saturday & Sunday the 26th, 27th & 28th at the Avalon Ballroom.
- Pinnacle Concerts presents Pink Floyd, Blue Cheer and introducing Jeff Beck on Friday & Saturday the 26th & 27th at the Shrine Auditorium in Los Angeles. **The Los Angeles Times** gives the Floyd a scathing review saying, "Pink Floyd on record is one thing: live, they're something else. Disappointing."
- The Retinal Circus in Vancouver, British Columbia features Papa Bear's Medicine Show and Winter Green on Friday & Saturday the 26th & 27th with lights by Addled Chromish.

27th July – 1968

- Middle Earth re-opens on Saturday the 27th at the Roundhouse with a performance from Traffic.
- The Free Concert in Hyde Park on Friday the 27th features Traffic, the Nice, Pretty Things, Action and Juniors Eyes.

30th July - 1968

- Bill Graham presents Paul Butterfield Blues Band, Santana and Hello People on Tuesday, Wednesday & Thursday the 30th, 31st & 1st at the Fillmore West. Lights by Holy See. This was Fillmore's debut of Santana.

31st July – 1968

• The Yardbirds along with Tom Northcott, Family Tree, Painted Ship and Magic Fern perform on Wednesday the 31st at the Kerrisdale Arena in Vancouver, British Columbia. Lights by Living Colour Mind Machine.

1st August – 1968

• There are now 541,0000 American troops in Vietnam.

2nd August - 1968

• Bill Graham presents Iron Butterfly, Canned Heat and Initial Shock on Friday, Saturday & Sunday the 2nd, 3rd & 4th at the Fillmore West. Lights by Holy See.
• The Family Dog presents the Holy Modal Rounders, Pink Floyd and Crome Syrcus on Friday, Saturday & Sunday the 2nd, 3rd & 4th at the Avalon Ballroom.
• The Grateful Dead, Curly Cooke's Hurdy Gurdy Band and Maya perform on Friday & Saturday the 2nd & 3rd at the Hippodrome in San Diego. Lights by Mirkwood.
• Muddy Waters performs on Friday & Saturday the 2nd & 3rd at the Vulcan Gas Company, 316 Congress Austin Texas.
• Bill Graham presents Big Brother and the Holding Company, the Staple Singers, Ten Years After and the Joshua Light Show on Friday & Saturday the 2nd & 3rd at the Fillmore East, New York.

3rd August – 1968

• Humble Harve presents the First Annual Newport Pop Festival on Saturday & Sunday the 3rd & 4th featuring, Tiny Tim, Jefferson Airplane, Sonny & Cher, Eric Burdon and the Animals, Country Joe and the Fish, the Byrds, Chambers Brothers, Quicksilver Messenger Service, Paul Butterfield Blues Band, Blue Cheer, James Cotton Blues Band, Grateful Dead, Electric Flag, Canned Heat, Iron Butterfly, Steppenwolf, Things to Come, and Illinois Speed Press! The event takes place at the Orange Country Fairgrounds in Costa Mesa.

5th August - 1968

• Ornette Coleman performs on Monday the 5th at the Fillmore West.
• The Marquee Club in London features the Nite People and the first appearance of Yes on Monday the 5th.

6th August – 1968

• Bill Graham presents the Chambers Brothers and the Charlatans on Tuesday,

Wednesday & Thursday the 6th, 7th & 8th at the Fillmore West. Lights by Holy See.
- The Retinal Circus in Vancouver, British Columbia features the Muddy Waters Blues Band and My Indole Ring from Tuesday the 6th through Friday the 16th with lights by Ecto Plasmic Assault.

8th August – 1968
- The Staple Singers and Bo Grumpus featuring Felix Pappalardi perform on Thursday, Friday & Saturday the 8th, 9th & 10th at the Boston Tea Party, 15 Lansdowne Street in Boston.

9th August – 1968
- Bill Graham presents Eric Burdon & the Animals, Blood Sweat & Tears and Gypsy Wizard Band on Friday, Saturday & Sunday the 9th, 10th & 11th at the Fillmore West. Lights by Holy See.
- The Family Dog presents Steppenwolf and the Siegal Schwall Band on Friday, Saturday & Sunday the 9th, 10th & 11th at the Avalon Ballroom.
- Russ Gibb presents Canned Heat, the Jagged Edge and Children Sun on Friday & Saturday the 9th & 10th at the Grande Ballroom, Detroit.
- Pink Floyd perform on Friday, Saturday & Sunday the 9th, 10th & 11th at the Eagles Auditorium in Seattle Washington with supporting act Blue Cheer and lights by the Retina Circus Light Company.

10th August - 1968
- Cream's **Wheels of Fire** reaches No.1 in the U.S album charts. It was a double disc with two of the four sides recorded live at the Fillmore West.
- The Band's **Music from the Big Pink** enters the charts heralding a return-to-roots musical style. The album title refers to house in Woodstock, New York, where it was recorded.
- The Doors hold down the No.1 spot on the U.S. singles chart with *Hello I Love You*.
- The Marquee Club in London features Neat Change and the Boots on Saturday the 10th.

11th August - 1968
- The West Coast Love In and Watermelon Feed is staged featuring Quicksilver Messenger Service, West Phoenix, Charlie Musslewhite Blues Band, the Youngbloods, Creedence Clearwater Revival and the Flamin' Groovies, in Santa Cruz on Sunday the 11th.

13th August – 1968
- Bill Graham presents the Who, James Cotton Blues Band and Magic Sam on Tuesday, Wednesday & Thursday the 13th, 14th & 15th at the Fillmore West with Lights by Holy See.
- The Retinal Circus in Vancouver, British Columbia features Tom Northcott and Mother Tuckers on Tuesday the 13th through Saturday the 17th with lights by Addled Chromish.

16th August – 1968

THE BANK PRESENTS THE FUGS, MT. RUSHMORE & GRAITY, TORRANCE CALIFORNIA

- Bill Graham presents Creedence Clearwater Revival, It's a Beautiful Day and Albert Collins on Friday, Saturday & Sunday the 16th, 17th & 18th at the Fillmore West with Lights by Holy See.
- The Family Dog presents Bill Haley and the Comets and the Drifters on Friday, Saturday & Sunday the 16th, 17th & 18th at the Avalon Ballroom.
- Russ Gibb presents in Detroit Country Joe and the Fish on Friday, Saturday & Sunday the 16th, 17th & 18th at the Grande Ballroom.
- The Bank presents the Fugs, Mt. Rushmore and Gravity on Friday, Saturday & Sunday the 16th, 17th & 18th at the Bank in Torrance California.
- Pink Floyd supported by Initial Shock and the A.B. Skhy Blues Band perform on Friday & Saturday the 16th & 17th at the Sound Factory, Sacramento, California.

17th August - 1968

- *Fire* by the Crazy World Of Arthur Brown reaches No.1 in the UK singles charts and stays there for the next 14 weeks.

20th August – 1968

- The USSR invades Czechoslovakia putting a halt to the liberalization-taking place there.
- Bill Graham presents the Grateful Dead, Kaleidoscope and Albert Collins on Tuesday, Wednesday & Thursday the 20th, 21st & 22nd at the Fillmore West with Lights by Holy See.

23th August – 1968

- Bill Graham presents the Quicksilver Messenger Service, Spooky Tooth and Cold Blood on Friday, Saturday & Sunday the 23rd, 24th & 25th at the Fillmore West with Lights by Holy See.
- The Family Dog presents Spirit, Sir Douglas Quintet Plus 2 and Notes from the Underground on Friday, Saturday & Sunday the 23rd, 24th & 25th at the Avalon Ballroom.

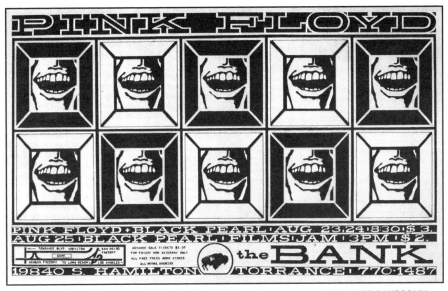

A CONCERT POSTER FOR PINK FLOYD PREFORMING AT THE BANK, TORRANCE CALIFORNIA

- H.P. Lovecraft and Kaleidoscope play on Friday & Saturday the 23rd & 24th at the Sound Factory, Sacramento with lights by The Light Brigade.
- The Bank presents Pink Floyd and Black Pearl on Friday, Saturday & Sunday the 23rd, 24th & 25th at the Bank in Torrance California.

24th August - 1968

- Country Joe and the Fish and Iron Butterfly perform on Saturday the 24th at the Merriweather Post Pavilion in Columbia, Maryland.
- The Free Concert in Hyde Park on Saturday the 24th features Fleetwood Mac, Family, Fairport Convention, Roy Harper, Eclection and Ten Years After.

26th August – 1968

- The Beatles release the first Apple singles, one of which is the seven-minute *Hey Jude*.

27th August 1968

- Bill Graham presents Steppenwolf, the Staple Singers and Santana on Tuesday, Wednesday & Thursday the 27th, 28th & 29th at the Fillmore West with Lights by Holy See.
- The Retinal Circus in Vancouver, British Columbia features Allmen Joy on Tuesday the 27th through Sunday the 1st. Lights by Addled Chromish.

28th August – 1968

- Jefferson Airplane perform on Wednesday the 28th at the Falkoner Centret in Copenhagen, Denmark.

29th August – 1968
• The Family Dog presents Youngbloods and It's a Beautiful Day on Thursday, Friday & Saturday the 29th, 30th & 31st at the Avalon Ballroom.

30th August – 1968
• Bill Graham presents the Grateful Dead, Preservation Hall Jazz Band and the Sons of Champlin on Friday, Saturday & Sunday the 30th, 31st & 1st at the Fillmore West with Lights by Holy See.
• The San Francisco Palace Of Fine Arts Festival takes place on Friday the 30th through Monday the 2nd featuring (amongst others) Kaleidoscope and Santana, with lights by the North American Ibis Alchemical Company, Holy See and Head Lights (30th). Linn County, A.B. Skhy, Ace of Cups, H.P. Lovecraft, Quicksilver Messenger Service, Big Mama Thornton and the Steve Miller Band, with lights by the North American Ibis Alchemical Company, Holy See and Head Lights (31st). S.F Mime Troupe, Crome Syrcus, Sons of Champlin, Country Weather, Randy Boone, Black Pearl and the Grateful Dead, with lights by Temporary Optics, Garden of Delights and Head Lights (2nd).

31st August – 1968
• The "Sky River Rock Festival and Lighter than Air Fair" is held at Betty Nelson's Organic Raspberry Farm in Sultan, Washington on Sunday, Monday & Tuesday the 31st, 1st and 2nd. Over 40 bands all showed up to perform for a crowd of over 10,000. Bands included Pink Floyd (first night only), Kaleidoscope, Muddy Waters, Peanut Butter Conspiracy, Santana, Country Joe and the Fish, H.P. Lovecraft, Steppenwolf, the Youngbloods and many others.
• The Marquee Club in London features the Boots and the Open Mind on Sunday the 31st.
• The Great South Coast Bank Holiday Pop Festival (The 1st Isle of Wight Pop Festival), Hayles Field, Ford Farm, near Godshill, Isle of Wight, UK is staged on Sunday the 1st and Monday the 2nd with Jefferson Airplane, Crazy World Of Arthur Brown, the Move, Plastic Penny, Pretty Things, Mirage, Aynsley Dunbar Retaliation, Fairport Convention, Orange Bicycle, Blonde on Blonde, Smile, The Cherokees and Halcyon Order.

1st September – 1968
• The "Oakland Pop Festival" is held on Monday the 1st at the Baldwin Pavilion on the Oakland University in Rochester, Michigan featuring Procol Harum, Pink Floyd, Howlin Wolf, Rationals, SRC Thyme, MC5, and the Frost Children. This was the last evening of Pink Floyd's U.S. tour.

4th September - 1968
• Pink Floyd play at the Middle Earth Club, London on Wednesday the 4th.

5th September – 1968
• The Grateful Dead begin recording the album **Aoxomoxoa**.

- Bill Graham presents Chuck Berry, the Steve Miller Band and Kensington Market on Thursday, Friday & Saturday the 5th, 6th & 7th at the Fillmore West with lights by Holy See.

6th September – 1968
- The Family Dog presents James Cotton Blues Band and Sir Douglas Quintet Plus 2 on Friday, Saturday & Sunday the 6th, 7th & 8th at the Avalon Ballroom.
- The Bank presents Moby Grape and FairBeFall on Friday, Saturday & Sunday the 6th, 7th & 8th at the Bank in Torrance California.
- The Doors and Jefferson Airplane perform at Middle Earth, the Roundhouse, Chalk Farm, London on Friday & Saturday the 6th & 7th. Support bands include Blossom Toes and Blonde on Blonde. Lights supplied by Glenn McKay's Headlights.

12th September – 1968
- Bill Graham presents Big Brother and the Holding Company, Santana and the Chicago Transit Authority on Thursday, Friday & Saturday the 12th, 13th & 14th at the Fillmore West with lights by Holy See.
- Pinnacle Concerts and the Free Clinic presents An American Music Show on Thursday the 12th through Sunday the 15th at the Rose Bowl in Pasadena California featuring Joan Baez, Everly Brothers, Big Brother and the Holding Company, the Byrds, Country Joe and the Fish, Jr. Wells with Buddy Guy, the Mothers of Invention, Buffy St. Marie and Wilson Picket.

13th September – 1968
- The Family Dog presents John Mayall and Big Mama Mae Thornton on Friday, Saturday & Sunday the 13th, 14th & 15th at the Avalon Ballroom.
- Bill Graham presents the Chambers Brothers, Blood Sweat & Tears and the Amboy Dukes on Friday & Saturday the 13th & 14th at the Fillmore East with lights by the Joshua Light Show.

14th September - 1968
- Golden Star presents Quicksilver Messenger Service and H.P. Lovecraft on Saturday the 14th at the Santa Rosa Fairground.

19th September – 1968
- Steppenwolf earns a Gold disc for the hit single *Born to be Wild*. The song would surface again in the movie **Easy Rider**.
- Bill Graham presents Albert King, Creedence Clearwater Revival and Black Pearl on Thursday, Friday & Saturday the 19th, 20th & 21st at the Fillmore West with lights by the Brotherhood of Light.
- The Marquee Club in London features the Nice and Yes on Thursday the 19th.

20th September – 1968
- The Family Dog presents the Steve Miller Band and Muddy Waters on Friday,

Saturday & Sunday the 20th, 21st & 22nd at the Avalon Ballroom.

- The Bank presents Quicksilver Messenger Service, Sons of Champlin, Ace of Clubs and Love Exchange on Friday & Saturday the 20th & 21st at the Bank in Torrance California.
- Bill Graham presents Traffic, Staple Singers and Chrome on Friday & Saturday the 20th & 21st at the Fillmore East with lights by the Joshua Light Show.
- The Marquee Club in London features Jethro Tull and Love Sculpture on Friday the 20th. The Love Sculpture featuring Dave Edmunds on vocals and guitar will make an additional 9 appearances at the Marquee.

22nd September – 1968

- The Autumnal Equinox Celebration featuring the Grateful Dead, Buddy Miles Express, Taj Mahal, Quicksilver Messenger Service, Sons of Champlin, Mother Earth, Curly Cooke's Hurdy Gurdy Band, Youngbloods, Ace of Cups and Phoenix is held on Sunday the 22nd at the Del Mar Fairgrounds, In San Diego. Sunday from Noon till Dusk.

24th September - 1968

- The Austin Love-In takes place on Tuesday the 24th at the Zilker Park Bandstand featuring Circus Maximus, Conquerod, Shiva's Head Band, the Thinges and Black Lace. This is a free event sponsored by the Austin Police Department, The Owl and the Vulcan Gas Company.

25th September – 1968

- A "Benefit for Peace and Freedom Cabaret" takes place on Wednesday the 25th at the Fillmore West featuring the Steve Miller Blues Band, Santana, Flamin' Groovies, It's a Beautiful Day, Country Weather, Fruminous Bandersnatch, Womb, and the Cleveland Wrecking Company with lights supplied by Garden of Delights.

26th September – 1968

- After Jefferson Airplane toured Europe with the Doors, they returned and threw a huge party, which in some ways was really a Wake for the San Francisco scene as most of the local bands had now moved away.
- Bill Graham presents the Super Session featuring Mike Bloomfield, Al Cooper & Friends, It's a Beautiful Day and Loading Zone on Thursday, Friday & Saturday the 26th, 27th & 28th at the Fillmore West with lights by Holy See.

27th September – 1968

- The Family Dog presents Flatt and Scruggs, Jack Elliott, Sons of Champlin and Country Weather on Friday, Saturday & Sunday the 27th, 28th & 29th at the Avalon Ballroom.
- The Bank presents John Mayall, C.T.A., Mug-Wumps, Maze and Flash Gordon on Friday, Saturday & Sunday the 27th, 28th & 29th at the Bank in Torrance California.
- Big Joe Williams and Sky Blues perform on Friday & Saturday the 27th & 28th at the Vulcan Gas Company, 316 Congress in Austin Texas.

- Russ Gibb presents in Detroit Spooky Tooth and the McCoys on Friday, Saturday & Sunday the 27th, 28th & 29th at the Grande Ballroom.
- Bill Graham presents Country Joe & the Fish, Ten Years After and Procol Harum on Friday & Saturday the 27th & 28th at the Fillmore East with lights by the Joshua Light Show.
- The Retinal Circus in Vancouver, British Columbia features the Collectors and Graeme Wafer on Friday, Saturday & Sunday the 27th, 28th & 29th. Lights by Addled Chromish.

28th September - 1968
- New York manager Albert Grossman announces that Janis Joplin will leave Big Brother and the Holding Company and strike out on a solo career. Insiders contend that Grossman was planning this since seeing her and the band perform at the Monterey Pop Festival in 1967.
- The Beatles *Hey Jude* reaches No.1 in the U.S charts. A landmark event given the song's seven-minute length.
- The Festival of Peace and Love is held on Saturday & Sunday the 28th & 29th at Live Oak Park, Berkeley with Rock Bands, Painting, Sculpture, Crafts and Lights.
- The Free Concert in Hyde Park on Saturday the 28th features the Move, Pete Brown's Battered Ornaments, Roy Harper, and Clouds.

3rd October – 1968
- Bill Graham presents Canned Heat, Gordon Lightfoot and Cold Blood on Thursday, Friday & Saturday the 3rd, 4th & 5th at the Fillmore West with lights by Holy See.

4th October – 1968
- The Family Dog presents Quicksilver Messenger Service, Black Pearl and Ace of Cups on Friday, Saturday & Sunday the 4th, 5th & 6th at the Avalon Ballroom. Lights by Vulcan.
- The Bank presents Country Joe and the Fish and A.B. Skhy Blues Band on Friday the 4th at the Bank in Torrance, California.
- Russ Gibb presents in Detroit a dance-concert featuring Ten Years After, Rationals, Dave Workman Band, and Orange Fuzz on Friday, Saturday & Sunday the 4th, 5th & 6th at the Grande Ballroom.
- Bill Graham presents Eric Burdon & the Animals, Sly & the Family Stone and Linn County on Friday & Saturday the 4th & 5th at the Fillmore East with lights by the Joshua Light Show.
- Pink Floyd perform on Friday the 4th at Mothers in Birmingham, England.
- The Retinal Circus in Vancouver, British Columbia features Mother Tucker's Yellow Duck and Mock Duck on Friday, Saturday & Sunday the 4th, 5th & 6th with lights by Addled Chromish.

5th October – 1968
- Cream begins a farewell tour of the United States with a concert in Oakland, California on Saturday the 5th.

- The Bank presents Hook and A.B. Skhy Blues Band on Saturday the 5th at the Bank in Torrance, California.
- A British package tour consisting of the Who, Small Faces, Crazy World of Arthur Brown and Joe Cocker kicks off with a concert in London on Saturday the 5th.

7th October – 1968

- KACY and Jim Salzer presents Jefferson Airplane on Monday the 7th at the Earl Warren Showground's in Santa Barbara, California.

10th October – 1968

- Bill Graham presents the Jimi Hendrix Experience, Buddy Miles Express and Dino Valenti on Thursday, Friday & Saturday the 10th, 11th & 12th at the Winterland with lights by Holy See.

11th October - 1968

- The Family Dog presents the Grateful Dead, Lee Michaels, Linn County and Mance Lipscomb on Friday, Saturday & Sunday the 11th, 12th & 13th at the Avalon Ballroom. Lights by the Garden of Delights.
- The Bank presents Canned Heat on Friday the 11th at the Bank in Torrance, California.
- Bill Graham presents the Beach Boys and Creedence Clearwater Revival on Friday the 11th at the Fillmore East with lights by the Joshua Light Show.

12th October – 1968

- John Sebastian quits the Lovin' Spoonful.
- GI's and War Veterans protesting the war in Vietnam march for peace from Golden Gate Park to the Civic Centre.
- Big Brother and the Holding Company's **Cheap Thrills** LP reaches No.1 in the U.S charts. The album is distinctive in its Robert Crumb drawn cover. It also contains the No.1 hit single *Piece of my Heart*.
- Bill Graham presents the Turtles, Creedence Clearwater Revival and the New York Rock and Roll Ensemble on Saturday the 12th at the Fillmore East with lights by the Joshua Light Show.
- The Bank presents Spirit on Saturday the 12th at the Bank in Torrance, California.

17th October – 1968

- Bill Graham presents Iron Butterfly, Sir Douglas Quintet Plus 2 and Sea Train on Thursday, Friday & Saturday the 17th, 18th & 19th at the Fillmore West with lights by the Brotherhood of Light.

18th October – 1968

- The Family Dog presents the Velvet Underground, Charlie Musselwhite and Initial Shock on Friday, Saturday & Sunday the 18th, 19th & 20th at the Avalon Ballroom. Lights by Jerry Abrams Headlights.
- The Bank presents the Grateful Dead, Cleveland Wrecking Company and Big

Mama Thornton on Friday & Saturday the 18th & 19th at the Bank in Torrance California.

- Bill Graham presents the Jeff Beck Group, Tim Buckly and Albert King on Friday & Saturday the 18th & 19th at the Fillmore East with lights by the Joshua Light Show.

- Led Zeppelin performs their first U.K. concert date at the Marquee Club in London on Friday the 18th. Coming out of the psychedelic Yardbirds, Led Zeppelin would go on to be one of heavy metal music's founding groups.

19th October - 1968

- Golden Star presents Canned Heat and Bronze Hog on Saturday the 19th at the Santa Rosa Fairgrounds with lights by the Light Brigade.

24th October – 1968

- Bill Graham presents Jefferson Airplane, the Ballet Afro from Haiti and A.B. Skhy on Thursday, Friday & Saturday the 24th, 25th & 26th at the Fillmore West with lights by Glenn McKay's Headlights. Jefferson Airplane were recording the evening live.

25th October – 1968

- The Family Dog presents the Buddy Miles Express, Dino Valenti and Country Weather on Friday, Saturday & Sunday the 25th, 26th & 27th at the Avalon Ballroom.
- Bill Graham presents the Moody Blues, John Mayall and Rhinoceros on Friday & Saturday the 25th & 26th at the Fillmore East with lights by the Joshua Light Show.

26th October – 1968

- Pink Floyd perform on Saturday the 26th at the new location of the Middle Earth Club, now located in the Roundhouse, Chalk Farm, London, England.

29th October – 1968

- Russ Gibb presents in Detroit a dance-concert featuring Quicksilver Messenger Service and Frost on Tuesday the 29th at the Grande Ballroom.

31st October – 1968

- The Motor City Five, better known as MC5 record their first album entitled **Kick out the Jams**. The live album was recorded at Detroit's Grande Ballroom.
- Bill Graham presents Procol Harum and Santana on Thursday, Friday & Saturday the 31st, 1st & 2nd at the Fillmore West.

151

November – 1968
- The first **Whole Earth Catalog** is published by Stewart Brand.

1st November – 1968
- The Family Dog presents the Byrds and Taj Mahal on Friday, Saturday & Sunday the 1st, 2nd & 3rd at the Avalon Ballroom.
- Russ Gibb presents in Detroit a dance-concert featuring Jeff Beck, Toad and McKenna Mendleson Mainline on Friday, Saturday & Sunday the 1st, 2nd & 3rd at the Grande Ballroom.
- Bill Graham presents the McCoys, Richie Havens and Quicksilver Messenger Service on Friday & Saturday the 1st & 2nd at the Fillmore East in New York City. Pink Floyd were to have been the headliners but cancelled with a weeks notice so the McCoys were booked in as last minute replacements.

4th November - 1968
- KACY and Jim Salzer present Buffalo Springfield, the Watts 103rd Street Band and the Lewis & Clark Expedition on Monday the 4th at the Earl Warren Showground's, Santa Barbara.

6th November – 1968
- The strike at the San Francisco State College begins on this day and ends on the 26th with the resignation of College president Robert R. Smith. S.I. Hayakawa is named acting president. The strike eventually ended March 21st 1969.

7th November – 1968
- Bill Graham presents Quicksilver Messenger Service, Grateful Dead and Linn County on Thursday, Friday, Saturday & Sunday the 7th, 8th, 9th & 10th at the Fillmore West with lights by the Brotherhood of Light.
- Pink Floyd perform with Barclay James Harvest and the Edgar Broughton Band on Thursday the 7th at Porchester Hall, London, England.

8th November – 1968
- The Family Dog presents Mother Earth and Kaleidoscope on Friday, Saturday & Sunday the 8th, 9th & 10th at the Avalon Ballroom.
- Bill Graham presents Steppenwolf, Buddy Rich & his Orchestra and Children of God on Friday & Saturday the 8th & 9th at the Fillmore East with lights by the Joshua Light Show.

9th November – 1968
- Moose Valley Farms presents Country Joe and the Fish and the Black Snake Blues Band on Saturday the 9th at the Sales Pavilion. Lights by Addled Chromish.

14th November – 1968
- Bill Graham presents Ten Years After, Sun Ra and Country Weather on Thursday, Friday, Saturday & Sunday the 14th, 15th 16th & 17th at the Fillmore West with lights by the Brotherhood of Light.

15th November – 1968
- The Family Dog presents Love and Lee Michaels on Friday, Saturday & Sunday the 15th, 16th & 17th at the Avalon Ballroom.
- The Bank presents Canned Heat, Linn County, Flamin Groovies and Harvey Mandel on Friday & Saturday the 15th & 16th at the Bank in Torrance California.

16th November - 1968

- **Electric Ladyland** by the Jimi Hendrix Experience reaches No.1 in the U.S album charts. The album contains the Hendrix classics, *Cross-town Traffic* and his classic reworking the Dylan song *All Along the Watchtower*.

21st November – 1968
- Bill Graham presents the Moody Blues, Chicago Transit Authority and Frumious Bandersnatch on Thursday, Friday, Saturday & Sunday the 21st, 22nd, 23rd & 24th at the Fillmore West with lights by Holy See.

22nd November - 1968
- The Beatles' **White Album** is released in America. The Beatles were becoming masters of many styles and released the double disc **White Album** containing a variety of styles including such psychedelic influenced pieces as *Revolution No.9*.
- Bill Graham presents Iron Butterfly, Canned Heat and the Youngbloods on Friday & Saturday the 22nd & 23rd at the Fillmore East with lights by the Joshua Light Show.
- Pink Floyd supported by Arcadium perform on Friday the 22nd at the Crawdaddy Club House, Richmond, England.

23rd November – 1968
- **Rolling Stone** magazine reports "the beginning of the end of an era" with the impending closure of the Avalon Ballroom.
- Tom Constanten joins the Grateful Dead in Athen's Georgia.
- Pink Floyd with Bobby Parker perform on Saturday the 23rd at the Regent Street Polytechnic, London, England.

24th November – 1968
- Russ Gibb presents in Detroit a dance-concert featuring Jefferson Airplane, Tim Buckley, Terry Reid and Blue Cheer on Sunday the 24th at the Grande Ballroom.

- Pink Floyd supported by Andromeda perform on Sunday the 24th at The Country Club, London, England.

26th November - 1968

- Cream performs their farewell gig at the Royal Albert Hall in London on Tuesday the 26th. The event is documented in Tony Palmer's film **Goodbye Cream**.

27th November – 1968

- Bill Graham presents the Incredible String Band on Wednesday the 27th at the Fillmore East with lights by the Joshua Light Show.
- The Marquee Club in London features Yes and Van Der Graaf Generator on Wednesday the 27th.
- Pink Floyd perform on Wednesday the 27th at the University of Keele, Newcastle, England.

28th November – 1968

- Bill Graham presents It's a Beautiful Day, Deep Purple and Cold Blood on Thursday, Friday, Saturday & Sunday the 28th, 29th, 30th & 1st at the Fillmore West with lights by Holy See.
- The final Family Dog dance-concert at the Avalon Ballroom takes place on Thursday, Friday & Saturday the 28th, 29th & 30th and features Quicksilver Messenger Service and the Sons of Champlin. According to many "the hippest" ballroom closes in part due to growing noise restrictions. Local residents complain that the Avalon regularly runs concerts past the 2am limit. The ballroom would hold a few more events under the ironic "Sound Proof Productions" moniker but failed to regain any of its original glory.
- Bill Graham presents Jefferson Airplane, Buddy Guy and Chuck Davis Dance Company on Thursday, Friday & Saturday the 28th, 29th, & 30th at the Fillmore East with lights by the Joshua Light Show.

29th November - 1968

- Lothar and the Hand People and Cloud perform on Friday & Saturday the 29th & 30th at the Boston Tea Party, 15 Lansdowne Street in Boston.
- Pink Floyd supported by Blonde on Blonde play at Bedford College, Bedford on Friday the 29th.

30th November – 1968

- Russ Gibb presents in Detroit a dance-concert featuring the Grateful Dead, Blood Sweat and Tears and the Rationals on Saturday the 30th at the Grande Ballroom.
- Big Brother and the Holding Company perform in Vancouver, British Columbia on Saturday the 30th.

4th December – 1968

- The Chambers Brothers earn a Gold record for sales of their album **The Time Has Come,** which contains the hit single *Time Has Come Today*.

5th December – 1968
- Bill Graham presents the Jeff Beck Group, Spirit, Sweet Linda Divine and Sweetwater on Thursday, Friday, Saturday & Sunday the 5th, 6th, 7th & 8th at the Fillmore West with lights by the Brotherhood of Light.

6th December – 1968
- Bill Graham presents the Chambers Brothers, Mother Earth and Country Weather on Friday & Saturday the 6th & 7th at the Winterland with lights by Holy See.
- The Quaker City Rock Festival is staged in Philadelphia featuring the Grateful Dead among others.
- Russ Gibb presents in Detroit Canned Heat, Hamilton Face and Teagarden and Vanwinkle on Friday & Saturday the 6th & 7th at the Grande Ballroom.
- Bill Graham presents Country Joe & the Fish, Fleetwood Mac, Kusama's Self Obliteration on Friday & Saturday the 6th & 7th at the Fillmore East with lights by the Joshua Light Show.

8th December – 1968
- Graham Nash quits the Hollies with the announcement that he intends to form a trio with David Crosby and Steve Stills.

12th December – 1968
- Bill Graham presents Country Joe and the Fish, Terry Reid and Sea Train on Thursday, Friday, Saturday & Sunday the 12th, 13th, 14th & 15th at the Fillmore West with lights by the Brotherhood of Light.

13th December – 1968
- The Bank presents the Grateful Dead, Magic Sam, Flash Gordon and Turnquist Remedy on Friday & Saturday the 13th & 14th at the Bank in Torrance California.
- Bill Graham presents the Sam & Dave Review, Super Session and Earth Opera on Friday & Saturday the 13th & 14th at the Fillmore East with lights by the Joshua Light Show.

15th December – 1968
- Jefferson Airplane make an appearance on the ill-fated Smothers Brothers Comedy Hour. Grace Slick appears in blackface and raises a black-gloved fist in a black-power salute. It's controversial incidents like this that would bring about the cancellation of the variety show.

17th December - 1968
- Pink Floyd release *Point Me At The Sky* b/w *Careful With That Axe Eugene*.

19th December – 1968
- Bill Graham presents Santana, the Grass Roots and Pacific Gas & Electric on Thursday, Friday, Saturday & Sunday the 19th, 20th, 21st & 22nd at the Fillmore West with lights by Little Princess No.109.

20th December – 1968

• Scenic Sounds presents a "Christmas Show" featuring Country Joe and the Fish, the Grateful Dead, Spirit, Pulse, Sir Douglas Quintet and Mint Tattoo on Friday & Saturday the 20th & 21st at the Shrine Auditorium in Los Angeles with lights by Jerry Abrams Headlights.

• Bill Graham presents Creedence Clearwater Revival, Deep Purple and the James Cotton Blues Band on Friday & Saturday the 20th & 21st at the Fillmore East with lights by the Joshua Light Show.

21st December – 1968

• The second annual Stax/Volt Yuletide Thing is staged in Memphis on Saturday the 21st with a host of Fillmore regular soul artists including Booker T and the MGs, Staple Singers, Albert King, Johnnie Taylor and Eddie Floyd. Of particular note is the appearance of Janis Joplin on the lineup. She is the only performer not from Memphis to appear on the bill.

26th December – 1968

• Bill Graham presents the Steve Miller Band, Sly and the Family Stone and Pogo on Thursday, Friday, Saturday & Sunday the 26th, 27th, 28th & 29th at the Fillmore West with lights by Optic Illusion.

27th December – 1968

• Bill Graham presents the Butterfield Blues Band, Crazy World of Arthur Brown, Super Session and Sweetwater on Friday & Saturday the 27th & 28th at the Fillmore East with lights by the Joshua Light Show.

28th December – 1968

• The first big East Coast rock festival, The Miami Pop Festival is held in Hallendale, Florida on Saturday and Sunday the 28th & 29th. One-hundred thousand individuals purchase the six and seven dollar tickets to see Jose Feliciano, Terry Reid, Procol Harum, Charles Lloyd Quartet, Ian and Sylvia, Buffy St. Marie, Pacific Gas & Electric, Country Joe and the Fish, Chuck Berry, Three Dog Night, Turtles, Canned Heat, Joe Tex, Sweetwater, McCoys, Steppenwolf, Booker T and the MGs, Marvin Gaye, Grateful Dead, Hugh Masakela, Paul Butterfield Blues Band, Joni Mitchell, James Cotton Blues Band, Junior Walker and the All Stars, Richie Havens, Box Tops, Grassroots and Iron Butterfly.

29th December – 1968

• A "Happy New Year" dance-concert featuring the San Francisco Sound of It's a Beautiful Day and Indian Puddin' and Pipe is held on Sunday, Monday & Tuesday the 29th, 30th & 31st at the Seattle Ballroom, Seattle Washington.

31st December - 1968

• Bill Graham presents a "New Years Eve Party" featuring the Grateful Dead, It's A

Beautiful Day, Quicksilver Messenger Service and Santana on Tuesday the 31st at the Winterland with the lightshow provided by the Brotherhood Of Lights. Following this performance Quicksilver vocalist and guitarist Gary Duncan quits the group to work with Dino Valente. The two spent much of 1969 just hanging out, riding across the country on their motorcycles. Upon returning to San Francisco they rejoined Quicksilver and went to record a new LP in Hawaii.

- Bill Graham presents the Chambers Brothers and Mother Earth on Tuesday the 31st at the Fillmore East with lights by the Joshua Light Show.

31st December – 1968

- Bill Graham presents a "New Years Eve Party" featuring Vanilla Fudge, the Youngbloods, Richie Havens and Cold Blood on Tuesday the 31st at the Fillmore West.

TIMELINE - 1969

2nd January – 1969

- Bill Graham presents the Grateful Dead, Blood Sweat & Tears and Spirit on Thursday, Friday & Saturday the 2nd, 3rd & 4th at the Fillmore West.

3rd January – 1969

- The Electric Theatre presents Muddy Waters and Fleetwood Mac on Friday & Saturday the 3rd & 4th at the Kinetic Playground, 4812 Clark Street in Chicago, Illinois.

9th January – 1969

- Bill Graham presents Country Joe and the Fish, Led Zeppelin and Taj Mahal on Thursday, Friday & Saturday the 9th, 10th & 11th at the Fillmore West with lights by the Brotherhood of Light.

10th January – 1969

- Bill Graham presents B.B. King, Johnny Winter and Terry Reid on Friday & Saturday the 10th & 11th at the Fillmore East with lights by the Joshua Light Show.
- The Electric Theatre presents Albert King and Lynn County on Friday & Saturday the 10th & 11th at the Kinetic Playground, 4812 Clark Street in Chicago, Illinois.

15th January –1969

- The Jimi Hendrix Experience perform on Wednesday the 15th at the Beethovensall, Stuttgart, West Germany.

16th January – 1969

- Bill Graham presents Creedence Clearwater Revival, Fleetwood Mac and Albert Collins on Thursday, Friday, Saturday & Sunday the 16th, 17th, 18th & 19th at the Fillmore West.

17th January – 1969

- Bill Graham presents Buddy Rich & his Orchestra, the Grassroots and Spirit on Friday & Saturday the 17th & 18th at the Fillmore East with lights by the Joshua Light Show.
- The Electric Theatre presents Buddy Rich and Genesis on Friday & Saturday the 17th & 18th at the Kinetic Playground, 4812 Clark Street in Chicago, Illinois.

18th January - 1969

- Pink Floyd along with Arcadium and Jimmy Scott & his Band play on Saturday the 18th at the Middle Earth Club, The Roundhouse, Chalk Farm, London.

22nd January - 1969

- The Byrds and Doug Kershaw play on Wednesday, Thursday & Friday the 22nd, 23rd & 24th at the Boston Tea Party, Boston.

23rd January – 1969

- Bill Graham presents Iron Butterfly, James Cotton Blues Band and A.B. Skhy on Thursday, Friday, Saturday & Sunday the 23rd, 24th, 25th & 26th at the Fillmore West.

24th January – 1969

- Sound Proof Productions presents the Grateful Dead, Sons of Champlin and Initial Shock on Friday, Saturday & Sunday the 24th, 25th & 26th at the Avalon Ballroom with lights provided by Garden of Delights.
- Bill Graham presents Blood Sweat & Tears, Jethro Tull and the Gay Desperados Steel Band on Friday & Saturday the 24th & 25th at the Fillmore East with lights by the Joshua Light Show. This is Jethro Tull's first U.S. concert date.
- The Electric Theatre presents Buddy Rich and his Orchestra, Buddy Miles Express and Rotary Connection on Friday & Saturday the 24th & 25th at the Kinetic Playground, 4812 Clark Street in Chicago, Illinois.

26th January – 1969

- The Vanilla Fudge (26th only), Siegal Schwall Blues Band and Glass Family perform on Sunday, Monday & Tuesday the 26th, 27th & 28th at Cheetah's in Venice, California.

29th January – 1969

- **Newsweek** magazine reports on the growing "Bosstown Sound" in Boston with the opening of clubs such as the Psychedelic Supermarket, the Catacombs and the Boston Tea Party.

30th January – February – 1969

- Bill Graham presents Chuck Berry, a musical jam featuring Mike Bloomfield, Nick

Gravenities, Mark Naftalin & Friends and Initial Shock on Thursday, Friday, Saturday & Sunday the 30th, 31st, 1st & 2nd at the Fillmore West with lights by Little Princess No.109.

31st January – 1969

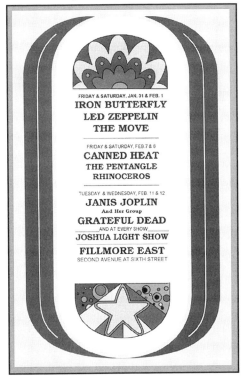

- Sound Proof Productions presents Van Morrison, Black Pearl, Saloom Sinclair and Mother Bear on Friday, Saturday & Sunday the 31st, 1st & 2nd at the Avalon Ballroom.
- Bill Graham presents Iron Butterfly, Led Zeppelin and Porter's Popular Preachers on Friday & Saturday the 31st & 1st at the Fillmore East with lights by the Joshua Light Show.
- The Electric Theatre presents the Grateful Dead and the Grassroots on Friday & Saturday the 31st & 1st at the Kinetic Playground, 4812 Clark Street in Chicago, Illinois.

2nd February – 1969

- Big Brother and the Holding Company, the Boxtops and Hook perform on Sunday & Monday the 2nd & 3rd at Cheetah's in Venice, California.

6th February – 1969

- Bill Graham presents the Byrds, a musical jam featuring Mike Bloomfield & Friends and Pacific Gas & Electric on Thursday, Friday, Saturday & Sunday the 6th, 7th, 8th & 9th at the Fillmore West with lights by Little Princess No.109.
- The Marquee Club in London features Locomotive and Tea and Symphony on Thursday the 6th.

7th February – 1969

- Sound Proof Productions presents the Youngbloods, Lee Michaels and Screamin Jay Hawkins on Friday, Saturday & Sunday the 7th, 8th & 9th at the Avalon Ballroom.
- The Grateful Dead, Fugs and Velvet Underground perform on Friday the 7th at the Stanley Theatre in Pittsburgh Pennsylvania.
- Bill Graham presents Canned Heat, Pentangle and Rhinoceros on Friday & Saturday the 7th & 8th at the Fillmore East with the Joshua Light Show.
- The Electric Theatre presents Vanilla Fudge, Led Zeppelin and Jethro Tull on Friday & Saturday the 7th & 8th at the Kinetic Playground, 4812 Clark Street in Chicago, Illinois.

8th February – 1969

- First Annual "KTBT Freak Fair" takes place on Saturday the 8th at the Orange County International Raceway.
- Eric Clapton, Ginger Baker, Steve Winwood and Rick Grech form Blind Faith.

11th February – 1969

- Bill Graham presents Janis Joplin & Her New Band and the Grateful Dead on Tuesday & Wednesday the 11th & 12th at the Fillmore East with the Joshua Light Show.

13th February – 1969

- Bill Graham presents Santana, the Collectors and Melanie on Thursday, Friday, Saturday & Sunday the 13th, 14th, 15th & 16th at the Fillmore West with lights by Brotherhood of Light.

14th February – 1969

- Sound Proof Productions presents It's A Beautiful Day, Country Weather and Big Mama Thornton on Friday, Saturday & Sunday the 14th, 15th & 16th at the Avalon Ballroom.
- Bill Graham presents Sam & Dave, Winter featuring Johnny Winter and Aorta on Friday the 14th at the Fillmore East with the Joshua Light Show.
- The Electric Theatre presents Tim Hardin, Spirit and the Move on Friday & Saturday the 14th & 15th at the Kinetic Playground, 4812 Clark Street in Chicago, Illinois.

15th February – 1969

- Bill Graham presents Chuck Berry, Winter featuring Johnny Winter, Savoy Brown and Aorta on Saturday the 15th at the Fillmore East with lights by the Joshua Light Show.

20th February – 1969

- Bill Graham presents the Move, Cold Blood and Albert King on Thursday, Friday, Saturday & Sunday the 20th, 21st, 22nd & 23rd at the Fillmore West with lights by Little Princess No.109.

21st February – 1969

- Sound Proof Productions presents Steve Miller, Allman Joy and Linn County on Friday, Saturday & Sunday the 21st, 22nd & 23rd at the Avalon Ballroom.
- Bill Graham presents the Mothers of Invention, Buddy Miles Express and Chicago Transit Authority on Friday & Saturday the 21st & 22nd at the Fillmore East with the Joshua Light Show.
- The Electric Theatre presents Jeff Beck, Savoy Brown and Mother Earth on Friday the 21st at the Kinetic Playground, 4812 Clark Street in Chicago, Illinois.

- Direct Productions presents Quicksilver Messenger Service, Boz Scaggs and Robert Savage on Friday the 21st at the Peterson Gym, San Diego State University.
- The Fugs and Shiva's Head Band perform on Friday & Saturday the 21st & 22nd at the Vulcan Gas Company, 316 Congress in Austin Texas.
- The Jimi Hendrix Experience, Woodys Truck Stop and Soft Machine perform on Friday & Saturday the 21st & 22nd at the Electric Factory in Philadelphia.

22nd February – 1969

- The Electric Theatre presents Blood Sweat and Tears, Savoy Brown and Mother Earth on Saturday the 22nd at the Kinetic Playground, 4812 Clark Street in Chicago, Illinois.

24th February – 1969

- The Jimi Hendrix Experience play their last British concert on Monday the 24th at London's Royal Albert Hall before calling it quits.
- Pink Floyd supported by Pretty Things and Third Ear Band perform on Monday the 24th at the Dome, Brighton, England.

27th February – 1969

- Bill Graham presents the Grateful Dead, Pentangle and the Sir Douglas Quintet on Thursday, Friday, Saturday & Sunday the 27th, 28th 1st & 2nd at the Fillmore West with lights by the Brotherhood of Light.

28th February - 1969

- Sound Proof Productions present Love, Mad River and Zephyr on Friday the 28th at the Avalon Ballroom.
- The Electric Theatre presents Paul Butterfield, B.B. King and Albert King on Friday the 28th at the Kinetic Playground, 4812 Clark Street in Chicago, Illinois.

28th February – 1969

- Bill Graham presents Ten Years After, John Mayall and Slim Harpo on Friday & Saturday the 28th & 1st at the Fillmore East with the Joshua Light Show.

1st March – 1969

- The Door's Jim Morrison is charged with indecent exposure after allegedly exposing himself during a concert at Miami's Dinner Key Auditorium. He's eventually convicted and sentenced to eight months hard labour and a $500 fine. He would appeal, but is found dead in Paris before coming to trial.
- The Electric Theatre presents Paul Butterfield, Bob Seger System and Lumpy Gravy on Saturday the 1st at the Kinetic Playground, 4812 Clark Street in Chicago Illinois.
- The Marquee Club in London features Spice and the Elastic Band on Saturday the 1st. The Elastic Band will make 4 more appearances at the Marquee.

6th March – 1969

- Bill Graham presents Spirit, Ten Years After and Country Weather on Thursday, Friday, Saturday & Sunday the 6th, 7th, 8th & 9th at the Fillmore West with lights by Little Princess No.109.

7th March – 1969
- Sound Proof Productions presents Moby Grape, A.B. Skhy and Gale Garnett on Friday, Saturday & Sunday the 7th, 8th & 9th at the Avalon Ballroom.
- Boyd Grafmyre and KOL Radio present Jethro Tull and MC5 on Friday & Saturday the 7th & 8th at the Eagles Auditorium in Seattle.
- The Electric Theatre presents John Mayall and Richie Havens on Friday & Saturday the 7th & 8th at the Kinetic Playground 4812 Clark Street in Chicago Illinois.
- Bill Graham presents Buffy Sainte Marie and Ian & Sylvia on Friday the 7th at the Fillmore East with lights by the Joshua Light Show.

8th March – 1969
- Bill Graham presents Vanilla Fudge, Amboy Dukes and Sirocco on Saturday the 8th at the Fillmore East with lights by the Joshua Light Show.

9th March – 1969
- The network cancels the Smothers Brothers Comedy Hour because it was becoming too controversial in matters dealing with politics and the war in Vietnam. Having run into trouble a number of times previously, the final straw is over the question of on-air censorship of guest Joan Baez.

11th March – 1969
- The Marquee Club in London features Bakerloo, Locomotive and Earth on Tuesday the 11th.

12th March – 1969
- Paul McCartney marries Linda Eastman.

13th March – 1969
- Bill Graham presents Creedence Clearwater Revival, Jethro Tull and Sanpako on Thursday, Friday, Saturday & Sunday the 13th, 14th, 15th & 16th at the Fillmore West with lights by Holy See.

14th March – 1969
- Bill Graham presents Procol Harum, Pacific Gas & Electric and the Collectors on Friday & Saturday the 14th & 15th at the Fillmore East with lights by the Joshua Light Show.
- Trans-Love presents MC5, the Congress of Wonder and Clover, with lights by Single Wing Turquoise Bird on Friday, Saturday & Sunday the 14th, 15th & 16th at The Straight Theatre.
- The Electric Theatre presents the Jeff Beck Group and Sweetwater on Friday & Saturday the 14th & 15th at the Kinetic Playground.

15th March – 1969
- **Rolling Stone** gives Janis Joplin a scathing review of her recent Fillmore East appearances.

20th March – 1969

- Bill Graham presents Janis Joplin with her new Kozmic Blues Band, Savoy Brown and Aum on Thursday, Friday & Saturday the 20th, 21st & 22nd at the Winterland in San Francisco with lights by the Brotherhood of Light. Response from the crowd was lukewarm at best, as many felt she'd betrayed Big Brother and the Holding Company by striking out on her own. Unknown to many of her fans was how Joplin's obsessive drinking habit was obscuring her increasing reliance on heroin. The performance on the evening of Sunday the 23rd was at the Fillmore West.

20th March – 1969

- John and Yoko fly to Gibraltar to get married. Then it was off to Amsterdam for one week for a "lie-in" for peace.

21st March – 1969

- Bill Graham presents Creedence Clearwater Revival, Spirit and the Aynsley Dunbar Retaliation on Friday & Saturday the 21st & 22nd at the Fillmore East with lights by the Joshua Light Show.
- Sound Proof Productions presents Santana and Sons of Champlin, with the Headlights lightshow on Friday, Saturday & Sunday the 21st, 22nd & 23rd at the Avalon Ballroom.
- Scenic Sounds presents the Paul Butterfield Blues Band, the Grateful Dead and Jethro Tull on Friday & Saturday the 21st & 22nd at the Rose palace in Pasadena, California.

22nd March – 1969

- Cream's final album **Goodbye** is the No.1 Pop album in the U.K. It holds that position for six weeks.
- The Electric Theatre presents the Sam and Dave Revue on Saturday the 22nd at the Kinetic Playground.

24th March – 1969

- Ralph Gleason writes in the **San Francisco Chronicle** that Janis Joplin should consider going back to Big Brother and the Holding Company, "If they'll have her."

27th March – 1969

- Bill Graham presents the Paul Butterfield Blues Band and Michael Bloomfield and Friends on Thursday, Friday Saturday & Sunday the 27th, 28th, 29th & 30th at the Fillmore West with lights by Little Princess No.109.
- The Winterland presents Bo Diddley, Muddy Waters, Otis Span and Magic Sam on Thursday, Friday & Saturday the 27th, 28th & 29th at the Winterland in San Francisco.

28th March – 1969

- Bill Graham presents Steppenwolf, Julie Driscoll & Brian Auger's Trinity and John

Hammond on Friday & Saturday the 28th & 29th at the Fillmore East with lights by the Joshua Light Show.
- The Electric Theatre presents Pacific Gas & Electric on Friday & Saturday the 28th & 29th at the Kinetic Playground.

29th March – 1969
- The Marquee Club in London features Country Joe and the Fish on Saturday the 29th.

1st April – 1969
- There are now 543,000 American troops in Vietnam.
- Janis Joplin begins a two-month European tour.

3rd April – 1969
- Bill Graham presents Procol Harum, Buddy Miles Express and Blues Image on Thursday, Friday, Saturday & Sunday the 3rd, 4th, 5th & 6th at the Fillmore West with lights by Brotherhood of Light.

4th April - 1969
- Bill Graham presents the Chambers Brothers, Hello People and Elephant's Memory on Friday & Saturday the 4th & 5th at the Fillmore East with lights by the Joshua Light Show.
- Sound Proof Productions presents the Grateful Dead, Flying Burrito Brothers and Aum on Friday, Saturday & Sunday the 4th, 5th & 6th at the Avalon Ballroom. This will be the last Grateful Dead performance at the Avalon and it is broadcast live on radio station KPFA-FM.

9th April – 1969
- Bill Graham presents Ten Years After, the Nice and Family on Wednesday & Thursday the 9th & 10th at the Fillmore East with the Joshua Light Show.

10th April – 1969
- Bill Graham presents the Jeff Beck Group, the Aynsley Dunbar Retaliation and Zephyr on Thursday, Friday, Saturday & Sunday the 10th, 11th, 12th & 13th at the Fillmore West.

11th April – 1969
- Bill Graham presents Blood Sweat & Tears, Jethro Tull and Albert King on Friday the 11th at the Fillmore East with lights by the Joshua Light Show.

12th April – 1969
- Bill Graham presents Blood Sweat & Tears and Savoy Brown on Saturday the 12th at the Fillmore East with lights by the Joshua Light Show.
- The SDS Ball takes place on Saturday the 12th at the University of Utah in Salt Lake

City with performances from the Grateful Dead and Spirit of Creation. Lights by Five Fingers.

14th April - 1969
• The "More Furious Madness From The Massed Gadgets Of Auximenes" event is held on Monday the 14th at the Royal Festival Hall, London with Pink Floyd.

15th April – 1969
• Claiming it's a public nuisance and provides a public gathering place for drug dealers city officials close down Philadelphia's most popular rock ballroom the Electric Factory.

17th April – 1969
• Bill Graham presents the Band, Sons of Champlin and Ace of Cups on Thursday, Friday & Saturday the 17th, 18th & 19th at the Winterland with lights by Little Princess No.109. This is the Band's first independent concert no longer a backing band for either Ronnie Hawkins or Bob Dylan and Bill Graham called it "An historic event."
• The Associated Students of the University of San Diego presents the Sons, Elvin Bishop and Stoneground on Thursday & Friday the 17th & 18th at the University of San Diego Gym.

18th April – 1969
• Bill Graham presents the Butterfield Blues Band, Foundations and Savoy Brown on Friday the 18th at the Fillmore East with lights by the Joshua Light Show.

19th April – 1969
• Bill Graham presents the Butterfield Blues Band and Savoy Brown on Saturday the 19th at the Fillmore East with lights by the Joshua Light Show.
• The Doves Inc. presents Country Joe and the Fish and H.P. Lovecraft on Saturday & Sunday the 19th & 20th at the Old Civic Auditorium, Honolulu, Hawaii.

20th April – 1969
• The Los Angeles Free Festival fails to get off the ground. After a number of injuries and 117 arrests, promoters bring the event to a speedy close. None of the scheduled bands played a note.

22nd April – 1969
• The Who give the first complete performance of their new recording, **Tommy** on Tuesday the 22nd at a concert in Dolton, England.

24th April – 1969
• Bill Graham presents Led Zeppelin, Julie Driscoll, Brian Auger & Trinity and Colwell – Winfield on Thursday & Sunday the 25th & 27th at the Fillmore West

with lights by the Brotherhood of Light. The evenings of Friday & Saturday the 25th & 26th were performed at the Winterland.

25th April – 1969
- Bill Graham presents Joni Mitchell, James Cotton Blues Band and Taj Mahal on Friday & Saturday the 25th & 26th at the Fillmore East with lights by the Joshua Light Show.

26th April – 1969
- Pink Floyd supported by East of Eden performs on Saturday the 26th at Bromley Technical College, Bromley Common, England. These shows were recorded and released on the **Ummagumma** album.

1st May – 1969
- Bill Graham presents Mongo Santamaria, Cold Blood and the Elvin Bishop Group on Thursday & Sunday the 1st & 4th at the Fillmore West with lights by the Brotherhood of Light. On Friday and Saturday the 2nd & 3rd Jefferson Airplane, Grateful Dead and Mongo Santamaria performed at the Winterland with lights by Glenn McKay's Headlights.

2nd May – 1969
- Bill Graham presents the Jeff Beck Group, Joe Cocker and NRBQ on Friday & Saturday the 2nd & 3rd at the Fillmore East with lights by the Joshua Light Show.

3rd May – 1969
- Jimi Hendrix is arrested coming into Canada at the Toronto International Airport. The charge is possession of narcotics. He is later released on $10,000 bail.
- Bob Harris presents the "Cow Rock Show" featuring Sir Douglas Quintet, Delaney and Bonnie, Guess Who, Youngbloods, Grassroots, Classics IV and People on Saturday the 3rd at the Cow Palace in San Francisco.
- The Marquee Club in London features the Klubs and the only appearance of the Turnstyle on Saturday the 3rd.

7th May – 1969
- The Grateful Dead and Jefferson Airplane perform on Wednesday the 7th at the Polo Field in the Golden Gate Park.

8th May – 1969
- Bill Graham presents Albert King, It's a Beautiful Day and Aum on Thursday, Friday, Saturday & Sunday the 8th, 9th, 10th & 11th at the Fillmore West with lights by the Brotherhood of Light.

9th May – 1969
- Bill Graham presents the Band and Cat Mother & the All-Night Newsboys on

Friday & Saturday the 9th & 10th at the Fillmore East with lights by the Joshua Light Show.
- Russ Gibb presents in Detroit the Who, Joe Cocker and the Grease Band and Mixed Generation on Friday, Saturday & Sunday the 9th, 10th & 11th at the Grande Ballroom.

10th May – 1969
- The Electric Flag, Hour Glass and Touch perform on Saturday & Sunday the 10th & 11th at Cheetah's in Venice, California.
- The Marquee Club in London features Procession and Mandrake Paddle Steamer on Saturday the 10th.
- The Nottingham 1969 Pop & Blues Festival is held at the Notts County Football Ground, Nottingham, England on Saturday the 10th. Bands performing include; Pink Floyd, Fleetwood Mac, Tremolos, Marmalade, Georgie Fame, Love Sculpture, Keef Hartley, Status Quo, Duster Bennett, Dream Police and Van Der Graaf Generator.

11th May – 1969

- The Cultural Arts Board of San Diego State presents Canned Heat, Grateful Dead, Lee Michaels, Santana and Tarantula on Sunday the 11th at the Aztec Bowl, San Diego State University.

13th May - 1969
- The "Out Now" Anti War demonstration in staged in Berkeley, California.

15th May – 1969
- Bill Graham presents Santana, the Youngbloods and Allmen Joy on Thursday, Friday, Saturday & Sunday the 15th, 16th, 17th & 18th at the Fillmore West with lights by Little Princess 109.

16th May – 1969
- Jefferson Airplane bassist Jack Casady is arrested in New Orleans on a charge of possession of marijuana. He receives a two and a half year suspended sentence.
- Bill Graham presents the Who, Sweetwater and It's A Beautiful Day on Friday, Saturday & Sunday the 16th, 17th & 18th at the Fillmore East with lights by the Joshua Light Show.
- The Marquee Club in London features the first appearance of King Crimson on Friday the 16th. They will go on to make 16 more appearances at the Marquee Club.

Bryan Morrison Agency presents . . .

**The Massed Gadgets of Auximenies
Some Musical Callisthenics**

from

THE

PINK
FLOYD

Featuring

The AZIMUTH CO-ORDINATOR

May 16	Town Hall, LEEDS
May 24	City Hall, SHEFFIELD
May 30	Fairfield Hall, CROYDON
June 8	Rex Cinema, CAMBRIDGE
June 10	Ulster Hall, BELFAST
June 14	Colston Hall, BRISTOL
June 15	Guildhall, PORTSMOUTH
June 16	The Dome, BRIGHTON
June 20	Town Hall, BIRMINGHAM
June 21	Royal Philharmonic, LIVERPOOL
June 22	Free Trade Hall, MANCHESTER

and

THE FINAL LUNACY

June 26, ROYAL ALBERT HALL, LONDON

(Box Office opens Monday, May 12)

(Concerts in 360° stereo)

• Pink Floyd kick off their first OFFICIAL U.K. Tour with a performance on Friday the 16th at the Leed's Town Hall, Leeds, England. Their tour would run for several weeks with a couple of trips to Europe in between.

20th May - 1969

• The "Festival of the Full Moon" is staged on Tuesday the 20th at Oak Island Stockton featuring Syndicate of Sound, Country Weather, Stuart Little.

22nd May – 1969

• Bill Graham presents Creedence Clearwater Revival, the Northern California State Youth Choir with Dorothy Morrison and the Bangor Flying Circus on Thursday & Sunday the 22nd & 25th at the Fillmore West with lights by Little Princess 109. The evenings of Friday & Saturday the 23rd and 24th were performed at the Winterland.

23rd May – 1969

• Bill Graham presents Sly & the Family Stone, Clarence Carter and Rotary Connection on Friday & Saturday the 23rd & 24th at the Fillmore East with lights by the Joshua Light Show.
• The Electric Theatre presents Led Zeppelin, Pacific Gas & Electric and Illinois Speed Press on Friday & Saturday the 23rd & 24th at the Kinetic Playground, 4812 Clark Street in Chicago, Illinois.

24th May – 1969

• Bill Graham presents the Incredible String Band for one night only, Saturday the 24th at the Fillmore West.
• The "Haight-Ashbury Festival at the Panhandle" is staged on Saturday & Sunday the 24th & 25th with a cast of thousands, including Country Joe and the Fish and many more.

28th May - 1969

• The "People's Park Bail Ball Benefit" is held on Wednesday the 28th at Winterland with Aum, Credence Clearwater Revival, Bangor Flying Circus, Grateful Dead, Jefferson Airplane and Santana with lights by Brotherhood of Light.

29th May – 1969

- Bill Graham presents the Steve Miller Band, Chicago Transit Authority and the Charlatans on Thursday, Friday, Saturday & Sunday the 29th, 30th 31st & 1st at the Fillmore West with lights by Little Princess 109.
- The "Memorial Day Ball" is staged on Thursday the 29th at the Rob Gym at the University of California in Santa Barbara. Performing are the Grateful Dead, Lee Michaels, and the Youngbloods. Lights supplied by Dry Paint.
- The Electric Theatre presents the Who, the Buddy Rich Orchestra and Joe Cocker and the Grease Band on Thursday, Friday & Saturday the 29th, 30th & 31st at the Kinetic Playground, 4812 Clark Street in Chicago, Illinois.

30th May – 1969

- Bill Graham presents Led Zeppelin, Woody Herman and his Orchestra and Delaney & Bonnie and Friends on Friday & Saturday the 30th & 31st at the Fillmore East in New York City with the Joshua Light Show.
- Russ Gibb presents in Detroit "The First Annual Detroit Rock and Roll Revival" featuring MC5, Chuck Berry, Sun Ra, Dr. John, Johnny Winter, Psychedelic Stooges, Terry Reid, Amboy Dukes, SRC, Frost, Rationals, Teagarden and Vanwinkle and many others on Friday & Saturday the 30th & 31st at the Michigan State fair Grounds.

31st May – 1969

- Country Joe and the Fish, Peanut Butter Conspiracy and Pacific Gas & Electric perform on Saturday & Sunday the 31st & 1st at Cheetah's in Venice California.

5th June – 1969

- Bill Graham presents the Grateful Dead, Junior Walker and the All-Stars and Glass Family on Thursday, Friday, Saturday & Sunday the 5th, 6th, 7th & 8th at the Fillmore West with lights by the Brotherhood of Light. On the evening of the 7th, Janis Joplin joins the Grateful Dead for a performance of "Turn on your Love light".

5th June – 1969

- Bill Graham presents the "Triumphant Return" of the Who with Chuck Berry and Albert King on Thursday & Friday the 5th & 6th at the Fillmore East with the Joshua Light Show.

6th June – 1969

- The Electric Theatre presents Vanilla Fudge, Muddy Waters and Rotary Connection on Friday, Saturday & Sunday the 6th, 7th & 8th at the Kinetic Playground, 4812 Clark Street in Chicago, Illinois.

7th June – 1969

- The Who release their rock opera **Tommy**. The double album is trend setting in its conception and execution. The album enters the charts at No.96 working its way up to the No.7 spot.

- A Free concert in Hyde Park, London on Saturday the 7th features the debut performance from Blind Faith. Also on the bill are, Richie Havens, Donovan, Edgar Broughton Band and the Third Ear Band. There are 120,000 in attendance.

8th June - 1969
- The "Benefit for the Fellowship Church" is held on Sunday the 8th at the Unitarian Center, San Francisco with Sons of Champlin, Freedom Highway, Ace of Cups, Phoenix, Morning Glory and many others.

9th June – 1969
- San Francisco favorites Moby Grape officially call it quits. The group members enter into a protracted legal battle with former manager Matthew Katz, who would later find some unknown Seattle musicians to perform as Moby Grape!

12th June – 1969
- Bill Graham presents the Byrds, Pacific Gas & Electric and Joe Cocker and the Grease Band on Thursday, Friday, Saturday & Sunday the 12th, 13th, 14th & 15th at the Fillmore West with lights by Little Princess 109.

13th June – 1969
- Pink Floyd release the soundtrack album **More**.
- Bill Graham presents the Mothers of Invention, Chicago and the Youngbloods on Friday & Saturday the 13th & 14th at the Fillmore East in New York City with the Joshua Light Show.
- The Family Dog presents Jefferson Airplane and the Charlatans in a live broadcast on KSAN direct from the Grand Opening of the Family Dog Ballroom at the Great Highway on Friday the 13th. By this time the Airplane were a huge headlining act and their appearance filled this opening. Their support band the Charlatans, the ones who many feel started the whole psychedelic movement, played their hearts out. Unfortunately their drummer went to jail the following week and the Charlatans never performed again. If Chet Helms needed another sign that the communal spirit was fading fast, as everyone left his new facility he found it stripped of every piece of furniture he had installed. Members of the audience had taken it all. Helms' was left with nothing but the bare floors! The Family Dog presentations at the Great Highway would continue until the weekend of August 21st, 1970.
- The Magic Circus presents the Who, Poco and the Bonzo Dog Band on Friday the 13th at the Hollywood Palladium.
- The Electric Theatre presents Eric Burdon, the Zombies and It's a Beautiful Day on Friday, Saturday & Sunday the 13th, 14th & 15th at the Kinetic Playground, 4812 Clark Street in Chicago, Illinois.

17th June – 1969
- Bill Graham presents the Who, Woody Herman & his Orchestra and A.B. Skhy on Tuesday, Wednesday & Thursday the 17th, 18th & 19th at the Fillmore West with lights by the Brotherhood of Light.

- The Marquee Club in London features the Spirit of John Morgan and the Mooche on Tuesday the 17th. The Mooche will make four more appearances at the Marquee.

20th June – 1969
- The Grateful Dead release **Aoxomoxoa**.
- Bill Graham presents Santana (Fri. Only), the Impressions, Ike & Tina Turner (Sat. & Sun. Only) and Blues Image on Friday, Saturday & Sunday the 20th, 21st & 22nd at the Fillmore West with lights by Little Princess 109.
- Bill Graham presents the Grateful Dead, Savoy Brown and Buddy Miles Express on Friday & Saturday the 20th & 21st at the Fillmore East in New York City with the Joshua Light Show.
- The 1969 edition of the Newport Rock Festival takes place in Northridge, California on Friday, Saturday & Sunday the 20th, 21st & 22nd. The performers include, Jimi Hendrix, Janis Joplin, Joe Cocker, Ike and Tina Turner, Creedence Clearwater Revival, Steppenwolf, Jethro Tull, the Rascals, the Byrds, Johnny Winter and Booker T and the MGs. Over one hundred and fifty thousand people are in attendance.
- The Electric Theatre presents the Crazy World of Arthur Brown and the Youndbloods on Friday, Saturday & Sunday the 20th, 21st & 22nd at the Kinetic Playground, 4812 Clark Street in Chicago, Illinois.

22nd June – 1969
- In Canada, the first Toronto Rock Festival is staged on Sunday the 22nd with performances from Steppenwolf, the Band, Procol Harum, Chuck Berry and Blood Sweat and Tears. Approximately fifty thousand show up for the violence free event.

24th June – 1969
- Bill Graham presents Iron Butterfly, Cold Blood and Sanpaku on Tuesday, Wednesday & Thursday the 24th, 25th & 26th at the Fillmore West with lights by Little Princess 109.

25th June – 1969
- The Doors, Lonnie Mack and the Elvin Bishop Group perform on Wednesday the 25th at the Cow Palace.
- The Marquee Club in London features Yes and Mandrake Paddle Steamer on Wednesday the 25th.

26th June – 1969
- Pink Floyd's first official U.K. tour comes to a close with a final night performance on Thursday the 26th entitled "The Final Lunacy!" at the Royal Albert Hall, London, England.

27th June – 1969
- Bill Graham presents Spirit, Lee Michaels and Pyewacket on Friday, Saturday & Sunday the 27th, 28th & 29th at the Fillmore West with lights by the Brotherhood of Light.

- Bill Graham presents Procol Harum, the Byrds and Raven on Friday & Saturday the 27th & 28th at the Fillmore East in New York City with the Joshua Light Show.
- The Denver Pop Festival is staged on Friday, Saturday & Sunday the 27th, 28th & 29th at the Mile High Stadium. Over fifty thousand show up see performances from Jimi Hendrix, Johnny Winter, Joe Cocker, Creedence Clearwater Revival, the Mothers of Invention, Tim Buckley, Poco, Iron Butterfly and Big Mama Thornton. Unlike the earlier festival in Toronto, Denver's event is marred by violence and police move in with clubs and tear gas. The festivals final day features the last performance of the Jimi Hendrix Experience.
- Jack Casady, Jorma Kaukonen (Hot Tuna), Joey Covington, the Grateful Dead and the Cleanliness & Godliness Skiffle Band, with lights by Marianne on Friday, Saturday & Sunday the 27th, 28th & 29th at The Barn, Rio Nido, Veterans Memorial Building, Santa Rosa.

29th June – 1969
- Jimi Hendrix announces his new formation will no longer go by the name the Jimi Hendrix Experience. He also announces his new bassist will be old army buddy Billy Cox.

July - 1969
- Big Brother guitarist James Gurley loses his wife to a heroin overdose while on a family campout.

1st July – 1969
- Bill Graham presents Johnny Winter, Lonnie Mack, Rockin' Foo on Tuesday, Wednesday & Thursday the 1st, 2nd & 3rd at the Fillmore West with lights by the Brotherhood of Light.

3rd July - 1969
- Brian Jones is found dead at the bottom of his swimming pool. The ex-Rolling Stone that'd recently quit the band, had a high level of alcohol and barbiturates in his system, but the coroner attributes his drowning death to "misadventure".
- Bill Graham presents the Jeff Beck Group, Jethro Tull and Soft White Underbelly on Thursday the 3rd at the Fillmore East in New York City with the Joshua Light Show.

4th July – 1969
- Bill Graham presents Eric Burdon, It's a Beautiful Day and Cat Mother on Friday, Saturday & Sunday the 4th, 5th & 6th at the Fillmore West with lights by the Brotherhood of Light.
- Bill Graham presents Iron Butterfly, Blues Image and Man on Friday & Saturday the 4th & 5th at the Fillmore East in New York City with the Joshua Light Show.
- The Saugatuck Pop Festival is held on Friday & Saturday the 4th & 5th featuring SRC, Procol Harum, MC5, Muddy Waters, John Lee Hooker, Amboy Dukes, Rotary Connection, Crazy World of Arthur Brown, Bob Seger, Frost, Stooges, Big Mama Thornton, Savage Grace and Caste all performing at the Potawatomi Beach in Saugatuck Michigan.

- The First Atlanta Pop Festival is held on Friday & Saturday the 4th & 5th at the Atlanta International Raceway in Atlanta Georgia. Performing are; Chuck Berry, Al Kooper, Blood Sweat and Tears, Canned Heat, Chicago Transit Authority, Creedence Clearwater Revival, Dave Brubeck, Delaney and Bonnie, Ian & Sylvia, Tommy James and the Shondells, Janis Joplin, Johnny Winter, Joe Cocker, Led Zeppelin, Pacific Gas & Electric, Paul Butterfield Blues Band, Johnny Rivers, Spirit, Staple Singers, Sweetwater, Booker T and the MGs, and Ten Wheel Drive.

5th July - 1969
- The Rolling Stones perform at a free concert in Hyde Park, London on Saturday the 5th as a tribute to Brian Jones. 500,000 people turn out to watch. Also on the bill are Family, Battered Ornaments, King Crimson, Roy Harper, Third Ear Band, Alexis Korner's New Church and Screw. Given the amount of violence that had taken place through the year this event came off in total peace. Many see this event as the last display of the "underground" spirit as rock music became a business and industry of its own.

8th July – 1969
- Bill Graham presents B.B. King, Aum and Frost on Tuesday, Wednesday & Thursday the 8th, 9th & 10th at the Fillmore West with lights by Little Princess 109.

11th July – 1969
- Bill Graham presents Santana, Taj Mahal and Flamin' Groovies on Friday Saturday

173

& Sunday the 11th, 12th & 13th at the Fillmore West with lights by Holy See.
- Bill Graham presents John Mayall, Preservation Hall Jazz Band and Spooky Tooth on Friday & Saturday the 11th & 12th at the Fillmore East in New York City with the Joshua Light Show.

12th July – 1969

- New York rock impresario Steve Paul closes his club called The Scene. This club gave birth to the careers of many bands during the sixties. It was also the sight of many famous jam sessions between the likes of Frank Zappa and the Monkees, Jimi Hendrix and the Doors, Jimmy Page and Jeff Beck, Janis Joplin and Eric Burdona and on one strange evening between Tiny Tim and the Doors.
- Blind Faith featuring the guitar work of Eric Clapton makes its U.S. debut on Saturday the 12th at Madison Square Gardens in New York City.
- It's a Beautiful Day and Aum perform on Saturday the 12th at the Bandshell in Waikiki, Hawaii.

14th July – 1969

- **Easy Rider** premieres in movie theatres.

15th July – 1969

- Bill Graham presents B.B. King, the Elvin Bishop Group and Love Sculpture on Tuesday, Wednesday & Thursday the 15th, 16th & 17th at the Fillmore West with lights by Holy See.

18th July – 1969

- Bill Graham presents Country Joe and the Fish, Joe Cocker and the Grease band and Country Weather on Friday, Saturday & Sunday the 18th, 19th & 20th at the Fillmore West with lights by Anathema.
- Bill Graham presents Creedence Clearwater Revival, Terry Reid and Aum on Friday & Saturday the 18th & 19th at the Fillmore East in New York City with the Joshua Light Show.

20th July - 1969

- Neil Armstrong becomes the first person to walk on the Moon.

22nd July – 1969

- Bill Graham presents Ten Years After, Ike & Tina Turner and Flock on Tuesday, Wednesday & Thursday the 22nd, 23rd & 24th at the Fillmore West with lights by the Brotherhood of Light.

25th July – 1969

- Bill Graham presents the Doors, Lonnie Mack and the Elvin Bishop Group on Friday the 25th at the Cow Palace in San Francisco.
- Bill Graham presents the Steve Miller Band, Albert King and Mountain on Friday, Saturday & Sunday the 25th, 26th & 27th at the Fillmore West with lights by Little Princess 109.

POSTER FOR THE FIRST SEATTLE POPS FESTIVAL

• Neil Young makes his first appearance with Crosby Stills and Nash at the Fillmore East.

• The Grateful Dead and It's a Beautiful Day perform on Friday, Saturday & Sunday the 25th, 26th & 27th at the Honolulu International Centre, Honolulu, Hawaii.

• The First Seattle Pops Festival is held on Friday, Saturday & Sunday the 25th, 26th & 27th at Goldcreek Park, Woodenville, Washington featuring Chuck Berry, Blacksnake, Tim Buckley, the Byrds, Chicago Transit Authority, Albert Collins, Alice Cooper, Crome Syrcus, Bo Diddley, the Doors, Floating Bridge, Flock, Flying Burrito Brothers, Guess Who, It's A Beautiful Day, Led Zeppelin, Charles Lloyd, Lonnie Mack, Lee Michaels, Rocking Fu, Retina Circus Light Show, Murray Roman, Santana, Spirit, Ten Years After, Ike & Tina Turner Revue, Vanilla Fudge and the Youngbloods. Upwards of seventy thousand are in attendance.

27th July – 1969

• KPRI and Hedgcock Piering present Jefferson Airplane, Sons of Champlin, Congress of Wonders and Ten Years After on Sunday the 27th at Balboa Stadium in San Diego.

29th July – 1969

• Bill Graham presents Canned Heat, Preservation Hall Jazz Band and Southwind on Tuesday, Wednesday & Thursday the 29th, 30th & 31st at the Fillmore West with lights by Little Princess 109.

1st August – 1969

• Bill Graham presents the Everly Brothers, Sons of Champlin and Baby Huey and the Babysitters on Friday, Saturday & Sunday the 1st, 2nd & 3rd at the Fillmore West with lights by Little Princess 109.

• Bill Graham presents Canned Heat, Three Dog Night, Santana and Sha Na Na on Friday & Saturday the 1st & 2nd at the Fillmore East in New York City with the Joshua Light Show.

• Jim Salzer presents Led Zeppelin, Jethro Tull and Fraternity Of Man on Friday the 1st at the Earl Warren Showground's, Santa Barbara.

- The three-day Atlantic City Pop Festivals is staged on Friday, Saturday & Sunday the 1st, 2nd & 3rd in Atlantic City, New Jersey. This is quite literally the first pop-music festival in the New York area and over 110,000 show up to see and hear performances from Jefferson Airplane, Creedence Clearwater Revival, B.B. King, the Byrds, Procol Harum, Iron Butterfly, Dr. John, Janis Joplin, Little Richard, Santana, Joe Cocker and others.

4th August – 1969

- Bill Graham announces for the first time that the music business has changed and he is not encouraged by the "big business" direction its heading in. His announcement states that new owners will take over the Fillmore West at the end of the year and he will be "through with San Francisco." As it turns out the new owners don't take over and Graham will continue to both the Fillmore West and East for a while yet.

5th August – 1969

- Bill Graham presents Fleetwood Mac and SRC on Tuesday, Wednesday & Thursday the 5th, 6th & 7th at the Fillmore West with lights by the Brotherhood of Light.

8th August – 1969

- Bill Graham presents Jr. Walker and the Allstars, Lee Michaels and Tony Joe White on Friday Saturday & Sunday the 8th, 9th & 10th at the Fillmore West with lights by the Brotherhood of Light.
- The Doors perform on Friday the 8th at the Electric Circus in New York City.
- Bill Graham presents Jefferson Airplane, Joe Cocker and Spontaneous Sound on Friday & Saturday the 8th & 9th at the Fillmore East in New York City with the Joshua Light Show.
- The Ninth National Jazz and Blues Festival, is held on Friday, Saturday & Sunday the 8th, 9th & 10th at Plumpton Race Track, Streat, East Sussex featuring Pink Floyd, Soft Machine, East Of Eden, Blossom Toes, Keith Tippet Jazz Group, Juniors Eyes, Village, Bonzo Dog Doo Dah Band, Roy Harper, Strawbs, Breakthru, Jigsaw, Peter Hammill, the Who, Chicken Shack, Fat Mattress, Aynsley Dunbar, Yes, Spirit Of John Morgan, King Crimson, Groundhogs, Dry Ice, Wallace Collection, Pentangle, Long John Baldry, Ron Geesin, Magna Carta, Jo-Ann Kelley, Noel Murphy, the Nice , Family, Chris Barber, Keef Hartley, Eclection, Blodwyn Pig, Circus, Hard Meat, Affinity, Babylon and Cuby's Blues Band.

9th August – 1969

- The Charles Manson murders are discovered.

12th August - 1969

- Bill Graham presents Chuck Berry, Jethro Tull and Loading Zone on Tuesday, Wednesday, Thursday the 12th, 13th & 14th at the Fillmore West with lights by Little Princess 109.
- Bill Graham presents Jefferson Airplane, B.B King and special guests the Who with the Joshua Light Show Tuesday the 12th at Tanglewood, Lenox, Massachusetts.

15th August – 1969

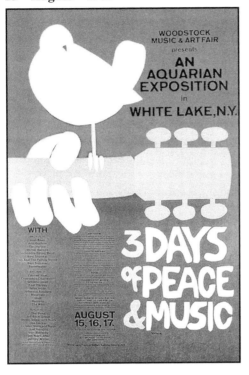

• Bill Graham presents the Chicago Transit Authority, the Youngbloods and Colosseum on Friday, Saturday & Sunday the 15th, 16th & 17th at the Fillmore West with lights by Little Princess 109.

• Mother Earth and Shiva's Head Band perform on Friday & Saturday the 15th & 16th at the Vulcan Gas Company, 316 Congress, Austin Texas.

• Woodstock Music & Art Fair Presents An Aquarian Exposition on Friday, Saturday & Sunday the 15th, 16th & 17th in White Lake, New York featuring Joan Baez, Arlo Guthrie, John Sebastian, Melanie, Tim Hardin, Richie Havens, Incredible String Band, Ravi Shankar, Sly and the Family Stone, Bert Sommer, Country Joe and the Fish, Sweetwater, Canned Heat, Creedence Clearwater, Grateful Dead, Keef Hartley, Janis Joplin, Jefferson Airplane, Mountain, Quill, Santana, the Who, the Band, Jeff Beck Group, Blood Sweat and Tears, Joe Cocker, Crosby Stills and Nash, Jimi Hendrix, Iron Butterfly, Ten Years After, Johnny Winter. While taking place on the East Coast, the event had a decidedly West Coast flavour, in particular because of the number of San Francisco bands. Of note was the fact that Bill Graham negotiated a slot for Santana who hadn't even recorded their album at that point. Anyone who was there or even seen the movie will attest to the fact Woodstock was a huge success. The festival was a unique and life changing experience to all who attended, and despite plenty of drugs, poor sanitation, three deaths, two births and four miscarriages, those three days continue to inspire the utopian vision of the Woodstock nation. Woodstock was also a monumental event in that by this time many of the hippie generation left the festival realizing they were going home to family and bills. In many respects a whole generation grew up at Woodstock.

16th August - 1969

• Jim Salzer presents Blind Faith featuring Eric Clapton, Steve Winwood, Ginger Baker, Rick Grech, Bonnie Delaney & Friends on Saturday the 16th at the Earl Warren Showground's, Santa Barbara.

19th August – 1969

• Bill Graham presents John Mayall, Mother Earth and the New York Rock & Roll

Ensemble on Tuesday, Wednesday & Thursday the 19th, 20th & 21st at the Fillmore West with lights by the Brotherhood of Light.

20th August – 1969
- Jasmine presents the Grateful Dead, New Riders of the Purple Sage, Sanpaku and Magic Theatre on Wednesday the 20th at the Aqua Theatre in Seattle Washington.

22nd August – 1969
- Bill Graham presents the Wild West on Friday, Saturday & Sunday the 22nd, 23rd & 24th at the Golden Gate Park with lights by the Brotherhood of Light.
- Wild West Festival at the Kezar Stadium is CANCELLED. The event was the brainchild of Quicksilver manager Ron Polte. This festival was to feature eight stages with performances from the Grateful Dead, Janis Joplin, Quicksilver Messenger Service, Turk Murphy, Mike Bloomfield, Nick Gravenites and Friends, Edwin Hawkins Singers, Fourth Way, Jefferson Airplane, Sons of Champlin, Country Joe and the Fish, Santana, Sly & the Family Stone, Steve Miller Band and the Youngbloods. Polte underestimated the bureaucracy involved staging such an event and was forced to cancel the event.

24th August – 1969
- The movie **Alice's Restaurant** staring Arlo Guthrie is released to in theatres.

26th August – 1969
- Bill Graham presents Ten Years After, Terry Reid and the Barkays on Tuesday, Wednesday, Thursday the 26th, 27th & 28th at the Fillmore West with lights by Little Princess 109.

29th August – 1969
- Bill Graham presents Spirit, Savoy Brown and Womb on Friday, Saturday & Sunday the 29th, 30th & 31st at the Fillmore West with lights by the Brotherhood of Light.

30th August - 1969
- The "Isle Of Wight Festival" is held on Saturday & Sunday the 30th & 31st featuring Blodwyn Pig, Blonde On Blonde, Bonzo Dog Doo Dah Band, Edgar Broughton Band, Joe Cocker, Aynsley Dunbar, Bob Dylan, Eclection, Family, Gary Farr, Fat Mattress, Julie Felix, Free, Gypsy, Richie Havens, Marsha Hunt and White Trash, Indo Jazz Fusions, Liverpool Scene, Mighty Baby, the Moody Blues, the Nice, Tom Paxton, Pentangle, Pretty Things, Third Ear Band, and the Who.
- The second Annual Sky River Rock Festival takes place near Seattle Washington on Saturday & Sunday the 30th & 31st featuring performances from Big Mama Thornton, Country Joe and the Fish, Quicksilver Messenger Service, the Steve Miller Band and others. There are 25,000 in attendance.
- The Texas International Pop Festival is staged on Saturday, Sunday & Monday the 30th, 31st & 1st at the Dallas International Motor Speedway. Some 120,000 attend to watch performances from Janis Joplin, Johnny Winter, Canned Heat, Chicago

Transit Authority, Santana, Led Zeppelin, Grand Funk Railroad, Sly and the Family Stone and B.B. King.

4th September – 1969
- Bill Graham presents Santana, Sea Train and Yuseff Lathf on Thursday, Friday, Saturday & Sunday the 4th, 5th, 6th & 7th at the Fillmore West with lights by the Brotherhood of Light.
- Bill Graham presents the Incredible String Band on Thursday the 4th at the Fillmore East in New York City with the Joshua Light Show.

5th September - 1969
- Bill Graham presents B.B. King, Albery King and Bobby Bland on Friday & Saturday the 5th & 6th at the Fillmore East in New York City with the Joshua Light Show.
- The Pure Filth Rock & Roll Club presents Moby Grape, Fields and Bicycle with lights by Deadly Nightshade on Friday the 5th at the Monterey Fairgrounds Horse Show Arena.

6th September - 1969
- A Free Concert in Hyde Park, London is held on Saturday the 6th featuring Crosby Stills and Nash and Jefferson Airplane. The Grateful Dead are booked, but cancel at the last minute.

7th September – 1969
- Bill Graham presents Ravi Shankar on Sunday the 6th at the Fillmore East in New York City with the Joshua Light Show.

10th September – 1969
- Bill Graham presents for one night only the Incredible String Band on Wednesday the 10th at the Fillmore West.

11th September – 1969
- Bill Graham presents the Steve Miller Band, James Cotton Blues Band and Keef Hartley on Thursday, Friday, Saturday & Sunday the 11th, 12th, 13th & 14th at the Fillmore West with lights by Little Princess 109.

12th September – 1969
- Bill Graham presents Ten Years After, Mother Earth and Flock on Friday & Saturday the 12th & 13th at the Fillmore East in New York City with the Joshua Light Show.

13th September – 1969
- Following up on their scorching performance at Woodstock, Santana release their first LP entitled **Santana**, which contains eventual hits *Evil Ways* and *Soul Sacrifice*.

14th September – 1969

- Bill Graham presents the Incredible String Band on Sunday the 14th at the Fillmore East in New York City with the Joshua Light Show.

18th September – 1969

- Bill Graham presents Taj Mahal, Buddy Guy and Spooky Tooth on Thursday, Friday, Saturday & Sunday the 18th, 19th, 20th & 21st at the Fillmore West with lights by the Brotherhood of Light.

19th September - 1969

- Bill Graham presents Crosby Stills Nash & Young and Lonnie Mack on Friday & Saturday the 19th & 20th at the Fillmore East in New York City with the Joshua Light Show.
- The Vulcan Gas Company presents Freddy King, Shepards Bush and Onion Creek on Friday & Saturday the 19th & 20th in Austin, Texas.

20th September - 1969

- While Blind Faith occupy the No.1 position on the American LP charts with their first release, it is pure bubblegum at the top of the singles charts in the U.S with the Archie's *Sugar Sugar*.
- Janis Joplin plays the Hollywood Bowl on Saturday the 20th.
- A Free Concert in Hyde Park, London is held on Saturday the 20th featuring Soft Machine, the Deviants, Al Stewart, Quintessence and the Edgar Broughton Band

23rd September - 1969

- The "Paul is Dead" hoax spreads. Everyone from fans to radio disc jockeys looks and finds clues demonstrating Paul actually died some time earlier and had been replaced by a double.
- The Marquee Club in London features Blossom Toes and Mike Hart and the Business on Tuesday the 23rd. Blossom Toes would play the Marquee three more times.

24th September – 1969

- The Bay Area Drug Committee presents "A Benefit Show To Save The Children" in Biafra, at Bill Graham's Fillmore West. Featuring Sanpako, Ace of Cups, Terry Dolan, It's a Beautiful Day, Sons of Champlin, Outlaws (featuring Gary Duncan and Dino Valenti) with lights by the Brotherhood of Light on Wednesday the 24th.

25th September – 1969

- Bill Graham presents Chuck Berry, Aum and Loading Zone on Thursday, Friday, Saturday & Sunday the 25th, 26th, 27th & 28th at the Fillmore West with lights by Little Princess 109.

26th September – 1969

- The Beatles release their last LP recorded together, **Abbey Road**. The album will sit at the No.1 spot on the charts for eleven weeks.
- Bill Graham presents the Grateful Dead, Country Joe and the Fish and Sha Na Na on Friday & Saturday the 26th & 27th at the Fillmore East in New York City with the Joshua Light Show.
- The original Fillmore vacated a year earlier by Bill Graham, re-opens as yet another rock ballroom under new management. It will be billed as the "New-Old Fillmore" in the posters advertising various performances.
- The Marquee Club in London features Vanilla Fudge and Grain on Friday the 26th.

1st October - 1969

- The Grape Workers Strike Benefit is held on Wednesday the 1st at the Fillmore West. On the bill are Santana, Mike Bloomfield and Friends, Tongue & Groove and Shades of Joy.

2nd October – 1969

- Bill Graham presents Crosby Stills Nash and Young, Blues Image and John Sebastian on Thursday, Friday, Saturday & Sunday the 2nd, 3rd, 4th & 5th at the Winterland with lights by the Brotherhood of Light. The show was originally only going to be a three-day run, one at the Fillmore West and two at the Winterland, but due to overwhelming response, Graham moved all the performances to the larger Winterland and added Sunday to the lineup. This is the first recorded rock act event where a group, in this case Crosby Stills Nash and Young, required a large Persian rug to cover the stage before they would perform!

3rd October – 1969

- Bill Graham presents Chuck Berry, John Mayall and the Elvin Bishop Group on Friday & Saturday the 3rd & 4th at the Fillmore East in New York City with the Joshua Light Show.

4th October - 1969

- The Goldrush Festival at Lake Amador is staged on Saturday the 4th featuring Santana, Taj Mahal, Bo Diddley, Albert Collins, Kaleidoscope, Al Wilson, Southwind, Ike & Tina Turner, Sons of Champlin, Country Weather, Cold Blood, John Fahey, Linn County and Daybreak.

9th October – 1969

- Bill Graham presents Country Joe and the Fish, Albert King and Blodwyn Pig on Thursday, Friday, Saturday & Sunday the 9th, 10th, 11th & 12th at the Fillmore West with lights by the Brotherhood of Light.

10th October – 1969

- Bill Graham presents Vanilla Fudge, Aum and Dr. John the Night Tripper on Friday & Saturday the 10th & 11th at the Fillmore East in New York City with the Joshua Light Show.

11th October – 1969

- Grand Fund Railroad release their first LP entitled **On Time** and it enters the charts at No.65. While critics unanimously eschewed it, within a year Grand Funk Railroad would become one of the best selling rock acts of all time.
- The Internationales Essener Pop & Blues Festival '69 is staged in Grugahalle, Essen, West Germany on Saturday, Sunday & Monday the 11th, 12th & 13th featuring Pink Floyd, Fleetwood Mac, Pretty Things, Yes, Muddy Waters, Alexis Korner, the Nice, Deep Purple and more.

15th October – 1969

- Today is World Peace Day and hundreds of thousands turn out in antiwar demonstrations across the country. More than 250,000 gather in Washington DC to protest the Vietnam War. It is the largest antiwar gathering ever and stimulates two further marches on November 14th and 15th.

16th October – 1969

- Bill Graham presents Joe Cocker and the Grease Band, Little Richard and the Move on Thursday, Friday, Saturday & Sunday the 16th, 17th, 18th & 19th at the Fillmore West with lights by Little Princess 109.

17th October – 1969

- Bill Graham presents Spirit, the Kinks and Bonzo Dog Band on Friday & Saturday the 17th & 18th at the Fillmore East in New York City with the Joshua Light Show.

20th October - 1969

- Bill Graham presents the Who for a six night stand Monday through Saturday the 20th – 25th performing Tommy at the Fillmore East, New York.

21st October – 1969

- Beat author Jack Kerouac, author of **On the Road**, dies of a stomach hemorrhage. While he was not at all sympathetic to the hippie ideals, his writings never the less inspired many of the Younger generation to become more socially and politically involved.

23rd October – 1969

- The Velvet Underground and Ramon, Ramon and the Four Daddyos perform on Thursday, Friday & Saturday the 23rd, 24th & 25th at the Vulcan Gas Company 316 Congress in Austin Texas.
- King Crimson makes their U.S. debut on Thursday the 23rd at Goddard College in Plainfield, Vermont. Bandleader Robert Fripp describes the crowd as "a peace-and-love crowd, sitting dreamily in lotus positions, probably expecting psychedelic folk or some such, after our first number there was dead silence. I looked up. The audience looked as if it had been squashed by a steamroller." King Crimson would form one of the core bands of the emerging Progressive Rock genre.

24th October – 1969

- Bill Graham presents Jefferson Airplane, Grateful Dead and Sons of Champlin Friday & Saturday the 24th & 25th at the Winterland. Lights supplied by Glenn McKay's Headlights.

25th October - 1969

- Pink Floyd play on Saturday the 25th at the Actuel Festival staged in Mont de l'Enclus, Amougies, Belgium. This was originally scheduled to be the First Paris Music festival but organizers were unable to secure proper permits and so the show was moved to Belgium.

30th October – November – 1969

- Bill Graham presents It's a Beautiful Day, Ike & Tina Turner and Alice Cooper on Thursday, Friday, Saturday & Sunday the 30th, 31st, 1st & 2nd at the Fillmore West with lights by Little Princess 109.

31st October – 1969

- Bill Graham presents Mountain, Steve Miller Band and the Steve Barron Quartet on Friday & Saturday the 31st & 1st at the Fillmore East in New York City with the Joshua Light Show.
- A Boogie-Man Halloween Ball is held on Friday & Saturday the 31st & 1st at the OLD Fillmore Auditorium at Fillmore and Geary. Performing are the Flamin Groovies, Commander Cody, Joy of Cooking, Canterbury Fair and Gold, with lights by Frank and Stein.
- Mike Quatro and Russ Gibb presents in Detroit "A Black Magic Rock and Roll Halloween" on Friday the 31st featuring Arthur Brown, Tim Leary, Frost, MC5, Bonzo Dog Band, Stooges, Coven, Pink Floyd, Savage Grace, Kim Fowley, Alice Cooper, Sky, Teagarden and Vanwinkle, SRC, Bob Seger, the Lonely People and Seekers at the Olympic Stadium in Detroit. A number of acts originally billed failed to appear because of missing contracts, including Pink Floyd.

1st November – 1969

- Pink Floyd release the double album **Ummagumma**. The album contains one disc of live recordings and one disc of studio efforts.

4th November – 1969

- The Final U.S. appearance of Cream takes place Tuesday the 4th at the Rhode Island Auditorium in Providence, Rhode Island with lights by the Road.

6th November – 1969

- Bill Graham presents Led Zeppelin, Bonzo Dog Band and Roland Kirk on Thursday, Friday & Saturday the 6th, 7th & 8th at the Winterland with lights by the Brotherhood of Light.

7th November – 1969

- The Grateful Dead, South Bay Experimental Flash Alligator and Crimson Madness perform on Friday & Saturday the 7th & 8th at the Old Fillmore on Fillmore and Geary.
- Bill Graham presents Santana, Humble Pie and the Butterfield Blues Band on Friday & Saturday the 7th & 8th at the Fillmore East in New York City with the Joshua Light Show.

9th November – 1969

- Bill Graham presents the Rolling Stones on Sunday the 9th at the Oakland Coliseum.

10th November – 1969

- Bill Graham presents the Rolling Stones on Monday & Tuesday the 10th & 11th at the San Diego International Sports Arena.

11th November – 1969

- The Who and Tony Williams perform on Tuesday & Wednesday the 11th & 12th at the Boston Tea Party, 15 Lansdowne Street in Boston.

13th November – 1969

- Bill Graham presents Crosby Stills Nash and Young, Cold Blood, Joy of Cooking and Lamb on Thursday, Friday, Saturday & Sunday the 13th, 14th, 15th & 16th at the Winterland with lights by Little Princess 109.

14th November – 1969

- Bill Graham presents Johnny Winter, Blodwyn Pig and Chicago on Friday & Saturday the 14th & 15th at the Fillmore East in New York City with the Joshua Light Show.

15th November – 1969

- Three hundred thousand anti-war protestors march in Washington DC while 150,000 participate in a peace march in San Francisco. The National Moratorium organization committee adopts the Plastic Ono Band's *Give Peace a Chance* as its anthem.
- Janis Joplin is arrested in Tampa, Florida for using vulgar and indecent language while arguing with police during a concert performance. She is released on $504 bail and all charges are eventually dropped.
- Country Joe and the Fish and Kaleidoscope perform on Saturday the 15th at the Concertgebouw, Amsterdam, Netherlands.

20th November – 1969

- Bill Graham presents Jethro Tull, MC5 and Sanpaku on Thursday, Friday, Saturday & Sunday the 20th, 21st, 22nd & 23rd at the Fillmore West with lights by the Brotherhood of Light.

THE DOORS—FRIDAY AUGUST 11967 ELECTRIC CIRCUS NEW YORK, N.Y.

LIGHT SHOW DANCE CONCERT

SEE HEAR FEEL

THE TRAUMA

HAPPENING EVERY FRI SAT SUN 2121 ARCH ST 9PM

COUNTRY JOE AND THE FISH

at WOOLSEY HALL in NEW HAVEN Sun., MAY 26 8 p.m.

Tickets $2.75, $3.50, $4.00 at Potpourri, Chapel Square; Hajian's Gifts, 1002 Chapel; Renaissance, 45 Whalley; and at door. Mail orders: Send payment and stamped, addressed envelope to The Spiral Staircase, 1232 Yale Station, New Haven.

FRIDAY & SATURDAY, JAN. 31 & FEB. 1
IRON BUTTERFLY
LED ZEPPELIN
THE MOVE

FRIDAY & SATURDAY, FEB. 7 & 8
CANNED HEAT
THE PENTANGLE
RHINOCEROS

TUESDAY & WEDNESDAY, FEB. 11 & 12
JANIS JOPLIN
And Her Group
GRATEFUL DEAD
AND AT EVERY SHOW
JOSHUA LIGHT SHOW
FILLMORE EAST
SECOND AVENUE AT SIXTH STREET

The Inner Mystique   Chocolate Watch Band

CROSBY, STILLS, NASH & YOUNG
with TAYLOR and REEVES
Guest Artist TAJ MAHAL

SATURDAY, DECEMBER 6, PAULEY PAVILION, UCLA – 8:30 P.M.

$6.00, 5.00, 4.00, 3.00 (2.00 students)

Andy Warhol

OH BOY!
IT'S ANOTHER
SEXSATIONAL
ISSUE!

JAGGER'S SADIST MOVIE FINALLY RELEASED

'PERFORMANCE' FOR U.K. SHOW

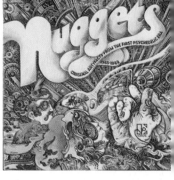

A HEAVY EVIL FILM, DON'T SEE IT ON ACID

PERFORMANCE, filmed some two years ago, is finally about to be unleashed on the British public. It's probably the heaviest movie ever made – a kaleidoscope of transvestitism, sado-masochism, deaths, bad fly, trips etc.

James Fox – Jagger as a retired rock star, and Fox as a thug on the run. Jagger is involved in a three—way relationship with two chicks at his Powis Square pad. Fox moves in and is gradually freaked—out and mentally demolished.

It's a totally illogical movie. A series of seemingly un—related incidents, and complex inter-relationships flashed across the screen at almost subliminal speed– Jagger/Fox Jagger/chicks Fox/chicks, and chick/chick. Chilling and very effective, with superb editing and camera work.

Jagger is outrageous. Any doubts about his acting ability that might remain after "Ned Kelly" are effectively dispelled. He parodies and caricatures himself; pouting, posturing grimacing and generally acting mean and ugly. The music comes from Jack Nitzche, Ry Cooder, and

the Merry Clayton Singers. The soundtrack album is now out and even taken out of the context of

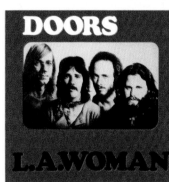

the film it's well worth hearing.

PERFORMANCE is an evil movie.

At times, it's almost pornographic and the violence scenes are sickeningly realistic. Warner Bros. are warning people not to see it while tripping – they could well be right. It'll be released in October/November this year.

The Stones have just started their first tour of Europe for 3½ years. Jagger was recently interviewed by the Copenhagen paper "Politiken", and came out with the following statement:-
"I want to earn money on our new records, not for the sake of the money but to invest it in other things, such as the Black Panther breakfast programme for ghetto children. We have already set aside some bread for them, in fact." He claimed that the profits of the big American companies went to buy arms and support right-wing organisations. "I want the money to fight this with" he finished.

FIVE BRIDGES   THE NICE

STEPPENWOLF
MONSTER

FRANK ZAPPA

HOT RATS

OZ 39   20p

THRILLING
MURDER
COMICS

NO. 1

TERRIFYING
TALES OF
TOTAL
PARANOIA

"ADULTS"
ONLY

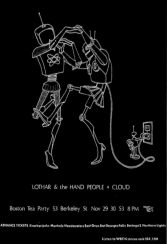

LOTHAR & the HAND PEOPLE + CLOUD

Boston Tea Party 53 Berkeley St Nov 29 30 53 8 PM

ADVANCE TICKETS Krackerjacks Manhole Headquarters East Onyx Bat Georges Folly Battega 2 Northern Lights

Listen to WBCN stereo rock 104.1 FM

WILDFLOWER

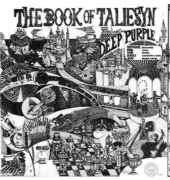

WE'VE JUST COME FROM

BILL GRAHAM'S

FILLMORE WEST

IT WAS NICE.

21st November - 1969

- Bill Graham presents Joe Cocker, Fleetwood Mac, King Crimson and the Voices of East Harlem on Friday & Saturday the 21st & 22nd at the Fillmore East in New York City with the Joshua Light Show.
- PAM Productions present It's A Beautiful Day, Cold Blood, Joy of Cooking and Magic Colours with lights by Deadly Nightshade on Friday the 21st at the Santa Rosa Fairgrounds.

27th November – 1969

- Bill Graham presents the Kinks, Taj Mahal and Sha-Na-Na on Thursday, Friday, Saturday & Sunday the 27th, 28th, 29th & 30th at the Fillmore West with lights by Little Princess 109.

28th November - 1969

FIRST ANNUAL INTERNATIONAL PALM BEACH MUSIC & ART FESTIVAL

THE ROLLING STONES ⋆ JANIS JOPLIN ⋆ CHAMBERS BROS. ⋆ SLY & THE FAMILY STONE ⋆ JEFFERSON AIRPLANE ⋆ THE BYRDS ⋆ STEPPENWOLF ⋆ SPIRIT ⋆ PACIFIC GAS & ELECTRIC ⋆ SWEETWATER ⋆ COUNTRY JOE & THE FISH ⋆ JOHNNY WINTERS ⋆ROTARY CONNECTION ⋆ GRAND FUNK RAILROAD ⋆ THE RUGBYS ⋆ KING CRIMSON ⋆ PLUS 10 MORE FAMOUS GROUPS ⋆ FOR INFO. CALL 305-832-9701

- Bill Graham presents Jefferson Airplane, the Youngbloods and Joseph Eger's Crossover on Friday & Saturday the 28th & 29th at the Fillmore East in New York City with the Joshua Light Show.
- First Annual Palm Beach Music and Art Festival at West Palm Beach, Florida is staged on Friday, Saturday & Sunday the 28th, 29th & 30th. Featuring the Rolling Stones, Janis Joplin, Chambers Brothers, Sly and the Family Stone, Jefferson Airplane, the Byrds, Steppenwolf, Spirit, Pacific Gas & Electric, Sweetwater, Country Joe and the Fish, Johnny Winter, Rotary Connection, Grand Funk Railroad, the Rubgys and King Crimson.
- The Brunel University Arts Festival is held on Friday the 28th in Uxbridge, England featuring Pink Floyd supported by Gracious and the Explosive Spectrum Lightshow.

4th December – 1969

- On the new release front Janis Joplin releases her **I Got Dem Ol' Kozmic Blues Again** and Sly and the Family Stone release **Stand**.

4th December – 1969

- Bill Graham presents the Grateful Dead, The Flock and Humble Pie on Thursday, Friday, Saturday & Sunday the 4th, 5th, 6th & 7th at the Fillmore West with lights by the Brotherhood of Light.

5th December – 1969
- Bill Graham presents Jethro Tull, Grand Funk Railroad and Fat Matress on Friday & Saturday the 5th & 6th at the Fillmore East in New York City with the Joshua Light Show.

6th – December – 1969

UCLA Committee on Fine Arts Productions in cooperation with College Concerts presents

CROSBY, STILLS, NASH & YOUNG
with TAYLOR and REEVES
Guest Artist TAJ MAHAL

SATURDAY, DECEMBER 6, PAULEY PAVILION, UCLA – 8:30 P.M.

$6.00, 5.00, 4.00, 3.00 (2.00 students)

Tickets are available at the UCLA Concert Ticket Office, 10851 LeConte Avenue, Westwood Village (opposite Bullocks), 825-2953, and all Mutual Agencies 627-1248 and Wallich's Music City Liberty Ticket Agencies 466-3553. Also available through Ticketron.

- Altamont! If Woodstock was three days of peace, love and music, Altamont turned into a one-day nightmare. In an effort to counter negative publicity, the Rolling Stones wanted to stage a free concert at Altamont Speedway. Unfortunately the Hells Angels handled security. While Jefferson Airplane were performing Marty Balin attempted to call the Angles on the level of violence. He was knocked unconscious for speaking out. The Grateful Dead opted not to perform at that point. The night ended with the Hells Angels stabbing Meredith Hunter at foot of the stage while the Stones performed. The decade ended on a very low note. In some peoples eyes this event actually marked the end of San Francisco rock era. It was never quite the same after the innocence was lost.

- UCLA Committee of Fine Arts presents Crosby Stills Nash and Young, with Taylor and Reeves and Taj Mahal on Saturday the 6th at the Pauley Pavilion, University of California, Los Angeles.

7th December – 1969
- Larry's Magic Productions presents in Baltimore, Janis Joplin and the Paul Butterfield Blues Band on Sunday the 7th at the Civic Centre in Baltimore, Maryland.

8th December – 1969
- Back in Toronto, Jimi Hendrix testified on his drug possession charges. After listing the times he's used drugs in the past, Hendrix claims he has now outgrown drugs. The jury finds him not guilty.
- Jethro Tull perform on Monday & Tuesday the 8th & 9th at the Boston Tea Party, 15 Lansdowne Street in Boston.

10th December – 1969

- Bill Graham presents for one night only the Incredible String Band on Wednesday the 10th at the Fillmore West.

11th December – 1969

- Bill Graham presents the Chambers Brothers, the Nice and King Crimson on Thursday, Friday, Saturday & Sunday the 11th, 12th, 13th & 14th at the Fillmore West with lights by Little Princess 109. It was during these shows that Greg Lake and Keith Emerson strike up a relationship that would eventually lead to the formation of Emerson Lake & Palmer.

12th December – 1969

- Bill Graham presents Richie Havens, Nina Simone and Isaac Hayes on Friday & Saturday the 12th & 13th at the Fillmore East in New York City with the Joshua Light Show.

14th December – 1969

- Bill Graham presents the Incredible String Band on Sunday the 14th at the Fillmore East in New York City with the Joshua Light Show.

18th December – 1969

- Bill Graham presents Santana, Grand Funk Railroad and Fat Matress with Noel Redding on Thursday, Friday, Saturday & Sunday the 18th, 19th, 20th & 21st at the Winterland with lights by the Brotherhood of Light.

19th December – 1969

- The Grateful Dead, Oceola and the Rhythm Dukes (Moby Grape) perform on Friday & Saturday the 19th & 20th at the Old Fillmore on Fillmore and Geary. It's now called the New-Old Fillmore! This turns out to be the Grateful Dead's last performance at the "old' Fillmore.
- Bill Graham presents the Byrds, the Nice, Sons of Champlin and Dion on Friday & Saturday the 19th & 20th at the Fillmore East in New York City with the Joshua Light Show.

26th December – 1969

- Bill Graham presents Sly & the Family Stone, Spirit, Southwind and Ballin' Jack on Friday, Saturday & Sunday the 26th, 27th & 28th at the Winterland with lights by Little Princess 109.
- Bill Graham presents Blood Sweat & Tears, Appaloosa and the Allman Brothers on Friday, Saturday & Sunday the 26th, 27th & 28th at the Winterland with lights by the Joshua Light Show.

29th December – 1969

- The Grateful Dead perform on Monday, Tuesday & Wednesday the 29th, 30th & 31st at the Boston Tea Party, 15 Lansdowne Street in Boston.

31st December - 1969

- Bill Graham presents Santana, It's a Beautiful Day, the Elvin Bishop Group and Joy of Cooking on Wednesday the 31st perform a New Years Show at the Fillmore West with lights by Little Princess 109.
- Bill Graham presents Jimi Hendrix and the Voices of East Harlem Wednesday the 31st at the Fillmore East in New York City with the Joshua Light Show.
- Bill Graham presents Jefferson Airplane, Quicksilver Messenger Service, the Sons and Hot Tuna on Wednesday the 31st perform a New Years Show at the Winterland with lights by the Brotherhood of Light.
- Bill Graham presents Lee Michaels, Love, the Youngbloods, Taj Mahal, Wolfgang and Southwind play a New Years Eve Party Wednesday the 31st at the Olympic Auditorium, Los Angeles.
- A "New Years Eve Bash" is held on Wednesday, Thursday & Friday the 31st, 1st & 2nd at the Armadillo World Headquarters featuring Doug Kershaw, Skyrocket and Tiger Balm, in Austin Texas.

TIMELINE - 1970

1st January – 1970

- Bill Graham presents the Band of Gypsies on Thursday the 1st at the Fillmore East. For this New Years Day concert Jimi Hendrix introduces his new band consisting of Billy Cox and Buddy Miles. The concert is recorded and released under the title **Band of Gypsies**.

2nd January – 1970

- Bill Graham presents the Grateful Dead, Lighthouse and Cold Blood on Friday & Saturday the 2nd & 3rd at the Fillmore East with lights by the Joshua Light Show.

2nd January – 1970

- Bill Graham presents the Byrds, Fleetwood Mac and John Hammond on Friday, Saturday & Sunday the 2nd, 3rd & 4th at the Fillmore West with lights by the Brotherhood of Light.

8th January – 1970

- Bill Graham presents Chicago, Guess Who and Seals & Croft on Thursday, Friday, Saturday & Sunday the 8th, 9th, 10th & 11th at the Fillmore West with lights by Little Princess 109.

9th January – 1970

- Bill Graham presents Ike & Tina Turner, Mongo Santamaria and Fats Domino on Friday & Saturday the 9th & 10th at the Fillmore East with lights by the Joshua Light Show.

10th January – 1970

- KQPI presents the Grateful Dead, Savoy Brown and Aum on Saturday the 10th at the Convention Hall Community Concourse in San Diego, California.
- Pink Floyd perform on Saturday the 10th at the University of Nottingham, Nottingham, England.

15th January – 1970

- Bill Graham presents B. B. King, Buddy Guy and the Allman Brothers on Thursday, Friday, Saturday & Sunday the 15th, 16th, 17th & 18th at the Fillmore West with Visionary Lights.

16th January – 1970

- Bill Graham presents Santana, James Gang and Catfish on Friday & Saturday the 16th & 17th at the Fillmore East with lights by the Joshua Light Show.
- Jim Felt presents the Grateful Dead and River on Friday the 16th at Springer's Ballroom in Portland Oregon.

22nd January – 1970

- Bill Graham presents Albert King, Savoy Brown and Zephyr on Thursday, Friday, Saturday & Sunday the 22nd, 23rd, 24th & 25th at the Fillmore West with lights by the Brotherhood of Light.

23rd January – 1970

- Bill Graham presents Quicksilver Messenger Service, Country Joe & the Fish and Eric Mercury on Friday & Saturday the 23rd & 24th at the Fillmore East with lights by the Joshua Light Show.

24th January – 1970

- Bill Graham presents Laura Nyro on Saturday the 24th at the Berkley Community Theatre.
- Musical inventor Robert Moog introduces his "Mini-Moog" available for about $2000. While the musician's union considers banning the instrument for its ability to duplicate sounds created by real musicians, the Mini-Moog and other synthesizers would go on to revolutionize the Creation of music.

24th January – 1970

- The "Free John Sinclair" Ralley is held in Detroit on Saturday & Sunday the 24th & 25th at the Grande Ballroom. It featured performances from; SRC, MC5, Up, Stooges, Scorpion, Commander Cody, Amboy Dukes, Bob Seger System, Mitch Ryder and the Detroit Wheels, Virgin Dawn, Wilson Mower Pursuit, Rationals, Jagged Edge, Richmond, All the Lonely People, Sky, Brownsville Station, Sunday Funnies, Shakey Jake, Blues Train and 3rd Power. Plus speeches from Abbie Hoffman, Ken Cockrell, Skip Taube and Ed Saunders.

28th January – 1970

- The Vietnam Moratorium Committee stage a seven hour benefit on Wednesday the 28th featuring the performances of Jimi Hendrix, the Rascals, Blood Sweat and Tears, Peter Paul and Mary, Judy Collins, Richie Havens, the Voices of East Harlem, Dave Brubeck, Harry Bellefonte, Mother Earth and the cast of Hair. The event raised $143,000 dollars in support of stopping the war in Vietnam.

29th January – February – 1070

- Bill Graham presents the Steve Miller Band, Sha-Na-Na and Ten Wheel Drive with Genya Ravan on Thursday, Friday, Saturday & Sunday the 29th, 30th, 31st & 1st at the Fillmore West with lights by Little Princess 109.

30th January – 1970

- Bill Graham presents Jack Bruce and Mountain on Friday & Saturday the 30th & 31st at the Fillmore East with lights by the Joshua Light Show.
- The Grateful Dead are performing at the Warehouse in New Orleans. After the performance Tom Constanten is busted by police. It is his last gig with the Dead.

February – 1970

- Janis Joplin flies to Rio, Brazil for a long vacation to "get off drugs and dry out."

5th February – 1970

- Bill Graham presents the Doors, Cold Blood, Doug Kershaw and Commander Cody on Thursday & Friday the 5th & 6th at the Winterland with lights by Holy See.
- Bill Graham presents the Grateful Dead, Taj Mahal and Big Foot on Thursday, Friday, Saturday & Sunday the 5th, 6th, 7th & 8th at the Fillmore West with lights by the Brotherhood of Light.
- The Cardiff Arts Centre project benefit Concert is held in Cardiff, Wales on Thursday the 5th featuring Pink Floyd, Quintessence, Daddy Longlegs, Gary Farr, Heaven, Ron Geesin, Tea & Symphony and Black Sabbath.

6th February – 1970

- Bill Graham presents Delaney & Bonnie with Eric Clapton, Wilbur Harrison and Seals & Crofts on Friday & Saturday the 6th & 7th at the Fillmore East with lights by the Joshua Light Show.

11th February – 1970

- Bill Graham presents the Magic Sam Memorial Concert on Wednesday the 11th at the Fillmore West. Performing are Paul Butterfield, Michael Bloomfield, Elvin Bishop, Charley Musselwhite and Nick Gravenites.
- Bill Graham presents the Grateful Dead, Love and Allman Brothers on Friday, Saturday & Sunday the 11th, 12th & 13th at the Fillmore East in New York City with the Joshua Light Show.
- Delaney and Bonnie with Eric Clapton and B.B. King perform on Wednesday the

11th at the Electric Factory in Philadelphia, Pennsylvania.
- Pink Floyd perform on Wednesday the 11th at the Birmingham Town Hall, England.

12th February – 1970
- Bill Graham presents Country Joe and the Fish, the Sons (of Champlin) and Area Code 615 on Thursday, Friday, Saturday & Sunday the 12th, 13th 14th & 15th at the Fillmore West.

19th February – 1970
- Bill Graham presents Delaney & Bonnie & Friends, Eric Clapton, New York Rock & Roll Ensemble and Golden Earrings on Thursday, Friday, Saturday & Sunday the 19th, 20th, 21st & 22nd at the Fillmore West with lights by Little Princess 109.

20th February – 1970
- Bill Graham presents Savoy Brown, Voices of East Harlem, Renaissance and Noonan on Friday & Saturday the 20th & 21st at the Fillmore East with lights by the Joshua Light Show.
- Middle Earth productions presents a "War over…Peace at Last" concert on Friday the 20th featuring the Quicksilver Messenger Service and the Grateful Dead at the Panther Hall in Fort Worth, Texas.

23rd February – 1970
- Bill Graham presents Jefferson Airplane, Quicksilver Messenger Service, Santana, It's a Beautiful Day and Dan Hicks and his Hot Licks on Monday the 23rd at the Winterland with lights by Glenn McKay's Headlights.

26th February – 1970
- Bill Graham presents Jack Bruce & Friends, Johnny Winter, Mountain, and Eric Mercury on Thursday and Sunday the 26th & 1st at the Fillmore West and Friday & Saturday the 27th & 28th at the Winterland with lights by Dry Paint.
- Bill Graham presents Ten Years After and Zephyr on Thursday the 26th at the Fillmore East in New York City with the Joshua Light Show.

27th February – 1970
- Bill Graham presents Ten Years After, John Hammond, Zephyr and Doug Kershaw on Friday & Saturday the 27th & 28th at the Fillmore East with lights by the Joshua Light Show.

3rd March - 1970
- The Benefit for Air Waves Peoples Radio is held on Tuesday the 3rd at the Carousel Ballroom with the Grateful Dead, Shades of Joy, the Gestalt Fool Theatre Family and the New Generation Singers.

5th March – 1970
- Bill Graham presents the Paul Butterfield Blues Band, Savoy Brown and Keith

Relf's Renaissance on Thursday, Friday, Saturday & Sunday the 5th, 6th, 7th & 8th at the Fillmore West with lights Brotherhood of Light.

6th March – 1970

- Bill Graham presents Neil Young & Crazy Horse, Miles Davis Quintet and the Steve Miller Band on Friday & Saturday the 6th & 7th at the Fillmore East with lights by the Joshua Light Show.
- Pink Floyd and Juicy Lucy perform on Friday the 6th at the Great Hall, Imperial College, London, England.

7th March – 1970

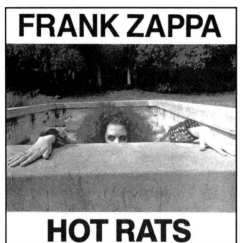

FRANK ZAPPA

HOT RATS

- Bill Graham presents Frank Zappa and Hot Rats and Johnny Winter on Saturday the 7th at the Olympic Auditorium in Los Angeles.
- Pink Floyd perform on Saturday the 7th at the University of Bristol Arts Festival, Bristol England.

11th March – 1970

- Pink Floyd embark on a two-week tour of Europe.

12th March – 1970

- Bill Graham presents Ten Years After, Buddy Rich and his Orchestra, Sea Train and Kimberly on Thursday, Friday, Saturday & Sunday the 12th, 13th, 14th & 15th at the Fillmore West with lights by Little Princess 109.

13th March – 1970

- Bill Graham presents John Mayall, B.B. King, Taj Mahal and Duster Bennett on Friday & Saturday the 13th & 14th at the Fillmore East in New York City with the Joshua Light Show.

15th March – 1970

- Bill Graham presents John Mayall, Taj Mahal and Leon Thomas on Sunday the 15th at the Fillmore East in New York City with the Joshua Light Show.

19th March – 1970

- Bill Graham presents It's a Beautiful Day, Chuck Berry and Loading Zone on Thursday, Friday, Saturday & Sunday the 19th, 20th, 21st & 22nd at the Fillmore West with lights by Deadly Nightshade.
- Bill Graham presents the Moody Blues, Lee Michaels and Argent on Friday &

Saturday the 19th & 20th at the Fillmore East in New York City with the Joshua Light Show.

23rd March – 1970
• Spencer Dryden quits Jefferson Airplane after an argument with Marty Balin.

26th March – 1970
• Bill Graham presents Chicago, James Cotton Blues Band, Family and Fritz on Thursday & Sunday the 26th & 29th at the Fillmore West and Friday & Saturday the 27th & 28th at the Winterland with lights by Brotherhood of Light.

27th March – 1970
• Bill Graham presents Joe Cocker, Ronnie Hawkins and Stone the Crows on Friday & Saturday the 27th & 28th at the Fillmore East in New York City with the Joshua Light Show.

April – 1970
• Janis Joplin disbands the Kozmic Blues Band and forms the much stronger Full Tilt Boogie Band.

2nd April – 1970
• Bill Graham presents Jethro Tull and Manfred Mann on Thursday, Friday, Saturday & Sunday the 2nd, 3rd, 4th & 5th at the Fillmore West with lights by Little Princess 109.
• Bill Graham presents the Moody Blues and Tom Rush on night only Thursday the 2nd at the Berkeley Community Center.

3rd April – 1970
• Bill Graham presents Quicksilver Messenger Service, Van Morrison and Brinsley Schwarz on Friday & Saturday the 3rd & 4th at the Fillmore East in New York City with the Joshua Light Show.

5th April – 1970
• Bill Graham presents Tom Paxton and Fraser & Debolt on Sunday the 5th at the Fillmore East in New York City with the Joshua Light Show.

9th April – 1970
• Bill Graham presents the Grateful Dead, Miles Davis Quartet and Stone the Crows on Thursday, Friday, Saturday & Sunday the 9th, 10th, 11th & 12th at the Fillmore West with lights by the Brotherhood of Light.
• Quicksilver Messenger Service, Sugar Creek and Roxy perform on Thursday, Friday & Saturday the 9th, 10th & 11th at the Boston Tea Party in Boston.
• Bill Graham presents Pink Floyd on Thursday the 9th at the Fillmore East in New York City. This is Pink Floyd's third U.S. tour and the first with the newly designed quad-sound Azimuth Controller.

10th April - 1970
- Paul McCartney announces the Beatles are finished, citing personal differences. He follows that up with the comment that he will no longer record with John Lennon.
- Bill Graham presents Santana, It's a Beautiful Day and American Dream on Friday, Saturday & Sunday the 10th, 11th & 12th at the Fillmore East in New York City with the Joshua Light Show.
- Pink Floyd perform on Friday the 10th with Rotary Connection, Mason Profit and Litter at the Aragon Ballroom, Chicago, Illinois.

11th April – 1970
- Bill Graham presents Richie Havens and Turley Richards for one night only Saturday the 11th at the Berkeley Community Center.
- Keith Emerson of the Nice and Greg Lake of King Crimson are currently auditioning drummers for the group that will eventually become Emerson Lake and Palmer.

12th April – 1970
- Bill Graham presents John Sebastian and Poco for one night only Sunday the 12th at the Berkeley Community Center.

16th April – 1970
- Bill Graham presents John Mayall, Larry Coryell and Argent on Thursday, Friday, Saturday & Sunday the 16th, 17th, 18th & 19th at the Fillmore West with lights by Little Princess 109.
- Bill Graham presents Pink Floyd on Thursday the 16th at the Fillmore East in New York City.

17th April – 1970
- Bill Graham presents Ray Charles and Dizzy Gillespie on Friday & Saturday the 17th & 18th at the Fillmore East in New York City with the Joshua Light Show.
- Pink Floyd supported by Insect Trust perform on Friday & Saturday the 17th & 18th at the Electric Factory in Philadelphia, Pennsylvania.

19th April – 1970
- Bill Graham presents Frank Zappa and his Hot Rats and Boz Scaggs for one night only Sunday the 19th at the Berkeley Community Center.

22nd April – 1970
- The first Earth Day is celebrated. Millions take part in activities.

23rd April – 1970
- Bill Graham presents Joe Cocker, Van Morrison and Stonemans on Thursday & Sunday the 23rd & 26th at the Fillmore West with lights by Dry Paint and the

evenings of Friday & Saturday the 24th & 25th at the Winterland with lights by Brotherhood of Light.
- Bill Graham presents the Incredible String Band and the Stone Monkey Mime Troup on Thursday – Sunday the 23rd – 26th at the Fillmore East in New York City with the Joshua Light Show.

25th April – 1970
- The "Brown Spring Weekend" takes place on Saturday & Sunday the 25th & 26th at Brown University in Providence Rhode Island, with performances from the Jefferson Airplane, Delaney and Bonnie and Friends, John Mayall, James Taylor, Ray Charles, and Judy Collins.
- The Marquee Club in London features the first headline of Status Quo on Saturday the 25th. They will make 10 more appearances at the Marquee.

29th April – 1970
- Bill Graham presents Pink Floyd on Wednesday the 29th at the Fillmore West.

30th April – 1970
- Bill Graham presents Jethro Tull, Fairport Convention, Salt'n Pepper and Clouds on Thursday, Friday, Saturday & Sunday the 30th, 1st, 2nd & 3rd at the Fillmore West with lights by Little Princess 109. Jethro Tull did not perform on Sunday.

1st May – 1970
- Bill Graham presents Mountain and Ambergris on Friday & Saturday the 1st & 2nd at the Fillmore East in New York City with the Joshua Light Show.

4th May – 1970
- Four students are killed at Kent State University when the National Guard opens fire. The students are protesting the escalation of the Vietnam War. Neil Young commemorates the event in his composition "Ohio".

6th May – 1970
- Bill Graham presents Jefferson Airplane and Manfred Mann: Chapter Three on Wednesday & Thursday the 6th & 7th at the Fillmore East in New York City with the Joshua Light Show.

7th May – 1970
- Bill Graham presents Lee Michaels, Small Faces, Catfish and Shorty on Thursday, Friday, Saturday & Sunday the 7th, 8th, 9th & 10th at the Fillmore West with lights by the Brotherhood of Light.

8th May – 1970
- Bill Graham presents the Mothers of Invention, Insect Trust and Sea Train on Friday & Saturday the 8th & 9th at the Fillmore East in New York City with the Joshua Light Show.

9th May – 1970

* 100,000 protesters attend an antiwar rally in Washington, DC.
* Pink Floyd perform with Blue Mountain Eagle on Saturday the 9th at the Terrace Ballroom, Salt Lake City, Utah.

11th May – 1970

* Bill Graham presents the Incredible String Band on Monday the 11th and Wednesday the 13th at the Fillmore West.

12th May – 1970

* Pink Floyd play in support of the Guess Who on Tuesday the 12th at the Municipal Auditorium in Atlanta, Georgia.

14th May – 1970

* Bill Graham presents Spirit, Poco and Gypsy on Thursday, Friday, Saturday & Sunday the 14th, 15th, 16th & 17th at the Fillmore West with lights by Little Princess 109.

15th May – 1970

* Iggy and the Stooges, Flamin Groovies, Alice Cooper, Commander Cody and Purple Earthquake, perform on Friday & Saturday the 15th & 16th at the New Old Fillmore on Fillmore and Geary.
* Bill Graham presents the Grateful Dead with New Riders of the Purple Sage on Friday the 15th at the Fillmore East in New York City with the Joshua Light Show.

16th May – 1970

* Jefferson Airplane singer Marty Balin is arrested for possession of Marijuana and the delinquency of a minor in Bloomington, Minnesota. He is eventually sentenced to a year of hard labour and a $100 fine. On appeal he ends up simply paying the fine.
* Bill Graham presents the Guess Who, Cold Blood and Buddy Miles on Saturday the 16th at the Fillmore East in New York City with the Joshua Light Show.
* Pink Floyd perform with the Allman Brothers Band and Country Funk on Saturday the 16th at the Warehouse, New Orleans, Louisiana. Following this performance that band's gear worth some $40,000 was stolen. The FBI recovered it within hours.

21st May - 1970

* Bill Graham presents B.B. King, Albert King and Mendelbaum on Thursday, Friday, Saturday & Sunday the 21st, 22nd, 23rd & 24th at the Fillmore West with lights by Crimson Madness.
* Mighty Baby, Hawkwind, Medicine Head and Innocent Child play on Thursday the 21st at the Casino South Shore, Blackpool with lights by the Lumina Lightshow.

22nd May – 1970

- Bill Graham presents Jethro Tull, Clouds and John Sebastian on Friday & Saturday the 22nd & 23rd at the Fillmore East in New York City with the Joshua Light Show.
- Pink Floyd play in support of Grand Funk Railroad on Friday the 22nd at the Houston Music Theatre, Houston, Texas. The following evening they played Dallas, Texas.

23rd May - 1970

- THE HOLLYWOOD FESTIVAL, Madeley, Newcastle-under-Lyme, Staffordshire is held on Saturday & Sunday the 23rd & 24th with (Saturday) Demon Fuzz, Trader Horne, Screaming Lord Sutch, Mungo Jerry, Family, Titus Groan, Mike Cooper, Ginger Bakers Airforce, Tony Joe White. (Sunday) The Flaming Groovies, Black Sabbath, Wildmouth, Quintessence, Colosseum, Free, Grateful Dead, Mungo Jerry, Jose Feliciano, Traffic. This is the Grateful Dead's first British concert. They played a FOUR-HOUR set.

28th May – 1970

- Bill Graham presents Country Joe and the Fish, Blues Image and Silver Metre on Thursday, Friday, Saturday & Sunday the 28th, 29th, 30th & 31st at the Fillmore West with lights by the Brotherhood of Light.

29th May – 1970

- Bill Graham presents James Taylor and Pentangle on Friday the 29th at the Berkeley Community Theatre.
- Bill Graham presents Nina Simone and Mongo Santamaria on Friday & Saturday the 29th & 30th at the Fillmore East in New York City with the Joshua Light Show.
- Direct Productions presents the Guess Who, Albert King and Taos on Friday the 29th at the Tarrant County Convention Centre in Forth Worth Texas.
- The Marquee Club in London features Arthur Brown and Pacific Drift on Friday the 29th.

30th May – 1970

- Pink Floyd appear on the film soundtrack **Zabriski Point** released on this day.
- Bill Graham presents Jimi

Hendrix with Mitch Mitchell and Billy Cox on Saturday the 30th at the Berkeley Community Theatre.

2nd June – 1970

- Bill Graham presents Crosby Stills Nash & Young on Tuesday – Sunday the 2nd – 7th at the Fillmore East in New York City with the Joshua Light Show.

3rd June – 1970

- The Jimi Hendrix album **Band of Gypsies** goes Gold.

4th June – 1970

- Bill Graham presents the Grateful Dead, New Riders of the Purple Sage and Southern Comfort on Thursday, Friday, Saturday & Sunday the 4th, 5th, 6th & 7th at the Fillmore West with lights by Dr. Zarkov.

7th June – 1970

- The final performances of **Tommy** by the Who take place Sunday the 7th at the Lincoln Centre in New York.

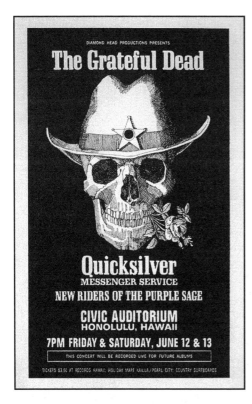

DIAMOND HEAD PRODUCTIONS PRESENTS

The Grateful Dead

Quicksilver
MESSENGER SERVICE
NEW RIDERS OF THE PURPLE SAGE

CIVIC AUDITORIUM
HONOLULU, HAWAII

7PM FRIDAY & SATURDAY, JUNE 12 & 13

THIS CONCERT WILL BE RECORDED LIVE FOR FUTURE ALBUMS

TICKETS $3.50 AT RECORDS HAWAII, HOLIDAY MART KAILUA / PEARL CITY, COUNTRY SURFBOARDS

10th June – 1970

- Bill Graham presents Traffic, Fairport Convention and Mott the Hoople on Wednesday & Thursday the 10th & 11th at the Fillmore East in New York City with the Joshua Light Show.

11th June – 1970

- Bill Graham presents John Sebastian, Buddy Miles & Rig on Thursday, Friday, Saturday & Sunday the 11th, 12th 13th & 14th at the Fillmore West with lights by Little Princess 109.

12th June – 1970

- Bill Graham presents Procol Harum, Rhinoceros and Seals & Crofts on Friday & Saturday the 12th & 13th at the Fillmore East in New York City with the Joshua Light Show.
- Diamond Head Productions presents the Grateful Dead, Quicksilver Messenger Service and New Riders of the Purple Sage on Friday & Saturday the 12th & 13th at the Civic Auditorium in Honolulu, Hawaii.

13th June – 1970

• American Tribal Productions presents Traffic, SRC, Bloomsbury People, and Edmunds and Curley on Saturday the 13th at the Aragon Ballroom 1106 West Lawrence in Chicago Illinois.

14th June – 1970

• The Grateful Dead release **Workingman's Dead** which features a more roots almost country flavour, a marked departure from their earlier psychedelic style.

16th June – 1970

• Woodstock Ventures, the people responsible for staging the Woodstock Festival report they lost $1.2 million dollars over the three days, but hope to recoup some of their investment from the revolutionary documentary film and various Woodstock memorabilia.

17th June – 1970

• Bill Graham presents Laura Nyro and Miles Davis on Wednesday-Saturday the 17th – 20th at the Fillmore East in New York City with the Joshua Light Show.

18th June – 1970

• Bill Graham presents Quicksilver Messenger Service, Don Ellis and his Orchestra and Rockwell on Thursday, Friday, Saturday & Sunday the 18th, 19th, 20th & 21st at the Fillmore West with lights by the Brotherhood of Light.

24th June – 1970

• Bill Graham presents Ten Years After, Illinois Speed Press and Catfish on Wednesday & Thursday the 24th & 25th at the Fillmore East in New York City with the Joshua Light Show.

25th June – 1970

• Bill Graham presents Sha-Na-Na, Pacific Gas & Electric and Dan Hicks & his Hot Licks on Thursday, Friday, Saturday & Sunday the 25th, 26th, 27th & 28th at the Fillmore West with lights by Ambercrombie.

26th June – 1970

• Bill Graham presents Chicago, Blodwyn Pig and the Jerry Hahn Brotherhood on Friday & Saturday the 26th & 27th at the Fillmore East in New York City with the Joshua Light Show.
• American Tribal Productions presents Ten Years After, B.B. King, Brownsville Station, and Mott the Hoople on Friday the 26th at the Aragon Ballroom 1106 West Lawrence in Chicago Illinois.

27th June - 1970

• The "Bath Festival Of Blues and Progressive Music '70" Bath and West Showground, Shepton Mallet is held on Saturday & Sunday the 27th & 28th.

Featured artists were: (Saturday 27th) John Mayall, Jack Bruce, Pink Floyd, Fairport, Colosseum, It's A Beautiful Day, Keef Hartley, Maynard Ferguson Big Band, Canned Heat and Johnny Winter. (Sunday 28th) Jefferson Airplane, Hot Tuna, Led Zeppelin, Frank Zappa, Steppenwolf, Moody Blues, Byrds, Flock, Santana, Dr. John and Country Joe. Pink Floyd take the opportunity to premier their latest concept, **Atom Heart Mother**. History shows this festival attracted twice the number expected as a rough estimate of 150,000 showed up to watch the distinctly "West-Coast" show. This festival would later inspire Michael Eavis to produce the Glastonbury Festival that continues to this day.

- Eaton-Walker Associates presents the Trans-Continental Pop Festival on Saturday & Sunday the 27th & 28th at the Canadian National Exhibition in Toronto. This two day event featured The Band, Janis Joplin, Grateful Dead, Delaney & Bonnie, Mashmakan, Cat, Ten Years After, Traffic, James and the Good Brothers, Charlebois, Ian and Sylvia with the Great Speckled Bird, Buddy Guy, Eric Anderson, Mountain, Tom Rush, Seatrain and Melanie. This tour would also perform in the Canadian cities of Montreal, Winnipeg and Calgary.

- The Holland Pop Festival '70 is held in Rotterdam, Netherlands on Saturday & Sunday the 27th & 28th featuring many of the same artists from the Bath Festival. Sponsored by Coca Cola performing artists included Pink Floyd, Jefferson Airplane, Santana, Flock, Canned Heat, Hot Tuna, Quintessence, East of Eden, Byrds, Family, Dr. John, Country Joe, Tyrannosaurus Rex, Renaissance, Third Ear band, Al Stewart, Soft Machine, Chicago Art Ensemble, John Surman, Caravan, Fairport Convention, Fotheringay and others.

30th June – July – 1970

- Bill Graham presents Traffic, John Hammond and Lamb in a mid-week special Tuesday, Wednesday & Thursday the 30th, 1st & 2nd at the Fillmore West with lights by the Brotherhood of Light.

3rd July – 1970

- American Tribal Productions presents, the Grateful Dead, It's a Beautiful Day and Rare Bird Friday the 3rd at the Aragon Ballroom, 1106 West Lawrence in Chicago Illinois.

- The 2nd Atlanta International Pop Festival is held on Friday, Saturday & Sunday the 3rd, 4th & 5th at the Middle Georgia Raceway in Atlanta. Performing are; Procol Harum, Allman Brothers, B.B. King, It's a Beautiful Day, Captain Beefheart and his Magic Band, Chambers Brothers, Mountain, Ginger Baker's Air Force, Richie Havens, Jimi Hendrix, Hampton Grease band, Taos, Ballin' Jack, Bloodrock, Lee Michaels, John B. Sebastian, Jethro Tull, Ten Years After, Spirit, Ravi Shankar, Terry Reid, Cactus, Gypsy and Johnny Winter. Of note here is that many years on from the heyday of the 1967 Summer of Love, the San Francisco bands were still much in demand. Of equal interest is that with the success of the two festivals in Atlanta, the world became aware of the growing "Southern-Rock" style. Some 200,000 would witness this festival, but as the festival draws to a close local authorities try to declare the area a health disaster area because of the rampant drug use.

7th July - 1970

- New Riders of the Purple Sage play on Tuesday the 7th at the Matrix Club, San Francisco.
- Bill Graham presents "The Fillmore at Tanglewood" featuring the Who, Jethro Tull and It's a Beautiful Day on Tuesday the 7th at Tanglewood in Lenox, Massachusetts, with a special giant screen magnification video from Joshua Television.

9th July – 1970

- Bill Graham presents Quicksilver Messenger Service, Mott the Hoople and Silver Metre on Thursday, Friday, Saturday & Sunday the 9th, 10th, 11th & 12th at the Fillmore West with lights by Brotherhood of Light.
- Bill Graham presents the Grateful Dead featuring the New Riders of the Purple Sage on Thursday, Friday, Saturday & Sunday the 9th, 10th, 11th & 12th at the Fillmore East in New York City with the Joshua Light Show.

10th July – 1970

- The "1st Open Air Pop Festival" is held in Aachen, West Germany on Friday, Saturday & Sunday the 10th, 11th & 12th. Featured artist were: Tase, Harden & York, Keef Hartley, If, Fat Matress, Champion Jack Dupree, Quintessence, Caravan, Golden Earing, Amon Duul II, Kevin Ayers & the Whole World, Traffic, Edgar Broughton Band, Tyrannosaurus Rex, Deep Purple and Pink Floyd.

12th July – 1970

- Janis Joplin plays her first performance with the new Full Tilt Boogie Band in Louisville Kentucky on Sunday the 12th.

14th July – 1970

- Euphoric Enterprises presents the Grateful Dead, New Riders of the Purple Sage and Rubberduck Company on Tuesday the 14th at the Euphoria in San Rafael California.

16th July – 1970

- Bill Graham presents the Steve Miller Band, Bo Diddley and Crow on Thursday, Friday, Saturday & Sunday the 16th, 17th, 18th & 19th at the Fillmore West with lights by Deadly Nightshade.

17th July – 1970

- Euphoric Enterprises presents the Youngbloods, Country Weather and Lambert & Nuttycomb on Friday, Saturday & Sunday the 17th, 18th & 19th at the Euphoria in San Rafael California.

18th July – 1970

- The Randall's Island Rock Festival turns into a disaster area when the gates are crashed and more than 30,000 slide in for free. The event is declared a financial disaster. Performing are Jimi Hendrix, Grand Funk Railroad, Little Richard, Elephant's Memory, Steppenwolf, Jethro Tull and others.

- A Free Concert in Hyde Park, London is held on Saturday the 18th featuring Pink Floyd, Roy Harper, Kevin Ayers, Edgar Broughton Band, Formerly Fat Harry and Lol Coxhill. Attendance is pegged at 20,000.

21st July – 1970

- Bill Graham presents the Fillmore at Tanglewood featuring Chicago, John Sebastian and the Preservation Hall Jazz Band on Tuesday the 21st at Tanglewood in Lenox, Massachusetts with a giant screen magnification video from Joshua Television.

23rd July – 1970

- Bill Graham presents Lee Michaels, Cold Blood and Brethren on Thursday, Friday, Saturday & Sunday the 23rd, 24th, 25th & 26th at the Fillmore West with lights by Little Princess 109.

24th July - 1970

- Bill Graham presents Hot Tuna, Leon Russell and Rig on Friday & Saturday the 24th & 25th at the Fillmore East in New York City with the Joshua Light Show.
- The "Phun City" event at Ecclesden Common, Worthing, Sussex is held on Friday, Saturday & Sunday the 24th, 25th & 26th. Organized by Mick Farren and artist Edward Barker and funded by the **International Times**. Originally intended to be a paying festival, Phun City turned into Britain's first free festival. The MC5 were on the bill but didn't play. Free were also on the bill but would not play for nothing and left the festival.... Stray, Wildmouth, J.J. Jackson, Pretty Things, Cochise, Mighty Baby, Demon Fuzz, Edgar Broughton, Kevin Ayers, Pink Fairies (playing naked!!), Quiver, Honks, Noir, Mike Chapman, Liverpool 8, Pete Brown, Sonia Christina, Roger Ruskin and Mungo Jerry do play.

28th July – 1970

- Bill Graham presents a Special Mid-Week show with Ten Years After, Cactus and Toe Fat on Tuesday, Wednesday & Thursday the 28th, 29th & 30th at the Fillmore West with lights by Anathema.

31st July – 1970

- Bill Graham presents It's a Beautiful Day, Elvin Bishop and Boz Scaggs on Friday, Saturday & Sunday the 31st, 1st & 2nd at the Fillmore West with lights by Anathema.
- Bill Graham presents Grand Funk Railroad, Pacific Gas & Electric and Bloodrock on Friday & Saturday the 31st & 1st at the Fillmore East in New York City with the Joshua Light Show.
- The Marquee Club in London features the MC5 on Friday the 31st.

3rd August – 1970

- Bill Graham presents Procol Harum, Leon Russell and Blodwyn Pig on Monday, Tuesday & Wednesday the 3rd, 4th & 5th at the Fillmore West with lights by San Francisco Light Works.

4th August – 1970

- Rocks first mobile rock festival takes the form of the Medicine Ball Caravan and starts out from San Francisco featuring the Grateful Dead. The mobile group weaves its way across the United States and ends up in the U.K.

5th August – 1970

- Bill Graham presents Jethro Tull and Cactus on Wednesday the 5th at the Fillmore East in New York City with the Joshua Light Show.

6th August – 1970

- Bill Graham presents Fleetwood Mac, Buddy Miles and Albert Collins on Thursday, Friday, Saturday & Sunday the 6th, 7th, 8th & 9th at the Fillmore West with lights by the San Francisco Light Works.
- The Tenth National Jazz and Blues Festival is held on Thursday, Friday, Saturday & Sunday the 6th, 7th, 8th & 9th at Plumpton Race Track, Streat, East Sussex. Featured acts include Jellybread, Fox, Samuel Purdy, Castle, Family, Groundhogs, Rare Bird, Steamhammer, Daddy Longlegs, Patto, Clark Hutchinson, Cat Stevens, Fotheringay, Strawbs, Magna Carta, Grannys New Intentions, Made In Sweden, Chicago Climax Blues Band, Gracious, Quatermass, Peter Green, Taste, Keef Hartley, Black Sabbath, Jackson Heights, Hardin York, Love Affair, East Of Eden, Wild Angels, Incredible String Band, Turley Richards, Every Which Way, Burnin' Red Ivanhoe, Van Der Graaf Generator, Colosseum, Yes, Juicy Lucy, Chris Barber, Caravan, Audience, Fat Mattress, Hard Meat and Tervor Bilmuss. Tickets are £2 for the weekend!!!

8th August – 1970

- Bill Graham presents Blodwyn Pig and Chicken Shack on Saturday the 8th at the Fillmore East in New York City with the Joshua Light Show.

10th August – 1970

- Bill Graham presents Santana, Ballin' Jack and the Voices of East Harlem on Monday, Tuesday & Wednesday the 10th, 11th & 12th at the Fillmore East in New York City with the Joshua Light Show.

12th August – 1970

- Janis Joplin gives her last concert performance at Harvard Stadium on Wednesday the 12th.

13th August – 1970

- Bill Graham presents the Byrds, Poco and Commander Cody on Thursday, Friday, Saturday & Sunday the 13th, 14th, 15th & 16th at the Fillmore West with lights by the Brotherhood of Light.

14th August - 1970

- Bill Graham presents Procol Harum, Country Joe McDonald and Toe Fat on Friday & Saturday the 14th & 15th at the Fillmore East in New York City with the Joshua Light Show.
- The Yorkshire Folk, Blues & Jazz Festival is held on Friday, Saturday & Sunday the 14th, 15th & 16th at Krumlin, Barkisland, Yorkshire featuring (Saturday) Atomic Rooster, Elton John, Juicy Lucy, Groundhogs, Pretty Things, Alexis Korner, Kinks, Fairport Convention, Pentangle, Ralph McTell, Pink Floyd, Taste. (Sunday) Ginger Baker's Airforce, Mungo Jerry, Taste, Edgar Broughton, Yes, Quintessence, Steamhammer, Mike Westbrook Concert Orchestra, National Head Band and Their Heavy Friends, Greatest Show On Earth, Jan Dukes De Grey and 70 Piece Choir. Pink Floyd's headlining appearance on the second day was cancelled due to heavy rain.

17th August – 1970

- Bill Graham presents the Grateful Dead and the New Riders of the Purple Sage on Monday, Tuesday & Wednesday the 17th, 18th & 19th at the Fillmore West.

18th August – 1970

- Bill Graham presents the Fillmore at Tanglewood featuring Santana, Miles Davis and Voices of East Harlem on Tuesday the 18th at Tanglewood in Lenox, Massachusetts, with a giant screen magnification video from Joshua Television.

20th August – 1970

- Bill Graham presents Albert King, Cold Blood and Mason Proffit on Thursday, Friday, Saturday & Sunday the 20th, 21st, 22nd & 23rd at the Fillmore West with lights by Crimson Madness.

21st August – 1970

- Bill Graham presents the Youngbloods, Blues Image and Tim Hardin on Friday & Saturday the 21st & 22nd at the Fillmore East in New York City with the Joshua Light Show.
- Ramon-Ramon and the 4-Daddyos, T. Thelonius Troll perform on Friday & Saturday the 21st & 22nd at the Armadillo World Headquarters in Austin Texas.

24th August – 1970

- Bill Graham presents Iron Butterfly, Aum and Black Oak Arkansas on Monday, Tuesday & Wednesday the 24th, 25th & 26th at the Fillmore West with lights by Little Princess 109.

26th August – 1970

- The 1970 Isle of Wight Pop Festival is held on Wednesday the 26th through Monday the 31st with performances from Jimi Hendrix, Bob Dylan, Joan Baez, Richie Havens, Joni Mitchell, Emerson Lake and Palmer and many others. The festival draws some 250,000-concert goers and is later released on record.

27th August – 1970

- Bill Graham presents John Mayall, Elvin Bishop and the Herbie Hancock Sextet on Thursday, Friday & Saturday the 27th, 28th & 29th at the Fillmore West with lights by Little Princess 109.

28th August – 1970

- Bill Graham presents Savoy Brown, Fleetwood Mac, Fairport Convention and Jake & the Family Jewels on Friday & Saturday the 28th & 29th at the Fillmore East in New York City with the Joshua Light Show.

30th August – 1970

- Bill Graham presents Van Morrison and John Lee Hooker on Sunday the 30th at the Berkeley Community Theatre.

30th August – 1970

- Bill Graham presents Savoy Brown, Fairport Convention and Chicken Shack on Sunday, Monday & Tuesday 30th, 31st & 1st at the Fillmore West with lights by Little Princess 109.

2nd September – 1970

- Bill Graham presents Led Zeppelin on Wednesday the 2nd at the Oakland Coliseum.

3rd September – 1970

- Canned Heat singer/guitarist, Al Wilson is found dead in a garden belonging to band member Bob Hite. An empty bottle of barbiturates is found by his side.
- Bill Graham presents Johnny Winter, Boz Scaggs and Freddie King on Thursday, Friday, Saturday & Sunday the 3rd, 4th, 5th & 6th at the Fillmore West with lights by Brotherhood of Lights.

5th September – 1970
- The No.1 album on the U.K. charts is the Moody Blues' **A Question of Balance** while in the U.S. the No.1 LP is Creedence Clearwater Revival's **Cosmo's Factory**.

10th September – 1970
- Bill Graham presents Santana, Dr. John the Night Tripper and Luther Allison on Thursday, Friday, Saturday & Sunday the 10th, 11th, 12th & 13th at the Fillmore West with lights by Heavy Water.

11th September – 1970
- Bill Graham presents the Byrds, Delaney & Bonnie and Friends and Great Jones on Friday & Saturday the 11th & 12th at the Fillmore East in New York City with the Joshua Light Show.

12th September - 1970
- A Free Concert in Hyde Park, London is held on Saturday the 12th featuring Canned Heat, Eric Burdon and War and John Sebastian.

14th September – 1970
- Bill Graham presents the Jefferson Airplane on Monday & Tuesday the 14th & 15th at the Fillmore West.

16th September – 1970
- A poll in the British music paper **Melody Maker** shows that for the first time Led Zeppelin has replaced the Beatles as Britain's most popular group.

17th September - 1970
- Jimi Hendrix dies from a combination of alcohol and barbiturates in his London apartment. He's 27 years old.
- Bill Graham presents Quicksilver Messenger Service, Buddy Miles and Robert Savage on Thursday, Friday, Saturday & Sunday the 17th, 18th, 19th & 20th at the Fillmore West with lights by Little Princess 109.
- Bill Graham presents the Grateful Dead featuring the New Riders of the Purple Sage on Thursday, Friday, Saturday & Sunday the 17th, 18th, 19th & 20th at the Fillmore East in New York City with the Joshua Light Show.

20th September – 1970
- In Miami Jim Morrison is acquitted of the charges of "Lewd and Lascivious" behavior, but is found guilty of indecent exposure and profanity.
- It's a Beautiful Day, the Byrds and Lamb perform on Sunday the 20th at the University of the Pacific in Stockton, California.

24th September – 1970
- Bill Graham presents Chuck Berry, Buddy Miles and Loading Zone on Thursday,

Friday, Saturday & Sunday the 25th, 25th, 26th & 27th at the Fillmore West with lights by Ambercrombie.

25th September – 1970

- Frank Zappa and the Mothers of Invention, Tim Buckley and Kindred perform on Friday & Saturday the 25th & 26th at Pepperland in San Rafael, California.
- Bill Graham presents Steve Miller, Mungo Jerry and Clouds on Friday & Saturday the 25th & 26th at the Fillmore East in New York City with the Joshua Light Show.

26th September – 1970

- Pink Floyd undertake their biggest tour of the United States and Canada. It will continue through to the 23rd of October.

1st October – 1970

- Pink Floyd release **Atom Heart Mother.**
- Bill Graham presents Eric Burdon and War, Seals & Crofts and Clover on Thursday, Friday, Saturday & Sunday the 1st, 2nd, 3rd & 4th at the Fillmore West with lights by the San Francisco Light Show.

2nd October – 1970

- Chicago's Aragon Ballroom bans all future rock and roll shows following an incident during a performance by the jazz-rock band Flock. A 19 year-old member of the audience under the influence of LSD, while detained broke through an upstairs window. In the fall he suffered serious injuries. Ballroom manager Scott Deneen issues a statement expressing the ballroom's concern about no longer being able to guarantee the safety and security of those attending rock performances.
- Bill Graham presents Johnny Winter & Buddy Miles and Tin House on Friday & Saturday the 2nd & 3rd at the Fillmore East in New York City with the Joshua Light Show.

4th October - 1970

- Janis Joplin dies from an overdose of heroin and alcohol, alone in the Landmark Hotel room in Hollywood. She had just finished recording her second solo album **Pearl**.
- The Grateful Dead, Jefferson Airplane, Quicksilver Messenger Service, Hot Tuna and the New Riders of the Purple Sage take part in the first-ever live Quadraphonic FM radio simulcast from the Winterland on Sunday the 4th. Before the series of performances were over, Marty Balin left Jefferson Airplane and John Cipollina left Quicksilver.

8th October – 1970

- Bill Graham presents Van Morrison, Captain Beefheart and his Magic Band and the Terry Hahn Brotherhood on Thursday, Friday, Saturday & Sunday the 8th, 9th, 10th & 11th at the Fillmore West with lights by Anathema.

9th October – 1970

- Bill Graham presents John Mayall, It's a Beautiful Day and Flock on Friday & Saturday the 9th & 10th at the Fillmore East in New York City with the Joshua Light Show.
- "Two Masters of the Blues" – Freddie King and Mance Lipscomb perform on Friday & Saturday the 9th & 10th at Armadillo World Headquarters in Austin Texas. Support provided by Storm, Wildfire, and Ginger Valley.

12th October – 1970

- Rock impresario Bill Graham holds an auction on Monday the 12th of assorted rock memorabilia to benefit the 1970 peace candidates. Among the many items auctioned off are a guitar smashed up by Pete Townsend, Ian Anderson's flute and a notebook that belonged to Joni Mitchel containing the lyrics to songs on her first album **Songs to a Seagull**.

15th October – 1970

- Bill Graham presents Leon Russell, Miles Davis, Sea Train and Hammer on Thursday, Friday, Saturday & Sunday the 15th, 16th, 17th & 18th at the Fillmore West with lights by Little Princess 109.

16th October – 1970

- Bill Graham presents B.B. King, Butterfield Blues Band and Elvin Bishop on Friday & Saturday the 16th & 17th at the Fillmore East in New York City with the Joshua Light Show.

20th October – 1970

- The Marquee Club in London features Judas Jump and Idle Race on Tuesday the 21st. This would be the only Marquee appearance by Idle Race and by this time Jeff Lynne had already joined the Move.

21st October – 1970

- Bill Graham presents an evening with Pink Floyd on Wednesday the 21st at the Fillmore West.

22nd October – 1970

- Bill Graham presents Bo Diddley, Lightning Hopkins and the New York Rock and Roll Ensemble on Thursday, Friday, Saturday & Sunday the 22nd, 23rd, 24th & 25th at the Fillmore West with lights by Front Lights.

23rd October – 1970

- Bill Graham presents Derek and the Dominoes with Eric Clapton, Ballin Jack and Humble Pie on Friday & Saturday the 23rd & 24th at the Fillmore East in New York City with the Joshua Light Show.
- Jet Productions presents Brooklyn Rock featuring the Byrds, Great Jones and

Cactus on Friday the 23rd at the 46th Street Rock Palace in Brooklyn New York.

28th October – 1970

- Bill Graham presents an evening with the Small Faces featuring Rod Stewart on Wednesday the 28th at the Fillmore West.

29th October – 1970

- Bill Graham presents Procol Harum, Poco and Mungo Jerry on Thursday, Friday, Saturday & Sunday the 29th, 30th, 31st & 1st at the Fillmore West with lights by Dr. Zarkov.

30th October – 1970

- Jim Morrison is sentenced to six month in jail and fined $500 for indecent exposure in Miami.
- Ike and Tina Turner, Spirit, Southwind and Bert Sommer perform on Friday & Saturday the 30th & 31st at the Winterland in San Francisco.
- Bill Graham presents Lee Michaels, Cactus and Juicy Lucy on Friday & Saturday the 30th & 31st at the Fillmore East in New York City with the Joshua Light Show.
- Jet Productions presents Brooklyn Rock featuring Iron Butterfly on Friday the 30th at the 46th Street Rock Palace in Brooklyn New York.

3rd November – 1970

- Magnus presents Jethro Tull and the Bob Seger System on Tuesday the 3rd at the Comerford Theatre in Wilkes-Barre, Pennsylvania.

4th November – 1970

- Jethro Tull and McKendree Spring perform at a sold out performance on Wednesday the 4th at Carnegie Hall in support of a drug-rehabilitation center.

5th November – 1970

- Bill Graham presents Frank Zappa and the Mothers of Invention, Boz Scaggs and Ashton, Gardner & Dyke on Thursday, Friday, Saturday & Sunday the 5th, 6th, 7th & 8th at the Fillmore West with lights by Little Princess 109. Frank Zappa and the Mothers did not perform on the Sunday evening.

6th November – 1970

- Bill Graham presents Albert King, New York Rock Ensemble and the Flying Burrito Brothers on Friday & Saturday the 6th & 7th at the Fillmore East in New York City with the Joshua Light Show.
- Jet Productions presents Brooklyn Rock featuring Country Joe, the Youngbloods and Big Brother and the Holding Company on Friday the 6th at the 46th Street Rock Palace in Brooklyn New York.

9th November – 1970

- The Moody Blues earn a gold LP for their fifth album **In Search of the Lost Chord**.

10th November – 1970
- Bill Graham presents the Small Faces with Rod Stewart, Black Sabbath and If on Tuesday the 10th at the Fillmore East in New York City with the Joshua Light Show.

11th November – 1970
- Jet Productions presents Brooklyn Rock featuring the Grateful Dead on Wednesday the 11th through Saturday the 14th at the 46th Street Rock Palace in Brooklyn New York.
- Pink Floyd undertake a European tour that runs through to the first week of December.

12th November – 1970
- The Doors make their last concert appearance as a foursome in New Orleans on Thursday the 12th. Opening for the Doors is Kansas.

12th November – 1970
- Bill Graham presents the Kinks, Elton John, Ballin Jack and Juicy Lucy on Thursday, Friday, Saturday & Sunday the 12th, 13th, 14th & 15th at the Fillmore West with lights by Little Princess 109. The Kinks and Elton John did not perform on Sunday evening.

13th November – 1970
- Bill Graham presents Frank Zappa and the Mothers of Invention, Sha Na Na, J.F. Murphy and Free Flowing Salt on Friday & Saturday the 13th & 14th at the Fillmore East in New York City with the Joshua Light Show.

16th November – 1970
- Bill Graham presents the Grateful Dead and Hot Tuna on Monday the 16th at the Fillmore East in New York City with the Joshua Light Show.
- Jet Productions presents Brooklyn Rock featuring Jefferson Airplane on Monday the 16th at the 46th Street Rock Palace in Brooklyn New York.

18th November – 1970
- Bill Graham presents Traffic, Cat Stevens and Hammer on Wednesday & Thursday the 18th & 19th at the Fillmore East in New York City with the Joshua Light Show.

19th November – 1970
- Bill Graham presents Love with Arthur Lee, James Gang and Black Sabbath on Thursday, Friday, Saturday & Sunday the 19th, 20th, 21st & 22nd at the Fillmore West with lights by Spontinuity.

20th November – 1970
- The Steve Miller Band, Country Joe McDonald, Ashton Gardner and Dyke and Big Brother and the Holding Company perform on Friday & Saturday the 20th & 21st

at the Winterland in San Francisco with lights by Holy See.

- Bill Graham presents Leon Russell, Elton John and McKendree Spring on Friday & Saturday the 20th & 21st at the Fillmore East in New York City with the Joshua Light Show.
- Jet Productions presents Brooklyn Rock featuring Savoy Brown, Buddy Miles and Haystacks Balboa on Friday the 20th at the 46th Street Rock Palace in Brooklyn New York.

25th November – 1970

- Bill Graham presents the Jefferson Airplane, Hot Tuna and Buddy Guy & Junior Wells on Wednesday, Friday & Saturday the 25th, 27th & 28th at the Fillmore East in New York City with the Joshua Light Show.
- Traffic and Cat Stevens perform on Wednesday the 25th at the Academy of Music in Philadelphia, Pennsylvania.

26th November – 1970

- Bill Graham presents Sha-Na-Na, Elvin Bishop and Tower of Power on Thursday, Friday, Saturday & Sunday the 26th, 27th, 28th & 29th at the Fillmore West with lights by Crimson Madness.

27th November – 1970

- Jet Productions presents Brooklyn Rock featuring Lee Michaels on Friday the 27th at the 46th Street Rock Palace in Brooklyn New York.

December – 1970

- Paul McCartney sues to dissolve the Beatles.

3rd December – 1970

- Bill Graham presents Savoy Brown, Sea Train, Ry Cooder and Humble Pie on Thursday, Friday, Saturday & Sunday the 3rd, 4th, 5th & 6th at the Fillmore West with lights by Sunburst.

5th December – 1970

- Bill Graham presents the Kinks, Love and Quatermass on Friday & Saturday the 5th & 6th at the Fillmore East in New York City with the Joshua Light Show.

6th December – 1970

- Close to 200 Public Broadcasting stations in the United States air a 60-minute radio special entitled **San Francisco Rock: Go Ride the Music**. The program features interviews and performances from Jefferson Airplane, Jerry Garcia of the Grateful Dead, Quicksilver Messenger Service and David Crosby.

7th December – 1970

- Bill Graham presents Tom Paxton for one night only Monday the 7th at the Fillmore West.

10th December – 1970

- Bill Graham presents Lee Michaels, Albert King and Atlee on Thursday, Friday, Saturday & Sunday the 10th, 11th, 12th & 13th at the Fillmore West with lights by Little Princess 109.

11th December – 1970

- Sly and the Family Stone, Pacific Gas & Electric, Dunn & McCashen and Little Sister perform on Friday & Saturday the 11th & 12th at the Winterland in San Francisco.
- Bill Graham presents Canned Heat, Allman Brothers and Dreams on Friday & Saturday the 11th & 12th at the Fillmore East in New York City with the Joshua Light Show.
- Pink Floyd undertake the "Atom Heart Mother is Going on the Road" U.K. Tour that will run through to December 22nd. The tour started in Brighton and ended in Yorkshire.

16th December – 1970

- Bill Graham presents the Incredible String Band on Monday & Wednesday the 14th & 16th at the Fillmore West.

17th December – 1970

- Bill Graham presents the Butterfield Blues Band, Buddy Miles and Quatermass on Thursday, Friday, Saturday & Sunday the 17th, 18th, 19th & 20th at the Fillmore West with lights by Orb.

18th December – 1970

- Bill Graham presents Savoy Brown, Poco, Gypsy and Jo Mama on Friday & Saturday the 18th & 19th at the Fillmore East in New York City with the Joshua Light Show.
- Laura Nyro and Jackson Brown perform Friday the 18th at the Convention Hall Community Concourse in San Diego, California.

22nd December – 1970

- Bill Graham presents Laura Nyro and Jackson Brown on Tuesday, Wednesday & Thursday the 22nd, 23rd & 24th at the Fillmore East in New York City with the Joshua Light Show.
- The Grateful Dead and New Riders of the Purple Sage perform on Tuesday the 22nd at the Memorial Auditorium in Sacramento, California.

26th December – 1970

- Bill Graham presents Delaney & Bonnie & Friends, Voices of East Harlem and Jam Factory on Saturday, Sunday, Monday & Tuesday the 26th, 27th, 28th & 29th at the Fillmore West with lights by Little Princess 109.

- Bill Graham presents Mountain, Mylon and David Rea on Saturday & Sunday the 26th & 27th and Wednesday & Thursday the 30th & 31st at the Fillmore East in New York City with the Joshua Light Show.

31st December – 1970
- Bill Graham presents New Years Eve with Cold Blood, Elvin Bishop, Boz Scaggs and the Voices of East Harlem on Thursday the 31st at the Fillmore West with lights by Missionary Lights.
- Bill Graham presents New Years Eve with the Grateful Dead, New Riders of the Purple Sage and Stoneground on Thursday the 31st at the Winterland with lights by Little Princess 109.

TIMELINE - 1971

1st January – 1971
- Bill Graham presents New Years Eve with Cold Blood, Boz Scaggs, Stoneground and the Voices of East Harlem on Friday, Saturday & Sunday the 1st, 2nd & 3rd at the Fillmore West with lights by Missionary Lights.

4th January – 1971
- Pink Floyd are back in Abbey Road Studios recording the follow-up to **Atom Heart Mother**. It will be called **Meddle**.
- A Benefit Concert for the Legalization of Marijuana featuring Commander Cody and the Lost Planet Airmen, Papa John Creech, Zulu and Steelwind all performing on Monday & Tuesday the 4th & 5th at the Village, 901 Columbus in San Francisco.

7th January – 1971
- Bill Graham presents Spirit, the Elvin Bishop Group and Kwane & the Kwan Ditos on Thursday, Friday, Saturday & Sunday the 7th, 8th, 9th & 10th at the Fillmore West with lights by the San Francisco Light Works.

8th January – 1971
- Bill Graham presents Buddy Miles, Big Brother and Sweetwater on Friday & Saturday the 8th & 9th at the Fillmore East in New York City.

14th January – 1971
- Bill Graham presents Free, Bloodrock and Edwards Hand on Thursday, Friday, Saturday & Sunday the 14th, 15th, 16th & 17th at the Fillmore West with lights by Wumberlog.

15th January – 1971
- Bill Graham presents Hot Tuna, Taj Mahal and Brethren on Friday & Saturday the 15th & 16th at the Fillmore East in New York City.

17th January – 1971

- Pink Floyd perform at an event called "The Implosion" on Sunday the 17th at the Roundhouse, Chalk Farm, London. Pink Floyd would continue touring Britain and Europe through much of year, performing **Atom Heart Mother** on many occasions with the addition of Brass and Choir.

21st January – 1971

- Bill Graham presents the Spencer Davis Group, Taj Mahal and Fox on Thursday, Friday, Saturday & Sunday the 21st, 22nd, 23rd & 24th at the Fillmore West with lights by Bob Holt Lights.
- The Grateful Dead and the New Riders of the Purple Sage perform on Thursday the 21st at the University of California in Davis, California.

22nd January – 1971

- Bill Graham presents Mason & Elliot, Livingston Taylor and Odetta on Friday & Saturday the 22nd & 23rd at the Fillmore East in New York City.

25th January – 1971

- The Jefferson Airplane's Grace Slick and Paul Kantner become the parents of a baby girl they name China.
- Bill Graham presents James Taylor and Victoria on Monday the 25th at the Fillmore East in New York City.

28th January – 1971

- Bill Graham presents Hot Tuna, Allman Brothers and the 24 Piece Trinidad Tripoli Steel band on Thursday, Friday, Saturday & Sunday the 28th, 29th, 30th & 31st at the Fillmore West with lights Little Princess 109.

29th January – 1971

- Bill Graham presents Spirit, Bloodrock and Cowboy on Friday & Saturday the 29th & 30th at the Fillmore East in New York City.

2nd February - 1971

- Jerry Garcia & Merl Saunders play the Matrix Club, in San Francisco on Tuesday & Wednesday the 2nd & 3rd.

4th February - 1971

- Bill Graham presents B.B. King, Ballinjack and Christian Rapid on Thursday, Friday, Saturday & Sunday the 4th, 5th, 6th & 7th at the Fillmore West with lights by Prigmatic Revenge.
- John Fahey plays at the Matrix Club in San Francisco on Thursday, Friday & Saturday the 4th, 5th & 6th.

5th February – 1971

- Bill Graham presents Steppenwolf, Ten Wheel Drive and Luther Allison on Friday & Saturday the 5th & 6th at the Fillmore East in New York City.

10th February - 1971

- Boz Scaggs formerly of the Steve Miller Blues Band, plays on Wednesday & Thursday the 10th & 11th at the Matrix Club in San Francisco.

11th February – 1971

- Bill Graham presents Fleetwood Mac, Tom Rush and Clover on Thursday, Friday, Saturday & Sunday the 11th, 12th, 13th & 14th at the Fillmore West with lights Crimson Madness.
- Bill Graham presents Taj Mahal, Roberta Flack and Leon Thomas on Thursday the 11th at the Fillmore East in New York City.

12th February – 1971

- Bill Graham presents Steppenwolf, Cold Blood, Sha-Na-Na and the Buddy Guy-Junior Wells Blues Band on Friday & Saturday the 12th & 13th at the Winterland with lights by Spontinuity.
- Bill Graham presents the Chambers Brothers, Taj Mahal and Spencer Davis Peter Jameson on Friday & Saturday the 12th & 13th at the Fillmore East in New York City.

16th February - 1971

- Larry Coryell plays at the Matrix Club in San Francisco on Tuesday & Wednesday the 16th & 17th.
- Bill Graham presents the Faces, Savoy Brown and the Grease Band on Tuesday & Wednesday the 16th & 17th at the Fillmore East in New York City with Joe's Lights.

18th February - 1971

- Bill Graham presents It's a Beautiful Day, Blues Image and Tower of Power on Thursday, Friday, Saturday & Sunday the 18th, 19th, 20th & 21st at the Fillmore West with lights by Front Lights.
- Ramblin' Jack Elliot plays the Matrix Club in San Francisco on Thursday, Friday & Saturday the 18th, 19th & 20th.

19th February – 1971

- Bill Graham presents Black Sabbath, J. Geils Band and Sir Lord Baltimore on Friday & Saturday the 19th & 20th at the Fillmore East in New York City with Joe's Lights.

20th February – 1971

- The Sons, Clover and Big Brother and Holding Company perform on Saturday & Sunday the 20th & 21st at Pepperland in San Rafael, California.

24th February – 1970

- Janis Joplin's **Pearl** is awarded a Gold record only four months following her death.

25th February - 1971

- Bill Graham presents the New Riders of the Purple Sage, Boz Scaggs and James & the Good Brothers on Thursday, Friday, Saturday & Sunday the 25th, 26th, 27th & 28th at the Fillmore West with lights by Little Princess 109.

26th February – 1971

- Bill Graham presents Fleetwood Mac, Van Morrison and Freeway on Friday & Saturday the 26th & 27th at the Fillmore East in New York City with Joe's Lights.

28th February – 1971

- Bill Graham presents Gordon Lightfoot and Happy & Artie Tatum on Sunday the 28th at the Fillmore East in New York City with Joe's Lights.

5th March – 1971

- Bill Graham presents Aretha Franklin, King Curtis & the Kingpins and Tower of Power on Friday, Saturday & Sunday the 5th, 6th & 7th at the Fillmore West with lights by Sunburst. Aretha recorded her performances at the Fillmore shows for a live album.
- Bill Graham presents Quicksilver Messenger Service and Eric Burdon & War on Friday & Saturday the 5th & 6th at the Fillmore East with Joe's Lights.

11th March – 1971

- Bill Graham presents Poco, Siegal Schwall and Wishbone Ash on Thursday, Friday, Saturday & Sunday the 11th, 12th, 13th & 14th at the Fillmore West with lights by Temporary Optics.

12th March – 1971

- Bill Graham presents Johnny Winter, the Elvin Bishop Group and the Allman Brothers on Friday & Saturday the 12th & 13th at the Fillmore East.

13th March – 1971

- The Allman Brothers record their breakthrough album **Live at the Fillmore East**.

18th March – 1971

- Bill Graham presents the Sons of Champlin, Mark Almond and Commander Cody on Thursday, Friday, Saturday & Sunday the 18th, 19th, 20th & 21st at the Fillmore West with lights by San Francisco Light Works.

19th March – 1971

- Bill Graham presents Cactus, Humble Pie and Dada on Friday & Saturday the 19th & 20th at the Fillmore East with the Pig Light Show.

20th March – 1971

- As of today Iron Butterfly's **In-A-Gadda-Da-Vida** has been on the charts for 138 weeks and sold more than three million copies.

23rd March – 1971
- The U.S. Congress votes to lower the legal voting age to 18.

25th March – 1971
- Bill Graham presents Eric Burdon & War and the J. Geils Band on Thursday, Friday, Saturday & Sunday the 25th, 26th, 27th & 28th at the Fillmore West with lights by Deadly Nightshade.

26th March – 1971
- Bill Graham presents Santana plus others on Friday & Saturday the 26th & 27th at the Winterland with lights by Heavy Water.
- Bill Graham presents Richie Havens, Mark Almond, Paul Siebel and Michael Grando on Friday & Saturday the 26th & 27th at the Fillmore East.

April – 1971
- Marty Balin leaves Jefferson Airplane. Unhappy and disgusted with the lack of togetherness and seeming futility of trying to change things prompts him to leave the group he founded six years previously.

1st April – 1971
- Six months after the death of Jimi Hendrix his album **Cry of Love** is certified Gold.
- Bill Graham presents Buddy Miles, Wayne Cochran and the C.C. Riders and Sugarloaf on Thursday, Friday, Saturday & Sunday the 1st, 2nd, 3rd & 4th at the Fillmore West with lights by Little Princess 109.
- Bill Graham presents Santana, Rahsaan Roland Kirk and Tower of Power on Thursday, Friday & Saturday the 1st, 2nd & 3rd at the Fillmore East with Joe's Lights.

5th April – 1971
- Bill Graham presents Cactus, Humble Pie, Edgar Winter's White Trash and Tin House on Monday & Tuesday the 5th & 6th at the Fillmore East with Joe's Lights.

8th April – 1971
- Bill Graham presents Johnny Winter, J. Geils band and Dreams on Thursday, Friday, Saturday & Sunday the 8th, 9th, 10th & 11th at the Fillmore West with lights by Optic Illusion.
- Bill Graham presents Elton John, Sea Train, Wishbone Ash on Thursday, Friday & Saturday the 8th, 9th & 10th at the Fillmore East.

9th April – 1971
- Bill Graham presents John Mayall, Sha-Na-Na and Randall's Island on Friday & Saturday the 9th & 10th at the Winterland with lights by Bob Holt.

10th April – 1971

- The Grateful Dead and New Riders of the Purple Sage perform on Saturday the 10th at the Franklin and Marshal College in Lancaster, Pennsylvania.

12th April – 1971

- Bill Graham presents Mountain, Mylon and T. Rex on Monday, Tuesday, Wednesday & Thursday the 12th, 13th, 14th & 15th at the Fillmore East.

15th April – 1971

- Bill Graham presents Van Morrison, Isley Brothers and Fanny on Thursday, Friday, Saturday & Sunday the 15th, 16th, 17th & 18th at the Fillmore West with lights by Abercrombie.

16th April – 1971

- Bill Graham presents John Mayall, Boz Scaggs and Elliott Randall's Island on Friday & Saturday the 16th & 17th at the Fillmore East.

18th April – 1971

- Bill Graham presents Grand Funk Railroad and Bloodrock on Sunday the 18th at the Winterland.

20th April – 1971

- Bill Graham presents Ten Years After and J. Geils Band on Tuesday the 20th at the Fillmore East in New York City with Joe's Lights.

22nd April – 1971

- Bill Graham presents Taj Mahal, Stoneground and Trapeze on Thursday, Friday, Saturday & Sunday the 22nd, 23rd, 24th & 25th at the Fillmore West with lights by Earth Light.
- Pink Floyd perform a track from their new recording for the first time called "Echoes".

23rd April – 1971

- Bill Graham presents Procol Harum, Winter Consort and Teegarden and Vanwinkle on Friday & Saturday the 23rd & 24th at the Fillmore East.

24th April – 1971

- Over 350,000 Veterans demonstrate against the Vietnam War with a march in Washington DC and in San Francisco. With antiwar demonstrations and rally's occurring regularly it's only a matter of time before their impact is felt.

25th April – 1971

- Bill Graham presents the Grateful Dead and New Riders of the Purple Sage on Monday-Saturday the 25th – 29th at the Fillmore East in New York City with Joe's

Lights. The 29th was the Grateful Dead's last appearance at the Fillmore East. They apparently played the 26th with special guest Duane Allman, the 27th with the Beach Boys and the 28th with Tom Constanten.

29th April – 1971
- Bill Graham presents Mike Bloomfield with Chicago Slim, Bola Sete, Mike Finnigan and Gold on Thursday, Friday, Saturday & Sunday the 29th, 30th, 1st & 2nd at the Fillmore West with lights by Dr. Zarkov.

30th April – 1971
- Rock impresario Bill Graham announces yet again he plans to close the Fillmore's. And while he's threatened to do it before many believe this time he is serious.
- Bill Graham presents Ten Years After, Cactus and Pot Liquor on Friday & Saturday the 30th & 1st at the Winterland.
- Bill Graham presents Emerson Lake & Palmer, Edgar Winter's White Trash and Curved Air on Friday & Saturday the 30th & 1st at the Fillmore East.

4th May – 1971
- Bill Graham presents Jethro Tull and Cowboy on Tuesday & Wednesday the 4th & 5th at the Fillmore East.

6th May – 1971
- Bill Graham presents Miles Davis, Elvin Bishop Group and Mandrill on Thursday, Friday, Saturday & Sunday the 6th, 7th, 8th & 9th at the Fillmore West with lights by Orb.

7th May – 1971
- Bill Graham presents Poco, Linda Ronstadt and Manhattan Transfer on Friday & Saturday the 7th & 8th at the Fillmore East.

13th May – 1971
- Recording sessions for the new Jefferson Airplane album are halted when lead singer Grace Slick smashes her Mercedes into a concrete wall near San Francisco's Golden Gate Bridge.
- Bill Graham presents Humble Pie, Swamp Dog and Shanti on Thursday, Friday, Saturday & Sunday the 13th, 14th, 15th & 16th at the Fillmore West with lights by Prismatic Revenge.

14th May – 1971
- Bill Graham presents Delaney and Bonnie, Mott The Hoople and Mandrill on Friday & Saturday the 14th & 15th at the Fillmore East.

17th May - 1971
- The Crystal Palace Garden Party is held on Monday the 17th featuring Quiver, Mountain, the Faces and Pink Floyd.

20th May – 1971
- Bill Graham presents the Rascals, Grootna and Grin on Thursday, Friday, Saturday & Sunday the 20th, 21st, 22nd & 23rd at the Fillmore West with lights by Garden of Delights.
- Bill Graham presents "The Final Concerts" featuring Leon Russell and Taj Mahal on Thursday, Friday, Saturday & Sunday the 20th, 21st, 22nd & 23rd at the Fillmore East with lights by Joe's Lights/Pig Light Show.

26th May – 1971

- Country Joe and the Fish perform on Wednesday the 26th at Woolsley Hall, Yale University in New Haven Connecticut.

27th May – 1971
- Bill Graham presents Cold Blood, Joy of Cooking, Sweathog and Frosty on Thursday, Friday, Saturday & Sunday the 27th, 28th, 29th & 30th at the Fillmore West with lights by Little Princess 109.

28th May – 1971
- Bill Graham presents the Grateful Dead, New Riders of the Purple Sage, R.J. Fox and James & the Good Brothers on Friday & Saturday the 28th & 29th at the Winterland. Roughly three-dozen Dead Heads are treated for hallucinations after they ingested LSD spiked apple juice served at San Francisco's Winterland. Band members are suspected but not accused.
- Bill Graham presents "The Final Concerts" featuring Lee Michaels, Fanny and Humble Pie on Friday & Saturday the 28th & 29th at the Fillmore East with lights by Joe's Lights/Pig Light Show.

30th May – 1971
- Bill Graham presents "The Final Concerts" featuring Laura Nyro and Spencer Davis Peter Jameson on Sunday the 30th at the Fillmore East with lights by Joe's Lights/Pig Light Show.

June - 1971
- The Eleventh National Jazz and Blues Festival, Reading featuring Bell & Arc, Armada, Demich Armstrong, Audience, Arthur Brown, Clark-Hutchinson, Clouds,

C.M.U., Colosseum, Colonel Bagshot, Country Joe, East Of Eden, Rory Gallagher, Peter Hammill, Hardin & York, Jon Hiseman, Al Kooper, Lindisfarne, Ian Mathews, Gillian McPherson, Ralph McTell, Medicine Head, Osibisa, Percussion Band, Terry Reid, Renaissance, Sha-Na-Na, Steel Mill, Storyteller, Stray, Van Der Graf Generator, Vinegar Joe, Warm Dust, Wishbone Ash and Pete York

3rd June – 1971
- A Party for Mother Earth featuring the New Riders of the Purple Sage, Country Joe McDonald, Stoneground, Grootna and Ace of Cups takes place on Thursday the 3rd at the Friends and Relations Hall in San Francisco.
- Bill Graham presents Albert King, Mott the Hoople and Freddie King on Thursday, Friday, Saturday & Sunday the 3rd, 4th, 5th & 6th at the Fillmore West with lights by Abercrombie.

5th June – 1971
- Bill Graham presents "The Final Concerts" featuring Frank Zappa and the Mothers of Invention, Hampton Grease Band and Head Over Heels on Saturday & Sunday the 5th & 6th at the Fillmore East with lights by Joe's Lights/Pig Light Show.

6th June – 1971
- John Lennon and Yoko Ono join Frank Zappa for a jam on stage on Sunday the 6th at the Fillmore East. Both remark how clean-cut the other looks.

9th June – 1971
- Bill Graham presents "The Final Concerts" featuring the Byrds and McKendree Spring on Wednesday the 9th at the Fillmore East.

10th June – 1971
- Bill Graham presents Cactus, Flamin' Groovies and Redeye on Thursday, Friday, Saturday & Sunday the 10th, 11th, 12th & 13th at the Fillmore West with lights by Sunburst.

11th June – 1971
- Bill Graham presents "The Final Concerts" featuring Bloodrock, Glass Harp and Alice Cooper on Friday & Saturday the 11th & 12th at the Fillmore East with lights by Joe's Lights/Pig Light Show.

17th June – 1971
- Bill Graham presents Boz Scaggs, Tower of Power and Mason Proffit on Thursday, Friday, Saturday & Sunday the 17th, 18th, 19th & 20th at the Fillmore West with lights by Crimson Madness.

18th June – 1971
- Bill Graham presents "The Final Concerts" featuring B.B. King, Moby Grape and

Grootna on Friday & Saturday the 18th & 19th at the Fillmore East with lights by Joe's Lights/Pig Light Show.

20th June – 1971

- Bill Graham presents Jethro Tull on Sunday the 20th at the Berkeley Community Theatre.
- The first Glastonbury Fayre is staged on Sunday the 20th through Thursday the 24th at Worthy Farm, Pilton, England. Featured bands included the Pink Fairies, Melanie, Fairport Convention, Gong, Family, Traffic, Quintessence, Traffic, Terry Reid - with David Lyndley and Linda Lewis, Hawkwind, Brinsley Schwarz, Arthur Brown, Skin Alley and David Bowie. Pink Floyd were scheduled to appear on the last night, but had to cancel as their equipment was still enroute to England from Rome, Italy the location of their final night of the European Tour. 12,000 people attend this event, which has become an annual institution.

23rd June - 1971

- Hells Angel's Annual party featuring Cold Blood, Cat Mother, Gold and Ghetto Fox on Wednesday the 23rd at the Longshoreman's Hall in San Francisco.

24th June – 1971

- Bill Graham presents the original Moby Grape, Spencer Davis & Peter Jameson and Flash Cadillac and the Continental Kids on Thursday, Friday, Saturday & Sunday the 24th, 25th, 26th & 27th at the Fillmore West with lights by Images.
- Bill Graham presents "The Final Concerts" featuring Johnny Winter and Edgar Winter's White Trash on Thursday the 24th at the Fillmore East with lights by Joe's Lights/Pig Light Show.
- Bill Graham presents Leon Russell on Thursday the 24th at the Berkeley Community Theatre.

25th June – 1971

- Bill Graham presents "The Final Concerts" featuring the Allman Brothers Band, Albert King and the J. Geils Band on Friday, Saturday & Sunday the 25th, 26th & 27th at the Fillmore East with lights by Joe's Lights/Pig Light Show. An emotional Bill Graham closes down the Fillmore East on Sunday the 27th. Everyone attending the closing nights finds red roses on their theatre seats and is given commemorative posters at the door.

30th June – 1971

- Bill Graham presents Cat Stevens on Wednesday the 30th at the Berkeley Community Theatre.
- Bill Graham presents "The Closing Week of the Fillmore West" featuring on day 1 - Boz Scaggs, Cold Blood, Flamin' Groovies and Stoneground on Wednesday the 30th at the Fillmore West with lights by the San Francisco Lightworks. Police had actually threatened to cancel Graham's permit for the Winterland when a drink was allegedly spiked with LSD.

1st July – 1971

- Bill Graham presents "The Closing Week of the Fillmore West" featuring on day 2 – It's a Beautiful Day, the Elvin Bishop Group, Grootna and Lamb on Thursday the 1st at the Fillmore West with lights by Little Princess 109.

2nd July – 1971

- Bill Graham presents "The Closing Week of the Fillmore West" featuring on day 3 – the Grateful Dead, New Riders of the Purple Sage and the Rowan Brothers on Friday the 2nd at the Fillmore West with lights by Heavy Water.

3rd July – 1971

- Bill Graham presents "The Closing Week of the Fillmore West" featuring on day 4 – Quicksilver Messenger Service, Hot Tuna and Yogi Phlegm on Saturday the 3rd at the Fillmore West with lights by Little Princess 109.

3rd July - 1971

- Jim Morrison of the Doors dies in Paris. Morrison had gone to Paris to relax and to write new material. The official cause of death is a heart attack.
- A Free Concert in Hyde Park, London is held on Saturday the 3rd with Grand Funk Railroad, Humble Pie and Head Hands & Feet.

4th July – 1971

- Bill Graham presents "The Closing Week of the Fillmore West" featuring on day 5 – Santana, Creedence Clearwater Revival, Tower of Power and the San Francisco Musicians Jam on Sunday the 4th at the Fillmore West with lights by Heavy Water.

12th July – 1971

- Creedence Clearwater Revival, Bo Diddley, and Tower of Power perform on Monday the 12th at the Cincinnati Gardens, Cincinnati, Ohio.

18th July – 1971

- Bill Graham presents Emerson Lake & Palmer on Sunday the 18th at the Berkeley Community Theatre.

31st July – 1971

- Pink Floyd depart for their first tour of the Far East.

2nd August – 1971

- Jefferson Airplane create their own record label called Grunt Records to be distributed by RCA.

6th August – 1971

- Procol Harum records a live concert album in Canada with the Edmonton

Symphony Orchestra. The single *Conquistador* from the album becomes a major hit for the band.

8th August – 1971

- The Marquee Club in London features the first appearance of Blonde on Blonde on Sunday the 8th.

26th August – 1971

- Gaelic Park in New York on Thursday the 26th marks the final performance of the original five-man Grateful Dead. Pig Pen leaves the band due to failing health.

27th August - 1971

- The Weeley Festival, Clacton On Sea, Essex is held on Friday, Saturday & Sunday the 27th, 28th & 29th featuring the Faces, Rory Gallagher, Groundhogs, the Grease Band, Quintessance, Colosseum, Edgar Broughton Band, Juicy Lucy, Arthur Brown, Mungo Jerry, Al Stewart, Argent, Barclay James Harvest, Assagai, Bell & Arc, Dave Edmunds, Caravan, Demon Fuzz, Fairfield Parlour, Formerly Fat Harry, Fusion Orchestra, Gnidrolog, Gringo, Hackenshack, Heads Hands & Feet, Jerry Lochran, Lindisfarne, Natural Acoustic Band, On, Principal Edwards Magic Theatre, Ricotti Albuquerque, Stray, Tir Na Nog, Steve Tilson, Third Ear Band and Van Der Graaf Generator. Lighting was by Heavy Light.

November – 1971

- Due in large part to the efforts of those involved in the many peace marches held throughout the sixties, U.S. President Richard Nixon begins withdrawing troops from Vietnam.
- Pink Floyd release **Meddle** on November 5th.

December – 1971

- Greenpeace is founded in Vancouver, Canada.

File No. 3

The Changing Face Of Concert Promotion With Psychedelic Posters

Nothing screams "psychedelic" like the wild and amazing series of posters created primarily in San Francisco from approximately 1965 through to the closing of the two Fillmore Auditoriums in 1971. They were colourful, they were bold, they were artistically groundbreaking but perhaps more than anything it was the sheer number of posters that attracted the attention. After all was said and done there were almost 150 Family Dog posters, almost 300 Fillmore posters and dozens of others for various events in San Francisco staged over the period. Yet psychedelic posters started showing up in cities everywhere. If you include posters created for a variety of smaller halls and events, including more prominent clubs such as the Grande Ballroom in Detroit, Michigan and the Vulcan Gas Company in Austin, Texas then you're talking about a body of work that amounts to something in the neighbourhood of 800 to 1000 posters.

The San Francisco posters created by the core artists of Wes Wilson, Stanley Mouse, Alton Kelly, Victor Moscoso, Rick Griffin, and others captured the period's complete nature, the wild shapes, the juxtaposition of traditional graphic icons and the revolutionary blending of colours that literally vibrated the images off the poster. The fact that the posters were difficult to read did not detract in any way. On the contrary it was this difficult-to-read aspect that proved to be the posters drawing power. In a community that claimed to be divesting itself of all things material, cars specifically, walking was very much in vogue. It was this kind of close contact on the street level that drew passers by into the wild images they saw in store-front windows and on telephone poles in the community. The posters conveyed the essence of the experience awaiting the reader at next dance-concert.

The reality was most of us never had the opportunity to visit a psychedelic ballroom like the Fillmore or the Grande, but we've all seen the posters. Apart from the music, the posters are the means by which most of us got a sense of what the period was like. To quote from **High Societies**, published by the San Diego Museum of Art for a special poster exhibition, *"The dance concerts became among the 1960s' most important contributions to American popular culture. They launched the careers of some of the most significant bands of the San Francisco sound...The events were also the forums in which the psychedelic light shows were perfected. The psychedelic rock posters are the graphic extensions of the dance-concert experience and the lasting documents of these events."* The posters said it all.

The September 1, 1967 issue of **Life** magazine ran a cover story on the burgeoning poster scene with the headline, "The Big Poster Hang-Up – Walls and Walls of Expendable Art". The article went on to explain how *"expendable graphic art"* had become America's biggest hang-up with more than a million posters every week being purchased and posted. The posters most in demand are the ones that *"jolt the eye or make the mind go topsy-turvy."* It's true that by the fall of 1967, posters were being collected all over the United States and Canada, even worldwide. These posters were so different from the "boxing-style" posters of the early sixties. They represented a whole new concept in music promotion. For most of us attending an event was out of the question but collecting the posters was the next best thing.

When Bill Graham first began using posters and smaller versions called handbills or flyers even he didn't foresee how popular they would become. In fact, the very first in the series were only printed in lots of three or four hundred. Graham would spend hours on his scooter going to various neighbourhoods convincing shop owners to put them in the windows. Or post them on telephone poles in and around the Haight-Ashbury area only to turn around and see them being carefully taken down and secreted away by hippies of all ages. He quickly realized he had a good thing going and looked for ways to turn the posters into incentives. Soon the size of the print orders increased to one and then two thousand per event. Each run had the initial printing, but then Graham would also offer posters to all who purchased advance tickets, or to shop owners who wanted some in exchange for posting the current weeks show. Still others were handed out at each weekend's performances.

Poster shops were opening all over the United States and Canada. In Chicago there was the Mole Hole, In New York's Greenwich Village it was the Infinite Poster and the Electric Lotus, in Houston it was the Mind Mart, in Washington DC it was the Yonder Wall and in my hometown of Saskatoon, Saskatchewan it was the Blown Mind. In the heart of it all was the Print Mint in Haight-Ashbury, a shop that specialized in posters of all kinds. It opened in December of 1966 and by the Fall of 1967 was selling 800 items a day!

In England the main poster artists were Martin Sharp, Michael English and Nigel Weymouth. English and Weymouth created Hapshash and the Coloured Coat and began designing everything from storefronts to album covers to posters. The primary difference with many of the British artists was their printing technique. While the San Francisco posters were offset printed, the British ones tended to use the silk-screen process. As a result they were able to use different metallic colours and because of the silk-screening process each poster tended to be unique in its coloration and saturation. In contrast to the other posters showing up around London, these new works with their bright colours and revolutionary use of graphics and lettering more than stood out. Unfortunately, for whatever reason there isn't as unified a body of British work as exists for the American ballrooms in San Francisco. The poster work in England seemed to be produced more haphazardly with few long consistent runs. Typical of this is how it's possible to find a sequence of only four posters for Sunday at the Saville even though there were more events. Similarly, not every event at the UFO or Middle Earth was advertised in poster form. It's quite possible that since the music tabloid business was so established in the U.K. small black and white print ads were used as the prime source of media exposure rather than the somewhat more expensive poster process.

The Seed…

I'm sure that when George Hunter and Mike Ferguson drew up the promotional poster to advertise their stint at the Red Dog Saloon in Virginia City in June of 1965, they had no idea they were setting in motion a whole new trend that would take on a life of its own. Looking back at their quaint poster it looks almost amateurish now, but it also boldly suggests the many elements we've come to accept as psychedelic art; the stylized lettering, the black-and-white line drawing, a doodling space-filling style, the old west motifs, the caricatures of the band members, the use of strange phrasing like "The Limit of the Marvellous" and the general busy-ness all set the groundwork for what was to follow. Their poster has since been given the name "The Seed" implying how it provided the origins of the poster-culture that followed.

Many of the early posters done by Alton Kelley and others for the initial Family Dog dance-concerts have been described as "kitchen table" doodles, with the poster-page containing an assortment of cartoon images, line drawings, doodles, silly expressions and lacking any real sense of traditional poster order and structure. Even these early efforts were undertaken with a desire to fill the page with images, more than with the desire to sell an event. In short order artists were able to bring their own unique ideas to the world of psychedelic poster design.

If we use the Fillmore poster series as a template for artists involved in the San Francisco psychedelic posters, Wes Wilson was one of the first to take up the challenge of translating the psychedelic experience into print. He had no formal art training, although he was working for a printer that did the very first Mime Troupe flyers for Bill Graham. As such Wilson made his limited skills known and was tagged to do many of the first posters for both the Avalon Ballroom and the Fillmore often times generating as many as six posters each month. After a few months of this he began to work exclusively for Bill Graham's Fillmore Auditorium. The Family Dog began sending their work to Stanley Mouse and Alton Kelley. Part of the reason for the move was that Graham didn't interfere much in Wilson's creative expression while Helm's having a background in poster production insisted on providing text and images for the Avalon posters. To hear Wilson's side of the story, *"The Good thing about Bill was he wasn't really that hung up on what he wanted in terms of graphics and he trusted me more in what I would come up with. I enjoyed and appreciated*

FD5 POSTER

that." Before parting ways with Helm's, Wilson created one of the era's most lasting visual images, the Family Dog logo, which ended up appearing on all 150 Family Dog posters. The image involved a photo of a longhaired "Indian" in formal dress appearing to be smoking a joint. The image made its initial appearance on FD5 a poster promoting the first Avalon Ballroom show featuring the Blues Project and the Great Society, a poster Wilson describes as one of his favourites. After creating FD5 Wilson stylized the image in a "button" form that stated "The Family Dog Presents" which other artists took great fun inserting in many unusual ways on all the follow-up posters.

Wilson's technique was perhaps the cornerstone of the psychedelic style, with highly stylized and distorted lettering filling the space of some invisible object or surrounding his own fine-art drawings of faces and figures. Many times the lettering was almost illegible and reading the poster became very much an effort. Wilson tells the story of calling Bill Graham late one night to explain the latest poster had been created for Bill's concept of the Sound, which eventually became poster BG29. Graham came over and studied it intently and said, *"Well, it's nice, but I can't read it."* To which Wilson responded, *"Yeah, and that's why people are gonna stop and look at it."* This in many ways sums up the psychedelic poster ethic. These posters were never meant to be easy to read. They were designed to be the visual representation of the acid experience to one degree or another. Or as Wilson said in the **Art of the Fillmore**, *"The Fillmore events that the posters advertised gave the posters meaning beyond just being pure decoration."*

By May of 1967, Wilson stopped creating posters for Graham when the two failed to come to an agreement on an increase in payment. By this time Graham was doing a booming business in the selling of posters and Wilson was more than aware of this but was still only receiving approximately $100 per design.

Bonnie MacLean, who at the time was Graham's girlfriend, took over. MacLean had already had a hand in some of the early flyers and was constantly creating her art in chalk on a blackboard at the top of the Fillmore stairs promoting upcoming events. To some degree her style started off looking similar to Wilson's, but she soon developed her own techniques. In particular she was most interested in capturing the subtleties of the human face and as a result virtually all of her works contain facial portraits of some kind. She said, *"What I was most interested in was the human face. I think I captured certain emotions relating to the times in those expressions."* Graham paid her the ultimate compliment in his summation, *"I can honestly say that if there was one person without whom the Fillmore wouldn't have happened; it was Bonnie. She was critical, and she was creative."* For her part MacLean sees the posters significance as, *"these posters were created with an intensity that was lived."*

Like Bonnie, Victor Moscoso came from an art education background, but he choose early on not to do any work for Bill Graham choosing instead to concentrate his efforts on the Avalon Ballroom, the Matrix and various other projects in Los Angeles. He arrived in San Francisco in the summer of 1966 and was teaching at the San Francisco Art Institute when he saw the first psychedelic posters. Oddly enough he was not impressed by what he saw. He believed with his training he could do better, and create something that looked more professional. What he found was just the opposite. The more he drew, the more he found it was his intuition that lead the way, not his training. In fact, Moscoso found that if he turned the rules upside-down they actually worked much better. Moscoso brought to postering a revolutionary sense of colour combining. Taking his cue from Josef Albers' book **Interaction of Colour**, Moscoso mixed colours that seemed to vibrate on the edges and practically jump off the page. Albers' wrote that conflicting colours that vibrated *"feels aggressive and often uncomfortable to our eyes."* In spite of this, Moscoso took bright pinks, purples or oranges and combined them with rich turquoise blues and emerald greens and made it all work. When all of the colours were combined with his skilled use of shaped lettering and image design, Moscoso took the art of postering to yet another level. Moscoso also treated the creation of posters as more of a business, and at the end of 1966 he started his own design company called Neon Rose and created a variety of posters under that banner for such diverse entities as the Matrix club and the Neiman Marcus Poster Show.

Stanley Mouse grew up in Detroit and came on the scene with a background of school graffiti, custom hot rod painting, pin striping and a host of other odds and ends. Mouse found himself in San Francisco in 1965 and soon struck up a partnership with Alton Kelley and in short order the two collaborated on 33 posters for the Family Dog's Avalon Ballroom, having taken over the poster when Wes Wilson choose to work exclusively for Bill Graham. Mouse's first poster for the Fillmore came in 1967 and by that time he was already recognized as one of the key players in the San Francisco poster scene. Mouse's collaborative efforts with Alton Kelley are one of those few times where artistic partnership worked as each brought something different to the table. Kelley had a keen eye for collage and had also spent time working around hot rods. Together they created a series of inventive posters combining Kelley's eye for collage and Mouse's hand for design. Kelley was also a founding member of the Family Dog. The partnership of Mouse and Kelley provided dozens of posters that took a much lighter tone than those of Wes Wilson. Their posters "borrowed" heavily from established icons such as the Zig Zag Man, Aunt Jamaima, Winnie the Pooh, photos from the San Francisco earthquake and many more easily recognizable images. These iconic images were usually placed in disconnected settings in an almost self-deprecating fashion. They were in-jokes that everyone in the hippie community seemed to get and their posters were well received. The two were also not above borrowing from the art-nouveau world and psychedelizised a number of classic designs from Alphonse Mucha, for their Family Dog posters FD29 (Jim Kweskin Jugband) and FD45 (Grateful Dead). While Wes Wilson may have been the first to use the skeleton image on a poster promoting the Grateful Dead. It was Mouse and Kelley who combined the skeleton image with roses to create the lasting Grateful Dead image on the poster FD26 created in September 16th 1966 for the Dead's Avalon Ballroom show. Kelley is also credited on 6 Fillmore posters including one as a solo artist.

With so many events needing posters it would be easy to think there was a lot of competition in the San Francisco postering community however that didn't seem to be the case, it was more about self-improvement. Kelly observed, *"It wasn't about competition with the other artists so much as it was about incentive. When Mouse and I saw a poster we thought was really far out, we'd say, 'Now we've gotta do one that good.'"* Ironically with all the creative outlandish, psychedelic posters surrounding him it surprised many to find out that Bill Graham's favourite turned out to be BG106 a rather simple design promoting John Mayall and Arlo Guthrie created by Stanley Mouse to resemble a English pub sign.

Rick Griffin arrived in San Francisco in 1966 from a background in the Los Angeles surfing scene, where he'd developed a following with his cartoons in various magazines. He brought yet another bizarre element to the poster style with his disembodied eyes, skulls, and limbs surrounded by flames as seen on countless hot rods in southern California. His first poster designed for the "Human Be In" makes use of his own fascination with Indian lore inherited from his amateur archaeologist father. Following this he began working with Mouse and Kelley at the Family Dog before lending his talents to the Fillmore. His assessment, *"In San Francisco, doing posters on a regular basis was like going to my own art school. I was educating myself about the basic principles involved in colour, how to mix colours, how to gear overlays, how to work up tones, and ultimately how to predict what the final version would look like."* Rick Griffin is best remembered for his uncanny wit and visual puns, which combined elements of the American old-west and the drug culture of the sixties.

The artist who came next is perhaps the one with the most bizarre images. Lee Conklin's detailed surrealistic, psychedelic visions set his style apart from everyone else and were the most directly expressive of the actual psychedelic experience. Conklin's visual imagery was at once dream-like and hallucinatory and packed with the drug-laden images of the late sixties. They also expressed a much darker tone than the earlier playful artists. By 1968 the overall tone of the world was changing and with the increasing number of riots and the growing student unrest, Conklin's posters captured the moment with their myriad of disembodied parts all searching for some sense of connectedness. Another technique used by Conklin was the mixing of foreground and background images, provoking the viewer to look past the obvious frontal images to actually read the lettering created by the background, almost looking inside the poster for the text. He came on the scene in early 1968 and packed his posters with intense detail. Imagine body parts melted into other body parts melted into the landscape and you begin to see the unusual nature of Conklin's efforts. He said, *"I made it my mission to translate experience onto paper. The afterglow was always the most creative time for me."*

There were a number of other artists of note; people like Bob Fried who was actually lured into the world of psychedelic posters and away from a master's program at the San Francisco Art Institute by his good friend Victor Moscoso. Much of Fried's work was for the Family Dog's Avalon Ballroom, where to hear him say it, *"I wanted the posters to have entrances and passages, to convey feelings of dimensional space like what you'd feel when you trip on acid, passing from one reality to another."* For all his emphasis on the "trip" aspect, Fried's posters tended to be more surreal than anything and stayed within more conventional visual elements of the Op Art world of the sixties.

THE PACK & MC5 AT THE GRANDE BALLROOM, DETROIT

Gary Grimshaw actually saw what was happening early on in San Francisco, following his discharge from the Navy. Grimshaw spent many an evening in early 1966 attending performances at both the Avalon and Fillmore ballrooms catching the mood of the growing psychedelic scene first hand. He remembers seeing posters everywhere including on the buses, *"And if you'd walk around anywhere, a third of the storefronts had a poster in them. You went to the hip record stores and they'd have a stack of them on the counter and you'd just take what you wanted, right off the press."* During this fertile time he was the art director for the first few issues of the **San Francisco Oracle**. He soon relocated to Detroit and began using his skills designing posters for Russ Gibb's Grande Ballroom. Initially his involvement with the Grande was as a light show artist, but he soon moved into designing the posters and handbills. Of all the poster artists outside of the San Francisco mainstream, Grimshaw's are the ones that best represent their style. His combination of photo images and highly stylized and flowing lettering display a keen sense of the psychedelic art.

Greg Irons, yet another self taught artists arrived in San Francisco in early 1967. His early days there were consumed with filling a sketch book with images of Haight-Ashbury, some of which would latter be incorporated into posters. With only one published poster in hand he visited Bill Graham. His timing couldn't have been better. Graham was in need of a poster fast and Irons was happy to oblige. With a style that borrowed elements of Griffin, Irons would go on to create eight posters for the Fillmore.

Around the same time Randy Tuten was putting his creative talents to use in a very different style. Tuten's penchant was to incorporate elements of transportation or industry such as trains, cars, Zeppelins etc. His lettering style incorporated aspects Mouse and Kelley and was only slightly more legible, although never clear enough to satisfy Bill Graham. Tuten was born in San Francisco, but moved to Los Angeles as a child and developed into a rebellious teenager there. By 1966 he was hitching rides back and forth between L.A. and San Francisco, taking acid and enjoying the growing ballroom scene. It was during these junkets that he kept seeing the various posters and eventually decided he wanted to try his hand at it. One might suppose great meaning or significance to the juxtaposition of such powerful images in Tuten's work, yet he's quick to downplay that notion, *"There really isn't any heavy meaning in my posters. What I did graphically was just a cross between what I liked and what fit."*

Bill Graham's experience with psychedelic posters in New York was very different from San Francisco. The localized Haight-Ashbury community and surrounding areas were all well travelled by foot, providing more of an opportunity to stop and read the posters. The lay of the land in New York was very different and postering was nowhere as effective. The Fillmore East just wasn't in the same kind of neighbourhood as the Fillmore West. That being said one of the artists that came to prominence was David Byrd. His designs for the few Fillmore East posters, flyers and programs shows a distinct skill. And in fact Byrd did have plenty of art schooling. Still when it came to psychedelic posters even he claims he was flying blind, *"It was my own interpretation of what they were doing out on the West Coast. I just did the best I could with the skills I had."* Byrd's style betrays his love of symmetry, whether it be the perspective looking down on the dancing human form, to the lines of an Egyptian tomb painting, to the hundreds of hand drawn circles of his Jimi Hendrix poster, he brought a certain structure and form that retained an organic human feel.

One of the last Fillmore artists was Norman Orr. His style was a blend of Griffin, Mouse and Kelly and his own unique quirks, and he created some of most striking posters. Orr said, *"In my mind Griffin was always the giant. The imagination he brought to the genre always went above and beyond. He made me want to be an artist."* Orr's use of few colours in combination with multiple font styles, and loads of tiny illustrations painstakingly hand drawn and crowded together make his efforts as difficult to wade through as those of the pioneers. Younger than many of the other poster artists, Orr remembers seeing the posters hanging on friends bedrooms walls and as a teenager, made up his mind that, *"Someday I'm gonna do Fillmore Posters."* He eventually got his wish and by 1970 he was fulfilling his dream.

The last artist to have a major impact on the poster scene was David Singer, who in the end produced more Fillmore West posters than anyone else. Singer's love was collage and lettering. His posters were produced on what can easily be described as the tail end of the whole psychedelic era. He typically created bold lettering placed around a strange mix of elements like classical statues, flowers and animals. Many times the images formed visual puns like the "two-lips" of BG180. In fact it was the collages that captured Graham's attention. On his first visit, after studying the various collage samples for 20 minutes, Graham asked, *"Do you do lettering?"* When Singer said yes, he was hired to do the next 12 posters. And in fact then went on to develop a love of lettering. According to Singer, *"By then the shock value and appeal of posters being illegible had worn off. Bill was tired of it and he was looking for something new."* Singer was the right person at the right time. His love of lettering allowed him to create a new "vocabulary" as often as he chose. He said, *"Lettering began to fascinate me because I realized I could take this alphabet, these 26 symbols and extend them in limitless ways."* Singer was called upon to design the last Fillmore West poster identified as BG287, again employing the visual images to tell a much deeper story than immediately meets the eye.

In England the creation of the most prominent psychedelic posters fell to individuals like Michael English, Nigel Weymouth and Martin Sharp. The designs are distinctly different from what was happening in the United States as was the actual printing process and yet in many respects created the same effect. Their posters incorporated more of an Eastern influence and because of their art school background the aspect of Op Art was incorporated more regularly. In fact some posters simply incorporated large letters to convey the message such as one promoting the Move's performance at the Marquee Club on July 11th, 1967.

Michael English left art school in the early sixties and after spending a few years as a commercial artist he met up with his eventual collaborator Nigel Weymouth. The two formed a design team with the name Hapshash and the Coloured Coat and set about designing posters for events at all of London's psychedelic clubs including UFO, Middle Earth, the Roundhouse and the Saville Theatre. Many of their posters, incorporate the use of the female form combined with flowing shapes and patterns incorporating English's distinctive lettering that was different from that used in San Francisco but just as illegible. The posters design was typically inked in black or blue with the colours laid over top allowing the line drawing to been seen through a variety of surface colours. The posters differed because they used the silk-screen process, which allowed them to employ many brighter and metallic colours. The process also allowed for colour variations with each poster run.

The other half of the Hapshash and the Coloured Coat team, Nigel Weymouth was born in India, which might have something to do with the strong Eastern influence in their poster designs. Weymouth was part owner in the fashionable hippie boutique, Granny Takes a Trip. His association with English lasted from 1966 through 1968.

Martin Sharp actually didn't create many event posters, his work was more to promote the visual identity of artists or activities and as such he got involved with the creation

WHEELS OF FIRE LP

of album graphics early on. It was while designing some of the early UFO events he came in contact with Eric Clapton and a strong artistic partnership ensued. It was his image-laden collage that graced the cover the Cream's **Disreali Gears** and **Wheels of Fire** LPs. He was even called upon to help write the lyrics for Cream's *Tales of Brave Ulysses.*

Poster artists ran into hard times when the ballrooms started closing. The face of concert promotion kicked into high-gear with the mass media. Some of the artists mentioned above moved into other artistic endeavours when the poster industry dried up. Wes Wilson and Bonnie MacLean moved away from San Francisco. Some who stayed like Lee Conklin and David Singer eventually moved into creating other forms of art. A number of artists like Stanley Mouse and Alton Kelley got heavily involved in album cover art and then commercial work. Sadly some like Rick Griffin and Greg Irons are no longer with us.

But is it Art?

Today the psychedelic poster has achieved the status of fine art having been the subject of displays at New York's Museum of Modern Art, Museum of Modern Art in California and the San Diego Museum of Art. Shows like these have pointed out how much psychedelic posters have in common with previous poster eras such as that of Toulouse Lautrec in the Moulin Rouge days. In fact the parallels are quite startling. As Alton Kelley says in **San Francisco Rock,** everything was done from a very spontaneous and natural feel, *"Nothing was preconceived. I don't think Lautrec did any serious thinking about what he was doing for the Moulin Rouge. I'm sure Lautrec had a good time at the Moulin Rouge. He was there on the scene. That was his world. And we were there on this scene. We went to all the dances, there was always a lot of stuff to do."*

A number of books have begun to shed increasing light on this aspect of the music scene from the sixties. The most authoritative volume is still Paul Grushkin's **Art of Rock** which is over 500 pages and reproduces over 1500 posters from the early Presley days to the late eighties but reserves the bulk of its pages to the psychedelic era. Now in its fourth printing this "encyclopaedia" is often referred to as the bible of postering. Each chapter is preceded by an extensive first-hand history of the times. What makes Gruskin's book so attractive are the sheer number of colour reproductions including the entire original Fillmore numbered series and virtually all the Family Dog posters as well. In addition, there are many sections devoted to hundreds of lesser know artists and areas where psychedelic posters played a part in the music scene.

Ted Owen's **High Art – A History of the Psychedelic Poster** is another excellent reference in that it reproduces some of the early writing of noted San Francisco poster and cultural historian Walter Medeiros along with many wonderful pages of poster reproductions in full colour. This book not only provides the detailed history of the psychedelic poster but also gives a detailed insight into the mechanics of many of the artists work with detailed profiles on many of the primary artists. Included in this group are some non-concert artists like the East Totem West Company who created psychedelic art posters. The book also details the work of British poster artists such as Michael English, Nigel Weymouth and Martin Sharp plus many of the lesser-known artists on both sides of the Atlantic. **High Art** also contains a valuable section on collecting psychedelic posters, which serves as a great introduction to the world of psychedelic memorabilia.

For those looking at the Fillmore Posters exclusively there is the **Art of the Fillmore** by Gayle Lemke. Bill Graham's Fillmore series with its run of almost 300 posters provides perhaps the most comprehensive overview of the many poster art styles. This full colour volume reproduces each and every poster, handout and in some cases variations in the art used for each event at the Fillmore. Many of these posters are reproduced to half or full page and provide the opportunity to study the posters in great detail. Not only does this volume provide brilliant colour reproductions, it includes a couple of excellent essays on the Fillmore's growth and how the poster work came about.

Other interesting, if somewhat difficult to track down books on posters include **High Societies**, published by the San Diego Museum of Art. This book was produced as the catalogue for the museums display of poster art that included Japanese block poster art, French dance-hall art of the Moulin Rouge hey-days and the psychedelic concert art of the sixties. The museum's display focused on the parallels between these eras and the catalogue contains many wonderful insights into the communities that helped create these works. Included are some interesting essays and comments from Walter Medeiros.

For those looking to collect works of specific artists there are books such as **Freehand: The Art of Stanley Mouse** that focuses on the work of Stanley Mouse, although books like this have become rather rare and difficult to locate.

For the longest time, a collector was able to pick up psychedelic posters for little more than pocket change. That all changed with the publication of Grushkin's book the **Art of Rock** in 1987. Overnight hundreds, if not thousands became attracted to these colours and swirls. As more and more people began tracking down posters, the market value for many of these items began to increase. Like so many things with the Baby Boom generation anything old…now has a value. It's not unusual to find hundreds of items listed on ebay.com or on-line at various poster shops selling for anywhere from $30 to well over $1000. And while most of these items are genuine a smart shopper will keep an eye out for the bogus reproductions sometimes passed off as originals.

It's not surprising that the prime source of these posters is San Francisco and that it's become quite a thriving industry there. Understand that many of those who collected the posters from the original concerts, and still have them squirreled away in the attic still reside in the Bay area. It is not unusual for small collections to regularly pop up. Dedicated museum/galleries are now open and even on-line to display these works of art. Two of the more prominent are Artrock on Folsom Street: *www.artrock.com* and SF Rock Posters and Collectibles on Powel Street. Both of these galleries have fine framed displays of original San Francisco psychedelic poster art and appear to be doing a booming business with collectors around the world. Outside of the San Francisco community collectors still have many reputable choices, one of the best being Peace Rock Posters in Florida *http://peacerock.com*. Having originally lived in the Bay area the company still maintains contacts there, and has a steady source of fine product.

For the serious collector, Eric King self-publishes **A Collectors Guide to the Numbered Dance Posters Created for Bill Graham and the Family Dog 1966 - 1973**. This self-produced, 640 plus page work is the result of over 30 years of studying posters, handbills and postcards and provides detailed descriptions of each and every version or printing of all the Fillmore, Avalon, Grande Ballrooms and Neon Rose items. Each poster, handbill and postcard is detailed with a small black and white print and a collector is able to determine the vintage of each item by such things as exact size, coloration, paper stock, paper colour and various, sometimes minute second or third printing changes to the original art. King also lists items known to be forgeries, bootlegged or pirate copies. This compendium is now in its 4th printing and is available direct from Eric King for $65.00 plus postage. King also maintains a website, which contains an on-going series of updates and corrections to the published text. The web site address is: ***http://home.earthlink.net/~therose7***. Kings book can be ordered either on line or at the following address:
Eric King
P.O. Box 4297
Berkeley, CA 94704

King's book avoids the issue of values. For this you will need a copy of Fred Williams' **5th Edition Rock Poster Price Guide**. This self-published book, like King's is in its 5th edition and provides valuable up-to-date information in regards to current values. What sets Williams' book apart from other such books, is his method of determining the values. The formula is simple and surprisingly accurate. Williams maintains an accounting of virtually all known sales so the prices he quotes are based, not on the sometimes inflated "asking" prices but on actual "sold" prices. When used in conjunction with Kings book any collector can be assured of staying on top of the market. The 5th Edition lists values for over 2000 posters, handbills and postcards from the 1960's to the 1980's.The book can be purchased direct from Williams for $25 plus postage. The website address is: ***http://www.rocknart2000.com***. Williams' book can also be purchased my mail at the following address:
Fred Williams
2313 East Willow Brook Way
Sandy, Utah 84092

The Changing Face Of Concert Lighting With The Psychedelic Light Shows

If the posters were the street-level artistic expression of the psychedelic music scene, the concert light show was clearly the organic, visual expression of the musical experience itself. The lightshows took the static ideas or images that appeared on the posters and transformed them into moving images saturated in colour. Like the bands of the day, the light show companies came with their own identities. Names like Glenn McKay's Headlights, the Holy See, the Brotherhood of Light, Little Princess 109, Dr. Zarkov and many more all shared billing with the top bands of the day on the dance-concert posters.

Light shows for rock concerts pre 1966 consisted of predominantly uniform stage lights that blanketed the entertainers in faint sheets of colour while the obligatory spotlights left the featured soloist bathed in white. The colours were used in the background and only for accents. The predominant view was that artists on stage want to be seen, why even consider disguising them in floods of colour.

All that changed in 1966 with the introduction of the psychedelic light show in both the United States and England. According to Haight-Ashbury historian Charles Perry, the experimentation with lightshows goes back to San Francisco State College in 1952 where a Professor Seymour Locks was using hollow slides filled with some kind of pigments and projecting them onto screens for special art classes. He initially was using a regular projector but soon changed over to the overhead projector to ad a further dimension. Jazz musicians typically accompanied these performances. The professor took the show to a special conference in Los Angeles and continued to teach Light and Art there. It was one of his students, Elias Romero who took the concepts back to San Francisco in the early sixties. Romero was living in a building that was managed by none other than Bill Ham. The two shared ideas and the rest is history.

The shows that came to light in San Francisco were perhaps the most representative of their kind. And while some would argue that better shows existed, in particular in New York at the Fillmore East, it was the Fillmore and Avalon shows that were the inspirational spring broad for the myriad of artists to follow.

The typical show at the Avalon didn't even feature a spotlight on the lead singer like at the Fillmore. The standard arrangement at both ballrooms consisted of a raised platform at the back of the hall where these light-artists were allowed to create live visuals in time to the music. The set-ups consisted of an array of overhead projectors, colour wheels, black lights, slide projectors, wet set-ups, film projectors, powerful coloured lights, plus any other fancy device created by these craftsmen to further their expression. The walls in the Fillmore were for the most part white, so while the dance floor may been somewhat dark, the walls and most particularly behind the performers on stage there was a mass of moving colours and images. These light artists, much like the poster artists, while not in competition with each other certainly took pains to out-do each other. At the Fillmore they went so far as to film dancers one weekend and then double expose the film and project it as part of the following week's show.

Some individuals like Bill Ham had been doing lights since 1965 following his meeting up with Elias Romero. Ham was a lightshow pioneer, one of the first to make liquid-lights work and had even taken his kinetic light sculpture to the Red Dog Saloon in Virginia City to provide the lights for the Charlatans. He was also the building manager for the Dog House where all the members of the original Family Dog collective lived. His early work took place in the Dog House basement, where local acidheads who lived on Pine Street gathered to trip out to his experimental light paintings usually to the sounds of someone on guitar or flute. It was no accident Ham was called upon to provide the lightshow at many of the early Avalon Ballroom Family Dog dance-concerts. Later he worked with partner Bob Cohen and created what they called the "magical light box" which actually changed colours to the music being played. By 1968 Ham created LSD Theatre. The LSD stood for Light and Sound Dimension.

AD FOR KRISHNA LIGHTS SHOP IN LONDON

In Britain the band most identified with the growing light-show industry was Pink Floyd. They first performed in front of a moving film in the early days of 1966. By March, they were using a combination of powerful blue and red floodlights combined with the projection film. Within a matter of months they had incorporated a slide projector that someone had seen used in San Francisco. The images were changed to coincide with the ebb and flow of the music.

At the height of their popularity the lightshows were seen to be a pivotal element of each evenings performance and in some cases even taking a mediocre musical performance over the top through the visual stimulation. On average working for Bill Graham at the Fillmore, the light show practitioners were paid anywhere from $250 to $750 a night and there were upwards of eighty different set-ups. These shows became finely tuned events.

Another one of the earliest light show pioneers was Ray Anderson who's Holy See began working performances at the Matrix before moving on to events at the Fillmore,

Avalon and California Hall. In an effort to create their own identity, Anderson worked with a number of the poster artists to obtain some of the poster elements for specific bands; these poster elements were then incorporated in an almost animated fashion in the evening's performances. Like the music, light shows were a spontaneous performance that required an almost invisible link between the musicians and the Holy See. When the two elements clicked it was a powerful visual enhancement.

The Holy See was soon providing the lightshows at the original Fillmore on a regular basis. One effect in particular is fondly remembered. Because of the clean walls and high ceilings of the Fillmore the Holy See were able to take a whole series of film and liquid images and create the effect where the images rush down a sidewall up the other side and finally ending up projecting on the stage. The overall vertigo created, as the room literally swam in a sea of lights, colour and fluid was a powerful effect that combined with the music to provide a sensory overload. Sadly the move to the new Fillmore West, the old Carousel Ballroom, with its lower ceilings meant that the light shows could only take effect on the stage. This reduction in overall image area significantly reduced the light shows effect and was perhaps one more reason why the focus turned more to just the performers on stage.

The light show set-ups in San Francisco, and in most other places were always at the back of the facility projecting onto the performers, Bill Graham was able to change this set-up when he opened the Fillmore East in February 1968 in New York City. The Fillmore East being an old movie house had a giant screen with room behind to set up the light show. This was significant for a number of reasons. It meant that the lights were now projected behind and didn't interfere with the performers. It also meant the images could be brighter and larger but perhaps most of all it allowed for a permanent set up, and in the case of the Fillmore East that fell to Joshua White and the Joshua Light Show, who were permanently billed with each show.

Bill Graham said in his autobiography, *"Joshua White added a visual element at Fillmore East far beyond what was available to me on the West Coast at the time. The West Coast light shows were beautiful slides and liquid projection. Joshua choreographed light shows to reflect the complexity of the music and the times we were living in."* For his part White saw his role as mediator between the performer and the audience, *"I could entertain that audience with slides. If the band was tuning, or something. We had visual tricks and gags. We had routines we would do. People began to look at the light show as sort of the emcee."* White took on the role of conductor and hired some extremely creative individuals to work specific components of the light rig.

The single most important element to the psychedelic lightshow that lives in our consciousness is the liquid effects. Who hasn't seen examples in movies, documentaries or even still-photos of bands performing before what appears to a wall of globular liquid suspended behind them and moving fluidly to the general tempo of the music, while bubbles are changing colours. It was like some primitive, flat lava lamp. In order to achieve this effect, light show practitioners secured two "clock-faces", like the old school wall clocks, and set the two convex faces inside each other, bowl side down. In between the two faces was poured a highly secretive mixture of water, oils and solvent-based pigments. The colours were not to mix and the oil and water were there to provide the bubbles. Movement was created by simply tapping the sides the "clock-faces". How much movement and how many bubbles were all created by the human touch of the wet-show operator, and how strong the colours were all relied on the amount of liquid they poured in. This whole unit was then placed on a regulation school overhead projector. It was truly revolutionary in its simplicity.

The radical effect of globs of colour moving and pulsating to the music is an image that remains truly unique in the world of light shows, because of its organic nature. The Joshua Light Show built their own special unit called the Tin Man. White explains, *"The basic effect everyone remembers was oil and water. We took an industrial clock face and we put oil and water in it and we coloured the oil and we coloured the water. We took another clock face and put it over the first and pressed down. It squeezed the oil and water out toward the edges. When you lifted up the clock face on top, the oil and water fell into the centre. Oil and water never mix. So what you got were different coloured bubbles. On the screen, the audience could not see the clock faces. All they saw were the bubbles keeping the rhythm of the music either by doing it very fast or very slowly."* Towards the end of the Fillmore East days, the Joshua Light Show was using ten different grades of oil to provide a full range of oil and water effects.

In addition to the wet effects the Joshua Light show incorporated a whole range of equipment designed to bend and shape light. Devices such as a "lumia" which created an effect similar to the aurora borealis, moving and shifting in sheets of colour. There was a wide assortment of projectors, both slide and film with an assortment of images and film loops to suit the moment, and at the controls was Joshua White. He was the visual conductor. While each artist was working their particular elements, White controlled what and how much the audience saw. He could allow only a small image or if the music was right he could display an explosion of colour and movement to assault the senses.

From their inception in 1965, the lightshows were seen as an integral part of San Francisco's psychedelic ballroom performances. But after years of working behind the scenes for what they felt was little financial reward, events came to a head with the big lightshow strike in August of 1969 spearheaded by Jerry Abrams among others. Basically the people involved with the various lightshows felt Bill Graham was too controlling of the music scene, so they planned to pull their services. It all culminated one evening at Chet Helm's Family Dog on the Great Highway. It was getting to the point where the lightshows were threatening to picket the Fillmore and Winterland shows. It was all down to money and they felt they weren't getting their share. In fact pickets did go up at one show where the Grateful Dead were supposed to play. Jerry Garcia who believed in the labour movement and came from a family who did likewise, refused to cross the picket line. The meeting at the Family Dog on the Great Highway provided the opportunity for all involved to vent, yell, and shout but in the end nothing much changed. Bill Graham stormed out. The lightshow groups were not going to get any more money from him. Helm's ever the idealist and mediator strived to provide the lightshow companies with the opportunity to create their own events devoted more to the light experience. They in fact did use Helm's facility for a few events, but the lighting guild quickly learned that people were coming to hear the music. The lights were nice but they had become an extra. A lot had changed from the early days of the psychedelic scene where each event was based on everyone's participation.

White says as far as the lightshow aspect, *"The great year for me was from when we re-opened [the Fillmore East] in 1968 until the summer of Woodstock. For me, that was one brilliant year. After Woodstock, all the famous things happened and then it went downhill."* Truly things changed dramatically after Woodstock. White explains, *"I stood on the stage at Woodstock, looking out and I knew that the Joshua Light Show was irrelevant there. No one needed us; we didn't need to be there, we didn't need to provide anything. It was such a visual event that the light show was no longer required to provide any visual stimulation."*

After 1969, lightshows did indeed begin to change their focus, perhaps because of the lightshow strike, perhaps not; the lightshow began to take on more of a support role until they disappeared entirely. Lights and visuals have always been important in rock theatre, but as lamps became more powerful and costs continued to rise, the lightshow artist set-ups gave way to other forms of lighting effects, which became more general sheets of colour with isolated accents. At the peak of their popularity there were over 80 different light shows operating, and to their credit they were a key element to creating the psychedelic scene. The sheer number of lightshow set ups created a very competitive market and it was impossible for all of them to work regularly. In the end the bands themselves chose to have more control over their own lights. Just like they began to have more say over the sound set up and even who the support acts would be, so they began planning their individual performances tied to specific lighting effects that were personalized for each tour. Sadly the lightshow artists became irrelevant.

The Changing Face Of The Musical Venues

Before the psychedelic era, that period from 1958 to 1965 there were countless clubs and coffee houses catering to either the jazz or folk scenes. As rock music and psychedelic music in particular became more popular many of these clubs began either devoting specific evenings or changing their format entirely to provide performance opportunities. Clubs in San Francisco included the Peppermint Tree, El Cid, the Purple Onion, the Coffee Gallery and Mother's, tagged by Joel Selvin as the country's first psychedelic nightclub that opened in 1965. In Los Angeles there was the Whisky A-Go-Go, the Trip, the Action, and the Troubadour to name a few. London, England has always had a rich musical history and the psychedelic scene was played out in venues like Blaises, where Hendrix played one of his first London gigs, Bag-o-Nails, the Upper Cut, the Speak Easy and the short-lived Tiles that opened in 1966 and closed a year later. Universities everywhere taking their cue from what they saw happening at the hip campuses, like Berkeley began staging dance-concerts and helped spread the musical word. But unlike the many typically smaller nightclubs there also arose designated facilities that for a time through the late sixties changed the face of musical venues. They were called "the ballrooms". Throughout cities in virtually every country there sprouted up medium sized venues that began catering specifically to the new music, many with in-house light shows and sound systems. Typical of the scene was what happened in Vancouver, Canada where venues of any decent size, especially if they were in the right neighbourhoods were adopted for use. In Vancouver there was the Afterthought, which was actually part of the Kitsilano Theatre located at 2114 W 4th Avenue. Then for a brief time there was a club called Dante's Inferno, then the Embassy Ballroom, which became the Retinal Circus. When the Retinal Circus started up, the action at the Afterthought closed down, partially because the Retinal Circus was bigger and could attract not only larger acts but also bigger crowds. This sequence was repeated over and over. The following list is a brief overview of some of the key venues that played a part in exposing new talent to the psychedelic counter-culture.

United States Venues:

The Matrix: Before the ballrooms there were a couple of smaller clubs such as Mother's or the Peppermint Tree, but the club that really started it off was the Matrix at 3138 Fillmore Street. It was an ex-pizza parlour that was remodelled by Marty Balin and friends as a place for his new band, the Jefferson Airplane to play. The club opened on September 13th, 1965 and became the home of Jefferson Airplane for the first months of the emerging psychedelic San Francisco scene. The Matrix showcased virtually all the Bay area bands and plenty of travelling outfits including the Doors. It closed for good in 1972.

Longshoremen's Hall: Located at 400 North Point, this odd-shaped hall was the sight of the first of three pivotal events that shaped the San Francisco psychedelic scene. On October 16th 1965 the "Tribute to Dr. Strange" was the first event staged by the Family Dog. It featured the Charlatans, fresh from the Red Dog Saloon, the Jefferson Airplane, performing for the first time outside of the Matrix, the Great Society, making only their second live appearance and the Marbles. This event along with the two that followed set the mould for the ballroom scene that soon followed. This hall was also the site of the Trips Festival in January of 1966 where Bill Graham was brought in as manager. That event led to the creation of the Fillmore and the rest is history.

The Fillmore: As already discussed the ballrooms in San Francisco were a facility in the right time and the right place. When we say the Fillmore we're actually talking about two facilities, the Original Fillmore and the Fillmore West. The original Fillmore Auditorium was located upstairs at 1805 Geary Street and was operated by Bill Graham from January 1966 to July 1968. It first opened as the Majestic Academy of Dancing in 1912 and its open dance floor had room for 1500. This is the ballroom most people think of when they think of psychedelic music. It became the focal point of the psychedelic genre by virtue of Graham's forceful business sense and his mission to expose young people to many different forms of music. In July of 1968 Graham relocated and renamed his ballroom the Fillmore West located upstairs on Market Street and Van Ness Avenue. He had recently opened the Fillmore East in New York and the renaming was smart packaging. The Fillmore West was originally know as the Carousel Ballroom until it changed hands to Graham, and had room for about 3000. It closed in June 1971. The original Fillmore on Geary and Fillmore had continued to put on rock shows with other promoters and was re-acquired by Graham after closing the Fillmore West. The refurbished original still operates as Bill Graham's Fillmore to this day with a regular schedule of contemporary artists.

Avalon Ballroom: Located at 1268 Sutter Street or for the posters sake, Sutter and Van Ness, the Avalon opened at the same time as the Fillmore and had room for close to 1500 people. The building had been constructed in 1911 as the Puckett Academy of Dance and opened as the Avalon Ballroom in April 1966. The Avalon was run in a much more relaxed fashion, in fact some say too relaxed. While Graham was constantly on the lookout for people slipping in without paying, Chet Helms thought nothing of offering a free nights entertainment for friends. It was after all, what friends do for friends. The Avalon Ballroom was always seen to be the true hippie ballroom. It eventually ceased being the home of Family Dog productions in November 1968 although it continued with shows under the name Soundproof Productions into April of 1969. The ballroom sat idle for some time before eventually being torn down and rebuilt as a multi-plex cinema in the seventies.

Winterland: As the bands got bigger and attendance grew Bill Graham started sharing time at the Winterland, which originally was an ice rink located on the corner of Post and Steiner. It was larger than the Fillmore seating a little over 5000 and became his main venue once he closed down the Fillmore West in 1971. In fact he spent most of 1968 and 1969 spreading performances between both the Fillmore and Winterland. The facility was used by many other independent producers and became a favourite for bands like the Grateful Dead, Janis Joplin, the Band, and even the Rolling Stones. The Winterland was used as the location for the Band's movie and recording, **The Last Waltz** and was also where Peter Frampton recorded his LP **Frampton Comes Alive**. The Winterland was demolished in 1985 to make way for a condominium project.

California Hall: Located at 625 Polk Street, Chet Helms used the California Hall for a couple of events in late 1965 before securing the Avalon as the home base for the Family Dog. For a short time, Big Brother and the Holding Company called California Hall home. During 1966 and 1967 it was in regular use with shows for all the key bands of the area including the Charlatans, Mystery Trend and the Grateful Dead. It was also used for one of the early Acid-Tests, but apart from the hey-days of 66-67, this officially recognized historic building played only a minor role on the music scene.

Carousel Ballroom: Located at Market Street and Van Ness Avenue, the Carousel has the distinction of having been changed to become the Fillmore West. It had originally been known as El Patio through the thirties and forties but came to prominence during the psychedelic era when in early 1968 the ballroom was taken over and managed by a partnership of the Grateful Dead, Jefferson Airplane and Quicksilver Messenger Service. Opened as an artist's alternative to both the Fillmore and even the Avalon, it suffered from an onerous lease arrangement and never made any money. While some interesting band line-ups were featured, the Carousel suffered from police pressure when a number of Hells Angel's gigs were staged. The lease was eventually taken over by Bill Graham who converted the facility to the Fillmore West in July 1968.

Continental Ballroom: Located at 1600 Martin Avenue in Santa Clara, the Continental was the South Bay's answer to the main San Francisco ballroom scene. And much like those other facilities, all the major bands performed regularly there. Given its location the Continental also provided a performance opportunity for many of the popular bands from the San Jose area like the Count Five and Harpers Bizarre.

Straight Theater: Located at 1702 Haight Street the Straight Theater was a local cinema built in 1910, but in 1967 it became a hippie owned and operated facility in the heart of Haight-Ashbury. The idea was to have an alternative to the Fillmore and the Avalon that was somewhat more people friendly. It had a superior sound system designed and installed by acid-king Owsley Stanley. The Grateful Dead adopted the theatre as their rehearsal hall and performed there, opening weekend in July 1967. Lacking the necessary business skills the theatre struggled along for a little over a year but finally had to close its doors by the end of 1968. It was torn down in 1978 to make way for new development.

The Shrine Auditorium was home to Pinnacle Productions staged by poster artist and concert promoter John Van Hamersveld. Hamersveld, who worked at Capitol Records and had contributed to the art-work art for the Beatles Magical Mystery Tour, began translating his skills to posters promoting events at the Shrine. The shows were highly influenced by what was happening in San Francisco at the time and featured many of the same performers and poster artists. The first shows began in 1967 and ran through to about 1969 before Pinnacle went bankrupt.

The Kaleidoscope: Located at 1228 Vine Street, very near the famous Hollywood and Vine corner in Los Angeles it was originally built in the 1930s and known as the Earl Carroll Theatre. The most unusual aspect to this facility was its eighty-foot revolving stage, which also featured a six-foot outer ring that could rotate in the opposite direction. Having been built to stage evening dinner club productions it also boasted such peculiar effects as a "rainfall" curtain, fire-jets and portions of the staging that elevated up and down. A capacity crowd at the Kaleidoscope was about 1000 people. It opened in April 1967 and ran through 1968 with weekly performances all promoted by posters that were cut to a circular shape.

The Grande Ballroom: It was opened by Russ Gibb who was greatly influenced by what he saw happening in San Francisco during his time there in early 1966. Pronounced "Grand-y", the Grande Ballroom became home base for bands such as the MC5 and the Stooges. Gibb employed artists such as Gary Grimshaw and Carl Lundgren and was able to recreate the San Francisco feel more effectively than most.

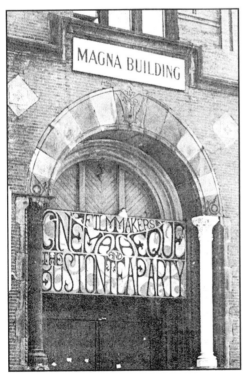

BOSTON TEA PARTY

Boston Tea Party: Originally an acoustic folk room called Club 47; the small facility was taken over by local rock entrepreneur Ray Riepen and renamed the Boston Tea Party to capitalize not only on the historical event but also the double meaning applied to tea and marijuana. Things moved into high gear in late 1967 when he began booking all the right acts both local and touring. A small club with seating capacity for 750 it forged alliances with local radio station WBCN and became the place-to-be in Boston's underground community. It befell the same fate as most other venues having to struggle with increasing talent fees and closed down in December of 1970.

Kinetic Playground: Located at 4812 North Clark Street in Chicago, the Kinetic Playground was better known to people in Chicago as the Electric Theatre. Like the San Francisco ballrooms it created weekly events running over two or three days featuring the typical wide mix of blues, rock and soul performers. Given its location the wealth of blues talent was first rate and they mixed well with the touring British bands.

Aragon Ballroom: Located at 1106 W. Lawrence in Chicago the Aragon has a rich history of staging rock performances which continues to this day. Built in 1926 it was one of the many large dance halls that featured ballroom dancing through until 1955 when the activity faded in popularity. It became a mod-discothèque in 1966 called the Cheetah Club. Its heyday as a psychedelic stop was from 1968 through to its initial closing in October of 1970. With a capacity of over 4000 it was a popular stop for all the touring bands from the Grateful Dead to Jethro Tull. It was also a hotbed for drug activity, which lead to a number of over-the-top crowd antics leading to its closure. Under new management it re-opened in 1972 and continues to host musical events to this day.

Vulcan Gas Company: Located in Austin it became Texas' first psychedelic ballroom. It opened in the Fall of 1967 and was an outgrowth of a club project called the Electric Grandmother. A capacity crowd on any given night was just under 1000 people providing a relatively intimate atmosphere very similar to what was happening at the Avalon Ballroom. In similar fashion the Vulcan Gas Company created approximately 100 posters to promote events through to early 1970 when it ceased to operate.

British Venues:

Marquee Club: This London club has a history that goes back many years and many locations having started out as a jazz and blues basement club on Oxford Street in the late fifties. By the early sixties it had developed a reputation for the blues. All that began to change by early 1964 as bands like the Yardbirds and Manfred Mann began putting in more regular appearances. The Marquee opened in a new location on Wardour Street in the middle of Soho in March of 1964 and immediately began booking many of the popular rock, mod and freakbeat bands. The Marquee was the home of some of the first psychedelic happenings in London with the five events known as the Spontaneous Underground. In addition to these totally unstructured affairs the club regularly booked the top psychedelic bands from the Pink Floyd to Cream regularly for one-night performances.

The UFO: This was the primary London underground club. It came to life on December 23rd 1966, at an old Irish club at 31 Tottenham Court Road called the Blarney that could hold roughly 600 people on the dance floor. Opening weekends featured two all-night raves on the 23rd and the 30th featuring Pink Floyd. The UFO (pronounced "You-Foe") was alcohol free and featured its own light show plus the usual sorts of underground arty-ness. Following some negative publicity the UFO was forced to relocate into the much less intimate Roundhouse at Chalk Farm in the Summer of 1967. It operated there until closing for good in October 1967.

Middle Earth: This underground (literally and figuratively) facility came into existence in early 1967 at 43 King Street, Covent Garden and was originally known as the Electric Garden. It soon changed its name to Middle Earth a name taken from the **Lord of the Rings** books. Much like the UFO, Middle Earth was forced to move in July of 1968 and the owners settled once again for the Roundhouse, Chalk Farm that had by now been vacated by the UFO people. At that location they not only presented the cream of the British psychedelic bands, but also many of the touring American groups like the Doors and Jefferson Airplane. Despite some Police intervention Middle Earth persisted until early 1969 when it too ceased operations.

The Saville Theatre: The Saville was a working theatre that had been in operation since 1931. Brian Epstein had been holding shows there since 1965 and by 1967 saw an opportunity to capitalize on the growing psychedelic scene so he began booking shows to suit the times. The Saville held roughly 1200 people and became London's main big-stage for the underground scene. Epstein started a Sunday Evening series that featured the top psychedelic bands including Hendrix, Traffic, Cream, Tomorrow and many others. Tragically when Brian Epstein died in the Summer of 1967 so did the events at the Saville.

Outdoor Festivals

Another aspect of the changing venues was the staging of elaborate outdoor festivals such as Monterey Pop, Woodstock, Altamont, etc. From the beginning there has been a tradition in pop music of creating package tours, where a group of artists would be contracted together to perform in a series of venues. Some of these venues would in fact take place outdoors at various fairs or summer events. This activity is realistically portrayed in the movie, **That Thing You Do**. In a small way these package tours can be seen as a precursor to the huge outdoor festivals that came to fruition during the psychedelic era.

The years 1967 to 1970 saw the development of sophisticated huge outdoor events where hundreds of thousands gathered with music as the focal point. For many commentators, the developmental or creative arc started with 1967's Monterey International Pop Festival, peaked with Woodstock in 1969 and in some respects died with the horrors of Altamont by the end of that year. These festivals were created with the idea of bringing together the various disparate bodies associated with or drawn together by the music of the radical sixties.

As explained elsewhere, the Monterey Pop Festival was an attempt to bring together the music scenes of San Francisco, London and Los Angeles and in many respects it succeeded in doing that. The success of this event pushed many of the groups involved and the whole psychedelic movement firmly into the media spotlight. In England there were outdoor festivals that pre-dated Monterey Pop such as the Jazz & Blues Festival that became the Reading Rock Festival, the Bath Arts Festival that became the Glastonbury Faire and so forth.

The fascination with large outdoor festivals took the world by storm, as events were staged around the world over the next couple of years. Festivals were held in Rome, Italy, Toronto, Canada, Paris, France, and even in Switzerland. But nowhere did they occur with such regularity as in the United States. In the years following 1967 it seemed there were a couple of large-scale events every few months taking place everywhere from Denver, Colorado to Atlanta, Georgia and many points in between. With the success of the first Woodstock in August of 1969 the impetus was there to go one better. But in the haste to do so, mistakes were made and events were ill planned or suffered from inclement weather resulting in some near disasters.

By the time of Altamont in December of 1969, and the following years Isle of Wight Festival in England in August of 1970 the entire mood of the counter-culture had changed. Charged by the political and military events of 1968 this group was in the mood for confrontation. There was the incessant demand for "free concerts" and "music is for the people" which constantly stirred up concert-goers. The sights of Hells Angels security resulting in the death of an audience member at Altamont, and Joni Mitchell's tearful plea for peace and understanding while concertgoers raged at the Isle of Wight clearly signalled a change from the peaceful early days of the Human Be-In.

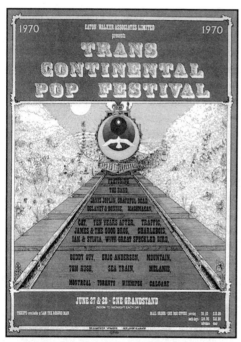

POSTER FOR TRANSCONTINENTAL POP FESTIVAL

Perhaps one of the most unusual undertakings for the psychedelic era was the 1970 Transcontinental Pop Festival express train tour that made four stops across Canada. Financially backed by members of the Eaton family the train was packed with bands and made stops in Montreal, Toronto, Winnipeg and Calgary. This was not some second rate show either, on board was the Band, Janis Joplin, the Grateful Dead, Traffic, Ten Years After, Buddy Guy, Ian & Sylvia, Mountain and many others. Over a dozen acts were booked to perform and travel on the train across Canada. The story is told of one stop in Saskatoon, Saskatchewan where a couple of individuals were sent to find a liquor store to replenish the train supplies, and in the process nearly cleaned out the entire store.

While festivals continue to this day, they have changed dramatically. This is best demonstrated in the comparing of two Woodstock events. On one-hand, festivals these days are staged with military precision having the benefit of years of experience in every department from food to porta-potties. The sound systems have improved immeasurably and the technical aspects of changing stages is now a fine-art and completed in minutes. Needless to say security is one of the highest priorities although it's not always foolproof. On the other hand, musically these events have evolved into cookie cutter affairs that in many ways mirror the pop package tours of the late fifties and early sixties more than they do the spirit of the psychedelic era. The original Woodstock of 1969 could proudly boast such diversity as solo folk artists like John Sebastian, Joan Baez or Richie Havens occupying centre stage along side performances from bands as Jimi Hendrix, Jefferson Airplane, the Who, Sha-Na-Na, Santana and Crosby Stills and Nash. Remember Santana had not even released their first album when they performed at the original Woodstock. Musical diversity was a cornerstone of those early events.

Today it's a whole different story. With corporate influence being exercised by the various management and record company executives the line-ups of today's festivals has been sterilized to a one-dimensional musical level witnessed by the 1999 version of Woodstock. On the main stage were Kid Rock, Korn, Offspring Metallica, Rage Against the Machine and a host of other so called alternative modern rock bands, all more or less cut from the same rock sub-genre. Consistency of "target audience" is now the key. Those other performers like Brian Setzer, Jewel, Elvis Costello or Bruce Hornsby were placed on the "other" stage. But artists aside there was something fundamentally different in spirit between these two events.

Between the two stages were the other tents, the video tent, the extreme sports tent and so on and so forth. What really separated Woodstock 69 from Woodstock 99 was how commercial it had become, and more than that how it appeared most of those in attendance were OK with that. In comparison to the original, Woodstock 99 had clearly "sold-out". The beer gardens were sponsored, there were logos and brand names everywhere, and food was even more over-priced. And it was all accepted as the way things are. Consumerism rules. Media coverage was everywhere. Everything was more "extreme" and there was "more" of everything.

Except for one thing. Sadly any spirit of peace, love and understanding was systematically extinguished over the three days of the 1999 Woodstock event, and the weekend degenerated into something resembling a burned out battlefield. Semi-trailer trucks were up-turned and set a-blaze, others looted the remaining tents and in the end the "lord of the flies" mentality reigned supreme. Without putting too fine a point on it, some will argue that the first Woodstock also had its share of problems and while that's true, what I would draw attention too is the changed spirit of the event. Woodstock 99 and events like that are no longer about peace and understanding. Long gone, it seems are the days when you made the trip to an event because you wanted to "make a difference". Today it's all about having a party and doing everything to the extreme. Some might argue that this is simply an updated version of the participatory dance-concerts of the ballroom era, but this fails to observe the obvious. The soul of these modern events has changed, but not for the better.

Yet reviewing the hundreds of photos posted on-line from Woodstock 99, within the thousands in attendance it was still possible to spot some who seemed to be there looking for that original spirit. Perhaps in time the cycle will turn and the original spirit of the sixties will return.

The Definition Of Psychedelic Music

Paul Kantner of the Jefferson Airplane once said, *"Nobody can define psychedelic music. Psychedelic is when the person that is listening to it is on acid."* To some degree this may true, however in this next section I plan to throw "caution to the wind" and do exactly that, attempt to define what psychedelic music really is. One-time guitarist for the British psychedelic band Tomorrow, Steve Howe begins the defining process, *"It's very hard to define what psychedelic music is. It's a certain kind of looseness with a certain kind of tightness. Certainly the lyrics had to be right. There had to be some kind of optimism, some sort of colouring or depth in the words that might surprise."* It is extremely difficult to put a clear and simple definition on this genre of music, more so than any other form. It's difficult because it's possible to play any number of other musical styles and still qualify to be a psychedelic band. Think about it; it is possible to be a psychedelic country band or psychedelic jug-band just as easy as it is to be a psychedelic rock band! After all it's worth remembering that the whole psychedelic genre began as a cultural movement. It was only as a result of this cultural movement that the music of the day was affected. But affected it was. More than ever before, the musician's of the psychedelic era developed a keen sense of real musical experimentation, exploration and innovation. What is also clear is that as bands influenced by the British Invasion of the early sixties started taking drugs such as LSD they sought to replicate the physical experience of that drug induced state through the music they created. The two bands most identified with this approach would be Pink Floyd and the Grateful Dead.

These two bands set the tone musically for much of the psychedelic music to follow. The Grateful Dead, an odd blend of schooled and self-taught musicians became known for their long drawn out, guitar laden musical trips, which became the soundtrack to the early Acid Tests conducted throughout many parts of the California coast in 1965. The Grateful Dead made an almost sacramental point of performing while high on LSD, at least at the beginning. Not only was the band stretching the length of the songs to suit the evening's mood they were also turning up the volume. Guitarist Bob Weir explains, *"We began turning up loud pretty quickly. From the start, it was faster, looser, louder and harrier. We were going for a ride. We were gonna see what this baby'll do. It helped that we were playing in an uncritical situation. What didn't help was the fact that we were so completely disoriented, so we had to fend for ourselves and improvise."* It was out of this open attitude that bands like the Dead began to mine other musical forms.

Pink Floyd meanwhile introduced the sensory overload of keyboards to the experience creating their own brand of extended flights of psychedelic fantasy. The Floyd even managed to craft a few hit singles through it all with *Arnold Layne* and *See Emily Play* which are now considered classics of the period from the pen of Syd Barrett. Barrett's obsession with LSD is well documented and it's accepted that it led to his creative downfall. Yet for a brief time it sparked a certain creativity that set the British Underground on its ear. Producer and friend Joe Boyd proclaimed, *"He set the tone for what people think of as psychedelic guitar playing. He wasn't as striking a technician as Gilmour, but he had a sound and a feeling that had all those qualities of spaciness and abstraction."*

The Times, they are a changing...

To help understand the times, it's important to realize that pop music of the early sixties was very much a carry-over from the late fifties. The songs were very superficial and relied in many cases on performers singing other people's material. The time of artists writing their own work hadn't yet occurred and wouldn't until the Beatles hit the stage. However, by the end of 1964 and early 1965 the notion of becoming a pop band had been revolutionized by the success of the Beatles. Remember pop music (initially there was no rock music) was still seen by many as somewhat shallow and not at all meaningful. The more serious writers were on the folk side of the musical tree. Here were people like Bob Dylan, Peter Paul & Mary, Pete Seeger, Phil Ochs, Joan Baez and a host of others who took their writing craft very seriously all with furrowed-brows and a studied earnestness in their acoustic presentation. In this world it was the words alone that were important. The musicianship provided merely a backdrop to create some sense of melody. In the time-honoured tradition of troubadours down through the ages, the melodies purpose was simply to make it easier for the words to be remembered and repeated. And all was well in this folk world, until one day when Bob Dylan met John Lennon. The two shared a musical epiphany. Dylan made the comment to Lennon that he thought the Beatles were in a wonderful position to have more of a social impact, but that their lyrics were for the most part meaningless. They didn't say anything. This hit John Lennon like a ton-of-bricks: so much so that he made an almost immediate change in his and even the other Beatles' lyrical content. Their next release, **Rubber Soul** displayed in full glory not only their initial psychedelic musical leanings but also showcased this new lyrical direction that went beyond the superficial pop norm.

For his part, Lennon introduced the electric guitar to Bob Dylan as the two of them casually jammed in the hotel room. This seemingly insignificant event left its mark with the budding folk-icon and would have greater impact in the coming months. Dylan, who was perhaps the most respected of the new folk performers, revered by some, astounded audiences a few months later at the 1965 Newport Folk Festival when he showed up on stage with an electric guitar. The audience, standing in the pouring rain were dumbstruck and outraged. The sheer volume shocked everyone at this very self-righteous and traditional event. In the end, Dylan was boo-ed off stage only to return with an acoustic guitar to perform a couple more numbers. Fittingly his closing numbers were *Mr. Tambourine Man* and *It's All Over Now, Baby Blue*. Needless to say the die had been cast.

What troubled those in the audience and virtually all the critical reviewers was the idea of change. Dylan challenged the long held belief that you could never be a serious writer AND play electric rock music. This notion was revolutionary in 1965. The conventional thinking said the Beatles may have been good pop/rock musicians but they didn't write about anything meaningful. Conversely Bob Dylan had lots to say but shouldn't stoop to using pop music methods or instrumentation to spread the message. And up till the 1965 Newport Folk Festival the line in the sand was clearly drawn. Suddenly Dylan was erasing the line. He opened the door to a new sound, one that combined both meaningful lyrics and electric music. He also opened the floodgates to a new musical experience by virtue of the volume of electric instrumentation.

Within a few short months the musical world had turned upside-down. Due in no small part to the growing counter-culture movement it was now accepted that you could actually write a song that said something, that had a message AND yes, used electric instruments that sounded loud. In fact, the counter-culture EXPECTED it to be so. In their world, there was so much to say and it was best expressed musically. By 1966 this new electric sound was something the counter-culture movement took for granted in their music. With this change to electric instrumentation and sound, virtuosity became a more important component of the composer's craft. This instrumental virtuosity became yet another means of self-expression. Learning your instrument and learning to play long and involved solos became the mainstay of the growing psychedelic musical movement. Even performers who played close to traditional blues learned to stretch the envelope and create startling nuances to tried-and-traditional musical motifs. The musical legacy that sprang from this adventurous outlook has never been paralleled for its uniqueness and originality since. This era was filled with such distinct and diverse sounds from contemporaries such as the Beatles, Jimi Hendrix, the Who, the Doors, the Byrds, Pink Floyd and so on. But more importantly, and this is the telling point, as different as they were from each other they all formed part of the youth cultures voice. It's doubtful we shall ever again see such diversity again as was witnessed on the stages of Monterey and Woodstock.

The Psychedelic Music Experience

At its' core, psychedelic music attempted to replicate some aspect of the drug-induced state of mind. It tried through the sensations of feedback, volume, arrangement, percussion, sonic-droning, raga rhythms and many other techniques to replicate a mood, sensation or experience. The instrument most associated with psychedelic music is without question the guitar. It was the instrument of choice. The guitar had developed to a critical point where the variety available, solid body, hollow body, six string, twelve string, acoustic and electric allowed for bands to, more than ever before, begin creating unique individual musical identities. Its perhaps not coincidental that the sitar being a "guitar-based" instrument was also looked to for musical inspiration. So much so that an electric equivalent was developed, known as the Coral Electric Sitar. In addition much of the ancillary equipment like the amplifier stacks and the pedal switches all allowed the players to modify even further the sound of their instrument. The guitar did for psychedelic music what the keyboards did for progressive rock. It opened the doors to enhanced musical self-expression.

What the psychedelic guitar players did generally was borrow the same chord boxes that had been used for years by many of the folk-rock players, but what they added was a sense of improvisation. It's in this space that the beat or rhythm is generally assumed by the bass, drums and keyboard while the guitarist is allowed to wander off into his own world. The music created during this highly experimental period was at times amazingly adventurous and at other times humorously naive. At least that's how we see it today as we attempt to read history backwards. The middle to late sixties was a very adventurous time for rock music in general and the psychedelic era allowed musicians to draw on many new or untried sources of inspiration such as improvisational jazz, jug-band, country, acoustic-folk or Middle Eastern music. This era, more so than any other was so open to new things that it was pretty much accepted that you play anything, call it rock and get away with it.

The drug element of psychedelia is the most obvious starting point in any discussion about the music. San Andrew co-founder of one of the genre's leading bands Big Brother and the Holding Company, quoted in **Guitar Player** agreed that the drug element was important. He rightly observed that psychedelic music was not powered by alcohol. But the drugs weren't the main driving force on the music's creation or performance side. *"In many ways it was a reaction to the beat era that came right before, which was an era of cynicism and despair and the humour that comes from having given up. The beat movement was a cool jazz thing and very literate and verbal. This all melted into that 'hippie' thing, which was a derogatory term used by the beats for younger people hanging around trying to crash the beat scene, like I was. We were all younger and hopeful and hand't given up. That sense of possibility had a big influence of psychedelic music."* These sentiments are echoed by Barry Melton of Country Joe and the Fish. Melton who turned to public defender work after the demise of his band, maintains there are other core reasons that helped create the psychedelic genre. *"Rather than being some drug induced thing, it was really a bunch of serious folkie musicologists who played blues and bluegrass joining forces with guys who played at the edge of town, chewed gum and couldn't put two sentences together – the rock & roll players. The real roots of psychedelic music was the end of the folk era. All of the guitar players would come to the little clubs around town and we'd all play together."* It was this mingling of diverse musical tastes from jug-band to bluegrass and blues to jazz at a time when it seemed not only okay but a righteous thing to do, that brought about the first electric psychedelic rock bands.

Critics today will point to jazz musicians like John Coltrane for his contribution to rock music in general and the psychedelic time specifically. It was Coltrane who opened a whole world of possibilities musically that had not been explored by the normally non-adventurous rock musicians. Coltrane's approach to traditional blues scales allowing for extended improvisation to occur, hit home with many coming on the scene. Guitarists like Big Brother's James Gurley in particular saw the opportunity to do more with the tried and tested rock & roll formula. *"I thought that if you could play guitar like John Coltrane played the sax, it would be really far out. That's what I was trying to do – of course, nobody understood it, especially me."* While that was going on advances were being made on the technological side, allowing for more to be done with the amplified instruments such as guitars, bass and even keyboards. An article by Jas Obrecht in a 1997 issue of **Guitar Player** detailed the new gadgets that were becoming available to guitarists, better amps, better pick-ups and of course loads of special foot pedals designed to deliver more echo, reverb or wah-wah at the flip of switch. These technological advances were widely used by many bands including Quicksilver Messenger Service's John Cipollina; *"My love for electronic gadgetry has been a shaping influence on my playing. The trick, however is learning how to use them just a little bit."* A point well taken, given the visceral nature of the psychedelic genre.

One of the first, if not *the* first psychedelic recordings available to American fans was the extended-play pressing of *Section 43* by Country Joe and the Fish. This odd piece along with its companion *Bass Strings* epitomized, early on the very nature of psychedelic musical experimentation. These two compositions were first released independently by the band and featured many aspects of the coming psychedelic musical era: changing tempos, unusual instrumentation, mixed musical styles etc. By the time it was re-released in June of 1966 the Byrds and the Yardbirds had already released their first nods to psychedelia. The Country Joe single being a limited release is often overlooked by most sources who go on to cite the Byrds and the Yardbirds as the first bands to officially usher in the recorded psychedelic era.

In Britain, the Yardbirds are cited primarily due to Jeff Beck's fuzzy guitar playing which is said to have laid the blueprint for psychedelic guitar performance. For many followers, their early 1966 hit *Shape of Things* is the first truly psychedelic rock song with its unusual tempo changes and searing guitar work. Not many months later in the United States the Byrds hit with the long extended *Eight Miles High*. To this day Roger McGuinn makes the point that the song was not about drugs. Interviewed in **Guitar** magazine in 2002 McGuinn stated: *"We never considered our own music psychedelic, though, even though we'd experimented with LSD by that point. We were never a singing commercial for drugs. Eight Miles High wasn't about getting high at all: it was a musical tribute to John Coltrane and Ravi Shankar, while the lyrics were literally about an airplane ride to the UK and our culture shock when we got there. People interpreted it in all sorts of ways, but that was just wishful thinking."* But while the band insisted it wasn't about drugs, the song captured the moment with its long meandering trippy solo that allowed the listener to escape into a world of their own making with drugs or not.

These influences were racing through the music world throughout the early days of 1966. The Beatles employed backward guitars on the single *Rain* and then released **Revolver**, with John actually quoting Timothy Leary. Many began incorporating the sitar into their work, like Donovan and even the Rolling Stones whose heavily R&B influenced material began incorporating subtle psychedelic influences, in particular their psychedelic masterpiece **Their Satanic Majesties Request**.

Everywhere bands began to alter the sound of their guitars, injecting more distortion or fuzz, adding a weedly Farfisa or Vox organ and then changing the structure of the normally short 2 ½ minute song to incorporate longer droning tuneless meanderings. Bands such as the Who, the Animals, the Small Faces and literally dozens of others modified their R&B roots and started displaying psychedelic trappings. The genre gave birth to a host of lesser know acts such the Creation, the Move, Tomorrow, Kaleidoscope, the Idle Race, the Smoke and many others.

The Early psychedelic sound

JEFFERSON AIRPLANE TAKES OFF

As already discussed the psychedelic scene really took hold in San Francisco. The Charlatans kicked the scene into high gear with their stint at the Red Dog Saloon, returning as some kind of heroes to San Francisco in late 1965. Their influence tends to be more as social figures than as significant musicians of the times. Their unusual blend of folk, blues and jug-band was never overtly psychedelic in and of itself, however it was the bands overall attitude that put them at the forefront of the growing scene. Their recorded material came far too late to have any impact. Instead, it was Jefferson Airplane who were the first Bay area band to have a major label release with their first album **Jefferson Airplane Takes Off** in 1966 and then **Surrealistic Pillow** with its' two hit singles surfacing in 1967.

The San Francisco Sound, as it's been dubbed, got its start with bands such as the Beau Brummels who were the first to successfully incorporate the British Invasion sound and make it their own. Bands that followed like the Vejtables and the We Five contributed their own sound mixing a strong folk influence with the combination of electric and acoustic guitars and the layered, harmonic blend of male and female vocals. This style which was just enough of a departure from the British Invasion sound, proved to be the stepping-stone that changed the course of the music being created in San Francisco. That change gave birth to the psychedelic acid-rock of the dance-concert scene growing in the community of Haight-Ashbury.

The music of the San Francisco ballroom era was typified by volume and long trippy excursions performed while the audience actively participated in the dance-concert events staged in multiple locations a number of times each week through 1966 to 1971. The fact that bands had places to play a few times a week helped provide an unusual bond between performer and audience that contributed to a sense of community. It didn't hurt that most everyone knew each other and were probably ingesting the same substances. Although it's interesting to hear Jerry Garcia, Captain

Trips himself, talking about the early days say, *"I don't think playing high ever yielded much of musical value, but it did instil in us a love for the completely unexpected. So right around then, the idea of having a set list, even having fixed arrangements, went completely out the window. We were playing to people who were taking LSD and dancing their hearts out, and it was easy, because we were playing from that flow."* The nurturing live-music environment of the San Francisco ballrooms was the most instrumental aspect to the creation of the psychedelic genre, as we know it today. In fact, it could be argued that the whole psychedelic music scene would never have happened had it not been for people like Chet Helms and Bill Graham who created the opportunity for the bands to hone their skills and develop rabid followings in their own community. That community consisted of, not only the music, but the fashions, posters, light shows underground comics everything…it was a lifestyle, a cultural movement. In the late sixties, if you were a band from San Francisco, you were something. It was something you put on the poster!

In England the psychedelic scene having been established by leading core bands such as Cream, Jimi Hendrix, Traffic and Pink Floyd sparked the imagination of dozens of others. Unlike the growing psychedelic garage band scene in the United States, the British scene took off with a more defined sound that tended to be lighter and more whimsical. British bands benefiting from a smaller country to cover also benefited from a stronger more defined production sense. The British recording studios excelled in the areas of studio gadgetry and their willingness to experiment with sound. At the height of the psychedelic period the British bands were prime exponents of unheard of levels of feedback, phasing and backward tape loops. Unlike what was happening in the United States where psychedelic bands were struggling to capture their trippy live sound on vinyl, the British studios became part of the process of pushing the envelope. Another difference between the two scenes was the level of radio airplay. In America there were hundreds of radio stations prepared to support the local bands. The British Broadcasting Corporation or BBC on the other hand was very tightly controlled and played little pop music. British psychedelic bands relied more on a constant touring schedule and a well-defined network of clubs to hone their chops. In addition, the British bands incorporated different instrumentation into their sound, such as the Mellotron, heard most notably in the early Moody Blues material.

Musically the psychedelic style peaked by the end of 1967, the year that featured the Summer of Love and the Monterey Pop Festival. During this time all musical genres seemed to be affected by a psychedelic style. However in retrospect psychedelia lasted only a short while. By late 1968 it all started to unravel as bands began shedding their psychedelic trappings and started to revert too more simplified styles as the music industry began to fragment into smaller, more distinct sub-genres. What had originally started out as a fusion of just a few primary styles such as folk, jazz, R&B, pop and some mixed ethnic genres had turned into something called rock as the music got louder and more electric. Rock music truly came into its own by 1968. Then within the space of less than two years the rock genre began to splinter into a myriad of different sub-genres. As 1969 rolled around we could see the beginnings of the hard rock or heavy metal, country rock, southern rock, bubblegum pop etc. Some bands that had flirted with psychedelia reverted back to R&B as their core sound; others became more pop and so on.

So What's It All About?

Before the psychedelic movement there was the garage band scene in the United States and the freakbeat movement in the U.K. Both these musical movements sprang out of the British Invasion, which had a huge impact during 1964 and early 1965. There is significant overlap between these musical movements owing to location and the spread or lack of, musical ideas over great distances. In the United States it was easier for localized musical movements to flourish and remain unheard of elsewhere because of the distance between major centres and the lack of a fully developed mass media. In England on the other hand, musical ideas spread and were assimilated much quicker. In any case it was about the middle of 1965 that things started to change. In America, the success of the British sound drove many novice musicians to their garages with guitar or drumsticks in hand. These rudimentary outfits incorporated small elements of the British Invasion style but charted a new course with music that even more immediate. It was raw energy condensed into just over two minutes with the emphasis on rock. And in the United Kingdom, the freakbeat sound, a precursor to the full-fledged psych movement, best described as a form of power-pop with the emphasis on pop spread throughout the land.

AN OLDER AD FOR A CLOTHING SHOP IN CALIFORNIA

To fully understand the psychedelic genre it's important to see this period of creativity as more than just the music. The music was a direct outgrowth of the newly established counter-culture. This music not only spoke directly to the youth movement it was by-and-large created by the youth that were involved in the movement. It's for that reason that we must always see psychedelic music as an expression of the time, more than just music. As an expression of the era's lifestyle, psychedelic music reflected four distinct aspects that help define it:

It's part <u>Music</u>: in terms of incorporating new styles, influences and instrumentation.

It's part <u>Fashion</u>: in terms of bands wearing certain clothing to appear to be a part of the scene.

It's part <u>Attitude</u>: in terms of taking drugs, freedom from rules, counter-cultural thinking.

It's part <u>Timing</u>: in terms of bands who participated in the psychedelic scene even though they existed before and after the key time period.

Sometimes it was just the name chosen by the group during the golden years of 1965 through 1969 that meant you were considered part of the psychedelic scene. The music may not have even resembled what was being done by the truly innovative bands of the time. Take for example bands such as the Chocolate Watch Band. Their musical approach more closely resembled a pop music style similar to the Mamas and the Papas and yet because of the all-encompassing scope of the music, as well as their name they are mentioned almost in the same breath as the Grateful Dead or Country Joe and the Fish.

Not all the bands that jumped to prominence in the early psychedelic days claimed to be proficient at their instruments. In fact as we've already pointed out the early psychedelic scene was based more on the live experience where volume, lights and drugs can mask many sins. Still there were some bands that took musicianship more seriously than others. The more experimental bands such as early Country Joe or later Spirit, H.P. Lovecraft, Steve Miller Blues Band or the Pretty Things reflected a whole different side. These bands were more proficient on their instruments at the outset and the music they created was in many ways technically superior to others of the day. H.P. Lovecraft's keyboardist David Michaels actually came to the band with some classical training providing a musical depth to the band's music that was missing in many other bands. Steve Miller is another example of skilled musicianship. Raised in Dallas, Texas he arrived in San Francisco in 1966 fresh from the blues circuit in Chicago. The story goes that when Miller witnessed bands such as the Grateful Dead and Jefferson Airplane performing traditional blues standards out of tune, he determined very quickly he couldn't miss. All he had to do was play in tune! And play he did. Miller lived near Haight-Ashbury and took the opportunity to perform at many of the free outdoor benefits that were staged in the early days.

Then there were bands such as the Charlatans, Sopwith Camel, Cuppa T and the Purple Gang whose musical style at times owed more to the Vaudeville stage or jug-band influences. They too have found a home in the psychedelic scene and played quite comfortably on the same bill as many of the more blues-based bands. Their musical style was lighter, even comical and in many cases simply more nostalgic. There is no question this nostalgic aspect played well with a counter-culture that looking back fondly on simpler earlier days.

Lastly there were many bands that had formed before the psychedelic revolution occurred and simply modified their writing style or incorporated varying degrees of psychedelia to suit their musical purposes. For example, the Who released *I Can See for Miles* and *Magic Bus*, the Beach Boys released *Good Vibrations* and *Heroes and Villains* and so forth. For some groups turning psychedelic simply meant adding a fuzz-box to the guitar. To others it might have meant securing a producer that was more adept at getting certain psychedelic effects from the studio production. Whatever it was bands everywhere were looking for ways to achieve their own version of this interesting musical genre. Certainly by 1967 the psychedelic influences had infiltrated the pop mainstream and was having its effect on groups such as the Monkees, the Lemon Pipers and even the Mamas and the Papas.

Robert Palmer wrote in **Rock and Roll: An Unruly History** about the beginnings of the Grateful Dead, *"Rock & roll has always thrived on a certain amount of musical* *diversity, most notably in the interaction of self-taught blues or country musicians with jazz-trained session players so characteristic of the fifties. But rarely had a rock or R&B band included musicians from so many different backgrounds, with such heterogeneous areas of expertise. In the sixties, such bands became the rule rather than the exception."* Lead guitarist for the "Dead", Jerry Garcia stood out among the new crop of psychedelic players, having lost the middle finger of his right-hand in a childhood accident. Garcia compensated for the loss of one picking-digit by carving out a distinct personal technique. Coming from a background of bluegrass banjo picking background he was quick to adopt the new influences of folk, jazz, blues, country and even Indian music.

The Psychedelic musical effect

Psychedelic music holds a special place for a number of succeeding genres that may never have come into being without its influence. Specifically if it weren't for bands like Spirit, H.P. Lovecraft, Pink Floyd and Procol Harum it's doubtful the progressive rock musical style would ever have coalesced into a genre that was greater than its origins. Even bands such as Cream, Arthur Brown's Kingdom Come and the Move helped shape a genre that took musical creation very seriously. Bands such as Yes, Emerson Lake & Palmer and King Crimson all grew out of psychedelic bands and for them creating more serious, technically adventurous rock music became paramount. The progressive bands that followed in the wake of the psychedelic era all took the psychedelic experience to the next level technically. Not to mention how bands such as Pink Floyd would later go on to create a whole sub-genre of progressive music called space-rock that would be perpetuated by others such as Hawkwind and Ozric Tentacles.

Without bands such as the Lemon Pipers, Bubble Puppy or Strawberry Alarm Clock we might never have seen the emergence of what became known as "bubblegum" music. Identified by its catchy up-beat pop style, immediately memorable melodies and many times simplistic lyrics. Over its short life-span this popular fad-driven sub-genre was popularized by bands such as Tommy James and the Shondells, and gave birth to groups such as the animated Archies and the Mathew Katz managed 1910 Fruitgum Company and Ohio Express. This sub-genre created such memorable tunes as *Yummy Yummy Yummy*, *1, 2, 3 Red Light*, *Sugar Sugar* and many others before it evolved into the next musical fad. As the number of adolescents grew larger in the United States the "bubblegum" sub-genre gave birth to the pre-teen idol music of groups such as the Cowsills, the Partridge Family and the Osmonds.

On another level completely, if it weren't for bands such as the Grateful Dead and The Band reverting to a more roots oriented style we may not have seen the surprising success of two separate and distinct Southern and Country rock sub-genres. The country rock element took off first with bands such as the Byrds, the Grateful Dead and Bob Dylan eventually evolving into the Flying Burrito Brothers, Poco and the Eagles. The southern rock style starting out with the Allman Brothers gave birth to others such as Lynyrd Skynyrd, Ozark Mountain Daredevils, Atlanta Rhythm Section, 38 Special and many others. To this day outfits such as the Dave Mathews Band and the Black Crows can trace their musical legacy to southern rock.

Clearly the psychedelic rock genre had its effect throughout the rock and pop sub-genres. There has never been a time where so many outside influences have been incorporated into a single musical style. As a result that "single musical style" created within itself many different sounds as seen by the various musical off-shoots discussed above. There was everything from acid-rock to pop-rock. It is perhaps no accident that music and music fans began to split into smaller sub-genres. Never before had so many well-defined musical styles been available to the masses.

It was also a time where the accepted Top 40 radio style of playing singles was for the most part abandoned. New, untried effects replaced traditional sounds as the development of musical technology kicked into high gear. Song lengths were stretched to unheard of lengths. All in an effort to break out of the traditional "established" approach. It's true that some psychedelic bands did have hits, most notably Jefferson Airplane, but initially the philosophy behind what most bands were into took a very anti-pop approach. In fact most bands felt out of place in the studio, their place was the dance hall. Psychedelic music was very much a live experience. It was only after 1967 and into 1968 that groups began to acknowledge the boost their careers would receive with mass media exposure. This period also saw tremendous growth in fringe groups, bands who were not part of the early counter-cultural aspects of the psychedelic movement but were simply interested in exploring the new musical sounds the psychedelic era had to offer.

It's interesting to note the cyclical nature of music and how musical trends repeat themselves. Just as the hundreds of "punk" garage bands of the early sixties, gave birth to the many more structured and well played forms of music, in the later sixties, so once the second wave of punk bands of the middle to late seventies died out, there arose many bands and musicians armed with more skill to once again mine the past. Suddenly the New Wave, Mod and Ska bands appeared on the scene to build on the musical shoulders of the past. And in amongst all these new musical sub-genres many of the original psychedelic elements continued to influence bands well into the eighties and beyond.

Coming To Terms With Terms

Before getting into defining what constitutes psychedelic music it's worth exploring some of the other familiar descriptive terms associated with this time period. Some of these terms are now used interchangeably and certainly represent a tremendous amount of musical overlap. Still each of these categories is home to bands that retained their specific category uniqueness and never crossed over. It's for that reason we identify them below.

Punk Rock: (Seeds, Stooges, MC5)

This term became popular with the mass-media during the mid to late seventies, but was actually coined much earlier to describe a generation of primitive rock & rollers who were long on attitude while short of skill. This umbrella term was used to describe a whole range of bands that sprang up across America in the wake the British

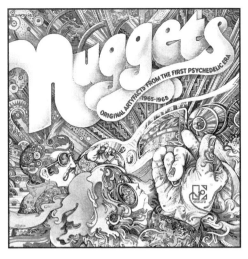

Invasion. The term was first used in the fall of 1972 by Lenny Kaye, former guitarist with the Patti Smith Group, in his essay that accompanied the first vinyl edition of the popular Rhino Records **Nuggets** series. Keep in mind this was a full five years before Sex Pistols burst on the scene. Gary Stewart of Rhino Records writing in the booklet that accompanied the **Nuggets** 4 CD box set clarified the term. He said, *"They weren't punks because they sported Mohawks and leather garb, knew their way around a mosh pit, or possessed the ability to incorporate nihilistic imagery and profanity into their lyrics, but because they had the nerve to pick up guitars, bass and drums, call themselves a band, play gigs, and make records."* Many of these groups also fall into other categories, or evolved into other styles but these initial bands merged the instrumental surf styles with a primitive vocal style that screamed of teenage attitude and angst.

Garage Rock: (Gestures, the Barbarians, the Chartbusters, the Standells)

COUNT FIVE - **PSYCHOTIC REACTION** LP

This largely North American musical movement occurred shortly after the first British Invasion. Mixing the instrumental surf rock music with the British sounds of bands like the Kinks and the Stones hundreds of bands formed overnight to create a style of music that was low on skill but high on energy. These bands were younger; less sophisticated, and put their attitude into simple songs that were then delivered with a sneering vocal style that at the time was mostly overlooked. The songs themselves were short blasts of sneering, loud, fuzzy guitar, bass and drum combinations. A style created to be heard above the current popular music. Given that most of these bands consisted of four or five white, suburban teenage males who practiced or in some cases performed only in neighbourhood garages, the name is more than appropriate. It's worth pointing out that a number of these bands crossed over into the psychedelic genre. Bands like the Count Five, Standells, the Seeds and even the Thirteenth Floor Elevators all moved into more experimental territory as their musical skills improved.

Freakbeat: (The Craig, Wimple Winch, Birds Birds, Masters Apprentices)

This relatively new term is for all intents and purposes the British equivalent to America's power pop. The most prominent musical period for freakbeat rests between the birth of the Beatles or the Merseybeat sound and the establishment of the underground music scene. This period of roughly late 1964 to 1966 featured a host of groups who were the true forerunners to the punk rock sounds of the seventies. These bands all attempted to merge the melodic elements of pop with the aggression of rock. The songs were usually tight, fast, and full of energy, bluesy angst, guitar feedback and attitude. The first known use of the term was on the sleeve of the 1984 **Rubble** compilation of obscure singles entitled the **Psychedelic Snarl** from the Bam-Caruso label.

San Francisco Sound: (Beau Brummels, Vejtables, We Five, Mystery Trend)

Four our purposes the San Francisco Sound is one that more rightly refers to the sounds that gave birth to the psychedelic scene. Bands such as those listed above all created a unique blend of folk and the British Invasion sounds. The material was typically strong on harmonies and melodies with, in many cases a blend of male and female vocals. The arrangements many times consisted of minor-key melodies, acoustic and electric guitars combined with hand held percussion instruments. Many of these bands strived to create material that was unique but still easily fit on the radio. As the blossoming San Francisco underground community grew and became a more cohesive body, these bands were seen to be un-hip as they catered to the commercial aspects of the music business. It was from this stance that the more psychedelic or acid-rock bands came into existence.

Acid Rock: (The Grateful Dead, Quicksilver Messenger Service, Jefferson Airplane)

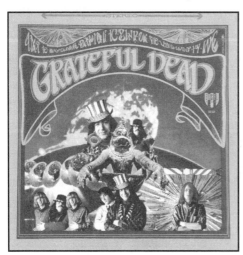

GRATEFUL DEAD LP

This term more than anything best describes the early San Francisco psychedelic bands that were performing at dance-concerts where LSD was plentiful, light shows were the standard and everybody danced. These events were designed to simulate the "trip" experience and featured bands performing long, extended, musical jam sessions designed to create a musical soundtrack to the night's drug induced activities. The music created was no longer pop influenced but loud rock music with plenty of feedback and loads of distorted fuzz-guitar solos.

A Comprehensive Psychedelic Rock Definition

Much like my previous book, **The Progressive Rock Files**, the definition for psychedelic music is one that can be used to create the music of the genre. I believe all musical forms contain in themselves the seeds to re-create their own form. All you need to do is take some or all the elements involved to re-produce the specific genre of music. It is a matter of understanding what those elements are and incorporating them in the same philosophical manner.

Some would suggest that this in and of itself is somewhat pretentious, but I contend it is no different than creating a Haiku or writing a march, etc. To compose a piece of reggae music you would follow certain parameters. The same would true if you were writing a piece of surf-music or a madrigal. The use of labels such as self-indulgent and pretentious are equally pointless when talking about psychedelic music as they are in reference to progressive rock.

It should be noted that this list of identifying criteria would not apply to all bands I've included in the A-Z listing. Remember there are a number of main criteria by which bands can be identified as psychedelic. Bands like the Purple Gang or Sopwith Camel who borrowed more from a Vaudeville dance hall style, or others like the Charlatans who incorporated a healthy dose of jug-band are simply a testament to the variety of distinct styles that were infused into the psychedelic genre. Unlike the later progressive rock many of these distinct styles retained their individuality and were not yet fully adapted or assimilated into the rock idiom. As such they remained identifiable outside the normal rock style at times falling more comfortably into the pop music world.

That being said here are the key descriptive **elements which best identify the psychedelic rock genre**:

- Longer songs became the norm in a live setting, performed to follow the ebb and flow of the crowd.
- Jamming or improvising became a core component of composition, particularly in the live setting.
- An almost independent rhythm section where bass and drums are allowed to percolate underneath different solo instruments.
- Repetitive elements, musical motifs or musical instrumentation were incorporated.
- Predominant use of early organs such as Farfisa or Vox creating a thin widdley or reedy organ sound.
- Fuzz-guitar effects best exemplified by Cream's *Sunshine of Your Love*.
- Longer lead-guitar solos are in the spotlight many times incorporating the new Wah-Wah pedal sounds.
- Trippy-spacey passages building in waves of intensity made popular by bands such as Pink Floyd.
- Creative use of feedback best exemplified by the work of Jimi Hendrix and the Who.
- Jangling guitar or 12 string guitar typified in the sound of the Byrds.
- Lyrically songs became more ambiguous and open to interpretation or associated with the psychedelic drug experience or in some cases focused on some utopian

quest or protest (influenced by the folk era).
- Recording studio experimentation with reverb, tape echo, tape flanging, backward tape loops, sound effects, stereo effects, etc.
- The introduction of non-rock instrumentation such as the Sitar, Tablas, harpsichords, glockenspiels, gongs etc.

Not withstanding Paul Kantner's comments that started this file, I believe a listener can identify psychedelic music. It is my hope this definition and the list of bands in the A-Z File aids you in your quest to discover more of the obscure and exciting bands from this unique period of rock music history.

The difference an ocean can make:

It's worth noting the different impact psychedelic music had on the respective musical cultures in the United States and in Britain, for the outgrowth of this experimenting period was very different on opposite sides of the Atlantic. Quoted in **Kaleidoscope Eyes**, Steve Howe makes the telling observation, *"Yes couldn't have played the kind of music it made without having the experience of developing the freedom and total nonconformist approach that came from the psychedelic bands."*

In **The Progressive Rock Files** I touched on how psychedelic and progressive rock evolved so differently in America than in Britain. It's interesting how many of the psychedelic bands in the United States, veered into other genres such as southern rock, hard rock, country rock and pop. While in Britain more than a few psychedelic bands took up the progressive rock mantra. None of the U.S. bands really followed that musical path in 1968 or 69. I believe the reason for this has a lot to do with the specific influences that were distinctly different to each country. For example, while the United States psychedelic bands incorporated a slight blues influence it was tempered by more regional influences such as jug-band, bluegrass, country and of course folk. In England the leading bands were far more steeped in R&B, pop, rock and a different kind of folk inspiration. It was this different foundation on which psychedelic grew and then splintered in different directions at a certain point of maturity.

The San Francisco bands like the Grateful Dead, the Charlatans, Big Brother and Quicksilver Messenger Service had been creating music to accompany the various acid tests and dance concerts that were happening in 1965 & 1966. These events featured long drawn out songs that created the prerequisite atmosphere for tripping on LSD. So the idea of long songs became accepted, albeit in the live arena more than on record at this point.

In England, Pink Floyd and Soft Machine picked up the extended song structure by 1967 at clubs such as UFO and at the Spontaneous Underground held at the Marquee club on Sunday afternoons and at the growing number of all night raves. It was not unusual for these bands to play only two or three songs in a forty-five minute set. Much like the San Francisco scene, the band was there to provide the soundtrack to the event, and the audience were the participants.

On both sides of the Atlantic, not only did the songs become longer, but the collective idealism of the period penetrated the lyrical content and many of the bands on both sides began writing lyrically in a more utopian fashion. If you compare the length of recorded songs you'll notice that by 1967, it was quite acceptable to break out of the two and a half-minute mould. Bands such as Velvet Underground, H.P. Lovecraft, Vanilla Fudge and the ones mentioned above were recording songs that were starting to edge over four or five minutes. Keep in mind playing long songs in a live setting was quite acceptable; recording them was another thing all together.

More importantly, in the case of many of these bands, the songs length allowed them to be more creative as they developed more complicated methods of musical arrangement, and as they explored incorporating many new influences and different genres including folk, blues, raga, East Indian, electronic etc. This not only made the songs more interesting, but it is also the obvious branching out of the whole progressive rock genre.

In the book, **I Want to Take You Higher** is a listing of the Top 50 psychedelic artists from each side of the Atlantic. This list reinforces what I'm referring to here.

First on the U.K. side among the 50 bands listed you had Pink Floyd, Family, the Yardbirds (who evolved into the first version of Renaissance), the Move and Idle Race (who melded into the Electric Light Orchestra), the Pretty Things (who created one of the first rock operas on disc), Simon Dupree and the Big Sound (who metamorphosed into Gentle Giant), Tomorrow (who's guitarist Steve Howe would go into Yes), the Crazy World of Arthur Brown (who created some excellent prog as Kingdom Come) and the Nice (who turned into Emerson Lake and Palmer).

On the U.S. side there were a few bands that started to do some creative things musically like, Spirit, Love, H.P. Lovecraft, Steve Miller Band, Country Joe and the Fish, and the Electric Prunes, however by late 1969 they had either disbanded or reverted back to a more blues-rock style.

It's clear there was something more at work here than just the drugs. There were the other obvious aspects of history and culture that caused more of the British psychedelic bands to look at the new musical opportunities available to them within the progressive rock genre. Progressive rock music would never have happened if it had not been for the psychedelic sixties, but it's clear that the impact of the psychedelic scene was assimilated very differently on opposite sides of the Atlantic.

In the end the psychedelic genre splintered into a number of primary directions. The more experimental adventurous side gave birth to the more complicated progressive rock genre. The more pop influenced side produced the whole bubblegum scene. The return to roots-oriented approach evolved quickly into country and southern rock, while the heavier side of psychedelia exploded into the guitar driven heavy metal genre.

There is yet another interesting parallel between the music of the late sixties and late nineties and that involves the youth cultures current fascination with raves. It's not something new by any means. In fact the closest parallel that exists between the music of the psychedelic ballrooms of the late sixties now exists in the all-night rave culture. These dancing orgies continue the tradition of the audience becoming participants in the evening's activities. As it was in the sixties, these dance marathons are propelled by music that takes on a hypnotic almost trancelike effect. Instead of the Grateful Dead providing the soundtrack, now it's the "acid-house" music of bands such as the Orb. The raves of the nineties continued to perpetuate all that was good and unfortunately all that was bad about the raves of the sixties.

In more ways than one the psychedelic influence of the late sixties has been pervasive and has pretty much been incorporated into whatever musical genre you were mining in the seventies and beyond. Music producer Joe Boyd quoted in **Rock and Roll: An Unruly History** asserts, *"So many of the fundamental assumptions behind the way people approach making music today wouldn't be there if it hadn't been for the music of the psychedelic era. The foundation of rock & roll was always this standard guitar-bass-drums structure, which came out of rhythm and blues and jazz. What psychedelic music did was to open the music up to Indian and Arabic influences – guitar solos based on modal scales replacing chord-based improvisation, the introduction of the drone. With Pink Floyd you had a definite classical influence coming in. You had an opening up to avant-garde jazz, so you had dissonances coming in. The long term effects have been so pervasive."* Modern music has benefited greatly from the experimentation with arrangements, technology and instrumentation that occurred during those heady days of the sixties. The assimilation of psychedelic into modern music has been so complete that you don't even notice it anymore unless you go looking for it. Joe Boyd again, *"They've [psychedelic influences] become so much a part of the musical landscape that they're just accepted as being part of the way music is played and recorded."* These sentiments are confirmed by many of today's current producers as well. Huw Price, known for his work with David Bowie, Primal Scream, My Bloody Valentine and others is also quick to point out how big a part the studio played in creating the psychedelic sound. Price recently wrote in **Guitar** magazine, *"Many of the wacky ideas for abusing technology that emerged through a fog of smoke in studio control rooms around the world have since become staples of the recording artist."* Certainly even a casual listening to the current crop of modern rock artists bears this out. Embedded in these new sounds are many of the hallmarks of the psychedelic era such as guitar tone, feedback, echo and phasing, composition and structure and even a subtle psychedelic feel. The psychedelic musical legacy is very much alive and well in much of today's modern rock music.

The Afterglow – Looking Back

You would be hard pressed to find many reviewers, critics or writers who would speak ill of the psychedelic era within the rock music literary world. For a variety of reasons, critics have generally been kind to this music unlike the venom they're known to expel on such genres as progressive rock. My belief is that in this case the critics "get it" and even look back on the era with a distinct fondness. I'm not sure if this overstates the point but there is a certain naiveté of the sixties that music critics cling too. After all pop music was just turning into rock, coming of age and it was taking a big step. It was becoming not only the voice of expression but in some cases the voice of dissent for a whole new generation. To some I'm sure the music was legitimised by its involvement with the many social and cultural movements or struggles that existed in the sixties. Its as if any music borne out of protest or a protesting-era has a worth beyond its own. That surely can't be said of progressive rock and perhaps is the reason why prog has always been seen as the "ugly step sister" to rock & roll.

There's more to it than that of course. The psychedelic era came out of the blossoming garage rock band era, highly admired for its rebellion, it's spontaneity; it's raw, course style and substance. It's seen as everything rock & roll is supposed to be. I tend to think that's at least one of the reasons rock historians look back fondly upon the psychedelic genre. We have a soft spot for its naïve motivation and short lived almost mythical free-lifestyle approach. So much so that I fear we've begun to read history backwards. And that can be a very dangerous thing, as it rarely gives us the real picture of then so much as it tells us how we want to see it now.

On the positive side of the equation, photographer, Gene Anthony who seemed to be everywhere during the height of the psychedelic sixties in San Francisco, is busier today on sixties related projects than ever before. The interest in the era is very high and Anthony works tirelessly to make sure his documentation of the period is available to those seeking a window into the past. Anthony was in the room when Bill Graham got his original dance permit for the Fillmore and managed to record the moment. He was at all of the events from the early Trips Festival to the Human Be In. He was there for many of the great early performances and he too looks back fondly on that period. But more than just looking back, Anthony is interested in the present and the future. Today in amongst all his projects he's begun a project called "The Sixties Foundation". He constantly runs into individuals young and old who are seeking a glimpse into the sixties. Not just people who are "stuck" in the sixties but those who are sincerely looking to recapture what it was that made that time so special. The older ones wonder what happened and why certain communal elements went away and the younger ones disillusioned by the mass commercialism they see around them are looking for a different path. The Sixties Foundation is a project that will attempt to identify what that "something" special is. And it will seek to re-establish the lasting spirit of the psychedelic sixties in this more modern time.

If there are critics of the psychedelic era they come from the community of those who created it. Those who were involved in the day-to-day aspects and saw how something so uniquely exciting, and I'm talking more specifically about the music, changed into the "same old, same old". The criticism however is not so much levelled at the psychedelic era itself but more at how it changed and what it became.

Selling Out!

Unfortunately when the psychedelic music scene died in the late sixties and early seventies, the "business" of rock & roll was born. This is something few commentators or rock historians talk about today. Throughout the sixties the credo of the counter-culture generation was, "Whatever you do man, DON'T SELL OUT!" And yet, this is precisely what happened to most involved in the music industry. They sold-out to the "business of rock" and the dream of stardom and in some cases the money consumed them. More than one participant from the psychedelic era has acknowledged that it changes you when suddenly you are no longer struggling to just make the rent, but now have enough money to buy anything you want.

Now let's be clear; it's not that being popular or making money in and of itself is wrong. Everyone has to eat and certainly you don't pick up a musical instrument and perform in front of people without some desire to be popular. No, the problem begins when the artist is no longer in control but when their manager, record label or booking agent has taken over. When he was alive, Lester Bangs made plenty of references to how rock & roll had changed. He saw first-hand how the business side of the music scene had completely taken control over the musical side. This is even truer today, with artists being pre-packaged with the right looks, the right clothes, the right video and so on. It's all very disheartening, but then that's only because I knew a time when it was different. Most kids today have no idea what they're missing, and that too is sad.

Bill Graham's distaste for the changes that were occurring in the music industry in the late sixties are well documented. What happened to Graham was in many ways symptomatic of the rock & roll industry in general. His opponents have argued that it was unfair that he, a producer should prosper at the hands of the artists, and that it was only fair that the artists should be the ones reaping the windfall of the growing rock & roll industry. Still there is something to be said for Graham's 'altruistic' approach to the music scene. He and others like Chet Helms, made sure that music was available to thousands and it was affordable.

Graham considered himself, and said so many times, a maitre d' whose job it was to serve a multi-course meal of music to his patrons. This he did as is documented elsewhere. Less well known were Graham's views of the music scene toward the late sixties. He was extremely critical of the direction the music industry was going, particularly post Woodstock, *"The entire monetary structure of rock has greatly changed, meaning that many groups can play a few large arenas and pocket enough money to live in luxury. It is not uncommon to find a twenty-two-year-old earning up to $1,000,000 a year. This emphasis on playing the big halls, taking your money and running has had a bad effect on rock. Many groups have priced themselves out of the medium-sized concert market and lost respect for the audience."*

Fans of Bill Graham will argue that his motivation was always to put on a good show for the audience. That meant having a good venue, good promotion, a good sound system, a resident light show and a good mix of performers. It also included not only motivating the artists to perform up to a certain level, but also keeping prices inline for the masses. When he opened the Fillmore Graham was charging $1.50 at the door and even by the end of 1971 his prices were $3.00.

He often called for some form of standards for the rock industry, citing that audiences could be quite fickle if they lost contact with the artist. And playing the larger halls was doing exactly that, creating distance between the growing stars and their fans. Graham said, *"Three-quarters of the groups around today are lousy. They just get out there and bang away to make a quick killing."* And yet when asked, what was keeping the rock industry going, Graham pulled no punches citing, *"The idiot mass. A majority of the people don't eat what they want to eat, only what they are fed, or can buy. The groups today know they don't have to be good, just gimmicky-give'em what they want."* It's telling that in a few short months after making this observation the music industry was at the height of the glam-rock period.

Playwright and one time Fillmore East stage hand, John Ford Noonan offers this observation, *"The thing that killed the Fillmore was this: If Santana got the closing act, and they were on Columbia, Columbia would dictate who went on before them. So they put acts that weren't any good. So by '69 there were no great new acts. All the great music came in '68 and early '69, and after that there was nothing."* Of course there was the aspect on money. Noonan says, *"Once the headliners began demanding money it got difficult...When the big bands wanted 20K for themselves, it became unprofitable. The musician's greed actually killed those kind of venues."*

Joshua White of the Joshua Light Show rightly pointed out, not with a little cynicism, *"When the Fillmore was open, all the best rock acts in the world played there, with few exceptions. But at the Fillmore every act would play four shows for twelve thousand dollars, and after Woodstock I knew bands weren't going to play four shows anymore. They were going to play one show for the big money. Everybody stood on the Woodstock stage and realized that nothing was going to be the same anymore."*

When Bill Graham held a news conference in New York to announce the closing of the two Fillmore auditoriums, he said running two halls had drained him. He was tired. But he took the time to read from a prepared statement that in many respects was his own version of the "state of the union" address. In it he outlined his reasons; the inflation of the concert scene, loss of booking control with concert packaging, the audiences' declining regard for quality, among other issues. Part of his address included the following, *"Two years ago I warned that the Woodstock festival syndrome would be the beginning of the end. I am sorry to say that I was right. In 1965 when we began the original Fillmore Auditorium, I associated with and employed "musicians." Now more often than not, it's with "officers and stockholders" in large corporations – only they happen to have long hair and play guitars. I acknowledge their success, but condemn what that success has done to some of them."*

The truth was by 1971 the economics of the rock market were shifting. Bands were asking for more money and that meant selling more tickets, which meant getting into larger halls. The original ballrooms fell out of favour; the places to play now were the sports arenas. After closing the Fillmore auditoriums, Graham went on to book acts into the larger facilities he hated so much. First it was the Winterland and then the Coliseum and even the larger outdoor events he initially detested. His explanation was that since that was the direction the music industry was going he would go there grudgingly. He explained that if those events were going to happen he may as well do it himself to ensure it was done right.

The 'Straight' business men

There was a point after the Monterey Pop Festival where the rock "industry" emerged. As people like Clive Davis and Albert Grossman began signing deals to represent artists or to put record deals together, the relatively "innocent" psychedelic scene turned its eyes to the money scene in Los Angeles and New York. You know what they say about the grass being greener. Davis and Grossman weren't the only ones involved in bringing about the change to a more business like structure, not by a long shot, but they certainly were representative of what was going on behind the scenes.

Albert Grossman was perhaps the first artist manager to change the nature of the business. Starting out as Bob Dylan's manager he cultivated and fostered the image of musician as "artist". Fred Goodman writing in **Mansion On The Hill** says, *"Grossman not only said his clients were artists, he believed it, and they, and not the manager or the record company, set the artistic and commercial agendas."* Grossman harboured a vision for each of his clients, it was true of Dylan and it was certainly true of Janis Joplin. After seeing her performance at the Monterey Pop Festival he quickly signed her and the band, but it was really Janis he was after and soon encouraged her to leave Big Brother. Her signing also prompted Grossman to have Janis and Big Brother do another set at the festival to ensure they would be included in the film. Remember, like the Grateful Dead they had refused to sign away the movie rights. Grossman saw her inclusion in the film as a major element to her future success. He also spoke to Clive Davis at the festival about a deal with Columbia.

Clive Davis had been rising the corporate ladder at Columbia records quite quickly and he was looking to make a name for himself. At the time Columbia was not exactly flush, but they were looking to find a position in the new emerging youth market. Clive was young, he liked rock music and he was at the Monterey Pop Festival. Davis turned out to be in the right place at the right time. As noted in Fredric Dannen's book **Hit Men**, Davis proclaimed Monterey was a creative turning point in his life and changed him as a person. He and Grossman eventually signed Janis Joplin to Columbia, but she wasn't the only one signed. In the aftermath of Monterey others followed, like Santana, Blood Sweat & Tears, Chicago, Johnny Winter and the Electric Flag. The key element noted by most record executives was the fact you had all these bands and a huge ready-made youth market. And to top it off the bands came cheap. In the case of Columbia they rarely paid more than $25,000 to sign a band, which ensured a high profitability. The bands were easily seduced and soon got caught up in the emerging business of rock & roll.

Yet another view from the inside can be glimpsed from the experience of Paul Rothchild, who while at Elektra Records during the sixties was responsible for signing and producing bands such as the Paul Butterfield Blues and the Doors. By 1969 a new breed of business savvy managers was on the loose in the rock & roll world. People like David Geffen. Rothchild saw individuals like Geffen and others like him emerging in the industry as a bad thing. Quoting Rothchild, Fred Goodman writing in **Mansion on the Hill** says, *"This was the beginning of the end of the love groove in American music. To me, that's the moment. When David Geffen enters the California waters as a manager. The sharks have entered the lagoon. And the entire vibe changes.*

It used to be, 'Let's make music, money is a by-product.' Then it becomes 'Let's make money, music is the by-product.'" Managers like Geffen preyed upon the artist's egos in a manner that blurred any loftier artistic goals by focusing on money as the end product. These managers may have talked-the-talk about 'art' but when it came to walking-the-walk it was all about making money. For a generation of artists, especially in the San Francisco area this was a radical paradigm shift.

Ḫas it really changed?

Some would suggest it has always been this way, that there has always been the "hit-making-machine". The business of pop or later still rock music. They will point to Tin Pan Alley, the Brill Building and the song writing machines of individuals like Don Kirshnir, whose job was to create the hit-song package for whoever it was he was contracted to work with. That might be Paul Anka or it might be the Monkees. To some degree it didn't matter who the artist was. Today this formula is alive and well with the current crop of cloned pop artists, be they the many "boy bands" or the myriad of chanteuses currently occupying the Top 40 charts. Tragically it's not much different with the new crop of harder edged pseudo-alternative bands that ply the "Modern Rock" radio station play lists. They too have fallen victim to an irritating sameness. A cookie cutter approach has been adopted by the record labels and mass media that has deprived listeners today of the opportunity to hear the variety of music available to them.

Again, some will charge that this too has always been the case. But that's simply not so. Back in the sixties it was infinitely easier to get home-grown talent played on the local radio stations. Today with many more radio and video stations than ever existed in the sixties it is now harder than ever to get local exposure. Today's stations stick to hand-me-down safe play-lists that provide exposure for only a select few. It's hard to believe that with so many socio-economic and cultural differences that spread across a country that only "one" song could be No.1 on the hit parade. With so many more stations broadcasting today you would expect there to be more diversity than ever, and yet it's just opposite. The odds of this boggle the mind unless it was manipulated to be so. To suggest that a song is No.1 across the country based on sales, fails to recognize that sales are driven by exposure and exposure on media is limited to what record companies choose to release and then promote.

What's missing today is, uniqueness and individuality. During the sixties we saw the birth of individuality with bands being as different from one another as people. The music created by the core San Francisco bands was entirely individual as was the music created by the British psychedelic bands. Take a look at the talent line-ups at the Monterey Pop Festival or Woodstock and compare the diversity to what's put together on today's festival stages. Being different today is almost frowned upon by the music packaging industry. Because being different means having to work harder than just selling a list of cookie-cutter artists under the guise of what's supposedly popular.

What's also missing is the opportunity to get on the radio, because as the rock music industry evolved (some might say devolved), so did the radio industry. After creating free-form FM with its laid-back approach of no talking over the music because that was too "Top 40", the radio industry fell victim in some respects to its own success. Formats once again became tighter; play-lists became shorter until by the mid seventies a whole new program format, Album Oriented Rock or AOR was born. The problem was it sounded in everyway like the Top 40 predecessors. Recent studies have pointed out that out of a possible 29 different radio formats available to stations, only 9 are used predominantly. These nine tend to include classic rock, adult contemporary, modern rock, oldies, news, talk and Top 40 or CHR (Contemporary Hit Radio) formats. The music that is played is only what can be squeezed onto these few formats. With video channels it's even more restrictive.

All of these changes and more took place with the underlying flawed premise that this is what the listener or buying public wants. Certainly the growing number of industry paid-for focus groups that have sprung up since the late seventies seemed to have provided research to back that up. Today a radio station doesn't even play something unless it scores a certain number of points on a preordained scale provided by national programmers, who are regularly serviced by record industry promo people in an effort to get their latest "cloned" find on the radio.

Now to some degree radio stations have always been pressured to play what the record labels have felt popular or what they wanted pushed. The big difference is that in the sixties radio stations played a great deal of independent local talent. That meant that in amongst all those big names it was still possible to take a tape or single that a local band had pressed and convince a local radio music director to play their song. Hundreds of artists took this route and successfully translated their efforts into sizable local hits. All of this no longer exists. It's troubling to consider that out of 5000 single releases each year only as many 200 might hit the airwaves. It's doubtful 4800 of these were bad! And yet, as stations became less autonomous, either because they've switched to tighter formats or because they were purchased by larger chains and fell under the control of national programmers, the opportunity to play local, home-grown talent fell by the wayside. Today many music directors even look askance at locally provided material, citing poor production values and no focus group scoring as reason enough to ignore it.

Until recently the last bastion of broadcasting uniqueness and creativity lies at the University or Campus radio station level. Primarily these stations are not concerned as much with generating revenue. This allows at least a portion of each station's play list to be inhabited by local independent artists. But even there the play-lists have begun to resemble the cookie-cutter nature of the mainstream broadcasting industry. This is because of the mass media's dominance in the entertainment world. The industry enjoys more control than ever before on who will be the next big star and who will be shunned from the play-lists. They deny it of course.

The truly "wide-open" format radio now exists on the Internet. Here diversity is king, and is a badge to be worn proudly. Each and every day new stations pop-up with the sole mission of playing material that fails to get any other mass-media exposure. It is now possible to hear many of those 4800 other songs by sifting through the various channels on web sites around the world. The beauty is, that if you can't find what you're looking for, you can always create your own radio show for a cost of next to nothing. It is not surprising that the record industry and mass-media outlets have focused their attention (as well as their legal departments) on the internet, because it is by the very nature of the internet that they can lose what they've struggled so hard to manufacture: control of the industry.

New bands just starting out rarely have the opportunity to hear as many outside influences as bands in the sixties did because most record stores only stock the mainstream releases. The music world today is ever more compartmentalized and most young musicians are exposed to what they're fed on the video channels or the music in their chosen sub-genre. They're allowed to see and hear little else. And in any case the major labels control what else is out there for the most part. Don't misunderstand. The other creative recordings are out there, distributed independently over the internet in most cases, but it takes very creative and determined individuals to cut through the existing norm to seek out and incorporate something new to their sound. As an example, most music purchasers have no idea that progressive rock continues to thrive because it has been ghettoized by the mainstream industry. Unless a fan or friend makes you aware of it, you'll probably never discover it.

Recently the keyboardist for Yes, Rick Wakeman talked about the state of music industry today and made the analogy that it's like going to the grocery store and you see three brands of coffee on the shelf. If you don't know which brand you'll like, you sample all three. In the end you determine brand A is the best and you keep buying that brand and telling your friends it is the best. But what you don't realize is that the grocery store has actually got 147 brands of different coffees in the back room that they never let you sample! You've only picked brand A out of the three they want you to pick from. They do this because then they can control what you see and ultimately what you buy.

The psychedelic music scene of the sixties can be viewed as both a "beginning" and an "end". What began as a vibrant localized music scene in 1965 grew into an industry, a business that by 1971 barely resembled its early nature. In the beginning there was a closeness to the audience that was fostered by playing smaller venues or clubs. The stages were never very high and members of the audience knew the performers. It was this familiarity that created community. As bands became more popular, they began spending less time in their own communities, the stages got higher putting them even more out of touch with their fans. The musicians became more isolated, and in the case of Haight-Ashbury even leaving the local scene altogether to find new digs in the more expensive neighbourhoods, which they could now afford thanks to lucrative record deals. By the seventies rock music became a business and adopted all that is good and bad about that. It's interesting to speculate how the psychedelic scene might have developed had the major bands not been signed to major label deals after Monterey. If Monterey had never happened would Woodstock have been staged? Who knows?

Psychedelic Rock Today

Psychedelic music has attempted to make numerous comebacks, most notably in the early eighties when a whole group of Los Angeles bands came to the fore giving rise to the term the "Paisley Underground". Bands such as Rain Parade, Three O'clock, Green on Red and a host of others that looked both backwards and forwards to craft a music that pushed, as much as possible those old psychedelic sounds to the fore. In England the psychedelic genre was resurrected in the "Manchester Sound" of the early eighties with bands such as Happy Mondays, EMF and the Charlatans UK. These bands soon gave birth to American bands such as Mercury Rev, Jane's Addiction, Soundgarden and many others. Perhaps the one distinguishing new characteristic of all these newer bands flying the psychedelic flag was their darker musical tone borrowing more from the avant-garde style of the Velvet Underground than the pop of the Strawberry Alarm Clock. The dilemma faced by the psychedelic genre is its ability to adapt to the current style. This is both a blessing and a curse because once you take psychedelic music out of the context of its hippie origins it easily loses its distinctiveness, only to become the sound of the day, whatever that is.

Unlike progressive rock that has flourished as an underground phenomenon, the psychedelic genre has been less successful. Primarily because the musical elements inherent in the genre have been so infused into the musical mainstream. All the elements detailed in the definition whether it be the fuzz-guitar, the playing style, the trippy lyrics or the reedy-organ sound have all either been appropriated by other bands to complete their sound, or have been used to foster many of the bands described above who tend be modern rock bands who push the psychedelic elements more to the surface. While progressive rock has been forcibly eradicated from the mass media consciousness, older psychedelic bands continue to hold an attraction for the media. They are strangely seen, not as a precursor to the genres logical musical extension, but rather as the last bands who performed in a supposedly "unpretentious" or "naively experimental manner".

Producer Joe Boyd's comment about how the psychedelic influence has been so assimilated can be applied too much more than just the music. Psychedelia has affected so many other aspects of culture it has left a lasting impact on such things as; our use of certain colours or the way we combine colours; lettering in advertising and design was set free in many respects; clothing both in terms of design, materials and colours, shoes and sandals; hair-length – longer for men and women; in short a whole lifestyle was affected by psychedelia. However, much like its presence in music today this psychedelic influence is almost invisible. We no longer even notice these influences except when they're specifically pointed out or when they're used in a blatant retrospective or tribute sense. We now see poster design as much more open to experimentation because of the psychedelic posters created during the sixties. We now see hairstyles as an unlimited pallet both in terms of colour and shape. And fashion continues to recycle what has gone before. All of what came to the fore during the height of the sixties is now a part of the fabric of culture, because it was about a time. And little of this stands out unless its supposed to.

In fact when it comes to music it could be argued, that other than specific tribute or original bands from the 1965 – 1969 era we no longer have true psychedelic bands.

The dilemma today goes to the crux of Boyd's comment about the defining elements of the genre having been so assimilated into the current music. Is there really such a thing as a psychedelic band today? It's a difficult question because many of the bands who "sound" psychedelic in some respect no longer consider themselves of that time, and are simply producing music that is the end-result of all those early influences. This is exemplified by bands like Beck who fuse a myriad of sixties styles into a modern potion, or Blur who use their high volume guitars and reverb much like the garage bands of the sixties, or Orb who do their own version of musical soundtracks for acid tests, except now the drug of choice might be Ecstasy. And then there are those who borrow from early Pink Floyd like Porcupine Tree and creative chaps like Moby, who dwell in modern electronic worlds. The list is endless and it's not that any of this is bad or wrong; it's just that it shows how psychedelic music has become so much a part of modern music both in terms of writing and studio production. Take away the musical experimentation of the psychedelic sixties and much of what we listen to today would simply disappear. By the same token the existence of bands such as those listed or many others who might fall into any falsely so-called "neo" psychedelic rock category are, I believe wrongly labelled. Unlike something like the progressive rock genre that continues to create within easily recognizable parameters, the psychedelic elements have been so fully integrated into modern rock that unless you're looking for them they are so easily missed. I'm sure few bands today would consider themselves "psychedelic". Today we have many bands that continue to interpret and incorporate the psychedelic genre in their own way creating modern or alternative music that is a distinct style of its own.

Just as some bands created music during the late sixties, that may not have been overtly psychedelic but were grouped in with others who were because they were "part of the scene". Today, out of the context of the psychedelic era, there are bands producing a music that is a reflection of what has gone before. But its not in-and-of-itself psychedelic. Without the surrounding social or counter-cultural environment it's hard to call it psychedelic just because it has some fuzz-guitar, feedback, jangly-guitar or whatever. It is now a product of those early influences but is not necessarily what it was. Because that time no longer is. This again is very different from the progressive rock genre, which is more about the music and less about the culture of the time. Progressive rock thrives today as a distinct musical genre based on a band's desire to create music that stretches the boundaries of modern rock music.

To clarify this point even further, this is different from what has happened to the progressive rock genre, where many of the defining elements have remained consistent and distinct from the pop and rock mainstream. Perhaps more to the point, progressive rock was less about the time and more about the music itself. It is relatively easy to distinguish a progressive rock song out of a batch of music, while it's not as easy to pick out the psychedelic material. Unless as stated above it's created in some sense of retrospective so that it in fact hearkens back to that earlier time. There are hundreds of bands creating progressive rock music today that have incorporated new technology and production but continue to create a genre of music that bears all the hallmarks of it's origins. Psychedelic music, as already stated, has been so assimilated as to be hardly distinguishable from the various modern rock styles.

For those who are a little more adventurous, wanting to check out some of the newer bands that might rightly be labelled as psychedelic, here is a list of some bands. I've already mentioned a few earlier in this section but here are a few more. This short list is highly subjective and includes groups of wide ranging styles: Absolute Grey, the Butthole Surfers, Julian Cope, the Chemical Brothers, Dream Academy, Flying Saucer Attack, Robyn Hitchcock, Loop, Moby, My Bloody Valentine, Oasis, Orbital, Plasticland, Portishead, Prince, the Psychedelic Furs, Sonic Youth, Space Time Continuum, Spiritualized, the Teardrop Explodes and Wire. Some of you will enjoy listening to these newer bands and some of you will not. If nothing else it demonstrates just how pervasive the psychedelic influence really has been.

A point should be made about the use of the word "psychedelic" or in some cases "psych" today. In certain circles this term has come to be used a descriptive less of the actual period discussed in this book and more about the style of music which has grown out of bands like Pink Floyd. Another words the use of the term has come to be blurred with the space-rock genre. It is distinguished by its floating trippy nature. If the piece incorporates any form of droning synth accompanied by a fuzz-toned, stinging guitar lead, the composition will in some cases be described as "psych". I don't share this approach, and feel compositions of this nature are better served by being included in the more descriptive space-rock genre.

Psychedelic Webster abounds on the Internet. Needless to say, the advent of the Internet has once again provided a window into the past (and the present) for many of the bands of the sixties. Now one is able to learn everything there is to know about many of the more popular as well as the more obscure artists of the period. The easiest thing is simply type in the name of the band you're looking for followed by a ".com" and chances are something will come up. Typically many of these sites are labours of love and rarely provide any form of income for their owners. As a result they are not always kept up-to-date, sometimes they change servers unexpectedly or even go dormant for a time. Still for anyone who's interested there's everything from sites devoted to a hippie lifestyle [hippy.com], to historical resources an all aspects of the sixties psychedelic movement [resinets.com/topics/the60s.htm, vcn.bc.ca/sig/htmlsig/psychome.htm], to genre-specific music sites devoted to British psychedelia or psychedelic music in general [marmalade-skies.co.uk, psychedelic-music.net]. Should you wish to explore more specific areas there are sites devoted just to Haight-Ashbury [sixties.com, sanfranciscobay.com/haightashbury/] or posters [artrock.com, peacerockposters.com]. Bottom line with the Internet, is that with a little digging and a good search engine you should be able to find something on what you're looking for.

Many psychedelic bands, including a good number of those listed in this book never released finished albums. Many of them only ever put out one or two singles before moving on to the next thing. As a result, trying to track down all these obscure recordings is nearly impossible. It can also become expensive, as the collectors market has ensured ever increasing values based on a records scarcity. Short of mortgaging the house to purchase the original vinyl LPs and singles, all of which have seen a significant increase in value, many record companies have seen fit to produce highly affordable CD re-issues. Labels as Rhino Records, Sundazed, Arf! Arf!, Collectibles,

Normal Records, Castle, plus many of the original record labels like Deram, Polygram and EMI have seen fit to repackage the more obscure psychedelic era bands. Sadly, quite a few of these compilations are also long out of print and difficult to track down, but will always be cheaper than trying to locate that obscure vinyl single. Plus new compilations continue to arrive on the scene as old masters are found and cleaned up. Fortunately psychedelic music fans have access to many excellent compilations. Once again your best bet is to visit the Internet to find what you're looking for.

For the vinyl purists who simply have to have the original, there is no shortage of retail outlets to satisfy the craving. Along with the CD reissues it's worth pointing out that a number of companies have taken to re-issuing the original recordings on higher-grade vinyl. While it's outside the scope of this work to include a listing of vinyl shops I want to focus on two. Ray Anderson who used to run the Holy See light show in the San Francisco ballroom era now runs Grooves on Market Street in San Francisco. He says every attempt to try and set up a dedicated psychedelic record display in the store is foiled, as the items are snapped up by the many younger patrons who are discovering the magic of the sixties for the first time. Ray's shop is small and packed with strictly vinyl. Another shop located in Victoria, British Columbia is called The Turntable. Run by Gary Anderson (no relation), The Turntable, like Grooves is a throwback to the sixties. I say throw-back not just because they both carry mostly vinyl, but because like so many of those early shops the walls and ceiling of both these shops are covered with either posters or album covers. It's safe to say there are shops like these in virtually every city where music fans congregate. Places like these are magnets for those recapturing recordings from their youth, or the younger ones searching out newly discovered music from the sixties or seventies. In many ways shops like this, and they are everywhere, carry on the legacy of the original Psychedelic Shop at 1535 Haight Street.

A-Z Listing

The leading question is always who to include and who not. It's a bit of a Pandora's Box as I found out with **The Progressive Rock Files**. There is a danger that if you are not specific enough in your categorization you can legitimately include just about everyone. Conversely if one is too selective it's just as easy to omit some who should rightfully be included. One of the things I've learned while researching and writing this book is that not every band included on every psychedelic compilation is in fact psychedelic. Just because a song has fuzz-guitar doesn't make it psych. As a result of this I've had to look more closely at my overall objective with this book.

This listing was perhaps the toughest list to narrow down. So many of the bands who were popular or who performed during the psychedelic era were not necessarily psychedelic bands themselves. Groups such as the Band, Santana, Paul Butterfield Blues Band, Blood Sweat & Tears are all bands that could rightly be found under more specific musical categories. Some of them are included here, some are not.

Bands such as the Beatles, the Kinks, the Who, the Rolling Stones, who had a career before the psychedelic period and in some cases after, are also listed but only with particular attention given to their input or influences during the period 1965 – 1969. In many cases I have chosen to list only the albums that are reflective of the psychedelic era, either by content or release dates. So albums released before roughly 1965 are omitted as are releases after the early seventies.

Some bands listed are "precursors" to the psychedelic movement. Bands such as the Shadows of Knight or even the Standells who played a kind of garage-punk style that was extremely popular in the United States following the British Invasion of 1964. Some of these bands either grew into psychedelic bands of the mid sixties or inspired others to do so. However that being said I have avoided including bands that legitimately fall into the garage-rock or garage-punk category, as I believe they would be better served in their own volume.

Suffice it to say everyone who is in here, is here because they would probably consider themselves either a psychedelic band or a band of the psychedelic era. Being psychedelic was after all a good part attitude. This list of bands represents the core of psychedelic music during those creative and productive years of 1965 through to about 1971. Despite having said what I said about not including certain bands, I have chosen to include some bands that were not in-and-of-themselves psychedelic but may have been a part of the scene. But first and foremost this is a book and list of the golden psychedelic era. I have not included many of the newer bands for much the same reasoning, only in reverse. Many who have been omitted may in fact carry over elements of the psychedelic sound but would not necessarily consider themselves psychedelic bands. They may include some of the defining characteristics, not the attitude.

So this list is an attempt to identify the psychedelic bands or those who at least performed within the genre. In that regard, many of the bands listed never created more than a few singles. While hard-core collectors will obviously be looking for those rare and obscure 45's many that read this will have a less determined approach. The sky-rocketing price of original material makes collecting cost prohibitive. But fortunately there have been some excellent compilation CDs assembled which include those rare releases for a fraction of the price. Some compilations even include rare alternate versions or even unreleased material, so they are definitely the way to go for casual collectors. For the most part, if the band's psychedelic work has been included on any kind of CD compilation I have included them here with the CD designation [Comp]. In some cases these compilations are exclusive to a particular band and they too will have the [Comp] designation. To help you separate the two, I've listed all the multiple-artist compilations in the Sources section under CD Compilations.

Is every psychedelic band listed here? Probably not, I'm sure I've missed some, but a good many of them are. My goal here is that if you only had the bands listed here you would have a more than comprehensive library of the psychedelic era. Hardcore collectors will undoubtedly point out bands or artists I've missed. Congratulations you are probably right. Some obscure bands who released a single or two will have been omitted. In some cases only one side of a single was psychedelic as the band was trying to cash-in on the craze and get some radio airplay. This is hardly what I'd call a psychedelic band. Still there are completists out there who will stop at nothing to find the most obscure psychedelic efforts, sincere or not. I would urge those rabid collectors to consult the fine series of books created by Vernon Joynson where even the most obscure acid-punk-garage recording will very likely have a listing. Joynson and his crew have done a spectacular job in tracking down and identifying even the most obscure one-sided releases. Alas that was not my intention here. So again, **The Psychedelic Rock Files** is somewhat more specific and intentionally so.

A-Z Listing

• A PASSING FANCY - Canada

Formed in 1966 in Toronto, Ontario; they were regulars in the underground coffee house scene and even had a couple of major regional hits in 1967. Musically they went in the psychedelic-pop vein with a bit of a garage feel. Lots of bright harmonies and fuzz-guitar. By 1970 they had disbanded.

A Passing Fancy (67), Made in Canada, Vol. 3 1961 - 1974 [Comp] (91)

• AARDVARK - UK

Formed in the late sixties their sole recording features an uncomplicated psychedelic almost progressive rock style with some early YES keyboard flavour. The album was produced by David Hitchcock who would later go on to work with GENESIS, CAMEL and CARAVAN. Overall not heavily prog sounding but good to capture the early seventies sound. It's worth pointing out the band did not have a guitarist but relied on keyboards as the lead instrument.

Aardvark (70)

• AARDVARKS - USA

Formed in 1968 in Florrisant, Missouri; the Aardvarks recorded one single officially but left a lot of stuff in the can on tape. Their sound is dominated by strongly fuzzed out lead-guitar power chords and some pleasant vocal harmonies. Based on the one single, they weren't afraid to be a little creative with their arrangements.

A Lethal Dose of Hard Psych [Comp] (99)

• A.B. SKHY - USA

Formed in 1968 in Milwaukee, Wisconsin; they originally went by the name New Blues, before relocating into the San Francisco psychedelic scene. Once there they played regularly on the ballroom circuit. Their musical style was not overtly psychedelic, but rather tended to be more electric blues with a healthy compliment of horns. They featured a full compliment of horns. They disbanded while working on their third LP.

A.B. Skhy (69), Ramblin' On (70)

• ABSTRACTS - USA

Formed in 1968 in Los Angeles but actually recorded in Texas. They created a one-off LP that was a product of the times showing a band capable of creating everything from light-weight pop influenced psychedelic to a more organ dominated acid-rock style like Iron Butterfly. They split up in the early seventies and guitarist Tony Peluso later turned up playing with the Carpenters.

The Abstracts (68)

• ACCENT - UK

Formed in 1966 in Yorkshire, they moved to London later in the year. The Accent released only one psychedelic single featuring some fuzzy guitar work and sound effects. Band member Rick Birkett later got involved with the Zombies.

The Great British Psychedelic Trip, Vol. 1 [Comp] (88), The Psychedelic Scene [Comp] (98)

• ACID GALLERY - UK

Formed in 1969 in London, the Acid Gallery was more of a studio project conducted by a band called the Epics with the assistance of Roy Wood. Their only single release called Dance Around The Maypole sounds like an obscure Move track as a result of Wood's strong involvement. Shortly after the song was released the band renamed itself Christie scoring the international Top 10 hit Yellow River.

Nuggets II Box Set [Comp] (01)

• ACT OF CREATION - USA

Formed in 1967 in Plymouth, Massachusetts; they released only one known single which featured a musical style more pop-oriented but still incorporating some of the psychedelic feel of the day.

• ACTION - UK

Formed in 1963 in Kentish Town they were originally known as the Boys and played beat music. They changed their name to Action in 1965 when their music took on more of a blue-eyed soul/Mod influence ala the Who. With the assistance of Beatles' producer George Martin, Action began to incorporate some psychedelic elements in 1966 with the release of their second single I'll Keep Holding On. You could call them psychedelic-lite.

The Ultimate Action [Comp] (81), Action Speaks Louder Than [Comp] (85), Brain (The Lost Recordings) [Comp] (96). Rolled Gold [Comp] (98), 16 Slices of ... [Comp] (01), Nuggets II Box Set [Comp] (01)

• ADAM - USA

Formed in 1966 in New York, they released only one official single. On the track Eve, Adam display their playing ability which borrows from the Byrds' Eight Miles High with its jangling lead guitar work. Loaded with lots of compression and fuzzy guitar they were a classic example of early psychedelic. Three of the members later went on to record two singles under the name Balloon Farm.

A Lethal Dose of Hard Psych [Comp] (99)

• AFFECTION COLLECTION - USA

Formed in the late sixties, this obscure outfit produced at least one LP of pop influenced psychedelia.

The Affection Collection (69)

• AFTERGLOW - USA

Formed in 1967 in Chico, California; they were originally known as the Medallions. The few obscure tracks Afterglow have left us, feature unusual trance like segments punctuated by spacey organ and unusual guitar and sound effects. Perhaps a hint of early Pink Floyd.

Afterglow (67), Beyond the Calico Wall [Comp] (93)

• AGGREGATION - USA

Formed in 1967 in Los Angeles they created one album of mellow Eastern influenced psychedelia that would appear to have been an influence on the style of bands like Ozric Tentacles. Lots of dreamy, moody passages.

Mind Odyssey (67)

• AGUATURBIA - Chile

Formed in 1968, Aguaturbia quickly became Chile's most prominent psychedelic band. With a female vocalist, and bluesy, acid-fuzz-guitar solos they quickly earned the title of "South America's Jefferson Airplane." They recorded two albums before splitting up in 1971.

Psychedelic Drugstore (70), Volumen 2 (70)

• ALEXANDER'S TIMELESS BLOOZBAND - USA

Formed in 1967 they released a couple of LPs that featured a basic blues style with a strong psychedelic influence on many of the tracks. It's worth pointing out a number of the songs featured the typical pop-psychedelic orchestration style of the day.

Alexander's Timeless Bloozband (67), For Sale (68)

• ALIBI - USA

Formed in 1968 in the New England area, they are known to have released at least one single of light flower-power pop.

• ALIENS - USA

Formed in 1968 in Norfolk, Virginia; this was an eight piece outfit with three dedicated vocalists. Their musical style featured on the two official single releases borrows heavily from the West Coast psychedelic and acid-rock style.

• ALLEN, DAEVID

An Australian who lived in England, he was a founding member of Soft Machine, before he encountered passport problems which led him to Paris where he formed GONG. Gong's psychedelic style is a mixture of spacey keyboard and guitar interplay with suitably trippy lyrics. He remained with GONG until the release of Gong Est Mort in 1977, before venturing off to pursue his solo efforts. He rejoined GONG in the nineties.

Magick Brother, Mystic Sister (70), Banana Moon (71, Good Morning (76), Now Is The Happiest Time (77), N'Existe Pas (79), About Time (80), Divided Alien Playbox 80 (80), Alien In New York (83), Death Of Rock and Other Entrances (84), Don't Stop (84), Trial By Headline (88), Stroking The Tail Of The Bird (89), The Australia Years (90), She/Australia Aquaria (90), Seven Drones (91), Magenta - She Made The World (93), Twelve Selves (93), Live (Recorded 1963) (93), Who's Afraid (93), Radio Sessions (94), Dreaming A Dream (95), Hit Men (96)

• ALLMAN JOYS - USA

Formed in 1966 in Daytona Beach, Florida; they established a solid reputation in the South East as a live outfit and even managed to tour out West putting in a few appearances in the San Francisco ballrooms. Their music was clearly blues based but contained elements of garage and psychedelia such as fuzz-guitar and folk inspired jangly guitar.

Early Allman (73)

• ALMENDRA - Argentina

Formed in 1968, Almendra in their early days created a psychedelic-pop style that borrows many psych elements from the Beatles including their use of strings and horns. By the turn of the decade they were finding their feet and producing tracks like "Obertura" with much more complicated rhythm patterns, Pink Floyd-ish crescendos and changes in tempo. Their fuzz-guitar remained front and centre.

Almendra (69), Almendra II (70), Love, Peace & Poetry: Latin American Psychedelic Music [Comp] (97)

• AMAZING BLONDEL - UK

Formed in 1969, they took a keen interest in early English medieval folk and incorporated it along some modern acoustic instruments to create a very unusual sound. Great medieval folk sound with acoustic guitars and flutes with a mix of short and long songs. Fans of GRYPHON and softer progressive rock will appreciate this style.

Amazing Blondel (70), Evensong (70), Fantasia Lindum (71), England 72 (72), Blondel (73), Mulgrave Street (74), Inspiration (75), Bad Dreams (76), Live in Tokyo (77)

• AMAZING FRIENDLY APPLE - UK

Formed in 1969, the music of Amazing Friendly Apple bridges the shores of psychedelic and progressive with its Mellotron and Hammond organ interludes. They produced one single in their time together, the 'A' side of which was a cover of Spirit's *Water Woman*.

The Great British Psychedelic Trip, Vol. 1 [Comp] (88), The Great British Psychedelic Trip, Vol. 2 [Comp] (88)

• AMBER ROUTE - USA

One of the USA's best known early-eighties space rock ensembles. Primarily a duo of Walter Holland on guitar and synth and Richard Watson on clarinet with other people augmenting on bass, guitar and drums etc. Their sound is somewhere between Pink Floyd and early to mid Tangerine Dream.

Snail Headed Victrolas (80), Ghost Tracks (83),

• AMBOY DUKES - USA

Formed in 1966 originally in Chicago but relocated to Detroit, the home of the MC5, SRC and the Stooges. The Amboy Dukes scored big in the summer of 1968 with the classic psychedelic single "Journey to the Centre of the Mind". Of note was the blistering guitar work of Ted Nugent. This was actually Nugent's third band. He later made a name for himself in the heavy metal world of the mid seventies.

The Amboy Dukes (68), Journey to the Centre of the Mind (68),

Migration (69), Survival of the Fittest (70), Marriage of the Rock - Rock Bottom (70), The Psychedelic Years Revisited [Comp] (92), Nuggets I Box Set [Comp] (98)

• AMERICAN BLUES - USA

Formed in 1967 in Dallas, Texas; they produced two albums of blues based rock full of psychedelic influences. After the second LP failed to sell they were dropped from the label and quietly disbanded in 1969. Two members, Frank Beard and Dusty Hill later went on to form ZZ Top.

American Blues is Here (68), American Blues Do Their Thing (69)

• AMERICAN REVOLUTION - USA

Formed in the late sixties in the Los Angeles area, this four-piece outfit released one album in 1968 that is best described as psychedelic-pop. Lots of sweet harmonies with nice orchestral arrangements on many of the tracks. By 1969 they'd faded from the music scene.

American Revolution (68)

• AMERICAN ZOO - USA

Formed in 1967 in the Los Angeles area, they produced two singles of pop psychedelia. As might be expected for the period the compositions come with flower-power lyrics and feature a nice organ sound.

• AMON DUUL II - Germany

Formed in 1968 in Munich, Germany they split off from the original Amon Duul to concentrate on the music rather than the politics. In many ways one of the first German rock bands to make any kind of impact on the rest of Europe. Many times described as foreboding and perhaps a little bleak, they forged their own sound based on a certain amount of electronic gadgetry. Some have put them in a group with bands like Faust and CAN but in many cases they are much more melodic and musical. Their brand of psychedelia came from the mid Pink Floyd period with the emphasis on the spacey side. While they had disbanded for a time in the nineties they were once again active as of this writing.

Phallus Dei (69), Yeti (70), Dance of the Lemmings (71), Carnival in Babylon (72), Wolf City (72), Vive La Trance (73), Live in London (74), Hijack (74), Lemmingmania [Comp](75), Made In Germany (75), Pyragony X (76), Almost Alive (78), Only Human (78), Vortex (81), Hawk Meets Penguin (83), Meeting With Men Machines (85), Full Moon (89), Die Losung (89), Surrounded by the Bars (93), Nada Moonshine # (95), Eternal Flashback (95), Kobe [Reconstruction's] (95)

• ANAN - UK

Little is known of this duo, other than they are listed in Record Collector's guide to British psychedelia. They recorded two singles in 1968.

Hot Smoke & Sassafras: Psychedelic Pstones Vol. 1 [Comp] (01)

• ANDROMEDA - UK

Formed in 1966 in London they began playing R&B influenced material but before long incorporated a fair dose of acid influenced psychedelia into their set. Following the recording of one single they recorded an LP but after failing to attract much attention disbanded

in 1969. Bassist Mick Hawksworth later turned up in Ten Years After while guitarist John Cann went to Atomic Rooster.

Andromeda (69), Anthology [Comp] (94), Live at Middle Earth [Live] (94)

• ANDWELLA'S DREAM - UK

Formed in 1968 in Northern Ireland they were originally known as the Method but changed their name and moved to London where they adopted a Hendrix-inspired form of psychedelic rock. Critical response to their 1969 LP **Love and Poetry** was positive however sales were minimal. In 1970 they shortened their name and moved more in the progressive rock vein along with bands like Traffic.

Love and Poetry (69), World's End (70), People's People (71)

• ANGEL PAVEMENT - UK

Formed in the late sixties in London, they crafted two baroque singles featuring nice harmony and pleasant melodies all in the Left Banke style. Danny Beckerman later turned up in Pussy.

The Best of and The Rest of British Psychedelia [Comp] (91)

• ANIMALS - UK

[see: ERIC BURDON AND THE ANIMALS]

• ANVIL CHORUS - Canada

Formed in 1967 in Vancouver, British Columbia; they crafted three singles with their Hendrix-inspired psychedelic guitar style. When they split up in late 1968, that guitarist, Jim Harmatta went to play in Scrubbaloe Caine.

• AORTA - USA

Formed in 1968 in Chicago, Illinois; Aorta evolved out of a band called Rotary Connection. Their sound featured a nice mix of organ and guitar with a strong psychedelic flow through the songs. After splitting up in 1970, two members Mike Been and Jim Donlinger joined H. P. Lovecraft.

Aorta (69), Aorta 2 (70)

• APHRODITE'S CHILD - Greece

A band of musicians from Greece who wound up recording in France. This was one of the first groups for, at the time unknown, keyboard player VANGELIS. The band has a strong jazz rock influence.

End of the World (69), It's Five O'clock (69), 666 (72), Aphrodite's Child (75)

• APOSTOLIC INTERVENTION - UK

Formed in 1966 in London's East End this obscure British psychedelic outfit is known to have produced only one single called (Tell Me) Have You Ever Seen Me that was produced on vinyl by Steve Marriott and Ronnie Lane of the Small Faces in the summer of 1966. If you listen carefully you'll even hear Marriott's distinctive backing vocals.

The Psychedelic Years 1966-1969 - Great Britain [Comp] (90), Psychedelic Perceptions [Comp] (96)

• APPLE - UK

Formed in 1968 in London they released a couple of psychedelic singles with a solid R&B foundation. Following this they worked on some covers of a couple Yardbirds' songs, all of which culminated in an LP, released in 1969. After garnering little attention they split up.

An Apple a Day… (69)

• APPLE-GLASS CYNDROM - USA

Formed in Clovis, New Mexico; this obscure psychedelic five piece released one known single in 1969 called *Someday* that is very reminiscent of early Pink Floyd.

• APPLE PIE MOTHERHOOD BAND - USA

Formed in 1964 in Boston they were originally known as C.C. and the Chasers. They moved to Greenwich Village where for a short time they called themselves the Sacred Mushroom. After securing a record deal with Atlantic they changed their name to the less 'drug' related Apple Pie Motherhood Band. Evolving out of a distinct garage style they adopted psychedelia in full force by the time they released their first album in 1968 and also played all the local halls like the Electric Circus and the Ark.

Apple Pie Motherhood Band (68), Apple Pie (69)

• APRYL FOOL - Japan

Formed in 1968, Apryl Fool used to be known as Floral. Musically the fuzz-guitar and organ trade off constantly building moods and intensity. Many of their compositions are low key trippy compositions with a vocal style that is reminiscent of Eric Burdon and the Animals, when it's not being heavily processed through phase controls. Haruomi Hosono later turned up in Yellow Magic Orchestra.

Apryl Fool (69), Love, Peace & Poetry: Japanese Psychedelic Music [Comp] (01)

• AQUARIAN AGE - UK

Formed in 1968 in London out of the ashes of Tomorrow, Aquarian Age consisted of bassist John Wood and drummer John "Twink" Alder who, under the production guidance of Mark Wirtz created the excellent single *10,000 Words In A Cardboard Box*. For all its studio gimmickry, the single failed to do well on the charts and Aquarian Age disbanded with Alder showing up later in the Pink Fairies.

Psychedelia at Abbey Road [Comp] (98)

• APASLAR - Turkey

Formed in the early-sixties, they started life playing surf music. By 1967, they found their voice as a full-fledged psychedelic band complete with the rolling bass and drums forming a foundation for the fuzz-guitar jamming on top. They parlayed their sound into a number of hits on local radio and developed a loyal following with their live gigs. They are seen as one of the top Turkish psychedelic outfits.

Hava Narghile, Vol. 1 [Comp] (01)

• ARBORS - USA

Formed in the early sixties they created a couple of obscure LPs. The first was more or less straight-ahead pop music with sweet harmonies while the second took their style more into the psychedelic realm.

Symphony For Susan (67), Arbors: featuring I Can't Quit Her (68)

• ARCH OF TRIUMPH - USA

Formed in the mid-sixties in Los Angeles this rather obscure outfit produced a couple of singles and one LP before disappearing from the music scene in 1970. Their music consisted of melodious psychedelic-pop heavy with orchestrations much like Left Banke.

Arch Of Triumph (70)

• ARS NOVA - USA

Formed in the mid-sixties, Ars Nova was one the early rock pioneers melding some rather obscure classical and folk styles into the psychedelic melting pot. Their first LP was on Elektra and produced by Paul Rothchild well known for his work with bands like the Doors. Their second LP was a little more straight-forward rock.

Ars Nova (68), Sunshine and Shadows (69)

• ART - UK

Formed in 1964 as the VIPs they changed their name to Art in 1967 and were signed to a subsidiary of Island records and released their first single in August of 1967 under the new name. They eventually issued one album entitled **Supernatural Fairy Tales** at which time they added American keyboardist Gary Wright. Shortly after the albums release they changed their name to Spooky Tooth and became part of progressive underground.

Supernatural Fairy Tales (67), The Psychedelic Years Revisited [Comp] (92)

• ARZACHEL - UK

They produced one LP that in some ways is similar to the psychedelic style of Pink Floyd, in particular the spacey or trippy side of things. However while the keyboards of Dave Stewart dominate the guitar parts of Steve Hillage are very tasty. Progressive fans will take note that this album was really recorded by Egg with help from Hillage.

Arzachel (69)

• ASHES - USA

Formed in 1966 in Los Angeles, this was Spencer Dryden's band before joining the Jefferson Airplane. They produced a couple of singles and one LP that was best described as early West Coast folk-rock hippie in style. They later evolved into the Peanut Butter Conspiracy.

Ashes (66)

• ASTRAL PROJECTION - USA

Formed in 1968 in New York City, they should not be confused with the more garage-oriented band out of Texas. These New Yorkers embarked on a studio project that resulted in a highly orchestrated stab at psychedelic flower-power music.

The Astral Scene (68)

• ASYLUM CHOIR - USA

Formed in 1968 in Los Angeles by Leon Russell and Marc Benno at the height of the psychedelic era and their first album bears all the trippy highlights. The second LP was less influenced by the times. After splitting up the first time in 1969, Russell went on to a very successful solo career and plenty of session work.

Look Inside the Asylum Choir (68), The Asylum Choir II (71)

• ATTACK - UK

Formed in 1966 in London they were originally known as Soul System but soon had a single out under the Attack name. Strangely each of the three singles they released was put out by another band, some at the same time and as a result the Attack failed to garner any attention. Original members Davey O'List split after the second single to join the Nice while Alan Whitehead joined Marmalade. One of the replacements Brian Davidson left after the third single to also hook up with the Nice and original guitarist John Cann joined up with Andromeda. The Attack called it quits in early 1968.

Magic in the Air [Comp] (90), The Psychedelic Scene [Comp] (98), Final Daze [Comp] (01)

• ATTIC SOUND - USA

Obscure band who recorded a single called *Look Straight Through You* in 1967.

A Heavy Dose of Lyte Psych [Comp] (96)

• AUGER, BRIAN - UK

After a history in the British soul and R&B community, organist Brian Auger had a brief fling in the psychedelic world after hooking up with Julie Driscoll in a second version of his original band Trinity. They released the popular single *This Wheels On Fire* which ended up being a UK Top 10 hit in 1968. A follow-up effort didn't do nearly as well and personal problems prompted the dissolution of this version of Trinity. They regrouped a few years later as more jazz influenced outfit.

Open (68)

• AUM - USA

Formed in the mid-sixties in San Francisco, this trio became regulars on the ballroom circuit playing long extended jams with a blues foundation. At times they were reminiscent of bands like Quicksilver. Shortly after recording their second LP for Bill Graham's Fillmore label they split up.

Bluesvibes (69), Resurrection (69)

• (AUSTRALIAN) PLAYBOYS - Australia

Formed in 1962 in Melbourne, Australia; the Playboys had a string of successful beat and R&B singles in their homeland before heading to Britain in late 1966. There they quickly fell in step with the happening freakbeat scene and began to incorporate the growing psychedelia of early 1967. They returned home in the middle of

1967 after failing to crack the British charts and split up shortly thereafter.

Nuggets II Box Set [Comp] (01)

• AUTO SALVAGE - USA

Formed in 1966 in New York, they were said to have been discovered by Frank Zappa. Not an unlikely story given the band's avant-garde approach to music, an approach that pretty much excluded them from the pop charts. The band's bassist Skip Boone was the brother of Lovin' Spoonful bassist Steve Boone. Their eclectic musical style borrowed from all over; folk, blues and even made room for string arrangements. Nothing much was heard from them after the release of their one and only album.

Autosalvage (68), Psychedelic Frequencies [Comp] (96)

• AYERS, KEVIN - UK

One of the premier members of the Canterbury sound that emanated from the area of England that gives its name to the music. Ayers helped form SOFT MACHINE in 1966 before going solo in 1968 with a style that focused on his over the edge writing style and very characteristic low monotone vocals and trippy guitar style. Ayers' compositional style is one that borrows plenty from the psychedelic or "hippie" era but then incorporates plenty progressive rock, jazz and electronic influences.

Joy of a Toy (70), Shooting at the Moon (71), Whatevershebringswesing (73), June 1, 1974 (74), Confessions of Doctor Dream (74), Sweet Deceiver (75), Yes, We Have No Mananas (76), Rainbow Takeaway (78), That's What You get Babe (80), Diamond Jack and the Queen of Pain (83), Too Old to Die Young (98)

• BACHS - USA

Formed in 1968 in Chicago, Illinois; the Bachs created one privately pressed, highly obscure LP featuring a variety of musical styles that bounce from a strong garage flavour to a more psychedelic approach.

Out of the Bachs (68)

• BACHDENKEL - UK

Early English heavy progressive sound, that borrows a lot from the psychedelic style of bands like Quicksilver Messenger Service.

Lemmings (73), Stalingrad (78)

• BALLROOM - USA

Ballroom put out only two singles although more was rumored to have been recorded. Produced by Curt Boettcher, better known for his work with the Association. The music created by Ballroom is all very spacey indeed, with plenty of repeated echo vocal treatments mixed with strange sound effects. Sort of like the middle bit of *Revolution No. 9* by the Beatles only with a little more rhythm.

A Heavy Dose of Lyte Psych [Comp] (96)

• BALLOON FARM - USA

Formed in 1967 in New York, they were originally known as Adam, before taking their name from a trendy local nightclub. They had great success with the single

"A Question of Temperature" in 1968, a pop song that oozed psychedelia featuring a swirling Hammond organ, fuzzed out guitar strange sound effects and clean production. A second single was released but missed the charts, as a result no time was spent on putting together an album. Mike Appel who helped write the hit single went on to write material for the Partridge Family and then became Bruce Springsteen's manager.

Nuggets I Box Set [Comp] (98)

• BANCHEE - USA

Formed in the late sixties in Boston, they took the more heavy approach at the tail end of the psychedelic era and produced a couple of albums full of extended guitar jams.

Banchee (69), Thinkin' (71), Psychedelic Frequencies [Comp] (96)

• BAROQUES - USA

Formed in 1967 in Milwaukee, Wisconsin; they created a psych influenced soul and R&B style that made it to vinyl on one obscure LP. Jam packed with light organ, fuzz-guitar and wild freakouts that detoured into other folk influenced territory they were quite popular on the local level but were never able to crack the big time. Another band that bridged the garage style to psychedelic.

The Baroques (67), Baroque Demos [Comp] (90), Purple Day [Comp] (95)

• BARRETT, SYD - UK

As everyone knows, Syd Barrett was a founding member of Pink Floyd and wrote most of their early psychedelic material, but he was shuffled out of the band during the recording of their second LP in 1968 when the effects of LSD started to take their toll. The stories of Barrett's constant high are endless, but soon after his departure from Pink Floyd he began working on his solo career. He eventually released two LPs before withdrawing from the music scene all together.

The Madcap Laughs (70), Barrett (70), Psychedelia at Abbey Road [Comp] (98)

• BEACH BOYS - USA

Formed in 1961 in Los Angeles, the Beach Boys shed their early 'surfing image' around the time of the recording of their revolutionary Pet Sounds created in response to the Beatles' Revolver. As founding member and main writer Brian Wilson began experimenting with drugs, this period of the Beach Boys became not only more creative but more turbulent. They released psyched out singles like "Good Vibrations" and "Heroes and Villains", which were going to be a part of an epic work being collaborated on with Van Dyke Parks entitled Smile. Word is that after the Beatles released Sgt. Pepper, the creative spark was extinguished and Wilson retreated into a creative cocoon, only to emerge years later. Fortunately much of the psychedelic material has surfaced on bootlegs over the years and rumours persist that Wilson still has plans to revive Smile.

Pet Sounds (66), Smiley Smile (67), Wild Honey (68)

• BEACON STREET UNION - USA

Formed in 1967 in Boston, Beacon Street Union were part of the "Bosstown Sound" which featured a host of home-grown talent that was springing up as part of the growing psychedelic scene in Boston. Their musical style like others of the era was part R&B, part acid-rock with a strong blues influence. They recorded two albums before changing their name to Eagle in late 1968.

The Eyes of the Beacon Street Union (68), The Clown Died in Marvin Gardens (68)

• BEATEN PATH - USA

Formed in 1966 in Brooklyn, New York; this garage/punk band released only one single and is not to be confused a similarly named outfit out of Reading, Pennsylvania.

My Rainbow Life: Psychedelic Microdots of the 60's, Vol. 3 [Comp] (92)

• BEATLES - UK

Formed in 1960 in Liverpool, the Beatles psychedelic era began with the LP Rubber Soul in 1965 which coincided with their first experiences with LSD and meeting Bob Dylan. In so many ways the Beatles set the bench mark for the pop psychedelic music scene, in that they were able to take their consummate writing skills and apply the greatest creative energy and studio gimmickry and were allowed the maximum opportunity to experiment. They went from strength to strength with the release of Revolver and then the epitome of pop-psychedelia, Sgt. Pepper's Lonely Hearts Club Band followed by The Magical Mystery Tour. While the psych influences became less overt in the releases following there is still a lot of magic right up their final effort Abbey Road.

Rubber Soul (65), Revolver (66), Sgt. Pepper's Lonely Hearts Club Band (67), Magical Mystery Tour (67), The Beatles (68), Abbey Road (69)

• BEAU BRUMMELS - USA

Formed in 1964 in San Francisco the Beau Brummels were the Bay areas answer to the British Invasion. They were signed to the Autumn Records label where their pre-psychedelic mood-shifting arrangements and strong harmonies gave them a number of decent hits including "Laugh Laugh" and "Just a Little" in 1965. As the psychedelic scene grew around them they adapted and produced singles like "Magic Hollow". Latter they reverted back to a folk-rock style and incorporated country influences before splitting up at the end of 1968. Many of the contemporary psychedelic era bands like the Monkees, the Byrds and even Jefferson Airplane credit the Beau Brummels with being a huge influence.

Introducing the Beau Brummels (65), Volume 2 (66), Beau Brummels 66 (66), Triangle (67), Bradley's Barn (68), Volume 44 (68), San Francisco Nights [Comp] (91), Psychedelic Visions [Comp] (96), Nuggets I Box Set [Comp] (98)

• BEAVERS - Japan

Formed in 1968, the Beavers were more of a flower-power band. Their material was produced with orchestral backing and they relied heavily on melodies and harmonies more so than fuzz-guitar and jamming. Lead guitarist Hideki Ishima later became a part of the Flower Travelling Band and after that he joined the Flowers.

Viva (68), Love, Peace & Poetry: Japanese Psychedelic Music [Comp] (01)

• BEN, TOBY - USA

From California this rather obscure artist released one LP with songs in a pop-psych style.

Wake Up to the Sunshine (68)

• BENT WIND - Canada

Formed in 1968 in Toronto, Ontario; they released one obscure LP that is distinguished by its classic psychedelic fuzz-guitar style.

Sussex (69)

• BERKELEY KITES - USA

Formed in 1967 in Florida they released at least four singles with a strong pop-psych flavour. Expect to hear some interesting, but subdued fuzz-guitar, Beach Boy style harmonies and a bit of pleasant flute work.

• BEVIS FROND - USA

Not really a group, Bevis Frond is actually the work of Nick Saloman. His long trippy guitar inspired work hearkens back to the acid-rock of the sixties but updates the overall sound with modern production and technology. The overall effect of the music is enhanced with an appropriate amount of melody and provides much adventurous listening. A bit of old and new with a strong Hendrix and Cream influence.

Inner Marshland (87), Miasma (87), Bevis Through the Looking Glass (88), Any Gas Faster (90), A Gathering of Fronds (92)

• BHAGAVAD GITA - USA

Obscure Mid-Western band who recorded at least one or two singles in 1967 of twin psychedelic guitar work. Lots of feedback and jamming with understated bass and drum rhythm section.

Beyond the Calico Wall [Comp] (93)

• BIG BOY PETE - UK

Obscure artist from Norwich, England; who released one single entitled "Cold Turkey" b/w "My Love is Like a Spaceship" in 1968. His other studio demos have since been released on CD compilations and feature all the psychedelic hallmarks and studio gimmickry so prevalent in the mid to late sixties.

Electric Sugarcube Flashbacks [Comp] (93), Homage To Catatonia [Comp] (96)

• BIG BROTHER & THE HOLDING COMPANY - USA

Formed in 1965 in San Francisco, their story is legend. Originally honing their chops playing the basement ballroom of their Victorian hippie mansion, they were managed by Chet Helms and soon were playing the ballroom circuit weekly. Early in their life span, Helms recruited lead vocalist Janis Joplin whom he knew from his days in Texas. With Joplin, Big Brother took off and created another chapter in the sound of West Coast acid-rock with their blues influenced style. After their powerful performance at the 1967 Monterey Pop Festival they were signed to Columbia records, primarily to secure Joplin and she left Big Brother in 1968 to form her own backing bands. Big Brother carried on for a time but while they remained a favourite in their home turf of San Francisco they never again made significant national coverage. They eventually split up in 1972.

Big Brother and the Holding Company (67), Cheap Thrills (68), Be a Brother (71), How Hard It Is (71), Psychedelic Perceptions [Comp] (96)

• BIRDS - UK

Formed in 1963 in West London, the Birds played the usual mix of R&B and soul tunes until firming up their own garage freakbeat style in early 1966. They signed to Decca records and released a number of singles which bore the hallmarks of contemporary bands such as the Stones and the Who. Their main claim to fame is that of being Ron Wood's first group. After failing to attract significant chart action they split apart in 1966 and bass guitarist Kim Gardner joined up with Creation and later became one third of Ashton, Gardner & Dyke. Ron Wood also spent time in Creation before going on to the Faces and then the Rolling Stones.

These Birds are Dangerous [Comp] (85), Say Those Magic Words [Comp] (97), The Collectors Guide to Rare British Birds [Comp] (99)

• BIRMINGHAM SUNDAY - USA

Formed in 1967 in Nevada they recorded one LP of flower-power pop in the same vein as bands like the Peanut Butter Conspiracy.

A Message From Birmingham Sunday (67)

• BLACK PEARL - USA

Formed in 1967 in San Francisco by the former members of the Barbarians. They featured a three guitar line-up spotlighting plenty of heavy psychedelic jams with a firm R&B foundation.

Black Pearl (69), Black Pearl Live at The Fillmore (70)

• BLONDE ON BLONDE - UK

Formed in 1968 in London it's the very early Blonde On Blonde that displays any real psychedelic influences. Their first single "All Day, All Night" released in December 1969, which topped off an attention getting performance at the Isle of Wight Festival, contained an Eastern influence along with their unusual blend of rock and classical influences. They quickly evolved into a fine example of early English style folk influenced progressive rock before disbanding in 1972.

Contrasts (69), Rebirth (70), Reflections on a Life (71), Hot Smoke & Sassafras: Psychedelic Pstones Vol. 1 [Comp] (01)

• BLOSSOM TOES - UK

Formed in 1967 in London, Blossom Toes saw the future of the growing psychedelic scene after hearing the Beatles' Sgt. Pepper LP and quickly left their soul and R&B origins behind. They were signed to a recording deal by the manager of the Yardbirds on his new Marmalade label and after one single they recorded their first LP complete with all the studio gimmickry and psychedelic embellishment allowed. Success eluded them and after recording a second LP they evolved into a band called B. B. Blunder in 1970. Guitarist Jim Cregan went on to play with Rod Stewart.

We Are Ever So Clean (67), If Only For a Moment (69), Collection [Comp] (88), Nuggets II Box Set [Comp] (01)

• BLUEBIRD - USA

Formed in the mid-sixties in Seattle, Washington; Bluebird's country-folk-rock style bore more than a little similarity to the fuzz-guitar and vocal harmony style of Buffalo Springfield.

The History of Northwest Rock Vol. 3: Psychedelic Seattle [Comp] (00)

• BLUE CHEER - USA

Formed in 1967 in San Francisco, they originally went by the name the San Francisco Blues Band and had six members. They saw the Jimi Hendrix Experience at the Monterey Pop Festival and immediately trimmed down to a more manageable trio and in 1968 had a huge national hit with their heavy fuzz-laden version of "Summertime Blues". Their first album nearly made the Top 10, but they failed to capitalize on any future releases. The band built a cult following based on their claim to being the "loudest" band in the world and boasting of a card carrying Hell's Angel as manager. The groups proto-heavy metal style help ed create the genre of the seventies later popularized by bands like Led Zeppelin. They disbanded in 1971.

Vincebus Eruptum (68), Outsideinside (68), New Improved Blue Cheer (69), Blue Cheer (70), The Original Human Beings (70), Oh! Pleasant Hope (71), San Francisco Nights [Comp] (91)

• BLU-EREBUS - USA

Formed in 1967 in Mt. Airy, North Carolina; they released only one single featuring some stellar fuzz-guitar and wah-wah pedal work. Throw in the harpsichord, some interesting vocal work and some trippy lyrics and you have a classic example of pop-psychedelia.

An Overdose of Heavy Psych [Comp] (97)

• BLUES CREATION - Japan

Formed in the late sixties, Blues Creation, as the name implies created a heavily blues based psychedelic style, with the emphasis on guitar. If you enjoy the Blue Cheer spectrum of psychedelia, this is your cup of tea.

Demon & Eleven Children (71), Love, Peace & Poetry: Japanese Psychedelic Music [Comp] (01)

• BLUES MAGOOS - USA

Formed in 1964 in New York they originally went by the name Trenchcoats before changing the name in 1966 to the creatively spelled 'Bloos Magoos'. By this time they had established quite a name for themselves on the Greenwich Village stages particularly for the emerging psychedelic influence which was manifesting itself in the groups use of sound effects, echo, feedback and well placed improvisational moments. After a

number of successful chart hits and five LPs they disbanded in 1971.

Psychedelic Lollipop (66), Electric Comic Book (67), Basic Blues Magoos (68), Never Going Back to Georgia (69), Gulf Coast Bound (70), Nuggets I Box Set [Comp] (98)

• BLUES MESSENGERS - USA

Formed in 1968 in Fort Lauderdale, Florida this obscure psychedelic outfit produced a couple of singles featuring a predominant acid-rock style with more than a little Vanilla Fudge or Iron Butterfly influence.

Psychedelic States: Florida Vol. 1 [Comp] (00)

• BLUES PROJECT - USA

Formed in 1964 in New York, the Blues Project was put together by guitarist Danny Kalb and included future star keyboard player Al Kooper. In short order they were playing the club circuit and developing their own style out of an R&B base, soon adding elements of folk, jazz and rock. By 1967 they had developed their own brand of psychedelia.

Live at the Au Go Go (66), Projections (66), Live at Town Hall (67), Planned Obsolescence (68), Nuggets I Box Set [Comp] (98)

• BOHEMIAN VENDETTA - USA

Formed in 1967 in New York City this obscure band created a couple of singles and even recorded a full album of psychedelic music in the mid-sixties which managed to hold on to a hint of the garage earnestness. Nice acid-laced fuzzy guitar and organ work.

Bohemian Vendetta (68), Beyond the Calico Wall [Comp] (93)

• BONDSMEN - USA

Formed in 1968 in Durham, North Carolina; the Bondsmen recorded a couple of singles released in 1969 that featured a soul vision loaded with the obligatory psychedelic trappings of fuzz-guitar and organ sound something like a garage version of the Music Express.

A Lethal Dose of Hard Psych [Comp] (99)

• BONZO DOG BAND - UK

Formed in 1965 in London they originally went by the extended name Bonzo Dog Doo-Dah Band and came out of an art school background. Their musical style was satirical and novelty laden with the best British dry humour. They fell into many of the psychedelic happenings of the day much for the same reason the Mothers of Invention did in the U.S. because they created challenging music with a large dose of fun. They split up in 1970, reforming briefly the following year to record their final LP before disbanding for good. Neil Innis would later resurface in the Beatles parody entitled the Rutles.

Gorilla (67), The Doughnut in Granny's Greenhouse (68), Tadpoles (69), Keynsham (69), Let's Make Up and Be Friendly (72)

• BOOTS - Germany

Formed in 1965 in Berlin, the Boots started out with an R&B style. As time progressed they incorporated their own elements of fuzz-guitar and organ to approximate a freakbeat almost psychedelic style. Following the release of a number of singles and two albums they disbanded in 1969.

Here are the Boots ( ), Nuggets II Box Set [Comp] (01)

• BOUGALIEU - USA

Formed in 1967 in Albany, New York; the Bougalieu played various Stones and Yardbirds cover tunes at just about any bar that would let them play. Their style being predominantly garage/punk. After a few poorly received singles the band relocated to Florida before falling off the radar screen.

My Rainbow Life: Psychedelic Microdots of the 60's, Vol. 3 [Comp] (92)

• BOW STREET RUNNERS - USA

Formed in the late sixties they were one of the bands who mixed the last hints of psychedelia with the coming progressive rock. A mixture of spacey Pink Floyd-ish sound and acid-tinged guitar work.

Bow Street Runners (70)

• BRAIN POLICE - USA

Formed in 1967 in San Diego, the Brain Police created one album of classic American flower-power rock tinged with the growing element of hard rock.

The Brain Police (68)

• BRAINSTORM - Australia

A nice blend of psychedelia with a hint of progressive rock, with the end result being a late sixties flavoured prog. Well developed themes with good clean guitar, analog synths and even a hint of Mellotron. The compositions when not being overly psychedelic tend to be melodic in an early Pink Floyd, Barclay James Harvest or Spring kind of way.

Tales of the Future (98), Brainstorm 2: Earth Zero (01)

• BRAVE NEW WORLD - USA

Formed in the mid-sixties in Seattle, Washington; Brave New World stuck out like a sore thumb in a world of garage bands. They took the basic garage sound and injected some searing acid-guitar leads and some suitably trippy lyrics to concoct their own version of psychedelia.

The History of Northwest Rock Vol. 3: Psychedelic Seattle [Comp] (00)

• BRITISH NORTH AMERICA ACT - Canada

Formed in 1968 in Montreal, Quebec; they toured the country extensively, playing in Vancouver on a number of occasions. Musically they were very eclectic and performed a mix of harmony pop with elements of psychedelia.

In the Beginning (69)

• BROWN, ARTHUR - UK

A product of England's psychedelic summer of 1967, Brown who'd spent his early years playing the London club circuit, enlisted organist Vincent Crane to help

form the Crazy World of Arthur Brown. After some regular dates at the underground club UFO they were invited to play at the seminal 14-hour Technicolor Dream event. They enjoyed tremendous success in 1968 with the strange hit *Fire* and an even stranger stage act which included a flaming helmet and a crucifixion. They eventually metamorphosed into the more progressive KINGDOM COME in the early seventies.

Crazy World of Arthur Brown (68), Galactic Zoo Dossier (72), Journey (72), Kingdom Come (73), Dance (75), Lost Ears (76), Chisholm in My Bosom (77), Faster than the Speed of Sound (80), Requiem (82), The Psychedelic Years 1966-1969 - Great Britain [Comp] (90), The Psychedelic Years Revisited [Comp] (92)

• BUBBLE PUPPY - USA

Formed in 1967 in San Antonio, Texas; they took their name from the writings of Aldus Huxley. Following a move to Houston in 1968 they released their first LP and the single *Hot Smoke & Sassafras*. The single did surprisingly well reaching into the Top 20 it featured a guitar based psychedelia just right for the times. While sales were respectable and the band toured in support of Steppenwolf they were never able to crack the big time. They eventually moved to California before disbanding in 1971.

A Gathering of Promises (69)

• BUCKLEY, TIM - USA

Hailed by many as one of the greatest songwriters of the psychedelic era, Buckley was signed to the Elektra label where he produced some stunning material. Born in Washington, Buckley combined a keen sense of lyrical skill with a vast knowledge of folk, jazz and blues musical inspiration. His latter work went even more into the avant-garde area. Commercial success eluded him and he ultimately took a job as a chauffer to Sly Stone. It was only after his death in 1975 that the critics took notice of his talents.

Tim Buckley (66), Goodbye and Hello (67), Happy - Sad (69), Blue Afternoon (70), Lorca (70), Starsailor (71), Greetings From L.A. (72), Sefronia (74), Look at the Fool (74), Psychedelic Perceptions [Comp] (96)

• BUFFALO SPRINGFIELD - USA

Formed in 1966 in Los Angeles consisting of Stephen Stills, Richie Furray, Neil Young, Dewey Martin and Bruce Palmer they took their name from a highway steamroller. They were a clash of powerful egos virtually from the beginning particularly between Stills and Young. While their music was never overtly psychedelic in style they none-the-less had one of the era's most significant hit singles *For What Its Worth,* a song about the Sunset Strip youth riots of late 1966. Stills and Young eventually morphed into Crosby Stills Nash and Young in 1969 while Furray formed Poco.

Buffalo Springfield (67), Buffalo Springfield Again (68), Last Time Around (68), Psychedelic Frequencies [Comp] (96)

• BULLDOG BREED - UK

Formed in the late sixties in London, Bulldog Breed bridged the gap between psychedelia and progressive rock and their one album displayed an equal amount of each style.

Made In England (69)

• BUMBLEBEES - Holland

Formed in the mid-sixties in Den Haag known as Holland's beat capital. Their 1967 single *Maybe Someday* is an odd affair featuring strange chanting background vocals and what sounds like a clarinet as the lead instrument.

Waterpipes & Dykes: Dutch Psychedelic Underground 1966 - 1972 Vol. 1 [Comp] ( )

• BUMPS - USA

Formed in the early sixties in Seattle, Washington; they retained a slight British Invasion sound but it was made blurry by the heavy fuzz-guitar and the reedy-organ laying in the background.

The History of Northwest Rock Vol. 3: Psychedelic Seattle [Comp] (00)

• BURNING RED IVANHOE - Denmark

Formed in the late sixties they combined elements of jazz-rock into a psychedelic style with just a few early progressive influences.

M144 (69), Burnin' Red Ivanhoe (70), 6 Elefantskovcikadeviser (71), WWW (71), Miley Smile (72), Right On (74), Burnin' Live 1970/72 (74)

• BYRD, JOE & THE FIELD HIPPIES - USA

Formed in 1968 in Los Angeles after the demise of the United States of America, Joe Byrd decided to take his musical leanings to the next level. Once again the music went in a somewhat avant-garde direction and lasted only a short time.

Joe Byrd and the Field Hippies (69)

• BYRDS - USA

Formed in 1964 in Los Angeles they were originally known as the Jetset. The Byrds along with the Yardbirds are credited with having the first psychedelic hits. It was *Mr. Tambourine Man* that brought them to public attention in the summer of 1965, but it was the overtly psychedelic *Eight Miles High* of 1966 that put them front and centre of the growing counter culture movement. The Byrds synthesised perfectly the British Invasion sound with a liberal dose of Americana folk set up by McGuinn's jangly 12-string guitar. In the early years they set the tone for dozens of bands that followed in the path they blazed. By 1967 the cracks were beginning to show and the group was starting to split. David Crosby was spending more time with Buffalo Springfield or in San Francisco wandering around Haight-Ashbury and was the first to leave the band. In the years that followed the Byrds went through a number of personel changes and shifting musical styles, including a return to roots country, in an attempt to find their former glory, but their time had passed and they never regained their prominent position.

Mr. Tambourine man (65), Turn! Turn! Turn! (66), Fifth Dimension (66), Younger than Yesterday (67), The Notorious Byrd Brothers (68), Sweetheart of the Rodeo (68), Dr. Byrd and

Mr. Hyde (69), The Psychedelic Years Revisited [Comp] (92), Psychedelic Perceptions [Comp] (96)

• BYSTANDERS - UK

Formed in the late sixties in Wales, the Bystanders released a number of singles that featured their close harmonies and special psychedelic take in arrangements. By the end of 1968 they'd gone through a number of personnel changes and then changed their name to Man.

Pattern People [Comp] ( ), Hot Smoke & Sassafras: Psychedelic Pstones Vol. 1 [Comp] (01)

• C. A. QUINTET - USA

Formed in 1967 in Minneapolis, Minnesota; the C.A. Quintet produced an unusual brand of psychedelia noted for its rather overall gloomy feel produced mainly by the overpowering organ. The primary influences seem to be elements of the Doors and a bit of the strangeness of Country Joe and the Fish.

Trip Thru Hell (68)

• CAGRISIM - Turkey

This obscure band from Bursa, Turkey; appeared in 1972 at the tail end of the psychedelic era. Their music is a mix of a spacey Pink Floyd-ish foundation with a West Coast trippy fuzz-guitar sound.

Hava Narghile, Vol. 1 [Comp] (01)

• CALEB - UK

Guitarist and vocalist Caleb Quaye is known to have recorded at least one single of saturated phased-out psychedelic splendour in 1967 entitled "Baby Your Phrasing is Bad". He later joined up with Hookfoot and session work with the likes of Elton John.

Nuggets II Box Set [Comp] (01)

• CALIFORNIA, RANDY - USA

[see: SPIRIT]

• CALIFORNIANS - UK

Obscure Midlands band whose first single was the Warren Zevon penned *Follow Me*. Over a period of three years they released eight singles. Their last single was released in January of 1969 and then they faded from the scene.

The Great British Psychedelic Trip, Vol. 1 [Comp] (88)

• CANTERBURY FAIR - USA

Formed in 1967 in Fresno, California; they moved to San Francisco in late 1968 only to return to Fresno a short time later. They stayed together till the eighties before disbanding. Their sound in the early psychedelic years was along the lines of bands like the Left Banke, kind of a poppy semi-orchestrated soft psych.

Canterbury Fair [Comp] (99)

• CAPES OF GOOD HOPE - USA

Formed in 1966 in Chicago, the Capes of Good Hope created a couple of splendid singles in 1966 which sound like a blend of the baroque Left Banke style with plenty of Eastern influences.

A Heavy Dose of Lyte Psych [Comp] (96)

• CAPTAIN BEEFHEART - USA

Born Don Van Vliet, he took the name Captain Beefheart from a short film he and FRANK ZAPPA had created. His family had originally settled in California when he was 13. He began playing in blues bands in 1959 and eventually met up with Zappa in 1963. The two shared an interest in music that stretched current convention and that said something in process. The two also battled over egos. While the music created by Captain Beefheart may not have fit the neat mould of psychedelia it none-the-less was very much a part of the musically adventurous sixties.

Safe As Milk (68), Strictly Personal (68), Trout Mask Replica (69), Lick My Decals Off, Baby (71), The Spotlight Kid (72), The Psychedelic Years Revisited [Comp] (92), Psychedelic Frequencies [Comp] (96), Nuggets I Box Set [Comp] (98)

• CARGO - Holland

Heavy sounding progressive rock with some long winded psychedelic guitar passages. Perhaps a little more like Golden Earring.

Cargo (72)

• CARDBOARD BOX - USA

Formed in 1967 in Pottstown, Pennsylvania; they were originally known as the Ethics, but soon adopted a psychedelic soul style as the Cardboard Box. Some have described their style as a funky-Iron Butterfly! They continued performing into 1969.

A Lethal Dose of Hard Psych [Comp] (99)

• CARDBOARD VILLAGE - USA

Formed in the late sixties in Massachusetts they crafted one album that's best described as acid-folk with female vocals.

Sea Change (69)

• CARPENTER, CHRIS - USA

From the Detroit area, Carpenter released a couple of singles, one sounding like a highly orchestrated psych-pop with plenty of echo and fuzz-guitar and the other a little more avant-garde full of rattles and chimes.

A Heavy Dose of Lyte Psych [Comp] (96)

• CATFISH KNIGHT & THE BLUE EXPRESS - USA

They released a couple of singles in 1968, one of which featured a horn arrangement sounding more like a TV theme song, and the other with a song called *Deathwish* which was jammed with thumping bass and drums and a bed of distorted fuzz-guitar.

A Lethal Dose of Hard Psych [Comp] (99)

• CEYLEIB PEOPLE - USA

Actually a group of Los Angeles session people including Ry Cooder, Jim Gordon, Larry Knechtal and others who created an album full of sitar and raga instrumental psychedelic-pop-rock that brings back sonic images of bands like Strawberry Alarm Clock.

Tanyet (68), Beyond the Calico Wall [Comp] (93)

• CHAMAELEON CHURCH - USA

Formed in 1967 in the Boston area, they crafted one album of pleasant flower-power pop along the lines of Left Banke.

Chameleon Church (68)

• CHAMBERS BROTHERS - USA

Formed in 1959 in Lee County, Mississippi; they were in fact four brothers who relocated to Los Angeles in 1961 at the time they were concentrating on gospel and folk music. By 1966 they began incorporating elements of psychedelic soul into the material and upon being signed to Columbia records they released *Time Has Come Today* which became a Top 10 hit. They played the ballroom circuit regularly. As the sixties came to a close, they moved more into a funk style but faded from the scene at the end of the sixties.

People Get Ready (66), The Chambers Brothers - Now Live (66), The Time Has Come (68), A New Time - A New Day (68),

• CHANGING TIMES - USA

This Texas band never actually recorded any official singles but some of their material recorded for a TV show has shown up on some psychedelic compilations. Their style was very garage/punk with a fair amount of fuzz-guitar thrown in.

Texas Twisted: Psychedelic Microdots of the 60's, Vol. 2 [Comp] (91)

• CHARLATANS - USA

Formed in 1964 in San Francisco, the Charlatans are acknowledged as the first underground or overtly psychedelic band. After making a name for themselves at the Red Dog Saloon they returned to San Francisco and played on bills with all the prime acid-rock bands. The Charlatan's style was more folk-jugband-blues-country but blended together with their turn of the century clothing style they presented a very psychedelic appearance. Unfortunately their vinyl recordings came so late in their career that the scene had passed them by. Band members Dan Hicks went on to fame with his Hot Licks and Mike Wilhelm found a home with the Flamin Groovies.

The Charlatans (69), San Francisco Nights [Comp] (91), Nuggets I Box Set [Comp] (98)

• CHEN, SHINKI - Japan

Chen was a prominent figure in the world of Japanese psychedelic music and as such he collaborated with the best of them for his recordings. Typical of Japanese psychedelia from the early seventies is its prominent heavy fuzz-guitar in blues based compositions.

Shinki Chen & his Friends (71), Love, Peace & Poetry: Japanese Psychedelic Music [Comp] (01)

• CHERRY SMASH - UK

Formed in 1967 in Gosport, Hampshire by Bryan Sebastian, the brother of Mike Hugg from Manfred Mann. Despite having the right connections the few singles released failed to attract any chart action and Cherry Smash disappeared quietly in 1969.

The Great British Psychedelic Trip, Vol. 1 [Comp] (88), The Great British Psychedelic Trip, Vol. 2 [Comp] (88)

• CHILDE HAROLD - USA

Formed in 1968 in New York, Childe Harold released a couple of singles, one produced by electronic artist Wendy Carlos. The music of Childe Harold is highly orchestrated and full of phased vocals, unusual tempo changes and a very whimsical British psychedelic style.

A Heavy Dose of Lyte Psych [Comp] (96)

• CHILDREN OF JUBAL - Holland

Formed in the late sixties they recorded a couple of singles in the early seventies which were very much like the droning, spacey style made famous by Pink Floyd. The sound of their instruments is different but the style is similar. Some interesting changes in timing and tempo, display how psychedelic was morphing into progressive in the early seventies. There are rumours of more recordings, but none have been released.

Waterpipes & Dykes: Dutch Psychedelic Underground 1966 - 1972 Vol. 1 [Comp] ( )

• CHIMERA - UK

Formed in England and signed to a small label they recorded upwards of twenty tracks, but little of it has seen the light of day even on current compilations. They created a folk inspired psychedelia that was both melodic and instrumentally well played. Word has it they were managed by Pink Floyd's Nick Mason and apparently both Mason and Richard Wright appear on some tracks.

The Best of and The Rest of British Psychedelia [Comp] (91)

• CHIMPS - USA

The Chimps were actually a spin-off project for the Thomas A. Edison Electric Band who recorded an album of strange pop in 1967. Although not all of it would be classed as psychedelic, one track in particular called Fifth Class Mail fits our needs here.

A Heavy Dose of Lyte Psych [Comp] (96)

• CHOCOLATE WATCH BAND - UK

Formed in 1967 in London they should not be confused with the American band of the same name. The UK version was decidedly more pop oriented with fuller arrangements. Lack of chart success following the release of two psychedelic-pop singles prompted them to disband in 1968.

The Great British Psychedelic Trip, Vol. 2 [Comp] (88)

• CHOCOLATE WATCH BAND - USA

Formed in 1965 in San Jose, outside of San Francisco they were managed by Ed Cobb who had also handled the Standells. The Chocolate Watch Band managed to retain all the best of the emerging edgy garage R&B music scene and blend it with the swirling sounds of the psychedelic movement. They recorded three albums before disappearing from the radar after the summer of 1968.

No Way Out (67), The Inner Mystique (68), One Step Beyond (69), Psychedelic Perceptions [Comp] (96), Nuggets I Box Set [Comp] (98)

• CHOIR - USA

Formed in 1965 in Cleveland, the Choir was part of the garage/punk scene. They recorded a number of singles incorporating a strong Brit-pop influence and had a local number one hit in Cleveland with It's Cold Outside in the spring of 1967. Following a short rise to fame, more singles, and a few disastrous tours they released the Left Banke influenced When You Were With Me which was ignored by everyone. The Choir carried on into the seventies on a local level. Guitarist Wally Bryson left to join Eric Carmen and eventually created the power pop band the Raspberries.

Choir Practice [Comp] (94), My Rainbow Life: Psychedelic Microdots of the 60's, Vol. 3 [Comp] (92), Nuggets I Box Set [Comp] (98)

• CHRISTMAS - Canada

Formed in 1969 in Oshawa, Ontario; where they had originally gone by the name Reign Ghost. Their musical style was folk oriented, psychedelic rock. After recording one album in 1970 they moved their music in a slightly more progressive rock vein ala Jethro Tull and recorded yet another LP in 1974 under the band name the Spirit of Christmas.

Heritage (71), Lies to Live By (74)

• CIRCLES END - Norway

Formed in 1997 this Norwegian five piece create a busy and somewhat complicated progressive rock with musical influences ranging from jazz to funk to fusion to psychedelic. With two guitarists the music is as expected more guitar driven. Keyboards appear on only a few tracks, provided by guests and generally take a back seat, although given the nature of the compositions, they're not always missed. Fans of the denser style of bands such as ANEKDOTEN should have no trouble appreciating what's going on here.

Circles End (98), In Dialogue With the Moon (01)

• CIRCUS MAXIMUS - USA

Formed in 1967 in Austin, Texas; they were a mix of folk-rock and hard rock but with an over-riding flower-power influence throughout their compositions. They produced a couple of albums and even performed at Carnegie Hall, but lack of sales caused the band to split up in 1968. Guitarist and vocalist Jerry "Jeff" Walker went on to fame with the solo single Mr. Bojangles.

Circus Maximus (67), Neverland Revisited (68)

• CLEAR LIGHT - USA

Formed in 1967 in Los Angeles, California; Clear Light were regulars for a time on the San Francisco ballroom scene. They were signed to the Elektra label and worked with producer Paul Rothchild who gave their sound some of the same nuances he gave other label-mates the Doors and Love. After recording one album in 1967 some of the band members went on to interesting projects. Doug Lubahn played bass on a couple of the Doors LPs, and drummer Dallas Taylor played with Crosby, Stills & Nash.

Clear Light (67), Black Roses [Comp] (87)

• CLIQUE - USA

Formed in 1968 in Austin, Texas; they created one album of flower-power pop, featuring a bright harmony style with some typical studio gimmickry. They had a Top 40 hit with *Sugar On Sunday*.

Happy Together: The Very Best of White Whale Records [Comp] (99)

• COLD BLOOD - USA

Formed in the late sixties in San Francisco they were not an overtly psychedelic band but rather more of a soul-funk band, especially after adding horns to the line-up in 1969. None the less they were part of the scene and regulars in the latter days of the ballroom circuit. Featuring the tiny in stature but big in voice Lydia Pense, they recorded a total of five albums but never really broke through to nationwide success.

Cold Blood (69), Sisyphus (70), First Taste of Sin (72), Thriller (73), Lydia (74)

• COLLECTORS - Canada

Formed in 1964 in Vancouver, British Columbia; they were originally called the Classics, but changed their name to the Collectors in 1965 and plunged headlong into the world of psychedelia. Prominent poster artist Bob Masse designed their first album cover. From that album they even had a hit in 1967 with the single *Fisherwoman*. After seven singles and two albums lead vocalist Howie Vickers left in 1969 at which time guitarist Bill Henderson took over, changing the bands name to Chilliwack, a town located near Vancouver and carried on as a hit making trio into the eighties.

The Collectors (67), Grass and Wild Strawberries (68), The History of Vancouver Rock & Roll, Vol. 4 [Comp] (91)

• COMFORTABLE CHAIR - USA

Formed in the late sixties in Los Angeles they were 'discovered' by Jim Morrison of the Doors and created one LP that was produced by Robbie Krieger and John Densmore of the Doors. Their musical style has been compared to bands such as the Peanut Butter Conspiracy.

Comfortable Chair (69)

• COMMON PEOPLE - USA

Formed in the late sixties in California they produced one album with a laid back acoustic psychedelic style.

Of the People by the People for the People from the Common People (69)

• CONQUEROO - USA

Formed in 1967 in Austin, Texas; the band is best remembered for being responsible for opening their own club called the Vulcan Gas Company in 1967. Their music was similar to much of the West Coast acid-rock scene best exemplified by bands like Grateful Dead. The band even relocated to San Francisco for a time in the late sixties but failing to find success they disbanded and returned to Texas.

From the Vulcan Gas Company [Comp] (87)

• CORPORATION - USA

Formed in 1967 in Milwaukee, Wisconsin, but soon relocated to Detroit where they recorded three albums during the late sixties.

Hassels in My Mind (68), Get on Our Swing (68), The Corporation (69)

• COSMIC ROCK SHOW - USA

Obscure mid-sixties band based out of Duluth, Minnesota; they created a trippy fuzzy guitar sound with strange organ, keyboard and bass work in the background. More than a hint of garage feel to this psychedelic sound.

Beyond the Calico Wall [Comp] (93)

• COTTON MOUTH - USA

Formed in 1968 in Olympia, Washington they released only a couple singles featuring a classic West Coast acid fuzz-guitar sound.

• COUNT FIVE - USA

Formed in 1965 in San Jose, California; they were originally known as the Squires. With all members still in their teens the Count Five created songs that represent the best of the early sixties garage/punk movement. Their skirting of the psychedelic era included an R&B base with liberal use of echo, reverb, feedback and stinging guitar solos. Their first single *Psychotic Reaction* was a huge hit in 1966, but even though the band released a string of follow-up singles none was able to make any impact and by 1968 the Count Five had split up. Guitarist Sean Byrne returned to Ireland to join the progressive rock group Public Foot The Roman.

Psychotic Reaction (66), Psychedelic Frequencies [Comp] (96), Nuggets I Box Set [Comp] (98)

• COUNTRY JOE & THE FISH - USA

Formed in 1965 in San Francisco they became known for their overtly more politicised musical direction. As such, they were befriended by the Berkeley crowd. After cutting a few minor singles they released one of the most psychedelic LPs with **Electric Music for the Mind and Body** in 1967. In the following year they recorded what has since become their signature tune *The Fish Cheer* a song that played off full audience participation. Its anti-war stance played well to the counter culture and was immortalized at Woodstock. Their music was the usual blend of folk-rock and a bit of country all electrified with plenty of experimentation. The band split up in 1970 and Country Joe McDonald went on to record many solo efforts.

Electric Music for the Mind and Body (67), I-Feel-Like-I'm-A-Fixin-To-Die (68), Together (68), Here We Are Again (69), C. J. Fish (70), San Francisco Nights [Comp] (91), The Psychedelic Years Revisited [Comp] (92)

• COUNTRY WEATHER - USA

Formed in 1967 in San Francisco, they used to be called the Virtues, but when the name changed so did their musical style. Featuring a blend of folk, pop, country and rock with an over-riding sense of West Coast psychedelia, they fit in to the scene perfectly and became regulars on the ballroom circuit. They managed to record one side of an LP and pressed some fifty copies. A long awaited record deal never came about and they disbanded in 1973.

Limited Edition One Side LP (68)

• CRASH - Holland

Formed in 1967 in Sneek, they display a keen soul-melody driven garage style that is mixed with psychedelic phased vocals and some unusual tempo shifts. As far as anyone knows they only recorded one single.

Waterpipes & Dykes: Dutch Psychedelic Underground 1966 - 1972 Vol. 1 [Comp] ( )

• CRAZY WORLD OF ARTHUR BROWN - UK

[see: BROWN, ARTHUR]

• CREAM - UK

Formed in July 1966 Cream were hailed as the first 'supergroup' consisting of Eric Clapton, Jack Bruce and Ginger Baker all having backgrounds in the 60's British R&B scene. The group's single, *I Feel Free* established them as pioneers in Britain's growing psychedelic scene. They were increasingly influenced by the popularity of the Jimi Hendrix Experience. Following the singles release they toured America twice, first in April and then in September of 1967 when they recorded their second album **Disraeli Gears** which contained the smash psychedelic hit *Sunshine of Your Love*. They employed poster artist Martin Sharp to design the LP's cover. Their third album, **Wheels of Fire** was a double, one disc recorded live at the Fillmore and contained the popular single *White Room*. At the height of their popularity the group disbanded in late 1968 and each went on to further solo adventures.

Fresh Cream (66), Disraeli Gears (67), Wheels of Fire (68), Goodbye (69), The Psychedelic Years 1966-1969 - Great Britain [Comp] (90), The Psychedelic Years Revisited [Comp] (92)

• CREATION - UK

Formed in 1961 in Middlesex, England; they were originally known as the Mark Four and they played London's club circuit regularly in the mid-sixties with a pop and R&B mix. In mid-1966 after a personnel shuffle they changed their name to Creation and their R&B musical style took a decidedly psychedelic twist. Best known for the blazing guitar work of Eddie Phillips who is one of the first to use a violin bow to create a unique buzzing sound that suited the times. They recorded a total of seven relatively successful singles in England and were quite popular on the European touring circuit, yet after a few line-up changes and internal squabbles they broke up in the spring of 1968.

How Does It Feel to Feel [Comp] (82), Psychedelic Visions [Comp] (96), Nuggets II Box Set [Comp] (01)

• CREATION OF SUNLIGHT - USA

Formed the late sixties in Southern California this obscure outfit recorded one LP featuring a psychedelic-pop style along the lines of Strawberry Alarm Clock.

Creation of Sunlight (68)

• CRESCENT SIX - USA

Formed in 1965 in New Jersey, Crescent Six recorded a couple singles that were primarily a British invasion/garage style with a slight psych influence.

A Heavy Dose of Lyte Psych [Comp] (96)

• CROCHETED DOUGHNUT RING - UK

Formed in 1960 in London they were originally known as the Whirlwinds, which then became Force Five, which by late 1966 became the Crocheted Doughnut Ring. They featured great harmonies with interesting guitar work, and stylistically they were from the same school as Cuppa T or Sopwith Camel. They eventually released three singles before calling it quits in 1969.

The Great British Psychedelic Trip, Vol. 2 [Comp] (88)

• CROME SYRCUS

Formed in 1965 in Seattle, Washington; they featured a very eclectic blues-based sound which included long acid-laced guitar and organ compositions. They built up a large following in the Pacific Northwest before venturing down to San Francisco where they played regularly at the Fillmore and Avalon performing with all the top bands of the era.

Love Cycle (68), The History of Northwest Rock Vol. 3: Psychedelic Seattle [Comp] (00)

• CROW - USA

Formed in the late sixties in Minneapolis, Minnesota; Crow crafted a blend of mid-sixties garage with a healthy dose of fuzz-ed psychedelia. They had originally gone by a few other names like South 40 and before that the Rave-Ons and Jokers Wild. Their R&B laced material can still be heard today as Crow continue to pound the boards as of this writing.

Crow Music (69), Crow by Crow (70), Mosaic (71), Best Of Crow (72), Evil Woman - Best of Crow [Comp] ( )

• CRYAN SHAMES - USA

Formed in 1965 in Chicago the Cryan Shames started off with a big hit in the Summer of 1966 called *Sugar and Spice* featuring a nice blend of British Invasion vocals and Byrds style folk-rock guitars. They eventually recorded three albums and a score of singles that became more and more orchestrated pop records before breaking up in 1970.

Sugar and Spice (66), A Scratch in the Sky (67), Synthesis (68), Sugar and Spice (A Collection) [Comp] (92), Nuggets I Box Set [Comp] (98)

• CRYIN' SHAMES - UK

Formed in 1966 in Liverpool they were originally called the Bumblies and created an American style garage rock sound before adopting a psychedelic flavour.

The Great British Psychedelic Trip, Vol. 1 [Comp] (88)

• CRYSTAL CIRCUS - USA

Formed in 1967 in Santa Barbara, California; they are

linked to the Strawberry Alarm Clock family and the rare and obscure LP produced but never officially released at the time bears all the pop-psychedelic elements of the bands such as those listed here.

In Relation to Our Time (67/01)

• CRYSTAL RAIN - USA

Formed in late 1968 in Dayton, Ohio; Crystal Rain released a couple of psychedelic singles very much in the Iron Butterfly vein. Lots of fuzz-guitar and heavy keyboard dominate an echo-soaked style.

A Lethal Dose of Hard Psych [Comp] (99)

• CUPPA T - UK

Formed in 1967 in London they adopted the name Cuppa T which was a pun on the phrase "cup of tea". They created a psychedelic style that took elements of Herman's Hermits and the Small Faces to create the single *Miss Pinkerton* released in September 1967. Masters of the flower-power pop style they failed to attract significant chart action and quietly disappeared.

The Great British Psychedelic Trip, Vol. 1 [Comp] (88)

• CURIOSITY SHOPPE - UK

Formed in Liverpool, the Curiosity Shoppe made their debut at the Cavern showing a psychedelic sound influenced by everyone from the Small faces to early Deep Purple. They are known to have recorded one single entitled *Baby I Need You.*

The Psychedelic Scene [Comp] (98)

• CYRKLE - USA

Formed in 1966 in Easton, Pennsylvania; the Cyrkle were managed by Brian Epstein in an attempt to secure a foothold in the burgeoning West Coast psychedelic scene. They created a melodic acoustic and electric folk-rock sound that was clearly more pop than rock but did approach what the Byrds were up to in Los Angeles. The Cyrkle had a huge hit in 1966 with *Red Rubber Ball* and made numerous live appearances on the same bill as the Beatles, even to the point of performing at the Beatles final live gig at Candlestick Park. None-the-less after the death of Epstein the band disbanded.

Red Rubber Ball (66), Neon (67), The Minx (70), Psychedelic Perceptions [Comp] (96)

• DAILY FLASH - USA

Formed in 1964 in Seattle, Washington; the Daily Flash incorporated a wide variety of influences including jazz, but their primarily influence was folk. By 1965 they had converted to electric but maintained a strong folk-rock arrangement in their material. They became regular players in the San Francisco ballroom scene. Failing to launch their career they split up in 1968.

I Daily Flash [Comp] (85), Nuggets I Box Set [Comp] (98)

• DAMNATION OF ADAM BLESSING - USA

Formed in 1968 in Cleveland, Ohio; they released three albums that featured a hard rock sound with a strong psychedelic influence carried over from the heydays of the Summer of Love. By the time of their third album a southern-rock influence was starting to creep in. Shortly after that they changed their name to Glory and moved further away from any psychedelic influence.

The Damnation of Adam Blessing (69), Second Damnation (70), Which is the Justice (71)

• DAMON - USA

This is actually the work of California based solo artist David Del Conte and features a classic psychedelic style with all the right sounds and influences. Lots of fuzz-guitar, trippy lyrics and Eastern musical motifs all combine in a manner that works.

Song of a Gypsy (70)

• DANCING, FOOD & ENTERTAINMENT - USA

Formed in 1968 in Berkeley, California, you may have seen their name on some San Francisco posters and missed the fact they were a real band by their strange name. They played a number of gigs at the Avalon Ballroom and other places on shows supporting the Grateful Dead. Their recorded output consists of a few tracks laid down in the studio but never released.

• DANTALIAN'S CHARIOT - UK

Formed in the early sixties in London, known as Zoot Money's Big Roll Band, they played a set full of the then popular soul and R&B tunes. By 1967 this style was out of fashion so they dropped the horns, trimmed down the line-up and created Dantalion's Chariot. Their new sound was classic British psychedelia, often compared with the best of early Pink Floyd or Tomorrow. Sadly they only released one official single in the fall of 1967. Their studio efforts for an album were left in the can when they split up in 1968. Guitarist Andy Somers later changed the spelling of his last name and resurfaced in the Police.

Chariot Rising [Comp] (95), Nuggets II Box Set [Comp] (01)

• DARK SUN - Finland

A mixture of psychedelic and progressive with material that is heavily influenced by Pink Floyd and Hawkwind.

Dark Sun EP (96)

• DAUGHTERS OF ALBION - USA

This obscure duo released one LP full of psychedelic Beatle influences resulting in a pleasant, harmonious psychedelic-pop sound.

Daughters of Albion (68)

• DAVE CLARK FIVE - UK

Formed in 1964 in London, the Dave Clark Five are not immediately known for their psychedelic leanings and yet during the heady days of 1967 and 68 they too ventured into the world of psychedelia with the release of the single *Maze of Love.* One never knows! They eventually split up in 1970 after having gone through a number of permutations.

Electric Sugarcube Flashbacks [Comp] (93)

• DAVID - USA

Formed in 1966 in Los Angeles, California; the David had no member named David. What they did have was an interesting blend of psychedelic influences including chanting, Eastern motifs and some psych-orchestration.

Another Day, Another Lifetime (67)

• DAWE, TIM - USA

Dawe produced an album in 1969 with plenty of classic psychedelic elements including great acid-guitar, organ, harpsichord etc. The album was released on Frank Zappa's Straight label. His 1976 LP still managed to retain a certain West Coast psychedelic feel although the time had obviously moved on.

Penrod (69), Timothy and Ms. Pickens with Natural Act (76)

• DAYBREAKERS - USA

Formed in 1966 in Muscatine, Iowa; the Daybreakers created a primarily garage/punk style even though the title of one of their few singles *Psychedelic Siren* of 1967 would have you think otherwise.

Orange, Sugar & Chocolate: Psychedelic Microdots of the 60's, Vol. 1 [Comp] (89)

• DEEP PURPLE - UK

Formed in 1968 they started out more of a hard rock band but quickly fell in line with the experimentation of the times. They were one of the first bands to play with orchestra. Only some of their earlier material qualifies as psychedelic while some material from their third and fourth albums leaned more in the progressive rock vein, the rest tended to be pretty much hard rock. Some great guitar playing interlaced with some great organ from Jon Lord. Although Lord always seemed to take a back seat in the band.

Shades of Deep Purple (68), Book of Taliesyn (68), Deep Purple (69), Deep Purple with the Royal Philharmonic (70), In Rock (70), Fireball (71), Machine Head (72), Who Do We Think We Are (73), Deep Purple in concert with The London Symphony Orchestra (00)

• DEL-VETTS - USA

Formed in 1963 in Chicago, Illinois; they started out playing the usual Stones covers until discovering the music of the Yardbirds in 1966 at which time their garage/punk style took a turn to the psychedelic. They did have at least one Top 30 hit in 1966 but then failed to capitalize on its success.

Nuggets I Box Set [Comp] (98)

• DEMONS OF NEGATIVITY - USA

Late eighties outfit based in the Boston area, their take on psychedelia is one that blends the spaced out lyrical delivery of Ursula Drabik spoken over a backdrop rolling organ and guitar with a pent up energy that just keeps on going. Psychedelia is not dead in the minds of these folks.

Beyond the Calico Wall [Comp] (93)

• DEVIANTS - UK

Formed in 1967 in London the Deviants took their cues from bands such as the Mothers of Invention mixed with the R&B sounds of the Yardbirds. This odd mixture borrowed a lot from the psychedelic scene in London during the heydays of 1967. Lots of social commentary mixed with wild blues based trippy guitar jams etc.

Ptooff! (67), Disposable (68), No. 3 (69)

• DIALOGUE - USA

A very obscure band from Pennsylvania who recorded a very psychedelic LP in 1973.

Dialogue (73)

• DIRTY - Holland

Formed in 1966 in Eindhoven they were originally called the Dirty Underwear. They shortened their name to Dirty in 1967 and a year later released their one and only single. The influences are obvious, fuzz-guitar, echo, phased and warbly vocals and tight harmonies. Failing to find success they split up in 1969.

Waterpipes & Dykes: Dutch Psychedelic Underground 1966 - 1972 Vol. 1 [Comp] ( )

• DISCIPLE - USA

Only the one known obscure LP containing a mixture of soft psychedelic-pop music.

Come and See Us As We Are (70)

• DR. STRANGELY STRANGE - UK

Formed in 1965 in London, they were contemporaries of the Incredible String Band. The duo of Tim Booth and Ivan Pawle was joined by Tim Goulding in 1969 by which time they were solidly ensconced in the British underground counter culture. More than most bands they were a part of the growing hippie community. Soon signed to Island Records their album displayed a unique blend of folk, mysticism and stream of consciousness lyrics. They disbanded in 1970.

Kip of the Serenes (69), Heavy Petting (70), The Psychedelic Years Revisited [Comp] (92)

• DR. WEST'S MEDICINE SHOW - USA

Formed in 1966 by Norman Greenbaum, Dr. West's Medicine Show & Junk Band crafted a distinctly West Coast style psychedelia, releasing three singles and then produced their only album in 1969. Following its release Greenbaum briefly retired to run his farm. see: [GREENBAUM, NORMAN]

The Egg Plant that Ate Chicago (69)

• DONOVAN - UK

Originally a folkie, Donovan was one of the first in Britain to discover the growing West Coast hippie scene in America and he quickly assumed the role of flower-power troubadour. He had originally had much success as a straight folk artist and even performed at the Newport Folk Festival in 1965 where a number of "Dylan" comparisons were made. None the less, Donovan's quirky blend of acoustic folk with psychedelic production compliments of Mickie Most landed him his first psychedelic hits in September of 1966 with *Sunshine Superman* and then in 1967 with *Mellow Yellow* followed by *Hurdy Gurdy Man* in 1968. Following his collaboration with Jeff Beck the 1969 LP

Barabajagal, Donovan left psychedelia behind.

Sunshine Superman (66), Mellow Yellow (67), Wear Your Love Like Heaven (67), For Little Ones (67), Hurdy Gurdy man (68), Barabajagal (69), Open Road (70), H.M.S. Donovan (71), Cosmic Wheels (73), The Psychedelic Years 1966-1969 - Great Britain [Comp] (90), Psychedelic Perceptions [Comp] (96), Psychedelia at Abbey Road [Comp] (98)

• DOORS - USA

Formed in 1965 in Los Angeles, the Doors settled on their line-up in 1966 and were recommended to Elektra records by Arthur Lee of Love. They hit big in 1967 with their first self-titled LP and the Top 10 single *Light My Fire*. The Doors sound was based around the poetic lyrics of Jim Morrison and an organ drenched rhythm backing centred on a blues foundation. Early on they were not averse to experimenting with convention writing long songs like the 11-minute *The End* or the side long *When the Music's Over*. Following a turbulent few short years of arrests, Morrison relocated to Paris in the spring of 1971 to recharge his creative energy. He was found dead in July of that year. The rest of the band carried on as trio for a short time but were never able to come out from Morrison's shadow.

The Doors (67), Strange Days (67), Waiting For The Sun (68), The Soft Parade (69), Morrison Hotel (70), L.A. Woman (71),

• DOUBLE FEATURE - UK

Formed in 1967 in Birmingham, they recorded a couple of singles identified best by their gritty soul influenced psychedelic-pop. Sonically there's lots of fuzz-guitar laid overtop of cello based orchestrations.

Great British Psychedelic Trip, Vol 2 [Comp] (88)

• DJAM KARET - USA

Formed in 1984 in Los Angeles, the band's name means "elastic time" in Indonesian. This four piece instrumental outfit produced two forms of music; one, a moody electronic style and the other a jagged edged progressive rock. Excellent guitar based instrumental material, with superb keyboards including Hammond and Mellotron. Much of their work contained hints of psychedelia, but it wasn't until the release of New Dark Age that the band seemed to put psychedelia front and centre. Highly recommended to fans of PINK FLOYD and KING CRIMSON.

McMusic For the Masses (82), No Commercial Potential (85), The Ritual Continues (87), Reflections From the Firepool (89), Burning the Hard City (91), Suspension & Displacement (91), Collaborator (94), The Devouring (97), Still No Commercial Potential (98), Live At Orion (99), New Dark Age (01)

• DRAGONFLY - USA

Formed in the late sixties in California they produced only one LP full of searing acid-fuzz-guitar mixed with many spacier moments.

Dragonfly (70)

• DRAGONWYCK - USA

Formed in the late sixties in Cleveland, Ohio; their first two albums, the second of which was never officially released, contain many great psychedelic moments. The second release leaned a little more in the progressive rock direction.

Dragonwyck (71), Dragonwyck (72)

• DREAM POLICE - UK

Formed in 1969 in Glasgow, the Dream Police were one of those bands who never seemed to know what style they really were. They released three singles which went from psychedelia to country-rock, none of which sold well. Hamish Stewart went on to form the Average White Band and later played with Paul McCartney while Ted McKenna joined the Sensational Alex Harvey Band.

The Great British Psychedelic Trip, Vol. 2 [Comp] (88)

• DREAM SYNDICATE - USA

Formed in the early eighties in Los Angeles, Dream Syndicate are one of the new breed of psychedelic bands that formed what was called the "Paisley underground". While other bands in this collective borrowed from the more popular West Coast bands like Jefferson Airplane or British bands like Pink Floyd, Dream Syndicate based their sound on the darker Velvet Underground. Their sound was packed with a dense psychedelic guitar sound that goes from mid-tempo rockers to ballads. Unlike the original bands of the sixties bands today don't shy away from creating radio friendly material. That success didn't come and they split up in 1989.

The Days of Wine & Roses (82), Medicine Show (84), This is Not the New Dream Syndicate (84), Dream Syndicate (85), Out of the Grey (86), 50 in a 25 Zone (87), Ghost Stories (88)

• DUFFY - USA

Obscure band based in the mid-western United States who recorded a few singles of driving psychedelic music in the vein of the Electric Prunes and Blues Magoos with lots of phasing and studio effects.

Beyond the Calico Wall [Comp] (93)

• DUG DUG'S - Mexico

Formed in the mid-sixties in Mexico they spent much of their early days in and around Tijuana. After a few years of playing Beatle covers, they moved to Mexico City in 1966 and were soon immersed in the growing psychedelic scene there. They hit the recording studio and released a couple singles, which added to their fame. After three albums they faded from the scene, but their legendary reputation followed them everywhere. The band still performs to this day.

Dug Dug's (71), Smog (73), Cambia Cambia (75), Love, Peace & Poetry: Latin American Psychedelic Music [Comp] (97)

• DUKES OF STRATOSPHERE - UK

Formed in 1987 in England, the Dukes are actually a side project for the modern pop band XTC. As such they've taken the XTC finely tuned pop writing sensibility and turned it on its psychedelic head, borrowing every studio gimmick in the book to create some wildly nostalgic psychedelia.

Chips from the Chocolate Fireball [Comp] (87)

• DUTCH MASTERS - USA

Formed in 1967 in Little Rock, Arkansas; the Dutch

Masters made a splash by dressing in period costumes, but their musical style was full-out psychedelic with a foundation of Hammond organ and searing fuzz-guitar. They released only a couple of singles.

A Lethal Dose of Hard Psych [Comp] (99)

• EARTH OPERA - USA

Formed in 1967 in Boston the two leading members coming out of a bluegrass background. They recorded a couple of albums with a myriad of folk, roots music influences with hints of psychedelia sprinkled throughout. By 1969 they split up with guitarist Peter Rowan going on to join Seatrain.

Earth Opera (68), The Great American Eagle Tragedy (69)

• EASYBEATS - Australia

Formed in 1965 in Sydney they hit the top of the Australian charts by the middle of 1965 and created quite a stir in their homeland. Following up on their local success they took their curious blend of pop-psychedelia and moved to England to start from scratch. They quickly released the popular *Friday on My Mind*. While it became a relatively successful worldwide single they were never able to follow up on its success and disbanded by the end of the sixties. Vanda and Young resurfaced in the eighties as the techno-pop Flash and the Pan.

Easy (65), It's 2 Easy (66), Volume 3 (66), Friday on My Mind (67), Falling Off the Edge of the World (68), Friends (69), Nuggets II Box Set [Comp] (01)

• EIRE APPARENT - UK

Formed in 1964 in Ireland they were originally known as Tony and The Telstars. In the spring of 1967 they had changed their name to People and moved to London. They were spotted by Jimi Hendrix's manager after playing a strong set in support of Procol Harum at the UFO club. Changing their name to Eire Apparent they jumped on the touring circuit in support of Hendrix and others. They recorded their first album **Sunrise** in 1968 in Los Angeles. The album was produced by Hendrix and he even supplied some distinctive guitar work. The band later returned to England in early 1969 but having been away for so long they were never able to re-establish themselves and ended up calling it quits at the end of 1969. Guitarist Henry McCulloch eventually joined Wings, while bass player Chris Stewart hooked up with Spooky Tooth.

Sunrise (69), The Psychedelic Years Revisited [Comp] (92), Psychedelic Visions [Comp] (96)

• ELASTIC BAND - UK

Formed in the late sixties they were originally known as Silvertone Set and played the Midlands club circuit before moving to London where they secured a deal with Decca, releasing their first single in 1968. The band's one and only LP was released in 1970 but failed to attract significant attention and the Elastic Band called it quits.

Expansions of Life (70), The Great British Psychedelic Trip, Vol. 2 [Comp] (88)

• ELASTIK BAND USA

Formed in 1967 in Belmont, California; their style was offbeat with the typical light-organ and fuzz-guitars. They recorded two odd singles before splitting up in 1968.

Nuggets I Box Set [Comp] (98)

• ELECTRIC PRUNES - USA

Formed in 1965 in Seattle, Washington; the Electric Prunes soon moved to Los Angeles. They came out of the garage/punk scene but quickly adopted a strong psychedelic stand both in terms of lyrics and sound. Lots of studio effects, wah-wah peddles and organ all went to creating hits like *I Had To Much To Dream Last Night* and *Gotta Get Me To The World On Time*. Their sound which was more rock than pop was perfect for the time. By the time of the third LP all five of the original members had been replaced and the psychedelic flavour was gone.

Electric Prunes (67), Underground (67), Mass in F Minor (68), Release of an Oath (69), Just Good Old Rock and Roll (69), The Psychedelic Years Revisited [Comp] (92), Psychedelic Perceptions [Comp] (96), Nuggets I Box Set [Comp] (98)

• ELLIE POP - USA

Formed in 1968 they produced one album of folk influenced psychedelic-pop music.

Ellic Pop (68)

• ELLISON, ANDY - UK

Ellison was originally the lead vocalist for the psychedelic John's Children before branching out on his own in 1968. He released at least three solid psychedelic-pop singles before eventually showing up in the 1970's band Jet and later still Radio Stars.

Electric Sugarcube Flashbacks [Comp] (93)

• EMTIDI - Germany

Formed in 1970 in Germany they released a couple of primarily acid-folk psychedelic albums with minor progressive rock influences. Their dreamy, spacey acoustic style featured beautiful female vocals.

Emtidi (71), Saat (72)

• END - UK

Formed in 1964 in Surrey, the End evolved out of Bobby Angelo & The Tuxedos. They took their beat style and turned it on its psychedelic head, but success eluded them. Managed by Rolling Stone Bill Wyman, the End recorded a couple of songs written by Wyman while working on the Stones' **Satanic Majesties Request** but not included on their own album. The songs failed to attract any significant chart action as did the LP Introspection released in September 1968. The band eventually evolved into the blues-rock Tuckey Buzzard with Wyman staying on as manager.

Introspection (69), The Great British Psychedelic Trip, Vol. 1 [Comp] (88), The Psychedelic Scene [Comp] (98)

• ENOCH SMOKY - USA

Formed in 1969 in Iowa City, Enoch Smoky 's style was

very garage punk with only slight psychedelic touches. The group relocated to Los Angeles where a few members wound up in the band Crabby Appleton.

A Lethal Dose of Hard Psych [Comp] (99)

• ETERNAL TRIANGLE - Canada

Formed in 1967 in Vancouver, British Columbia; the Eternal Triangle was an unusual outfit in that it consisted of three people who actually were in other bands at the time. They were, Tom Northcott, who had a solid solo folk-rock career going, Howie Vickers, who was lead vocalist of the Collectors and Susan Jacks who was about to join the Poppy Family. The group's folk-rock style had a lot in common with many of the San Francisco bands such as the Vejtables. In the end they recorded three singles under this name.

The History of Vancouver Rock & Roll, Vol. 4 [Comp] (91)

• EPISODE SIX - UK

Formed in 1964 in London, Episode Six were regulars on the London Club circuit playing a mix of R&B, raga flavoured rock and by 1967 were busily incorporating the prevalent psychedelic influences of the day. Despite a string of nine singles in a short period of three years they failed to crack the big leagues and split up 1969. Following the demise of Episode Six, two members, namely Ian Gillan and Roger Glover went on to form Deep Purple.

Put Yourself in My Place [Comp] (87), The Complete Episode Six [Comp] (94), Hot Smoke & Sassafras: Psychedelic Pstones Vol. 1 [Comp] (01), Nuggets II Box Set [Comp] (01)

• ERIC BURDON & THE ANIMALS - UK

Formed in 1964 in London they were originally known as the Animals. Their first hit *House Of The Rising Sun* showed them clearly inspired by the blues. After a string of hit singles, Eric Burdon and the Animals re-located to Los Angeles in 1967 to take full advantage of the growing psychedelic scene. With a wardrobe that now consisted mostly of Nehru jackets and beads they hit the charts in rapid succession with a series of hits, *San Francisco Nights*, *Monterey*, and the epic *Sky Pilot* intended to be one of the first stereo singles. The new psychedelic Animals made their debut at the Monterey Pop Festival.

Eric Is Here (67), Winds of Change (67), The Twain Shall Meet (68), Love Is (68), The Psychedelic Years 1966-1969 - Great Britain [Comp] (90), The Psychedelic Years Revisited [Comp] (92)

• ERIC, MARK - USA

Eric produced one LP in 1969 that was full of an orchestrated psychedelia, but also borrowed slightly from the Pet Sounds era Beach Boys vocal style.

A Midsummer's Day Dream (69)

• ERICKSON, ROKY - USA

[see: 13TH FLOOR ELEVATORS]

• EVERPRESENT FULLNESS - USA

Formed in 1965 in Los Angeles, they were part of the psychedelic scene playing the ballroom circuit in L.A. and San Francisco. Their musical style was a West Coast blend of pop and country rock that went over well in the live jam environment.

Everpresent Fullness (70), Happy Together: The Very Best of White Whale Records [Comp] (99)

• EYES - UK

Formed in 1963 in London they were originally known as the Renegades. After a few name changes they settled on the Eyes in late 1964. Their musical style was based on a solid R&B footing featuring a lot of guitar feedback and such, which incorporated mostly a Mod influence with many hints of the Who. They only flirted with a psychedelic style retaining more of the pop influences. They gigged steadily in the clubs and in the end they released a total of five singles but failed to garner much attention on the charts and disbanded in 1966.

Blink [Comp] (84), Scene But Not Heard [Comp] (87), Nuggets II Box Set [Comp] (01)

• EYES OF DAWN - Canada

Formed in 1967 in Ottawa, Ontario; they produced a couple of singles in the classic psychedelic style loaded with pleasant harmonies and jangling guitars. Together for only a short time they split up after releasing the second single.

• F.A.B. COMPANY - USA

Formed in the late sixties in Denver, Colorado; they created one LP in a psychedelic-pop vein featuring some well crafted male and female vocals.

Take Time (70)

• 49TH PARALLEL - Canada

Formed in 1966 in Calgary, Alberta; they were originally called Shades of Blonde. Soon they changed some personnel and their name, adopting the 49th Parallel moniker to signify the border between Canada and the United States. They quickly hit the charts with a couple of hits like *Labourer*, *She Says* and *Blue Bonnie Blue* all displaying a strong psych-pop style based around the echoey, fuzzy guitar sound and reedy organ. More personnel changes followed and by 1970 they had changed into Painter having few more rock oriented hits in the seventies before turning into Hammersmith who then faded from the music scene in the late seventies.

49th Parallel [Comp] (97)

• FACTORY - UK

Formed in 1968 in London this obscure trio originally went by the name the Souvenir Badge Factory before adopting just the Factory tag. They recorded a couple of singles displaying influences such as Cream and Pink Floyd before fading into obscurity. The first of their singles featured the often-used 'megaphone' vocal style made popular by number pop-psychedelic bands. They disbanded in 1969.

Path Through the Forest [Comp] (95), Nuggets II Box Set [Comp] (01)

• FACTORY - USA

Formed in 1966 in Los Angeles, Factory included a pre-

Little Feet Lowell George. The band's musical foundation was a mixture of blues-rock with a heavy dose of the folk-psychedelia that was so prevalent in L.A. at the time. They released only two singles of psych-pop during their short existence. They evolved into the Fraternity of Man in 1968.

Lightning-Rod Man [Comp] (93)

• **FACTREE - Canada**

Formed in 1968 in Welland, Ontario, the Factree produced a single called *Kaleidoscope* that features clean as a whistle, up-front vocals over a bed of fuzzy guitar and almost a raga beat. Nice blend of an almost Hendrix solo with a bit of strange jamming in the songs bridge and end.

A Lethal Dose of Hard Psych [Comp] (99)

• **FAIRYTALE - UK**

Formed in 1967 in Warrington, Lancashire; Fairytale created a soft pop psychedelic sound that suited the flower-power of 1967's Summer of Love. Lack of commercial success caused them to split up in 1968.

The Psychedelic Scene [Comp] (98)

• **FAMILY - UK**

Formed in 1967 in Leicester, Family never dallied long in the psychedelic world although they did record one single in 1967 entitled *Scene Thru The Eye Of A Lens* which was full of eastern influences, sitars, bells and raga percussion. It turned out to be their only effort in this direction and Family soon became one of Britain's first successful progressive rock groups before splitting up in 1973.

Music In A Dolls House (68), Family Entertainment (69), A Song For Me (70), Anyway (70), Fearless (71), Bandstand (72), Electric Sugarcube Flashbacks [Comp] (93)

• **FAMILY TREE - USA**

Formed in 1965 in San Francisco out of the remains of the Brogues. Their material was influenced by the psychedelia around them but featured a strong folk-rock emphasis.

Miss Butters (68)

• **FANKHAUSER, MERRELL - USA**

[See: FAPARDOKLY]

• **FAPARDOKLY - USA**

Formed in 1966 in California, Fapardokly was put together by Merrell Fankhauser and recorded only one album of classic West Coast psych-pop-folk. The material produced for their one and only LP was never intended to be a unified work, rather it was the result of Fankhauser and various group permutations. But in the end it was he who chose the name and decided to put the record out. Soon after its release they evolved into HMS Bounty and then into MU in 1971.

Fapardokly (66)

• **FEATHER - USA**

Formed in the late sixties in Los Angeles, Feather crafted a musical sound that was along the same lines as Crosby Stills Nash & Young. Their strong harmonies

were mixed with some interesting West Coast style guitar jamming.

Happy Together: The Very Best of White Whale Records [Comp] (99)

• **FELIUS ANDROMEDA - UK**

Formed in 1967 this London based band fit neatly into the Procol Harum psychedelic style. They recorded at least one single entitled *Meditations*.

The Psychedelic Scene [Comp] (98)

• **FENWYCK - USA**

Formed in 1966 in Los Angeles, their single of 1967 *Mindrocker* is a splendid example of folk-rock with psychedelic influences such as neatly layered harmonies, an early synthesizer loop and a simulated 12-string sitar guitar sound. They evolved into Back Pocket in 1968.

The Many Sides of Jerry Raye featuring Fenwyck (67), Orange, Sugar & Chocolate: Psychedelic Microdots of the 60's, Vol. 1 [Comp] (89), Nuggets I Box Set [Comp] (98)

• **FEVER TREE - USA**

Formed in 1967 in Houston, Texas; they started out creating music more in the garage-psych vein until they signed to Uni Records in 1968. Once there they threw their hat completely into the psychedelic world and produced the regional hit *San Francisco Girls* in 1968. Much of their music was fleshed out with strings and orchestra, providing a lush overall feel. The band soldiered on into the late sixties before experimenting with a more progressive rock style. They eventually disbanded in 1970.

Fever Tree (68), Another Time, Another Place (68), Creation (70), For Sale (70), Psychedelic Perceptions [Comp] (96)

• **FINAL SOLUTION - USA**

Formed in 1965 in San Francisco, They were a band who never fit in style wise at least. Musically they crafted long-guitar filled jam fests that were typical of the West Coast psychedelic sound. They never committed anything to vinyl.

• **FINGERS - UK**

Formed in 1966 in South London, Fingers are reportedly the first band to actually call themselves psychedelic. They recorded a couple of singles, most notably *Circus With A Female Clown* released in early 1967, but while they found some radio airplay, the band split up soon after its release.

Psychedelia at Abbey Road [Comp] (98)

• **FIRE - UK**

Formed in 1966 in Hounslow, Middlesex; the trio was originally known as Friday's Chyld. They soon changed their name to Fire. The trio consisted of Dick Dufall, Bob Voice and Dave Lambert. They hit the scene with a number of psychedelic singles before eventually putting together the concept LP entitled **The Magic Shoemaker** in 1970. While by this time their music was leaning more in a progressive rock vein they managed to retain some psych elements. Shortly after the LPs release they split up with Lambert joining progressive rockers the Strawbs while the trio's other members Dick Dufall and Bob Voice went over to Paul Brett's Sage.

The Magic Shoemaker (70), Underground and Overhead: The Alternate Fire [Comp] (97), Hot Smoke & Sassafras: Psychedelic Pstones Vol. 1 [Comp] (01), Nuggets II Box Set [Comp] (01)

• FIRST CROW ON THE MOON - USA

Formed in 1967 in Brooklyn, New York; their sound was a combination of acid-punk and a liberal dose of psychedelia. They were originally called the First Crew to the Moon but due to a miss-type at the Roulette Records label they were mistakenly called "First Crow to the Moon". The name stuck. Recent records indicate a young Chris Stein, later to show up in Blondie got his start with this band.

My Rainbow Life: Psychedelic Microdots of the 60's, Vol. 3 [Comp] (92)

• FIVE FIFTEEN - Finland

They create a style that incorporates psychedelic, hard rock and a very keyboard driven progressive rock.

Progressive Hardrock Beyond the Mainstream (94), Armageddon Jam Session #4 (95), Psychedelic Singalongs for Stadiums (97), Six Dimensions of the Electric Camembert (98)

• FLAMIN' GROOVIES - USA

Formed in 1965 in San Francisco they were originally called the Chosen Few, then the Lost and Found finally adopting the name Flamin' Groovies in 1967. Their characteristic style of garage-punk persisted well into the psychedelic period. They played the ballroom circuit towards the early seventies, then got caught up in the second punk/new wave movement of the mid seventies. They eventually disbanded in 1979, reforming for one live LP in 1987. Fans of psychedelic should look to their early work.

Sneakers (67), Supernazz (70), Flamingo (71), Teenage head (71)

• FLEUR DE LYS - UK

Formed in 1964, Fleur De Lys left home in Southampton and moved to London and began playing the club circuit. They were quickly signed to the Immediate label. Their second single, *Circles* caused quite a stir with the rumour their producer, a young Jimmy Page also provided some guitar work. After leaving the Immediate label they recorded a number of singles for Polydor and then Atlantic where they had reverted to putting out soul inspired releases. All their efforts failed to attract significant attention and they eventually disbanded in 1969.

The Psychedelic Years Revisited [Comp] (92), Electric Sugarcube Flashbacks [Comp] (93), Les Fleur de Lys Reflections 1965 - 1969 [Comp] (97), Nuggets II Box Set [Comp] (01)

• FLIES - UK

Formed in 1966 in London, the Flies were purveyors of American style garage-punk and recorded three singles complete with searing guitar and sneering vocals. The Flies skirted around the fringes of the flower-power scene, as their sound was more akin to bands like the Count Five.

The Great British Psychedelic Trip, Vol. 1 [Comp] (88)

• FLOWER POT MEN - UK

Formed in 1967 in London this was essentially a group of four studio session players throwing their hat into the psychedelic scene. They had a reasonable hit with their first single *Let's Go To San Francisco*. Musically they borrowed all the key flower-power elements to craft some decent pop psychedelia. They split up in 1969 and vocalist Tony Burrows showed up in Edison Lighthouse.

Let's Go To San Francisco [Comp] (93)

• FLOWER POWER [1] - USA

Formed in Louisiana, Flower Power's music was based on a strong melodic foundation but could turn aggressive and just downright weird. This band's sound featured very nice organ backgrounds and underplayed guitar.

Beyond the Calico Wall [Comp] (93)

• FLOWER POWER [2] - USA

Formed in Florida, this Flower Power recorded a couple of tracks in 1967 that have since found their way onto a couple of different compilations. Their sound is based on an R&B or soul foundation with some high-energy fuzz-guitar work. Overall their style shows some risk taking arrangements but sticks pretty close to a garage-punk style rather than tripping.

A Lethal Dose of Hard Psych [Comp] (99)

• FOCUS 3 - UK

Formed in 1967, Focus 3 were a studio project created by Liza Strike, Larry Steele and Tony Wilson all who had previously been involved in soul acts. This experiment in psychedelia was short lived, as they all were more interested in pursuing other musical styles.

Psychedelia at Abbey Road [Comp] (98)

• FOODBRAIN - Japan

This one-off project is essentially a Japanese supergroup of prominent psychedelic musicians. Bands represented here include Apryl Fool, Powerhouse, Strawberry Path and others. The music is fuzz-guitar heavy with lots of guitar and organ interplay plus the obligatory spacey echo inserted at the appropriate moments.

Social Gathering (70), Love, Peace & Poetry: Japanese Psychedelic Music [Comp] (01)

• FORRAY, ANDY - UK

Forray was an American who moved to London in 1966 and who over the next couple years tried his hand at hit making. His dabbling in psychedelia produced a couple of interesting singles but no hits. He joined the cast of Hair in late 1968.

The Psychedelic Scene [Comp] (98)

• FORTES MENTUM - UK

Formed in 1968 they recorded three singles with a

piano and organ dominated psychedelic style with an overall strong pop sensibility. They evolved into the band Pussy.

The Best of and The Rest of British Psychedelia [Comp] (91)

• FORUM QUORUM - USA

Formed in 1968 in New York City they released one LP, which featured a host of psychedelic influences built upon a soul foundation. The overall effect is a pleasant pop-psychedelia with some Middle Eastern influences.

The Forum Quorum (68)

• FOURTH WAY - USA

Obscure group who recorded a couple of singles in 1968, one of which features an Eastern flavoured rolling rhythm section of weedy-organ, bass and marimbas overtop of which is featured a trancey female narration of trippy lyrics!

A Heavy Dose of Lyte Psych [Comp] (96)

• FOX - UK

Formed in 1970 in London, Fox created a post-psychedelic folk style that is similar to bands like the British Nirvana. They released one LP and then disappeared.

For Fox Sake (70)

• FREE FOR ALL - USA

Formed in the mid-sixties in Canada they originally went by the name the Great Scots before heading to New York and eventually Los Angeles. This obscure garage/punk band featured a strong folk-rock influence and had some regional success with a single called *Blue Monday* b/w *Show Me The Way* a song which also displayed a strong British Invasion influence.

Orange, Sugar & Chocolate: Psychedelic Microdots of the 60's, Vol. 1 [Comp] (89)

• FREEBORNE - USA

Formed in 1967 in Boston, Freeborne created a lighter style psychedelic music that was strong on melody but loaded with strange shifts in tempo and adventurous vocal arrangements. Lead guitarist Bob Margolin went on to play with Johnny Winter before pursuing a solo career in the blues.

Peak Impressions (68), A Heavy Dose of Lyte Psych [Comp] (96)

• FREEDOM HIGHWAY - USA

Formed in the mid-sixties in San Francisco, Freedom Highway played regularly at the Avalon Ballroom for a number of years before disbanding. Their long drawn out West Coast jams never made it to vinyl in the studio although one live recording has surfaced.

Made in '68 (01)

• FREUDIAN COMPLEX - USA

Obscure American band that recorded four tracks for Buddha Records in the late sixties.

The Psychedelic Years Revisited [Comp] (92)

• FRESH AIR - UK

Obscure British band that recorded at least three singles for Pye records in 1969 but failed to ignite any interest.

Hot Smoke & Sassafras: Psychedelic Pstones Vol. 1 [Comp] (01)

• FRUMIOUS BANDERSNATCH - USA

Formed in 1966 in Oakland, California; they played all the Bay area ballrooms for a number of years but never cracked the big time. Over the years they recorded fleetingly. All these tracks have been assembled on a CD compilation. The band split up for good in 1969.

A Young Man's Song [Comp] (96)

• GALES, ERIC - USA

One of the new breeds of psychedelic guitarists, the Eric Gales Band, a trio, borrows heavily from the Jimi Hendrix school of psychedelia. What's more his approach is not only sincere, but well played. While only 16 at the time of his first album in 1991, Gales shows he's serious.

The Eric Gales Band (91), Picture of a Thousand Faces (93)

• GAME - UK

Formed in 1964 in Mitcham, Surrey; they started out by borrowing from the freakbeat scene, but soon the Game came into their own and created a psychedelic style that was similar to that of the Small Faces and Creation. In total they released four singles.

The Great British Psychedelic Trip, Vol. 2 [Comp] (88),

• GANDALF - USA

Formed in 1968 in New York, they created a softer, laid back kind of pop-psychedelic music that may be in part due to their producers who were better known as having worked with the Lovin' Spoonful and Sopwith Camel.

Gandalf (69), Psychedelic Frequencies [Comp] (96)

• GANDALF THE GREY - USA

Formed in 1972 in New York, this obscure effort seems to bear no relation to the other Gandalf listed. The music here is a mix of progressive folk and some interesting psychedelic guitar work.

The Grey Wizard I Am (72)

• GARDEN ODYSSEY ENTERPRISE - UK

Based in Manchester, It's suspected that Garden Odyssey Enterprise was more of a studio project for future 10CC member Graham Gouldman who already had a thriving song writing catalogue to his credit. Under this guise he released the 1969 single *Sad & Lonely* displaying Gouldman's penchant for writing trippy pop songs.

The Psychedelic Scene [Comp] (98)

• GENESIS - USA

Formed in 1967 in Los Angeles this obscure outfit played a number of times in the San Francisco area, as well their home-town of Los Angeles. After the group disbanded their guitarist Kent Henry went to Steppenwolf.

In The Beginning (68)

• GENTLE INFLUENCE - UK

Formed in 1968 in Oxfordshire they played a late sixties psychedelic style that bordered on progressive rock. They released at least two singles in 1969.

Hot Smoke & Sassafras: Psychedelic Pstones Vol. 1 [Comp] (01)

• GENTLE SOUL - USA

Formed in 1966 in California, their one and only recording was produced by Terry Melcher and is a fine example of the softer flower-power pop psychedelia that was coming out of California at the time. The group consisted of a who's-who of local talent with the likes of Ry Cooder, Paul Horn, Larry Knechtel, Van Dyke Parks and others.

Gentle Soul (68)

• GEORGE, LOWELL - USA

Before coming to prominence in Little Feat, George first spent time in an R&B group called the Factory, who mixed up blues and folk to create a psychedelic style that was far more laid back than material produced by contemporaries the Count Five or even Moby Grape. Following a couple of single releases with a flower-power feel, George joined up with the Mothers of Invention before forming Little Feat in 1969.

Psychedelic Frequencies [Comp] (96)

• GHOST - UK

Formed in 1969 in Birmingham, England, Ghost was spearheaded by guitarist and vocalist Shirley Kent. Their blues-rock style borrowed heavily from the West Coast American sound and the album they created also included a strong psychedelic folk and blues influence. They evolved into a band called Resurrection in late 1970.

When Your Dead - One Second (70)

• GLASS FAMILY - USA

Formed in 1967 this obscure California three-piece band is known in psychedelic circles for their flower-power songs.

An Electric Band (68), Psychedelic Visions [Comp] (96)

• GLASS MENAGERIE - UK

Formed in 1967 in Lancashire they made the move to London in 1968 and quickly produced a number of cover-version psychedelic-pop singles. In 1969 they acquired new management with Chas Chandler and a few more attempts at the singles charts went unnoticed and the band split. Lead vocalist Lou Stonebridge went to Paladin for a while and then session work. Guitarist Al Kendal moved on to Toe Fat for a time before landing a gig working with the Bee Gees.

The Glass Menagerie [unreleased], Hot Smoke & Sassafras: Psychedelic Pstones Vol. 1 [Comp] (01)

• GODS - UK

Formed in 1965, the Gods consisted of Ken Hensley,

Joe Konas, John Glascock, and Lee Kerslake. They shared much in common when it came to creating music and after one single in 1967 they created a concept album entitled **Genesis** plus a number of adventurous singles and then yet another LP. That second LP, **To Samuel A Son** was released prior to the band splitting up in two directions. The core of the band formed Toe Fat while Hensley created Uriah Heep. It's interesting that all members of the Gods eventually played in Uriah Heep at some point.

Genesis (68), To Samuel A Son (70), Psychedelia at Abbey Road [Comp] (98)

• GODZ - USA

Formed in 1966 in New York, they are often compared to the Fugs, primarily because of their psychedelic style that leaned heavily to the dissonant avant-garde. Add in just a small dose of acid influenced folk and you may begin to hear the unusual mixture they created. After failing to attract much chart action they disbanded in late 1969.

Contact High With the Godz (66), Godz II (67), The Third Testament (68), Godzhunheit (69)

• GOLDEN DAWN - USA

Formed in 1967 in Austin, Texas; their psychedelic style was similar in technique to their friends the 13th Floor Elevators.

A Power Plant (67)

• GONG - France

Formed in 1970 in Paris by main pixie Daevid Allen following his extended visits with the likes of Allen Ginsberg and William Burroughs in various Parisian Beat cafes. They quickly became a pioneering psychedelic-progressive band working in the jazz-rock, space-fusion, and percussive side of things. Excellent musicians playing in an adventurous format. Critically acclaimed, and highly popular, especially in Europe. They went through many different group formations; the discography is based on releases for both GONG and Pierre Moerlen's Gong. Their most popular psychedelic material would include their early years especially the Radio Gnome Invisible Trilogy.

Magick Brother (70), Camembert Electrique (71), Continental Circus (71), The Flying Teapot (72), Angels Egg (73), You (74), Shamal (75), Gazeuze [Expresso] (76), Live Etc. (77), Gong est Mort (77), Floating Anarchy (77), Expresso 2 (78), Downwind (79), Time is the Key (79), P. Moelen's Gong Live (79), Leave it Open (80), Radio Gong Pt. 1 (84), Radio Gong Pt. 2 (84), The Owl and the Tree (86), Breakthrough (86), Second Wind (88), The History & Mystery of Planet Gong (90), Gong Live on TV (90), Live at Bataclan 73 (90), Live at Sheffield 1974 (90), Je N'Fume pas de Bananes (92), Shapeshifter (92), Camembert Eclectique (95), The Birthday Party: Oct. 8th, 9th 1994 (95), The Peel Sessions 1971-1974 (96), Pre-Modernist Wireless [early BBC sessions] (96), Family Jewels (99), Zero to Infinity (00)

• GRATEFUL DEAD - USA

Formed in 1965 in San Francisco they were originally known as the Warlocks but changed their name for one of the early Kesey run Acid-Tests for which they became the house band. The group was a mix of trained and untrained musicians coming from a wide background of styles including everything from bluegrass to blues. When introduced to LSD the members and the styles metamorphosed into the classic West Coast trippy psychedelic style. The music broke convention and formed a musical 'soundtrack' to the dancing events they played for, where one song could become as long as it needed to be. They also set the framework for sound, being backed technically by the acid-king Owsley Stanley, that being said they were also LOUD. Benefiting from a long career and a relatively stable lineup the Grateful Dead created many successful albums and to this day have perhaps one of the most loyal group of fans in rock. In 1995 founder Jerry Garcia died of heart failure. The Grateful Dead decided to call it a day.

The Grateful Dead (67), Anthem of the Sun (68), Aoxomoxoa (69), Live/Dead (70), Workingman's Dead (70), American Beauty (70, Grateful Dead (71), Wake of the Flood (73), From the Mars Hotel (74), Blues for Allah (75), Terrapin Station (77), Shakedown Street (78), Go to Heaven (80), Reckoning [Live] (81), Dead Set [Live] (81), In the Dark (87), Built to Last (89), Without a Net [Live] (90)

• GREAT SOCIETY - USA

Formed in 1965 in San Francisco. It's said that Darby and Grace Slick were sitting in the audience of opening night at the Matrix club in San Francisco and while watching the new Jefferson Airplane perform they immediately decided to form a band. Their band called the Great Society figured prominently in the early psychedelic San Francisco scene and they shared the bill with many of the musical leaders of the day until Grace Slick was asked to join the Airplane. She brought with her two Great Society songs, *Somebody To Love* and *White Rabbit* and both became huge hits for the Airplane. The Great Society split up shortly after in September 1966. Two albums of material were released following their break-up.

Conspicuous Only in it's Absence (68), How it Was (68), Live at The Matrix (88), San Francisco Nights [Comp] (91), Psychedelic Visions [Comp] (96)

• GREEK FOUNTAINS - USA

Formed in 1965 in Louisiana, the Greek Fountains took a stab at recording a couple of strange tripped out pieces of music with loads of odd musical effects, backward tapes, and little musical motifs thrown together. If you're a fan of bands like Red Krayola you should appreciate what's going on here.

Beyond the Calico Wall [Comp] (93)

• GREENBAUM, NORMAN - USA

Following the demise of his first band Dr. West's Medicine Show and a brief career running a dairy farm, Norman Greenbaun returned to the music scene with the captivating single *Spirit In The Sky* which still managed to evoke many aspects of psychedelia for its 1969 release date. This pop-psychedelic song was a distinct hand clapper and rocketed to No.1 when it was re-released in the spring of 1970. After two more albums Greenbaum retired from the music business.

Spirit In the Sky (69), Back Home Again (70), Petaluma (72)

• GROUP 1850 - Holland

Formed in the early sixties they played mostly beat music, turning to a more psychedelic style in 1967. They mixed a bit of Pink Floyd and a bit of the Mothers of Invention to create a whimsical, utopian, shifting tempo style that at one point may be dark and gloomy but changing to something lighter. Their material hinted at the coming progressive rock style. Even though they sang in English they failed to make much of an impact and disbanded in late 1969.

Agemo's Trip to Mother (68), Paradise Now (69), 1967 - 1968 [Comp] (93)

• GROWING CONCERN - USA

Formed in 1967 they recorded one LP of rockier psychedelic songs. Lots of good harmonies and plenty of searing guitar work.

The Growing Concern (68)

• GUNN - UK

Formed in 1968 in Ilford, Essex; this trio played a hard rock blues type of music with a plodding psychedelic style. Jon Anderson, lead vocalist of Yes sang briefly for Gunn in their very early days. They went on to play with Moody Blues drummer Graeme Edge on his solo LPs. Their first album featured one of the first Roger Dean cover designs.

Gunn (68), Gunnsight (69)

• GURUS - USA

Formed in 1966 in New York, the Gurus produced a couple of singles on the United Artists label. Their style was a mix of garage and psychedelic-pop with well defined harmonies and sitars. It appears any plans for promoting the band's album were shelved after the second single failed to do anything on the charts.

The Gurus Are Here (67), A Heavy Dose of Lyte Psych [Comp] (96)

• GYPSY - UK

Formed in 1969 in Leicester, England; this five-piece created two albums of decidedly West Coast influenced hippie psychedelia. A few singles were thrown to the charts and the band toured heavily but failed to attract any attention to their efforts and called it quits in early 1973.

Gypsy (71), Brenda and the Rattlesnake. (72)

• H.M.S. BOUNTY - USA

Following the release of one album under the name of Fapardokly, founder Merrell Fankhauser moved to Los Angeles in late 1967 and put together H.M.S. Bounty which proved to be yet another excellent example of the West Coast folk influenced psychedelic style. The music they produced is in the same league as contemporaries Moby Grape and Buffalo Springfield. A short time later they evolved yet again into a band simply called MU.

Things (68)

• HAPPENINGS FOUR - Japan

Formed in the late sixties, Happenings Four, borrowed

many psychedelic aspects of the Beatles' Sgt. Pepper era to craft their own vision of psychedelia. Singing in Japanese their work also contains the influences of prominent British bands such as Procol Harum.

Magical Happenings Tour (68), Love, Peace & Poetry: Japanese Psychedelic Music [Comp] (01)

• HAPSHASH & THE COLOURED COAT - UK

Formed in 1967 in London by poster artists Michael English and Nigel Weymouth they called on a host of friends including Mike Batt and Tony Mcphee to create a couple of experimental albums loaded with the free-form psychedelia of the day. The LPs were well received in the hippie community but didn't provide any kind of income and the pair returned to their first love designing posters and store fronts for London's psychedelic underground.

Hapshash and the Coloured Coat (68), Western Flyer (69)

• HARBINGER COMPLEX - USA

Formed in 1966 in Fremont, California; the Harbinger Complex released at least two singles which reflected a strong Stones R&B influence all masked with the typical psychedelic fuzz-guitar a prerequisite for the times.

Nuggets I Box Set [Comp] (98)

• HAWKWIND - UK

Formed in 1969 in London, England; Hawkwind have the distinction of surpassing GONG and Soft Machine for personnel changes with ex-members of Amon Duul, GONG and the Pink Fairies passing through the ranks. Hawkwind's first album was produced by the Pretty Thing's Dick Taylor and was compared immediately to Pink Floyd. Hawkwind helped define the term space-rock, with their long spacey, improvisational musical jams and science-fiction lyrics. While the keyboards are ever present the Hawkwind sound was based more Dave Brock's searing guitar work.

Hawkwind (70), In Search of Space (71), Doremi Fasol Latido (72), Space Ritual (73), Hall of the Mountain Grill (74), Warrior on the Edge of Time (75), Road Hawks (76), Masters of the Universe (77), Quark Strangeness and Charm (77), PXR5 (78), Live 79 (79), Levitation (80), Sonic Attack (81), Choose Your Masques (82), Friends & Relations (82), Friends & Relations II (83), Zones (83), Stonehenge (This Is Hawkwind Do Not Panic) (84), Chronicle Of The Black Sword (85), Friends & Relations III (85), Live Chronicles (86),Angels Of Death (86), Out & Intake (87), The Xenon Codex (88), Space Bandits (90), Palace Springs (91), Electric Tepee (92), California Brainstorm (92), It is the Business of the Future to be Dangerous (94), Psychedelic Warriors The White Zone (95), Alien 4 (95), Love In Space (96), Future Constructions (96), Live In Chicago 1974 (97), Distant Horizons (97), The Elf and The Hawk (98)

• HAYMARKET RIOT - USA

Formed in the late sixties in Monroe, Missouri; Haymarket Riot played a garage-punk style that had a lot in common with bands like MC5. Officially they only released one single that was very intense, very loud, very fast!

A Lethal Dose of Hard Psych [Comp] (99)

• HEAD SHOP - USA

Little known psychedelic band from 1969 whose members are listed on their only LP release as Drew, Jesse, Joe, Geoff and Danny.

The Head Shop (69), Psychedelic Visions [Comp] (96)

• HEAVY JELLY - UK

Heavy Jelly was formed in 1968 in an attempt to cash in on the publicity surrounding the name when a popular London magazine featured the fictitious group's album on the cover. They were actually Skip Bifferty, a band who were in dispute with their manager at the time. The single released by the band, *I Keep Singing That Same Old Song* became one of the longest singles ever at 8:22. They split up soon after their debut as Heavy Jelly.

Take Me Down to the Water (69/84), The Psychedelic Years Revisited [Comp] (92)

• HENDRIX, JIMI - USA

[see: JIMI HENDRIX EXPERIENCE]

• HERBAL MIXTURE - UK

Formed in 1966 in London as the Groundhogs, they took a slight musical detour from the blues to a more psychedelic style and released a couple of wacky singles under the name Herbal Mixture. Neither of the two singles managed to make any impact on the charts so the band reverted back to being the Groundhogs and carried on well into the seventies by that name.

Electric Sugarcube Flashbacks [Comp] (93)

• HERE AND NOW - UK

Similar in nature to the type of psychedelic music produced by GONG.

What You See is What You Get (78), Give and Take (78), A Dog in Hell (78), All Over the Show (79), Fantasy Shift ( ), Theatre ( )

• HOLLIES - UK

Formed in 1961in Manchester as part of the beat boom and British Invasion. Although they more than dabbled in the world of psychedelia, most notably with songs like *King Midas In Reverse* written by Graham Nash and *Dear Eloise* and *Jennifer Eccles*. Sadly, not all members of the Hollies shared Nash's interest in psychedelia, and after two mildly psychedelic albums Nash left towards the end of 1968. He would then join up with David Crosby and Stephen Stills in the folk-rock influenced Crosby Stills Nash and eventually Young.

Stop, Stop, Stop [For Certain Because - UK Title] (66), Evolution (67), Butterfly (67), Psychedelic Frequencies [Comp] (96), Psychedelia at Abbey Road [Comp] (98)

• HONEYBUS - UK

Formed in 1967 in London they are most remembered for their one and only hit entitled *I Can't Let Maggie Go*, but along the way they crafted many more singles that never made it and even released an LP in 1970. Trouble was, the band had actually split up in late '69.

Their style is best described as classic British psychedelic-pop.

Story (70)

• HOOK - USA

After the demise of the Leaves and then the New Leaves, the members regrouped under the name Hook in 1968 and recorded three singles and two albums on the UNI label.

The Hook Will Grab You (68), Hooked (69), Psychedelic Perceptions [Comp] (96)

• H. P. LOVECRAFT - USA

Formed in 1967 in Chicago, Illinois; H. P. Lovecraft were an in interesting blend of folk and classical music, featuring two lead singers supported by haunting arrangements, quite experimental for the time. Taking their name from a science fiction/horror writer they produced their first album featuring songs inspired by his writings. They moved to the San Francisco area in 1968 to take advantage of the many live venues in the area and became regulars on the ballroom circuit. Their second LP, H. P. Lovecraft II was recorded in L.A. in September 1968. This second release displayed their original influences but also integrated the West Coast trippy sound they'd experienced since relocating.

H. P. Lovecraft (67), H. P. Lovecraft II (68), The Psychedelic Years Revisited [Comp] (92)

• HUMAN BEINZ - USA

Formed in 1965 in Youngstown, Ohio; they released their first single *Gloria* in 1966. The single failed to attract much attention but their constant live performances did and they were signed to Capitol Records in 1967. They originally spelled their name the Human Beingz, but when the Capitol Records psychedelic-pop single of *Nobody But Me* was released the name had been misspelled as Human Beinz. Further singles made little impact in America, but their career took off in Japan. In 1969 they toured Japan and recorded a couple of rare albums there.

Nobody But Me (68), Evolution (68), Nuggets I Box Set [Comp] (98)

• HUMAN EXPRESSION - USA

Formed in 1966 in Los Angeles, Human Expression were a classic example of L.A.'s Sunset Strip psychedelic sound with loads of reverb and fuzz and songs not unlike what the Seeds were creating. They incorporated the prevalent folk-rock sounds supported by the weedy-organ in the background blended together with unusual sound effects designed to create the trippy psychedelic atmosphere of the times. They released five singles in total before splitting up in late 1967.

Live at Psychedelic Velocity [Comp] (94), Nuggets I Box Set [Comp] (98)

• HUMAN INSTINCT - New Zealand

After experiencing three number one hits in the mid-sixties in their native New Zealand, Human Instinct picked up sticks and moved to London, arriving in September 1966 in the midst of the growing psychedelic scene. After recording three singles for

Mercury they were signed by Deram where one single was released by the name of *Day In My Mind's Mind* which was then followed up with a reworking of the Byrd's *Renaissance Fair* in March of 1968. Before long they gave up on London, returned home and recorded a number of highly regarded albums, which were eventually released on a compilation disc in 1988.

The Great British Psychedelic Trip, Vol. 1 [Comp] (88), Human Instinct 1969-1971 [Comp] (88), The Psychedelic Scene [Comp] (98)

• HUSH - UK

Formed in 1968 in Manchester, this obscure five-member group produced only one known recording. Highly sought after this recording is one of the better psychedelic-pop singles recorded.

• I NUMI - Italy

A band that created mostly psychedelic shorter songs heavily influenced by the Beatles.

Alpha Ralpha Boulevard (71), Stroia Di Zero ( )

• ICE - UK

Formed in 1967 in London, or more specifically at Sussex University, Ice recorded two singles that were soft pop with nice harmonies and psychedelic influences

The Great British Psychedelic Trip, Vol. 1 [Comp] (88), The Great British Psychedelic Trip, Vol. 2 [Comp] (88), The Psychedelic Scene [Comp] (98)

• ID - USA

Formed in 1967 in San Diego, the Id created a psychedelic style that was influenced by the Beatles in many ways. The album displays all the elements of Eastern mysticism, fuzz-guitar and a trippy vocal style.

The Inner Sounds of the Id (67), A Heavy Dose of Lyte Psych [Comp] (96)

• IDLE RACE - UK

Formed in 1967 in Birmingham, Idle Race was led by Jeff Lynne and evolved out of a band called the Night Riders. They released a number of singles such as *Impostors Of Life Magazine* and *Skeleton & The Roundabout*. Their style is classic English psychedelic incorporating a whimsical air, heavy production and searing guitar work. Despite being received well by the major critics of the time, they failed to achieve commercial success. Lynne left in 1970 and joined forces with Roy Wood's Move for a short time before the pair invented the Electric Light Orchestra. The remaining members carried on for a short time releasing one more LP and a couple singles.

The Birthday Party (68), Idle Race (69), Time Is (71), The Psychedelic Years 1966-1969 - Great Britain [Comp] (90), Psychedelic Visions [Comp] (96), Nuggets II Box Set [Comp] (01)

• IGRA STAKLENIH PERLI - Yugoslavia

Psychedelic flavoured progressive rock with hints of Hawkwind and Meddle era PINK FLOYD.

Igra Staklenih Perli (79), Vrt Svetlosti (80), Inner Flow [recorded 75] (9?), Drives [recorded 78] (9?), Soft Explosion Live [recorded 78] (9?)

• ILLINOIS SPEED PRESS - USA

Formed in 1968 in Chicago, Illinois; this band included H. P. Lovecraft guitarist Kal David. Their music was based on a country-rock or folk-rock foundation with a psychedelic strain running throughout. After recording two albums and even a couple gigs at the Fillmore East they split up in 1971.

Illinois Speed Press (69), Duet (70)

• ILLUSION - USA

Formed in 1968 in New York this Illusion (not to be confused with Keith Relf's Illusion in Britain) hit the charts with the Top 40 single *Did You See Her Eyes* which was a classic piece of psychedelia but failed to capture much further attention. In the end they released a handful of singles and three albums but disbanded in 1971 without much of a trace.

Illusion (69), Together (As a Way of Life) (70), If it's So (71)

• INCREDIBLE - Holland

Formed in 1963 in Nieuwkoop they originally were called Sounding Rockets. They changed their name to Incredible in 1967 and recorded only one single. They mix a haunting vocal harmony style with a very baroque Left Banke psychedelic-pop sound.

Waterpipes & Dykes: Dutch Psychedelic Underground 1966 - 1972 Vol. 1 [Comp] ( )

• INCREDIBLE STRING BAND - UK

Formed in 1966 in Glasgow, the Incredible String Band featured the multi-instrumental talents of Mike Heron and Robin Williamson. Their eclectic material drew its prime inspiration from a strong folk background. They were not above including some bluegrass or even an American West Coast feel to their material. The band made a number of appearances in the San Francisco ballrooms and their hippie lifestyle endeared them to the psychedelic community. They recorded fully through to 1974 before Heron and Williamson went on to solo careers.

The Incredible String Band (66), The 5000 Spirits or The Layers of the Onion (67), The Hangman's Beautiful Daughter (68), Wee Tam (68), The Big Huge (68), Changing Horses (69), I looked Up (70), U (70), Be Glad For The Song Has No Ending (71), Liquid Acrobat As Regards The Air (71), Earth Span (72), No Ruinous Feud (73), Hard Rope and Silken Twine (74), The Psychedelic Years 1966-1969 - Great Britain [Comp] (90), The Psychedelic Years Revisited [Comp] (92)

• INDESCRIBABLY DELICIOUS - USA

Formed in 1965 in Torrance, California; they recorded on the same label as Strawberry Alarm Clock and even worked with various members of that group in different incarnations. The music created on their only album is along the same lines, kind of pop-psychedelia.

Good Enough to Eat (69)

• INFLUENCE - Canada

Formed in 1966 in Montreal, Quebec; Influence crafted a soul guitar style with the usual psychedelic studio touches. Their one and only album showed them being as adventurous as the mid-sixties could get, producing a mini-opera entitled *Man Birds Of Prey*. Despite a rigorous touring effort the band split up shortly after the LPs release. Guitarist Walter Rossi later showed playing with Luke and the Apostles and the Buddy Miles Express.

Influence (68)

• INITIAL SHOCK - USA

Formed in 1966 in Montana, they moved to San Francisco in 1967 where they played a few gigs at the Avalon Ballroom and other smaller clubs in the area. They recorded two singles in the psychedelic-pop style.

• INNER LIGHT - USA

Formed in the late sixties in Page, North Dakota; Inner Light released a single of fuzz loaded, Vox organ psychedelia in 1969 sounding a little like Iron Butterfly 'lite'.

A Lethal Dose of Hard Psych [Comp] (99)

• IRON BUTTERFLY - USA

Formed in 1966 in San Diego, California; Iron Butterfly have the distinction of being the first psychedelic act to hit Platinum status selling in excess of 3 million copies of the classic **In-A-Gadda-Da-Vida** in 1968. The album's proto-heavy metal seventeen minute title track took up one whole side of the recording. In fact quite a case can be made for Iron Butterfly having a major influence on the new, at the time, heavier guitar style bands that were emerging on the scene. They were never able to follow-up on this success and by 1971 looked at calling it quits with members going on to Alice Cooper and Captain Beyond. They reformed briefly in 1974 to record two more albums that did poorly on the charts before splitting up once more in 1976. That however was not the end as Iron Butterfly reformed once again in early 1989 to do mostly live performances..

Heavy (68), In-A-Gadda-Da-Vida (68), Ball (69), Iron Butterfly Live (70), Metamorphosis (71), Scorching Beauty (75), Sun and Steel (75), Psychedelic Visions [Comp] (96)

• IT'S A BEAUTIFUL DAY - USA

Formed in 1967 in San Francisco, It's a Beautiful Day was fronted by classically trained violinist David LaFlame which gave the group a unique and original sound on the ballroom circuit. The band's mix of West Coast psychedelia and classical flourishes won them high praise and they achieved early success with the single *White Bird,* which became a staple on underground radio stations everywhere. Following up on this early success proved difficult and while the band gigged steadily sales eluded them. Falling victim to a major dispute with their manager they decided to call it quits in 1974.

It's a Beautiful Day (69), Marrying Maiden (70), Choice Quality Stuff/Anytime (72), At Carnegie Hall Live (72), Today (73), 1001 Nights (74)

• IT'S ALL MEAT - Canada

Formed in 1969 in Toronto, Ontario; they worked their psychedelic sound mostly around the keyboards.

Overall there is a mix of psychedelia and a rougher garage influence to their material.

It's All Meat (70)

• IVORY - USA

Formed in 1968 in California, this little known group recorded one LP that bears a striking similarity to psychedelic bands with strong female lead vocalists ala Jefferson Airplane. Lots of interesting fuzz-guitar and organ interplay.

Ivory (68)

• JACKAL - Canada

Formed in 1971 in Toronto, Ontario; they created a heavy psychedelic progressive rock similar to Deep Purple only more complex. A mix of prog and psychedelic incorporating good guitar and organ interplay.

Awake (73)

• JACKS - Japan

Formed in the late sixties, the Jacks most prominent sound was the over-the-top expressiveness of their vocalist. The project was a melting pot of Japanese psychedelia including members of Apryl Fool and Blues Creation.

Vacant World (68), Love, Peace & Poetry: Japanese Psychedelic Music [Comp] (01)

• JADE, FAINE - USA

Jade was playing guitar for the East Coast garage band the Rustics in 1966 but then went off under his own name to record a highly sought after psychedelic album replete with Syd Barrett and early Pink Floyd influences.

Introspection: A Faine Jade Recital (68)

• JAMES, TOMMY & THE SHONDELLS - USA

Formed in 1960 in Niles, Michigan; their early material was more of a pop-beat blend with a hint of garage edgy-ness. As the sixties progressed that garage sensibility came more into play as did a feel for the emerging bubblegum sound with hits like *Hanky, Panky* and *Mony, Mony*. The psychedelic influence came more into play, especially on the production side when they created songs like *Crimson & Clover*, *Crystal Blue Persuasion* and the LP **Cellophane Symphony**. Following their flirtation with the psychedelic side of things, they went back to creating more pop oriented hit songs. Tommy James retired from the music business in the early eighties.

Crimson and Clover (69), Cellophane Symphony (69)

• JAMME - USA

Formed in the late sixties in California, they created one LP, which was produced by John Phillips of the Mamas and the Papas. The musical results were a pleasant mix of folk-rock and psychedelia.

Jamme (70)

• JARVIS STREET REVIEW - Canada

Formed in 1970 in Thunder Bay, Ontario; they produced one LP that was a mix of heavy rock and psychedelia. The guitar shows a distinct Hendrix influence and the lyrics tend to focus on some socially conscious issues.

Mr. Oil Man (70)

• JASON CREST - UK

Formed in 1967 in Tonbridge, Kent; and had worked under a couple different names before landing a recording contract at EMI. They released a total of five singles featuring a psychedelic-pop style that was heavy on keyboards. Their compositions have elements of Procol Harum on the lighter side and Deep Purple on the heavier side. A lack of commercial success contributed to the band's break-up in 1969.

• JASPER WRATH - USA

Formed in 1969 in Hamden, Connecticut; they produced one LP during their hippie-psychedelic days which was primarily a softer, acoustic affair with bits of Left Banke baroque keyboards and jangling 12-string guitars. In the mid seventies they produced a further effort that leaned more in the progressive rock vein. They evolved into the more art-rock oriented Archangel.

Jasper Wrath (71), Jasper Wrath Anthology 1969 - 1976 [Comp] (97)

• JEFFERSON AIRPLANE - USA

Formed in 1965 in San Francisco by Marty Balin, Jefferson Airplane became one of the classic psychedelic bands of the sixties. They were also the first of the Bay area bands to release an LP with **Takes Off** in September of 1966. Following the release of that LP, Grace Slick formerly of the Great Society joined as did former Peanut Butter Conspiracy drummer Spencer Dryden. Slick brought two songs with her that became strong chart placers, *Somebody To Love* and *White Rabbit* both of which ended up in the Top 10. The Airplane started off as the house band at the Matrix club but quickly became regulars on the ballroom circuit and were one of the first local psychedelic bands to go on longer national tours. Through the seventies and eighties they went through many personnel permutations releasing a number of albums with various member combinations. They became Jefferson Starship in the early nineties.

Jefferson Airplane Takes Off (66), Surrealistic Pillow (67), After Bathing at Baxter's (68), Crown of Creation (68), Bless Its Pointed Little Head [live] (69), Volunteers (70), Bark (71), Long John Silver (72), 30 Seconds over Winterland [Live] (73), Jefferson Airplane (89), Psychedelic Frequencies [Comp] (96)

• JIMI HENDRIX EXPERIENCE - USA

Originally from Seattle, Hendrix was playing in a group called Jimmy James and the Blue Flames in New York in early 1966, when he was seen by ex-Animal bass player Chas Chandler. Chandler quit and became Hendrix's manager, taking him out of New York to the more open psychedelic world of London. It's said on the flight over, Jimmy James changed his name to 'Jimi' Hendrix. In 1967 they charted with the Top 10 hit *Hey Joe*, which was followed by *Purple Haze* and shortly thereafter the album **Are You Experienced** was released. Following his knock-out performance at the Monterey Pop Festival, witnessed by Mickey Dolenz, Hendrix was hired to open for the 1967 national tour of the Monkees, which he did for five perfomances before storming off stage and quitting the tour. By the summer of 1968, Hendrix was living the high life with success on both sides of the Atlantic. All of this came to an abrupt end when he died of a drug overdose in September of 1970. Many maintain that Hendrix revolutionized guitar playing with his blues technique and ear splitting feedback. His influence is felt in modern rock music to this day.

Are You Experienced (67), Axis: Bold As Love (67), Electric Ladyland (68), Band of Gypsies [Live] (70), Cry of Love (71), The Psychedelic Years Revisited [Comp] (92)

• JK & CO. - Canada

Formed in Vancouver they released a concept album in 1969 created by 15 year old Jay Kaye that captures the times with a mix of Beatles psychedelic influences. Kaye traveled up from Las Vegas and worked with a number of top Vancouver session people to create a generally obscure psychedelic masterpiece. His low-key almost melancholy vocals are placed over layers of orchestrated psych.

Suddenly One Summer (69), A Heavy Dose of Lyte Psych [Comp] (96)

• JOHN'S CHILDREN - UK

Formed in 1965 in Ashtead, Surrey they were originally known as the Clockwork Onions, then the Silence and finally as 1966 rolled around they changed their name to John's Children. They crafted a half-dozen singles during the British freakbeat era, which featured a certain R&B and Yardbirds influence, but failed to generate any significant interest. Of note was the inclusion of Marc Bolan as their guitarist who joined in early 1967 leaving later in the year to form Tyrannosaurus Rex. Founding member Andy Ellison formed Jet in the early seventies, a band that evolved into the new wave band Radio Stars in 1977.

Legendary Orgasm Album [Comp] (82), Instant Action [Comp] (85), Midsummer Night's Scene [Comp] (87), Happy Together: The Very Best of White Whale Records [Comp] (99), Nuggets II Box Set [Comp] (01)

• JOPLIN, JANIS - USA

Originally from Texas, Joplin first travelled to San Francisco in 1963 with Chet Helms, only to return home with a critical drug addiction. She was coaxed back to Frisco to become the lead singer for Big Brother and the Holding Company in 1966, giving up a similar spot with the emerging 13th Floor Elevators. Her rise to prominence was swift once she joined Big Brother and they became regulars at all the local Bay area haunts. Her appearance with the band at the Monterey Pop Festival was the final push to stardom and she soon shed Big Brother in favour of forming her

own Kosmic Blues Band. Her return to San Francisco was treated coolly as many fans disapproved of her treatment of hometown favourites Big Brother. She later formed the Full Tilt Boogie Band and had just completed most of the recording of the album Pearl when she died of an accidental drug overdose.

I Got Dem Ol' Kozmic Blues Again Mama! (69), Pearl (71)

• JUDE - UK

Her real name is Judy Willey and her one single *Morning Morgan Town* is included on a couple of psychedelic compilations of the sixties. Her style is clearly psychedelic-pop heavy with orchestration in the Left Banke style.

The Best of and The Rest of British Psychedelia [Comp] (91)

• JULY - UK

Formed in 1966 in Ealing they were originally known as the Tomcats. By 1968 they'd changed their name to July. Over their short career they released a couple of singles and one very psychedelic LP. By late 1968 they evolved into the more progressive Jade Warrior.

July (68), The Psychedelic Years 1966-1969 - Great Britain [Comp] (90)

• JUSTIN HEATHCLIFF - Japan

Formed in the early seventies, Justin Heathcliff was the brainchild of Osamu Kitajima. Having spent time in London he was keenly aware of the British Invasion style and the psychedelic scene. Merging the two he created Justin Heathcliff with the hope of being mistaken as a British outfit.

Justin Heathcliff (71), Love, Peace & Poetry: Japanese Psychedelic Music [Comp] (01)

• KAK - USA

Formed in 1968 in Sacramento, California, when guitarist Dehner Patten emerged from ballroom regulars Oxford Circle and joined up with Gary Yoder. Kak benefited from great guitar work from both Patten and Yoder. They created a trippy laid-back easy going style popular in the Bay area. Yoder went on to join BLUE CHEER in 1969 when KAK disbanded.

Kak (69), The Psychedelic Years Revisited [Comp] (92)

• KALEIDOSCOPE - Mexico

Formed in 1969, Kaleidoscope's psychedelic style is infused with strange studio echoes and sound effects, stinging acid fuzz-guitar laid overtop of a foundation of haunting organ. The band's sound failed to catch on and they split up shortly after their album was released.

Kaleidoscope (69), Love, Peace & Poetry: Latin American Psychedelic Music [Comp] (97)

• KALEIDOSCOPE - UK

Formed in 1964 in London they were originally called Side Kicks creating the typical R&B influenced pop music of the day. Following a name change to the Key in 1966, they became Kaleidoscope in 1967 and released two albums, which featured more of a spacey Pink Floyd influence. By 1970 they were on to other things, including recording but never releasing the obscure White Faced Lady LP. After that they changed their name to Fairfield Parlour and began incorporating a more progressive rock style releasing From Home to Home in 1970.

Tangerine Dream (67), Faintly Blowing (69), White Faced Lady (70/91), Nuggets II Box Set [Comp] (01)

• KALEIDOSCOPE - USA

Formed in 1963 in Los Angeles, California; by ex-folkie David Lindley and Turkish born Solomon Feldthouse. They were originally called the Rodents changing their name to Kaleidoscope in 1966. The band featured a huge assortment of unusual ethnic instrumentation and incorporated many diverse folk influences from around the world creating an interesting psychedelic-folk sound. They recorded four albums. After breaking up in 1970, David Lindley went on to play with Jackson Browne. They reformed for a one-off project released in 1977.

Side Trips (67), A Beacon From Mars (68), Incredible Kaleidoscope (69), Bernice (70), The Psychedelic Years Revisited [Comp] (92), Psychedelic Frequencies [Comp] (96)

• KAWACHI, KUNI - Japan

The psychedelia here is all heavily blues based with prominent fuzz-guitar flourishes.

Kuni Kawachi & Friends (70), Love, Peace & Poetry: Japanese Psychedelic Music [Comp] (01)

• KAYGISIZLAR - Turkey

Formed in the mid-sixties these guys were legends of the Turkish underground music scene.

Hava Narghile, Vol. 1 [Comp] (01)

• KENNY & THE KASUALS - USA

Formed in 1963 in Dallas, Texas; Kenny and the Kasuals spent a lot of time listening to bands like the Kinks and the Yardbirds. Their sound is one of many that bridged the gap between the garage-punk style and the emerging psychedelic genre. The band released a total of seven singles and two albums but failed to garner significant attention and after a rather topsy-turvy period they split up in 1968.

Impact (65), Live at the Studio Club (66), Nothing Better to Do [Comp] (83), Things Getting' Better [Comp] (84), Nuggets I Box Set [Comp] (98)

• KENSINGTON MARKET - Canada

Formed in 1967 in Toronto, Ontario; one of their first members was Luke Gibson of Luke and the Apostles. They were one of the main psychedelic bands working out of Toronto's Yorkville district. Their musical style when not focusing on psychedelic-pop would veer into folk or even heavier acid-rock. After three singles, a couple albums and two gruelling US tours they split up in 1969. Keyboardist John Mills Cockell turned up in the electronic progressive outfit Syrinx.

Avenue Road (68), Aardvark (69), Made in Canada, Vol. 4 1961 - 1974 [Comp] (91)

• KINGDOM - USA

Formed in the late sixties in the Los Angeles area they featured twin lead guitars in a classic psychedelic West Coast rock style.

Kingdom (70)

• KINGSTON WALL - Finland

Spacey psychedelic rock in the Ozric Tentacles vein.

Kingston Wall (92), II (93), III Tri-logy (94)

• KINKS - UK

Formed in 1963 in the Muswell Hill part of London, it was their third single, 1964's You Really Got Me that got everyone's attention. While the band came out of a traditional English pop R&B or beat style, the Kinks venture into psychedelia often goes unnoticed. But singles such as Lazy Old Sun and Waterloo Sunset contain all the hallmarks of a band reflecting the mood around them. Even more unnoticed are the solo psychedelic efforts of Dave Davies who attempted to move out from under the shadow of brother Ray with a couple of personal releases that reflected an even stronger psychedelic flavour.

Face to Face (66), Something Else by The Kinks (67), The Kinks are the Village Green Preservation Society (68), Arthur (69), Lola Versus Powerman and the Moneygoround Part One (70), Hot Smoke & Sassafras: Psychedelic Pstones Vol. 1 [Comp] (01)

• KINSMEN - UK

Formed in early 1967 as the Four Kinsmen, they released one single before dropping the 'Four' and turning to a more flower-power psychedelic-pop sound.

The Great British Psychedelic Trip, Vol. 2 [Comp] (88), Electric Sugarcube Flashbacks [Comp] (93)

• KIPPINGTON LODGE - UK

Formed in 1967 in London, Kippington Lodge produced at least five singles, most notably Shy Boy which was a sort of travelogue of London in 1967. Two of the members included Nick Lowe and Brinsley Schwartz and their early style fused the beat sound with psychedelia. Their psychedelic efforts failed to create any significant impact, so in the early seventies they renamed themselves 'Brinsley Schwartz' and went in a pub-rock direction while Nick Lowe pursued a solo career.

The Psychedelic Years 1966-1969 - Great Britain [Comp] (90), Kippington Lodge '67 - '69 [Comp] (98)

• KISSING SPELL - Chile

Formed in the early seventies, their vocal style is very reminiscent of that laid-back San Francisco minor-note harmony style over a dreamy organ or piano foundation interspersed with searing fuzz-guitar and horns.

Los Pajaros (70), Love, Peace & Poetry: Latin American Psychedelic Music [Comp] (97)

• KNOWBODY ELSE - USA

Formed in the late sixties they featured a mix of folk or country influenced hippie rock and roll that surged into some heavy psychedelia by virtue of some solid guitar playing. They recorded one LP in 1969 and then in the early seventies evolved into Black Oak Arkansas.

The Knowbody Else (69)

• KOOBAS - UK

Formed in 1964 in Liverpool, the Koobas moved to London in 1965 where they were soon managed by Tony Straton Smith's agency. Shortly after they were off to Hamburg, then a tour with the Beatles and eventually signed to EMI in 1966. Throughout 1967 and 68 they played regularly on London's club circuit and appeared with many of the eras top psychedelic bands such as Pink Floyd. After releasing a total of seven poorly received singles, the band released their one and only album in 1969 providing just a glimpse of the creativity present had they been allowed to chart their own musical path. By the time the LP came out the band had split up. Bass player Keith Ellis went on to join Van Der Graaf Generator.

The Koobas (69), Psychedelia at Abbey Road [Comp] (98), Nuggets II Box Set [Comp] (01)

• KORAY, ERKIN - Turkey

In 1967 psychedelia was spreading the world over and in Turkey, pop artist Erkin Koray even threw his hat into the ring. Complete with an authentic Eastern influences and instrumentation and subtle electric guitar, it's a classic hippie sound.

Hava Narghile, Vol. 1 [Comp] (01)

• KRAVITZ, LENNY - USA

One of the newer artists whose musical accomplishments are littered with the influences of the psychedelic era. And it sounds great. Starting with the foundational elements of soul and R&B, Kravitz melds a little Hendrix and a little Beatles and a whole lot more to craft some highly original sounding modern rock that still manages to maintain a strong psychedelic feel. In the process he's had a number of significant hit singles and strong selling albums.

Let Love Rule (89), Mama Said (91), Are You Gonna Go My Way (93)

• LA DE DAS - New Zealand

Formed in 1964 in Auckland, they were originally called the Mergers but changed their name to La De Das in 1965. Playing in an R&B style they became one of New Zealand's most popular rock acts. They incorporated new gear such as a guitar fuzz box, which had them flirting with a mixture of Mod and psychedelic sounds. In 1968 they recorded their most psychedelic LP entitled **The Happy Prince**. They eventually changed into more of a hard rock outfit and after recording three rather obscure LPs and a few singles they split up in the early 70s.

La De Das (66), Find Us a Way (67), The Happy Prince (68), Nuggets II Box Set [Comp] (01)

• LA VIDA - Mexico

Formed in the early seventies they released one album that combined a Byrds-like influence with a rougher garage feel. The album is noted for the unusual syncopated organ that weaves through virtually all the tracks.

La Vida (72)

• LADIES W.C. - Venezuela

Formed in the late sixties, Ladies W.C.'s musical style is very reminiscent of bluesy psychedelic bands such as Quicksilver Messenger Service and even the Grateful Dead. The guitar style goes from stinging fuzz to acid-wah-wah and the vocals run from dreamy trippy chanting to minor note refrains.

Ladies W.C (70), Love, Peace & Poetry: Latin American Psychedelic Music [Comp] (97)

• LAGHONIA - Peru

Formed in the early seventies their sound revolved a strong fuzz-guitar sound with neat little atmospheric organ introductions giving that dreamy spacey psych flavour.

Etcetera (71), Glue (71), Love, Peace & Poetry: Latin American Psychedelic Music [Comp] (97)

• LAMB - USA

Formed in 1969 in San Francisco they crafted an interesting West Coast hippie styled psychedelia with plenty of soul influence. The group incorporated an unusual assortment of instruments in their mix including cello, oboe and classical guitars. They were signed to Bill Graham's Fillmore label and played the Bay area ballrooms regularly developing quite a following. After some limited success Lamb split up in 1973 when founder and lead vocalist Barbara Mauritz went solo.

A Sign of Change (70), Cross Between (71), Bring Out the Sun (71)

• LAZY NICKELS - USA

Formed in the late sixties in Michigan, the Lazy Nickels recorded only one single that might conceivably be considered psychedelic due to its phased production and sound effects.

A Lethal Dose of Hard Psych [Comp] (99)

• LAZY SMOKE - USA

Formed in 1967 in Massachusetts, Lazy Smoke borrowed heavily from the Beatles style of psychedelia, lots of harmonies and catchy melodies intertwined with some great guitar work. Sadly by the time the LP was released the band had already split up.

Corridor of Faces (69)

• LEAVES - USA

Formed in 1964 in the Los Angeles area the Leaves were led by Jim Pons and crafted a folk-rock style which incorporated a healthy dose of fuzz-guitar and protest lyrics. They were originally known as the Rockwells and were greatly influenced by the folk-rock style of the Byrds. By early 1966 they'd changed their name to the Leaves and lead guitarist Bobby Arlin had bought a fuzz-box and then they recorded *Hey Joe* which became a Top 40 hit. Unfortunately it was also their last hit. Pons left the band just after they signed to Capitol Records to join the Turtles then later Flo & Eddie and Frank Zappa.

Hey Joe (66), All the Good That's Happening (67), Psychedelic Perceptions [Comp] (96), Nuggets I Box Set [Comp] (98)

• LEFT BANKE - USA

Formed in 1966 in New York the band scored a hit single early in their career with *Walk Away Renee* and then followed that up with *Pretty Ballerina*. Left Banke created an interesting blend of pop music and classical touches that had many describing them as a "baroque rock." Their style of composition seemed to blend in well with the experimentation going on during the "hey day" of psychedelia. They disbanded in 1970, with founding member and keyboardist Michael Brown later forming Stories in 1972, hitting the charts again with *Brother Louie*.

Walk Away Renee...Pretty Ballerina (67), The Left Banke Too (68), The Psychedelic Years Revisited [Comp] (92)

• LEGEND - USA

Legend formed in 1968 and created an almost British style of psychedelic music, strong on melody and harmony. They recorded a couple of singles and one album of garage flavoured guitar driven songs with a nice organ support and plenty of echo and even some sitar sounds. They evolved into a band called Dragonfly.

Legend (68), A Lethal Dose of Hard Psych [Comp] (99)

• LEMON DROPS - USA

Formed in 1966 in Chicago, the Lemon Drops were a group of teenagers who made music that was pure flower-power psychedelic. They officially recorded only one single called *I Live In The Springtime* which featured the prerequisite fuzz-guitar, jangling rhythm section and up-beat harmonies. They seemed to have everything together except the promotion side. Even though they recorded more material in the studio they failed to make the next leap and disbanded in 1968.

Crystal Pure [Comp] (85), Second Album [Comp] (87), Nuggets I Box Set [Comp] (98)

• LEMON PIPERS - USA

Formed in 1967 in Oxford, Ohio; they soon moved to New York where they scored big in 1968 with the hit *Green Tambourine*. Their particular style of psychedelic folk-pop led to the creation of what eventually became bubblegum music although they managed to create some classic psychedelia like the nine minute *Thru With You* off their first album. While their music was well received by the public, critics hated its' seeming 'light-ness' and the Lemon Pipers disbanded in 1969.

Green Tambourine (68), Jungle Marmalade (68), The Psychedelic Years Revisited [Comp] (92), Psychedelic Visions [Comp] (96)

• LEMON TREE - UK

Formed in 1968 in Birmingham, the Lemon Tree had a lot in common with other bands in the area, namely the Move and Idle Race. Not only did they cover many of the Move's songs, albeit in a more pop style, Lemon Tree used the same producer. One of their members left to join Idle Race and then had their drummer later join

Roy Wood's Wizard. They only ever released two official singles before splitting up.

Electric Sugarcube Flashbacks [Comp] (93)

• LEVIATHAN - UK

Formed in 1968 this obscure and short-lived British outfit released a total of three psychedelic singles with lots of great fuzz-guitar, phasing and unusual lyrics. They split up by the end of 1969 with one member winding up in Jason Crest.

• L'EXPERIENCE 9 - Canada

Formed in the late sixties in Montreal, Quebec; they made one album, that as the title implies is a psychedelic overload.

Freak Out Total (70)

• LIFE 'N' SOUL - UK

Formed originally in 1966 in Liverpool, they moved to London in 1967 and developed a style that is part Spencer Davis Group and part Fifth Dimension. Their first single was a remake of *Ode To Billie Joe* and while one further single followed the band split up shortly after its release in early 1969.

The Great British Psychedelic Trip, Vol. 2 [Comp] (88)

• LIGHT - USA

Formed in 1967 in Riverside, California; they recorded at least one single which has much in common with bands like Music Machine. The single *Back Up* features a high energy foundation with a powerful folk-influenced chorus line.

A Lethal Dose of Hard Psych [Comp] (99)

• LINDY BLASKY & THE LAVELLS - USA

Formed in 1966 in New Mexico, Lindy Blasky and the Lavells ventured only slightly out of their familiar garage-punk style but did record a number of singles such as *You Ain't Tuff* and *Let It Be* that were well received on local radio stations.

Orange, Sugar & Chocolate: Psychedelic Microdots of the 60's, Vol. 1 [Comp] (89)

• LINN COUNTY - USA

Formed in the late sixties they were originally from Cedar Rapids, Iowa; but eventually relocated to San Francisco where they played regularly at the various venues in the Bay area. Their musical style was primarily a mixture of jazz and blues worked into the West Coast psychedelic sound of the day. They disbanded in 1971 and members went to play with Elvin Bishop, the Full Tilt Boogie Band and Gainsborough Gallery.

Proud Flesh Soothseer (68), Fever Shot (69), Till Break of Dawn (70)

• LIQUID SMOKE - USA

Formed in the late sixties in New York their musical style was centred on a heavy mix of guitar and organ, not unlike Iron Butterfly or Vanilla Fudge. They managed a minor hit with the song *I Who Have Nothing*.

Liquid Smoke (70)

• LITTER - USA

Formed in 1966 in Minneapolis, Minnesota; their goal was to become the loudest garage-punk-psych rock band in the area. Borrowing influences from bands like the Who and the Yardbirds, they set on a quest recording their first single in early 1967. While it did well locally, it never caught the ears of national radio programmers. The band eventually recorded their first LP in 1967 and followed that up with two more in later years before breaking up in 1970.

Distortions (67), $100 Dollar Fine (68), Emerge (69), Nuggets I Box Set [Comp] (98)

• LIVING END - USA

Formed in early 1966 in Amarillo, Texas; they're known to have recorded a number of tracks in a Dallas studio including a remake of Creation's *Making Time*.

Texas Twisted: Psychedelic Microdots of the 60's, Vol. 2 [Comp] (91)

• LOCKSLEY HALL - USA

Formed in 1968 in the Pacific Northwest they became relatively popular on the local circuit. Their musical style is typical West Coast guitar oriented psychedelia with echoes of Quicksilver Messenger Service and Big Brother.

Locksley Hall (69)

• LOCOMOTIVE - UK

Formed in 1967 in Birmingham by guitarist/vocalist Norman Haines, they started out in the tried and true R&B pop style releasing a couple of singles. It was with their third single from late 1968 that the band changed their musical focus. Entitled *Mr. Armageddon* it bears an almost gothic feel. Locomotive then began creating a psychedelic music that was closer to progressive rock than whimsical pop. They eventually recorded one LP before splitting up, with Haines forming the Norman Haines Band.

We are Everything You See (69), Psychedelia at Abbey Road [Comp] (98)

• LOLLIPOP SHOPPE - USA

Formed in 1965 in Las Vegas they were originally known as the Weeds. They soon moved to Portland, Oregon, there they were signed to a management deal by Lord Tim Hudson an English Disc Jockey who also managed the Seeds. That's when they changed their name. Taking the name Lollipop Shoppe in 1967 to avoid confusion with the similarly named Seeds. The band's harder edge psychedelic-punk style points to the coming hard rock sounds of the later sixties and early seventies. After a disappointing response to one single and a follow-up LP the band split in 1969.

Just Colour (67), Psychedelic Visions [Comp] (96), Nuggets I Box Set [Comp] (98)

• LONG TIME COMIN' - Canada

Formed in the early seventies in Vancouver, they came on the scene late and only recorded three singles in the early seventies, the third of which was called *Part of the Season* and featured the same type of psychedelic phasing and guitar style as *Pictures of Matchstick Men*. The band eventually went their separate ways before finding fame.

The History of Vancouver Rock & Roll, Vol. 4 [Comp] (91)

• LOOK - Canada

Formed in 1967 in Vancouver, the Look featured a classic folk-rock style that was punctuated with tight Beatle-ish harmonies. They only recorded one extended single with four songs on it. The band eventually included Rob and Barry Rowden, both original members of Painted Ship who were known in Vancouver for their garage-punk style.

The History of Vancouver Rock & Roll, Vol. 4 [Comp] (91)

• LORDS OF LONDON - Canada

Formed in 1966, they were originally called Nucleus, but as they changed their music style to a more psych-pop they adopted the new name Lords of London. Their first hit was *Cornflakes & Ice Cream* in 1967. They carried on for a time before going through a number of personnel changes and eventually became A Foot In Cold Water.

Made in Canada, Vol. 3 1961 - 1974 [Comp] (91)

• LOS CHIJUAS - Mexico

Formed in 1967 in Mexico, Los Chijuas incorporated all the right elements to create a flower-power sound with a slight Latin flavour. They incorporated the reedy organ and jangling guitars popular with many psychedelic bands that worked from a folk-rock base.

Los Chijuas (68), Los Chijuas (69), Nuggets II Box Set [Comp] (01)

• LOS GATOS - Argentina

Formed in 1968 they created a haunting style built around strange organ and rhythm patterns.

Seremos Amigos (68), Love, Peace & Poetry: Latin American Psychedelic Music [Comp] (97)

• LOS MAC'S - Chile

Formed in 1967 Los Mac's became one of the pre-eminent psychedelic bands in Chile. They featured the obligatory reedy, psychedelic organ sound, nice echoey harmonies and cantering drumming patterns so prevalent with the early San Francisco bands. Mixing psychedelic and pop their albums also contained many Beatle or British Invasion sounds as well. They travelled to Italy to record their fourth LP, but failing to find a following, they disbanded in 1969.

Go Go 22 (66), GG Session (67), Kaleidoscope Men (67), Los Mac's (68), Love, Peace & Poetry: Latin American Psychedelic Music [Comp] (97)

• LOS SHAKERS - Uraguay

Formed in 1963 in Montevideo they started out playing a beat or surf style and released their first LP as such but all that changed when the Beatles came on the international scene. Los Shakers soon began adopting the various psychedelic elements heard on Rubber Soul and Revolver to create two LPs with their own take on psychedelia. The record company was urging them to become more commercial, but the band resisted. Lack of promotional support and a delayed fourth LP release all spelt disaster. By the time their fourth LP was released the band had all but disbanded.

Los Shakers (65), For You (66), La Conferencia Secreta Del Toto's Bar (68), In the Studio Again (71), Nuggets II Box Set [Comp] (01)

• LOS SPEAKERS - Columbia

Formed in 1965 they started out playing straightforward beat music before adopting a rougher garage style. Fans of psychedelia will want to explore their last two albums recorded in 1967 and 1968.

Los Speakers (65), La Casa Del Sol Naciente (66), Tuercas, Tornillos Y Alicates (66), Los Speakers (67), En El Maravilloso Mundo de Ingenson (68)

• LOS VIDRIOS QUEBRADOS - Chile

Formed in 1965, they created a psychedelic musical style that at times was very reminiscent of many of the British psychedelic flower-pop. Light and whimsical being the key trademarks. While moderately successful they eventually split up shortly after the release of their one and only LP.

Fictions (67), Love, Peace & Poetry: Latin American Psychedelic Music [Comp] (97)

• LOST AND FOUND - USA

Formed in 1965 in Houston, Texas; they were originally called the Misfits. By 1967 they had befriended Roky Erikson of the 13th Floor Elevators and had gigged steadily at local clubs where their garage-psych style was well received. After recording two singles and one album, plus a month long tour with the Music Machine, the band were exhausted and called it quits.

Everybody's Here (67)

• LOTHAR & THE HAND PEOPLE - USA

Formed in 1965 in Denver, Colorado; Lothar and the Hand People were the first band to popularize the synthetic electronic sounds of the Theremin, an instrument that changed sound and pitch based on your hand movements used to great effect on the Beach Boy's *Good Vibrations*. This innovative experimentation was mixed with their folk-influenced rock style. The band soon relocated to New York City but after releasing six singles and two albums that failed to place on the charts the band split up in 1970.

Presenting… Lothar and The Hand People (68), Space Hymn (70), Psychedelic Frequencies [Comp] (96)

• LOVE - USA

Formed in 1965 in Los Angeles, Arthur Lee the band's founding member, having relocated to L.A. from Memphis soon heard the music of the Byrds and set to work to create his own blend of the blues, folk and acid rock in a band he called Love. They were signed to the Elektra label and created an impressive LP entitled **Forever Changes** featuring a host of unique influences. The album has since become a classic of Los Angeles psychedelic sound. After the break up of the original

lineup, Lee put together a whole new band in early 1969. Unfortunately, while many of the contemporary bands had moved to a harder musical sound, Love had not and the band's seceding albums were not well received. Following the break up of Love in 1971, Lee recorded a solo album in 1972 and then reformed a version of Love in 1975 before once again pursuing a solo path in the early eighties. The recorded results of these later incarnations were received rather luke warmly.

Love (66), Da Capo (67), Forever Changes (68), Four Sail (69), Out There (69), False Start (70), The Psychedelic Years Revisited [Comp] (92), Psychedelic Perceptions [Comp] (96), Nuggets I Box Set [Comp] (98)

• LOVECHAIN - USA

Formed in the late sixties in Ohio, Lovechain released at least one single in 1969 with a trippy minor key vocal delivery like some of the West Coast acid-rock bands. They've spiced it up with some interesting guitar and organ work and added a vocal delivery loaded with tremolo.

A Lethal Dose of Hard Psych [Comp] (99)

• LOVE CHILDREN - UK

Formed in the late sixties, the emphasis with this British group was on harmony vocals mixed with the prevailing folk tinged psychedelic style in much the same manner as the Kinsmen and Tinkerbells Fairydust. They released two singles before disbanding in 1970.

The Great British Psychedelic Trip, Vol. 2 [Comp] (88)

• LOVE EXCHANGE - USA

Formed in 1967 in Los Angeles their sound is a classic example of the lighter L.A. flower-power pop style. Nice breezy vocals with great studio arrangements.

Love Exchange (68)

• LOVE SCULPTURE - UK

Formed in 1967 in Wales, they originally went by the name Human Beans but after releasing one single changed their name to Love Sculpture. They proceeded to have a serious hit with the rock reworking of the classical piece *Sabre Dance*. Their first LP was more or less a straight-ahead blues rock effort but their second release in 1969 entitled **Forms and Feelings** contained some interesting pop-psych. The band split in 1970 when Dave Edmunds briefly pursued a solo career before teaming up with Nick Lowe in Rockpile.

Blues Helping (68), Forms and Feelings (69), Nuggets II Box Set [Comp] (01)

• LOVIN' SPOONFUL - USA

Formed in 1965 in Greenwich Village, New York; the Lovin Spoonful was fronted by folkie John Sebastian and Canadian Zal Yanovsky. They broke out of the folk scene with the 1965 hit **Do You Believe In Magic**." This led to string of Top 10 pop hits. But it was their folk-jug-band background that endeared them to the early psychedelic crowds much like the Charlatans or Sopwith Camel. By late 1967 and 1968 the Lovin Spoonful's style was firmly entrenched in the pop music world.

Do You Believe in Magic (66), Daydream (66), Hums of the Lovin Spoonful (66), Everything Playing (68), Revelation: Revolution '69 (69)

• LUKE & THE APOSTLES - Canada

Formed in 1966 in Toronto, Ontario, Luke and the Apostles hold the distinction of having performed with the Jefferson Airplane and the Grateful Dead when Bill Graham produced the Sounds of San Francisco tour in 1967. The band were favourites on the local coffee house circuit playing regularly but failed to generate their live success into anything major on the radio. They released three singles before splitting up in late 1967. Luke Gibson went to Kensington Market, Mike McKenna turned up with the Ugly Ducklings for a time before forming the blues rock outfit McKenna Mendelson Mainline and Pat Little turned up in Neil Young's Crazy Horse. A one off reunion in 1970 also failed to go anywhere.

Made in Canada, Vol. 3 1961 - 1974 [Comp] (91)

• LYME & CYBELLE - USA

This duo released a total of three singles on the White Whale label in 1966. They were actually an unknown (at the time) Warren Zevon and female partner Violet Santangelo. Together their sound has been likened to a more psychedelic Sonny and Cher. After recording the singles each went their separate ways.

Nuggets I Box Set [Comp] (98), Happy Together: The Very Best of White Whale Records [Comp] (99)

• MAD RIVER - USA

Formed in 1967 in Yellow Spring, Ohio; they eventually found their way to San Francisco where they became regulars on the ballroom circuit. Their music was the embodiment of West Coast psychedelia with a blend of acid-folk and a hint of country. Their compositions featured plenty of minor-key guitar jamming mixed with periods of frenetic tripping. They disbanded in 1969 when drummer Greg Dewey went to Country Joe and the Fish.

Mad River (68), Paradise Bar and Grill (69)

• MAGIC CYCLE - Canada

Formed in 1966 in Toronto, Ontario; they hit the recording studio and released a number of singles like *Doctor Lollipop* and *Groovy Things* all displaying the typical psych-pop style of the flower-power era. In 1970 they changed their name to the Cycle and released a couple LPs.

Saturday Afternoon Rummage Sale (70), Magic Music (73)

• MAGIC FERN - USA

Formed in 1966 in Seattle, Washington; they started out playing gigs on the University of Washington campus. Their musical style was straight ahead hippie-folk that went over well as a counterpoint to the heavier electric blues psychedelic bands. If you enjoy the Lovin' Spoonful or the Youngbloods you'll like Magic Fern.

Magic Fern [Comp] (80), The History of Northwest Rock Vol. 3: Psychedelic Seattle [Comp] (00)

• MAGIC MIXTURE - UK

Formed in 1967 in London, this obscure group existed on the scene for a very short time releasing only one LP with a mixture of many psychedelic elements from pop to jazz. They disbanded shortly after the release of their album.

This Is (68)

• MAGIC MUSHROOMS - USA

Formed in 1966 in Philadelphia, the Magic Mushrooms hit with a freak-out psychedelic style that would have made Frank Zappa proud. Borrowing a searing fuzz-toned Yardbirds guitar style, they released a single called *It's A Happening* that seemed to be at least two years ahead of everyone else's place in the psychedelic scene.

Nuggets I Box Set [Comp] (98)

• MAGIC WORMS - UK

This obscure outfit produced a couple of singles that are best described as "classic" British pop psychedelia.

The Best of and The Rest of British Psychedelia [Comp] (91)

• MAGICIANS - USA

Formed in 1965 in New York, the Magicians were a product of Greenwich Village and shared the stages with bands like the Lovin' Spoonful and the Blues Magoos. They released their first single in 1965 called *An Invitation To Cry* betraying a little Young Rascals influence. They failed to attract any attention and split up in 1966. Two members, Gary Bonner and Alan Gordon continued writing and came up with some hits for The Turtles including *She'd Rather Be With Me* and *Happy Together*.

Nuggets I Box Set [Comp] (98), An Invitation to Cry: The Best of The Magicians [Comp] (99)

• MAJORITY - UK

Formed in 1965 in Hull, but shortly after relocated to London. They were originally known as Barry Graham & the Mustangs and were known for their fine vocal style and arrangements similar to those made popular by groups such as the Fortunes. Over the course of three years they released no less than eight singles with only moderate success. What success they had came mostly from the continent and the band continued recording there into early seventies under the name Majority One.

The Great British Psychedelic Trip, Vol. 2 [Comp] (88), Nuggets II Box Set [Comp] (01)

• MAMAS AND THE PAPAS - USA

Formed in 1964 they went through a number of folk permutations before becoming the Mamas and the Papas in 1966 after relocating to Los Angeles. They hit the charts running with *California Dreaming*, *Monday Monday* and many others all displaying a keen folk-pop-rock sensibility loaded with hummable melodies and superlative harmonies. By the time of the Monterey Pop Festival, where they were one of the headliners, they were already on the downward spiral, but it was internal personality crises that eventually brought them to an end in late 1968. Mama Cass carried on as a solo artist for a while before experiencing a heart attack in 1974. The others continued popping in and out of the music scene.

If You Can Believe Your Eyes (66), Cass John Michelle Denny (67), Deliver (67), Presenting The Mamas and The Papas (68)

• MAMMOTH - USA

Formed in either Texas or California in the late sixties, Mammoth released at least one single called *Mammoth* that bore more than a striking resemblance in vocal style and song structure to Buffalo Springfield's *Mr. Soul*. Lots of stinging fuzz-guitar work.

A Lethal Dose of Hard Psych [Comp] (99)

• MAN - UK

Formed in 1968, in Swansea, this Welsh band was strongly influenced by the West Coast bands such as Quicksilver Messenger Service. In fact in a surprising move Quicksilver guitarist John Cippolina even joined the group for the recording of the **Maximum Darkness** LP. Their first album entitled **Revelation** was released in 1969 and was a concept album about evolution. Man developed a hugely loyal cult following for their guitar oriented sound but never cracked the mainstream. They eventually released many albums before splitting up in 1977. The reformed in the early eighties and have been seen performing ever since.

Revelation (68), 2 Ounces of Plastic With a Hole In The Middle (69), Man (70), Do You Like It Here Now, Are You Settling In? (71), Be Good To Yourself At Least Once A Day (72), Back Into The Future (73), Rhinos, Winos and Lunatics (74), Slow Motion (74), Maximum Darkness (75), The Welsh Connection (76), All's Well That Ends Well (77), The Psychedelic Years Revisited [Comp] (92)

• MAN MADE - Canada

Formed in the early seventies in Montreal they produced one album on the tail end of the psychedelic golden era. The album has plenty of transitional psych influences, borrowing a bit of electronic keyboard space-y-ness from Pink Floyd and some rather folk-ish elements similar to Tim Buckley's trippy efforts.

Man Made (72)

• MANCO, BARIS - Turkey

Manco teamed up with the popular Turkish band Kaygisizlar to create some classic psychedelic rock in 1968. As expected the use of authentic Eastern tones and instruments mixed with a strong West Coast, laid-back trippy style both musically and vocally created a classic psychedelic style.

Hava Narghile, Vol. 1 [Comp] (01)

• MANDALA - Canada

Formed in 1966 in Toronto, Ontario; they were originally called the Rogues. Fronted by guitarist Dominic Troiano, the Mandala had a big hit with *Opportunity* in 1967 but they were never able to follow it up. After releasing one LP they changed some personnel and took the name Bush. Their style was a mixture of soul influenced garage-psych.

Soul Crusade (68), Mandala Classics (86), Made in Canada, Vol. 4 1961 - 1974 [Comp] (91)

• MANDRAKE MEMORIAL - USA

Formed in 1967 in Philadelphia they opened for all the major acts coming through town. At the time they were as popular as the Nazz especially on their first LP, however they are not remembered as much today. Their brand of psychedelia which really came into its own on their second and third releases incorporated more than a hint of middle Eastern and jazz influences.

Mandrake Memorial (67), Medium (69), Puzzle (70)

• MANDRAKE PADDLE STEAMER - UK

Formed in 1968 in London, the band consisted of Brian Engle, Martin Briley, Martin Hooker, Paul Riodan and Barry Nightingale. Their sound was a British approximation of the San Francisco West Coast style of psychedelia. They were one of the first groups to use Abbey Road's new 8-track facilities and there they created one of the gems of late sixties British psychedelia in *Strange Walking Man*. Despite receiving their share of exposure the band failed to hit it off and eventually disbanded in 1970. Members of Mandrake Paddle Steamer wound up in a variety of British bands such as Prowler, Greenslade and Pickettywitch, while Martin Briley went on to a solo career in the United States.

Mandrake Paddlesteamer [Comp] (91), Psychedelia at Abbey Road [Comp] (98)

• MAQUINA - Spain

One of the better psych-prog bands from Spain. Lots of great fuzz-guitar.

Why? (71)

• MARMALADE - UK

Formed in 1961 in Glasgow, Scotland; they were originally called the Gaylords and played the usual Brit pop and R&B mix of styles. Marmalade had a string of pop influenced psychedelia including *I See the Rain* in 1967 and *Lovin' Thing* in 1968 and of course the huge international hit *Reflections Of My Life* in 1970. By that time the trippy influence was wearing off and they reverted to more of straight forward pop approach to writing.

There's a Lot of it About (68), Reflections of The Marmalade (70), Songs (71), Electric Sugarcube Flashbacks [Comp] (93), Nuggets II Box Set [Comp] (01)

• MASADA - USA

Obscure band reportedly from New England who recorded one single with a low-key plaintive vocal delivery over top of a subdued pop-psych musical style.

A Heavy Dose of Lyte Psych [Comp] (96)

• MASKERS - Holland

Formed in 1962 in Amsterdam they released a couple of folk oriented singles in their early days before adopting a little more R&B feel in the mid-sixties. By 1968 they were fully immersed in the psychedelic underground. They released one single as such, with loads of guitar distortion and feedback and a mournful vocal style.

Failing to find success they split up in 1969 after releasing about thirty singles and four LPs.

Waterpipes & Dykes: Dutch Psychedelic Underground 1966 - 1972 Vol. 1 [Comp] ( )

• MASTERS APPRENTICES - Australia

Formed in 1963 in Adelaide, Australia; they were originally called the Mustangs, playing an instrumental guitar style much like the Shadows. In late 1964 they changed their name and began to play more R&B material. Before long they were bitten by the freakbeat and psychedelic influences to release their first LP. By the early seventies and their second release they began moving more in the progressive rock direction musically but failed to generate success and eventually split up in 1972.

The Master's Apprentices (67), A Toast to Panama Red (72), Nuggets II Box Set [Comp] (01)

• MATADORS - Czechoslovakia

Formed in 1965 in Prague, they were originally known as the Fontanas but changed their name by the end of that year. Formed originally to play music with an R&B feel, they couldn't help but be influenced by what little Western sounds they heard and that included the obligatory fuzz-guitar and reedy organ. They recorded a couple singles but never made much impact outside their homeland.

The Matadors (68), Nuggets II Box Set [Comp] (01)

• MAVI ISIKLAR - Turkey

Formed in 1965 they adopted a strong Eastern or Turkish ethnic sound by 1968 that blended in well with the growing world of psychedelia.

Hava Narghile, Vol. 1 [Comp] (01)

• MAZE - USA

Formed in the late sixties in Fairfield, California; they recorded their one and only album in San Francisco. Musically they run the gamut from laid back hummable acid-pop to more fuzz-guitar laden jams.

Armageddon (69)

• MCKENZIE, SCOTT - USA

McKenzie's main claim to fame was his smash hit of 1967 entitled San Francisco (Be Sure to Wear Flowers In Your Hair). There are some in the psychedelic community who look down on this effort and yet there is no denying the impact the song had on promoting the positive side of the Summer of Love. The flip side of course is that it helped draw thousands of youth into an already crowded Haight-Ashbury. McKenzie had originally played in a folk trio called the Journeymen which also included John Philips of the Mamas and the Papas and it was Philips who actually wrote the tune specifically for McKenzie to record. An album followed, but the song proved to be McKenzie's only chart success and by the end of 1967 he moved on to other things including help ing to write the 1988 hit song Kokomo for the Beach Boys.

The Voice of Scott McKenzie (67)

• MCWILLIAMS, DAVID - UK

From Ireland, McWilliams released his first single in 1966 before charting with the heavily psychedelized underground hit single Days of Pearly Spencer. Continually dogged by hype and an uneasiness about performing live hindered any chance of success. While McWilliams recorded a healthy number of singles and albums into 1980, mostly with a decidedly folk influence, chart success eluded him and he retired from the business in 1982

Singing Songs of David McWilliams (67), David McWilliams Vol. 2 (67), David McWilliams Vol. 3 (68), Psychedelic Perceptions [Comp] (96)

• MELLOW CANDLE - UK

Formed in 1968 in Ireland, Mellow Candle released one album with a psychedelic-acid-folk influenced style that bordered on progressive rock. Their style was not dissimilar to early Fairport Convention. The LP failed to catch much attention and they disbanded shortly after.

Swaddling Songs (72)

• MENERALS - USA

Formed in the mid-sixties in a Northern suburb of Dallas, Texas; the Menerals never recorded any significant singles, but a couple demos were taped in the television studio while recording the popular Sump'n Else TV program. Style wise they retain the garage-punk sensibility.

Texas Twisted: Psychedelic Microdots of the 60's, Vol. 2 [Comp] (91)

• MET & ZONDER - Holland

Formed in 1967 in Amsterdam, they created a whimsical, British influenced psychedelic-pop music. After three official singles they called it quits.

Waterpipes & Dykes: Dutch Psychedelic Underground 1966 - 1972 Vol. 1 [Comp] ( )

• MICAH - USA

Formed in the late sixties in New York City they recorded only one known album that consisted of extended psychedelic guitar and organ jams with a blues foundation.

I'm Only One Man (70)

• MICHAELS, LEE - USA

Lee Michaels was a keyboardist who came to prominence in the psychedelic San Francisco ballroom scene playing the local venues regularly and recording a number of albums on the A&M label. He even scored a Top 10 single with Do You Know What I Mean in 1971. His musical style was much more elaborate than the single betrayed and Michaels was more at home in the studio creating longer well constructed organ/piano/harpsichord musical jams than he was writing hits. After failing to follow-up on the success of the single Michaels retreated from the scene, doing a little session work before fading away entirely.

Carnival of Life (68), Recital (68), Lee Michaels (69),

• MICHELE - USA

Formed in the late sixties in California the band included Lowell George on vocals. Musically their one and only album was classic West Coast psychedelic folk-rock even down to some Eastern influences.

Saturn Rings (69)

• MICKEY FINN - UK

Formed in 1961 in London, they were originally called the Strangers playing a mix of R&B standards. By 1965 they had adopted the name Mickey Finn and were moving towards a Mod, freakbeat direction. These early influences allowed them to flirt with the growing psychedelic scene with a number of singles that failed to generate much interest. Try as they might success eluded them and they split up in 1971. The guitarist and keyboard player later turned up in the Heavy Metal Kids.

Keep Moving [Comp] (97), Nuggets II Box Set [Comp] (01)

• MIGHTY BABY - UK

Formed in 1968 in London after the demise of Action, Mighty Baby crafted a psychedelic sound that was vaguely reminiscent of the guitar oriented West Coast sound. With two guitars plus some woodwinds they created some moody almost jazzy musical flavours.

Mighty Baby (69), A Jug of Love (71)

• MIKE STUART SPAN - UK

Formed in 1966 in Brighton, they started out as a soul band but then moved to London in 1967 and quickly fell into the psychedelic scene happening at the time. They played in all the hot spots and released a few singles into 1968 before disbanding only to re-emerge later as a group called Leviathon.

Electric Sugarcube Flashbacks [Comp] (93), Timespan [Comp] (95)

• MILLER, PETE - UK

[see: Big Boy Pete]

• MILLER, STEVE - USA

Born in Texas, blues trained in Chicago, Steve Miller arrived in San Francisco in 1968 where he soon put together the Steve Miller Blues Band. They quickly were playing the ballroom circuit and anywhere else they could. More proficient at the guitar than most of the Bay area bands, Miller soon built up a loyal following and after the band's appearance at the Monterey Pop Festival were signed to Capitol Records. Their early albums not only show cased some excellent blues guitar but they also displayed lots of the studio experimentation so prevalent with the early psychedelic bands. After shedding the 'Blues' portion of the name, the Steve Miller Band went on to record many albums and began having a string of hit singles in 1973 through to the early eighties. Steve Miller continues recording to this day.

Children of the Future (68), Sailor (69), Brave New World (69), Your Saving Grace (70), Number 5 (70), Recall the Beginning…Journey From Eden (72), The Joker (73)

• MIND GARAGE - USA

Formed 1968 in Morgantown, West Virginia; Mind Garage released a couple of singles full of intense fuzz-toned garage-punk with screaming sneering vocal style. They were signed to RCA and released a couple of albums but appeared to lose their way and failed to capture the aggression present on their early discs.

Mind Garage - An Electronic Rock Mass (69), Again - Electric Liturgy (70), A Lethal Dose of Hard Psych [Comp] (99)

• MISTY WIZARDS - USA

Formed in Ann Arbor, Michigan; the Misty Wizards also recorded as Spike Drivers. Their two Reprise singles were loaded with the obligatory psychedelia required for 1967. Everything from feedback, sitars, echo, trippy lyrics and shuffling beat its all there.

A Heavy Dose of Lyte Psych [Comp] (96)

• MISUNDERSTOOD - USA

Actually formed in Riverside, California, in early 1965 they played a garage style rock influenced by many of the R&B and surf bands of the day. Their career took a bit of a boost when they relocated to London, England in June of 1966. They were quickly signed to Fontana records and released a half a dozen singles in rapid succession. Their live performances were seen by many of the leading psychedelic bands in London but just as it appeared the band were about to make it big and they were deported back to America. The bands guitar player Glenn Ross Campbell returned to England with a completely new line-up but this second version never made it and eventually became Juicy Lucy who did in fact enjoy some success in the seventies.

Before the Dream Faded [Comp] (82), Golden Glass [Comp] (84), The Psychedelic Years Revisited [Comp] (92), Nuggets II Box Set [Comp] (01)

• MOBY GRAPE - USA

Formed in 1966 in San Francisco. Led by ex-Jefferson Airplane drummer Skip Spence Moby Grape created one of the classic West Coast psychedelic recordings. Its release was surrounded by never before seen publicity and five singles were released simultaneously. This 'over-exposure' didn't help the band. While "Omaha" managed to get some airplay most of the other singles suffered from programmers confusion over what to play. More unfortunately was the fact the band were arrested the night of the launch party with teenage girls and charged with contributing to the delinquincy of minors. In some respects the band never recovered and spent much of the rest of the year partying when not on the road. In November of 1967 they were summoned to New York by the record company to record their second album WOW. Unfortuantely they returned to San Francisco before supervising the mixing and all were unhappy with the finished results. Spence soon develped drug related problems and left the band eventually going solo after some hospitalization. The remainder of the band released a couple more roots-ier LPs before running into legal problems with their manager Matthew Katz.

Moby Grape (67), WoW (68), Moby Grape 69 (69), Truly Fine Citizen (69), The Psychedelic Years Revisited [Comp] (92), Psychedelic Frequencies [Comp] (96)

• MOCKINGBIRDS - UK

Formed in 1964 in Manchester, the Mockingbirds members included Graham Gouldman and Kevin Godley. Gouldman had great success writing songs for bands like the Yardbirds, the Hollies, and Herman's Hermits, unfortunately his songs recorded by his band the Mockingbirds were viewed by more than one label as not commercial enough. Both Gouldman and Godley would later form half of 10cc.

Nuggets II Box Set [Comp] (01)

• MOCK DUCK - Canada

Formed in 1967, in Vancouver, Mock Duck were one of the psychedelic regulars in the Vancouver club scene. Their West Coast guitar style and high-pitched organ jazzy sound was the epitome of the Vancouver psychedelic style. They recorded a few singles plus a limited edition live LP. Leader Joe Mock later went on to front the hippie oriented folk group Pied Pumpkin.

The History of Vancouver Rock & Roll, Vol. 4 [Comp] (91)

• MODULO 1000 - Brazil

Formed in the early seventies these guys created a busy-spacey psychedelic sound with instrumental solos weaving in and out of the compositions.

Nao Fale Com Peredes (71), Love, Peace & Poetry: Latin American Psychedelic Music [Comp] (97)

• MOGOLLAR - Turkey

Formed in the mid-sixties, Mogollar developed a reputation for infusing traditional Turkish instruments and melodies with English lyrics. The music has that Eastern influence with an overriding acoustic feel. In some ways it's a more authentic version of what Strawberry Alarm Clock were trying to achieve. As the sixties faded into the seventies, Mogollar began to experiment with even more adventurous ethnic rhythms and styles all blended with a psychedelic folk-rock sensibility.

Hava Narghile, Vol. 1 [Comp] (01)

• MOJO MEN - USA

Formed in 1965 as a male four-piece the Mojo Men released a number of singles before adding Jan Errico from the Vejtables to their line-up. The Mojo Men were one of those pre-psychedelic San Francisco bands that quickly adapted the folk and rock style to great effect having a nation wide hit in 1967 with the Stephen Stills penned Sit Down I Think I love You. The single was produced as a mini symphony by Van Dyke Parks, a full year before his work with Brian Wilson of the Beach Boys. Strong harmonies and a pleasant mix of male and female vocals are the hallmarks of the Mojo Men. Their later work benefited from more complicated arrangements borrowing from groups such as the Mamas and the Papas but they failed to make a dent in the charts and split up in the late sixties.

Mojo Magic (68), Dance With Me [Comp] (84), San Francisco Nights [Comp] (91), Nuggets I Box Set [Comp] (98)

• MOLES - UK

Formed in 1968 in London, the Moles were actually the transition from Simon Dupree and the Big Sound into Gentle Giant. The band was tired of the flower-power label and Derek Shulman was growing tired of everyone calling him Simon Dupree, so they quickly put the Moles together and under the production of George Martin created the single We Are The Moles (Pt. 1). The Moles sound displayed less of a flower-power sound but retained a psychedelic influence with compressed guitars and phased vocals. They eventually split up in 1969 making way for the creation of progressive rockers Gentle Giant.

Psychedelia at Abbey Road [Comp] (98)

• MONGRELS - Canada

Formed in 1967 in Winnipeg, the Mongrels recorded five singles during their time together. Their early material displayed a distinct Sgt Pepper influence. They disbanded in 1970.

A Heavy Dose of Lyte Psych [Comp] (96)

• MONKEES - USA

Formed in 1965 in Los Angeles, the story of the Monkees is well known. Four individuals selected out of over 400 who auditioned for a TV show about a pop group. Much like a fairy tale the TV group became a real group had an amazing string of hit singles and LPs. Their most psychedelic material comes off the Pisces, Aquarius, Capricorn and Jones Ltd. LP and the soundtrack to their psychedelic movie Head. Both albums featured plenty of studio gimmickry and even some very early synthesizer work on the former release. But it's worth pointing out how much of their music has stood the test of time and the band continues to perform to a loyal fan base to this day.

The Monkees (67), More of The Monkees (67), Headquarters (67), Pisces, Aquarius, Capricorn and Jones Ltd. (68), The Birds, The Bees and The Monkees (68), Instant Replay (69), Head (69), The Monkees Present (69), Changes (70)

• MOOCHE - UK

Formed in the late sixties in East Anglia, the Mooche recorded one single that failed to generate any interest in the charts and disbanded in the early 1970s.

Hot Smoke & Sassafras: Psychedelic Pstones Vol. 1 [Comp] (01)

• MOODY BLUES - UK

Formed in 1964 in Birmingham, they worked in the traditional beat and R&B world with their original line-up having a hit with Go Now before losing Denny Laine and Clint Warwick. The new line up with addition of Justin Hayward and John Lodge to the remaining Mike Pinder, Ray Thomas and Graeme Edge launched at the beginning of the psychedelic era in Britain. The Moody Blues soon became the epitome of dreamy-trippy-spaced out music with their symphonic psychedelic material. They released one single at the height of the Summer of Love entitled Love & Beauty a psychedelic-pop classic that then led to their prodigious album work starting with **Days of Future Past**. They maintained this image for a full seven albums before splitting up in 1973. They reformed in 1978 and virtually picked up where they left off with a long succession of orchestrated pop-prog-rock that continues to sell well to this day.

Days of Future past (67), In Search of The Lost Chord (68), On the Threshold of a Dream (69), To Our Children's Children's Children (69), A Question of Balance (70), Every Good Boy Deserves favour (71), Seventh Sojourn (72), The Psychedelic Scene [Comp] (98)

• MOONKYTE - UK

Formed in the late sixties in Bradford, this obscure outfit produced one LP full of trippy, softer psychedelia in the early seventies.

Moonkyte (71), Electric Sugarcube Flashbacks [Comp] (93)

• MOPS - Japan

Formed in 1966 in Tokyo, they began by playing many Beatles and Animals cover tunes before developing their own style. They were eventually billed as "The First Psychedelic Band in Japan" and added the obligatory fuzz-guitar and raga style. Moving along with the trends they gravitated to a heavier sound in 1969 and continued performing until splitting up in 1974. Their recorded output includes 11 albums.

Psychedelic Sounds in Japan (68), Love, Peace & Poetry: Japanese Psychedelic Music [Comp] (01), Nuggets II Box Set [Comp] (01)

• MORE-TISHIANS - USA

Formed in 1966 in Stillwater, Minnesota; the More-Tishian's main claim to fame was a single of 1967 called *Nowhere To Run* that featured a stong garage guitar sound but bright British Invasion style harmonies. As you might expect, they travelled to their live gigs in a hearse!

Orange, Sugar & Chocolate: Psychedelic Microdots of the 60's, Vol. 1 [Comp] (89)

• MORGEN, STEVE - USA

Formed in Long Island, New York; this band recorded just one LP which featured some great psychedelic guitar.

Morgen (69)

• MORNING GLORY - USA

Formed in 1967 in San Francisco, this short-lived outfit were regulars on the ballroom scene for a time. They created one LP with a classic laid-back West Coast hippie feel featuring some well placed sound effects and acid guitar solos.

Two Suns Worth (68)

• MOTHER EARTH - USA

Formed in 1966 in San Francisco, Mother Earth maintained their R&B musical foundation, embellishing it with the hippie flower-power elements of the day. They were regulars on the Bay area ballroom scene and recorded a couple of albums. Failing to make any significant impact on the charts, their lead vocalist, Tracy Nelson departed for Nashville and the band faded

from the scene shortly after.

Living with the Animals (68), Make a Joyous Noise (69)

• MOTHERLIGHT - UK

Formed in the late sixties, Motherlight recorded one album and are sometimes referred to by the name of the album. The material is full of moody, trippy songs all with a bit of a dark foreboding psychedelic edge.

Bobak, Jons, Malone (70), The Best of and The Rest of British Psychedelia [Comp] (91)

• MOTHERLOAD - Canada

Formed in 1968 in London, Ontario; with members coming from some of the more popular groups in the area, they are considered by some to be one of Canada's first supergroups, although their originating bands had only regional success. Their musical style borrowed heavily from the soul library of sounds which was very much in evidence on their first hit single *When I Die* released in 1969. Success was hard to follow-up and they split up in 1971.

When I Die (69)

• MOTHERS OF INVENTION - USA

[see: ZAPPA, FRANK]

• MOTHER TUCKERS YELLOW DUCK - Canada

Formed in 1967 in Vancouver, British Columbia; they were one of the key psychedelic bands in Vancouver's active hippie club scene, and played regularly at places like the Retinal Circus. They released a total of seven singles, and one LP before calling it a day in 1971. Their guitarist Donny McDougall then joined the Guess Who.

Home Grown Stuff (69), Starting a New Day (70)

• MOTHER'S LOVE - Holland

Formed in 1967 in Tiel they released a couple of psychedelic singles with an almost pop feel yet retaining a certain weirdness in the vocal delivery and instrumental style. The reedy organ that rambles around in the background makes for interesting listening on the track *Highway To Heaven*. After a few more singles they changed their name to Dream only to release a few more singles. Various band members were active in the music business well into the eighties.

Take One (67), Waterpipes & Dykes: Dutch Psychedelic Underground 1966 - 1972 Vol. 1 [Comp] ( )

• MOTIVES - Holland

Obscure Dutch band with at least one single released in the early seventies displaying many psychedelic folk-rock hallmarks.

Waterpipes & Dykes: Dutch Psychedelic Underground 1966 - 1972 Vol. 1 [Comp] ( )

• MOURNBLADE - UK

Formed in 1982 they crafted a heavier guitar oriented musical style with a strong space rock influence ala Hawkwind.

Times Running Out (85)

• MOUSE AND THE TRAPS - USA

Formed in 1965 in Tyler, Texas; Mouse & the Traps hit big with their first single sounding like a psychedelic clone of Bob Dylan and then went on to release 9 more singles each taking on more of acid-garage flavour before splitting up in 1969.

The Fraternity Years [Comp] (97), Nuggets I Box Set [Comp] (98)

• MOVE - UK

Formed in early 1966 in Birmingham. Leader Roy Wood pulled members together from existing outfits and then made the move to London where the band established themselves as the wild men of psychedelic rock. In August of 1966 they took over the Who's weekly spot at the Marquee Club. While their destructive stage antics included breaking almost anything in sight, their music was at times in the same spacey style as contemporaries Pink Floyd. As the band developed its style their music moved more in a pop-psychedelic direction with singles like *Flowers In The Rain* and *I Can Hear The Grass Grow*. In 1970 Jeff Lynne joined and when the Move finally disbanded in 1972 he and Wood created the Electric Light Orchestra.

The Move (68), Shazam (70), Looking On (70), Message From The Country (71), The Psychedelic Years 1966-1969 - Great Britain [Comp] (90), The Psychedelic Years Revisited [Comp] (92), Nuggets II Box Set [Comp] (01)

• MOVING SIDEWALKS - USA

Formed in the late sixties in Houston, Texas; Moving Sidewalks crafted a blues based garage style rock that leaned heavily in the psychedelic direction. Their biggest claim to fame was opening locally for Jimi Hendrix but the band failed to gain much attention outside of Houston and split up in the early seventies. Lead guitarist Billy Gibbons went on to form ZZ Top.

Flash (69), 99th Floor [Comp] (82)

• MU - USA

Formed in 1970 in California, MU evolved out of Fapardokly and then HMS Bounty. They recorded two albums of obscure experimental underground psychedelic music that featured some speedy fuzz-guitar, Beach Boy style harmonies and a loose trippy-hippie Grateful Dead rhythm style.

Mu (71), Lemurian Music (74), The Last Album (74/82), End of an Era [Comp] (88)

• MUSIC MACHINE - USA

Formed in 1965 in Los Angeles they were originally called the Ragamuffins and consisted mostly of disaffected folkies. With the addition of an organist they changed their appearance and their musical style to a more psychedelic garage flavour and had an almost immediate hit with a single called *Talk Talk* in 1966. They were never able to follow up this success and after a number of line-up changes they disbanded in 1969.

Turn on...The Music Machine (66), Bonniwell Music Machine (68), Close (69), Nuggets I Box Set [Comp] (98)

• MYSTERY TREND - USA

Formed in 1964 in San Francisco, Mystery Trend were one of the first bands on the psychedelic scene playing at a number of the early Fillmore gigs. Stories abound about how their equipment got even more use by other bands as it was used for gigs all over town. They spent a lot of time in the studio recording a folk influenced West Coast acid rock but little of their material has surfaced and they only released one official single before disbanding in late 1967.

San Francisco Nights [Comp] (91), Nuggets I Box Set [Comp] (98), So Glad I Found You [Comp] (99)

• MYSTIC TIDE - USA

Formed in 1966 in New York, Mystic Tide crafted a dark and foreboding style of psychedelia that borrowed elements of the Doors and Velvet Underground. They incorporated a mysterious Eastern influence, minor key melodies and heavily distorted guitar breaks into a number of self produced singles. Vaguely audible are other influences such as early Pink Floyd and Jimi Hendrix. Failing to garner much attention they disbanded in 1967.

Solid Ground [Comp] (94)

• MYTHOS - Germany

Formed in 1969 in Germany their style is perhaps more progressive rock but it contained more than a hint of a psychedelic space-rock sound.

Mythos (72), Dreamlab (75), Strange Guys (78), Concrete City (79), Quasar (80), Grand Prix (81)

• N' BETWEENS - UK

Formed in Birmingham, they moved down to London in 1966 and met up with American producer Kim Fowley. After recording a couple of singles released in 1967, they changed their name to Ambrose Slade, which was then just shortened to Slade, a band that found fame in the Glam Rock era of platform boots and glitter.

Psychedelia at Abbey Road [Comp] (98)

• N.V. GROEP '65 - Holland

Formed in the mid-sixties they developed a reputation as an exciting live act, adopting a number of garage-psychedelic influences, although they only recorded a couple of songs in 1966. Their sound is raw and devoid of much in the way of studio production.

Waterpipes & Dykes: Dutch Psychedelic Underground 1966 - 1972 Vol. 1 [Comp] ( )

• NASHVILLE TEENS - UK

Formed in 1962 in Weybridge, Surrey; and under the production skills of Mickie Most scored a Top 10 hit in 1964 with *Tobacco Road*. The single's aggressive guitar stance and hesitant arrangement made it a standout on the charts. They continued in a psych-R&B style through the height of 1967 and 1968 playing the clubs constantly. Through a myriad of personnel changes they persisted through to 1984 releasing eighteen singles but only one LP. Two members, Michael

Dunford and John Hawken both left in the late sixties and joined the progressive Renaissance.

Tobacco Road (64),

• NAZZ - USA

Formed in 1968 in Philadelphia and led by Todd Rundgren, the Nazz borrowed their name from a Yardbird's song and then adopted a style from the British psychedelic bands like the Move and Idle Race to create their own brand of psych-pop music. Great production, Beatle-esque harmonies and accomplished song writing set them in place to be the leaders of the emerging power-pop style. Rundgren departed in 1970 and began a solo career that continues to this day.

Nazz (69), Nazz Nazz (69), Nazz III (70), Nuggets I Box Set [Comp] (98)

• NEAT CHANGE - UK

Formed in 1968 in London, this short-lived and obscure outfit is most noted for its guitarist, Peter Banks. The group produced one single that was in a psychedelic-pop vein. Banks went on to play in the progressive rock bands Yes and Flash.

The Great British Psychedelic Trip, Vol. 2 [Comp] (88)

• NEIGHB'RHOOD CHILDR'N - USA

Formed in 1968 in San Francisco they were one of the more obscure bands playing the ballroom circuit. Musically they created a spacey style that was complimented by rather trippy vocals and lyrics. Psychedelic guitar jams are kept to a minimum although there are a few. They disbanded shortly after the release of their one and only LP.

Neighb'rhood Childr'n (68), Long Years in Space [Comp] (97)

• NEO MAYA - UK

An offshoot of Episode Six, Neo Maya turned out to be a one off effort by guitarist Graham Carter-Dimmock during the psychedelic Summer of Love in 1967. The adventurous single I Won't Hurt You went all out with full orchestral accompaniment and backing vocals from Episode Six band mate Roger Glover. The singles lack of success guaranteed the demise of future Neo Maya projects.

Hot Smoke & Sassafras: Psychedelic Pstones Vol. 1 [Comp] (01)

• NEW DAWN - UK

Formed in 1968, this English outfit produced one LP of heavier psychedelic music. The album contains a few folk influenced tunes but is primarily on the heavy rock side with trippy tunes driven by an overpowering organ style.

Mainline (69)

• NEW FORMULA - UK

Formed in 1967 In Corby in the North of England they released a handful of singles, not all of which would qualify as psychedelic, some even leaning more to the burgeoning progressive rock scene. Still they managed to incorporate some excellent flute and guitar interplay in these singles before finally fading from the scene.

Sax Player Ricky Dodd eventually resurfaced in Tucky Buzzard.

Hot Smoke & Sassafras: Psychedelic Pstones Vol. 1 [Comp] (01)

• NEW SALVATION ARMY BANNED - USA

[see: SALVATION]

• NEW TWEEDY BROTHERS - USA

Formed in 1966 in Portland, Oregon; they played a fair bit in the San Francisco area and established quite a name for themselves. Their one and only LP release in 1968 featured a mix of pleasant harmonies loaded with echo, punctuated by psychedelic guitar jams. A classic West Coast folk-rock piece of psychedelia.

New Tweedy Brothers (68)

• NEW YORKERS - USA

Formed in the mid-sixties in Portland, Washington; they were quickly signed to a semi-major label but failed to make any significant impact with their psychedelic-pop style. They eventually changed their name and landed their own TV show using their family name called The Hudson Brothers.

The History of Northwest Rock Vol. 3: Psychedelic Seattle [Comp] (00)

• NICE - UK

Originally the back-up band for P.P. Arnold, they took off on their own in October of 1967 and quickly became one of the favourite, adventurous underground psychedelic bands. They were soon signed to the Immediate label. The Nice was fronted by Keith Emerson, whose classical training leant a certain structure to their compositions. The band spend most of the psychedelic years performing outlandish stunts which included burning an American flag while performing the song America at the Royal Albert Hall in London. After failing to make the desired inroads in the United States, the band split up after 1970, which led to the formation of the progressive trio Emerson Lake and Palmer.

The Thoughts of Emerlist Davjack (67), Ars Longa Vita Brevis (68), The Nice (69), Five Bridges Suite (70), The Psychedelic Years Revisited [Comp] (92), Psychedelic Perceptions [Comp] (96)

• NICHOLS - Holland

Formed in 1967 they released four singles with a strong harmony driven garage style with a slight psychedelic influence.

Waterpipes & Dykes: Dutch Psychedelic Underground 1966 - 1972 Vol. 1 [Comp] ( )

• NICO - USA

Part of the New York proto-punk movement Nico joined the Velvet Underground in 1965 where her mysterious persona was quickly mined to project the bands avant-garde stance. She left the group in 1967 when it was feared she might have been stealing the band's limelight. She later hooked up with John Cale and others making a series of recordings that featured her unique anti-pop melancholy vocal style. She died of a brain haemorrhage in 1988 after falling off her bike and striking her head.

Chelsea Girl (68), The Marble Index (69), Desertshore (71), The End (74), The Psychedelic Years Revisited [Comp] (92), Psychedelic Frequencies [Comp] (96)

• NIRVANA - UK

Formed in late 1965 in London's West End, Nirvana was created by multi-instrumentalists Patrick Campbell-Lyons, Alex Spyropoulos and guitarist Ray Singer. Their dream-like material was filled with interesting baroque and classical touches. The partnership fell apart in early 1968 just after their one and only hit *Rainbow Chaser* settled in at number 34 on the UK charts and Singer departed to a career in studio work. Campbell-Lyons and Spyropoulos soldiered on with guests through to 1972 before disbanding altogether. New material was recorded in 1993 and put together with tracks from 1969.

The Story of Simon Simopath (68), All of Us (68), To Markus III (70), Local Anesthetic (71), Songs of Love and Praise (72), The Psychedelic Years Revisited [Comp] (92), Psychedelic Perceptions [Comp] (96)

• NOBODY'S CHILDREN - USA

Formed in 1968 in Dallas, Texas; this obscure sixties garage-punk band featured a style loaded with bad attitude, sneering vocals and only a hint of psychedelia. Their only single release *Good Times* came out June of 1968 and was shunned by radio stations everywhere for its bleak sound.

Orange, Sugar & Chocolate: Psychedelic Microdots of the 60's, Vol. 1 [Comp] (89)

• NOCTURNS - UK

Formed in 1967 in Birmingham this obscure psychedelic-pop band is mostly known for their 1968 reworking of *Carpet Man* written by Jim Webb and originally recorded by the Fifth Dimension. Drummer John Camp later turned up in Renaissance while two other members became part of the New Seekers.

Psychedelia at Abbey Road [Comp] (98)

• NORTHWEST COMPANY - Canada

Formed in late 1966 in a small town outside Vancouver, British Columbia called Haney, they were originally called the Bad Boys but changed their name to the Northwest Company in flurry of patriotism in 1967. Their music was always harder edge, not far removed from the garage scene, with plenty of Kinks references. They recorded seven singles between 1967 and 1971.

The History of Vancouver Rock & Roll, Vol. 4 [Comp] (91)

• TOM NORTHCOTT TRIO - Canada

Northcott from Vancouver, British Columbia is one of the founding artists for the Canadian West Coast folk-hippie scene. He started singing in clubs in 1963 and by 1966 was part of a trio that played a number of gigs in San Francisco at the Matrix and the Avalon in 1966. His relaxed folk-psych style got him a few hits on the radio but Northcott eventually took a step back from the live

scene in 1973 to concentrate on studio efforts.

Upside Downside (71)

• NUCLEUS - Canada

[see: LORDS OF LONDON]

Nucleus (69), Made in Canada, Vol. 3 1961 - 1974 [Comp] (91)

• OBSCURED BY CLOUDS - USA

Formed in 1997 in Portland, Oregon; this trio have taken the Pink Floyd spacey style of songs like *Breathe* and *Cymbaline* and pushed it in their own direction. As a new-ish band many of the tunes on their first release are covers but you can see how this influence is shaping their own compositions that in many respects pays homage to one of psychedelic's founding bands.

Bleed (98)

• ODYSSEY - USA

Formed in the late sixties in Brentwood, Long Island, New York; they are one of those bands that bridged the divide between psychedelia and progressive rock. There is plenty of psychedelic acid-guitar spread throughout the compositions but more time is spent of making the arrangements a little more complicated.

Setting Forth...Improvising Against the Future (71)

• OMNI OPERA - UK

This newer band is clearly inspired by the likes of Ozric Tentacles and creates a spacey psychedelia with roots in bands like Pink Floyd and Hawkwind.

• ONE WAY STREET - Canada

Formed in 1966 in Vancouver, British Columbia; One Way Street created their own brand of garage-punk influenced psychedelia until 1968 when the band split up. They played around Vancouver a lot but only ever recorded two singles.

The History of Vancouver Rock & Roll, Vol. 4 [Comp] (91)

• ONYX - UK

Formed in 1966 in Cornwall, Onyx were originally known as Rick and the Hayseeds and developed quite a loyal following based on their live act. A short-lived outfit that took the time to create a pop-psychedelic sound with elements of both the Beach Boys and the Beatles. After six singles that went nowhere they decided to call it a day. They returned briefly in the early seventies under the name Salamander.

Hot Smoke & Sassafras: Psychedelic Pstones Vol. 1 [Comp] (01)

• OPAL BUTTERFLY - UK

Formed in 1968 in London, this obscure outfit was home briefly to Lemmy (from Hawkwind) after leaving Sam Gopal. Of note is that the group also had future members of not only Hawkwind but also of the Nice and Arthur Brown. They only ever recorded three singles but their music can be described as the organ drenched sound of Vanilla Fudge mixed with the vocal style of the Moody Blues with some wild guitar thrown in the mix.

Electric Sugarcube Flashbacks [Comp] (93)

• OPEN MIND - UK

Formed in 1968 in London they originally went by the name Drag Set, before adopting the more psychedelic Open Mind. They took a freakbeat sound and injected the pre-requisite psychedelic sounds like fuzz, wah-wah pedals and interesting harmonies.

The Open Mind (69), Nuggets II Box Set [Comp] (01)

• ORANGE BICYCLE - UK

Formed in 1967 in London they originally were called Robb Storme and the Whispers. Musically their music consisted of cleverly crafted psychedelic-pop tunes with strong harmonies and melodies.

The Orange Bicycle (70), The Best of and The Rest of British Psychedelia [Comp] (91)

• ORANGE MACHINE - UK

Formed in 1968 in Ireland, Orange Machine created a psychedelic sound similar to Tomorrow. The two singles released feature some searing psychedelic guitar work. They failed to attract much attention and the band split apart in mid 1969.

Hot Smoke & Sassafras: Psychedelic Pstones Vol. 1 [Comp] (01)

• ORANGE SEAWEED - UK

Formed in 1968 Orange Seaweed was originally known as the Kingpins. Their distinctly British freakbeat sound quickly evolved into a psychedelic style to release the single *Stay Awhile* b/w *Pictures In The Sky* in April of 1968. It went unnoticed, and much later lead guitarist Ray Neale worked briefly with Screaming Lord Such in the early 1980s.

Hot Smoke & Sassafras: Psychedelic Pstones Vol. 1 [Comp] (01)

• ORCHIDS & VINES - Canada

Formed in 1994 in Vancouver, British Columbia; Orchards & Vines had taken the route of self-promotion and distribution. Featuring powerful female vocals in the finest Jefferson Airplane tradition their compositions evoke all the finest of the psychedelic era without sounding like a tribute band. Hardly retro, Orchards & Vines craft trippy songs powered by a tightly knit unit of guitar, bass, cello and drums.

Tomorrow's Yesterday (00)

• ORGANGRINDERS - USA

Formed in 1969 in Baltimore, Maryland; they produced one album that featured a classic flower-power pop style. Lots of nice harmonies and catchy melodies.

Out of the Egg (70)

• ORKUSTRA - USA

Formed in 1965 in San Francisco, they had the distinction of being David LaFlame's (It's a Beautiful Day) first group and also featured the notorious San Francisco Digger Emmet Grogan on vocals. Their musical efforts leaned more to the avant-garde and while they played the local ballrooms they failed to produce any recordings.

• OS MUTANTES - Brazil

Formed in 1966 in Brazil, this art collective released upwards of five albums before disbanding in 1973. They incorporated a myriad of influences including a strong ethnic flavour. Imagine a mix of Beatle-ish harmonies and orchestrations and strange sound effects all blended together with electric and local traditional instrumentation with a strong garage-psychedelic theme.

Os Mutantes (68), Mutantes (69), A Divina Comedia ou Ando Meio Desligado (70), Jardim Electrico (71), Nuggets II Box Set [Comp] (01)

• OTHER HALF - USA

Formed in 1966 in Los Angeles, the Other Half came out of the psychedelic Sunset Strip scene but retained a strong garage-punk, R&B style which only added to their Yardbirds influenced material. Lead guitarist Randy Holden had previously played with the Sons of Adam and then left the Other Half to replace Leigh Stephens in Blue Cheer in 1968.

The Other Half (68), Mr. Pharmacist [Comp] (82), Nuggets I Box Set [Comp] (98)

• OUTCASTS - USA

Formed in 1965 in San Antonio, Texas; they were part of a group of Texas bands that created a powerful psychedelic garage sound that inspired dozens of others. Their material is primarily fast-paced shorter songs complete with lots of echo, weedy-organ and fuzz-guitar. They eventually recorded some five singles before splitting up in 1967.

I'm in Pittsburgh and it's Raining [Comp] (95)

• OUTER LIMITS - UK

Formed in 1967 in Leeds, the Outer Limits evolved from the skiffle group, Three Gs Plus One. Musically they retained a rough-edge, garage feel to their music but placed a strong emphasis on their harmonies. In the end they released four singles that failed to attract much notice.

The Great British Psychedelic Trip, Vol. 1 [Comp] (88)

• OUTSIDERS - Holland

Formed in 1964 in Holland while still in their teens, they released a number of singles through the next couple years and by 1966 they were one of Holland's most recognized psych-garage bands. What made the Outsiders unique was their broad range of psychedelic influences including the Pretty Things, the Byrds, Tim Hardin as well as local folk traditions. Instrumentally they included a host of odd items including mandolin and Harpsichords. Their musical style took into account the many diverse elements available going from folk to rock to a trippy spaciness. Following many singles and three albums they split up in 1969 with some members pursuing solo careers.

The Outsiders (67), CQ (68), Best of The Outsiders [Comp] (79), CQ Sessions [Comp] (94), Nuggets II Box Set [Comp] (01)

• OXFORD CIRCLE - USA

Formed in 1966 in Sacramento, California; they were soon regulars on the San Francisco ballroom circuit. Their time together was short and their psych-garage style was recorded for posterity on only one single release in 1966 entitled, *Foolish Woman*. Guitarist Dehner Patten joined up with Gary Yoder to form Kak in 1969.

Live at the Avalon '66 [Comp] (98)

• OXPETALS - USA

Formed in the late sixties in upstate New York they produced one album that's best described as hippie-folk crossed with flower-power pop. It manages to display the return to roots musical attitude so prevent at the time.

The Oxpetals (70)

• OZRIC TENTACLES - UK

Formed in 1982 in London they've developed a loyal following over the many independent cassette and now CD releases featuring sprawling trippy jams that feature an equal mix of keyboards and acid-guitar. The band's entire image is based on a hippie ethic in name and style. They've even been described as a "hipper" Hawkwind in some circles.

Pungent Effulgent (89), Erpland (90), Strangeitude (91), Jurrassic Shift (93), Arborescence (94), Become the Other (95), Curious Corn (97), Waterfall Cities (99), The Hidden Step (00), Pyramidin ((01)

• P205 - Germany

A mixture of heavy psychedelic and progressive rock, with spacey-ness of PINK FLOYD and heavy guitar style of BLACK WIDOW.

P205 (75/93), Vivat Progressio Pereat Mundus (78)

• PH PHACTOR JUG BAND - USA

Formed in 1964 in California they relocated to Portland, Oregon in 1965. As you might expect from their name their music was somewhat bluegrass influenced psychedelic rock that fit well with the whole flower-power era. They recorded only one official single, but much of their studio tapes have been assembled on the compilation listed. As their popularity increased they returned to San Francisco where they became popular on the Fillmore and Avalon Ballroom circuit.

Merryjuana [Comp] (80), The History of Northwest Rock Vol. 3: Psychedelic Seattle [Comp] (00)

• PACIFIC DRIFT - UK

Formed in 1969 in London they were originally known as Sponge. When Sponge split up, saxophonist Jack Lancaster left to form Blodwyn Pig, leaving Lawrence Ardenes to put Pacific Drift together. Ardenes had originally been in the freakbeat group Wimple Winch and recorded a few unsuccessful singles before creating the slightly more psychedelic Sponge. Pacific Drift cut one single for Deram and an LP. Due to a lack of interest the band split shortly after the albums release in 1970.

Feelin' Free (70), The Great British Psychedelic Trip, Vol. 2 [Comp] (88)

• PAINTED FACES - USA

Formed in 1966 in Fort Meyers, Florida; Painted Faces recorded at least three singles of psych-garage songs. They incorporated a host of prevalent influences including folk-rock, soul and even a hint of pop-ness. Their drummer was drafted in 1968 and the band split up shortly after.

Anxious Colour [Comp] (94)

• PAINTED SHIP - Canada

Formed in 1966 in Vancouver, British Columbia; Painted Ship recorded two official singles that typified the early psychedelic-garage style prominent for the day.

Afterthought: The History of Vancouver's Rock and Roll, Vol 3 [Comp] ( )

• PALMER, BRUCE - Canada

After a career that included stints in Jack London & the Sparrows, Buffalo Springfield and Crosby Stills Nash & Young, Palmer decided to go solo. He enlisted a host of old friends including Rick James and members of the L.A. based Kaleidoscope to create an LP consisting of four long tracks of Eastern influenced trippy psychedelia. He later went on to join a Sikh sect.

The Cycle is Complete (69)

• PANDEMONIUM - UK

Formed in 1964 in Kent, they were originally called the Pandas, changing their name to the more fitting Pandemonium soon after. This obscure pop-psychedelic British band managed to put out three singles but failed to attract any attention to themselves and disbanded in 1967.

Electric Sugarcube Flashbacks [Comp] (93), Nuggets II Box Set [Comp] (01)

• PAPA BEARS MEDICINE SHOW - Canada

Formed in 1968 in Vancouver, British Columbia; their musical style was a blend of West Coast acoustic flavoured hippie-folk.

A Memory Album of Papa Bears Music (70)

• PAPER BLITZ TISSUE - UK

Formed in 1967 in London, this obscure outfit produced one single *Boy Meets Girl* in the classic whimsical psychedelic-pop style with a great psychedelic introduction. Although popular as a live act in the London clubs they disbanded shortly after the singles release.

• PAPER GARDEN - USA

Formed in the late sixties in New York they created one LP that has since been reissued a couple of times. The musical style was very Eastern influenced.

The Paper Garden Presents... (69)

• PARK AVENUE PLAYGROUND - USA

Formed in 1967 this obscure band from the Chicago

area created a trippy hard edged psychedelic music complete with spaced out lyrics, prominent Vox style organ plus loads of fuzz-guitar work.

Beyond the Calico Wall [Comp] (93)

• PAUPERS - Canada

Formed in 1965 in Toronto, Ontario; they were originally called the Spats. They became a five-piece band and changed their name in 1966. Bob Dylan's manager, Albert Grossman picked them up and soon had them playing in all the hippie ballrooms across America including the Fillmore, the Whisky A-Go-Go and the Boston Tea Party. In 1967 they hit the big time when they opened for Jefferson Airplane in New York. Drummer and founding member Skip Prokop left in 1968 and did loads of session work with everyone from Richie Havens to Mike Bloomfield. Bassist Brad Campbell left to join Janis Joplin's new band and soon Prokop met up with Paul Hoffert to form Lighthouse in 1969.

Magic People (67), Ellis Island (68), Made in Canada, Vol. 3 1961 - 1974 [Comp] (91), Made in Canada, Vol. 4 1961 - 1974 [Comp] (91)

• PEANUT BUTTER CONSPIRACY - USA

Formed in 1966 in San Francisco, they used to be called Ashes and their original drummer was none other than Spencer Dryden who later found a spot in Jefferson Airplane. The Peanut Butter Conspiracy created a lush full, heavily produced sound that while very popular at the live club level never translated into any mainstream hits. They split up after the release of their third LP.

The Peanut Butter Conspiracy is Spreading (67), The Great Conspiracy (68), For Children All Ages (69), Psychedelic Visions [Comp] (96)

• PEARLS BEFORE SWINE - USA

Formed in the mid-sixties in New York by folkie Tom Rapp, Pearls Before Swine created a type of acid-folk psychedelic sound heavily influenced by the early work of Bob Dylan. They released six drug-laced albums before Rapp moved on to a solo career under his own name. He then recorded three more LPs before relocating to Holland.

One Nation Underground (67), Balaklava (69), These Things Too (69), The Use of Ashes (70), City of Gold (71), Beautiful Lies You Could Live In (71), The Psychedelic Years Revisited [Comp] (92)

• PEBBLE EPISODE - USA

Formed in 1967 in Brooklyn, New York; this obscure group managed to record at least one single that stepped out of the garage feel and landed squarely in the world of psychedelia. Who knows maybe there was more.

Beyond the Calico Wall [Comp] (93)

• PERTH COUNTRY CONSPIRACY - Canada

Formed in 1969 in Stratford, Ontario; they created a number of albums that were their own special take on psychedelic hippie-folk music. Their music is not dissimilar to the Incredible String Band at times. They disbanded in the late seventies.

Mushroom Music (69), Cabin Fever (69), Perth Country Conspiracy Does Not Exist (70), Alive (71)

• PESKY GEE - UK

Formed in 1968 In Leicester, Pesky Gee's first attempt at the charts was a reworking of the Vanilla Fudge track *Where Is My Mind?* in 1969. Failure to crack the charts led to the early demise of Pesky Gee with most of the members showing up in the 1970's Black Widow.

Exclamation Mark (69), Hot Smoke & Sassafras: Psychedelic Pstones Vol. 1 [Comp] (01)

• PHANTOMS - USA

Formed in 1967 in Portland, Oregon; they recorded a couple of singles that featured a Beatles influenced psychedelic style.

• PHLUPH - USA

Formed in 1967 in Boston, they recorded one LP of pop-psychedelia that is awash in the mood of the day. They split after the release of the LP.

Phluph (68)

• PICCADILLY LINE - UK

Formed in 1967 in London they produced four singles and one LP that captures the psychedelic-pop and flower-power music of the times.

The Huge World of Emily Small (67)

• PICTURE - USA

Formed in the late sixties in Milwaukee, Wisconsin; this obscure band were known to have recorded at least one single in the Nashville area. Lots of spacey phasing, echo and a trippy vocal style are the things to look out for.

A Heavy Dose of Lyte Psych [Comp] (96)

• PINK FLOYD - UK

Formed in 1965 in London, Pink Floyd soon became the musical leaders of the London underground movement and then progressed musically as did the technology around them. They were the first to perform at the Marquee's Spontaneous Underground incorporating their own lightshow setup and then became the house band at the UFO for a time. After a couple of psychedelic albums they moved beyond Syd Barrett who was consumed with LSD. Dave Gilmore was brought in as a replacement and they settled into some dreamy spacey soundscapes and then created Dark Side of the Moon. What followed were a series of great concept albums that in many ways set the example for many bands. They continue to be an influence on both psychedelic and progressive rock bands to this day. Their last studio recording was released in 1995 and the tour in support was sold-out worldwide showing the staying power of Pink Floyd. Great material, excellent production and fine musicianship.

Piper At the Gates of Dawn (67), A Saucerful of Secrets (68), More (69), Ummagumma (69), Atom Heart Mother (70), Meddle (71), Relics (71), Obscured by Clouds (72), Dark Side of the Moon (73), Wish You Were Here (75), Animals (77), The Wall (79), The Final Cut (83), Works (83), Momentary Lapse of Reason (87), Delicate Sound of Thunder (88), The Division Bell (94), Pulse (95),

• PLAGUE - UK

Formed in the late sixties this obscure band released one psychedelic single entitled *Looking For The Sun* in 1968.

The Psychedelic Scene [Comp] (98)

• PLASTIC CLOUD - Canada

Formed in 1968 in Bay Ridge, Ontario; they recorded one LP that is now highly sought after as representative of some of the best psychedelia of the times. Lots of fuzz-guitar and Easter influences along with some rather trippy lyrics.

The Plastic Cloud (69)

• PLASTIC PENNY - UK

Formed in 1967 in London they were originally known as the Universals. They created a number of singles, their first *Everything I Am* turned out to be a Top 10 hit. The remainder failed miserably. Their three LPs display the band's pop influenced psychedelia and stand up reasonably well as markers of the time. After splitting up in 1970, most of the members landed with their feet in other groups, Mick Grabham showed up in Procol Harum, Paul Raymond joined Chicken Shack, and Nigel Olsson went to the Spencer Davis Group and then Elton John.

Two Sides of a Penny (68), Currency (69), Heads You Win, Tails I Lose (70)

• PLEASURE FAIR - USA

Formed in 1967 in Los Angeles this four-piece crafted one LP with a classic psychedelic-pop style. The LP was produced by David Gates before he put his band Bread together.

Pleasure Fair (67)

• POETS - UK

Formed in 1964 in Glasgow playing in an R&B and beat style with a distinctive 12-string guitar jangle. They were signed by Rolling Stones manager Andrew Loog Oldham but despite such help in high places they failed at every corner. Shifting personnel plagued them and by 1967 there were no original members left. While they released upwards of nine singles between 1964 and 1971 they never fulfilled the promise held out for them and they disbanded in 1970.

The Great British Psychedelic Trip, Vol. 1 [Comp] (88), The Great British Psychedelic Trip, Vol. 2 [Comp] (88), In Your Tower [Comp] (97), The Psychedelic Scene [Comp] (98), Nuggets II Box Set [Comp] (01)

• PRETTY THINGS - UK

Formed in 1963 in London, they started life as an R&B group following in the style of the Rolling Stones. In fact their image was somewhat even wilder than that of the Stones. Chart success eluded them and as they saw the changing musical landscape in early 1967, they decided to throw their hat in the psychedelic ring. Singles such as *Talking About the Good Times* b/w

Walking Through My Dreams provided a foretaste of the more progressive material they would create. Their first true psychedelic album was Emotions in 1967. The Pretty Things have the distinction of being somewhat ahead of their time by writing the first rock opera, concept album entitled SF Sorrow in 1968. Their later albums tended to be simply straight-ahead rock.

The Great British Psychedelic Trip, Vol. 1 [Comp] (88), The Great British Psychedelic Trip, Vol. 2 [Comp] (88), In Your Tower [Comp] (97), The Psychedelic Scene [Comp] (98), Nuggets II Box Set [Comp] (01)

• PRINCIPLE EDWARD'S MAGIC THEATRE - UK

Formed in 1969 at Exeter University by a group of hippie students they quickly fell in with the original psychedelic underground scene creating an unusual acid-folk-spacey-psychedelia. Their live show incorporated performance theatre, lights, costumes, dancing, the works. Their third and last LP **Round One** was produced by Pink Floyd's Nick Mason. They never really survived the transition to progressive rock, but got lost in their music, dance, lights and poetry. Unusual!

The Great British Psychedelic Trip, Vol. 1 [Comp] (88), The Great British Psychedelic Trip, Vol. 2 [Comp] (88), In Your Tower [Comp] (97), The Psychedelic Scene [Comp] (98)

• PROCOL HARUM - UK

Formed in 1967 originally as an R&B band called the Paramounts, Procol Harum had a huge hit in 1967 called *Whiter Shade of Pale* which was inspired musically by Bach. The single became a classic during the Summer of Love. Procol Harum carved out their style through the crafty combination of the individual differences. They were certainly one of the first bands to create musical epics, long and winding stories that held your attention throughout. Keith Reid's lyrics and Gary Brooker's distinctive voice created some amazing aural images. Procol Harum were one of the core bands to make the move to progressive rock. After recording some ten albums they disbanded in 1977 only to reform in the nineties for a couple of recordings.

Procol Harum (67), Shine on Brightly (68), A Salty Dog (69), Home (70), Broken Barricades (71) Live In Concert (72), Grand Hotel (73), Exotic Birds and Fruit (74), Procol's Ninth (75), Something Magic (77), The Psychedelic Years 1966-1969 - Great Britain [Comp] (90), Prodigal Stranger (91)

• PROFESSOR MORRISON'S LOLLIPOP - USA

Formed in 1967 in Lincoln, Nebraska; they were originally known as the Coachmen and played a garage-rock before psychedelia hit them. They changed their name and their fashion sense and created some psychedelic-pop material that followed in the footsteps of bands like the Strawberry Alarm Clock.

Happy Together: The Very Best of White Whale Records [Comp] (99)

• PRUDENCE - Norway

Guitar dominated progressive material that falls into the folk-psychedelic mould.

Takk Te Dokk ( ), Drunk and Happy ( ), No. 3 ( ), 11 12 75 Live (75), Tomorrow Maybe Vanished ( ), The Legendary Tapes Vol. 1 ( )

• **PULSE - USA**

Formed in New Haven, Connecticut; they were originally called Bram Rigg Set and the Shags, eventually taking the name Pulse. Their music was primarily a harder edged psychedelic sound but also included a number of strange and unusual spoken word creepy elements.

The Pulse ( ), Beyond the Calico Wall [Comp] (93)

• **PURE LOVE AND PLEASURE - USA**

Formed in 1968 in San Francisco they recorded one LP that was a mix of the laid back hippie-rock style with a more upbeat flower-power pop.

A Record of Pure Love and Pleasure (68)

• **PURPLE GANG - UK**

Formed in 1965 in Stockport, they took their name from some obscure group of gangsters in Detroit. They were signed to the folkie Transatlantic label and soon produced the kind of songs that got them labelled as Britain's answer to the Lovin' Spoonful. Their playful, jug-band influenced single *Granny Takes A Trip* was banned by the BBC for potential drug references. The Purple Gang performed at all the usual psychedelic haunts including UFO and the 14-hour Technicolor Dream. They were generally included in the underground scene even though their one and only LP took a more straight forward hard rock approach. They split up in 1968 after the release of the LP.

The Purple Gang Strikes (68), The Psychedelic Years Revisited [Comp] (92)

• **PUSSY - UK**

Formed in Hertfordshire, Pussy was originally known as Wc Shake Milk. Their music in typical British psychedelic fashion went from bright and sunny psych-pop one minute to dreamy, spacey Pink Floyd style episodes the next minute. To their credit they were capable of writing nice melodies and delivering pleasant harmonies however they never really cracked the charts and faded from the scene.

Pussy Plays (69), The Best of and The Rest of British Psychedelia [Comp] (91)

• **QOPH - Sweden**

Formed in 1994 they're a modern psychedelic band, with a strong West Coast acid-rock style. The compositions are long, jam-filled blues based affairs with many guitar solos. Qoph have injected a fair share of prog elements to keep the music interesting for prog fans.

Kalejdoskopiska Aktiviteter (99)

• **QUEEN'S NECTARINE MACHINE - USA**

Formed in 1968 in New York this band came out of the Kasenetz-Katz stable of psychedelic-bubblegum bands. Their one and only album has a little bit of both

including some rather strange freak out sessions.

The Mystical Powers of Roving Tarot Gamble (69)

• **QUICKSILVER MESSENGER SERVICE - USA**

Formed in 1964 in San Francisco, Quicksilver Messenger Service became known for their fiery acid-rock guitar work and were favourites on the ballroom circuit. Two members, Greg Elmore and Gary Duncan originally played with the pre-psychedelic garage-punk band the Brogues. Following their performance at the Monterey Pop Festival they were signed to Capitol Records and while hit singles eluded them, they scored respectably in LP sales. In fact their second LP which contained a 25 minute rendition of Bo Diddley's *Who Do You Love* is perhaps the best example of what was experienced on any given night of the heydays of the San Francisco ballroom days.

Quicksilver Messenger Service (68), Happy Trails (69), Shady Grove (69), Just For Love (70), What About Me (71), Quicksilver (71), Comin' Thru (72), Solid Silver (75), San Francisco Nights [Comp] (91), Psychedelic Visions [Comp] (96)

• **QUINTESSENCE - UK**

Formed in 1968, in London, Quintessence emerged from the Landbroke Grove area, London's answer to Haight-Ashbury. They played a unique blend of Eastern-flavoured jazz-rock with a heavy dose of East Indian inspiration. They became known for their hippie-lifestyle inspired live events, where they toured with as many as fifty people creating huge pick-nick like affairs. Their music soon took on more of a hypnotic or trance feel as they strived to become what they referred to as a "good vibrations" band. They eventually disbanded in 1973.

In Blissful Company (69), Quintessence - Open Up To You (70), Dive Deep (71), Self (72), Indweller (73), The Psychedelic Years Revisited [Comp] (92)

• **RABBLE - Canada**

Formed in 1966 in Montreal, Quebec; they started out as the typical cover band playing everything from the Beatles to Dylan. In time they developed their own unique psychedelic-pop style and recorded a couple of albums. As you might expect lots of fuzz-guitar with some Sgt. Pepper influences.

The Rabble Album (68), Give Us Back Elaine! (69)

• **RAIK'S PROGRESS - USA**

Formed in 1966 in Fresno, California; Raik's Progress featured a strong folk feel in the vocal department, with blended voices and harmonies, but underneath the fuzzed-out rhythm guitar work and tremolo laden lead guitar were all psychedelic. They were known to have recorded only one single.

Beyond the Calico Wall [Comp] (93)

• **RAIN PARADE - USA**

Formed in the early eighties in Los Angeles, Rain Parade were a major player in the so-called "paisley underground' psychedelic revival happening in LA at the time. Borrowing heavily from the past they created an updated style that attempted to reflect a psychedelic attitude in lyrics as well as musical style. Vocalist and guitarist Dave Roback left in 1984 to form Opal. Rain Parade carried on for a time, and were signed to Island Records. Failing to gain success they split up in 1988.

Emergency 3rd Rail Trip (83), Beyond the Sunset (85), Crashing Dream (86), Explosions in the Glass Palace (88)

• RAINBOW FFOLLY - UK

Formed in 1967 in London by brothers John and Richard Dunsterville. They created a psychedelic-pop style that was along the lines of what the Beatles were doing during 1967, in that they placed emphasis on melodies and harmonies and incorporated all kinds of studio gimmickry and sound effects. They recorded one LP before splitting up. The brothers later turned up doing some session work for Rick Wakeman early in his solo career.

Sallies Fforth (68)

• RAINY DAZE - USA

Formed in 1965 in Denver, Colorado; they were originally known for more of an R&B sound. Later they became involved with Phil Spector and treated to his special production style and were set to have a huge national hit with *That Acapulco Gold* in the summer of 1967 until radio programmers realized what the song was about. The album contains a variety of psychedelic influenced pop songs. The band split up in 1968, with songwriters John Carter and lead vocalist Tim Gilbert writing the hit *Incense and Peppermints* for the Strawberry Alarm Clock.

That Acapulco Gold (67), Psychedelic Visions [Comp] (96)

• RASCALS - USA

Formed in 1964 in New York City they evolved out of a group called the Starlighters and first went by the name the Young Rascals and based their early hits on an R&B or soul foundation. That all changed in 1967 as demonstrated by a string of hits starting with *Groovin'*, *How Can I Be Sure* and *It's Wonderful*. By the end of 1967 they changed their name to just the Rascals and were fully into flower-power. The hits kept coming and the Rascals proved to have great staying power as well as writing ability. They eventually disbanded in 1972 when all members took up positions in other lesser known groups.

The Young Rascals (66), Collections (67), Groovin' (67), Once Upon A Dream (68), Freedom Suite (69), See (69), Search and Nearness (71), Peaceful World (71), The Island of Real (72)

• RASPUTIN & THE MAD MONKS - USA

Formed in 1967 in Massachusetts, this obscure band only recorded a few tracks, mostly British Invasion material but also a strange take on the Electric Prunes' *I Had Too Much To Dream* full of strange sound effects and studio production. Bizarre stuff!

Beyond the Calico Wall [Comp] (93)

• RAVES - USA

Formed in 1967 in Brooklyn, New York this obscure group recorded at least three singles of melodic psychedelic-pop music. The Raves maintained a smooth, pronounced British Invasion harmonic feel in the vocals overtop of the raga beat and trippy organ work.

Beyond the Calico Wall [Comp] (93)

• RED CRAYOLA - USA

Formed in 1966 in Houston, Texas; they were quickly signed to a local label to record a couple of albums that were part psych-garage and part avant-garde. Their time together was short but various member combinations continued to record together well into the nineties.

Parable of Arable Land (67), God Bless The Red Crayola and All Who Sail With Her (68)

• REIGN GHOST - Canada

Formed in 1969 in Toronto, Ontario; they recorded two albums featuring Lynda Squires on vocals. Both albums feature that latter day psychedelic sound of a ringing guitar laid overtop of organ. Lots of electronic droning, acid-fuzz-guitar breaks with some great Squires led harmonies.

Reign Ghost (69), Reign Ghost Featuring Lynda Squires (71)

• RENAISSANCE - Mexico

Formed in the early seventies, Renaissance incorporated many diverse musical influences to produce one album that bridged the space between psychedelic and progressive rock.

Renaissance (71)

• REVOLUCION DE EMILIANO ZAPATU - Mexico

Formed in the early seventies their psychedelic musical style hearkens back to the hey-days of the San Francisco sound with guitar work strongly reminiscent of bands like Quicksilver Messenger Service. Their second released incorporated a female vocalist and even longer jam-filled compositions.

La Revolucion de Emiliano Zapata (71), Hoy (72)

• RIBA, PAU - Spain

He's been called the Spanish Daevid Allen.

Diopria 1 (69), Dioptria 2 (70), Jo, La Donya I el Gripau (71), Electriccid Alquimistic Xoc (75), Licors (77), Dioptria [comp.] (78)

• RIDERS OF THE MARK - USA

Formed in 1967 in Arizona, Riders of the Mark recorded a couple of singles which featured an instrument sound that was all psychedelic with backward fuzzy guitar loops and blurry organ and bass work with shouting vocals delivered with loads of garage band angst.

Beyond the Calico Wall [Comp] (93)

• ROAR - Germany

Semi symphonic progressive material with some folk and psychedelic influences.

The Roar of Silence (91)

• ROCKADROME - Canada

Formed in 1969 in Toronto, Ontario; they played a blues-rock foundation but incorporated many aspects of psychedelia into their sound. As might be expected those influences stem mostly from the Beatles psychedelic period.

Royal American 20th Century Blues (69)

• ROLLING STONES - UK

Formed in 1962 in London the Rolling Stones were essentially an R&B and blues outfit. Like the Beatles they scored with many hits during the rise of the British Invasion and with the earlier beat boom. The Rolling Stones and psychedelia collided in 1967 with the release of **Their Satanic Majesties Request,** which everyone saw as their response to the Beatles **Sgt. Pepper**. Truth is the Stones never dallied long in the world of psychedelics and returned to their R&B roots relatively quickly after this release.

Between The Buttons (67), Their Satanic Majesties Request (67), Beggars Banquet (68)

• ROOSTERS - USA

Formed in the mid-sixties in Los Angeles they recorded a couple of singles featuring a Byrds influenced folk-rock sound. Lots of jangling guitar and harmonica.

• ROTARY CONNECTION - USA

Formed in 1967 in Chicago, Illinois, the Rotary Connection had an unusual take on psychedelia, relying on the arty-ier aspects of orchestration and arrangements to flesh-out their rock compositions. This approach provided the necessary frills and even added a more progressive element to their risk taking. They eventually split up in 1971. A couple members had actually left in 1968 to form Aorta. Lead vocalist Minnie Ripperton went on to a solo career.

Rotary Connection (68), Aladdin (68), Sings (69), Dinner Music (69), Hey Love (71)

• RUPERT'S PEOPLE - UK

Formed in 1967 in London, Rupert's People was put together following the success of the single *Reflections of Charles Brown* in July of 1967. The song had originally been recorded by session players, most of whom were in Les Fleur De Lys. After forming a completely new group to tour under the name Rupert's People they recorded a couple more relatively successful singles (three in total) before dropping "below the radar." Their psych-pop musical style bears a striking resemblance to early Procol Harum. After disbanding in 1968, keyboardist John Tout turned up in Renaissance.

Nuggets II Box Set [Comp] (01)

• RYAN, PAUL & BARRY - UK

They've been called the British equivalent to the Walker Brothers, Paul and Berry recorded quite a few singles beginning in the sixties through to the mid seventies. Their psychedelic style was of a pop variety containing lush orchestral arrangements but with all the right guitar, organ and production to match.

Electric Sugarcube Flashbacks [Comp] (93)

• RYE - USA

Formed in the late sixties in Los Angeles they recorded one LP that falls squarely into the psychedelic-pop category.

The Beginning (69)

• SAGITTARIUS - USA

This studio project of 1967, was directed by producer Gary Usher who had worked with the Byrds, Chad and Jeremy and others. For his own project he relied on some of the best LA studio session people and crafted a British orchestrated psychedelic style. The LP was heavily orchestrated and loaded with a very delicate style that bore a Beach Boys *Pet Sounds* influence. The single *My World Fell Down* featuring vocals and guitar work from Glen Campbell was a moderate hit in 1967.

Present Tense (68), The Blue Marble (69), Nuggets I Box Set [Comp] (98)

• ST. GILES' SYSTEM - Holland

Formed in the late sixties they produced only one official single of deranged, orchestrated psychedelic rock. A trippy affair that changes tempo and is driven by a droning organ that slides away only to be replaced by some powerful vocals and an early synthesizer.

Waterpipes & Dykes: Dutch Psychedelic Underground 1966 - 1972 Vol. 1 [Comp] ( )

• SALVATION - USA

Formed in 1967 in San Francisco they got their start playing a number of free concerts in the Bay area before signing a record deal. They originally went by the name The New Salvation Army Banned, but upon signing a record deal changed the name to Salvation to avoid potential legal problems. Their trippy West Coast style went over well as they played regularly on the ballroom circuit. In the end they recorded two albums before splitting up in 1969.

Salvation (68), Gypsy Carnival Caravan (68)

• SANDS - UK

Formed in 1964 in Middlesex, England; Sands came out of an R&B background before adopting the sounds of the psychedelic sixties. They recorded two singles, one in 1967 and the other in 1970 before fading from the scene.

Nuggets II Box Set [Comp] (01)

• SANTANA - USA

Formed in 1966 in San Francisco, Santana's origins are steeped in legend. As best as can be ascertained Carlos Santana used to sneak into the Fillmore and had put together the Santana Blues Band. One evening Graham needed a support act and knew of Santana's desire to perform. The opportunity was offered and he never looked back. Under Graham's direction the band flourished and were given a prime slot on the stage at Woodstock without even having secured a record deal. Santana's unique Latin tinged psychedelia was perfect for the times revealing yet again just how well the psychedelic style took to incorporating influences.

Santana continues to record and perform successfully to this day.

Santana (69), Abraxas (70), Santana III (71), Caravanserai (72)

• SAPPHIRE THINKERS - USA

Formed in the late sixties in California they recorded one LP with a very West Coast psychedelic sound along the same lines as Jefferson Airplane. Standout attributes include some nice harmonies and the obligatory fuzzy guitar sound.

From Within (69)

• SAUTERELLES - Switzerland

Formed in Switzerland they tried to take their popularity to Britain in 1968 by relocating to London. Their mellow psychedelic style was similar to that of bands like the Moody Blues. They failed to make any significant impact and so returned to Switzerland where their popularity remained strong.

View to Heaven (68), The Great British Psychedelic Trip, Vol. 1 [Comp] (88)

• SAVAGE RESURRECTION - USA

Formed in 1967 in Richmond, California; they released one LP featuring a classic psychedelic West Coast jamming guitar style with a hint of Eastern influence creeping through from time to time.

Savage Resurrection (68)

• SAVAGE ROSE - Denmark

Formed in 1967 in Denmark, Savage Rose is one of the most internationally well-known Danish psychedelic acts. Their early material features a quirky mix full of the psychedelic flavour of the times. The compositions are replete with influences such as the Doors, Pink Floyd and even Jefferson Airplane, not the least because of Savage Roses' splendid female vocalist. The band featured three keyboard players and an assortment of other odd instruments including an unusual sounding organ. Their later material moved more in the progressive rock vein.

Savage Rose (68), In the Plain (68), Travellin' (69), Your Daily Gift (70), Refugee (71), Doden's Triumf (72), Babylon (73), Wild Child (73), I'm Satisfied (7?), En Vugge Af Stal ( ), Solen Var Ogsa Din (77), Oden's Triumph ( )

• SCRUGG - UK

Formed in 1966 in London, they originally released a single under the name of Floribunda Rose, which went no where. Under the leadership of John Kongos they changed their name to Scrugg in early 1968 and proceeded to put out three more barely noticed single releases that reverberated with British psychedelia. They ended up releasing some three singles, all of which failed to set the world on fire and they ultimately split up in 1969. Kongos would have to wait a while before the release of He's Gonna Step On You Again in 1971 for his name to be reckoned with on the charts.

Hot Smoke & Sassafras: Psychedelic Pstones Vol. 1 [Comp] (01), Nuggets II Box Set [Comp] (01)

• SEATRAIN - USA

Formed in 1969 in San Francisco, by various musicians who'd worked together in other groups such as the Blues Project or other individuals like bluegrass king Bill Monroe. It was this diverse blend of styles that allowed Seatrain to stand out briefly from the crowd. In particular their use of violin gave them a very distinctive sound. They faded from the scene by the mid seventies.

Seatrain (69), Seatrain (70), Marblehead Messenger (71), Watch (73)

• SECOND-HAND - UK

Formed in 1967 Second-Hand even in their early days seemed to be bridging the gap between psychedelic and progressive rock. Their first album certainly maintained a closer link to the world of psychedelia with its influences being Hendrix and a bit of Arthur Brown. The material is highlighted with some dramatic Mellotron, which gets even more play by the time of the second release. By this time the line-up had changed considerably and the focus was more along the lines of Kingdom Come.

Reality (68), Death May Be Your Santa Claus (71)

• SEEDS - USA

Formed in 1965 in Los Angeles by lead vocalist Sky Saxon, the Seeds worked the live scene very hard and soon earned a reputation for being one of the most exciting and popular bands in the region. Their single, Pushin Too Hard was released in 1966 and became a big hit. The Seeds are credited with bridging the gap between the garage-punk and the emerging psychedelic scene of 1967. It wasn't until their third LP, Future that they really incorporated any amount of psychedelia. Saxon folded the Seeds in 1972 before going on to a variety of solo efforts.

The Seeds (66), A Web of Sound (66), Future (67), A Full Spoon of Seedy Blues (67), Raw and Alive (68), Nuggets I Box Set [Comp] (98)

• SERPENT POWER - USA

Formed in 1966 in San Francisco, they established a strong local following playing for various benefits in the Bay area. Their musical style was more along the lines of softer hippie-folk with some pleasant guitar added. Adding spice to the mix are the vocals from Tina Meltzer and a mystical Eastern influence on a couple tracks.

Serpent Power (67)

• SHADES OF BLUE - USA

Formed in 1966 in Detroit they were strong contenders on the local Top 40 charts and produced one album in the psychedelic-pop vein.

Happiness is the Shade of Blue (66)

• SHADOWS OF KNIGHT - USA

Formed in 1965 in Chicago, Illinois; the Shadows of Knight went through a number of personnel changes before settling into a steady line-up by 1965 by which time they were gigging steadily in the clubs and signed a record deal releasing the single Gloria. The band were always listening to material from England before anyone else and quickly developed a reputation for playing this blues influenced material in a raucous live setting. They became pioneers of early sixties garage-punk style. They eventually disbanded in 1970, but before that guitarist Jerry McGeorge had left to join H. P. Lovecraft in 1967.

Gloria (66), Back Door Men (67), The Shadows of Knight (69), Nuggets I Box Set [Comp] (98)

• SHIELDS, KEITH - UK

With a background that included performing in Marty Wilde's backing band the Wildcats, Keith Shields a Newcastle native produced three moderately successful singles and as a song like *Deep Inside Your Mind* from February 1967 shows he was not adverse to showing his psychedelic style.

The Great British Psychedelic Trip, Vol. 1 [Comp] (88), The Psychedelic Scene [Comp] (98)

• SHIVA'S HEADBAND - USA

Formed in 1967 in Austin, Texas; they were regulars on the Texas ballroom circuit playing regularly at the Vulcan Gas Company. They were put together by violinist Spencer Perskin who'd spent time in San Francisco and had a clear idea of the type of psychedelic band he wanted. After honing their West Coast psychedelic style they moved to San Francisco for a time before eventually returning to Austin. Though they were signed to a major label, their records failed to sell well. They continued recording into the mid eighties before splitting up in 1985.

Take Me To The Mountains (70), Comin' To A Head (72), Psychedelic Yesterday (77), In The Primo of Life (85)

• SHOCKERS - Canada

Formed in 1965 in Vancouver, British Columbia; the Shockers were firmly in the garage-soul vein with plenty of fuzz-guitar effects. Word has it their live presentation was pretty spectacular. They wound up recording one single for RCA entitled *Somebody Help Me*.

The History of Vancouver Rock & Roll, Vol. 4 [Comp] (91)

• SHORT 66 - Holland

Formed in 1964 in Amsterdam they were originally called the Golden Corvairs. They took their British Invasion Mod style and adopted it to a very flower-power psychedelic-pop style in 1967 during the Summer of Love.

Waterpipes & Dykes: Dutch Psychedelic Underground 1966 - 1972 Vol. 1 [Comp] ( )

• SHYSTER - UK

This band is actually the Fleur de Lys and recorded a single called *Tick Tock* in 1968 under the name of Shyster.

• SIDDHA - USA

Formed in the mid-seventies by Ian Underwood after leaving the Mothers of Invention, this band's sole release is an interesting mix all the West Coast psychedelic style including some great guitar playing.

A Very Gentle Force (75)

• SIDELLS - USA

Formed in 1968 in Durham, North Carolina; the Sidells recorded at least one single of strange, almost progressive material that featured shifts in tempo and some rather strange sound effects. Needless to say their sound included the weedy-organ and fuzz-guitars of the period.

A Lethal Dose of Hard Psych [Comp] (99)

• SIEGAL-SCHWALL BAND - USA

Formed in 1966 in Chicago, they played regularly in San Francisco and developed quite a following for their heavily blues-based psychedelic style.

Siegal-Schwall Band (66), Say Siegal-Schwall (67), Shake (68), Siegal-Schwall 70 (70), The Siegal-Schwall Band (71), Sleepy Hollow (72)

• SILVETLER - Turkey

Formed in the mid-sixties, this was the first band to create significant impact in the world of Turkish rock and roll. Their early sixties garage sound melded elements of Turkish ethnic music and a growing sense of psychedelia.

Hava Narghile, Vol. 1 [Comp] (01)

• SIMON DUPREE & THE BIG SOUND - UK

Formed in 1965 in Portsmouth by the Shulman brothers, Derek, Ray and Phil, they were originally known on the beat club circuit as Howlin' Wolves and Roadrunners. They changed their name to Simon Dupree and the Big Sound in 1966 and had a string of unsuccessful singles to their credit. Then, unlike much of their earlier R&B material they released the song *Kites* at the end of 1967. Its dreamy psychedelic flow captured the moment and the single proved to be a Top 10 hit. In 1969, after a total of ten singles and one LP the band evolved into progressive rockers Gentle Giant.

Without Reservations (67), Amen [Comp] (82), The Psychedelic Years 1966-1969 - Great Britain [Comp] (90), Psychedelic Visions [Comp] (96), Psychedelia at Abbey Road [Comp] (98)

• SILVER APPLES - USA

Formed in 1967 in New York by Dan Taylor and Simeon. They were early experimenters with electronics mixed with drums and unusual vocals. Their musical style while strong on melody was a mixture of quasi-sci-fi movie music mixed with the typical psychedelic trippyness of the spacey variety. After the release of their second LP in 1969 they retired from the music scene for over twenty years only to resurface in 1996 with a new recording.

Silver Apples (68), Contact (69)

• SIX FEET UNDER - USA

Formed in 1968, in New Jersey, Six Feet Under recorded at least one single but spent plenty of time in the studio leaving hours of demos in the can. This included their own relatively faithful cover of the classic *In-A-Gadda-Da-Vida* with the prerequisite fuzzed out guitars, wah-wah pedals and dominating organ work. After releasing the one single they added a female vocalist and they adopted more of a Jefferson Airplane musical style.

In Retrospect 1969 - 70 [Comp] (98), Beyond the Calico Wall [Comp] (93)

• SKIP BIFFERTY - UK

Formed in 1966 in Newcastle, they were originally known as the Chosen Few before changing their name. Skip Bifferty eventually recorded at least three singles in a psychedelic-pop vein plus one album. As noted elsewhere, they adopted the name Heavy Jelly at the end of their career to capitalize on some free publicity and released one single as such. None of these singles efforts had any lasting impact and they later evolved into Bell & Arc in early 1971.

Skip Bifferty (68), Electric Sugarcube Flashbacks [Comp] (93)

• SLY AND THE FAMILY STONE - USA

Formed in 1966 in San Francisco, Sly Stone had been a busy record producer and DJ before creating his own band with a decidedly "psychedelic soul" approach to the music of the day. Stone took elements of Hendrix and Motown and created a kind of flamboyant African-American hippie image that worked well for him. Their first single and LP slipped out with barely a ripple, however their single *Dance to the Music* rocketed into the Top 10 in 1968. They were successful in following that up with a string of hits plus a standout performance at Woodstock. Following his move to Los Angeles in 1970 Stone became enmeshed in drugs and his music suffered. They recorded until 1975 when Stone went solo for a time. He reformed the Family Stone in 1976 and recorded a couple more albums before quietly disappearing from the scene in 1981.

A Whole New Thing (67), Dance to the Music (68), Life (69), Stand (69), There's a Riot Goin' On (72), Fresh (73), Small Talk (74)

• SMALL FACES - UK

Formed in 1965 in the East End of London the Small Faces played a Mod, R&B style in their early days but really came into their own in early 1967 having discovered LSD. They created a kaleidoscopic range of singles, the first of which was *Here Comes the Nice* then *Itchycoo Park* and *Tin Soldier*. With its tongue-in-cheek lyrics and revolutionary phasing the song was a instant psychedelic-pop smash hit. Their 1967 album Ogden's Nut Gone Flake is sort of a loose concept-come psychedelic-arty album. Good fun! When Steve Marriott left to form Humble Pie in 1969 the rest of the band shortened the name to just the Faces, changed their musical style back to R&B laced rock and hooked up with Rod Stewart. The Small Faces reformed briefly in 1977 but they no longer reflected a psychedelic influence.

Small Faces (66), From the Beginning (67), These are but Four Small Faces (68), Ogden's Nut Gone Flake (68), The Autumn Stone (69), The Psychedelic Years 1966-1969 - Great Britain [Comp] (90), The Psychedelic Scene [Comp] (98), Nuggets II Box Set [Comp] (01)

• SMELL OF INCENSE - Norway

As the name might imply there is a strong psychedelic influence in this folk oriented progressive rock. Instrumentation highlights include sitar, organ and Mellotron.

All Mimsy ( )

• SMITH, BOB - USA

More of a studio project; Smith assembled at least eight other musicians to create some fascinating psychedelia with an Eastern mystical flavour particularly on his second LP release. The foundation is blues based but with the addition of violin and Mellotron there's a lot happening.

The Lid (68), The Visit (70)

• SMOKE - UK

Formed in 1965 in Yorkshire out of two bands known as the Shots and Chords 5, the Smoke had a sizable psychedelic hit with the well crafted *My Friend Jack*. Unfortunately the BBC took offence to the suggested drug reference and banned the single so it received only pirate station airplay in Britain. The band eventually signed to Island records, but despite support from their peers, they failed to make any further commercial inroads in Britain. Looking elsewhere they continued to record and released a couple of albums in Germany up to 1974!

My Friend Jack (67), The Best of and The Rest of British Psychedelia [Comp] (91), Electric Sugarcube Flashbacks [Comp] (93), It's Smoke Time [Comp] (94), Psychedelic Perceptions [Comp] (96), Nuggets II Box Set [Comp] (01)

• SMOKE - USA

Formed in 1967 in Los Angeles they recorded one LP featuring some flower-power pop with pleasant orchestration on a few of the tracks showing some inspiration from the Beatles. After a brief tour supporting the West Coast Pop Art Experimental Band, the group disbanded with each member pursuing other activities.

The Smoke (68)

• SNELLING, ALVA - USA

Snelling was a student in Baton Rouge, Louisiana who had the opportunity to record a couple of obscure singles with a garage-psych feel.

Beyond the Calico Wall [Comp] (93)

• SOCIETIE - UK

Formed in 1967 in Glasgow, Societie created a melodic, low-key almost melancholy vocal style much like some of the Hollies material. Poor sales after the release of their one and only single caused the break up of the group, with two of the members landing in the progressive Andwella.

The Psychedelic Scene [Comp] (98)

• SOFT MACHINE - UK

Formed in 1966 in Canterbury they grew out of a band called the Wilde Flowers. The Soft Machine's first LP shared a lot in common with the psychedelic style of London in 1967. They along with Pink Floyd shared the stage at many of those early all-night raves and like the Floyd developed a loyal following. These two bands essentially set the tone for the British psychedelic movement. Following a gruelling tour in America in support of Jimi Hendrix the first of many personnel changes took place. With these changes came a shift in musical direction. Their style became much more experimental with a stronger jazz and avant-garde influence. By the time of their LP they were clearly more in the progressive rock world. They continued recording in various permutation until 1981.

The Soft Machine (68), Soft Machine Vol. 2 (69), Third (70)

• SOMA - UK

A newer band that creates a psychedelic style much like OZRIC TENTACLES, only with vocals. Musical influences will include Pink Floyd and Hawkwind.

Epsilon (91), Dreamtime (9?)

• SOM IMAGINARIO - Brazil

Formed in 1967 at the height of the Summer of Love, they incorporated many of the studio gimmicks like phased vocals, feedback and strange talking interludes all adding to the trippyness of their music which generally revolved some catchy ethnic rhythms.

Son Imaginario (70), Son Imaginario (71), A Matana Do Porco (72), Love, Peace & Poetry: Latin American Psychedelic Music [Comp] (97)

• SONS OF ADAM - USA

Formed in 1965 in Los Angeles, the Sons of Adam had a reputation for being one of the better, if not the best garage bands on the scene. They incorporated an increasing psychedelic influence and even performed at some of the early San Francisco ballroom gigs. By 1967 after three unsuccessful singles vocalist Dave Peters left to join Love and following two more unsuccessful singles they became the Other Half for a short while before Randy Holden left to become part of Blue Cheer.

Sons of Adam [Comp] (80)

• SONS OF CHAMPLIN - USA

Formed in 1965 in San Francisco, the Sons of Champlin were strong on harmonies and purveyors of that typical laid-back folk influenced jamming West Coast style and were also one of the first rock bands in the area. In fact their music tended to contain more complicated arrangements based on a soul foundation. They were regulars on the ballroom circuit although problems with shifting personnel (15 different lie-ups are recorded!) never helped them break out of the local scene. After releasing 3 albums they disbanded, only to form again under the name Yogi Phlegm for a short time in the early seventies, although that didn't speed success their way either. They reverted back to just the Sons in 1973 and carried on in various permutations well into the eighties.

Loosen Up Naturally (68), The Sons (69), Follow Your Heart (71), San Francisco Nights [Comp] (91), Best of The Sons of Champlin [Comp] (93)

• SONSET - Puerto Rica

Formed in 1967 they recorded one LP that brought together a mix of psychedelic and rawer garage band influences.

Discoteca (67)

• SOPWITH CAMEL - USA

Formed in 1965 in San Francisco, Sopwith Camel were the second of the San Francisco bands to have a hit single (Jefferson Airplane were the first) with the 'vaudevillian' single *Hello Hello* in 1967. The song however was not totally indicative of the band's style, as they were able to produce a West Coast flower-power acid rock with the best of the San Francisco bands. The group's singer and main writer, Peter Kraemer had been at the forefront of the psychedelic movement in San Francisco and the band became a regular favourite on the ballroom circuit. They split following the release of their first album. Drummer Norman Mayell joined Blue Cheer. They reformed a recorded a second poorly received LP in 1973.

Sopwith Camel (67), Hello Hello (73), The Miraculous Hump Returns from the Moon (73), San Francisco Nights [Comp] (91), The Psychedelic Years Revisited [Comp] (92), Psychedelic Frequencies [Comp] (96)

• SORROWS - UK

Formed in 1963 in Coventry, the Sorrows were part of Britain's great R&B boom. They issued their main claim to psychedelic fame in June 1967 with *Pink, Purple, Yellow, Red*. The single went nowhere and the original band split up in 1967. A number of personnel shifts later saw the band move to Italy where some single success ensued. Some of the original members continued on as solo artists in England.

Take a Heart (65), In Italy [Comp] (83), The Sorrows [Comp] (91), Hot Smoke & Sassafras: Psychedelic Pstones Vol. 1 [Comp] (01), Nuggets II Box Set [Comp] (01)

• SOUND SYSTEM - USA

Formed in 1967 in Greenville, North Carolina; Sound System released at least one single with a nice early psychedelic mix of weedy-organ and fuzz-guitar. Their compositional style and vocals hearkened back to a strong garage influence.

A Lethal Dose of Hard Psych [Comp] (99)

• SOUTHWEST FOB - USA

Formed in 1967 in Dallas, this Texas band scored a minor hit in 1968 with the *Smell Of Incense* distributed nationally by Stax records. Their early psychedelic-pop-ish style is loaded with Farfisa organ and fuzz-guitar. The band included future mellow seventies rockers England Dan Seals and John Ford Coley.

The Smell of Incense (68), Orange, Sugar & Chocolate: Psychedelic Microdots of the 60's, Vol. 1 [Comp] (89), Texas Twisted: Psychedelic Microdots of the 60's, Vol. 2 [Comp] (91)

• SPARROW - Canada

Formed in 1965 in Toronto, they were joined by John Kay in 1966. They performed regularly in the Yorkville scene and gained a loyal following however chart success eluded them. The group moved to California in early 1967 and played around the San Francisco area before disbanding briefly only to reform as Steppenwolf by the end of the year. In this incarnation they released a number successful psychedelic singles such as *Born To Be Wild* and *Magic Carpet Ride*.

Presenting Jack London and the Sparrows (65), John Kay and the Sparrows (66), The Psychedelic Years Revisited [Comp] (92)

• SPEED, GLUE & SHINKI - Japan

Formed in the early seventies this trio, augmented from time to time by guest musicians, created a much more blues-based psychedelia along the lines of the emerging heavier San Francisco bands like Blue Cheer.

Eve (71), Speed, Glue & Shinki (72), Love, Peace & Poetry: Japanese Psychedelic Music [Comp] (01)

• SPENCE, SKIP - USA

Canadian born, Spence was originally recruited to play drums in the early Jefferson Airplane only to leave after their first LP to help form the seminal West Coast psychedelic outfit Moby Grape as guitarist. Following the legal hassles that led to the demise of Moby Grape, Spence, who's often compared to Syd Barrett in more ways than one, became a casualty to the volume of LSD he'd been ingesting. After a period of enforced hospitalization he went to Nashville and recorded a solo album, which contained the less than optimistic *War In Peace*.

Oar (69), Psychedelic Frequencies [Comp] (96)

• SPIDERS - Mexico

Formed in the late sixties, the Spiders created one LP with that distinctive West Coast psychedelic sound. The compositions are full of atmospheric, dreamy organs mixing it up with fuzz-guitar solos. Sung in English the tunes are strong on melody.

Back (70)

• SPINDLE - USA

Formed in 1967 in Bremerton, Washington; they recorded three singles with a West Coast hippie-folk vibe. Overall their style was a blend of British Invasion vocals and early San Francisco folk-rock.

The History of Northwest Rock Vol. 3: Psychedelic Seattle [Comp] (00)

• SPIRIT - USA

Formed in the spring of 1967 in Los Angeles. Four of these musicians had earlier played in a band called the Red Roosters. Drummer Ed Cassidy had played in a wide variety of bands and styles including folk, jazz and R&B. It was this variety of musical influences that made the music of Spirit so compelling. Cassidy's 16 year old stepson Randy California (Randy Wolfe) was brought in to play guitars. Interestingly, California had spent time in New York playing in a band called Jimmy James and the Blue Flames. Jimmy James would later change his name to Jimi Hendrix. The music of Spirit displayed a wide range of influences and styles that played well with the psychedelic idea of stretching the music. Spirit disbanded for the first time in 1972, reforming in 1975 and recording through to 1981. After that Spirit became more or less a project that Randy

California returned to in between solo efforts. California himself died in a drowning accident in Hawaii in 1997.

Spirit (68), The Family that Plays Together (69), Clear (69), Twelve Dreams of Dr. Sardonicus (71), Feedback (72), The Psychedelic Years Revisited [Comp] (92), Psychedelic Visions [Comp] (96)

• SPONTANEOUS GENERATION - USA

Formed in 1966 in Atlanta, Georgia, this obscure band recorded a garage-psych fuzzed-out single replete with loads of rumbling bass and wah-wah guitar.

Beyond the Calico Wall [Comp] (93)

• SPOOKY TOOTH - UK

Formed in late 1967, they were originally known as Art but after adding keyboardist Gary Wright changed their name and moved their musical style ever slightly more away from psychedelia and more towards a blues influenced progressive rock. They stayed together the first time until 1970 at which time members went to Frampton's Camel, Stone The Crows and Illusion. They reformed in 1973 and carried on till 1975 before splitting up for good. Gary Wright went on to fame with the hit *Dream Weaver*.

It's All About A Roundabout (68), Spooky Two (69), Ceremony (70), The Last Puff (70)

• SPRINGFIELD RIFLE - USA

Formed in 1966 in Seattle, Washington; Springfield Rifle crafted a folk-rock flower-power psychedelic style. Imagine the Beatles vocal style harmonies mixed in with a more psychedelic Association.

The Springfield Rifle (68), The History of Northwest Rock Vol. 3: Psychedelic Seattle [Comp] (00)

• SRC - USA

Formed in 1967 in Detroit, Michigan; home of such bands as the Stooges and MC5, SRC created a psychedelic style that was as adventurous as it was trippy. Compositionally you hear the obligatory sustain-laden distorted guitar, punctuated by short blasts of organ. By the time of their third LP they were moving more into the world of neo-classical composition and as a result of poor sales were dropped by their label. They faded from view shortly after.

SRC (68), Milestones (69), Traveller's Tale (70)

• STACCATOS - Canada

Formed in 1963 in Ottawa, Ontario; the Staccatos were part of the Canadian garage band scene. Under the guidance of founder Les Emmerson they achieved a number of hit singles early in their career. In 1968 they recorded their second LP entitled **The Five Man Electrical Band**, a name they adopted for the group from that point on. Their sound evolved into less garage and more straight-forward pop-rock and had a string of hit singles in Canada.

Initially the Staccatos (65), The Five Man Electrical band (68)

• STANDELLS - USA

Formed in 1962 in Los Angeles, the Standells made a name for themselves on the club circuit playing an

R&B influenced garage style. In 1965, following an appearance on the TV show The Munsters, the Standells switched their hair and clothing style to reflect the tail end of the British Invasion and then switched their music to a more edgy, fuzz-guitar psychedelic style. They disbanded in 1968.

Standells in Person at P.J.s (65), Dirty Water (66), Why Pick on Me (66), Hot Ones (66), Try It (68), Nuggets I Box Set [Comp] (98)

• STATUS QUO - UK

Formed in 1962 in London they were originally known as the Spectres. Fronted by the guitar duo of Francis Rossi and Rick Parfitt they changed their name to become the Status Quo in 1967and hit the psychedelic scene with the Top 10 hit single *Pictures Of Matchstick Men*. They retained the psychedelic feel only a short time before reverting to a more blues based rock.

Picturesque Matchstickable Messages From the Status Quo (68), Spare Parts (69), Ma Kelly's Greasy Spoon (70), Psychedelic Visions [Comp] (96), Hot Smoke & Sassafras: Psychedelic Pstones Vol. 1 [Comp] (01), Nuggets II Box Set [Comp] (01)

• STEAMHAMMER - UK

Formed in 1968, out of London's answer to Haight-Ashbury, Ladbroke Grove Steamhammer's take on the psychedelic sound was more influenced by the blues and as a result tended to have a sound that was closer to the West Coast American bands. Popular as a live band, they failed to have a successful record and eventually split up in 1971.

The Psychedelic Years Revisited [Comp] (92)

• STEPPENWOLF - USA

Formed in 1965 in Toronto, originally called the Sparrow, they moved to San Francisco and after playing the ballroom circuit for a time regrouped and changed their name to Steppenwolf. Their sound was more on the heavier side of rock for its day and the band are even credited with being one of the first to coin the term "heavy metal" which appeared in their first big hit *Born To Be Wild*. Despite the heavier style Steppenwolf were able to inject a strong psychedelic influence easily seen in the follow up hit, *Magic Carpet Ride*. They disbanded in early 1972. John Kaye went solo for a time but reformed variations of Steppenwolf as projects between his other solo efforts and together they continued releasing records into the nineties.

Steppenwolf (68), Steppenwolf The Second (69), At Your Birthday Party (69), Monster (70), Steppenwolf 7 (70), For Ladies Only (71), Psychedelic Perceptions [Comp] (96)

• STEWART, Al - UK

Stewart came out of the folk scene in Scotland during 1966 and landed himself a folk-psychedelic single called *The Elf*. Showing his influences Stewart later recorded *Turn To Earth* with a decidedly Yardbirds feel partially because of Paul Samwell Smith's production. Stewart later became a superstar in his own right during the soft-rock hey-day of the middle-to-late seventies.

Bedsitter Images (67), Love Chronicles (69), Zero She Flies (70), Orange (72), The Great British Psychedelic Trip, Vol. 1

[Comp] (88), The Great British Psychedelic Trip, Vol. 2 [Comp] (88), The Psychedelic Scene [Comp] (98)

• STILLROVEN - USA

This teen sensation band from Minneapolis formed in late 1966. Their main claim to fame was having a huge local hit with *Hey Joe* in June 1967. After a few unsuccessful singles the band loaded up their van and moved to California. They called it a day when the van, with all their gear caught fire and everything was lost.

Cast Thy Burdon Upon… [Comp] (96), My Rainbow Life: Psychedelic Microdots of the 60's, Vol. 3 [Comp] (92)

• STIRLING, PETER LEE - UK

Primarily known as a songwriter, he fronted a band in Birmingham called the Bruisers in the early sixties. Stirling attempted to chart some of his own success during the highly experimental days of 1967. But while he was able to craft an excellent pop song the magic wasn't there and after a couple of singles he returned to writing only. That was until the mid seventies when once again he tried his hand at singing and had a hit with *Beautiful Sunday* going by the name of Daniel Boone.

The Great British Psychedelic Trip, Vol. 2 [Comp] (88)

• STRAWBERRY ALARM CLOCK - USA

Formed in 1966 in Santa Barbara, California; they were originally called Thee Sixpence, but changed their name to Strawberry Alarm Clock. This band was one of the first truly psychedelic bands to have a nation-wide hit with *Incense and Peppermints* which became a No. 1 hit in September 1967 and has become a classic from the Summer of Love. The band also were featured in the movies **Psych-Out** and **Beyond the Valley of the Dolls**. In latter years they experienced many line-up changes before officially splitting up in 1971. Lead guitarist Ed King went on to play in Lynard Skynard.

Incense and Peppermints (67), Wake Up, It's Tomorrow (68), World In A Sea Shell (68), Good Morning Starshine (70), Psychedelic Visions [Comp] (96), Nuggets I Box Set [Comp] (98)

• SUGAR SHOPPE - Canada

Formed in the mid-sixties in Toronto, the Sugar Shoppe consisted of four very young performers and started out in a pop style in early 1967 but soon adopted a myriad of psychedelic influences to their pop and had a significant hit with a song called *The Attitude*.

The Sugar Shoppe (68)

• SURPRIEZE - Holland

Formed in 1970 in Breda, Surprieze incorporated a bizarre number of effects, instruments and influences to craft their psychedelic mix. Based mostly around the fuzz-guitar jamming performances of leader Eddy van der Meer, he is know for using only three strings and playing in a tuning style that sounded like a sitar loaded on echo. They recorded a number of records all of them released privately and highly sought after now.

Waterpipes & Dykes: Dutch Psychedelic Underground 1966 - 1972 Vol. 1 [Comp] ( )

• SVENSK - UK

Formed in 1967 in Bournemouth this trippy duo were actually "discovered" by Roy Orbison and recorded two wonderful singles of moody, ballad-like, organ filled psychedelia. A third single appeared in 1969.

Electric Sugarcube Flashbacks [Comp] (93)

• SWEET - UK

Formed in 1968 they were originally known as the Sweet Shop. By 1969 they had dropped the "Shop" portion of their name but were still producing some masterful psychedelic-pop music such as the overlooked b-side *Time*. Success eluded them in this style and they reverted to a harder edged brand of power-pop-rock in the seventies and had a long string of successful hits.

Funny How Sweet Coco Can Be (71), Electric Sugarcube Flashbacks [Comp] (93)

• SWEETWATER - USA

Formed in the late sixties in the Los Angeles area their music was a psychedelic blend of folk, jazz and even some Latin rhythms. They recorded three albums but perhaps their main claim to fame was being the second act at Woodstock following Richie Havens.

Sweetwater (69), Just For You (70, Melon (71)

• SYN - UK

Formed in 1967 in London, the Syn were originally known as the Selfs and like so many bands of the time played an R&B influenced pop music. They adopted psychedelia early in 1967 and recorded a couple of singles that sold quite well. The Syn disbanded in early 1968 and members Chris Squire and Peter Banks went on to form Mabel Greer's Toyshop and then later Yes.

The Psychedelic Scene [Comp] (98), Nuggets II Box Set [Comp] (01)

• T.C. ATLANTIC - USA

Formed in the mid-sixties in Minneapolis, Minnesota; T.C. Atlantic for a time were one the areas most popular local psychedelic outfits. Combining their psychedelia with a garage foundation they blended some nice guitar work and hooky melodies to craft some gems of the era. They failed to crack the singles market and disbanded by the late sixties.

Live at The Bel Rae Ballroom (67), T.C. Atlantic [Comp] (84)

• TAGES - Sweden

Formed in 1963 in Gothenburg, the Tages evolved with the musical styles of the day, going from R&B to Mod and then incorporating the growing freakbeat and psychedelic influences. By 1968 their style was classic pop influenced psychedelia. They split up at the end of 1968 and regrouped as a band called Blond in 1969.

The Tages 1964-68! [Comp] (83), Nuggets II Box Set [Comp] (01)

• TALES OF JUSTINE - UK

Formed in 1965 in Potter's Bar, Hertfordshire where they originally were called the Court Jesters. It was their most recent member David Daltry, a distant cousin to Roger who brought in the Mellotron, Celeste and sitar and pointed the band in a psychedelic direction. They changed their name to Tales of Justine in 1967 then won a deal with EMI. They recorded a number of singles with Andrew Lloyd Weber as musical arranger and Tim Rice as producer. None of their material seemed to stir up much attention and even though they persisted for a time the band eventually called it quits in 1969.

Petals From a Sunflower [Compilation] (97), Psychedelia at Abbey Road [Comp] (98)

• TANGERINE PEEL - UK

Formed in 1968, Tangerine Peel were a band that tried to capitalize on the psychedelic explosion of the late sixties. They recorded 8 singles over a span of two years and released one LP all with the prerequisite psychedelic-pop feel. Sadly no one took notice and they disappeared quietly in 1970.

Soft Delights (70)

• TAXI - UK

Formed in the late sixties in Ireland, Taxi managed only one shot at vinyl with a Jethro Tull inspired composition. Despite strong local coverage and exposure they failed to further their goals musical and disbanded.

Hot Smoke & Sassafras: Psychedelic Pstones Vol. 1 [Comp] (01)

• TEA COMPANY - USA

Formed in 1967 in Queens, New York; the Tea Company created one album featuring a number of Beatle-inspired psychedelic flavoured compositions that were saturated with echo, tape-loops, and lots of stereo panning intended to simulate the psychedelic experience.

Come Have Some Tea with The Tea Company (68), A Heavy Dose of Lyte Psych [Comp] (96)

• TEDDY & HIS PATCHES - USA

Formed in 1966 in San Jose, they tended to stay more firmly planted in a garage-rock style with a tiny bit of West Coast acid-rock guitar work. Short lived they only released a couple singles, one of which displayed some imaginative work.

A Heavy Dose of Lyte Psych [Comp] (96)

• TER - Turkey

Formed in 1971 by Erkin Koray, Ter was influenced by the growing heavy blues psychedelic sound. Here the ethnic influence is reduced to the performance style of the lead guitar. The drums and bass propel the song along in typical blues fashion.

Hava Narghile, Vol. 1 [Comp] (01)

• THINGS TO COME - USA

Formed in 1966 in Los Angeles, they cut three official singles that fused a British Invasion vocal sound with the prevailing garage style of the day. The Farfisa organ and fuzz-guitar were perhaps the most prominent psychedelic touch. By all accounts they split up in 1968.

I Want Out [Comp] (94)

• THIRD BARDO - USA

Formed in 1966 in New York, the Third Bardo created only one single during their time on the scene that's become a classic in the acid-punk style with loads of fuzz.

The Third Bardo [Comp] (94), My Rainbow Life: Psychedelic Microdots of the 60's, Vol. 3 [Comp] (92), Nuggets I Box Set [Comp] (98)

• THIRD POWER - USA

Formed in 1968 in Detroit, Michigan they produced one album of predominantly heavy acid rock.

Believe (70)

• THIRD RAIL - USA

This was a studio project for Joey Levine and the single created, *Run, Run, Run* became a minor hit during the Fall of 1967 with its catchy, upbeat style. In some respects the sound was reminiscent of the English psychedelic style, but in America it soon gave birth to the Bubblegum style. In fact Levine became the lead vocalist of the Ohio Express.

ID Music (67), Nuggets I Box Set [Comp] (98)

• THIRTEENTH FLOOR ELEVATORS - USA

Formed in 1965 in Austin, Texas; the band's cornerstone member was 17 year old guitarist Roky Erickson. He'd originally been in an outfit called the Spades before joining up with the Lingsmen who then mutated into the Thirteenth Floor Elevators. In addition to Erickson's fiery guitar style the band featured an "electric liquor jug" providing an unusual rhythmic element to their music. They proved to be a big hit on their first visit to San Francisco but failed to translate their live popularity into commercial or recording success. Drug problems ensued and in 1968 Erickson, following intense police pressure pleaded insanity and was sent to a hospital for the criminally insane. The band carried on without Erickson half-heartedly until 1969. Erickson was released in 1972.

The Psychedelic Sounds of the Thirteenth Floor Elevators (66), Easter Everywhere (67), Bull of the Woods (68), Texas Twisted: Psychedelic Microdots of the 60's, Vol. 2 [Comp] (91), Nuggets I Box Set [Comp] (98)

• THORINSHIELD - USA

Formed in 1967 in Los Angeles they produced one LP filled with a flower-power psychedelic-pop style similar to groups like Sagittarius. A nice mix of folk-rock with psychedelic touches and some pleasant orchestrations. Drummer Terry Hand had previously been in the band Everpresent Fullness.

Thorinshield (67)

• THREE'S A CROWD - Canada

Formed in 1964 in Vancouver, British Columbia; they were part of a flourishing folk-rock community that played regularly at all the coffee houses. They relocated to Toronto in 1965 and made a name for themselves in the budding Yorkville underground. Their maturing folk-rock style was spotted by Mama Cass who helped get them a record deal, which led to four singles and an LP. After a major US tour in the 1969, the band drifted apart with many members going on to solo careers. The prominent members of Three's A Crowd included Bruce Cockburn and Colleen Peterson.

Christopher's Movie Matinee (68)

• THUNDER AND ROSES - USA

Formed in the late sixties in Philadelphia, this trio produced one album that displayed a certain debt of gratitude to Jimi Hendrix in terms of combo style. They created a heavier sound with plenty of psychedelic or acid-guitar trimmings.

King of the Black Sunrise (69)

• TICKLE - UK

Formed in 1967 this obscure British outfit produced only one single, but many historians cite it as a true psychedelic gem worthy of greater attention than it received at the time. The single *Subway* b/w *Good Evening* contained some searing guitar and distorted vocals, and was actually part of a longer demo that has never surfaced.

• THUNDERCLAPP NEWMAN - UK

Formed in 1969 in London, the band was actually the brainchild of Pete Townsend of the Who. The trio clicked right away and had a No. 1 single in Britain with *Something In The Air* in early 1969. By the time of their next release, a year later they failed to attract much chart activity. The album that followed also failed to chart and they split up in 1971. Vocalist Andy Newman went solo, while guitarist Jimmy McCulloch spent time with Stone the Crows and then Wings before committing suicide in 1979.

Hollywood Dream (70)

• TIFFANY SHADE - USA

Formed in 1967 in Cleveland, Ohio; this four piece sounded more English than most with a bright, pop-psychedelic style

The Tiffany Shade (68)

• TINKERBELLS FAIRYDUST - UK

Formed in 1967 they were called Rush at first before changing their name just in time for the release of their first single in 1967 called *Lazy Day*. Their psychedelic-pop style mixed a vocals that were equal parts Turtles and Association with some low key studio effects. In the end they recorded three singles before splitting up in 1969. The album they recorded just before their break-up was eventually released in 1998.

Tinkerbell's Fairydust (69/98), The Great British Psychedelic Trip, Vol 2 [Comp] (88)

• TIMEBOX - UK

Formed in 1965 in Southport, they were originally called Take Five, but moved to London in 1966 and took the name Timebox. It was in London that they recruited lead vocalist Mike Patto, a veteran of several R&B groups. Timebox incorporated a soul-jazz influence into their psychedelic sounds. They initially recorded their first single on the Piccadilly label before moving to the more experimental Deram for five psych-influenced singles. In late 1969 after releasing many singles that failed to rise high on the charts, Timebox evolved into Patto.

The Great British Psychedelic Trip, Vol. 1 [Comp] (88), The Great British Psychedelic Trip, Vol. 2 [Comp] (88), The Psychedelic Scene [Comp] (98), Nuggets II Box Set [Comp] (01)

• TIMON - UK

Originally part of the Liverpool folk scene, Timon, who's more recently gone by the name Tymon Dogg had recorded a couple of odd pop-psychedelic singles one of which was the unusual *The Bitter Thoughts Of Little Jane*. He was signed to the Apple label but the proposed LP failed to materialise. He did record one more single for the Threshold label before fading from the scene. He later re-emerged with the help of his pal Joe Strummer of the Clash in the early eighties.

Nuggets II Box Set [Comp] (01)

• TINTERN ABBEY - UK

Formed in 1967 in London they created one tasty bit of psychedelia in the form of the single *Bee Side* b/w *Vacuum Cleaner* featuring some excellent fuzz-guitar and Mellotron. The band's four members were from North Africa, Vienna, Yorkshire and London providing quite a cosmopolitan mix of influences. A follow-up single and LP were never released and they split up in 1968. Guitarist Paul Brett went on to Velvet Opera for a short time for creating the more progressive Paul Brett's Sage.

The Great British Psychedelic Trip, Vol. 1 [Comp] (88), The Psychedelic Scene [Comp] (98), Nuggets II Box Set [Comp] (01)

• TOBY TWIRL - UK

Formed in 1966, and after working the Northern club circuit for a number of years known as Shades of Blue, they adopted the Toby Twirl moniker and plunged into the world of psychedelia with three interesting singles. Long seen as classic examples of UK acid-pop, the band failed to have a hit single. They eventually disbanded in 1969.

The Great British Psychedelic Trip, Vol. 1 [Comp] (88), The Great British Psychedelic Trip, Vol. 2 [Comp] (88)

• TOM DAE TURNED ON - USA

Tom Dae was from Rockville, Connecticut; and he created a number of different garage or psych outfits going back to 1966. Over the years he recorded almost a dozen singles under these different banners. His most psychedelic would be a track called *I Shall Walk* from the mid seventies loaded with phased vocals and fuzz-guitar effects.

Tommy Dae (70), A Lethal Dose of Hard Psych [Comp] (99)

• TOM THUMB & THE CASUALS - USA

Formed in 1964 in Seattle they made only a couple of recordings that featured the traditional sax-and-organ sound of many of the early garage bands. Their psychedelic influence really surfaced in some of their more unusual lyrics.

The History of Northwest Rock Vol. 3: Psychedelic Seattle [Comp] (00)

• TOMORROW - UK

Formed in 1966 in London, Tomorrow along with Pink Floyd were considered to be part of "swinging London's" leading psychedelic lights. Originally called the In Crowd they played a mix of R&B standards, however when the underground scene hit they changed their name to Tomorrow and incorporated no end of studio gimmickry to create some of the finest psychedelic-pop music of the era. They play regularly on the underground club scene. After a couple of unsuccessful attempts at the charts with singles like *My White Bicycle* they split up in 1968. Keith West went to a pop solo career while guitarist Steve Howe found fame and fortune in progressive rockers Yes.

Tomorrow (68), The Psychedelic Years 1966-1969 - Great Britain [Comp] (90), Psychedelic Visions [Comp] (96), Psychedelia at Abbey Road [Comp] (98), Nuggets II Box Set [Comp] (01)

• TOUCH - USA

Formed in 1968 in Portland, Oregon; before which time they were known as Don and the Good Times. The "good-time" sounds changed to psychedelic in 1967 and Touch was born. Their first single combined equal amounts of pop and psychedelia however their album reflected more of a jazz influenced progressive rock style. A lack of critical response led to them splitting up in 1969.

This is Touch (69)

• TRAFFIC - UK

Formed in 1967 out of the ashes of the Spencer Davis Group, Traffic consisted of Steve Winwood, Dave Mason, Jim Capaldi and Chris Wood all from around Birmingham. They were the first band signed to the new Island label and started a trend for bands to retreat to the countryside to get their material together. The first formation of Traffic eventually broke up at the end of 1968 with Winwood joining the "supergroup" Blind Faith. Traffic were one of the bands that really captured the spirit of the psychedelic era and the Summer of Love in Britain with their slightly experimental music and trippy lyrical style. In 1970 a reformed Traffic came on the scene and recorded six more albums but by this time they had clearly moved out of their psychedelic phase.

Mr. Fantasy (67), Traffic (68), Last Exit (69), The Psychedelic Years Revisited [Comp] (92)

• TRAFFIC SOUND - Peru

Formed in 1968 and singing in English, their style hearkens back to a bit of the melodic, harmony driven British Invasion sound that's spiced up with some long (for the time) acid-guitar solos. Their later work took on a more acoustic element including the use of woodwinds and stronger Latin influences.

A Bailar Go Go (68), Virgin (70), Traffic Sound (70), Lux (72), Love, Peace & Poetry: Latin American Psychedelic Music [Comp] (97)

• TRANSATLANTIC RAILROAD - USA

Originally formed in 1965 in Marin County, north of San Francisco, they were one of the more obscure Bay area bands. They managed to play around the scene even getting to some of the Wednesday night Fillmore audition sessions, as well as many of the local festivals where they played on the same bill as bands like the Grateful Dead and Jefferson Airplane. During their time together they recorded a number of demos all featuring that laid back West Coast psychedelic guitar jamming style.

Express to Oblivion [Comp] (01)

• TRIPSICHORD - USA

Formed in 1967 in the North West they were originally called Ban and then Now before moving to San Francisco. They soon came under the management of Matthew Katz. Musically they shared a lot in common with Quicksilver Messenger Service's twin guitar style. Lots of extended West Coast acid guitar jamming was a prerequisite. When Katz lost control of the original Moby Grape, he used Tripsichord to fill in using the Grape name. The band never felt good about this and it eventually let to them breaking up in the early seventies.

Tripsichord (71)

• TROGGS - UK

Formed in 1965 in Andover, the Troggs emerged out of a couple local bands one of which was called Ten Feet Five. Their first single *Lost Girl* was released in early 1966. While that first single failed to get noticed, their second *Wild Thing* took everyone by storm. They went on to have a number of hit singles including their big hit of January 1968, *Love Is All Around*. This song seemed to fit the flower-power era, but was certainly a far cry from the garage-punk style of their earlier hit *Wild Thing* which Jimi Hendrix later covered quite successfully in a psychedelic vein. The Troggs in some version were performing and recording into the early nineties.

From Nowhere...The Troggs (66), Wild Thing (66), Trogglodynamite (67), Cellophane (67), Love is All Around (68), Mixed Bag (68), Nuggets II Box Set [Comp] (01)

• TROLL - USA

Formed in 1966 in Chicago, Illinois; they recorded a half dozen singles and one LP with a predominantly psychedelic rock style.

Animated Music (68)

• TRUTH - USA

Formed in 1968 in Los Angeles, Truth recorded one single that had all the hallmarks of the classic West Coast acid rock style. Of note is that they were produced by Dave Hassinger who's known for his work with the Electric Prunes.

A Heavy Dose of Lyte Psych [Comp] (96)

• TURNSTYLE - UK

Formed in 1968 in London this obscure band recorded

a psychedelic-pop single for Pye records in the late sixties entitled *Riding A Wave*. Drummer Mark Ashton went on to join Rare Bird for their progressive release Sympathy in 1969.

Hot Smoke & Sassafras: Psychedelic Pstones Vol. 1 [Comp] (01)

• TURQUOISE - UK

Formed in 1968 in the Muswell Hill area of London home to the Kinks, so it's no surprise to hear a hint of the Kink's sound in their style. Their sound is typified by strong melodies, tight harmonies and a West Coast jangling psychedelic guitar sound. They recorded two singles before calling it a day.

The Great British Psychedelic Trip, Vol. 1 [Comp] (88), The Great British Psychedelic Trip, Vol. 2 [Comp] (88), The Psychedelic Scene [Comp] (98)

• TURTLES - USA

Formed in 1961 in Los Angeles, they were originally called the Nightriders. A couple years later with addition of new members they became the Crossfires and finally in 1965 they took the name the Tyrtles with a spelling to compete with the Byrds. Their musical style evolved out of a strong garage sensibility combined with a love of folk and pop music. All was neatly wrapped up with some very effective vocal harmonizing and arranging. They quickly hit the charts with a string of successful singles that took them through to 1970. Leaders Mark Volman and Howard Kaylan went solo working with Frank Zappa and under the name Flo and Eddie.

It Aint Me Babe (65), You Baby Let Me Be (66), Happy Together (67), The Turtles Present The Battle of the Bands (69), Turtle Soup (69), Wooden Head (70), Nuggets I Box Set [Comp] (98), Happy Together: The Very Best of White Whale Records [Comp] (99)

• 23RD TURNOFF - UK

Formed in 1966 in Liverpool, and named after the exit off the M6 that led to Liverpool, they evolved out of a beat band called the Kirkbys. Their psychedelic style was evidenced on only one single release before splitting up. The 'A' side *Michael Angelo* displayed a keen sense of trippyness but failed to attract any attention.

The Great British Psychedelic Trip, Vol. 1 [Comp] (88), The Psychedelic Scene [Comp] (98)

• TWILIGHTS - Australia

Formed in 1964 in Adelaide as a trio, they joined forces with another local group the Hurricanes to become a six-piece. Their rise to fame was fast and furious on a slew of singles that captured the right elements of pop to play well on the local radio. They toured England in 1967 and soon adopted the psychedelic trappings of fuzz and sitar and returned home to another hit single. After five years together they decided to split up in 1969. Vocalist Glenn Shorrock later found fame in the Little River Band while lead guitarist Terry Britten became a successful pop song writer.

Nuggets II Box Set [Comp] (01)

• TWINK - UK

Twink, whose real name is John Alder was the drummer in a number of early sixties beat bands, but came to prominence for his work in the psychedelic band Tomorrow. When they split in 1968 he joined the Pretty Things and recorded S.F. Sorrow with them. After leaving that band in 1969 he formed Pink Fairies. During this time he recorded a solo LP full of late sixties psychedelia including Eastern influences, sitars, backward loops etc.

Think Pink (70)

• UGLY DUCKLINGS - Canada

Formed in 1965 in Toronto, they were the prime movers of the growing garage-psych scene in the emerging hippie community of Yorkville. Their first recording, the raw and abrasive guitar heavy *Nothin* became a national hit, but it was their more psychedelic *Gaslight* released in 1967 that became their calling card. Sadly they split by the end of the year having only released four singles and one LP.

Somewhere Outside (66), Made in Canada, Vol. 3 1961 - 1974 [Comp] (91), Made in Canada, Vol. 4 1961 - 1974 [Comp] (91), Nuggets II Box Set [Comp] (01)

• ULTIMATE SPINACH - USA

Formed in 1967 in Boston, they were part of a local psychedelic scene known as the "Bosstown Sound". Loaded with flower-power philosophy the band reflected the mood of the day. They recorded three albums but after the third failed to bring them the fame they desired, they disbanded. Jeff "Skunk" Baxter who'd joined for the third LP went on to fame with Steely Dan and the Dobbie Brothers.

Ultimate Spinach (68), Behold & See (68), Ultimate Spinach (69), The Psychedelic Years Revisited [Comp] (92)

• UNITED EMPIRE LOYALISTS - Canada

Formed in 1967 in Vancouver, British Columbia; they soon acquired the reputation of being the local answer to San Francisco's Grateful Dead as a result of their seemingly endless live jamming. Only one official single was released before they disbanded and two members went on to form Mock Duck.

Afterthought: The History of Vancouver's Rock and Roll, Vol 1 [Comp] ( )

• UNITED STATES OF AMERICA - USA

Formed in 1968 in Los Angeles they took the psychedelic approach to its logical conclusion and recorded an album dense with avant-garde electronics and quirky acid-rock that was perhaps a little too adventurous for the times. Their sharp musical style was softened slightly by the vocals of Dorothy Moskowitz. Band leader Joe Byrd was a respected contemporary composer and he brought his skills to bear in a rock format with some very "modern" instrumentation. At best their style can be described as a mixture of the spaciness of Pink Floyd and the darkness of Velvet Underground.

The United States of America (68)

• VAMP - UK

Formed in 1968 this obscure British band included two former members of Sam Gopal's Dream, Viv Prince and Pete Sears. They recorded two singles, one of the tracks from 1968 entitled *Floating* is as you might expect from the title a laid back spacey sound full of the prerequisite drug-influenced lyrics.

Electric Sugarcube Flashbacks [Comp] (93)

• VANILLA FUDGE - USA

Formed in 1965 in New York City they originally went by the name the Pigeons but took the name Vanilla Fudge in late 1966 when they appeared at the Village Theatre. They combined elements of early heavy metal with long symphonic psychedelic organ drenched passages. They had an interesting approach of taking established hits outside of the psychedelic genre and putting their own trippy embellishments in place. The first such epic was the seven minute plus version of The Supremem's *You Keep Me Hangin' On* which went to No. 67 on the United States charts but did even better overseas rising into the Top 20 in Britain. Their albums were adventurous musical excusions and most placed in the upper regions of the charts. Interestingly, Vanilla Fudge replaced Jimi Hendrix as the opening act for the Monkees 1967 tour. The band originally folded in 1969 when Tim Bogart and Carmine Apice formed Cactus in 1970. The original members reformed Vanilla Fudge to record yet another album in 1984.

Vanilla Fudge (67), The Beat Goes On (68), Renaissance (68), Near The Beginning (69), Rock & Roll (69)

• VEJTABLES - USA

Formed in 1965 in San Francisco they were signed to the Autumn Records label along with the Beau Brummels. The Vejtables were like many bands in the mid-sixties fusing elements of folk-rock and the British Invasion incorporating pleasant harmonies in catchy melodies. They and a few others were instrumental stepping stones to the more overt psychedelic sound that was just around the musical corner. They recorded only three singles before splitting up with members going the Mojo Men and the Syndicate of Sound.

San Francisco Nights [Comp] (91), Feel the Vejtables [Comp] (96)

• VELOSO, CAETANO - Brazil

This Brazilian artist produced three albums that at times bordered on soft folk psychedelia. On the whole the material on the three albums incorporates a wide variety of psychedelic elements including some flower-power orchestration, sound effects, the obligatory reedy organ and even some Eastern influences.

Caetano Veloso (67), Araca Azul (68), Caetano Veloso (69)

• VELVET OPERA - UK

Formed in 1966 in London they started out with the full name Elmer Gantry's Velvet Opera recording one LP as such. They added Paul Brett on guitar and lost vocalist Elmer Gantry necessitating a shortening of the name to just Velvet Opera. When the name changed they altered their psychedelic-soul style into more of a progressive rock approach. They eventually split up in 1969, when John Ford and Richard Hudson joined Strawbs.

Elmer Gantry's Velvet Opera (68), Ride a Hustler's Dream (69)

• VELVET UNDERGROUND - USA

Formed in 1965 in New York City by Lou Reed and John Cale they became the darlings of the New York underground and avant-garde music scenes. Their brand of music was far removed from the peace-love-and flower-power that was prevalent elsewhere. Instead they took a darker and almost disturbing musical approach to the issues of the day. It was because of their underground style and the fact they spoke to contemporary issues that they fit in with psychedelia. They endured many personnel shifts, first with vocalist Nico leaving in 1967, then founder Cale departing in 1968. After a few more turbulent years the band folded in 1973 only to reform twenty years later in 1993 for one recording.

The Velvet Underground and Nico (67), White Light/White Heat (68), The Velvet Underground (69), Loaded (71), Squeeze (73), The Psychedelic Years Revisited [Comp] (92)

• VILLAGE - UK

Formed in 1969 this obscure venture consisted of Peter Bardens formerly of Them and bassist Bruce Thomas who would go on to work in Quiver. They managed to release one very trippy single called *Man in the Moon* which is best described as a jazz influenced piece full of Hammond organ, echo, reverb and some interesting wah-wah guitar. They split up in early 1970 and Barden's helped form progressive rockers Camel.

Electric Sugarcube Flashbacks [Comp] (93)

• VIRGIN SLEEP - UK

Formed in 1967 in South London under the name Themselves, they soon adopted the moniker Virgin Sleep but sadly recorded only two psychedelic-pop singles in early 1968. Their first single *Love* was full of the sound of sitars and then *Secret* was released with a string laden, Mellotron-ish Moody Blues style.

The Great British Psychedelic Trip, Vol. 1 [Comp] (88), The Great British Psychedelic Trip, Vol. 2 [Comp] (88), The Psychedelic Scene [Comp] (98)

• VIRUS - Germany

Formed in 1970 in Germany they released a couple of albums that were harbingers of the growing progressive rock genre. Their first LP certainly retained more of a psychedelic feel while by the time of their second release they were working on longer and more involved arrangements. They disappeared from the radar screen following the release of their second LP.

Revelation (70), Thoughts (71)

• WADE, CLIFF - UK

This rather obscure vocalist surfaced in the late sixties and released at least one psychedelic-pop single entitled *You've Never Been To My House*. The material has that distinctive whimsical British psych-pop style. He's known to have recorded other material, some of which has surfaced on other compilations.

The Best of and Rest of British Psychedelia [Comp] (91)

• WAITE, MICHAEL - Canada

A strange mixture of progressive and psychedelic rock that was clearly a hold-over from the sixties.

Cosmic Wave (83)

• GARY WALKER & RAIN - UK

The convoluted history of Gary Walker & Rain begins with American Gary Walker getting ousted from the Walker Brothers, then changing his name to Gary Leeds and spending time in the Standells before moving to England in 1966. Changing his name back to Walker he formed this group and recorded a string of psychedelic singles between 1966 and 1974 as Gary Walker & Rain. They also recorded one album, which was only released in Japan.

Gary Walker & Rain ( ), Electric Sugarcube Flashbacks [Comp] (93)

• WARM SOUNDS - UK

Formed in 1967 this duo consisting of Denny Gerrard and Barry Younghusband displayed an uncanny ability to write catchy melodies with lush harmonies all blended together in an off-kilter manner. It was always more than just a catchy pop song with them. At the height of the Summer of Love their first single *Birds & Bees* hit the top of the pirate radio charts. Unfortunately their next two singles failed to chart as well and they split up. Younghusband, or Young as he was then known went on to play with Hapsash and the Coloured Coat.

The Psychedelic Scene [Comp] (98)

• WATERMELON - USA

Formed in the late sixties in Illinois they were first called the Lemon Drops. They relocated to San Francisco in search of fame, which unfortunately eluded them. Their music runs the gamut but is primarily based around a West Coast acid guitar jamming style.

From the Lemon Drops to Vibration of Sequence in Order [Comp] (96

• WATERPROOF TINKERTOY - USA

Formed in 1967 in Springfield, Massachusetts; Waterproof Tinkertoy recorded five different singles in their lifetime. One cut featured a strange instrumental excursion full of discordant plucking and banging. Far out stuff, but their other tracks fall into the fuzz-guitar garage-psych mould.

Beyond the Calico Wall [Comp] (93)

• WE ALL TOGETHER - Peru

Formed in the early seventies in Peru consisting of members from Traffic Sound and Laghonia, We All Together managed to distil a number of Beatle and psychedelic influences to craft an interesting South American take on the genre. Their single *Tomorrow* bears all the hallmarks of Paul McCartney and Wings. Nice harmonies, swirling organs and fuzz-guitar come together in a sound that could have been created four years earlier.

We All Together (72), Love, Peace & Poetry: Latin American

Psychedelic Music [Comp] (97), Nuggets II Box Set [Comp] (01)

• WE FIVE - USA

San Francisco band whose folk-rock style gave them a big hit in 1965 with *You Were On My Mind*. Stylistically they were very representative of the layered vocal folk-rock or pop that was very much an influence on the coming jangly psychedelic style. To some degree they even influenced the sound of the first Jefferson Airplane LP. Not overtly psychedelic themselves they certainly played a part in shaping the sound.

You Were On My Mind (65), Make Someone Happy (67), The Return of We Five (69), Catch the Wind (70), San Francisco Nights [Comp] (91)

• WE THE PEOPLE - USA

Formed in 1965 in Orlando, Florida; We the People featured a strong hint of garage-punk mixed with the growing psychedelic fuzz tones. These five talented teenagers soon had a minor local hit on their hands with their self penned *Mirror Of Your Mind*. The band played locally and in the end recorded over half a dozen tracks on a variety of labels including RCA, but with no major hits to their credit the band split up in 1968.

Orange, Sugar & Chocolate: Psychedelic Microdots of the 60's, Vol. 1 [Comp] (89), Declaration of Independence [Comp] (93), Mirror of Our Minds [Comp] (98), Nuggets I Box Set [Comp] (98)

• WENDY AND BONNIE - USA

The two sisters here were just 18 and 15 when they recorded their one and only LP and stylistically it's best described as flower-power folk-rock. It's a very bright harmonious sound with some subtle orchestration and a few tracks with some well placed acid-guitar. Overall very representative of the period.

Genesis (69)

• WEST COAST EXPERIMENTAL POP ART BAND - USA

Formed in 1964 in Los Angeles, they first went by the name Snowman but changed their name in 1966 with the release of their first LP. They were as the name implies a highly experimental outfit and thanks to an understanding record company were given a lot of freedom in the studio. What they produced bore all the hallmarks of the era, long guitar jams, sprinkled with serious freakouts, the typical trippy lyrics all performed with an underpinning of a Los Angeles folk-rock style. They disbanded in 1969.

West Coast Pop Art Experimental Band (66), Part One (67), Vol. 2 - Second (67), Vol. 3 - A Child's Guide to Good & Evil (68), Where's My Daddy (69)

• WHISTLER, CHAUCER, DETROIT & GREENHILL - USA

Formed in 1967 in Fort Worth, this group created a classic psychedelic LP with some obvious Beatles influences. The music is primarily folk-rock with some interesting guitar solos and some rather trippy lyrics. An interesting piece of psychedelia.

The Unwritten Works of Geoffrey, etc... (68)

• WHITE ROOM - USA

Formed in 1968 in the New York area, White Room created a psychedelic-pop style that had much in common with bands like Strawberry Alarm Clock and the Lemon Pipers.

A Heavy Dose of Lyte Psych [Comp] (96)

• WHO - UK

Formed in 1964, they originally called themselves the High Numbers but by 1965's *I Can't Explain* had changed their name to the Who. Taking their cues from the Mod scene both in dress and musical style they had a long string of hit singles. Their excursion into the world of psychedelia began with the release of *Happy Jack* and culminated with the trippy *I Can See For Miles* and *Magic Bus*. It was at this point Pete Townsend set his sights in a more progressive vein and created the concept LP **Tommy** and then a few years later **Quadrophenia**. By the mid seventies the Who reverted back to their own identifiable brand of rock. Having attempted to break up many times, the Who continue to perform as of this writing. Bassist John Entwhistle passed away in 2002.

My Generation (65), Happy Jack (66), The Who Sell Out (68), Magic Bus (68), Tommy (69), Live at Leeds (70), Who's Next (71)

• WILDE FLOWERS - UK

Formed in 1966 they were the precursor to bands like Soft Machine and Caravan. The original members drifted in and out of various formations putting some material on tape in demo fashion but never releasing anything on vinyl at the time. While the band gave birth to the famous progressive *Canterbury* sound, the Wilde Flowers musical style borrowed more from the beat era with a healthy jazz influence, but given the times it was unavoidable that there wouldn't be just a hint of psychedelia involved.

Tales of Canterbury: The Wilde Flowers Story [Comp] (94)

• WILDFLOWER - USA

Formed in 1966 in San Francisco this was a folk-rock outfit that made the rounds in the early days playing places like the Matrix club and the Bay area ballrooms. Popular at the time they only recorded two singles.

• WILDFLOWERS - USA

Formed in Phoenix, they released two singles in 1967, one of which seemed highly influenced by the Beatles *Rain*. Guitarist Michael Bruce later went on to play in the Nazz.

A Heavy Dose of Lyte Psych [Comp] (96)

• WILLIAM TELL & THE MARKSMEN - Canada

Formed in 1965 in Vancouver, British Columbia; William Tell and the Marksmen were fixtures on the Vancouver music scene. Their music incorporated more of a folk feel than their contemporaries. Two members Lindsey Mitchell and Jeff Edington went on to front the legendary Seeds of Time in the late sixties.

The History of Vancouver Rock & Roll, Vol. 4 [Comp] (91)

• WIMPLE WINCH - UK

Formed in 1961 in Liverpool, Wimple Winch had previously gone by the names Four Just Men and then Just Four Men, and before that the Silhouettes. By 1966 they were one of front runners in the short-lived freakbeat scene. They recorded at least three singles for Fontana Records but failed to hit it big finally splitting up in early 1967. Lawrence Ardenes changed his name to Lawrence King and joined up with Pacific Drift.

The Wimple Winch Story - Volume Two '66-'68 - The Psychedelic Years [Comp] (92), The Wimple Winch Story 1963-1968 [Comp] (94), Nuggets II Box Set [Comp] (01)

• WINSTON'S FUMBS - UK

Formed in 1966 in London by ex-Small Face-er Jimmy Winston they were originally known as the Reflections, but by 1967 they'd changed their name to Winston's Fumbs and were creating a freakbeat and psychedelic influenced music. Nice searing fuzz leads over waves of Hammond organ assembled with the appropriate studio gimmickry. The band split up after releasing only one single. Keyboardist Tony Kaye soon landed a spot with Yes.

Nuggets II Box Set [Comp] (01)

• WINTER'S GREEN - Canada

Formed in the mid-sixties in Vancouver, British Columbia; they recorded at least one official 45 with a keyboard styled Doors sound. They later became pop stars Trooper under the guidance of Randy Bachman.

Afterthought: The History of Vancouver Rock and Roll Vol. 2 [Comp] ( )

• WIRTZ, MARK - UK

Wirtz is remembered more for his studio production work than his personal recording although he did a fair share of both. Wirtz is also known for creating the "Teenage Opera" featuring Keith West. Wirtz was employed at Abbey Road and worked with a variety of bands such as the In-Crowd which became Tomorrow, which is how he met West. His style was like that of Phil Spector, where he employed the studio and its effects to the maximum. As everyone knows the Teenage Opera was less than successful and Wirtz resumed his studio work well into the seventies.

A Teenage Opera: The Original Soundtrack Recording [Comp] (96), Psychedelia at Abbey Road [Comp] (98)

• WITNESS INC. - Canada

Formed in 1966 in Saskatoon, Saskatchewan; the obscure Witness Inc. were a classic garage-psych band heavily influenced by the British Invasion vocal style. They produced five regional hit singles, the biggest being *Jezebel* in 1967.

• WOMB - USA

Formed in 1969 in San Francisco they produced two psychedelic albums with an eclectic mixture of styles including horns and woodwinds. Lots of longer songs full of improvisation that would have gone over well in a live format.

Womb (69), Overdub (69)

• WOODY KERN - UK

Formed in the late sixties, Woody Kern were on the scene as psychedelic rock was morphing into progressive rock. As such Woody Kern released a couple of singles to little notice before putting out an LP that cemented their fate. Of note is that bassist Rik Kenton joined Roxy Music for a short time performing on Virginia Plain before going off to do some solo work.

The Awful Disclosures of Maria Monk (68), Hot Smoke & Sassafras: Psychedelic Pstones Vol. 1 [Comp] (01)

• WOORDEN - Holland

Formed in the mid-sixties, the Woorden were an obscure outfit that released a highly sought after LP in 1967. A single released from that LP features some strange "stream-of-consciousness" spoken trippy lyrics. The musical background is totally improvised. Perhaps it's their own drug-induced trip committed to vinyl!

Waterpipes & Dykes: Dutch Psychedelic Underground 1966 - 1972 Vol. 1 [Comp] ( )

• WORLD OF OZ - UK

Formed in 1967 in Birmingham, World of Oz created a light psychedelic-pop style best represented by their early 1968 single *Muffin Man*. They released two other singles with some interesting instrumentation including an East Indian influence. After recording their first and only LP they disbanded in 1969.

World of Oz (69), The Great British Psychedelic Trip, Vol. 1 [Comp] (88), The Psychedelic Scene [Comp] (98)

• XHOL - Germany

Formed in 1967 in Germany their music leaned heavily in the Pink Floyd spacey vein as one can surmise from the title of their second LP, Electrip. This emerging style pf jazz-fusion-psychedelia and progressive rock led to the emergence of a whole sub genre called Krautrock. They split up and disappeared from the music scene in late 1970.

Get in High (67), Electrip (69), Hau-Ruk (70)

• XIT - USA

Formed in 1966 in Albuquerque, New Mexico they originally went by the name Lincoln St. Exit and at the time focused their style in the garage rock vein. In 1971 they changed their name to XIT and altered their musical direction adding orchestration and elements of psychedelia to craft a very unique style. Their prime recordings as XIT came between 1972 and 1974 after which they became a trio releasing one more LP in 1978 before breaking up for good.

Plight of the Red Man (72), Silent Warrior (73), Entrance (The Sound of Early XIT) [Comp] (74)

• YABANCILAR - Turkey

Formed in 1966 in Ankara, Turkey; their sound is moody, atmospheric, spacey and very similar to some of the trippier moments of Pink Floyd.

Hava Narghile, Vol. 1 [Comp] (01)

• YANKEE DOLLAR - USA

Formed in 1968 in San Luis Obispo, California; they released three singles and one LP best described as West Coast flower-power pop. The songs are bright, harmonious with a healthy dose of fuzz-guitar thrown in for good measure.

Yankee Dollar (68)

• YARDBIRDS - UK

Formed in 1963 in Richmond, Surrey; the Yardbirds are credited by some with having one of the first overtly psychedelic singles in the 1966 *Shapes Of Things To Come* their fourth UK Top 10 single. Their experimentation with the world of psychedelia is credited to their bassist and producer, Paul Samwell-Smith who recorded the single in October of 1965 in Chicago while the group were on tour. The move towards a more psychedelic sound had started in early 1965 when the group replaced guitarist Eric Clapton with Jeff Beck who began moving the group away from its blues roots. Later Jimmy Page was brought in to play bass replacing Samwell-Smith. In short order he picked up the guitar and with both Page and Beck on guitar the Yardbirds created *Happenings Ten Years Time Ago* a delicious slice of psychedelia. Jeff Beck left following this release and Page took over and had his fling with psychedelia. Soon however, Page created the New Yardbirds, which then quickly became Led Zeppelin.

Five Live Yardbirds (65), For Your Love (65), Over Under Sideways Down (66), Little Games (67), The Psychedelic Years 1966-1969 - Great Britain [Comp] (90), Psychedelic Frequencies [Comp] (96)

• YELLOW PAYGES - USA

Formed in 1966 in Torrance, California; they recorded some ten singles and one LP over the period 1967 - 1970 most of which were a blend of slow folksy-psychedelic-ballads or straight ahead harder rock. They eventually split up in 1970.

Volume One (69)

• YOUNGBLOODS - USA

Formed in 1965 in New York City, the Youngbloods became favourites on the San Francisco ballroom scene, due in no small part to their recording of the anthemic 1967 hit *Get Together* a song that landed in the Top 10 and epitomized the mood of the era. The song was penned by Dino Valenti a prominent fixture in the San Francisco scene. The song had been recorded by no less than three other groups including the Jefferson Airplane. The Youngbloods continued working together until 1972. Leader Jessie Collin Young later went on to a relatively successful solo career and although radio hits were never a part of the picture, his albums did consistently bounce into the Top 50.

The Youngbloods (67), Earth Music (68), Elephant Mountain (69), Rock Festival (70), Good and Dusty (72), High on a Ridgetop (72), San Francisco Nights [Comp] (91)

• YUYA UCHIDA & THE FLOWERS - Japan

Formed in the late sixties, they had originally gone by the name Flowers and released two albums under that name. In their later incarnation they created a classic West Coast fuzz-guitar jamming style with a slight Japanese feel. Uchida's role as the band's producer is at its strongest for their Challenge LP, with the music going off in many directions all at once, but all working to maintain that rolling collective energy.

Challenge (69), Love, Peace & Poetry: Japanese Psychedelic Music [Comp] (01)

• ZAPPA, FRANK - USA

Originally born in Maryland, Zappa settled in Los Angeles in 1950. In 1956 he put the Blackouts together with buddy Don Van Vliet who later became Captain Beefheart. In the early sixties Zappa's band the Souljants slowly evolved into the Mothers of Invention and produced their first single, *Help , I'm A Rock* in 1966. The already eccentric Zappa took to making his 'political' and 'social' comments with songs that defied description. At times bordering on the avant-garde and at other times playing humorous homage to any and all musical styles, his music took an even more adventurous tone (if that's possible) with the advent of psychedelia. Zappa, a non-drug user, preferred to inflict musical highs on his listeners that started with 1967's **Freakout**. Ever the non-conformist, Zappa did much to lead others into musically challenging areas. His recording career continued up until his death in 1993.

Freak Out (67), Absolutely Free (67), We're Only In It For The Money (68), Lumpy Gravy (68), Cruising with Ruben and the Jets (69), Uncle Meat (69), Hot Rats (70), Burnt Weeny Sandwich (70), Weasels Ripped My Flesh (70), Chunga's Revenge (70), Fillmore East (71), 200 Motels (71), Waka/Jawaka (72)

• ZIPPS - Netherlands

Formed in 1965 in Holland, they were the result of the merger of the Beattown Skifflers and the Moving Strings. They rose to prominence provoked in part by their outspoken attitude towards various drugs including LSD which they wrote a song about. Their early days saw them develop a following with the local beats before incorporating the new hippie attitudes in their lyrics. They recorded a couple of singles and remained staunchly underground until their break-up in 1971.

Nuggets II Box Set [Comp] (01)

• ZOO - USA

Formed in 1968 in California, this obscure outfit recorded one LP that displays some psychedelia, but refuses to let go of a rawer mid-sixties garage-punk style. The LP was produced by Ed Cobb.

...Presents The Chocolate Moose (68), Psychedelic Perceptions [Comp] (96)

• ZOSER - USA

This obscure band was believed to be from the Minneapolis area, and recorded one mid-tempo single released in 1971. Their style featured a subdued, breathy, falsetto vocal delivery and the double tracked guitars verge on a country-rock flavour.

A Lethal Dose of Hard Psych [Comp] (99)